An Illustrated History of British Theatre and Performance

An Illustrated History of British Theatre and Performance chronicles the history and development of theatre from the Roman era to the present day. As the most public of arts, theatre constantly interacts with changing social, political and intellectual movements and ideas, and Robert Leach's masterful work restores to the foreground of this evolution the contributions of women, gay people and ethnic minorities, as well as the theatres of the English regions, and of Wales and Scotland.

Highly illustrated chapters trace the development of theatre through major plays from each period; evaluations of playwrights; contemporary dramatic theory; acting and acting companies; dance and music; the theatre buildings themselves; and the audience, while also highlighting enduring features of British theatre, from comic gags to the use of props.

This first volume spans from the earliest forms of performance to the popular theatres of high society and the Enlightenment, tracing a movement from the outdoor and fringe to the heart of the social world. The *Illustrated History* acts as an accessible, flexible basis for students of the theatre, and for pure fans of British theatre history there could be no better starting point.

Robert Leach has been schoolteacher, political activist, teacher of acting, freelance theatre director and academic. Not only has he taught at Birmingham, Edinburgh and Cumbria universities, he has also acted professionally in Britain and the USA, directed plays in Russia and Britain and has published five volumes of poetry.

Robert Leach

An Illustrated History of British Theatre and Performance

Volume One – From the Romans to the Enlightenment

Routledge
Taylor & Francis Group

LONDON AND NEW YORK

First published 2019
by Routledge
2 Park Square, Milton Park, Abingdon, Oxon, OX14 4RN

and by Routledge
711 Third Avenue, New York, NY 10017

Routledge is an imprint of the Taylor & Francis Group, an informa business

British Library Cataloguing-in-Publication Data
A catalogue record for this book is available from the British Library

Library of Congress Cataloging-in-Publication Data
Names: Leach, Robert, 1942– author.
Title: An illustrated history of British theatre and performance / Robert Leach.
Description: First edition. | Abingdon, Oxon ; New York, NY : Routledge, 2019– |
    Includes bibliographical references and index.
Contents: volume 1. From the Romans to the Enlightenment.
Identifiers: LCCN 2018015345 | ISBN 9780815374824 (hardback : alk. paper) |
    ISBN 9780429463686 (ebook)
Subjects: LCSH: Theater—Great Britain—History.
Classification: LCC PN2581 .L43 2019 | DDC 792.0941—dc23
LC record available at https://lccn.loc.gov/2018015345

ISBN: 978-0-8153-7482-4 (hbk)
ISBN: 978-0-429-46368-6 (ebk)

Typeset in Frutiger
by Apex CoVantage, LLC

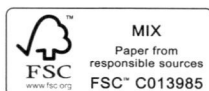

MIX
Paper from
responsible sources
FSC
www.fsc.org
FSC™ C013985

Printed in the United Kingdom
by Henry Ling Limited

This book is dedicated to

Natasha, Nicholas, Rebecca and Daniel

Contents

Illustrations

INTERLUDE: THE QUEEN'S MEN

PART TWO: OPEN AIR PUBLIC THEATRES

INTERLUDE: THE BOYS' COMPANIES

PART THREE: CAVALIER THEATRE

INTERLUDE: DRAMATICK OPERA

PART FOUR: THEATRE AND BOURGEOIS SOCIETY

INTERLUDE: EIGHTEENTH-CENTURY AMATEUR THEATRICALS

PART FIVE: THEATRE AND ENLIGHTENMENT

INTERLUDE: GARRICK'S SHAKESPEARE JUBILEE

Preface

This book, the first of two volumes, is an attempt to establish a credible narrative for the British theatre through history. It does not include the history of Irish theatre, though the influences across the Irish Sea in both directions are considerable, and it omits any detailed discussion of those important performance forms, opera and ballet.

The narrative is new in that it attempts to incorporate the results of much recent research into British theatre history. In this regard it attempts especially to restore to the story the contributions of women, gay people and black theatre practitioners, and, in what is usually a London-centric narrative, it tries to reassert the importance of regional, Welsh and Scottish theatres.

It certainly bears the marks of the author's presuppositions, assumptions and unspoken prejudices, some of which are laid out in this Preface. The theatre is seen as a specialised branch of social history, which explains why there is a constant effort to relate developments in theatre to the social, intellectual, cultural and political movements of the times.

This volume is divided into five sections, but it should be remembered that such divisions reflect the historian's desire for order and for the allocation into manageable boxes of too-often unruly happenings. Of course this desire cannot be met honestly, and in consequence a few unboxable practitioners, forms or events have been given their own interludes and the parts of this history overlap and inter-penetrate each other. The theatre of the Cavaliers, for example, existed side by side with the open air public theatre associated with the Elizabethan age for decades. Should Richard Tarlton be categorised as a late medieval clown or as an early exponent of the 'Shakespearean' theatre? And so on.

Historical 'truth' is thus always subject to different interpretations, and if not all interpretations are equally valid, any single one – including this one – must be regarded as partial and certainly not immutable. In this sense, history writing is like acting, which is a particular focus of this book:

> An actor is soon forgotten – he reigns as a king awhile:
> He's feted and cheered and honoured, and he basks in the public's smile,
> But the moment his work is over, and gone is the power to please,
> He has drained the cup of pleasure, and come to the bitter lees.[1]

Like the actor, this history will be superseded. But any history is useful as a dialectical interaction between past and present, and it is hoped this one serves such a purpose.

One of the problems – or opportunities – for the theatre historian is that this elusive phenomenon, the theatre, is simultaneously an art form and a business. The art itself is extraordinarily complex, embracing poetry, speech, dance, music, the visual arts and much more, but so is the business side of it, including as it does matters of investment, the business process, the Box Office, employment law, shareholding, selling, speculating and so on. While this book aims to take note of all these, and more, those facets of theatre history which are emphasised here will not be emphasised by another historian. Everything is provisional.

What is clear is that the theatre is a natural forum for the airing of matters of public concern and for public debate. It is no surprise to learn that the Roman theatre building was situated adjacent to the temple and the forum. Theatre has always been a space where identities, especially social and national identities, have been rehearsed and defined. While John Bale was strutting the stage asserting the Protestant narrative of English history, in many towns and cities the old mystery cycles were affirming a quite different story. Moreover, the theatre itself is a potent metaphor for society and social identity. Performances present kings, processions, riots, love-making, arguments, while in its configuration the space where these things are shown mirrors the social context, whether spectators gather round informally or are segregated into private boxes, a pit and a gallery. British theatre exhibits changing British identities.

These identities express the ideologies which parade on the stage. The theatre does not merely express these identities or ideologies, however; rather it is a battleground for competing identities and ideologies, which constantly conflict and destabilise one another: they change, and adapt and fade. At different times, and in different ways, the theatre reinforces or challenges prevailing ideologies. For in the theatre ideas are embodied and made immediate and potent. It is part of the quest of this book to explore how this happens.

The British theatre has suffered from a confusion between text and performance: the written play text has too often been accorded primacy over the performance. This perhaps derives from the eighteenth-century scholars who produced editions of Shakespeare's and other 'old plays', and allowed supremacy to the lexicographer Samuel Johnson. Such an approach makes it difficult to understand why Shakespeare was so careless about the publication of his written texts. But Shakespeare, even if his poetic gifts were unique, was a theatre practitioner before everything, and he knew that the written text was no more than a blueprint for performance, and probably in his eyes for performance by a particular company, the King's Men. Perhaps Ben Jonson may be held responsible for the long-standing supremacy of the word on the British stage, since he was the first to publish his plays in a scholarly edition, thereby making them into literary 'works'.

On the stage, words interact with what is seen, and what is seen often bears more weight in the imagination. Indeed we say we go to 'see' a play, and theatregoing could be regarded as a specialised form of voyeurism. Spectators sit in the dark (at least in the modern theatre), solitary in public, neither private nor sociable, gazing at the bodies performing in front of them. Performance is fluid, elusive and dissolves distinctions between fantasy and reality. It has its own relationship with theatre, the two circling one another like boxers. This book, a history of theatre *and performance*, aims to see where the punches land.

Performance is framed in time and space. It has its own conventions and techniques. Its authorship belongs to the actors and also to the designers, costumiers and others. The playwright's contribution is inflected by intertextuality: meaning is enriched by a knowledge of earlier productions of the play, as well as of others in a similar *genre*. 'Performance' and 'theatre' merge in the theatrical event.

The theatrical event consists of everything that happens in and around the presentation of the play, from the moment the first person involved in it, performer or spectator or other functionary, leaves home for the theatre; perhaps even from the moment the first ticket is bought, or from the moment it is decided to present the play. It lasts until the theatre is empty again, or the last participant is at home, in bed and asleep. But who knows what dreams will occur then? Seventeenth- and eighteenth-century practitioners knew something of how a performance must be led into and, at the end, laid aside, as their Prologues and Epilogues attest.

The audience completes the performance. If the performance embodies ideas, the ideas are tested against the audience's responses, and it is the audience which finally constructs the meaning. One strand in the history of the British theatre is the contest for who owns the theatre. Is it the management, the performers, the spectators, a combination of these or the prevailing larger political government with its urge to censor and forbid? The question is urgent because the performance liberates fantasy, fear, laughter, at deep levels; it provokes pleasure or shame, or it energises spectators almost as no other art form. What the long-term effects of any playgoing may be has never been calculated – perhaps it never could be.

Spectators are thus in a liminal mode, accepting the events on stage as both not real and real. They operate on several levels at once, as S.L. Bethell noticed almost a century ago[2] simultaneously following the play as story, admiring (or criticising) the acting, suffering with the characters, and yet aware all the time that they are in a theatre.

Theatre is a collective creation, involving not only all the elements of performance, context and presentation, but also the audience's imaginations, in differing social and political circumstances. Complex, fascinating and elusive as all this is, it is the subject of this book.

*   *   *

It is hoped that the illustrations in this book will illuminate the subject. But they should be regarded with care. Paintings do not have the accuracy which we look for in photographs, but even photographs are constructed from contemporary critical ideas, aesthetic prejudices, commercial motivations and so on. They, like paintings and other forms of illustration, also respond to the conventions of both the theatre itself and of pictorial art.

*   *   *

The author of a study of this length owes an incalculable debt to many people who have discussed, debated and argued with him. Sometimes they have read and criticised draft chapters. I wish to record my sincere thanks to all of them. A special debt of gratitude is owed to the staff at Routledge for their patience, encouragement and tact: to Talia Rodgers for having the nous or nerve to commission the book in the first place; to my editor, Ben Piggott; to Harriet Affleck and Kate Edwards; and to all those who have helped the book on its way. Some of the illustrations were found by Paul Brotherston, but the vast majority were discovered and tracked down by Jo Walton. Without her persistence, knowledge, sheer hard work and indulgence of a demanding author, this book would simply not be what it is. My thanks to her are immeasurable. A huge debt is also owed to the staff at the National Library of Scotland, whose Reading Room I have haunted for years. And my deep gratitude goes to a few people whose interest and encouragement have sustained me through many an arduous search or self-doubting season, and who have often supplied invaluable words of advice or nuggets of information, including Angela Bull, Peter Hoad, John Milligan, Claire Pençak, Olga Taxidou, John Topping and, above all, Joy Parker.

NOTES

1 John M. East, *Neath the Mask*, London: G. Allen and Unwin, 1967, p. 76.
2 S.L. Bethell, *Shakespeare and the Popular Dramatic Tradition*, London: Staples Press, 1944.

Prologue: The Romans in Britain

The Romans loved theatre. Wherever they went they built theatres (and circular amphitheatres for games, gladiator contests, chariot races and so on), and Britain was no exception.

ROMAN THEATRES IN BRITAIN

Traces of up to ten built theatres have been found here. The oldest, which is mentioned in Tacitus's account of Boudicca's revolt, is in Colchester in Maidenborough Street and may have been built around 50AD before the conquest was complete. Another is nearby at Gosbeck's Farm. St Alban's had a theatre built around 150AD. There were two theatres in Canterbury and others in Faversham in Kent, Cirencester, Brough-on-Humber, Catterick in Yorkshire and Caister-by-Norwich in East Anglia.

Like other theatres across the Roman Empire, these buildings were largely modelled on the theatres at Rome, like Pompey's 55BCE theatre-cum-temple complex dedicated to Venus Victrix, which was set beside a new Senate House, gardens, shops and statues in what David Wiles calls 'the world's first arts centre'.[1] Julius Caesar's, later Augustus's, Theatre of Marcellus was linked to the temple to Apollo, and it is recorded that Antony and Octavius sat on their thrones in triumph in the orchestra of this theatre after the defeat of Pompey.

These links to temples and politics were significant. The Romans did not separate theatre from politics or religion, and the story of British theatre for the following two millennia reveals similar constant, if often denied, links. At Canterbury, the theatre was adjacent to the *temenos*, the sacred enclosure or precinct of the temple, to its west; the forum, the place where political debate was conducted, to the north west; and the public baths to the north. Similar dispositions were common throughout the empire, and in Britain the theatres at St Alban's, Colchester, Gosbeck's Farm and Caistor-by-Norwich were all situated close to political, religious and social places.

THE ARCHITECTURE OF THE ROMAN THEATRE

The ground plan of these theatres was D-shaped. The semi-circular *cavea*, or auditorium, was steeply banked and seated up to ten thousand spectators. It was divided by a central corridor from the orchestra to an exit at ground level at the back, which was useful for processions. In front of these seats was the D-shaped orchestra which was backed by the stage, which was raised nearly

Figure 0.1
Remains of the Roman theatre at St Alban's
Source: Photo Carole Raddato

two metres from the orchestra. Because the seating ran round to the edges of the stage, the stage itself was often twice the width of the orchestra, its depth being about a quarter of its length. The stage itself was walled off at the back and on both sides, the side walls often containing doors, perhaps to foyers, and it was covered with a roof. The frontage of the stage building formed the rear of the stage. It was as high, sometimes higher, than the tallest point of the *cavea*, that is, ten metres or more, and usually had two or even three storeys of columns as well as three doors giving onto the stage itself. The central door was reserved for the leading actor, the one to the right for the second actor and the left-hand one for any other actors. In front of the stage building, however, was sometimes a curtain which was lowered at the beginning of the performance and raised at its conclusion. The stage building contained dressing rooms, storage space and so on.

PERFORMANCES

These theatres staged rituals like animal sacrifices, religious processions and incense burning, but also concerts, debates and, of course, plays. It is highly unlikely that any of the dramas of Plautus or Seneca were seen here. The productions were probably more like variety shows, with acrobats, jugglers and singers appearing beside entertainments which later ages would more easily recognise as drama, but it should be remembered that for the Romans, theatre performances did not involve Greek *mimesis*, but rather consisted of *ludi*, games.

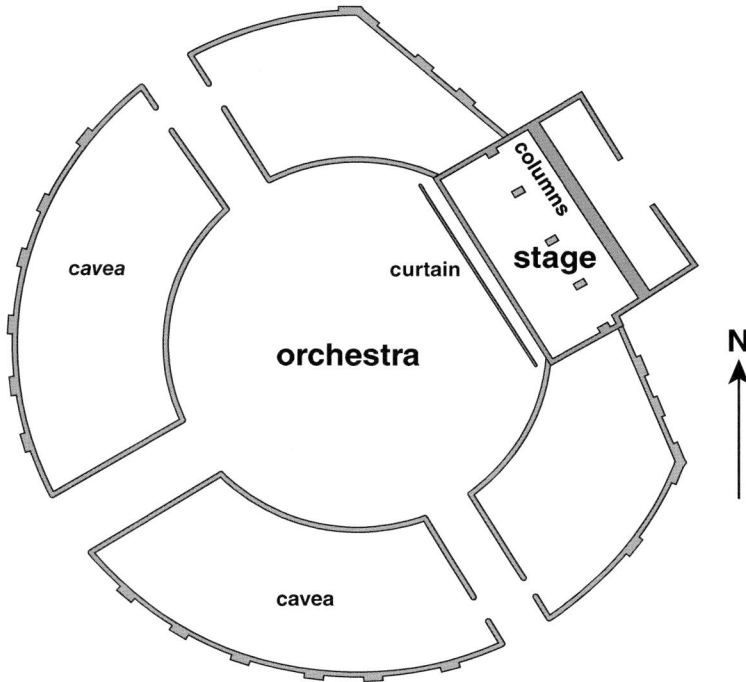

Figure 0.2
Plan of the Roman theatre at St Alban's. The D-shaped orchestra is surrounded by the *cavea*, where the audience was situated, and gave onto the raised stage with its columns

Tragedies were sung by solo performers like storytellers or ballad singers. *Mimes* were spoken plays which *mimicked* life and sometimes involved large casts and violent action. *Pantomimes*, often satirical or even blasphemous, were solo performances, danced or mimed to spoken or sung commentary or explanation. Pantomime performers could become stars in their own right, with large popular followings.

PERFORMERS

Perhaps Vecunda, an actress whose name has fortuitously been preserved on a shard of pottery found near Leicester, was such a star. She was, interestingly, a woman, when most performers were male. She was almost certainly a member of one of the surprisingly large strolling companies which performed in these theatres, as well as in the homes of aristocrats and other venues. They wore large, grotesque masks, happy or sad, up to a dozen of which have been found in Britain, including a small ivory tragic mask found at Caerleon. Their costumes were symbolic, not realistic. Thus, upper-class characters sported purple, while the poor wore red. A soldier was recognisable from his cloak and a slave from his short tunic.

THE END OF THE ROMAN THEATRE

With the collapse of the Roman Empire around 400AD, the theatres fell into disuse, the strolling companies broke up, and – though probably itinerant entertainers were never absent from life in the post-Roman period – it would be centuries before anything which could properly be called theatre again took hold in Britain.

NOTE

1 David Wiles, *A Short History of Western Performance Space*, Cambridge: Cambridge University Press, 2003, p. 177.

SELECT BIBLIOGRAPHY

Millett, Martin, Revell, Louise, and Moore, Alison, *The Oxford Handbook of Roman Britain*, Oxford: Oxford University Press, 2016
Sear, Frank, *Roman Theatres: An Architectural Study*, Oxford: Oxford University Press, 2006
Wacher, John, *A Portrait of Roman Britain*, London: Routledge, 2000
Wiles, David, *A Short History of Western Performance Space*, Cambridge: Cambridge University Press, 2003

PART ONE

THEATRE BEFORE THEATRES

Timeline

	Society	Theatre
c.1300		Anon, *The Interlude of the Student and the Girl*
1328	Birth of John Wycliffe	
1343	Birth of Geoffrey Chaucer	
1348	The Black Death	
1351	Statute of Labourers	
1376		Earliest reference to York mystery play
1377	Poll Tax	
1381	Peasants Revolt under Wat Tyler	
c.1397		Anon, *The Castle of Perseverance*
1399	Richard II deposed by Henry IV	
1414	Sir John Oldcastle's rebellion	
1420s		Lydgate's mummings
1422		Earliest reference to Chester mystery play Earliest reference to Robin Hood play, Exeter
1450	Jack Cade's rebellion	
c.1461		Anon, *The Play of the Sacrament*
c.1465		Anon, *Mankind*
1473		W. Woode, actor, leaves Sir George Paston's service
1485	Death of Richard III: accession of Henry VII	
1488	Accession of James IV of Scotland	

1492	Columbus reaches America	Roger Marchell as Robin Hood charged with threatening a riot
c.1497		Henry Medwell, *Fulgens and Lucres*
c.1500		Anon, *The Summoning of Everyman* Anon, *Mary Magdalene*
1501	Katherine of Aragon's entry into London	
1503		English King's Men perform at the wedding of King of Scotland to Margaret Tudor
1509	Death of Henry VII: accession of Henry VIII	
1513	Death of James IV: accession of James V of Scotland	
1516	Erasmus, *The Education of a Christian Prince* Thomas More, *Utopia*	
c.1519		John Skelton, *Magnificence*
1520	Field of the Cloth of Gold	Thomas Heywood, *The Four PP*
1527		*Love and Riches* staged at Greenwich
1530	Death of Cardinal Wolsey	
1533	Henry VIII marries Anne Boleyn Patch, Henry VIII's Fool, dismissed for denigrating Anne Boleyn and Princess Elizabeth	
1535	Sir Richard Morrison urges the use of drama for anti-Catholic propaganda	John Kyllour, *History of Christ's Passion*, Stirling, Scotland
1537–40		John Bale leads Cromwell's Men, performing Protestant plays
1538		John Bale, *King Johan*
1542	Birth of Mary, Queen of Scots Death of James V of Scotland: regency	
1540	Fall and execution of Thomas Cromwell	
1547	Death of Henry VIII: accession of Edward VI	
1548		Hereford City Council abolishes its mystery play
1552	John Bale appointed Bishop of Ossory	Sir David Lindsay, *Ane Satire of the Thrie Estaitis*, Cupar, Fife George Ferrers Lord of Misrule at Greenwich

1553	Death of Edward VI: accession of Mary	Mr S. Master of Art, *Gammer Gurton's Needle*
1554	Birth of Sir Philip Sidney	
1558	Death of Mary; accession of Elizabeth I	
1560		Death of the clown, Will Somer
1561		Thomas Norton and Thomas Sackville, *Gorboduc* Edinburgh attempts to ban Robin Hood plays
1567	Mary, Queen of Scots, replaced by her son, James VI	
1568		W. Wager, *The Longer Thou Livest*
1575	Elizabeth I's visitation to Kenilworth, Woodstock, etc.	Probable last performance of Chester mystery play

Chapter 1: The earliest British performances

The Roman theatre was essentially an import. The indigenous theatre's beginnings are, as may be expected, often cloaked in fragmentary documents and disputed records. But that there was theatrical life in Britain after the Romans left can hardly be doubted. Itinerant jongleurs – singers, musicians, dancers – were probably roaming the country before the Norman invasion, and later we hear of 'goliards', entertainers who were formerly monks or clerks, but who perhaps preferred an alternative lifestyle. The first workable evidence probably comes from the palace of Northumbrian King Edwin at Yeavering in the seventh century. Here there are what appear to be the remains of a theatre, and there is some difficult evidence to suggest that Christian dramas may have been performed here.

'QUEM QUAERITIS'

More certainly, the earliest record of the 'Quem quaeritis' trope – the dialogue spoken by priests enacting the visit to Christ's empty tomb after the resurrection – occurs at Winchester towards the end of the tenth century. A hundred years later there is recorded in Canterbury a trope concerning Christ's Ascension. And there is more from the twelfth century: plays based on the Biblical stories performed outside churches, a play of St Catherine given at Dunstable before King Henry I, and by the middle of the century fragments of a dramatic dialogue, perhaps written by a clerk, Laurentius, who thus is probably our earliest known dramatist. Some years later, miracle and saints plays were staged in London, and other religious dramas in Lichfield and Eynsham. Elsewhere clerks presented imitations of Latin plays, such as *Babio*, probably written by Walter Map.

DRAMA AND DANGER

In the thirteenth century the records become fuller. There was the case of a peasant called Thurkill in Stistead, Essex, who had a vision much like a stage play, in which sinners were compelled to act out their sins watched by an audience of devils 'as if at a merry show'. A very few years later the subdeacon of Salisbury condemned performers in masks who performed plays of 'dishonest imaginings' and sang indecent satirical songs. King John watched what was probably a secular play in 1210, and in 1214 Alexander II of Scotland refused to watch a play because he was in mourning. At the same time there are records of civic pageantry, as in London at the royal entry in 1207, and increasingly sophisticated tournaments, with the participants costumed and playing the parts of various famous

Figure 1.1
The early sixteenth-century Easter altar piece at St Margaret South Elmham, typical of those before which the climax of the earliest liturgical dramas was performed

Source: Photo David/CC BY-SA 2.0

champions. The rulers were learning that theatrical performance was a useful way of demonstrating their power, a lesson which would be put to uncompromising use in the following two centuries.

SOME EARLY INTERLUDES

Dramatic activity increased in the fourteenth century. *The Interlude of the Student and the Girl*, dating from about 1300, consists of two fragments of dialogue, in the first of which the student protests his love to the unsympathetic girl, while in the second he seeks help with his suit from 'Mother Eloise'. This seems to be what could be termed an 'interlude'. In 1323 Edward II kept a group of four clerks to perform interludes for him, and a few years later a performance of the interlude, *Pride of Life*, is recorded. Groups of itinerant players who presented 'clerk's plays', probably similar to these, were found at Oxford in 1360, Reading in 1382 and New Romney in 1387. On the other hand, the clerks of Exeter were recorded behaving less properly in 1333, when they appeared in masks and disrupted the Feast of the Holy Innocents with 'shrieks of laughter, obscene gestures and drunken revelry'.

More seemly miracle plays were also being performed in the fourteenth century – at Lanercost Priory near Carlisle, for instance, before the Queen in 1307, and in the market place at Carlisle in 1345. The earliest morality plays date from a little later: the York Paternoster play was performed around 1385 and *The Castle of Perseverance* in East Anglia in about 1397.

The variety and range of these references demonstrate an impressive – if now largely lost – theatrical and performing culture at all levels of society in the early middle ages.

Chapter 2: Performing power

MUMMINGS

Theatre is the most public of the arts. This gives it greater potential than any other art form for intervention in public affairs. It is not surprising therefore that many of the earliest records of theatrical activity in medieval Britain involve a theatricalisation of political power.

One example was the visit during the extended Christmas celebrations of January 1377 of the Lord Mayor and 130 leading citizens to the young prince who in a few months would become Richard II. They set out from London in the dead of night, in flamboyant costumes, carrying flaming torches and accompanied by suitable music. They reached Kennington, where Richard was staying, and seemingly spontaneously engaged in a 'mumming': they played dice with the prince, with equipment loaded to ensure he won the golden trophies – cup, ball and ring – as well as other prizes won for the queen and the Duke of Lancaster. Then they joined the royal party in dancing and feasting. But they never revealed their identities and left as unknown, apparently, as when they arrived. The effect of the event was to reinforce the prince's potency, and the dependence of the others on his authority.

This event used the convention known as 'mumming', when disguised visitors called on a house, or mansion, played dice for food or money, and then, after dancing and eating, departed. They had to keep their masks on at all times, and indeed keep silent, or 'mum', for if they were recognised, they got no prizes. Mummings varied according to circumstances: they might be little more than we would expect from three or four Hallowe'en trick-or-treaters today, or they might present something highly elaborate, with staged effects and spectacular moving scenery; and they might perform to music or even in silence, or employ a Presenter or Narrator to give their exhibition a more dramatic character.

Such disguisings were often attached to royal progresses, as well as to civic pageants, religious festivals and so on. There were, for example, further mummings for Richard II at Christmas 1392 at Eltham Palace in Kent, in 1393 at Westminster, and again in 1395. And when Henry IV replaced Richard, he was greeted by Londoners in a Christmas mumming. The best known mummings date from the 1420s when the court poet, John Lydgate, devised several, some of which have been preserved. Devised for Henry VI or for the Lord Mayor of London or one or other of the livery companies of the capital, Lydgate's narrations accompanied the shows. In *A Mumming at Eltham* he used a classical story and the mummers were disguised as Ceres, Juno and Bacchus; his *Mumming* at *Bishop's Wood* featured the god Flora and a personification of Spring; *A Mumming for the Goldsmiths* used Fortune as Narrator, and introduced a group of Levites who sang while the Ark of the Covenant was brought in as a gift to the mayor; and *A Mumming for the Mercers* included the group of mummers entering the hall in a huge (presumably wheeled) ship. Best known is Lydgate's *Mumming at Hertford* in which six peasant husbands, with names like Robin the Reeve, Colin Cobbler and Bartholomew the Butcher, complained to the King about their wives, named as Beatrice Bittersweet, Cicely Sourcheer and so on. One of the women rebutted the husbands' claims, and at the end, all twelve were enjoined to return in a year to hear the monarch's judgement. His wisdom, as well as his power, were implicitly acknowledged.

Yet perhaps these mummings were not always what they seemed. In 1414 the Lollard leader, Sir John Oldcastle, plotted to take advantage of the Twelfth Night mumming at Eltham to capture the king and seize power himself. The plot was discovered and Oldcastle fled into hiding, but his adventure suggests the inherent danger in troupes of men going about disguised after dark.

And even the acceptable face of mumming could be more ambivalent than it seemed. Lydgate's civic mummings, for instance, seemed to present overtly benign attitudes to immigrants. Foreigners were welcome to London, the performances seemed to say. Thus, the *Mumming for the Mercers* presented Jupiter who had travelled across Africa and Europe to London, and now brought with him three ships with immigrants who greeted the Mayor. All was harmony. *The Mumming for the Goldsmiths* presented Levites – foreigners – who would keep London safe with their Ark. But this was 1429, when other attitudes to foreigners were held by powerful people. England was at war. An invasion from France was feared. The mummings put perhaps the guilds' alternative view to the imperialist ambitions of the king and court: these were, after all, people with whom they wanted to do business. But the matter was still more complicated than this. The London merchants paradoxically were also keen to exclude foreigners from membership of their guilds, and thereby freeze them out of business.

In the mummings, the characters were not real foreigners: members of the Guild had dressed up as aliens. They were welcomed, but in the subordinate position of those bearing gifts and greetings. The threat from foreign competitors was thereby reduced. Indeed, the foreigners were objectified in a classic example of 'Orientalism': they represented not real Dutch or Spanish merchants in competition with Guild members, but distant Africans or figures from the Old Testament. Moreover, the fact that these visitations occurred not during business hours but during a festival further diluted any threat they might seem to carry. In other words, Lydgate offered an ambivalent resolution to the pressing conundrum of how to expand foreign trade yet maintain a practical monopoly.

PROCESSIONS AND ENTRIES

Mummings were complemented by more formal processions and entries into the city. For instance, exactly contemporary with Lydgate's mummings, in 1426, the Duke and Duchess of Bedford were welcomed into London, he being Lord Protector of the realm during Henry VI's minority, with a spectacular pageant on London Bridge: children as angels sang from two specially constructed towers, while giant puppets of Biblical figures, heroes from Greek mythology and, finally, the Duke himself, were paraded before him. In 1494 Henry VII attended a spectacular Twelfth Night

Figure 1.2
This illustration from *The Romance of Alexander* conveys the splendour of some royal pageants

Source: Pictures From History/akg-images

pageant about St George which was specifically 'designed to exhibit the power and magnificence of the monarch'.[1]

PAGEANTS FOR KATHERINE OF ARAGON

Over the next half century a series of astonishing shows were mounted to welcome the Tudor queens to London. When Katherine of Aragon arrived in 1501 to marry Prince Arthur, she was greeted by 'perhaps the most original and complex essay in the pageant medium ever presented in England'.[2]

As she was escorted into the city, she stopped six times before different pageants which dramatised a mythical quest for 'Honour'. In the first pageant, presented on London Bridge, St Katherine, supported by St Ursula, reminded the would-be princess that her first 'mate' must be Christ, but that Prince Arthur would be her second. Adherence to these two would bring her honour:

> With the second, an Honour temporal;
> And with the first, Glory perpetual.

In the pageant, St Katherine was seated in a kind of tabernacle, accompanied by a host of virgins. The tabernacle was decorated with images of the Trinity and an image of the garter and the Tudor rose. Posts at each side sported ostrich feathers and portcullises with rampant lions bearing the shield of England, and all were painted gilt and gold and blue.

In Gracechurch Street, the second pageant presented 'The Castle of Policy, Noblesse and Virtue', whose players welcomed Katherine from a castle of wood and canvas surmounted by a golden crown, garters, fleur-de-lys, a golden portcullis, white harts and peacocks and clouds pierced with sunbeams. Next, at the Conduit in Cornhill, was a scene of imitation marble pillars, dragons, lions, a huge zodiac and a blue 'sphere of the moon'. And so it continued until she reached 'The Throne of Honour', where two empty thrones were seen, 'one for your noble spouse, and that other for you'.

ANNE BOLEYN AND HENRY VIII

This splendour was virtually matched in 1533 when Anne Boleyn, on the day before her coronation, arrived in London by boat, with an accompanying barge in which a huge dragon continually breathed real fire as it swung on deck among monsters and wildmen. In a separate barge, maidens sang and played music, while in another, decked in cloth of gold and fine silk, were trumpeters and tinkling bells. In 1540, Anne of Cleves, Henry's fourth wife, was welcomed in similarly superb fashion when she arrived in London.

Such shows were only part of the Tudor exhibition of power. More like dramas, perhaps, were entertainments like that at New Year, 1512, when six captive ladies were revealed in an elaborate castle; six men, including Henry VIII himself, attacked the castle and rescued the ladies, whom they invited to dance with them. In 1514 the famous Field of the Cloth of Gold was an almost unparalleled display of regal magnificence, and at the height of the formal ceremonies an enormous puppet serpent, spouting fire, appeared in the air, terrifying many of those who were present. And in 1527, the entertainment for the French Ambassadors at Greenwich Palace included an address by an actor dressed as Mercury, a 'dispute' between Love and Riches, six lords descending from a stage scenery rock to dance with ladies in the hall and maskers who also danced before revealing their identities. There followed a huge banquet.

QUEEN ELIZABETH I AND THE ROYAL PROGRESS

But surely the most notable of all these theatricalised displays of Tudor magnificence and political power were those granted to Queen Elizabeth I as she made her lengthy progresses through England. Wherever she went she was presented with more or less dramatic entertainments, in which she was celebrated as quasi-divine, or else made the object of near religious adoration. The Virgin Queen seemed almost to be replacing the Catholic Virgin Mary whose pre-eminence had been destroyed when the Roman Catholic Church was uprooted. So at Sudely, she was greeted by an ancient shepherd who offered her gifts and everlasting obedience, and she was asked to offer her protection to Daphne against the passionate pursuit of the god Apollo. At Kenilworth, she was greeted by giant trumpeters – actually men behind, or perhaps within, enormous puppets – and she watched an Italian tumbler 'whose feats of agility' included 'goings, turnings, tumblings, castings, hops, jumps, leaps, skips, springs, gambado, somersaults, caprettie and flights: forward, backward, sideways, downward, upward and with sundry windings, gyrings and circumflexions; also lightly and with such easiness'.[3] She watched an Italian *Commedia dell'arte* troupe, probably the famous Gelosi, with a band of black musicians, and later, the Lady of the Lake, on a moveable island blazing with torches, drifted towards her and offered her obeisance.

Perhaps most famously, at Woodstock, a pair of linked dramas, presented on successive days, employed music, dramatic texts and visual and emblematic images to assert the royal power and dignity which she embodied. She herself took a symbolic but central role in the proceedings. On the first day was recited *The Tale of Hermetes*, concerning the adventures of three questing knights. Their seeking was only resolved when the 'most virtuous lady in the world' (that is, Elizabeth herself)

Figure 1.3
A *commedia dell'arte* performance by the Gelosi troupe

Source: Musée Carnavalet, Paris

appeared. Then the Queen of the Fairies was drawn in on her wagon of state, complete with six children. The Fairy Queen addressed the real queen, offered her a rich embroidered gown and her court ladies each a nosegay with an appropriate verse attached. A larger bouquet, with lines of Italian verse, was presented to Elizabeth herself. As the queen left the scene of this triumph, the twilight was filled with strange music made apparently from an old oak tree. The following day she was presented with an acted comedy with nine characters, concerning the conflict between love and riches. She was, apparently, highly pleased.

THE USES OF ENTERTAINMENT

It was above all the *usefulness* of these forms of entertainment which made them so attractive to power. They demonstrated dominion vividly and unequivocally. But the potential ambivalence of performative embodiment also enabled some entertainments to make more than merely laudatory statements. Glynne Wickham has drawn attention to the gorgeous entry of Richard II into London in 1392, after he had transferred his court to York and sacrificed certain of London's traditional liberties in the process. Patriotic pageants on Cheapside and Temple Bar struck a cautionary tone which advised the king to return to former – to them, more satisfactory – arrangements. He did. And a hundred years later, in Bristol, a pageant featuring the legendary King Bremius appealed for help against a slump in trade, to which Henry VII immediately responded.

GORBODUC

Most interesting in this respect, perhaps, was the performance of Thomas Norton and Thomas Sackville's *Gorboduc, or The Tragedy of Ferrex and Porrex*, probably the first blank verse tragedy in English. It was presented privately to Queen Elizabeth at Westminster by 'the gentlemen of the Inner Temple' in January 1562. The two authors were ardent Protestants, who had both seen the inside of a gaol in consequence of their beliefs. Norton probably chaired the Committee of MPs, which in 1563 recommended the Queen to marry. These were troubling times for the Protestant masculine hegemony: Elizabeth, like her predecessor, her half-sister Mary, was female and without an heir, unless it were Mary, Queen of Scots, another woman, and a Catholic to boot. If the queen's gender was a problem for Norton and Sackville, her unmarried state was perhaps worse and seemed to them to threaten the very stability of the state. She needed a man, and if possible, an Englishman. Robert Dudley, who presided over the Inner Temple's Christmas revels that year, and who was available since the mysterious death of his wife two years earlier, was implicitly the authors' choice of husband for Elizabeth. *Gorboduc* tells the story of a monarch who divided his kingdom between his two sons, Ferrex and Porrex, an action which led inevitably to division and civil war, evoking memories of the bloody Wars of the Roses, concluded less than a century previously. The urgings of the Dudley-Norton-Sackville faction were underlined with a short piece which was performed with *Gorboduc* before the Queen, *Beauty and Desire*, a story of courtly wooing which ended with marriage and carried clear reference to Dudley as a potential consort for the queen. The whole performance, therefore, not only flattered the ruler, it also urged a particular course of action on her.

Figure 1.4
Title page of *The Tragedie of Gorboduc*, 1562

CIVIC SHOWS

Nor must it be imagined that performances of power and political contention were confined to royal matters. Anne Lancashire has described, for instance, the London Midsummer Watch, which until at least about 1550 provided the opportunity for different livery companies to flaunt their civic influence through shows, pageants and other presentations. Meanwhile, the increasingly significant Lord Mayor's Show was subsidised and produced, not by the royal household, but by the powerful city livery companies. These shows, too, exhibited a similar form of social, political and religious display which enhanced the importance of the patrons, and reconstructed, and perhaps idealised, the ideology underpinning the governance of city and country.

These forces are not yet dead. Even today in events like the Lord Mayor's Show, the state opening of Parliament and the Trooping of the Colour, pageantry and display help to ensure the continuance of the status quo. Whether other contemporary pageants, such as the Notting Hill Carnival, serve the same or a more subversive purpose may be disputed.

NOTES

1 Clifford Davidson, *Festivals and Plays in Late Medieval Britain*, Aldershot: Ashgate, 2007, p. 14.
2 Sydney Anglo, *Spectacle, Pageantry and Early Tudor Policy*, Oxford: Oxford University Press, 1969, p. 58.
3 Philip Butterworth, *Magic on the Early English Stage*, Cambridge: Cambridge University Press, 2005, p. 37.

Chapter 3: Playing and performing

The court was not the only early performance site. In the greater world beyond, there were professional strolling entertainers like tumblers, rope-dancers and jugglers, for whom records go back beyond the sixteenth century, as well as performances by local people at festivals usually tied to the agricultural calendar. Evidence for these is often scantier even than for court performances, and what there is frequently partial or partisan. Nevertheless, we can glimpse some vibrant popular dramatic activity.

The agricultural year was marked by a large number of traditional festivals, which the church often appropriated for a particular saint or Christian happening. Celebrations on these dates regularly took on a dramatic expression. The main festivals were, first, those clustered round Christmas and the New Year; then, Easter and the end of winter; and, finally, Whitsun, May Day, and midsummer.

BOY BISHOPS

The most notable of the winter performatives were those of the Boy Bishop and the Lord of Misrule. Boy Bishop festivities were to be found from the thirteenth century or earlier in many cathedrals and parishes across Britain. They usually began on St Nicholas's Day and involved choosing a boy chorister to act as bishop for three weeks or more, often ending on Holy Innocents Day. The boy chosen fulfilled all the duties and enjoyed all the privileges of the genuine bishop, including wearing his splendid robes of office, carrying the symbolic crozier and preaching significant sermons. In 1222 there were Boy Bishops in Salisbury, Oxford, Cambridge, Bristol, Lincoln and elsewhere. In 1283 a play was performed before the Boy Bishop in Gloucester. In 1299 the Boy Bishop said vespers before Edward I in Heton, near Newcastle-upon-Tyne. The custom continued until well into Tudor times. The Renaissance humanist and scholar, John Colet, who founded St Paul's School, expressly stated in the statutes of 1512 that on every Holy Innocents Day the pupils should 'come to St Paul's Church and hear the Child Bishop's sermon, and after be at the high mass, and each of them offer a penny to the Child Bishop'.

LORDS OF MISRULE

The Christmas Lord of Misrule, or 'master of merry disports' as Stubbs called him, was perhaps a kind of secular equivalent to the Boy Bishop. He presided over the Christmas entertainments in

Figure 1.5

Fools, musicians, dancers and other entertainers depicted on a five-hundred-year-old window at Betley in Staffordshire, now in the Victoria and Albert Museum, suggest the vibrant popular performance culture which existed before 1500

Source: British Library, London

the royal household most years during the reigns of Henry VII and Henry VIII, and the Mayor and sheriffs of London each supported their own Lords of Misrule. A little lower down the social scale, at the Inns of Court, for instance, and at many colleges, the position was often elective and lasted for twelve days when the Lord of Misrule instigated and superintended the seasonal diversions, which often had a burlesque or topsy-turvy flavour. Thus, George Ferrers, a respectable lawyer of Lincoln's Inn, was Lord of Misrule for the twelve days of Christmas when Edward VI's household was at Greenwich in 1551–2, and he spent over £500 producing a 'drunken masque', jousting, a mock midsummer night and a play with masks, as well as a spectacular entry into London. In 1562 Robert Dudley was Lord of Misrule in the Inner Temple, when Norton and Sackville's blank verse tragedy, *Gorboduc*, was presented before an audience including Queen Elizabeth I.

In his *Anatomy of Abuses* of 1583, Philip Stubbs described more popular Lord of Misrule playing. The 'Lord' and his followers dressed in gaudy and flamboyant costumes, with handkerchiefs 'borrowed for the most part of their pretty Mopsies and loving Bessies for bussing them in the dark'. Then

> their pipers piping, drummers thundering, their stumps dancing, their bells jingling, their handkerchiefs swinging about their heads like madmen, their hobby horses and other monsters skirmishing amongst the throng . . . they go to the church (though the minister be at prayer or preaching) . . . like devils incarnate, with such a confused noise that no man can hear his own voice. Then the foolish people, they look, they stare, they laugh, they fleer, and mount upon forms and pews, to see these goodly pageants . . . (then) they go into the churchyard where they have commonly their summer halls, their bowers, arbours and banqueting houses set up.[1]

Though Stubbs is an angry crusader against such popular pastimes, and is probably exaggerating to make his point, the nature of the play is plain and his general description probably accurate enough: the Lord of Misrule's play at Shrewsbury in 1525 had actors in false hair and beards, one wearing a jester's mask, and there were explosions and artificial smoke.

FESTIVALS AND DRAMA

Easter and springtime dramatic pastimes also often included dressing up and invading the church's space. The grounds claimed for this invasion may have been that money was being collected for the church, as in the Palm Sunday rituals when singers appeared as prophets for a musical performance which concluded with the tossing of flowers and cakes to the people, and the Hock Monday entertainments, which sometimes included scenes in which costumed knights battled one another or rescued imprisoned ladies. A more dubious Hocktide entertainment in Worcester in 1451 involved the women tying up the men one day and the men tying up the women the following day. It seems these were sexual games carried out in full view of passers-by: the players were 'pretending to increase church profit but earning a loss for the soul under false pretences'.

WOMEN AND FESTIVE DRAMA

Notable in the Hocktide entertainments is the fact of women performing, because their contribution to early drama has often been ignored or overlooked. In fact, evidence of the equal participation of women in these pastimes is quite extensive and should be borne in mind when considering many of the manifestations discussed here. In Lincolnshire, for example, women participated in traditional entertainments in Gainsborough, Boston, Stamford and Lincoln itself. The socio-religious St Anne's Guild of Lincoln included equal numbers of men and women, and their costumed processions took in not only display for its own sake but probably also tableaux and perhaps actual scenes presented on floats or small pageant wagons. There is plenty of evidence of women participating across the country: in rushbearing in Preston in Lancashire, for instance, or in the Christmas celebrations, May games and Whitsun ales throughout Gloucestershire, perhaps like Perdita's participation in the sheep-shearing festival in Shakespeare's *The Winter's Tale*. The subsequent sixteenth-century assault on traditional culture was probably undertaken at least partly because of female participation.

ST GEORGE

Somewhat better documented are the St George and the dragon 'ridings' which were fairly prevalent across the country in the fifteenth and sixteenth centuries. One version of this equestrian pastime was watched by Henry VII at Hereford in 1486, and random examples of recorded ridings include those in Woodbridge in Suffolk between 1475 and 1500, in Salisbury between 1478 and 1524, in Leicester (where citizens were instructed to 'attend' the mayor for the riding) around 1530 and in Stratford-upon-Avon between 1541 and 1557. The Norwich 'Snap Dragon', relic of

Figure 1.6
The famous Norwich 'Snap Dragon'
Source: Norfolk Museums Service (Norwich Castle Museum and Art Gallery)

the pageant of the Guild and Fraternity of St George, in which the giant puppet reputedly flapped its wings and breathed fire and smoke, is still preserved in the city's Castle Museum. At Reading in 1536, St George triumphed on a raised platform and the churchwardens paid for a special coat for the hero, as well as for 'roses, bells, girdle, sword and dagger', all 'at the charge of St George'.

ROBIN HOOD PLAYS

All these playings seem to offer an alternative set of values to those conventionally preached to the people – what may be called the values of holiday. And these are seen supremely to govern the most popular of the summer playings, the May games, or King games or Robin Hood games, which happened on May Day, or at Whitsun, or midsummer in very many different places. Stephen Knight has argued that those specifically connected to Robin Hood, the first of which is recorded at Exeter in 1422, were largely confined to the south and west of England (Scotland is a partly different case) because they derive from the French *pastourelle* tradition, and these were areas with French trading connections. But May games, which find their clearest expression in Robin Hood plays, were probably held virtually everywhere. Sir Richard Morrison wrote to Henry VIII in 1535:

> In summer, commonly upon Holy Days in most places of your Realm, there be plays of Robin Hood, Maid Marian, Friar Tuck wherein besides the lewdness and ribaldry that there is opened to the people, disobedience also to your officers is taught, whilst these good bloods go about to take from the Sheriff of Nottingham one that for offending the laws should have suffered execution.[2]

Morrison was of course making a special argument to do away with old forms of drama to make way for a new Protestant repertoire, but his reference to 'most parts' of the king's realm is clear. The implication of a letter from Sir John Paston, dated 16 April 1473, also challenges the idea that Robin Hood plays were confined to the south and west. Writing from his home in Norfolk, Paston regrets that his servant, W. Woode, is to leave him, since he had 'kept him this 3 year to play *St George* and *Robin Hood and the Sheriff of Nottingham*'.

The Robin Hood plays seem to have had three sections (or acts, perhaps). First, the young men in their green costumes entered the village. Perhaps they had been in the woods overnight, or they may have arrived from a nearby village, but their processional entry was significant. They seemed to represent a freer, unenclosed, 'natural' world. They brought with them the bounty of summer – blossom, greenery – and set up a 'bower' and perhaps a maypole. How elaborate this was might vary, but in 1566 the churchwardens in St Helen's, Abingdon, paid as much as eighteen pence 'for setting up Robin Hood's bower'. Even more splendid was the one Henry VIII and his queen were invited to in 1515. Hall's chronicle recorded that 'there was an arbour made of boughs, with a hall and a great chamber and an inner chamber very well made and covered with flowers and sweet herbs'.

The second act seems to have had a set core, but plenty of scope for improvisation. In the earliest Robin Hood play to survive, dating from about 1475, a knight and a sheriff plot to capture Robin Hood. Robin and the knight then compete at archery, at stone throwing, at tossing a heavy pole and at wrestling, finally drawing their swords and fighting to the death. Robin is triumphant. It is these contests, athletic or combative, which form the heart of the plays. In the second play, preserved on the same scrap of manuscript as the first, the central act is an archery contest between Little John and Friar Tuck, a skirmish in which the sheriff captures them both, and then their rescue by Robin. In *Robin Hood and the Friar*, published about 1600, there is a series of confrontations between Robin and a Friar: the Friar throws Robin into a stream, fights him with quarterstaffs and after a general melée is rewarded with membership of the band as well as a 'lady free' which much delights him. In the perhaps incomplete *Robin Hood and the Potter* Robin breaks the pots of Jack, the potter's boy, and when the potter himself arrives, he fights Robin. The outcome is unclear.

If the centre of this act is the contest in which Robin competes with his adversary, it seems probable that the local villagers could pit their strength against him, too, in a kind of come-all-ye challenge like that in *As You Like It* when Orlando challenges Charles, the Duke's wrestler. By participating in the loosely controlled drama, spectators could identify themselves with the young men who were performing. There are hints of social protest: Robin defeats authority in the person of the knight; the Dionysian Friar escapes his Order to find food, drink and sexual adventure; the potter, a representative of money-based trade, a sort of embryonic capitalist, perhaps, has his wares destroyed. The villager who participated in the sports was often given a badge to show he was a member of Robin's band, thereby tacitly endorsing the implied social critique.

The third act of the Robin Hood game was the *quête*, the communal celebratory dancing and feasting after the entertainments and competitive sports were over. Communal feasting is an important means of expressing togetherness, and contemporary records, like that of 1505, when the Robin Hood troupe from Finchhamstead were provided with 'supper' at Reading, make this clear. One of the features of Henry VIII's 1515 Robin Hood adventure was the venison and wine that were served. The second part of the *quête*, before the procession's final departure, was also important: it involved the collection of money.

As suggested, the Robin Hood plays, like the ceremony of the Boy Bishop and the entertainments of the Lord of Misrule, carry a hint of political or social dissidence. Jack Cade, leader of the 1450 defeated rebellion, performed his power like a kind of Summer King of Misrule, dressing in flamboyant finery and having an unsheathed sword carried before him as he moved about. These carnivalesque merrymakings may be clownish, unpredictable and violent, but they also suggest the world turned upside down. In the plays we have, Robin Hood frequently disguises himself – he dons the defeated knight's horse-hide garments, he pretends to be the potter, and he is in disguise when he first meets the Friar – behaviour which implies danger or subversion. And occasionally we see tangible evidence of this: in 1492, at the Court of the Star Chamber, a complaint was brought against Roger Marchell of Wednesbury in the West Midlands, that he, as Robin Hood, with a hundred men, had descended on Willenhall Fair where he had met William Milner, impersonating the Abbot of Marham, and eighty of his followers and threatened a riot. This sounds like a blockbuster version of the Robin Hood play described earlier, though it may be that Milner's band joined Marchell's and real insurrection was threatened. Marchell's defence, however, was that they were raising money for the church. And indeed the money raised by these summer games seems usually to have gone on such admirable projects as repairing the church roof, mending the local roads or providing relief for the poor. The Robin Hood Guild in Woodbury, Devon, made a series of surprisingly large donations to the local church between about 1475 and 1520.

The way Robin Hood emerges from the forest, with his men in green, his sprigs of blossom and his maypole, suggests another association, one with disturbing pagan deities like the Green Man, or Wildman or Robin Goodfellow. The poet Langland identified Robin Hood with a deadly sin, Sloth, and the obsessively reforming Bishop Latimer agreed. Intending to preach one Sunday in the 1549, he found the church closed and locked.

> I tarried there half an hour or more, at last the key was found, and one of the parish comes to me and says, 'Sir, this is a busy day with us, we cannot hear you, it is Robin Hood's day. The parish are gone abroad to gather for Robin Hood. I pray you, let (obstruct) them not'. I thought my rochet (priest's surplice) should have been regarded, though I were not, but it would not serve, it was fain to give place to Robin Hood's men.

However, it is also true that the Robin Hood games seem very often to have been organised by the parish guilds and, as has already been noted, to have been associated with the local church. Certainly, in one incarnation, the elusive Robin was a noted devotee of the Virgin, whose cult was at its height in the thirteenth century. Though it is true that the cult became noted for social conviviality in its later manifestations, it is also true that in at least some stories Robin Hood is renowned for his piety. The contradiction is encapsulated in the report from Stratton in Cornwall in 1535 when the churchwarden played Little John, yet the bower was filled with 'maidens', whose behaviour seems to have been less than wholly decorous. And there is a corbel in Exeter Cathedral which depicts the Virgin and child standing above the head of the Green Man. One critic suggests that

> this image integrally weds the iconography of the Virgin with that of the Green Man in a positive rather than ominous symbiosis. . . . (It) celebrates her motherhood, as her child chucks her chin and Mary herself smiles just as much as the 'happy' Green Man who supports her.[3]

But another critic simply describes this as the Virgin treading the Green Man underfoot.[4]

Robin Hood plays were clearly dynamic and hugely popular. Like the Christmas Lord of Misrule entertainments and perhaps the spring Saint George ridings, too, they released working people from poverty and their day-to-day drudgery. They brought a whiff of holiday to those whose toil was long, and sometimes they seemed to flout authority. There may have very rarely been any overt or articulated political agenda – Robin Hood players were not required actually to rob the rich and give to the poor, nor to embrace the tenets of Lollardism, nor to endorse the aims of Wat Tyler and the peasants in revolt. But the plays did free often deadened imaginations, and they did offer a glimpse of alternative possibilities.

NOTES

1 Philip Stubbs, *Anatomy of Abuses*, 1583.
2 Glynne Wickham, Herbert Berry and William Ingram (eds), *English Professional Theatre 1530–1660*, Cambridge: Cambridge University Press, 2000.
3 Thomas Hahn (ed), *Robin Hood in Popular Culture: Violence, Transgression and Justice*, Cambridge: D.S. Brewer, 2000, p. 247.
4 A.J. Pollard, *Imagining Robin Hood*, London: Routledge, 2004, p. 77.

Chapter 4: The Christian epic

The so-called 'mystery plays' were for long the best-known medieval dramas in Britain; but in fact they were only one form among many in the pre-Elizabethan period, and they comprised a comparatively small proportion of performed medieval drama. However, it must be added that they are as spectacular and impressive as anything from the period.

ONE CYCLE, MANY PAGEANTS

The mystery play, or 'cycle', consisted of a number of short plays, or 'pageants', each telling one incident in the whole Biblical story from the creation of the world through the stories of the Old Testament, Christ's Nativity, His passion, resurrection and ascension, to Doomsday, or the Final Judgement. Each pageant in this vast story was self-contained, but each one – and there might be as many as forty, fifty or even more of them – was part of the overall 'cycle', which in performance might last for many hours.

Their religious subject matter encouraged earlier critics to imagine that they had evolved over centuries, deriving initially from the tenth-century *Visitatio Sepulchri* ('Quem quaeritis in sepulchro, o Christicolae?'). Christian drama, it was said, had moved 'from minster to market place'. But such cultural Darwinism is now rejected.

These works are sometimes known as 'Corpus Christi' plays, largely because the biggest and best-known cycle was performed annually on Corpus Christi day, the first Thursday after Trinity Sunday. Glynne Wickham has argued forcefully that the shape of the cycles derives precisely from this feast, which was only instituted in 1264 to celebrate the Eucharist, the Catholic doctrine of transubstantiation. Wickham argues:

> We are taken out of ritual time into universal time: for the Eucharist has no significance in this context of man's salvation without taking account of the Fall of Lucifer and Adam on the one hand and of Christ's Harrowing of Hell and Doomsday on the other, and thus of the judgement of man himself.[1]

This is a neat argument, but it has been rejected by some recent scholars, who point out, for instance, that the 'N-Town' cycle has no discernible connection to Corpus Christi, that Chester's cycle transferred from Corpus Christi day performances to Whitsun sometime around 1500, and so on.

More persuasive may be the argument which suggests that people always inclined to dramatising stories from the Bible, and this natural predisposition received an urgent impetus from the disaster of the Black Death, which devastated Britain in 1348 and 1349. Although this outbreak reduced the country's overall population drastically, paradoxically many towns and cities saw an increase in their numbers: the Black Death drove many off the land. The expanding cities attained new self-confidence, and they instituted or developed all manner of pageantry, processions and festivities to assert themselves. The mystery cycles were developed as part of this communal assertiveness. The streets became, in new ways, a kind of stage for the citizens – the mayor, the aldermen, the civic corporation, but also the ordinary people – to act upon. And it should be stressed that the citizens participating always included women, who were involved in financing, planning, production, stage managing and audience control at all levels; though they seem usually to have been banned from acting.

SOCIAL FACTORS

These factors must also be set beside the drastic sharpening of social conflict which was discernable after the Black Death. Partly because of the plague's destructiveness, but partly also as a result of the kings' never-ending wars in France, and, more subtly, because feudalism was slowly, almost imperceptibly, breaking apart and a new kind of money economy was gradually usurping it, the ruling élite felt an increasingly desperate need to exert its grip on the people. Thus, the Statute of Labourers (1351) tried to hold down wages; the sumptuary laws (1363) told people what clothes they could wear; and the Poll Tax (1377) took unfair taxation to new levels. All this led to renewed and harsher calls from the oppressed lower classes for an end to corruption, for freedom and justice. And while social strife was thus becoming crueller, the old spiritual certainties the church had preached for so long were also fracturing. John Ball's extreme communistic Christianity struck a fresh and appealing note, while John Wycliff and the Lollards, a sort of organised clerical opposition, gained many followers. Lollardism viewed the Pope as anti-Christ and denied the central Catholic doctrine of transubstantiation. And its growth at this time was hardly hindered by the split in the papacy itself: from 1378 to 1429 there were two Popes, one based in Rome, the other in Avignon.

In 1381, around Corpus Christi day, things reached a climax. The peasants revolted. In fact, it was not so much a peasant's revolt as a revolt among the discontented lower and middle orders, plebians, artificers, yeomen, craftsmen, servants, even apprentices. They were led by a former soldier, Wat Tyler, and for a brief period, they threatened both the state and the church. Though Tyler professed loyalty to the king, he was fiery in his demands for the king's advisers, henchmen and ministers to be thrown down and executed; and he advocated the seizure of church property and the abolition of all clergy except mendicants. The revolt was stopped by a mixture of royal trickery and the honest naiveté of Tyler and his fellows, but active discontent rumbled on and flared up frequently, most notably in the Lollard uprisings of 1414 and 1431, and the rebellion of Jack Cade, which also took place around Corpus Christi day, in 1450.

MYSTERY CYCLES AS DEFENCE OF TRADITIONAL CHRISTIANITY

The political and ecclesiastical powers responded to this ongoing disaffection and unrest in a number of ways, perhaps one of the least expected being the endorsing of the mystery cycles. In this view, the cycles, huge demonstrations of the eternal verities of the Christian faith, appear as a conservative reaction to the threats to the Church's trembling authority, an attempt to re-assert long-revealed truths especially against the Lollards, but also against other popular diversions, from preaching friars to Robin Hood plays and folk games. And by encouraging the people to act in the mystery cycles, it may have hoped to keep them from the barricades.

The form this defensive reaction took suggests the relationship between the cycles as Christian drama and the Corpus Christi day celebrations, which often included processions with floats sporting static or moving *tableaux vivants*. Thus, Lydgate's *A Procession of Corpus Christi* included a series of such tableaux, beginning with the Crucifixion, then a sequence of Old Testament scenes (Isaac, Jacob, David and Goliath and others), then scenes of evangelists and Christian Fathers. The mystery cycles, too, at least in some places, were taken through the streets in procession on huge 'pageant wagons', which halted at predetermined stopping places so the actors could perform. Whether the cycles developed from the processions, which continued to exist in parallel though increasingly separately, well into the fifteenth century, or vice versa, or, more likely, they developed simultaneously, cannot now be known. Rosemary Woolf suggested that the cycles may have been performed at Corpus Christi 'not because they were appropriate, but because they were not inappropriate'.[2] It may also be noted, however, that Corpus Christi was the time when, in 1381, 1450 and in other years, revolt seemed feasible: play performance may have used energies which could otherwise have become more dangerous.

SURVIVING CYCLES

The mystery cycles seem to attract such speculation, perhaps because what survives from them is both surprisingly extensive and annoyingly elusive. Four more or less complete cycles have survived. The original locations of two is known – York, a centre of rebellion in 1381, and Chester. The two others are the so-called Towneley Cycle, which takes its name from the fact that the manuscript containing the playscripts was sold in 1814 by the Towneley family, in whose library it had resided perhaps for centuries, and the 'N-Town' Cycle, once thought to be from Coventry but now known to be of East Anglian origin. The York cycle was played from at least 1376 to about 1570; the Chester cycle is first recorded in 1422 and continued to 1575. The other two complete cycles were written down about 1500, but where they were performed, and when, is not known. Perhaps indeed they are not cycles in the true sense at all, but are rather collections of disparate pageants.

Other cycles or pageants included Clerkenwell in London's 'play of the Passion of our Lord and the Creation of the World'. This was performed over at least three days, sometimes before the king, between 1384 and 1409, though it may be noted that not every historian accepts this as a proper mystery cycle. Unfortunately, no script survives. New Romney's 'Whitsun Play' dramatised Christ's passion over four days in most years between 1483 and 1561, two pageants by Robert Croo were performed in Coventry, and there are surviving *Abraham and Isaac* plays from Brome and Northampton. Only the Norwich *Adam and Eve* pageant survives from at least twelve which were performed here in the 1530s, and there are records of performances at Beverley ('Creation to Doomsday') in 1375, at Durham in 1403, Exeter before 1413, Ipswich before 1422, Worcester in 1424 and Newcastle in 1426. Later performances include the mystery cycle at Chelmsford between 1562 and 1576, the cycle which was banned in Hereford in 1548, those at Preston and Lancaster which were both continuing in 1603 and Kendal's 'Corpus Christi play', which was perhaps the last to still be performed, in 1612.

GUILD PLAYS AND CITY CYCLES

In many but not all of these, the town's trade guilds seem to have been involved, often one guild being responsible for one pageant. The members were responsible for the creation of scenery, costumes and more. They could use the performance as a kind of advertisement. Probably the guild also provided most of the actors from among their members (though it is also known that sometimes good actors who were not guild members were hired to perform major roles, as John Careless was in 1553, and released from prison to do so). Each individual pageant was subsidised and guaranteed by its own guild, sometimes ironically appropriate, as the water leaders and drawers of Dee were responsible for the Chester play of Noah and the Flood, sometimes in curious combinations, as with the hat makers, labourers and masons who together mounted the Annunciation in York.

THE YORK CYCLE

At least in York, the whole performance of about fifty plays was under the final control of the City Corporation, who perhaps hoped thereby to strengthen community identity, or perhaps to improve the city's spiritual health. They may also have been spurred to rival similar European displays of civic magnificence. Alternatively, the whole festival might simply reinforce their political grip.

Whatever the motive or motives, the performance of the whole cycle in a single day at York represents an enormous logistical achievement. At the first performing site, or 'station', the first pageant was performed; when it was finished, it moved on to the second 'station' and the second pageant wagon with its performance on board stopped to perform at the first station. As the first finished its performance at the second station, so the second moved to that station and the third pageant began at the first station. And so on. The pageant wagons were manoeuvred through the narrow streets first at the south western corner of the city, next to Holy Trinity Priory in Micklegate, up Micklegate and across the river, during which journey they performed probably three more times, before turning left towards and then past the Minster, giving more performances here, before turning right along Petergate and right again to All Saints Pavement and back to the river, giving yet more performances on the way. In total each of up to fifty pageant wagons stopped to perform perhaps twelve times in a single day. At Chester, with considerably fewer wagons, there were only five stations. The wagons were all different, but on average they may have been 2.5 metres wide, four or more metres long, with a stage floor about a metre and a half from the ground, and some being 'double deckers'. Was it really possible for such monstrous wagons to negotiate those medieval streets with their overhanging upper storeys? And if a single wagon could do this, could fifty? In a single day? In Newcastle, the wagons paraded through the streets but only performed at the final stopping place. Could York have followed a similar pattern, perhaps stopping at the various stations to present simply a tableau? Even if the first of the fifty wagons had begun its performance at four-thirty in the morning, the whole performance would still have had some way to go at midnight. It is hard to believe that every pageant was performed at every station. Perhaps one can understand those who have tried to argue that the whole cycle could only have been performed indoors and probably to an elite audience of civic dignitaries.

Figure 1.7
Conjectural reconstruction of the pageant wagon of the Mercers of York

Source: Alexandra F. Johnston and Margaret Dorrell, The York Mercers and their Pageant of Doomsday, Leeds Studies in English

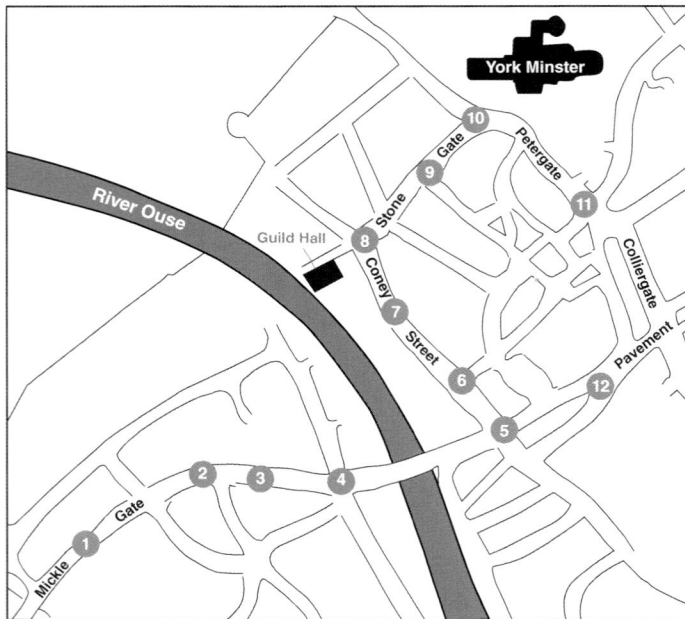

Figure 1.8
Map of the possible route of the pageant wagons, with performance 'stations' marked, in medieval York

THE CHESTER CYCLE

The Chester cycle was written down some years after the final performances in 1575 and seems to possess a kind of unity which may not accurately reflect what was ever actually presented. It owes something to French originals, *Le mystère du viel testament*, for the Old Testament pageants, and the *Stanzaic Life of Christ* for those of the New Testament. The original Corpus Christi Day performances at Chester were changed to Whitsun sometime between 1475 and 1521, and by the 1530s the cycle was being performed over three days, rather than one, perhaps in response to the problems posed by pageant wagons in the streets discussed earlier.

THE TOWNELEY CYCLE

The other two extensive cycles are more problematic. The Towneley Cycle, which some would say now was not a true cycle at all, was once thought to be associated with Wakefield, but this attribution is no longer accepted. Its thirty-two pageants seem to be of three kinds – up to ten which derive in often considerable measure from the York cycle, six or more written by the so-called Wakefield Master, a playwright with a distinctive style, and the others which are more or less original. It is also now generally accepted that the Towneley cycle was not performed from pageant wagons, that it would require what is known as a 'place-and-scaffold' production, which meant being staged at a single venue, using a number of discrete booth stages around a more generalised acting area, as discussed in more detail next. Davidson has suggested that perhaps Britain's favourite medieval single drama, the Towneley *Second Shepherds Pageant*, may have been devised, not for a cycle at all, but as a freestanding contribution to some civic or parish event.

THE 'N-TOWN' CYCLE

The 'N-Town' cycle might also require a form of place-and-scaffold staging. This collection of forty-two pageants seems unusually disparate, and it is not surprising perhaps that its provenance is unknown. The old attributions to Coventry or Lincoln have long since been refuted: the cycle seems to be an eclectic compilation by a monk or scribe from either Thetford or Bury St Edmunds, and to have been used perhaps as a sort of touring production around the villages of East Anglia, or perhaps more likely as a kind of script bank from which individual village groups or others could hire one or more pageants for performance.

THE PLAYWRIGHTS

Little is known of the authors of these pageants, though most of them were probably clerks in orders. Two anonymous writers whose work has been identified are the 'York Realist', author of several of the York pageants of the Passion, who has a vigorous alliterative writing style and is able to characterise his villains particularly effectively, and the 'Wakefield Master', who seems to have written up to half a dozen of the Towneley plays. He uses a distinctive stanza form and blends comedy, satire and tragedy into a unique and very actable dramatic form.

EPIC DRAMA

More important than the individual playwrights, however, is the overarching achievement of this epic drama. Ruskin suggested that the overwhelming impression created by a Gothic cathedral came not from some unified whole, but rather from the diverse, distinct details, each vivid in its own right, and apparently owing nothing to any other detail: the gargoyles, the misericords, the stained glass, the archways, the recesses and so on. The unity was in the variety. And so it is perhaps with the mystery cycles. Each includes scenes of realism, scenes of social satire, scenes of broad comedy and scenes of devotion and piety. Some include scenes from the life of Christ – His baptism, His Temptation by the devil, His raising of Lazarus and so on; some move straight from the Nativity to the Passion. Each deals with the key moments in the story differently – one sequence of the Passion of Christ, for instance, emphasises the cruelty of the soldiers, another the suffering and lamentations of Mary and a third the serene composure of Jesus Christ himself; one version of the Resurrection centres on the miraculousness of the action, another on the personal story of Mary Magdalene. There are varieties of style and metre, contrasts, repetitions and prophesies. It is in the juxtapositioning of the pageants and their different concerns that the overall impact is achieved. The subtle, often perhaps unintentional use of thematic patterning is also striking: there is an implicit comparison between Eve and the Virgin, for instance, and this also illuminates the actions of Mrs Noah, or Mary Magdalene. Again, the similarities and differences between Lucifer on the one hand, and Pharaoh and Herod and Pilate and Judas on the other are endlessly provocative.

THEATRICALITY

The cycles are also highly theatrical. There is, for instance, the use of conventional Christian iconography which turns here into effective tableaux which act like punctuation marks through the drama: the expulsion from Eden, Abraham poised to kill Isaac, the Annunciation, the crucifixion and the taking of Jesus from the cross, known as the Pièta. In Christian iconography the devil may be half-man half-beast, with claws, or horns, or bats' wings or a tail. He is almost always hairy. The managers of the mystery cycles tried to reproduce this: the York Drapers play, for instance, lists a devil's mask and hairy coat among its costumes. It is known that all supernatural creatures wore masks of some sort. This is helpful, perhaps, to the spectators when Jesus, for instance, appears in play after play, portrayed by different actors: if they all wear a golden mask, an acceptable kind of continuity is established.

Set against these solemn concerns are the comic resources of the cycles. Thus, there is lavatorial humour – N-Town's Lucifer trembles: 'For fear of fire, a fart I crack!' and Cain murderously mumbles 'Kiss my arse' whenever he is vexed. Cain's servant, the cheerfully cheeky Pick-Harness in the Towneley pageant, mocks his master like a fly mocking a grazing cow. In York, Cain's servant is Brewbarret ('Make-Trouble'), who appears to much the same effect. Then there is Joseph, who when he learns of Mary's pregnancy, expresses his doubt like a traditional stage cuckold. The Towneley shepherds' pageants contain a great deal of comedy, from the whole adventure of Mak the Sheep Stealer to, in the First Shepherds' pageant, Gyb's extraordinary fantasy as he herds his purely imaginary sheep.

The humour is often set against social satire: Cain is not only funny, he is also a good example of a bad master (which explains the strength of Pick-Harness's or Brewbarret's part); the shepherds in the field provide not only humour, they complain bitterly of the harshness of their lives. Meanwhile the soldiers who slaughter the children or nail Christ to the cross are cruelly typical of law enforcement agents throughout history, and Annas and Caiaphas are examples of the self-serving bishops who bore down so hard on the poor.

Finally mention should be made of the way the various pageants interact with each other, echoing, prefiguring and reminding the audience of the cycles' central concerns. The Ark prefigures the cross. The argument between Moses and Pharaoh is renewed in Christ's argument with Satan in *The Harrowing of Hell*, and the exodus from Egypt is echoed, too, in the *Harrowing of Hell* when the faithful are led forth. The audience should remember, too, in this connection, the flight into Egypt by Joseph, Mary and the infant Jesus, as well as His triumphant entry into Jerusalem in Holy Week. In *The Harrowing of Hell*, Jesus's disruption of Hell is a mirror image of Lucifer's disruption of Heaven in the pageant of the Fall. It is also a mirror image from a different angle of the *Ascension*.

THE EPIC ACHIEVEMENT

Distilled from its different and distinct variations, the whole cycle can be seen as a vast epic of Christianity: at first, there is a series of apparently unconnected Old Testament scenes which challenge our identity and ideas of morality; then comes the intimate story of the Nativity, told in close-up, almost Bruegel-like in its detail; and, finally, there is Christ's Passion, Crucifixion and Resurrection, which has the finest attributes of tragedy, until the Doomsday finale turns this to a kind of release. The whole is a uniquely powerful achievement. It is both a fine story and an intensely spiritual journey. For audiences who respond to these plays, there is a transcendent cleansing and, equally important, an assurance that every individual has a place in the operation of universal destiny.

NOTES

1 Glynne Wickham, *The Medieval Theatre*, London: Weidenfeld and Nicolson, 1974, p. 61.
2 Rosemary Woolf, *The English Mystery Plays*, London: RKP, 1974, p. 70.

Chapter 5: Didactic drama

MORALITIES AND MIRACLE PLAYS

If the mystery cycles were defensive in their Christian intent, there were other plays of the fourteenth, fifteenth and early sixteenth centuries which were much more aggressive. These may loosely be grouped as morality plays, which illustrate an argument about sin, repentance and salvation through largely abstract characters, and miracle plays, or saints' plays, which mostly have a saint as protagonist and include a miracle or religious conversion (or both) in the action. Even fewer of these moralities and miracles have survived than pageants from the mystery cycles: there are only five definite morality plays extant – *The Pride of Life*, actually only a fragment of the play which was probably originally composed around the time of the Black Death about 1350; *The Castle of Perseverance*, dating from fifty years later; *Mankind* and *Wisdom Who Is Christ, or Mind, Will and Understanding*, usually known simply as *Wisdom*, both of which were composed around 1465; and still probably the best-known morality play, *The Summoning of Everyman*, which is actually a translation from Dutch, made about 1500. The number of miracle plays is even fewer, the only certain survivals being *The Play of the Sacrament*, dated about 1461; *The Conversion of St Paul* and *Mary Magdalene*, both about 1500; the slightly later Cornish play, written in Cornish, *Saint Meriasek*; and *The Interlude of St John the Evangelist*, about 1550.

Both morality plays and miracle plays derived from popular sources. Dialogues and disputations were popular from Anglo-Saxon times, and many preaching friars and other predicants made their sermons into quasi-theatrical happenings. The moralities especially seem to be derived from such preaching: they are didactic, involved in argument and controversy and rooted in disgust at the Church's obvious corruption, its worldliness and political entanglements, its pastors' absenteeism and pluralism, simony (buying and selling of preferment) and benefit of clergy, which gave priests virtual legal immunity. After the Black Death especially, a new emphasis was laid on the individual soul: anyone, it was argued, could be tempted, and all were sinners, but redemption could be found through penitence and Divine Grace. This pattern – temptation, sin, despair, repentance, Divine Grace and salvation – gave a clear structure to the morality plays. Meanwhile, the saints' plays came at the same subject matter from a different angle. Stories and ballads, church windows with their story-board-like sequences and popular preachers told abundant tales of the saints, their lives, their conversions and the miracles connected with them. For the makers of miracle plays, these accessible stories were illustrations of the progression to salvation and were thus appropriate bases for pseudo-biographical dramas.

This difference in approach explains other differences: the central figure in the morality plays was usually an abstract generalisation with whom the spectator could identify – Mankind, or Everyman,

Figure 1.9
Death confronts Everyman in the Anglo-Dutch morality play, *The Summoning of Everyman*

for example. This character was asked to choose between virtue and vice, before he (and it always was 'he') faced the Final Judgement. The miracle plays told the stories of those who had made their choice and been canonised for it. They were therefore exemplars. And whereas the action of the morality plays took place outside the specifics of time and place, the miracle plays had a concrete historical or pseudo-historical reality in where and when they were set, their characters and so on.

THE FORM OF MORALITY PLAYS: THE VICE

As already noted, in the morality plays the characters were embodied abstract qualities, not just Mankind or Everyman, but also lesser characters like Good Deeds, Understanding or New

Guise. The aim of this was to make vivid the dilemmas the plays wished to explore. Sins, or vices, became perhaps especially immediate and there developed in these plays a sort of generalised Vice character, like a devil's lieutenant, who often instigated the plot against the protagonist, whispered temptations in his ear, amused him and offered him luxury, indulgence, fun – things too often missing from the drudgery of quotidian life and absent, too, from virtuous living. For this to convince, Vice had to be portrayed as attractive, which was dangerous enough for a preacher, but for a play was contentious indeed. It was doubly controversial, of course, when the Vice character hit on a genuine problem in contemporary life, as when he voiced the common disapproval of much priestly behaviour. His appeal was enhanced by his dramatic *persona*: he tended to be jaunty, energetic and charismatic. This was why he attracted the central figure and of course the spectator, too. But perhaps he was too attractive: it was easy for the opponents of the theatre to point out that by making Vice so seductive, the theatre was leading the spectator towards damnation, however much the performers or playmakers intended to point towards salvation.

Thus in *Wisdom*, Lucifer appears as 'a proud gallant' and prompts Mind, Will and Understanding to enjoy themselves, to stop being so serious and miserable, till Will decides no longer to 'row against the flood', but to 'set my soul on a merry pin'. We may imagine the delightful *frisson* of genuine terror which this Lucifer arouses. He is the devil; but he is in fact an actor. When he sweeps up the little boy and bears him off on his back, it is genuinely terrifying, yet it is also pleasurably exciting, like a twenty-first century spectator's response to a horror film, except that the medieval spectator really did believe in the devil. In *The Castle of Perseverance*, Backbiter is a sort of Mercury in reverse, the devil's 'mad messenger', who whenever two or three people are gathered together stands by to make a third (or fourth), simultaneously comic and sinister. It is Backbiter who conducts Mankind to Avarice and later he who reports Mankind's defection to the castle of perseverance to Belial. In *Mankind*, the three Vices, New Guise, Nowadays and Nought, bamboozle the audience, conducting them in some notably dubious community singing and taking a collection among them before agreeing to bring up the Devil. This last action raises extremely uncomfortable questions: by paying to see the devil, is the audience endorsing evil? Is the play offering a moral lesson or an entertainment? Is morality compatible with entertainment? This is a critical and theoretical crux which the theatre continued to grapple with for centuries.

MANKIND

Mankind is now often regarded as the best example of an English morality play. It is racy, scatological and comic. Though derived from *The Book of Job*, the play is notably theatrical, from the cutting of Mankind's costume with each of his mistakes, to the trial scene near the end. And it contains one of the medieval theatre's most memorable scenes when the devil, Titivillus, teases Mankind; it is theatrically conceived and greatly discomfiting to the audience, who are caught between laughter and tears. The dramatic rhythm, too, is masterly: after the raucous mock trial, for example, there is the quiet of Mercy's meditation, which is interrupted when the others burst back on stage half drunk. The ending has Mankind, in despair, about to hang himself (his tormenters have brought in 'the tree shaped like a gibbet'), when Mercy arrives in the nick of time, drives out the Vices and rescues the hero like the US Cavalry in some hackneyed western film.

OTHER MORALITY PLAYS

Of the morality plays, *The Castle of Perseverance* is perhaps the most impressive – a huge play aimed at a popular audience which is played out on a large open field with a series of scaffolding structures round the playing area. It opens before the birth of its protagonist, Mankind, and traces his journey through life, climaxing with a staged battle between the forces of good and evil for his soul. *Wisdom*, despite its dances and disguising, is a more sophisticated theologically conceived piece, while *Everyman* is probably the most austere of these plays. Pessimistic (life is illusory, the only reality is death) and serious, this play seeks to define goodness, as it traces its protagonist's last journey towards death. Nevertheless, it too contains striking dramatic moments, as when Death confronts Everyman early in the play, or when Everyman comes to his grave.

THE MIRACLE PLAYS

Despite the very small number of miracle plays which have survived (there are records of many more which have not survived), those which are extant show a surprising range. *The Play of the Sacrament* contains a number of spectacular miracles in its narration of the conversion of a group of Jews. *The Conversion of St Paul*, too, employs a highly theatrical device for Paul's conversion, and is notable for its use of a Poet as Narrator. *Mary Magdalene*, on the other hand, is a long, complex epic drama with Mary Magdalene at its centre. Her soul's progress is contextualised by scenes involving Tiberius, Herod and Pontius Pilate and – on another level – Christ's crucifixion and resurrection. The play is exciting partly because it is so ambitious: very episodic, it uses over twenty actors and is challenging both intellectually and theatrically. Competing with it as a long, elaborate epic is the Cornish play, *St Meriasek*, which also follows the life of its protagonist through a series of varied experiences.

The moralities and miracles which have come down to us thus provide a tantalising sample of a kind of drama we know little about. But the fact that they engage so fiercely with the controversies of their day suggests not just their importance, but the significance of theatre itself.

Chapter 6: Outdoor performance

There were two forms of outdoor staging common in medieval Britain – that which used pageant wagons in the streets of cities to present the mystery cycle, and the more common 'place-and-scaffold' form.

PAGEANT WAGONS

Only the cities of York and Chester certainly employed pageant wagons in their streets. Whether the plays were presented with the wagons side-on or end-on (or indeed some plays presented in one way, and others in the other) is a question still unanswered, and the way these massive wagons were manoeuvred through the streets is also still unknown. Most of them were probably custom-built and were astounding, ostentatious, immense and colourfully painted and curtained. Whatever their difficulties in negotiating the city streets, they provided versatile conditions for acting. Most of the action was likely to take place on the main floor of the wagon, but there was often an upper deck of some sort, for God or specific scenes 'above'. There was also a room 'below', probably used as a dressing room or Green Room, but also available for the appearance of devils or other monsters. And of course, there was always the possibility of actors descending to the street itself, though how often they availed themselves of this has been much disputed. It seems likely that tableaux would be notably potent on such wagons, but they were also capable of including several separate locations, as in the York play of the Jews' Exodus from Egypt, which has scenes in Pharaoh's court, near Mount Sinai and by the Red Sea. No doubt trapdoors and stairs were put to good use here. Modern reconstructions have shown how the pageant wagon enables both large-scale acting and much more intimate scenes equally to make their mark with an audience which is gathered informally round the wagon.

'PLACE-AND-SCAFFOLD'

'Place-and-scaffold' staging was widely used in outdoor performances. This system used space in two ways simultaneously: centrally, the *platea*, or place, was an unlocalised acting space, not limited by concerns of place or time, and at the edges of this open space, or around it, the *loci* (plural of *locus*), or scaffolds, which represented particular locations, specific in time and place. Thus, a character moving from one house to another, would enter from one scaffold, cross the empty acting space and mount the other scaffold. The *platea*, or place, might be the ocean, a battlefield, a market square or nowhere in particular. It changed according to need. The individual *locus*, or scaffold, on the other hand, was always throughout the performance one predetermined location.

The scaffolds were usually booth stages, probably with curtains which remained closed when the action was elsewhere. They could be large interiors, or small cubby-holes, but they were usually higher than the level of the *platea* (Chaucer's Absolon in *The Miller's Tale* has played Herod 'on a scaffold high'). The 'place-and-scaffold' arrangement allows for – indeed, encourages – extreme fluidity of staging, and frees the spectator's imagination to enter the created world of the play. Its effectiveness can be seen, for instance, in the Towneley Noah play, when Mrs Noah sits firmly in her scaffold house, while Noah himself rushes back and forth across the *platea* between the built ark and her *locus*, trying to persuade her to come aboard; or in *The Second Shepherd's Pageant*, when the action moves rapidly from the open fields, the *platea*, to the scaffolds which represent Mak's house, the stable in Bethlehem, and so on; or in the Cornish *Death of Pilate*, when the Messenger goes to Pilate's scaffold, and Pilate tells him to 'go into the country and walk a little while' – '*and then the Messenger shall go and walk about in the plain a little, and Veronica shall meet him*'.

In the Digby *Killing of the Children*, at the end of the first scene, the 'place' is specifically recognised: '*The knights and Watkin walk about the place till Mary and Joseph be conveyed into Egypt*'. In *Christ's Resurrection*, the Angel takes the three Maries across the *platea* to show them the scaffold which represents the empty tomb:

> Come hither and behold with your eye
> The place where the body did lie!

The Play of the Sacrament has three scaffolds – the Jews' house, the merchant's house and the church – where the miracles are performed, but the comic interlude with the Doctor and his boy, for instance, takes place on the *platea*. *Mary Magdalene* presents a more complex case, since it seems there are simply too many scaffolds required. It has been suggested that some of them might double as more than one location. Mary's journey across the sea, however, takes place on the *platea*, where there is at least one rock which threatens the ship she is travelling in, whereas her temptation and fall takes place in a tavern, a specific *locus* or booth stage.

The 'place-and-scaffold' arrangement is seen most intriguingly in *The Castle of Perseverance*, the text of which is accompanied by a teasing diagram of the original acting space. This consists of the Castle of Perseverance itself, at the foot of which is a bed, surrounded by a circular ditch, outside which are five scaffolds. The castle is a tower made, presumably, of wood and canvas, which does not reach the ground so as not to conceal Mankind's bed. Four of the five scaffolds are at the cardinal points of the compass. At the top of the diagram (actually the South) is Flesh's stage, where he waits with Gluttony, Lechery and Sloth. Opposite him, on the North stage at the bottom of the diagram, sits Belial with his immediate followers, Pride, Anger and Envy. To the left, or east, is God's scaffold, and opposite that the World, with Lust-Liking, Folly and the Boy. To the northeast, at the bottom left of the diagram, is Avarice's stage, where the Vice, Backbiter, is also stationed. The ditch itself is supposed to be filled with water. Exactly how this functioned has been much debated. Did the ditch mark the boundary of the stage? Was the earth thrown up from digging it heaped into a circular bank upon which the audience sat to watch the play? Were the scaffolds actually inside the ditch? The interpretation of the plan most favoured by modern scholars suggests that the ditch was actually much closer to the castle than appears in the diagram, so that it was in effect a moat, which

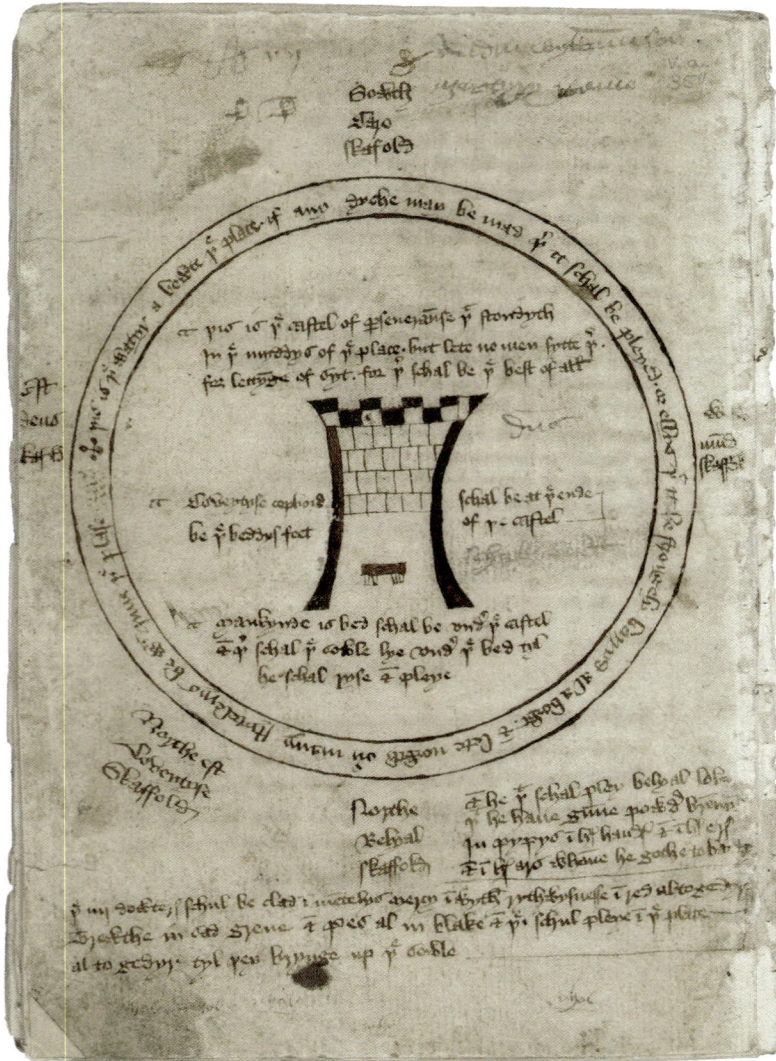

Figure 1.10
Diagrammatic representation of the place-and-scaffold staging for the fifteenth-century *Castle of Perseverance*
Source: By permission of the Folger Shakespeare Library

comes into its own when Belial's forces attack the castle. Whatever the precise ordering of these elements, it is clear that the castle in the middle of the place provides the central image and is itself a scaffold stage. When the castle is assaulted in a spectacular scene worthy of a film blockbuster, this took place with Belial's army approaching across the *platea*.

Many plays were adaptable to different conditions and were probably toured to different villages but the basic arrangement of *platea* and *locus* seems always to have pertained. Plays might have been performed in churchyards, on village greens, at crossroads and at least two possible specific sites have been discovered, one at Walsham-le-Willows in Suffolk, the other at Great Yarmouth. In Cornwall, there are play venues, known as 'rounds', as at St Just and near Perranporth. The stage plan for *St Meriasek* survived, and it looks rather like the plan for *The Castle of Perseverance*, being a circular *platea*, surrounded by no fewer than thirteen scaffolds.

THE ACTOR: DEMONSTRATIVE AND EXPLICIT

This arrangement of the stage space offers the actor particular kinds of freedom. What he cannot achieve is detailed realism: the very existence of the *platea* excludes that. In any case, a character's motivation is not important to the playwright, so it need have no importance for the actor. And despite the presence in many mystery cycle presentations of a 'property-player', a kind of well-paid, professional actor-director-producer, most actors in these outdoor dramas were amateurs. But it was not a case of allowing any willing body onto the stage. At York in 1476, it was

> ordained and established by the full consent and authority of the Council (that) four of the most cunning,
> discreet and able players within this city (will) search, hear and examine all the plays and players and pageants
> throughout all the artificers belonging to Corpus Christi play, and all such as they shall find sufficient in
> person and cunning to the honour of this city and the worship of the crafts to admit and enable, and all other
> insufficient persons either in cunning, voice or person to discharge, amove and avoid.[1]

A hundred years later in York they were still demanding 'expert and meet players . . . for the cunning handling of the play'.

The 'expert and meet' actors were required above all to stand still and speak clearly and intelligently. The scripts called for acting which was formal and rhetorical, or else energetic and 'broad', even 'ham', but never naturalistic. Herod strutted about absurdly, or frighteningly, but certainly energetically, and comedy similarly required energy. Mak the sheep stealer was tossed in a blanket. Watkin, the comic and cowardly soldier who boasts how he will kill babies, is actually scared of the mothers of his victims and creeps under a bench to hide. But he is discovered and beaten with the women's distaffs.

This style of acting may be described as demonstrative, gestural and explicit. It is easily noticed in the York pageants, for instance. In *Adam and Eve*, the Angel presents Adam with a spade:

> Adam, have this: look how ye think;
> With sorrow must ye sweat and swink.

Abraham tells Isaac, in *Abraham and Isaac*:

> Lay down that wood even here,
> Till our altar be prepared.

And when the shepherds arrive in Bethlehem:

> FIRST SHEPHERD: Brethren, be all live and glad;
>   Here is the borough where we should be.

2ND SHEPHERD: In that same steading now are we stood,

     Therefore I will go seek and see.

     Such hap of health never herdsmen had!

     Lo, here is the house, and here is he!

3RD SHEPHERD: Yea, forsooth; this is the same.

     Lo! Where that lord is laid

     Betwixt two beasts so tame.

REPRESENTATION

The action is always representational, never illusionistic. Death meets Everyman in a confrontation which easily becomes a self-explanatory tableau. *The Castle of Perseverance*'s Mankind stands between Good Angel and Bad Angel, who cajole, urge, counsel and tempt him. The women's parts are played by young men: women are thus *represented*; no-one believes they *are* women. This distancing effect is enhanced by the episodic nature of the mystery cycle's construction. The part of Jesus, notably, is represented by different actors in the several pageants He appears in. A sort of generalised Jesus is thus presented, and the spectator is consequently more likely to understand His role in the story than to empathise with His dilemmas. This practice, in other words, strengthens the role at the expense of the character's motivation or the individual's sensibility.

The necessary detachment is apparent in other ways, too. Thus, in *The Conversion of St Paul* and in *The Killing of the Children*, we find a Poet as narrator. In *The Killing of the Children*, this figure addresses the audience, telling them what is to come in the play. Having explained the plot, which many in the audience probably knew anyway, he concludes:

Friends, this process we purpose to play

As we can, before you all, here in your presence,

To the honour of God, Our Lady, and Saint Anne,

Beseeching you to give us peaceable audience.

The presentational style is above all concrete, as a brief summary of the Chester *Noah* play indicates. This description relies heavily on the text-given stage directions, and one should note that it is never wholly clear whether these are based on a particular performance, or whether they are imagined by the writer, and indeed how accurately they are expressed. With this caveat, this pageant script is still illuminating. The building of the ark is an intensely interesting sequence of stage 'business'. When the animals enter the ark, they are large pictures handed up from below: '*Then Noah shall go into the Ark, and his family shall give to him and call out all the animals painted on cards; . . . and the animals as painted must coincide with the words*'. A little later Noah sends forth the dove, which must return with an olive branch. Again, the stage direction gives us an idea how this might happen: '*Then he shall send forth the dove, and there will be in the ship another dove bearing an olive branch in its beak. This Noah will send by a rope attached to the mast into his hands*'. In a final spectacular effect at Chester, a rainbow is created over the pageant wagon.

MUSIC, DANCE AND SONG

The acting style is expanded by frequent use of dance and song. There are so many examples of singing in these plays that illustration is hardly necessary. But we may notice the Angels in the first York pageant singing '*Te Deum Laudamus*' and '*Sanctus, Sanctus, Sanctus*' before anyone except God has even spoken. At random we may add from York the Jews singing when they have left Egypt in the *Exodus* or the Shepherds singing on their way to Bethlehem. The mothers in the Towneley cycle sing perhaps the best known medieval carol of all, the Coventry carol. A stage direction in the Digby *Killing of the Children* notes: '*Here shall Simeon bear Jesus in his arms, going a procession round about the temple, and all this while the virgins sing:* Nunc dimitis'. And in the Chester *Harrowing of Hell*, the saved souls are led forth in a procession, singing 'We praise thee, O God'. These processions remind us of the importance of movement and the concrete use of the stage space. In the same play, the Poet-Narrator asks the virgins to dance, and in the N-Town pageant of the crucifixion the Jews dance round the crucified Christ even as He is on the cross. This is almost like a children's ring game, but with a thoroughly unsettling centrepiece. Instead of poor Mary sitting a-weeping in the middle of the ring, it is Christ crucified there.

COSTUME

In such a theatre, costumes assumed a clear importance. They were emblematic, not realistic and the producers of plays spent a good deal of money on them. Account books which survive record purchases of fur, gloves, hats and footwear. In 1476, the York authorities made payments to no fewer than three felt hat makers as well as two 'seamters'. At other times, they paid for such matters as the 'painting of shirts' and the mending of an angel's coat. Indicative costumes included God in white leather, angels with wings, kings with crowns and devils with horns, a hairy coat and bells.

Figure 1.11
Medieval musicians, such as played in dramatic performances

Source: British Library, London

ius: et plantauit radices eius. um

Figure 1.12
Four dancers of the kind who performed in medieval drama
Source: British Library, London

Devils and Vices always had exciting costumes, and changing their dress was an obvious way of dissembling for them. Thus, when Lucifer appears to Eve in the Garden of Eden, he notes:

> A manner of an adder is in this place,
> That wings like a bird she has,
> Feet as an adder, a maiden's face,

and he slides into this costume. Exactly what an adder's feet are like, by the way, is not clear: perhaps he wears the adder's skin like a pair of trousers.

N-Town's demon in *The Council of the Jews* drew the audience's attention to his fashionable clothes 'from the sole of his foot to highest ascension', which he used as a disguise. He wore long pointed shoes made of goat skin, crimson hose made of the costliest cloth held up by braces of kid's leather and silver buckles. His shirt was of fine Holland linen, whose cost he had not bothered to calculate, and he wore a waistcoat of cloth from Rennes. And to make a greater impression, he stuffed the clothes with cotton wool, that he should seem more svelte and shapely! The gallant who seduces Mary Magdalene in her play also wore a shirt of expensive Rennes cloth, with wide sleeves and with a silk lace presumably at the neck. By contrast, the four daughters in *The Castle of Perseverance* are dressed symbolically, but simply – Mercy in white, Righteousness in red, Truth in 'sad green' and Peace 'all in black'.

MASKS AND MAKE-UP

To complement the effect of costuming, the outdoor plays also used masks and face-painting. It seems that supernatural characters, for instance, were always masked: God and Jesus wore gold masks, angels red and devils or demons black. The devil's mask might also have been two-faced as at York. Thus in mystery cycle pageants like *The Fall* and *Doomsday* which deal exclusively with supernatural events, all the characters probably wore masks. To us, the idea of Christ in a golden mask hanging on the cross may be incongruous, but the medieval spectator expected it, and it probably aided a serious appreciation of the action.

The blackened faces of the demons may also cause us to pause, but for different reasons. There is a niggling undercurrent here which depends on the unspoken idea that black people are funny, or odd or despicable. The blackface throughout theatre history has been seen as comic, but here there is a hint that it implies mental deficiency or physical deformity. The most dramatic presentation of blackness comes in the plays of *The Fall* when Lucifer and his followers leave Heaven, where they were angels in red masks, and reach hell as devils, now in black masks: 'Now are we waxen black as any coal'. When Cain's sacrifice fails, the smoke from his fire blows in his face, and blackens it: we know instantly that he is odd, other and probably allied to the devil. And in *The Castle of Perseverance*, the devil introduces himself with these words:

> Now I sit, Satan, in my sad sin,
> As devil doughty, in draf *(filth)* as a drake *(dragon)*.
> I champ and I chafe, I choke on my chin,
> I am boisterous and bold, as Belial the black.

The behaviour he claims is that associated with the mentally unstable.

STAGE PROPS

As for stage props, these performances used few, and they were likely to be symbolic and conventional rather than realistic. Thus Adam usually carried his spade; Mary wore a tiara; and so on. Nevertheless, very little is known in detail of the practicalities of how props were used in these outdoor performances. No doubt the medieval stage creators were as theatrically lucid or alternatively as ingenious as those of any other age. We know the York Red Sea, for example, was made of half a yard of red cloth, split in the middle: presumably it was simply opened like a curtain for Moses to pass through. This is imaginative and unambiguous. But more complicated was the Hell Mouth, which seems often to have needed a complicated apparatus to work. Thus, a windlass might open the jaws, a bellows blew out fire and smoke, and some kind of thunder machine made it boom like an earthquake. It is not clear how Noah's rainbow was made, but in 1433 an inventory from York included 'a cloud and two pieces of rainbow of timber', as well as 'two pieces of red clouds and stars of gold belonging to heaven; two pieces of blue clouds painted on both sides; three pieces of red clouds with sunbeams of gold and stars for the highest of heaven'. Though there are reports of pantomime-style camels and donkeys, real animals also featured, as in the Towneley plays of the three kings, who rode horses, and the *Resurrection*, in which the Centurion rode a horse. In *The Conversion of St Paul*, Saul is lent a 'palfrey' to go about his business: when lightning flashes in front of him on the road to Damascus, he falls off.

SPECTACULAR EFFECTS

This is a typical effect which the medieval open air theatre delighted in. In the same play, Gluttony, Wrath and Covetousness 'vanish away with a fiery flame and a tempest', and in an interpolation, taking its cue perhaps from this, Belial appears 'with thunder and fire' and a few moments later another devil, Mercury, appears not only with fire but 'crying and roaring' as well. Belial leads the assault on the Castle of Perseverance, and is instructed to 'look that he have gunpowder burning in pipes in his hands and in his ears and in his arse when he goes into battle'. In the Chester *Harrowing of Hell*, when Christ arrives 'a clamour shall be made, or a loud sound of things striking together', and in the N-Town *Doomsday*, '*all the souls rise from their graves, whilst the earth quakes and the world is consumed by fire*'. Finally, one might note the extraordinary stage direction in the Cornish play of *The Death of Pilate*: '*And then they shall put him in the ground, and he shall be thrown up again*'.

There are plenty of other examples of the medieval theatre's delight in the astonishing on stage.

In the *First Shepherds Pageant* from Towneley, Slow-Pace, the third shepherd, enters with a sack which he shakes like a conjuror to show it is empty. Only a few moments later he opens it again and it is full of food. In fact, he has probably had time to change it while the audience's attention was taken up by the entrance of Jack, the boy, but it has a powerful on-stage effect. Elsewhere, Moses shakes his stick at Pharaoh, only for it to turn into a snake; and when Jesus is on the cross, blood spurts from his side.

Miracle plays need miracles, and *The Play of the Sacrament* probably contains more, and more astonishing, miracles than any other extant play. In it we see Christ's hand nailed to a post, and it comes off! The Communion wafer is laid on the table and stabbed, and it spurts blood. It is put in a cauldron which boils over, and the oil turns to blood. And when the bread is put into the oven, the oven door bursts open and blood gushes out. The image of Christ magically appears and then turns back to bread.

There is much that remains obscure about the performance of the plays, pageants and cycles of the high middle ages. But the texts we do have show a huge variety of stage effects and theatrical moments, certainly enough for us to be able to say with confidence that here was a performance tradition which was widespread, inventive and popular.

NOTE

1 J.S. Purvis, *From Minster to Market Place*, York: St Anthony's Press, 1969, p. 63.

Chapter 7: The beginnings of professional theatre

From the second half of the fifteenth century, theatrical activity saw a slow but steady drift away from presentations by amateurs in open spaces, and towards smaller scale, indoor performances. Tudor 'interludes' were plays with or without a moral purpose, which were usually, but not necessarily, comedies in the broadest sense. They were interludes in that they were often played in great halls at a time of festivity, when they might be presented between the courses of a banquet. They were secular, used smallish casts and were often (though by no means always) performed by professional companies.

SIR THOMAS MORE

In the play *Sir Thomas More* by Anthony Munday and others (including William Shakespeare), written in the early 1590s, a group of players come to More's house. They have a repertoire of seven plays, and More chooses one for performance. The company consists of four men and a boy who plays the women's parts. Though *Sir Thomas More* was written seventy years after the event, the incident seems true to the life of a Tudor acting company. The work of these companies was clearly popular. Among the earliest troupes were Lord Neville's Players who performed at King's Hall, Cambridge in 1361, and from then the numbers of such companies grew steadily. By the sixteenth century some were taking on more actors so that by Elizabeth's reign there might be seven or eight of them in a troupe, though the boy was still an important member: the cast list of John Heywood's 1530s *Play of the Weather* asks for 'A Boy, the least that can play'.

THE KING'S PLAYERS

The best known, and perhaps the best, of these troupes were the King's Players, a sort of equivalent to the modern National Theatre. In the 1490s they consisted of four men, led by John English. They were given a livery and paid a retainer of five marks each, but they were encouraged to travel and find paying audiences. In 1503 they were at the King of Scotland's court playing at the wedding celebrations of Henry VII's daughter to the King of Scotland. Their number increased to six and then eight actors, under Henry VIII, but probably split into two separate troupes, one still led by John English and the other consisting of John Slye, who later led Queen Anne Boleyn's troupe, Thomas Sudborough, William Rutter and John Scott. During this period they toured all over the country – they appeared in places as far apart as Bristol, Barnstaple, Worcester, Boston, Shrewsbury, Dover, Coventry, Sandwich and even Calais.

In the 1530s the company included Richard Hinstock, George Birch and George Maller, whose place was taken by Richard Parrowe about 1540. In 1528 Maller had taken his apprentice, Thomas Arthur, to court for breaking the terms of his apprenticeship: Arthur and three others of the 'king's interluders', having agreed to go on tour with Maller, seem to have got rid of him and continued the tour without him, making over thirty pounds by their performances. In the late 1530s the King's Men's leader seems to have been Thomas Yely. The group are recorded as performing at Beverley, Bristol, Norwich, Shrewsbury, Canterbury and other places during this period. Their repertoire included *The Market of Mischief*, which they played in 1546, *The Dragon with Seven Heads* in 1549 and *Aesop's Crow* and *The Play of Self Love* in 1551. By now the company had grown to seven men: Richard Hinstock, George Birch, John Birch, Henry Harriott, Richard Skinner, Richard Coke and Thomas Southey, though in 1552 Hinstock had been replaced by John Browne.

Edward VI, a keen supporter of the drama, paid the company a fee of £6-13s-4d, plus £3-6s-8d for each player, as well as their liveries. In 1553, when Edward died, they became the Queen's Men under Mary, who was also something of an enthusiast for the drama: she had employed the company many times in the 1540s when she was still Princess Mary. Their repertoire now included *Roister Doister*, *Respublica* and *Wealth and Health*, and they were found touring to Shrewsbury, Bristol, Beverley, Dover and other towns. After Mary's death, they became Elizabeth's Queen's Men.

OTHER ACTING TROUPES

Through these years there were also very many other itinerant acting troupes travelling the country. Glynne Wickham recorded how in the single year 1479–80, Selby Abbey in Yorkshire paid seven different visiting troupes for performances. One of these was given by the Earl of Northumberland's players who were contracted to play for him at Christmas and Shrove Tuesday, but at other times found audiences where they could.

The earliest records of performances in Wales are probably those of similar companies – in 1503 a Welsh company was performing in Shrewsbury; in 1540, a company from Wrexham, north Wales, presented plays, again in Shrewsbury.

Charles Brandon, Earl of Suffolk, had a prominent company who were seen across the country between 1520 and 1540. Other troupes included Arthur Plantagenet's, which flourished between 1526 and 1542, the Earl of Derby's Men, touring through the 1530s, the Marquis of Dorset's Men between 1536 and 1552, and, either side of 1550, companies patronised by Henry Ratcliffe, Viscount Fitzwalter and the Earl of Sussex.

One prominent woman patron was Katherine Willoughby, Duchess of Suffolk, whose troupe visited Canterbury, Peterborough, Long Sutton, Dover, Belvoir Castle and other venues during the reign of Edward VI. Queen Katherine of Aragon's Players were on the road between 1529 and 1532; perhaps they became Queen Anne Boleyn's Men, under John Slye, who were seen at Worcester in 1534 and at Battenhall in 1535, and seem indeed to have become Queen Jane Seymour's Players later still, for John Slye was leading her company in 1536.

The London livery companies were significant patrons of these small professional groups, hiring them annually to perform at functions like election feasts from about 1400 well into Elizabeth's reign. Thus, the Drapers Company hired a different group almost every year: the King's Men

Figure 1.13
Katherine Willoughby, Duchess of Suffolk, a prominent woman patron of an acting company in the mid-sixteenth century

Source: Art Collection/Alamy Stock Photo

appeared seven times for them between 1517 and 1541, the Duke of Suffolk's Men appeared in 1531 and 1532, and the Queen's Men in 1539. The Goldsmiths, the Mercers and the Merchant Taylors all hired theatre companies at different times. The King's Men appeared for the Grocers' Company on three different occasions between 1514 and the mid-1530s, and for the Bakers in 1536.

These performances were presumably comparatively uncontentious, but some troupes seem to have courted controversy. Fiercest of these was probably the company whose patron was Thomas Cromwell and whose leader was John Bale, the belligerent Protestant propagandist whose group was at Shrewsbury, Coventry, Leicester and Oxford in 1537–8, at Ipswich, Yarmouth, Norwich, Thetford and Cambridge the following year, and in 1540 at Cambridge, Stanford, Lincoln, Doncaster and York. At Cromwell's fall, the company seems to have hurriedly dispersed. Less fanatical perhaps were Sir Francis Leke's Men who however still got into trouble in the 1550s for presenting Protestant drama in the north of England when Mary was furiously trying to impose her Catholic Counter-Reformation on the country.

TOURING

The companies' usual practice seems to have been a first presentation of any new production for their patron, or perhaps at the Royal Court itself or an Inn of Court. This production would then be added to the repertoire, and the troupe would set out on the road, probably going by foot, though with a wagon or packhorse to carry their costumes, props and other stage equipment. Their itinerary would be set before they started out, and when they arrived at one of their planned destinations they would first visit the mayor to ask permission to perform. Perhaps the first performance would be a private presentation for the mayor and his guests for which the company would receive a fee: provincial authorities seem usually to have been happy to patronise the players, especially if they wore the livery of some important politician or lord. The troupe would then perform, probably several times in the town, for the public, in the guildhall, perhaps, or a livery hall, perhaps in a churchyard or an innyard, and, of course, as in the play *Sir Thomas More*, for any local magnate who would have them. At each performance, they would hope to generate money, either through a collection or, more reliably, a fee from their host. The productions must have been adaptable to fit such different venues, and the actors versatile to cope with the various stages.

JOHN RASTELL AND THE BUSINESS OF THEATRE

The actors did not perform throughout the year; most had other trades to fall back on between tours, though some found employment assisting amateur groups, including groups in rural districts and villages. But a few, like John Rastell, seem to have made a good living from the theatre. Rastell's activities included stagework: he was involved in building the splendid stage settings for the Field of the Cloth of Gold in 1520, the Calais Roundhouse the same year and the pageant staged to welcome the Emperor Charles V to England in 1522. He was also responsible for the design of the royal pageant, *Love and Riches*, which he probably wrote, too, staged at Greenwich in 1527. Even more intriguingly, Rastell seems to have built a theatre in Finsbury in his own house or grounds, in the 1520s, perhaps used to stage his own plays, perhaps hired out to other companies as part of his commercial activities.

These were furthered by an extensive costume hire business, for which Rastell's wife was a leading seamstress. His was not the only such business in London in Henry VIII's reign, but it must have been one of the most flourishing. He paid a tailor four pence per day, as well as giving him food and drink: costumes were not only made new, they were also altered and recycled. The more expensive costumes in his wardrobe were worth over a pound. The hirer was charged between two and four shillings per costume for a 'play', and eight pence for one for an 'interlude', though the distinction is not always clear. The business was profitable enough for him to sue a long-standing colleague, Henry Walton, a stage carpenter with whom he had worked on the Greenwich project as well as the building of his Finsbury theatre. When Rastell was in France, he seems to have left the costume business in Walton's hands, and Walton had failed to return everything in good order.

Rastell, who was married to Thomas More's sister, was also a playwright. His work includes *The Four Elements* (c.1519), *Calisto and Melibea* (c.1524) translated from Spanish and perhaps *Gentleness and Nobility* (c.1523). Perhaps more importantly he published plays, including *Fulgens and Lucres*. The scripts may have been for hire by aspiring groups, who could then have produced the plays in Rastell's theatre, dressing the actors in Rastell's costumes. At all stages of the venture, Rastell stood to gain.

Chapter 8: Secular drama

THE INTERLUDES

Supporting an acting troupe gave an aristocratic patron status, but it also offered him the opportunity to prosecute a political agenda. Tudor interludes often retained the morality play structure (the prosperous protagonist succumbs to temptation, despairs but just in time repents, recovers and returns to moral health) but were usually more political in their implications. The politics of the time of course was rooted in religion, which provided the ideological underpinning for much political action. But some interludes were neither particularly political nor particularly religious.

However, as productions over decades since the Second World War have shown repeatedly, these Tudor interludes were fast-paced, lively and fun. Their humour was often broad, and might be scatological and earthy, but they could also encompass abstract debate. They were usually quite short – perhaps an hour is the average – though occasionally they were longer, like Skelton's *Magnificence*. Though these plays were not tied to any religious or calendar festivals, they often retained features from morality plays: the names of the *dramatis personae* of the 1570s interlude, *The Marriage between Wit and Wisdom*, for example, are abstract qualities – Idleness, Wantonness, Good Nurture, Irksomeness and so on. For economic reasons casts were small, and authors were rarely interested in the nuances of their characters' psychological states. But the plays were usually socially aware, sometimes bitingly satirical and they often included comic horseplay.

FULGENS AND LUCRES

One of the earliest Tudor interludes is *Fulgens and Lucres* (c.1497) by Henry Medwell, chaplain to the Archbishop of Canterbury, and it demonstrates how politics can form part of the fabric of these plays. On the surface, it concerns the wooing of Lucres by two suitors, Cornelius and Gaius. Cornelius bases his suit on the fact that he comes from a long line of noble ancestors. Gaius, on the other hand, is from the rising middle class. Henry Tudor was busily advancing such men at the expense of the old aristocracy. Consequently, the play's contest, entertaining as it is as drama, and containing significant contemporary echoes as it does, is really no contest at all.

THE INTERLUDE OF YOUTH AND HICK SCORNER

The Interlude of Youth, presented in 1513 or 1514 by the Earl of Northumberland's Men, concerns a sort of Prodigal Son seen roistering with characters called Riot and Pride. His homosocial world is

Chere is cõteyned a godely interlude of Fulgens Cenatoure of Rome. Lucres his doughter. Gayus flaminius. ꝓ Publi9. Corneli9. of the disputacyon of noblenes. ꝓ is deuyded in two ptyes/to be played at ii.tymes. Cõppled by mayster Henry medwall. late chapelayne to þ ryght reuerent fader in god Johan Morton cardynall ꝓ Archebysshop of Caũterbury.

PD

Figure 1.14
Title page of *Fulgens and Lucres*, published about 1512 by John Rastall, showing Lucres and one of her suitors. In fact, the woodcut is entirely conventional and had been used in earlier books.

destabilising and irresponsible, and its social implications dangerous. But finally Youth is saved by Charity: 'All sin I forsake And to God I me betake'. The play's subtext presents Northumberland's warning to the young energetic Henry VIII, whom some in the provincial aristocracy saw as being led astray by high-spirited and irresponsible courtiers. It was answered by the Duke of Suffolk's Company's *Hick Scorner*, which gives us the view of a London insider. Hick Scorner is a ship's master, but he is also an image of the Yorkist pretender, Richard de la Pole, who was even then attempting to land an invasion force in England. Free Will, like a character in a morality play, is traduced by Hick Scorner, and brawls, boasts and blasphemes, but Contemplation and Perseverance bring him to his senses, he is symbolically given a new coat, and his problems are left behind. Henry, in other words, must be allowed some of the joys of youth: when it is necessary, he will be there to do his duty. The

Figure 1.15
Title page of *Hick Scorner*, published about 1515 by Wynkyn de Worde, purporting to show (top row, left to right) Contemplation, Pity and Good Will (bottom row, left to right), Imagination, Hick Scorner and Perseverance. However, these woodcuts are conventional and were also used in other printed books.

plays conduct a kind of coded argument about a king's experience and his responsibilities from the points of view of Henry's supporters and his opponents.

MAGNIFICENCE

Another play from the same period with a political subtext is the poet John Skelton's *Magnificence* (c.1519), written during the period of the rise of Cardinal Wolsey. Skelton, a grumpy conservative and a brilliant poet, had no time for Wolsey. Yet what exactly his play is saying has caused much argument. Whether Skelton's protagonist, Magnificence, who gets into such difficulties, represents the king or Wolsey is not completely clear. Is the play simply anti-Wolsey, or does it seek to inform, is it 'official' history which dramatises the expulsion of certain courtiers from Henry's inner circle? It plainly addresses questions such as what makes a suitable courtier, and how should a king rule? Highly stageable, the play teases and fascinates, partly because of Skelton's sophisticated use of language, and the extraordinarily versatile way he employs only five actors to cover the eighteen parts.

DOUBLING

This typical use of doubling – and trebling and more – of roles was a feature of the plays the small professional companies presented in the sixteenth century. It seems likely that it was not something to be covered up but rather the actors were proud of it. After all, an actor who could play several different parts in the course of a single performance possessed an enviable versatility, and in all probability audiences enjoyed this, too. And for the purposes of understanding the play, the spectator, aware of conventions, noted the costume, not the player. Consequently we find in the published text of *Lusty Juventus* (c.1550) a note appended to the cast list that 'four may play it easily, taking such parts as they think best'. John Rastell's *The Four Elements* required five actors in its uncut version but Rastell suggested cutting the text according to the performance circumstances and the number of actors available. *The Marriage between Wit and Wisdom* (c.1579) divides its nineteen parts between no more than six actors. Even more impressively, the printed text of *Cambyses* (c.1568), a tragedy which takes itself extremely seriously, shows how to divide the thirty-eight roles between a mere eight actors.

JOHN HEYWOOD

The earliest playwright whom we know wrote several plays is John Heywood. He was a musician who played the virginals and sang in the King's Singers. He also taught at St Paul's School and some of his short, anecdotal plays written between 1518 and 1533 may have been intended for his pupils. The exact constitution of his canon is disputed, but he is acknowledged as the author of *The Four PP* in which a Pardoner, a Palmer and a Pothecary, ironically observed by a Pedlar, compete to find which is the biggest liar; *The Pardoner and the Friar*, which shows these two rogues each haranguing half the audience simultaneously till the local curate and 'Neighbour Pratt' interrupt them and a slapstick battle ensues; and *John John, Tib and Friar John*, which dramatises the plight of a henpecked husband whose wife flirts with the local friar till he finally asserts himself. These short farce-like pieces are complemented in Heywood's canon by *The Play of Love*, a disputation exploring love in intellectual terms, and *The Play of the Weather*, in which various characters beg Jupiter for weather to suit their occupations (the Gentleman wants good hunting weather, the merchant wants wind to blow his ships, the laundrywoman wants a drying sun, the boy wants snow to make snowballs): Jupiter represents Henry VIII. The play suggests that courtiers cannot have all they want, only the king has a viable social or political overview, though there is a further implication that Henry, too, should not necessarily get all he wants – Anne Boleyn or a son, perhaps – for Heywood was no supporter of Henry's political manoeuvrings of the late 1520s.

Heywood may also be the author of *Witty and Witless*, another disputation about wisdom and folly, and *Gentleness and Nobility*, though this seems more likely to be by John Rastell. In it, interestingly enough, a ploughman gets the better of a knight and a merchant. Heywood and Rastell were part of a politically committed Catholic circle centred on Thomas More, Heywood having married Rastell's daughter, and their reforming social stance can be seen in their plays: *The Four PP*, for instance, denounces Catholic priests' deceit and charlatanism, and *The Pardoner and the Friar* does the same, with especial focus on the Pardoner's practices. But the reforms they sought were moderate: they condemned the Catholic church's corruption but refused to countenance Reformism or a break with Rome. In the end, More was executed; Rastell fell foul of Thomas Cromwell, was imprisoned and died in gaol; and Heywood effectively retired. Though he resurfaced in Mary's reign, he left England for good when she died and spent his final years in exile on the continent.

DRAMA AND THE ENGLISH REFORMATION

By 1529 it was clear enough that Henry VIII was aiming to terminate England's relationship with the Catholic Church. The controversy provided new matter for plays. One of the earliest was the anonymous *Good Queen Hester* (c.1528) which told the Biblical story of Esther so that it supported Katherine of Aragon's position and attacked Wolsey.

JOHN BALE

The most virulent dramatist who participated in this political upheaval, however, was John Bale, who has clear claims to be regarded as England's first major playwright. He may have written as many as twenty-one plays, though only half a dozen survive. He was born in 1495 and educated at Jesus College, Cambridge, before becoming a Carmelite monk. In 1535 he renounced his Orders, married and became an ordinary parish priest at Thorndon in Suffolk. But he was already engaged in controversy. In 1536 he was examined for heresy, and though he disowned his earlier play, *The Harrowing of Hell*, he was thrown into prison. Released the following year, he attached himself to Thomas Cromwell and by 1538 he was leading Cromwell's Players who presented the plays he wrote. These included *Three Laws*, *God's Promises*, *The Temptation of Our Lord*, *John the Baptist*, *The Conversion of St Paul* and most controversially, *King Johan*, which was presented at St Stephen's, Canterbury in September 1538, and again before Archbishop Cranmer in January 1539.

The company consisted of five men (or perhaps four men and a boy), probably ex-monks like Bale, whose repertoire of seven plays were all by Bale. Bale himself played the central role in the plays, even sometimes doubling this with the Prologue (or Prolocuter, as he tended to call the part). On the extremist wing of the Reforming party, he even aimed to create a new cycle of Protestant mystery plays, in which the devil was the pope and the cardinals, priests and others his agents.

But when Cromwell fell in 1540 and a much more moderate Protestantism was installed, Bale fled to the continent. In 1547, however, when Edward VI succeeded Henry VIII and a more radical Protestantism was ushered in, he returned to England, published a collection of his plays and after holding a series of positions was appointed Bishop of Ossory in 1552. Catholic Ireland was perhaps not the most fertile ground for him to present his plays, but still, he attempted to do so, including three of them on the day Edward VI's half sister, the Catholic Mary, acceded to the throne. Soon after he left for exile on the continent again, but when Mary died in 1558 he returned to England and became a prebendary at Canterbury Cathedral where he continued to revise his plays till his death in 1563.

Figure 1.16
John Bale, fanatical Protestant and perhaps Britain's first major playwright

Bale's plays are revolutionary, both dramatically and in terms of their content. The Prolocuter in the plays (the author himself) was to tell the audience what would happen in the drama and thus indicate how the spectator should respond. This technique helps an audience concentrate, not on the moment-to-moment excitement of the drama, but on *how* the events happen. Bale's *King Johan* especially is extraordinarily original. The first serious history play in the language, it constructs an alternative narrative for English history in which King John tries to free the Widow England from her Catholic oppressors. Bale's characters exist on both real and allegorical planes: Stephen Langton, the Archbishop of Canterbury, is effectively a mask donned by Sedition. But he is also a real historical person, who is (in Bale's view) seditious. Similarly, Dissimulation is also Simon of Swynsett who poisons King John. Thus Bale finds a way of converting the old morality play method to one which serves the purposes of historical drama. History is seen as a way of telling who we are, and so what we need to do. Not only that, but Bale finds a way in which to replace the generalisation of Catholicism, which saw salvation as a matter for the church, by Protestantism's new focus on the individual. No longer does human fate depend on theological abstractions; it becomes an individual's responsibility. His innovations ensured that English drama would follow a different path to that of other European countries.

LATER INTERLUDES

One play which may be seen as a riposte to Bale was *Respublica*, a strongly pro-Catholic play produced by Queen Mary's Players at her court in 1553. In this, Lady Respublica is the counterpart to Bale's Widow England, and the Vices – Avarice, Intolerance and Oppression – are Protestants enriching themselves at the country's expense. In the end they meet Nemesis, a woman, perhaps an incarnation of Mary herself, who causes their downfall.

Other interludes from the 1550s like *Lusty Juventus* and *Nice Wanton*, on the surface fast-moving comedies, actually carry a Protestant implication – indeed, Barnabus, the hero of *Nice Wanton*, seems like a sort of embryonic Puritan. He is a good boy who goes to school while his sister Delilah becomes a 'nice wanton': the different moral consequences need no spelling out. Other interludes suggest the range and variety of this dramatic form. *Roister Doister*, for instance, by Nicholas Udall, a Headmaster of Eton with, however, a sense of humour, is a brilliant farcical comedy, witty, knockabout and satirical, and *Gammer Gurton's Needle* by the unknown 'Mr S. Master of Arts' has many of the same qualities, and is perhaps even better. Its social dilemma – that Gammer Gurton has lost her needle which must be found so Hodge's split trousers can be mended – is actually rooted in reality: these people's livelihoods depend on the results of the action. *Jack Juggler* is perhaps less comic but it raises real questions about individual identity as Jack Juggler 'steals' Jenkin Careawaie's selfhood. Careawaie's gradual loss of self-confidence is truly pitiable. All these plays have a Bruegel-like intimacy, peasant earthiness and pungency.

THE VICE IN LATER INTERLUDES

A favourite character in many of these interludes is the Vice. Developed along secular lines from the diabolical character in the religious moralities, the Vice still exercises malign control over events in some plays. Matthew Merrygreek in *Roister Doister*, for example, seems almost like a puppet master. Somewhat similar are Covetousness in *Enough Is as Good as a Feast* (c.1569) and Nichol Newfangle in *Like Will to Like* (c.1568), both of whom carry wooden knives, the 'daggers of lath' described by Shakespeare's Feste. Diccon in *Gammer Gurton's Needle* is a bedlam, a sower of discord among other characters, and in this is rather like Ambidexter in the tragedy, *Cambyses*. Others, like Jack Juggler, Avarice in *Respublica* and Merry Report in *The Play of the Weather* are more comic, mocking and quick-witted. Some Vices have distinctly mixed fortunes: Iniquity in *Nice Wanton* gets a kiss from the seductive Delilah, but most of his plots are actually thwarted; and Idleness in *The Marriage between Wit and Wisdom* (c.1579) is made fun of, beaten and robbed. Nevertheless, the Vice is a compulsive dramatic figure: he dances metaphorically, and sometimes literally, round the protagonist, teasing, tempting and tormenting him.

ACADEMIC DRAMA

Though many interludes were designed for performance by companies of boys, or perhaps students at an Inn of Court, they were also often taken up by professional troupes. George Gascoigne's *Supposes*, derived from Ariosto's *I Suppositi*, and first performed at Gray's Inn in 1566, is a case in point. This is also true of the few tragedies of the time. *Gorboduc* has already been mentioned. It is notorious as the first English tragedy to employ blank verse, even if that is often declamatory and long-winded as it unreels its tale of fratricide, rebellion and civil war. *Cambyses* employs rhyme and would-be, high-flown language in preference to blank verse, but is actually little more than a hotchpotch of low comedy and gratuitous violence. However, both these plays, as well as other tragedies like *Horestes* (1567) perhaps by John Pickering and *Apius and Virginia* (c.1564) by 'R.B.', owe a debt to Senecan tragedy, at least as far as it was understood at the time, just as some of the comic dramas owe a debt to Plautus: *Jack Juggler*, for instance, is partially derived from *Amphitrion*, while *Roister Doister* is partly descended from *Miles Gloriosus*.

SCATOLOGY

Cambyses also partakes of the cheerful scatology which is common to so many Tudor interludes: Ambidexter promises to overcome his enemy 'with a fart'. Moros, in *The Longer Thou Livest*, is so afraid that 'at every word I am like to fart'. In many plays the Vice asks his intended victim or another to 'kiss his arse', as Diccon gets Hodge to do in *Gammer Gurton's Needle*. In Heywood's *The Four PP* the Pardoner produces a jawbone for his hearers to kiss. But it stinks, and the Pothecary shies away:

> Foh, by St Saviour, I never kissed a worse;
> Ye were as good kiss All-Hallows' arse

The Pardoner then produces a buttock-bone, which the Pothecary rejects outright:

> By Christ, and yet for all your boast,
> This relic hath beshitten the roast.

In *Like Will to Like*, Hance is made to dance:

> *He danceth as ill-favoured as may be devised, and in the dancing he falleth down, and when he riseth he must groan.*
> NICHOL NEWFANGLE: Rise again, Hance, thou hadst almost got a fall:
>> But thou dancest trimly, legs and all.
>> Body of me, Hance, how doth thy belly? Canst thou tell?
>> By the mass he hath berayed his breeches, me think, by the smell.

W. WAGER

Like Will to Like dates from approximately 1568, by which time the Tudor interlude had all but run its course. Perhaps the last playwright in this form of whom notice should be taken is W. Wager, a well-connected teacher and preacher. His two extant plays, *The Longer Thou Livest* and *Enough Is as Good as a Feast*, both dating from about 1569, are remarkable achievements. They employ the basic morality structure, but now the certainty of theology has been replaced by something much closer to social satire. Wager's drama exposes the greedy landlord and the hard struggles of the poor. *The Longer Thou Livest* traces the life of Moros, his youth, adulthood and old age. Moros has attractive features, but he wastes his life and at the end literally goes to the devil. *Enough Is as Good as a Feast* is even more pessimistic. In it, Worldly Man is corrupted, understands his evil, but the plague strikes him down before he can even make a will. A Calvinist gloom hangs over these plays, but they are undeniably powerful. In them, the moral interlude, a form developed for its happy ending designed to comfort the Christian, has become bleakly tragic.

Chapter 9: Theatre in Scotland before 1600

THE FIRST PLAYS PRESENTED IN SCOTLAND

Because of the massive destruction of Scottish documents and records from guilds, burghs, churches and courts – worse destruction even than in England – the story of Scottish theatre before 1600 is difficult to trace with certainty. There were possibly mystery plays or pageants performed in Aberdeen and Dundee, as well as Perth and Edinburgh, in the fifteenth century. But no texts or descriptions have come down to us, though sites of outdoor performance exist at Windmill Hill, Aberdeen and Greenside in Edinburgh.

The text of a Plough Play dating from approximately 1500 has survived. What happens in this little drama is not wholly clear, but it seems that the dying plough ox must be killed. The participants then play the part of a new ox team and drag the plough in procession through the lanes of the village, presumably in celebration of a new agricultural season.

BLACK COURT ENTERTAINERS

What may have been the first troupe of black entertainers in Britain appeared at the court of James IV around 1504. They were probably seized from a Portuguese slaver by Scottish privateers. One was a drummer and choreographer who devised a dance for twelve dancers in black-and-white checked costumes on Shrove Tuesday 1505. He seems to have been a special favourite of the king.

Also in the troupe was a female performer. Her most significant performance came in a pageant presented in Edinburgh in 1504, and repeated three years later, in which she guarded the Tree of Esperance where the knights hung their shields. In the ensuing tournament, the victor, of course, was the king, and he was rewarded by this lady with a tight embrace and kisses on the lips. Her beauty was recorded by William Dunbar: she had full lips, a snub nose and her skin gleamed like tar more splendid than the sun in her brilliant costume, damask flowered with gold, green and yellow taffeta, gauze-covered sleeves, soft leather gloves. Attended by two females in green Flemish taffeta trimmed with yellow, and two males dressed all in white, she was carried in a 'chair triumphale'. At the end of the show a cloud descended from the roof of the palace, and the lady was taken in it up to heaven.

ROBIN HOOD GAMES

There are at least a dozen references to Robin Hood games or plays in Scotland between 1492 and 1612 at Aberdeen, Arbuthnott, Ayr, Dumfries, Edinburgh, Lasswade, Linton and Perth. Scotland's

Reformation Parliament voted to suppress many traditional folk festivities, including Robin Hood games, but the Edinburgh craftsmen and apprentices went ahead anyway in July 1561, only for their elected Robin Hood, James Gillone, a shoemaker, to be arrested, thrown into prison and sentenced to be hanged. His fellows rebelled. In the name of Robin Hood, they 'dinged down' the gallows and barricaded the Tollbooth, and the Constable of Edinburgh Castle was forced to intervene.

DRAMA AND THE SCOTTISH REFORMATION

It seems that Gillone was reprieved, but the incident reminds us of the ferocity of the struggle between John Knox and the Scottish Reformers on the one hand, and tradition, including Catholic tradition upheld by, among others, Mary Queen of Scots, on the other. As with John Bale in England, the Scottish Reformers used the stage to propagandise their beliefs. At Stirling in 1535 a friar, John Kyllour, presented his *History of Christ's Passion* before James V, and in Dundee in the early 1540s James Wedderburn mounted productions of his dramas, including the tragedy, *The Beheading of John the Baptist* and a comedy *Dionysus the Tyrant*. He also seems to have been responsible for a piece of very broad satire, a counterfeit conjuring of a ghost in imitation of the king's former confessor, Friar Laing. But the two men suffered grievously for their activities. Kyllour was taken and burned at the stake by the Catholic hierarchy, and Wedderburn was forced to flee to the continent, where he died after ten years in exile. His dramatic cast of mind seems to have stayed with him, however, for he is reputed to have told his son on his death bed: 'We have been acting our part in the theatre; you are to succeed; see that you act your part faithfully'.[1]

ANE SATIRE OF THE THRIE ESTAITIS

The religious-political debate in Scotland was dramatised most tellingly in *Ane Satire of the Thrie Estaitis* by the courtier, scholar and diplomat, Sir David Lindsay. The play, an enormous 'state of the nation' epic which lasts well over six hours in performance, has demonstrated its stageworthiness in various shortened productions since 1949, as well as a full version given at Linlithgow Castle in 2013. The first half of the play tells how King Humanity is led astray into a passionate relationship with Dame Sensuality. The kingdom descends into disarray, until Divine Correction arrives to urge the king to summon Parliament. The second half shows the three estates – the clergy, the nobility and the burghers – in Parliament. Their corruption is confronted by John the Commonweal, representing the poor, and his intervention leads to them being hanged or banished. Ambiguously enough, Folly is left at the end to preach the sermon-lesson.

The play – or something sounding very like it – was produced in a first short version on 6 January 1540 before James V at Linlithgow, when it so impressed the king that he was immediately stirred to harangue the assembled episcopate on the need for spiritual renewal. The play was then greatly expanded and given, again before James V, in an outdoor performance at Cupar in Fife in 1552. It was preceded by a sort of farcical prologue which, among other facetiousnesses, warned the women spectators to empty their bladders before the play began (at seven in the morning) so as to avoid getting a 'wet shirt'. A third performance after James's death was given on 12 August 1554 on Calton Hill in Edinburgh before Mary of Guise, mother of Mary, Queen of Scots, and at this time Queen Regent. This performance lasted from nine in the morning to six in the evening.

Figure 1.17
Sir David Lindsay's *Ane Satire of the Thrie Estaitis*, performed at the Edinburgh International Festival, 1984, with Caroline Kaart as Dame Sensuality and David Rintoul as King Humanity

Source: Topfoto/ArenaPAL

Lindsay, unlike Kyllour or Wedderburn (or Bale), was a liberal. His monumental play argues for reform, certainly, but the satire ultimately urges moral reform rather than any political change. It is however surprisingly materialistic. The battle is for the king's body, which is perhaps understandable only when Lindsay's own fate is remembered: when James V was kidnapped in 1524 by the Earl of Arran, Lindsay lost his position in the royal household; when James was free again four years later, Lindsay was reinstated. In other words, Lindsay's own livelihood depended on the fate of the king's body. Perhaps not unexpectedly, therefore, bodily functions are much in evidence in the play, and there are a multitude of references to eating, drinking, shitting, pissing, fucking and farting. The Fool's sermon at the end of the play has been likened to a French *sotie*, a kind of short satirical farce in which the Fool turns the world upside down. Despite some *longeurs*, *Ane Satire of the Thrie Estaitis* is an impressive achievement. As one critic noted: 'Its vernacular Scots can express fluently its angry compassion for the poor and powerless, the bawdy colloquialism of arse-kissing farce, virtuoso satirical wordplay and comic routines of the courtly vices, and the formal rhetoric of parliament

Figure 1.18
Linlithgow Palace where the first performance of Sir David Lindsay's *Ane Satire of the Thrie Estaitis* took place in 1540

Source: Sir Gawain/Wikimedia Commons/CC BY-SA 3.0

and preacher'.[2] Its song, music and spectacle provide an exciting release from some of the more closet-like domestic Tudor interludes.

ENTERTAINMENTS AND MASQUERADES

Nothing quite like *Ane Satire of the Thrie Estaitis*was recreated in later years in Scotland: it stands as a solitary high peak of achievement. There were court entertainments and masquerades under James IV and James V, which became more masque-like entertainments for Mary, Queen of Scots, when she briefly reigned. Mary enjoyed 'mirth and pastime', including puppet shows and female jesters, and when her grandson, Prince Henry, was born, a huge public pageant was staged, including a black performer dressed as a lion pulling a decorated chariot.

Figure 1.19
Sir David Lindsay, author of *Ane Satire of the Thrie Estaitis*

Such entertainments were fiercely condemned by the implacable John Knox, though he is reported to have attended a play by John Davidson at St Andrews in 1571 which promulgated the Knoxian faith. Writers for the Queen's entertainments included Alexander Montgomerie and Robert Semple, as well as her old tutor, George Buchanan. Buchanan was a writer who proved unexpectedly influential for European drama, though his work was intended for reading, not performance. He translated Euripides and wrote at least two own original plays in Latin, *Jephthes* about the Biblical Jephthah, and *Baptistes* about John the Baptist.

TWO PLAYS

Two other Scottish plays of the late sixteenth century, the anonymous *Philotus* (c.1585) and *Pamphilus* (c.1590) by John Burel were more comic. *Philotus*, though probably intended for an élite audience, yet resembles a popular *commedia dell'arte* scenario. It is a verse comedy about an old man, Philotus, who wants to marry a young girl. She however manages to escape with her lover despite her father's conniving with the eighty-year-old suitor. Full of fun, chases and slapstick, the play manages to incorporate virtually every plot expedient and stock character the drama has ever known – disguises and cross-dressing, mistaken identities, comic servants, identical twins and traditional gags, all performed by conventional types like the old man, the young lover, the courtesan and the long-lost brother. *Pamphilus*, probably translated from a late Latin play, is a tale of intrigue with a not unhappy ending – the power of sex effectively overwhelms romantic love. Though probably intended only for reading, the play has in fact been staged successfully.

In 1603 the drama-loving James VI of Scotland became James I of England in a union of crowns, but not yet of kingdoms. He brought south with him an enthusiasm for all forms of drama which was crucial to the theatre of the seventeenth century.

NOTES

1 Bill Findlay (ed), *A History of Scottish Theatre*, Edinburgh: Polygon, 1998, p. 19.
2 Ian Brown (ed), *The Edinburgh Companion to Scottish Drama*, Edinburgh: Edinburgh University Press, 2011, p. 19.

Chapter 10: Indoor performance

VENUES

Most performances of Tudor interludes took place in the Great Halls which were the centre of royal palaces, castles, private mansions, guildhalls, school buildings and colleges. This central feature of such buildings was the venue for all sorts of entertainments, especially feasting, but also concerts, dances, masquerades and more, so that drama rubbed shoulders with all sorts of other forms of entertainment. Plays were usually only a part of any festive evening, and the players had to be ready to cut or expand their performances at the shortest notice, or to include intervals between scenes so that those who were there for convivial reasons could get on with their eating and drinking. Some playscripts, indeed, forewarn of this: Rastell includes a note addressed to actors in his published script of *The Four Elements* that 'if ye list ye may leave out much of the sad matter' in the play.

GREAT HALLS

Great halls were fairly similar in layout, though they could vary in size from the huge to the intimate. They were usually rectangular in shape with a dais at one end with a high table, behind the centre of which sat the host, the king or lord or mayor, flanked by the chief guests. At the other end was a lobby, with ways to the kitchens as well as to outside, and partitioned off from the main hall by more or less solid walls. In this partition were two doorways, or openings, through which, for instance, the servants brought food, and the actors in the play entered. The floor of the body of the hall was strewn with rushes, there was a fireplace, probably in one wall, and a number of long tables with benches on either side at right angles from the high table. These might be pushed to the side if necessary for the play to be performed or a dance to be held in the centre of the hall. The whole would be lit by a mass of candles. Usually no scenery was required for the plays, for a specific location for the action is rarely specified, and the centre of the hall functioned like the *platea* of the open air performance spaces. Of course, the two openings in the screen partition opposite the high table could indicate specific houses – Ralph's and Christian Custance's houses in *Roister Doister*, for example, or Gammer Gurton's and Dame Chat's in *Gammer Gurton's Needle*.

Some great halls had the potential for spectacular scenic effects. Lydgate's mummings, for instance, in the 1420s abounded in a certain sort of extravagance. One scholar has proposed for

Figure 1.20
The Great Hall at Eton College, not untypical of the type of venue where many Tudor interludes were performed

Source: Heritage Images/The Print Collector/Diomedia

the *Mumming at Windsor* the need for God, a dove and the angel all to descend from the heavens, and the dove to be on some sort of wire and bearing an ampulla. The action also called for a font for baptism, and a flash of light perhaps through the use of gunpowder. Besides these, there were a large number of splendid costumes, a choir of angels, and much music and singing. A hundred years later, Rastell's staging of the Greenwich pageant included a tiltyard barrier falling from the ceiling when six mounted knights were to do battle, and a huge construction which was wheeled in, with towers and battlements, apparently set on red rocks with flowers and fruit, upon which reclined richly dressed young men, who descended and each invited a lady to dance.

ACTING IN A GREAT HALL

The typical great hall encouraged the actor to develop a strong intimacy with the spectators. In the interludes it is noticeable that many characters push through the audience to enter the playing space, as Youth does in *The Interlude of Youth*: 'Aback, fellows, and give me room, Or I shall make you to avoid soon!' and Ambidexter in *Cambyses*: 'Stand away, stand away, for the passion of God!'

At the beginning of the second half of *Fulgens and Lucres*, B actually gets stuck behind the door when he is due to enter. Earlier it was A who realised that the audience needed a break:

> These folk that sit here in the hall
> May not attend thereto (i.e. to the next part of the story).
> We may not, with our long play,
> Let them from their dinner all day!
> They have not fully dined!

He goes on to order the usher to fill the wine glasses and announce that they will finish the piece once the audience is refreshed.

In *Hick Scorner*, Free Will and Imagination imagine that Hick is hiding among the watchers, while the Prologue to *Jack Juggler* teases the audience that they do not know Latin:

> *Interpone tuis interdum gaudia curis,*
> *Ut possis animo quemvis sufferrer laborem.*
> Do any of you know what Latin is this,
> Or else would you have an *expositorem*
> To declare it in English *per sensum planiorem*?

We may imagine the amused curl of the actor's lip as his sarcasm in the last three of these lines registers. In both *Fulgens and Lucres* and in Heywood's *The Four PP* the audience is made to join in singing organised by particular characters. And pickpockets are another means of involving the audience. In *Cambyses*, Ambidexter warns: 'Take heed for his hand is groping even now' while in *Like Will to Like* Nichol Newfangle admonishes the spectators:

> See to your purses, my masters, and be ruled by me,
> For knaves are abroad; therefore, beware:
> You are warned; and ye take not heed I do not care.

A few moments later, however, we see him seeking to share the pickpockets' ill-gotten takings.

ACTING SKILLS

In this context, the success of the performance depended hugely on the vigour and commitment of the actors. Their performances had to be more nuanced than those of the outdoor players, because they were closer to the spectators, and the action was happening virtually among them. They were helped by the plays which use stock types, and conventional gags, relationships and motifs, but the player had still to be quick-witted and versatile. George Maller, a King's Player in the 1520s and 1530s, talked of the 'feat and cunning' of the actor which his apprentices had to learn. The skills needed included the ability to improvise, speak, sing, dance, tumble, clown, fence, play an instrument or perhaps walk a rope or juggle. Plays could be cut or expanded at the last moment, and the actor had to be ready for this. He would also be expected to find opportunities for music or a song, a comic improvisation or a spectacular insertion. Sometimes this is evident in play texts. Thus, in *The*

Four PP, the Pothecary hopes to show how a lie can leap off his tongue. Sedition in *King Johan* pulls props out of his bag like a conjuror pulling rabbits out of his hat:

> Here is first a bone of the blessed Trinity,
> A dram of the turd of sweet Barnabe;
> Here is a feather of good Saint Michael's wing,
> A tooth of Saint Twide, a piece of David's harp string,

And much more of the same.

ACTING IN *MAGNIFICENCE*

Most interesting from this point of view, perhaps, are the stage directions in Skelton's *Magnificence*, which give us a glimpse of the performances which Tudor actors might aspire to. For instance, Skelton indicates how characters should enter: '*Here let Cloaked Collusion enter with a lofty expression, pacing up and down*', and later '*Here cometh in Crafty Conveyance and Cloaked Collusion with a lusty laughter*'. Other directions are more complex: '*Here let Collusion introduce Measure, while Magnificence stares with a lordly expression*', or, still more interestingly,

> *Here let him act as though he is quietly reading the letter. Meanwhile let Counterfeit Countenance arrive singing and hopping, and when he sees Magnificence let him draw back for a moment. But after a short delay let Counterfeit Countenance approach Magnificence looking at him and speaking from a distance: and Fancy motions him to silence with his hand.*

This asks for extremely sensitive acting and suggests that these play texts must be seen as vehicles for performance even more clearly than is usually the case.

MUSIC AND SONG

The plays abound in music and song. Juventus sings a notably charming Tudor ballad:

> In Herber green asleep where as I lay,
> The birds sang sweet in the midst of the day,
> I dreamed fast of mirth and play,
> In youth is pleasure, in youth is pleasure,

whereas in *Nice Wanton* Delilah and Ismael sing hedonistically:

> Farewell, our school!
> Away with books and all,
> I will set my heart
> On a merry pin,
> Whatever shall befall!

More sophisticated dramatically is the interruption of King Johan's intense prayer by Dissimulation's absurd drinking song:

> JOHAN: From this habitation, sweet Lord, deliver me,
>> And preserve this realm, of thy benignity.
>
> DISSIMULATION (*sings offstage*): Wassail wassail, out of the milk pail,
>> Wassail wassail, as white as my nail,
>> Wassail wassail, in snow, frost and hail,
>> Wassail wassail, with partridge and rail.

DANCE

Like Will to Like shows how dance, too, is often integrated into the musical texture of the plays, when the devil in a bear's costume, the Vice and Tom Collier dance together:

> Nichol Newfangle must have a gittern or some other instrument (if it may be): but if he have not they must dance about the place all three, and sing this song that followeth –which must be done also although they have an instrument.

SET SCENES

The plays also offer actors what might be called 'set scenes' – the courtroom, for instance, as when Nichol Newfangle assumes the role of judge in *Like Will to Like*, or the quasi-rituals in *Gammer Gurton's Needle*. Gammer Gurton makes her friends swear on their knees to seek the needle, and a little later Diccon conjures Hodge so intensely that he fouls his trousers. These scenes recall the ritualised excommunication with 'cross, book, bell and candle' in *King Johan*, for here too the ritual is satirised, even ridiculed, not least when immediately afterwards the Pope sings a jolly song. More serious, but still requiring concentration and precision from the actors is the scene in *The Marriage between Wit and Wisdom* when Wit is sent to sleep:

> Here shall Wantonness sing this song to the tune of 'Attend thee, go play thee'; and having sung him asleep upon her lap, let him snort; then let him set a fool's bauble on his head, and colling (blacking) his face; and Idleness shall steal away his purse from him, and go his ways.

DUMB SHOWS

The dumb shows in *Gorboduc* similarly require considerable skill from the actor:

> First, the music of hautboys began to play, during which there came forth from under the stage, as though out of hell, three furies . . . clad in black garments sprinkled with blood and flames, their bodies girt with snakes, their heads spread with serpents instead of hair, the one bearing in her hand a snake, the other a whip, and the third a burning firebrand: each driving before them a king and a queen; which, moved by furies, unnaturally had slain their own children . . . after that the furies and these had passed about the stage thrice, they departed, and then the music ceased.

EROTIC SCENES

There are erotic scenes, too, tricky to play between two men, which of course also gives them an extra – perhaps unintended – ambiguity, but the authors' frequent insistence in the stage directions on the actors 'kissing' is noteworthy. Among the most interesting of the carnal women to be played by men are the louche temptress Dame Sensuality in *Ane Satire of the Thrie Estaitis*, the siren-like Abominable Living who kisses lusty Juventus, Delilah, the 'nice wanton', and Wantonness, who seduces Wit in *The Marriage Between Wit and Wisdom*. Comedy is not necessarily excluded from these scenes, of course: in *Fulgens and Lucres* B is just kissing Joan when his rival, A, arrives.

COMIC SCENES

Comedy of all kinds suffuses these plays. In *Roister Doister*, Marjorie Mumblecrust is a delightful old woman who belongs to the same tradition as *Romeo and Juliet*'s Nurse. Ralph himself is the centre of much knockabout comedy: he says he will die if Constance refuses him, prompting Merrygreek to exaggerated sympathy, which stretches even to the point of composing a comic funeral song. And when Ralph and his servants, intending to capture Constance by main force, march on her home to the sound of the drum, Ralph suddenly realises he has forgotten his helmet. Dobinet brings him a bucket which he puts on his head. Constance and her servants attack Ralph's 'army' with wooden spoons and saucepans, and after a farcical battle, Ralph and his 'army' retreat defeated.

The actor of the Vice had repeated comic opportunities in the interludes. One contemporary commentator recalled that

> it was a pretty part . . . when the nimble Vice would skip up nimbly like a jackanapes into the devil's neck, and ride the devil a course, and belabour him with his wooden dagger till he made him roar, whereat the people would laugh.

This scene, derived from the moralities, occurs at the end of *Like Will to Like* when Nichol Newfangle 'rideth away on the Devil's back', and in Wager's plays. Moros departs thus in *The Longer Thou Livest*, and at the end of *Enough Is as Good as a Feast* the Devil bears the Vice, Covetousness, 'out upon his back'.

COSTUMES

The Devil and the Vice were instantly recognised by their costume and though many costumes were simple and contemporary, many companies preferred costumes which had symbolic or emblematic overtones. Thus, Money's coat in Thomas Lupton's *All for Money* (1577) was half yellow and half white, upon which were sown gold and silver coins. In *Wisdom*, the king wore a rich purple robe of cloth of gold, while Anima had a white garment, also of cloth of gold, under a black cloak. Costumes, such as these and those made by John Rastell's company, rich and denotative of the symbolic movement of the play, were clearly part of the attraction of many of the better productions. The changes to Moros's beard and his clothes are highly indicative in *The Longer Thou Livest*, as when Ignorance adjusts his clothes ('I would trim you in your gear') or when he is stripped of his outer garments to reveal the Fool's costume beneath. When Youth in the interlude named after him repents and returns to virtuous ways, Charity and Humility give him a 'garment' and a rosary respectively, and when Free Will repents in *Hick Scorner*, he too is given 'a new coat' by Contemplation.

Most telling in terms of symbolic costuming, perhaps, are Bale's 'apparelling of the six vices' for his play, *Three Laws*:

> Let Idolatry be decked like an old witch, Sodomy like a monk of all sects, Ambition like a Bishop, Covetousness like a Pharisee or spiritual lawyer, False Doctrine like a Popish Doctor, and Hypocrisy like a grey friar.

But Sodomy was seen as something of a fool, too:

> This fellow is well decked,
> Disguised and well necked,
> Both knave bold and pie-pecked,
> He lacketh nothing but bells.

STAGE PROPS

As for the few props which the companies used in performance, these too were often symbolic, as with Titivillus's net and satchel in *Mankind* and Mankind's spade. Ambidexter, the Vice in *Cambyses* appears 'with an old cap case on his head, an old pail about his hips for harness, a scummer and a potlid by his side, and a rake on his shoulder'. This play includes the stage direction: '*Strike him with a sword to signify his death*', which could be made so much more splendid by apparently real blood and gore. A few minutes later, the stage direction reads: '*A little bladder of vinegar pricked*'. But props, too, could be more ambiguous. The most obvious example, perhaps, was Gammer Gurton's needle itself. This must have been comically large for the audience to have seen it. Thus it became a kind of phallic symbol, and indeed it is used for anal penetration. Yet a needle is an almost quint-essentially female object. The play, like the best drama of all times, leaves us just a little puzzled.

Chapter 11: Theorising Tudor theatre

While the drama was used mainly to express orthodox religious views it hardly needed justifying. As it became increasingly secularised in the fifteenth century, however, there was a growing need to theorise its purpose and practice.

HUMANIST IDEAS

Initial attempts to do this were associated with Thomas More and the group of humanists surrounding him. More himself was fascinated by drama, as Anthony Munday's play indicates, and as we may infer from the fact that he amended a play about the wise King Solomon, possibly for performance at Magdalene College, Oxford, in 1501. This triggered a trend at both Oxford and Cambridge. A stage was erected for plays at Peterhouse, Cambridge, in 1562 and again in 1571 and 1572. Pembroke College, Cambridge, had plays in 1582 and 1585, though in the first of these years, it is recorded that Miles Moses, a fellow of Pembroke, broke the head and shed the blood of Robert Thexton of Corpus Christi College, 'while the stage production was being put on'.

More's friend Erasmus, author of *The Education of a Christian Prince*, published in 1516, argued that performance provided a means of learning. It taught the value of memorising, speaking and rhetoric, as well as voice training and role playing. He also emphasised its value in understanding and learning how to use gesture and movement, and also prosopopoeia, identifying with the speaker and exploring the emotion behind rhetoric. Acting itself in the sixteenth century came to bear the mark of Erasmus's precepts in its presentational style and it is noticeable that many schoolteachers after Erasmus pursued an active interest in performance, including John Heywood, Nicholas Udall and Richard Edwards.

The humanist scholars advocated performing the comedies of Plautus and Terence, rather than simply reading them, and a production of a play by Terence at Cambridge in 1510 or 1511 may have been the first such in England. By 1520 Henry VIII was watching Plautus, and in 1527 and 1528 the pupils of St Paul's presented plays by both Plautus and Terence. This educational drive was continued by Sir Thomas Elyot, author of *The Book Named the Governor*, published in 1531, in which he emphasised the usefulness of comedy. It was, he said, 'a mirror of man's life' in which

> evil is not taught but discovered, to the intent that men beholding the promptness of youth unto vice, the snares of harlots and bawds laid for young minds, the deceit of servants, (and) the chances of fortune contrary to men's expectations.

Comedies, Elyot asserted, helped audiences to be ready for the vicissitudes of fortune. Roger Ascham, tutor to Princess, later Queen, Elizabeth, and author of *The Schoolmaster*, which largely expressed ideas from Erasmus, took much the same line. Ascham recalled how he enjoyed discussing dramatic theory at St John's College, Cambridge, with Sir John Cheke and Thomas Watson, author of the play, *Absolom*.

PLAY PUBLICATION AND ITS PURPOSES

A further consequence of this interest in drama as a humanist discipline was that plays began to be published. John Rastell, More's brother-in-law, was instrumental in this development, which changed the visibility and status of drama. Not only did the printing of texts disseminate knowledge of plays, it also suggested that these were works dedicated to the teaching of philosophy or morality. Rastell himself indicates some of this in his Prologue to *The Four Elements*:

> . . . because some folk be little disposed
> To sadness, but more to mirth and sport,
> This philosophical work is mixed
> With merry conceits, to give men comfort
> And occasion to cause them to resort
> To hear this matter, whereto if they take heed
> Some learning to them thereof may proceed.

Other playwrights agreed that learning and laughter were the twin pillars of comedy. Thus Udall, in *Roister Doister*, first declared his belief in laughter, claiming he knew

> . . . nothing more commendable for man's recreation
> Than Mirth which is used in an honest fashion:
> Mirth recreates our spirits and voideth pensiveness,
> Mirth increaseth amity, not hindering our wealth . . .

This refreshingly open attitude ('Mirth recreates our spirits') was, however, modified:

> The wise poets long time heretofore,
> Under merry comedies secrets did declare,
> Wherein was contained very virtuous lore,
> With mysteries and forewarnings very rare.

W. Wager, in *The Longer Thou Livest*, articulated the same idea, but the other way round: his comedies contained 'wholesome lessons' delivered via 'honest mirth' which would lead to 'the shame of vice'.

STEPHEN GOSSON

None of this quite answered the increasingly ferocious attacks on the inherent depravity of the drama, as writers like Stephen Gosson saw it. Gosson, a playwright and actor, educated at Corpus

Christi College, Oxford, renounced the theatre in favour of Puritan religiosity and denounced his old colleagues and their profession. According to him, plays corrupted the nation, led to effeminacy and licentiousness and 'rocked us asleep in all ungodliness'. He clearly enjoyed imagining the sins of playgoers:

> In our assemblies at plays in London, you shall see such heaving, and shoving, such itching and shouldering to sit by women: such care for their garments, that they be not trod on: such eyes to their laps, that no chips light in them: such pillows to their backs, that they take no hurt: such masking in their ears, I know not what: such giving them pippins to pass the time: such playing at foots aunt without cards: such tickling, such toying, such smiling, such winking, and such manning them home when the sports are ended, that it is a right comedy to mark their behaviour.[1]

LATER HUMANIST DEFENDERS OF THE DRAMA: EDWARDS, WHETSTONE, SIDNEY

Gosson is important partly because he dedicated his work, probably without permission, to Sir Philip Sidney, author of *The Defence of Poesy* and a critic of some standing. Sidney never supported Gosson, but he took issue with a basic idea of Richard Edwards, a musician and playwright who was Master of the Children of the Royal Chapel. Edwards wrote the play, *Damon and Pithias* (1564), which survives, though his later *Palamon and Arcite*, which may stand behind *Measure for Measure*, is lost. In the Prologue to *Damon and Pithias* Edwards explains that the only fair term he can find to describe his play is 'tragical comedy', the word 'tragicomedy' not having yet been coined. In it, he says he mixes 'mirth and care' rather as Nicholas Grimald had in his 1540 Latin play, *Christus Redivivus*, which he too had labelled a 'tragic comedy'. It was the kind of play English (and Scottish) authors had developed, mixing merriments with serious content, but it enraged critics like Sir Philip Sidney. He likened such drama to 'hornpipes and funerals' and his older contemporary, George Whetstone, observed testily how English dramatists, 'many times, to make mirth . . . make a clown companion with a king'.[2] Whetstone was a friend of the dramatist, George Gascoigne, and wrote at least one play, *Promos and Cassandra*, himself. He insisted on the prime importance of literary decorum, that characterisation and dialogue must reflect the characters' social status. A 'tragic comedy' could surely not achieve this.

Sidney agreed, but went further:

> how all their plays be neither right tragedies, nor right comedies, mingling kings and clowns, not because the matter so carrieth it, but thrust in clowns by head and shoulders, to play a part in majestical matters with neither decency nor discretion, so as neither the admiration and commiseration, nor the right sportfulness, is by their mongrel tragicomedy obtained.[3]

Sidney's comments contained an important kernel. Disagreeing with Edwards's other contention that tragedy, unlike comedy, should be rooted in history by arguing that tragic truth is poetic not historical, he asserted that tragedy 'stirs the affects of admiration and commiseration'. Sidney probably knew Aristotle, if only at second hand (he advocated a rather crude version of the 'three unities' of action, place and time for tragedy), but his variation on the more familiar 'fear and pity' is surely piquant.

These critics also addressed problems of characterisation, which for them was never a matter of psychology, but rather of decorum. Edwards asserted the need

> . . . to frame each person so
> That by his common talk you may his nature rightly know.
> A roister ought not preach, that were too strange to hear.
> But as from virtue he doth swerve, so ought his words appear.
> The old man is sober: the young man rash: the lover triumphing in joys:
> The matron grave: the harlot wild and full of wanton toys.[4]

Effectively this meant the dramatist employing stock types in his plays, and Whetstone endorsed this: 'To work a comedy kindly', he wrote, 'grave old men should instruct, young men should show the imperfections of youth, strumpets should be lascivious, boys unhappy, and clowns should speak disorderly'.[5]

Figure 1.21
Sir Philip Sidney, a prominent theorist of Tudor theatre

Source: Art Collection 3/Alamy Stock Photo

Sidney believed in decorum rather than realism, too. He admitted to being not greatly attracted by the drama, though he approved of *Gorboduc* and liked the works of George Buchanan. He was probably present at the entertainment presented to the Queen at Kenilworth in 1575, and himself wrote an interesting court masque, *The Lady of May*. He was heavily influenced by the Italian critical tradition and though his sister, the playwright and drama patron, Mary, Countess of Pembroke, probably understood the drama better than he did, he was responsible for one apparently unpremeditated but extremely lucid insight into dramatic convention: 'What child is there that coming to a play, and seeing *Thebes* written in great letters upon an old door, doth believe that it is Thebes?' Yet curiously, and disappointingly, he failed to comprehend the open stage, the *platea*, and grumbled at it like a nineteenth-century naturalist playwright:

> You shall have Asia of the one side and Afric of the other, and so many under-kingdoms that the player, when he comes in, must ever begin with telling where he is or else the tale will not be conceived. Now ye shall have three ladies walk to gather flowers and then we must believe the stage to be a garden. By and by, we hear news of shipwreck in the same place and then we are to blame if we accept it not for a rock.[6]

The remarks of these critics as they begin to wrestle with the problems of drama remain interesting, but they are unable to take the debate much further. They all concur on the moral purpose of comedy. Thus Whetstone admired the Roman audiences who 'won morality (from a play) as the bee sucks honey from weeds', but it was Sidney who made the humanist case in the plainest terms: 'comedy is an imitation of the common errors of our life . . . in the most ridiculous and scornful sort that may be; so as it is impossible that any beholder can be content to be such a one'.[7]

NOTES

1 Stephen Gosson, *Plays Confuted in Five Actions*, 1582.
2 George Whetstone, 'Epistle Dedicatory', *Promos and Cassandra*, 1578.
3 Sir Philip Sidney, *The Defence of Poesy*, 1595.
4 Richard Edwards, *Prologue to Damon and Pithias*, 1564.
5 George Whetstone, *op.cit.*
6 Sir Philip Sidney, *op.cit.*
7 *Ibid*.

Chapter 12: Fooling and clowning

KINGS AND FOOLS

George Whetstone's objection to seeing a clown as 'a companion with a king' flew in the face of all English and Scottish theatre practice of his time. The clown was a real-life entertainer of kings who also found his way into very many stage plays.

Pace Whetstone, almost every English king kept a fool. Roger Follus and Roland le Pettour entertained the court of Henry II, William Picol was King John's fool, Tom le Fol amused Edward I, Robert Bussard was Edward II's, Jakeman was Edward III's, Richard II's fool was named William. Later, one Woodhouse was a witty fool to Edward IV and Henry VII's fools included Peche in 1492 and Dick in 1493. And they were well looked after: the perhaps appropriately named William Worthy was 'Keeper of the King's Fools'. Some queens had fools of their own, too. Anne Boleyn had a female fool and so did Queen Mary in the 1550s. In Scotland, Mary, Queen of Scots, had a series of female fools, including the French 'La Jardinière' who wore a green plaiding coat, Jane Colquhoun whose costume was red and yellow, and Nichola 'La Folle', also from France, who stayed with Mary even when she was imprisoned, though later she returned to France.[1]

WISE FOOL AND SIMPLE FOOL

Fools were of two sorts. There was, first, the wise or witty fool, like Edward IV's Woodhouse, or, later, Patch, fool to Henry VIII. Though it would be dangerous to generalise, and in any case fashions changed, it seems that the witty fool often wore a costume of more than a single colour, 'motley', and perhaps a cock's comb or fantastical hat, and he often carried either a slapstick, a stick with a split end so that when he banged it on something or somebody, it made a resounding slap even if the blow was not severe, or a 'bauble', a stick with a head – perhaps his own, perhaps the king's – in miniature at its end. This fool was in contrast to the simpleton, or clown, or 'natural'. He was the 'fall guy', 'he who gets slapped', who often wore a rustic smock and a slouch hat, and was sometimes genuinely mentally or physically disabled. A definition of this clown from 1802, describes

> a rustic appearance, vacant or gazing eyes, an open mouth, arms dangling, yet shoulders raised, the toes turned inwards, a shambling gait with a heavy step, great slowness of conception, and apparent stupidity of mind and manner.[2]

Figure 1.22
A clown entertains the king, his wife and perhaps his two daughters as servants wait on them at table: woodcut from Wynkyn de Worde, *Book of Kerving* (carving), 1508

Source: Granger Historical Picture Archive/Alamy Stock Photo

The fact that this description was written three hundred years after Henry VII's time suggests the enduring appeal of the clown. Throughout the history of comedy and foolery, these two characters, the wit and the natural, have worked together as a double act, and this certainly occurred during Tudor times.

HENRY VIII'S FOOLS

Henry VIII had a fool of his own, John Goose, at the age of ten. Lob, a 'natural', was his fool when he became king, and he was complemented by 'Master Sexton', known as Patch, who was presented to Henry by Cardinal Wolsey. Patch wore a coat of Kendal green, twilled mock-velvet hose and a fancy hat to cover his baldness. An amusing poem indicates the sort of illogical foolery Patch indulged in:

> Master Sexton, a person of known wit,
> As he at my Lord Cardinal's board did sit,
> Greedily raught at a goblet of wine:
> 'Drink none', said my lord, 'for that sore leg of thine'.
> 'I warrant your Grace', quoth Sexton, 'I provide
> For my leg; for I drink on t'other side'.[3]

Figure 1.23
Will Somer, King Henry VIII's jester or 'natural'

Patch seems to have been unable to accept Henry VIII's discarding of Katherine of Aragon and her daughter Mary, and apparently referred to Anne Boleyn as 'ribald' and her daughter Elizabeth as a bastard. He was fired and replaced with James Lockwood who, after Henry died, continued his career as an itinerant solo performer into the 1570s.

Henry VIII appointed Will Somer as his 'natural' fool, perhaps in succession to Lob, in the 1530s, and it may be assumed that Somer and Lockwood on occasion formed a double act. Somer was kindly and simple, his humour expressed, for instance, in word-jumbling: 'Frauditers, Conveyers and Deceivers' he said, instead of 'Auditors, Surveyors and Receivers'. Somer continued in favour after

Henry's death. He attended on George Ferrers when the latter was Lord of Misrule at Christmas 1552 and participated in the mock combat dressed in cardboard armour. Under Queen Mary he found a new and original partner for a double act – Mary's female fool, Jane: Mary seems to have appreciated each of these equally. In 1559 Will Somer was at Queen Elizabeth's coronation, and he died in June 1560. However, his fame lived on, and he was resurrected as a character in Thomas Nashe's 1592 pastoral, *Summer's Last Will and Testament*. The title of this play depends on a pun: the central character is Summer who is fading into autumn and needs to make a will, while the narrator, or author's mouthpiece, is Will Somer. Somer here stands between the audience and the actors, mediating the proceedings with sardonic asides. After one scene, he springs up: 'Heigh ho. Here is a coil indeed to bring beggars to stocks. I promise you truly, I was almost asleep; I thought I had been at a sermon'.

CLOWNS AND THE STAGE

It is hardly surprising therefore that many dramatists wished to make clowns companions to their kings. We see the clown edging towards the stage in the person of Kelsey, who was playing the part of the Vice in a performance at Bungay in 1566, but who was paid also 'for his pastime before the play, and after the play'. In Heywood's *The Play of the Weather*, Merry Report may have been played initially by John Scott, probably a dwarf who was a fool at the court of Henry VII in the 1490s and subsequently joined the King's Players as their comic man. He seems to have been a tumbler, juggler and dancer, as well as a clown. Merry Report is a witty fool, fast on his feet, manipulative and cunning. He frequently appeals to the audience, as clowns often do, and, indeed, quite early in the play comes among them and knocks them about:

> Now, sirs, take heed! For here cometh God's servant!
> Avaunt, carterly caitiffs, avaunt!
> Why, ye drunken whoresons, will it not be?
> By your faith, have ye neither cap nor knee?
> Not one of you that will make curtsy
> To me, that am squire for God's precious body?

This is traditional stuff for a clown. Equally traditional is Folly at the end of *Ane Satire of the Thrie Estaitis*. He enters the pulpit to preach an 'upside-down' sermon on the text, 'Infinite are the number of fools', during which he hands out fools' caps to his social superiors. Similarly, conventional is Wager's treatment of Moros in *The Longer Thou Livest*. Moros, the central figure, is disrobed near the end of the play to reveal a Fool's motley under his garments. He has shown the validity of this transformation a little earlier when he fights himself – a traditional *lazzo* stolen from *commedia dell'arte*.

DOUBLE ACTS

Traditional double acts are also prevalent in Tudor drama. The Croxton *Play of the Sacrament* has the doctor and his servant wisecracking with the audience about their ailments. The Pardoner and the Friar, in Heywood's play of the same name, fall to in an absurd slapstick combat. In *Magnificence*, Folly enters 'shaking his bauble and making much ado by beating drums and such like'. He

Figure 1.24
Clown depicted in the St Jerome Great Bible, c.1410, entertaining the people and perhaps God

Source: British Library, London/Diomedia

is the witty fool, and he indulges in a good deal of cross talk with the slower clown, Fancy. He takes Fancy's dog amid much amusing 'business' and tricks Fancy into swapping his purse, which contains forty marks, for his own, which holds only an old shoe buckle. All this is carried through with comic patter and probably a fair amount of extemporising. A little later Folly pretends to extract a louse from Crafty Conveyance's gown. Crafty takes the gown off, and in the ensuing mayhem, he and Crafty may somehow even manage to get each an arm through the gown's different sleeves. Fancy laughs uproariously at a physical gag still being used by Laurel and Hardy over four hundred years later.

Matthew Merrygreek and Ralph form another kind of double act in *Roister Doister*. The crafty Merrygreek contrasts with the roistering Ralph, the butt of his companion's jokes because he is lugubriously, and inappropriately, in love. They, too, follow classic comic routines, such as when Merrygreek slaps Ralph. Ralph asks why he has hit him. Merrygreek tells him there was a feather on his coat. He slaps him again. This time Merrygreek says an insect was crawling on him. And a third time. When Ralph protests again, Merrygreek tells him 'it was a lousy hair from your mastership's beard'.

In the double act between the nimble-witted Jack Juggler and the slower, more deliberate Jenkin Careawaie, Jack Juggler pretends to be Careawaie. Careawaie repudiates him: *he* is Jenkin Careawaie, page to his kindly Master Boundgrace. For this defiance, Jack Juggler strikes him. 'Art thou Master Boundgrace's page?' Careawaie asserts he is. 'Dar'st thou to my face say thou art I?' Jack Juggler strikes him again. Careawaie again protests he is Jenkin Careawaie. Jack Juggler strikes him again. And a fourth, fifth, sixth and seventh time, until Careawaie is psychologically bamboozled, and admits he does not know who he is. Careawaie's comic bafflement is voiced with exaggerated weeping, in another Stan Laurel-like performance:

> Good Lord of Heaven, where did I myself leave?
> Or who did me of my name by the way bereave?

Figure 1.25
Fool on a hobby horse, from an English psalter, late fourteenth century
Source: Granger Historical Picture Archive/Alamy Stock Photo

Dame Coy hits him, too. Careawaie is surely the ultimate fall guy who gets slapped. Finally, when he is asked where Careawaie is, he suggests that maybe he is in the hall: Master Boundgrace and Careawaie himself charge into the audience to seek him, to no avail. When Careawaie tries to explain, even Boundgrace slaps him!

CLOWNS: SUBVERSIVE OR RIDICULOUS?

Are these clowns subversive or merely ridiculous? Boundgrace asserts the prerogatives of the master. Matthew Merrygreek and Skelton's Folly may be clever, but they are surely no threat. Yet clowning can be disruptive, and the absurdity of the Pardoner and the Friar, supposedly reverent fathers, fighting over trivialities, may convey the implicit truth embedded in foolery. As Sir David Lindsay's Folly insinuates, we are all foolish, and none more so than our betters. That is why Whetstone is wrong and why clowns make particularly fitting companions for kings.

NOTES

1 Antonia Fraser, *Mary Queen of Scots*, London: Weidenfeld and Nicolson, 1994.
2 Anon, 'The Art of Acting', *The Theatrical Recorder*, London, 1802, p. 66.
3 John Southworth, *Fools and Jesters at the English Court*, Stroud: Sutton Publishing, 2003, p. 85.

Chapter 13: The struggle for control

THE THEATRE OF THE 1520S

Before the reign of Henry VIII, little attempt was made by the secular authorities to control the drama, and in the 1520s a remarkably dynamic theatrical culture flourished. In pride of place, at least for the authorities, were the spectacular entertainments of various sorts mounted by the royal household. These were complemented by city processions, mummings, pageants and the like. In the country there were May games, Robin Hood plays, Boy Bishops, as well as plenty of strolling entertainers and small but sturdy troupes of four or five actors with their costumes and props loaded on a pony or wagon. These companies performed a rich repertoire of plays with often quite sophisticated political content. Amateur groups in towns and country were often serviced by such professionals, and companies like that of John Rastell existed to help them, as well as to make a profit for themselves. And in schools and colleges there were productions of Latin plays and classes in speaking, acting and singing.

This was not entirely without its problems, of course: theatrical entertainments are always potential battlegrounds. In 1527, the player and dramatist, John Roo, presented a satirical play at Gray's Inn which dramatised how misgovernment sparks popular rebellion, which so offended Cardinal Wolsey that Roo was flung into the Fleet Prison and the student actors roundly rebuked. Ten years after this there was the case of a play given in Suffolk about 'a king, (and) how he should govern his realm'. In the performance, the actor playing the part of Husbandry said 'many things against gentlemen, more than was in the book of the play', a clearly subversive undertaking.

POLITICS AND RELIGION: DRAMA AGAINST CATHOLICISM

But still, the situation seemed set fair until, in 1529, Henry VIII, who loved the drama as well as any British monarch, began divorce proceedings against Katherine of Aragon, and in view of the Pope's intransigent opposition to his plans, he took the government of ecclesiastical affairs into his own hands. To understand these happenings, it is crucial to understand that politics and religion were two sides of one coin: political struggles were religious struggles, and over the next decades, indeed over the next century and a half, the political-religious battles were bitter and often vicious. More Roman Catholics were burned in Tudor and Stuart England than in any other European country, and plenty of Protestants and Puritans were also burned or otherwise judicially assassinated during this period. The theatre was swept willy–nilly into the ensuing controversy.

There were straws in the wind. In 1532 the City of Chester had demanded the removal from the mystery cycle performances of all references to papal supremacy. But the critical moment for the theatre came, perhaps, in 1535 when Sir Richard Morrison urged the king to use drama as a propaganda weapon against Catholicism, and for the next thirty years the theatre was the site of constant strife.

In 1536 Henry pushed the justices in York to imprison those staging Catholic plays, presumably referring to the mystery cycle. His Chancellor, Thomas Cromwell, a man known to enjoy good food and to employ his own jester, supported the radical preacher-cum-dramatist John Bale who was happy to compose and present vitriolic anti-Catholic plays. And though Cromwell fell from power and was executed in 1540, the theatrical reformation continued. In 1541 the producer of an ideologically misconceived play in Shoreditch was prosecuted, and a troupe of actors in Wiltshire were burned to death because of their work. In 1542 the Protestant bishops advised Henry to 'correct public plays and comedies which are acted in London, to the contempt of God's word', and the next year an Act of Parliament 'for the Advancement of True Religion' attempted to define what was permissible subject matter for drama. In 1545 there was a notorious controversy in Cambridge after the staging of an anti-Catholic play, perhaps one of John Bale's, and the same year the office of the Master of Revels was reorganised, and he was provided with a comptroller and a yeoman to assist him and the Lord Chamberlain to oversee drama throughout the country.

THE STRUGGLE IN THE TIME OF EDWARD VI

The death of Henry VIII in 1547 only exacerbated the struggle. The advisers to the young Edward VI were clear that the stage was potentially subversive and must be controlled. In Norfolk, a crypto-Communist revolution led by Robert Ket was said to have been fomented when many poor people attended a play: they laid down their tools and sought redress for their wrongs through non-cooperation rather than violence. It did them little good, for the government's Italian and German mercenaries quickly destroyed them along with their ideals. But it seemed to underline the danger of the drama.

In 1548 Hereford City Council abolished their Corpus Christi mystery play in perhaps the first example of a political closing down of this long-lasting form. Over the next thirty years, most of the mystery cycles were banned or strangulated out of existence. Its supporters sometimes seemed to adapt: in Norwich in 1565 the Grocers Company staged a 'reformed' version of *Adam and Eve*, but the tide was running against them. It was reinforced by the intellectual case against the mystery cycles being made by Humanist scholars who advocated the staging of classical plays and held up Terence and Seneca as right dramatic models for a drama with wider subject matter than the simple Bible stories, and a more sophisticated form than the medieval pageants.

QUEEN MARY: THE CATHOLICS FIGHT BACK

This is not to say, however, that there was no attempt at a counter-reformation in the drama. Edward VI's death in 1553 led first to the brief near-reign of Lady Jane Grey and then to the accession of the Catholic Queen Mary. Now the politics of religion swung the other way and Protestant performers were in danger as she made energetic attempts to reverse the anti-Catholic trend. She saw to the

Figure 1.26
The Catholic Queen Mary Tudor, who inaugurated a purge of Protestant drama

Source: Museo del Prado, Madrid

banning of specific Protestant plays, the arresting and imprisonment of recalcitrant actors and the prohibition on performing on Sundays. Thus in April 1557 the Lord President of the North received instructions from the Privy Council to summarily ban the company belonging to Sir Francis Leke because 'their plays and enterludes' contained 'very naughty and seditious matter touching the King and Queen's majesties, and the state of this realm, and . . . slander Christ's true and Catholic religion'. Such plays were menacing, for through them 'the people may . . . be stirred to disorder'.[1] Similar directives were sent to Canterbury, Essex and several places in London.

ELIZABETH I: ATTEMPTS TO CONTROL

In the year following this injunction to the Lord President of the North, however, Mary died, and her half-sister Elizabeth, a staunch Protestant, ascended the throne. Her first instincts were to fetter the theatre still more closely. Her Parliament quickly passed an Act which permitted acting companies to perform only so long as their plays did not treat of 'matters of religion or the governance of the estate of the common weale'. These were 'no mete matters to be written or treated upon, but by men of authority, learning and wisdom, nor to be handled before any audience but of grave and discreet persons'.

Elizabeth's settlement seemed, perhaps unintentionally, to give licence to the Puritan campaign against drama in all its forms. The City of London struggled to regulate the players. It said they defied their legitimate authority over inns and gardens, they caused traffic jams around the performance venues, people went to plays instead of to church on Sundays and the crowds inevitably helped to spread plague. An outbreak of plague seemed almost welcome to these campaigners against theatre, as it allowed them to inveigh against the perceived evil. For others, stage performers of any kind were simply public nuisances: 'almost all places in these our days', said John Northbrooke in 1577, 'are replenished with jugglers, scoffers, jesters, and players, which may say and do what they list, be it never so filthy and fleshly, and yet are suffered, and heard with laughing and clapping of hands'.[2]

These ongoing struggles, the swaying back and forth over what was permissible and what was not, during the thirty or more years after Henry VIII sued for divorce, encapsulate the seemingly eternal divisions and struggles over the licensing of drama. They certainly have a resonance not just for Tudor theatre, but for virtually all the ensuing history of the British theatre.

NOTES

1 Glynne Wickham, Herbert Berry and William Ingram (eds), *English Professional Theatre 1530–1660*, Cambridge: Cambridge University Press, 2000, p. 43.
2 Glynne Wickham, Herbert Berry and William Ingram, *op.cit.*, p. 160.

Select bibliography

Beadle, Richard, and Fisher, Alan J. (eds), *The Cambridge Companion to Medieval English Theatre*, 2nd edn, Cambridge: Cambridge University Press, 2008

Betteridge, Thomas, and Walker, Greg (eds), *The Oxford Handbook of Tudor Drama*, Oxford: Oxford University Press, 2012

Brown, Ian (ed), *The Edinburgh Companion to Scottish Drama*, Edinburgh: Edinburgh University Press, 2011

Brown, Pamela Allen, and Parolin, Peter (eds), *Women Players in England, 1500–1660*, Aldershot: Ashgate Publishing, 2005

Davidson, Clifford, *Festivals and Plays in Late Medieval Britain*, Aldershot: Ashgate Publishing, 2007

Happé, Peter, *English Drama Before Shakespeare*, London: Longmans, 1999

Holland, Peter, and Orgel, Stephen (eds), *From Script to Stage in Early Modern England*, Basingstoke: Palgrave Macmillan, 2004

Lancashire, Anne, *London Civic Theatre*, Cambridge: Cambridge University Press, 2002

Lancashire, Ian, *Dramatic Texts and Records of Britain: A Chronological Topography*, Cambridge: Cambridge University Press, 1984

Milling, Jane, and Thomson, Peter, *The Cambridge History of British Theatre*, vol 1, Cambridge: Cambridge University Press, 2004

Southworth, John, *Fools and Jesters at the English Court*, Stroud: Sutton Publishing, 2003

White, Paul Whitfield, *Theatre and Reformation: Protestantism, Patronage and Playing in Tudor England*, Cambridge: Cambridge University Press, 1993

Wickham, Glynne, Berry, Herbert, and Ingram, William (eds), *English Professional Theatre 1530–1660*, Cambridge: Cambridge University Press, 2000

Interlude: The Queen's Men

POLITICAL DANGERS

By 1580, the political stability of England seemed increasingly imperilled by resurgent Catholic enemies. At home, although the queen's cousin, Mary, Queen of Scots, was imprisoned, her existence gave a focus to disaffected Catholic plotters who were determined to replace Elizabeth with Mary. Abroad, the Catholic threat was fiercely embodied in the Spanish, who were gearing up to invade England with their fearsome Armada.

The regime's basic ideological stance was 'reformed Protestant': that is, not Catholic, but not Puritan either. The Puritans provided another sort of threat, not perhaps as dangerous as that of the Catholics, but still they had no intention of endorsing Elizabeth's middle-of-the-road compromises. Elizabeth was thus walking something of a political tightrope, and to maintain her balance she needed to know precisely what plots were hatching, where new plots might emerge and exactly what they would consist of. She needed detailed, accurate, up-to-date information about what was going on in the country.

THE QUEEN'S MEN: AIMS AND OBJECTIVES

In 1582 Francis Walsingham, the Queen's principal secretary, was put in charge of a sizeable budget to be spent gathering such informations, that is, effectively, on spying. Interestingly, a portion of this budget went on establishing a new theatre company – the Queen's Men. At its simplest level, the new company would tour the country as a kind of substitute for the queen herself since she had given up her royal progresses. They would, as it were, fly her flag and be the visible face of the monarchy to the people. And the success of this policy can be judged from Thomas Nashe's famous anecdote: when the audience at a country performance roared with laughter at the clown, Dick Tarlton's, antics, the local magistrate laid about them with his stick for disrespecting the queen's representatives.

They offered further advantages, too. Theatre troupes were proliferating, their rivalries becoming too fierce. There was an almost anarchic free-for-all among them, often springing from the vicious competition between different lordly patrons who, as courtiers, wished to see their own stars in the ascendant. For the queen's government, it was therefore worth creating a single troupe of the best players who would outshine all the others. They alone would provide the royal entertainment at festivals such as Christmas, and thus they would cow and reduce all the other troupes. It would be infinitely preferable for the authorities to deal with a single company: it made censorship easier, and arranging court performances simpler. Furthermore, it allowed the court to assert itself in the face of the city authorities' campaign against the theatre, and it gave them direct access to, if not perhaps total control over, this growing and unruly form.

Walsingham also had deeper, less overt purposes. The company could become the regime's most effective means of propaganda for the monarch and the *status quo*. Their message would be cunningly embedded in the dramas they presented, of course, but it would definitely be there. Besides, company members could, on their travels, keep a sharp eye and ear open, they could collect all sorts of possibly useful information and relay that information back to Walsingham. It seems they did so. John Garland, a comic actor of some stature within the group, for example, was awarded a special pension by the queen of two shillings per day in 1595 for his political usefulness.

THE FORMATION OF THE QUEEN'S MEN

Thus, the formation of a Queen's company would fulfil many telling functions. In early 1583, a nucleus of twelve of the best actors were brought from other troupes and contracted as sharers in

Figure 1.27
Dick Tarlton, the star and leading comedian of the Queen's Men
Source: British Library, London

the new, unusually large, company. Some of them, including John Towne, Lionel Cooke, William Johnson, John Dutton and John Garland, stayed with the company for many years, well into the 1590s. The others remained Queen's Men for shorter periods, but they were all notable performers: Tobias Mills; John Bentley, who played leading tragic roles; John Adams, an athletic man who specialised in loveable or clever rogues and was still remembered three decades later in Ben Jonson's *Bartholomew Fair*; John Lanham, who was to lead half the company when it was desirable – as it sometimes became – to appear in two different places at once; John Singer, who played dolts and dullards, but was renowned for his *ad-libbing*; and the two biggest stars, Robert Wilson and Richard Tarlton. Wilson, also famed for his ad-libs, combined playwriting with acting and had, according to one critic, 'a quick, delicate, refined extemporal wit'. He seems to have partnered Tarlton and also later Will Kemp, perhaps as the straight man to their comic, like Ernie Wise to Eric Morecombe. More will be said of Tarlton in the section on the Elizabethan jig that follows: he was the star of the Queen's Men, the most famous and best loved performer of the time.

The company was well paid and highly regarded. Thomas Heywood, a generation later, recorded that 'by the report of many judicial auditors, their performances of many parts (were) so absolute that it were a kind of sin to drown their worths in Lethe, and not commit their (almost forgotten) names to eternity'. And because they were privileged, the City of London complained to the Privy Council, that 'all the places of playing were filled with men calling themselves the Queen's players'.

CHANGING PERSONNEL

But they were not a stable group for long. John Bentley and Tobias Mills died within two years of the troupe's establishment. Bentley's place was taken by William Knell, and Lawrence Dutton, John Dutton's brother, was also an early recruit, perhaps Tobias Mills's replacement. But Knell did not last long, either. For some reason, in 1587 he tracked and attacked his colleague, John Towne, but was himself killed in the ensuing scuffle. (His widow, by the way, then married John Hemminges, Shakespeare's colleague, who edited his First Folio thirty-five years later.) In 1588 the company suffered their most grievous loss when Tarlton died. Some good actors joined them – Francis Henslowe, George Attewell, Robert Nicholls, William Smith, John Shank and John Cowper – and in 1592 they were still good enough to tempt Cambridge University students out to the village of Chesterton to see them, but they gave their last performance at court in 1594 and spent the last decade of the queen's reign almost entirely in the provinces.

IN THE PROVINCES

But that, of course, was where Walsingham wanted them. Immediately on their formation in 1583 they had set off for East Anglia, where they made good money, being paid officially forty shillings in Norwich, twenty shillings in Aldeburgh, forty shillings in Ipswich and so on, as well as moneys collected at other public performances. In Norwich, Bentley and Singer were involved in a fracas when a man with his servant refused to pay the admission price and began acting aggressively while the play was in progress. Despite Tarlton's attempts to intervene, Bentley, in full beard and carrying his stage sword, and with Singer backing him, flew at the man. He ran off, but the actors caught him, a fight ensued and the servant, named George, was killed. Bentley and Singer were apprehended and imprisoned though (perhaps because they were the Queen's servants) only for a short period.

In June and July 1583 the company were touring Bristol and the south west, in August and September they were in the south east. Later this same year they may have split into two groups for the first time: in London for the winter, they occupied both the Theatre and the Curtain, and gave three performances at court, too. When they split in later years it seems that Lanham led one group and the Dutton brothers the other. But the tours continued inexorably: in 1583–4 they were seen at Bath, Cambridge, Marlborough, Norwich, Saffron Walden and Southampton among other places; in 1587–8 they played in Bath, Coventry, Exeter, Faversham, Hythe, Lydd, Maidstone, Southampton and Saffron Walden; and so on. In 1589 they visited both Ireland and Scotland.

The pattern was that they toured the provinces through the summer and autumn, were in London in the winter so as to be available for the court's Christmas call for entertainment; there were no performances in Lent, but immediately after it they set off once more for the provinces. After 1590 their prestige in London began to fade, and their last court appearance was in 1594, though in April that year they joined forces with Sussex's Men to present eight performances at the Rose Theatre, including *Friar Bacon and Friar Bungay* and their version of *King Leir*, to considerable acclaim. And they continued to tour widely, sometimes linking up with other popular entertainers, such as the acrobat they worked with at Shrewsbury in July 1590, who was 'as nimble as if he had been an eel', performing 'in such wonderful manner that the like was never seen by the inhabitants there before that time'. Their ubiquity reminded civic and other leaders of the queen's continued long reach, and their life on the road was still lively: in 1597 a spectator at Canterbury was arrested for attacking one of the actors. But by the end of the century, the old queen was dwindling fast and the company's last recorded performance was at Congleton in Cheshire in early 1603, a few weeks before Elizabeth I passed away.

THE REPERTOIRE

To the end it seems that the Queen's Men preserved the repertoire which they had largely built up in the 1580s, which may be one reason why they lost ground with London audiences who had moved through the plays of Marlowe to Shakespeare, Jonson and others. The more conservative people of the provinces continued to savour the old plays. These were designed for travelling: they rarely call for a scene 'above', nor do they ask for stage trapdoors, and where these do feature in the scripts they could usually be otherwise accommodated. The surviving plays often do ask for a curtained space – a cell, a study, a pavilion – but these can easily be provided, perhaps with portable screens or other tent-like structure.

The repertoire was tried and trusted to articulate a specific political ideology, so that when something like the Marprelate controversy blew up, they were likely to become involved. In 1588 and 1589, an anonymous Puritan calling himself Martin Marprelate published a series of satirical and polemical attacks on the established church. The Queen's Men were dragooned into staging a reply, *Martin's Mouth's Mind*, on behalf of their masters. Sadly the play has not survived, and the controversy died down quite quickly.

But several of the Queen's Men's plays were published and have survived, though they do not read particularly well. They were designed for brilliant actors who could improvise and ad-lib, and they are probably best seen as part of a popular, non-literary culture rather than as adding to the stock of long-lasting dramas. They often have apparent gaps, where it may be assumed the clowns would entertain, though it should be added that the scripted passages for the clown characters are often funny and usually suggest possibilities to the imaginative or experienced theatre performer.

The Queen's Men's plays tend to be constructed scene by scene, rather than as a closely knit whole: each scene makes its own impact which does not depend on what has gone before or what is to come. The play is thus a 'medley', or, as one twentieth-century practitioner called such dramatic construction, a 'montage of attractions'. *Three Lords and Three Ladies of London* by Robert Wilson, for example, is a revue-like piece which moves unpredictably between the solemn, the comic, the histrionic and the sententious, while the anonymous *True Tragedy of Richard III* is similarly a series of more or less self-contained episodes.

HISTORY PLAYS

The history play, which the Queen's Men pioneered, demonstrates precisely how this repertoire is politically charged. Several history plays assert that they will be 'true' (a common propaganda stratagem: 'The fact is . . .') even before a word has been spoken or an actor has donned a costume: they are called *The True Tragedy of Richard III* or *The True Chronicle History of King Leir* – even though the latter tells a legendary story. These plays, and others from the repertoire, especially perhaps *The Famous Victories of Henry V* and *The Troublesome Reign of King John*, demystify history through the physicality of performance: history is embodied before us in the actors, allowing the past to acquire a kind of reality in the present. Thus *The Troublesome History of King John's* anti-Catholicism is neatly embodied in one of the most memorable moments in the play, when the Friar is discovered to be harbouring a nun secretly in his clothes chest. In *King Leir*, it is the murderer seeking to assassinate Leir who is most discountenanced by the storm. These narratives promote the mystique of the crown, civil obedience and Protestantism, in more or less obvious ways. Here, for instance, is the Bastard speaking at the coronation of King John:

> Let England live but true within itself,
> And all the world can never wrong her state
>
> . . .
>
> If England's peers and people join in one,
> Nor Pope, nor France, nor Spain can do them wrong.

The history plays encourage a particular kind of public identity. Richard III, King Leir, Henry V, King John: some scholars have speculated that Shakespeare may have joined the Queen's Men around 1587, since his familiarity with these plays is remarkable. But there is no hard evidence for this.

Many of these history plays include, perhaps surprisingly, clowns. It is reported that at one performance of *The Famous Victories of Henry V*, Tarlton stood in for an absent actor, and played the part of the Judge as well as that of the clown, Derick. In the trial scene, Tarlton's deliberate incompetence led to Knell, as King Henry, striking him a sharp blow on the cheek. When in the next scene Tarlton reappeared as Derick, he remarked that he was amazed the king could strike a judge – he (Derick) could even feel the blow on his own cheek, it burned so! The comic scenes parody or comment on the main action, as when Derick steals the dead Frenchmen's shoes just as Henry is intent on stealing their kingdom. But their jokes and merry tricks bring the historical stories close to us, make them accessible and therefore more potent as propaganda.

The dominant Elizabethan ideology is also dramatised in other, more tendentious ways. Marlowe's *Tamburlaine the Great* (not a Queen's Men's play) had presented a mighty rebel conquering kingdoms. The company replied with Robert Greene's *Selimus* which purported to show the reality – political and social chaos – which Tamburlaine left. Greene's play implicitly reveals the reality of overweening ambition and suggests that ruthless aspiration which leads to the overthrow of monarchies, initiates civil war and social dislocation. We are kept alive to the ideological message partly by Greene's typical episodic structure of the play, which is evident in his other dramas for the Queen's Men, *Alphonsus*, *King of Aragon*, *Friar Bacon and Friar Bungay* and *James IV*.

FOLK COMEDIES

These last two (though *James IV* may not have belonged to the Queen's Men) are really only partially history plays. They also partake of the nature of folk comedies, or pastorals, which form provides the other strand of the Queen's Men's repertoire (and again Shakespeare's canon). These plays give their audiences a warm sense of belonging, they reassure as to the benefits of being part of a strong traditional culture, of which the Queen is head. Later, such orthodoxy was repudiated by writers like John Fletcher, who damned the pastoral as 'a play of country hired shepherds in grey cloaks, with curtailed dogs in strings, sometimes laughing together, and sometimes killing one another'. But for the Elizabethans the pastoral conventions were meaningful: Elizabeth herself as the faithful shepherdess was a well-known trope in the poetry and prose of the period.

Some of these plays must have seemed old fashioned when they were first performed. Yet they have the distinct charm of the folk tradition which is far from naïve. They are often emblematic in their presentation, mixing ceremony with comedy, folk songs and dances with wonders and amazing feats of magic. There is homespun philosophy, riddles, incantations and laughter. They usually employ stock characters – long-lost brothers, wise elders, magicians, questing knights, forlorn maidens, fairies – all familiar from traditional tales and ballads. In short, they provide the sort of drama which is easy – and enjoyable – to relate to.

For example, *Clyomon and Clamydes*, in the company's repertory from 1583, is fantastic and exotic, and has a cast list which mixes abstract morality figures with 'real' characters. The play 'feels' medieval partly because of its alliterative and rhyming verse. But it also includes the old figure of the Vice, Subtle Shift:

> And as it is my name, so it is my nature also,
> To play the shifting knave wheresoever I go.

When he is first called he is offstage, apparently stuck in the mud:

> If I get out one of my legs as fast as I may,
> Ha lo, a! my buttock, the very foundation thereof doth break.
> Ha lo, once again, I am as fast, as though I had frozen here a week.

The stage direction asks for a traditional piece of stage business: '*Here let him slip onto the stage backwards, as though he had pulled his leg out of the mire, one boot off, and rise up to run in again*'. But whereas the Vice exists in a context which asks for moral judgements, the clown, who in the Queen's Men's repertoire supersedes the Vice, exists in a social context. Thus in Greene's *Orlando Furioso* (which was perhaps not a Queen's Men's play and in which Will Kemp is reputed to have played the clown), when Orlando is mad and meets the clown dressed in his beloved Angelica's clothes, he mistakes him for her:

ORLANDO: Are not these beauteous cheeks,
    Wherein the lily and the native rose
    Sit equal suited with a blushing red?
CLOWN: He makes a garden plot in my face.
ORLANDO: Are not, my dear, those radiant eyes
    Whereout proud Phoebus flashes out his beams?
CLOWN: Yes yes, with squibs and crackers bravely.

This is laughter-provoking mockery with no pretence of morality about it. Even more is this true of Adam, the clown in Lodge and Greene's tellingly titled *A Looking Glass for London and England*. Adam is wooed by his master's wife. When her husband, his master, discovers them together, Adam gives him a thorough beating with his slapstick in a scene which is gloriously amoral, but which also parodies the trouble and strife of the more serious scenes.

THE OLD WIVES' TALE

Best of all these comedies which the Queen's Men presented is *The Old Wives' Tale* by George Peele. The story is begun by the old wife to amuse two young men lost in the forest. The story is acted out for them: they are spectators, forming a subtle frame for what is in effect a play within a play. It includes all the best ingredients of the folk tale – riddles, lost relatives, a quest for a magic well and even a cheerful and pro-active ghost. Interestingly, much of the stage is taken up with particular locations which do not change – Madge's house, the crossroads, Sacrapant the magician's study and so on – but the stage here does require a trapdoor, since Jack leaps into the grave at the end. How the Queen's Men managed this on tour is not clear. Nevertheless, Peele organises all this material with a masterly hand, so that the overall effect is hugely satisfying: old fashioned it may be, but old fashioned in the manner many people appreciate.

The Old Wives' Tale hardly conforms to Walsh's remark about these plays, though there is more than an element of truth generally in what he called them: 'Knockabout entertainment laced with Tudor propaganda'.

SELECT BIBLIOGRAPHY

Walsh, Brian, *Shakespeare, the Queen's Men and the Elizabethan Performance of History*, Cambridge: Cambridge University Press, 2009

Ostovich, Helen, Syme, Holger Scott, and Griffin, Andrew (eds), *Locating the Queen's Men 1583–1603*, Farnham: Ashgate, 2009

McMillin, Scott, and MacLean, Sally-Beth, *The Queen's Men and Their Plays*, Cambridge: Cambridge University Press,1998

PART TWO

OPEN AIR PUBLIC THEATRES

Timeline

	Society and politics	Theatre
1558	Accession of Elizabeth I	
1567		Theatre built in Red Lion Inn, Mile End
1572	Act for the Punishment of Vagabonds St Bartholomew's Day Massacre, Paris	
1574		Patent granted to Earl of Leicester's Men
1576		The Theatre, Finsbury Fields, opened
1577		The Curtain, Finsbury Fields, opened
1579		Gosson, *School of Abuse*

1580	Francis Drake completes his voyage
	    round the world
	Jesuit mission to re-convert
	    England to Catholicism	

1581		Master of the Revels appointed to licence all plays
1582	Francis Walsingham sets up advanced spy network	
1583		Queen's Men established Amalgamated boys' company at Blackfriars Theatre
1587	Execution of Mary, Queen of Scots	Kyd, *The Spanish Tragedy* Marlowe, *Tamburlaine*, Part 1 Rose Theatre, Bankside, opened
1588	Spanish Armada defeated Marprelate controversy	Death of Richard Tarlton
1589		Greene, *Friar Bacon and Friar Bungay*
1591		Peele, *The Old Wives Tale*
1593		Death of Christopher Marlowe

1594	Greene's *Groatsworth of Wit*	Lord Chamberlain's Men and Lord Admiral's Men granted patents to perform at the Theatre and the Rose
1595	Riots in London over price of butter Ulster rebellion	Swan Theatre opened Shakespeare, *A Midsummer Night's Dream*
1596		Lord Chamberlain's Men leave the Theatre
1597		Death of James Burbage
1598	Death of Lord Burghley	
1599		Globe Theatre opened St Paul's Boys company re-established
1600	East India Company founded	Fortune Theatre opened Shakespeare, *Hamlet* Dekker, *The Shoemaker's Holiday*
1601	Essex rebellion	
1603	Death of Elizabeth I: accession of James I	Edward Alleyn finally retires Lord Chamberlain's Men become the King's Men Admiral's Men become Prince Henry's Men Worcester's Men become Queen Anne's Men
1605	Gunpowder Plot	
1606		Middleton, *The Revenger's Tragedy* Shakespeare, *Macbeth* Jonson, *Volpone*
1608	New Exchange, The Strand, built	King's Men begin performing at Blackfriars Fletcher, *The Faithful Shepherdess*
1609	Shakespeare, *Sonnets* published	Children of the Queen's Revels open Whitefriars Theatre
1610		Jonson, *The Alchemist*
1611		Cooke, *Greene's Tu Quoque*
1612	Death of Prince Henry	Shakespeare, *The Tempest* Heywood, *Apologie for Actors*
1613		Globe Theatre burns down
1614		Webster, *The Duchess of Malfi*
1616	Prince Charles invested as Prince of Wales Ralegh's expedition to Guiana	Death of William Shakespeare Jonson, *Works*

1617		Cockpit Theatre opened and damaged by riots
1618	Execution of Sir W. Ralegh	
1619	Death of Queen Anne	Death of Richard Burbage
1621		Fortune Theatre burns down
1623	Prince Charles and Duke of Buckingham visit Spain *incognito*, seeking a bride for Charles	Shakespeare, *Comedies, Histories and Tragedies* (the 'First Folio')
1624		Middleton, *A Game at Chess*
1625	Death of James I: accession of Charles I Charles I marries Henrietta Maria	
1626		Death of Edward Alleyn
1627		Death of Thomas Middleton
1628	Murder of Duke of Buckingham	
1629		Salisbury Court Theatre opened
1634	William Laud becomes Archbishop of Canterbury	Prynne, *Histrio-Mastix* Heywood, *The Late Lancashire Witches*
1637		Death of Ben Jonson
1640	Rebellions in Scotland and Ireland	
1642	English Civil War begins	All theatres are closed

Chapter 14: Queen Elizabeth and the drama

QUEEN AND PEOPLE

> My loving people, we have been persuaded by some that are careful of our safety, to take heed how we commit ourselves to armed multitudes, for fear of treachery; but I assure you I do not desire to live to distrust my faithful and loving people. Let tyrants fear; I have always so behaved myself that under God, I have placed my chiefest strength and safeguard in the loyal hearts and good will of my subjects . . . I know I have the body of a weak and feeble woman; but I have the heart of a king, and of a king of England, too.[1]

Queen Elizabeth stood at Tilbury in 1588 surrounded by people fearful of the approaching Spanish Armada. She made a speech equal to any of the finest pieces of rhetoric given to a stage hero in a contemporary tragedy. Whether she actually spoke these words, and however they may read to a feminist historian, they somehow embody the heart of the Elizabethan paradox: the queen seemed weak, she was assailed by dangers, tragedy threatened, but somehow she sailed through and contrived continual happy endings.

THE QUEEN'S REIGN: PROGRESS AND PROBLEMS

It was a theatrical moment in a theatrical reign. Elizabeth loved drama, and indeed identified with it. 'We princes are set on stages in the sight and view of all the world', she said.[2] She welcomed professional and amateur performances (even attending the Westminster school play) both at her court and on her royal progresses through her realm, progresses which were themselves highly theatricalised demonstrations of her regality and power. Her presence in the shires exhibited the blessings of peace. But she lacked an heir, and this provoked the terrible dangers of civil war, dramatised forcefully on the stage, not only in Shakespeare's extraordinary sequence of plays about English history, but also for instance in Thomas Lodge's *The Wounds of Civil War* (c.1588). The question of the succession was always perilously open. But her settlement after the rigours of her half-sister Mary's Catholic fervour was widely and gladly accepted. Hers was an undogmatic Protestantism: she was the 'Supreme Governor' of a remodelled Church of England which reinstated the 1552 Prayer Book.

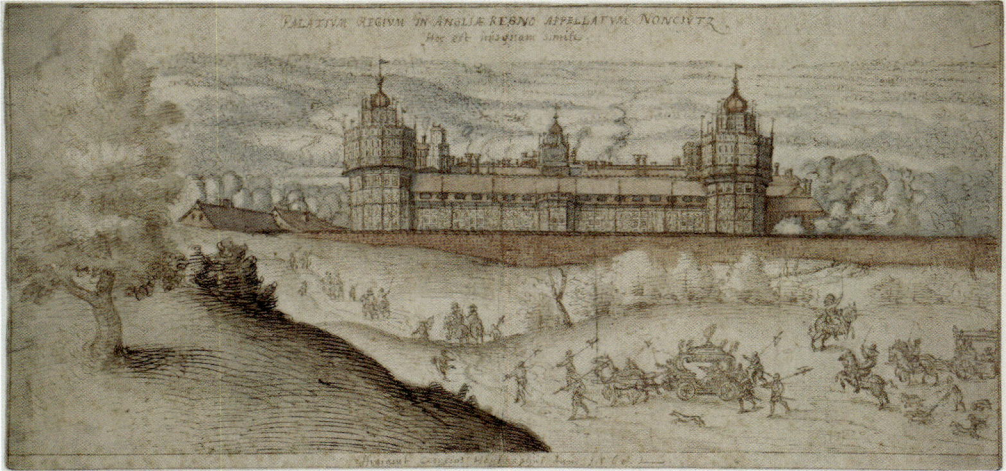

Figure 2.1
The progress of Queen Elizabeth I to Nonsuch Palace. The palace was built for her father, Henry VIII, near Ewell, Surrey
Source: The Trustees of the British Museum

THE ENGLISH CATHOLICS

With religion still the fiercest driving force in politics, her opponents were mostly either Catholic or Puritan. Initially apparently accepting of Elizabeth, English Catholics were perhaps unsettled by the arrival in England from her turbulent northern kingdom of Mary, Queen of Scots, in 1568. Ardently pro-Catholic and Francophile, and the heir to Elizabeth's throne, Mary seemed extraordinarily complacent concerning her co-religionists' opposition to Elizabeth. In 1569 Catholics rebelled. The following year, the Pope excommunicated Elizabeth and urged further insurrections. In 1570 the Ridolphi plot to place Mary on the English throne was defeated. Meanwhile the potential horrors of Catholic rule for Protestant subjects seemed to be graphically illustrated when France was convulsed by the St Bartholomew's Day massacre in Paris, which Christopher Marlowe dramatised in his last play, *The Massacre at Paris* (c.1592), surely one of the bloodiest in the canon.

Elizabeth was reluctant to take drastic steps against Mary, who was, however, disgraced and imprisoned. But the Catholics were not to surrender so easily. From 1570 they sent missionaries to England to bring the country back under the Pope's dominion. Their machinations were increasingly daring, and Elizabeth's government's responses were equally convoluted. Parliament passed anti-Catholic measures – their priests were outlawed, and they were barred from schools and universities – while Archbishop Whitgift campaigned tirelessly in the church against them, and Walsingham established his spy network, which went so far as to include the Queen's Men theatre troupe as described in the previous section of this book. Their play, *The Troublesome Reign of King John* (c.1590), was typical anti-Catholic propaganda: John ransacks the Catholic abbeys and priories, and declares patriotically:

The Pope and Popelings shall not grease themselves
With gold and groats that are the soldiers' due.

SPAIN AND CATHOLICISM

It was not until 1587 that Mary was executed. By then the Catholic Spanish were threatening the country with their Armada, the immediate cause of the Queen's speech at Tilbury. Spain had been especially stirred into action against England by the activities of English buccaneering pirates like Sir John Hawkins and Sir Francis Drake, who made huge profits from their privatised war on Spain. Hawkins particularly had been heavily involved in the slave trade from the 1560s, and he and Drake had tangled with the Spanish repeatedly. While Drake sailed round the world, Hawkins was incorporated officially into the government to rebuild the English navy, and it was his creation which faced and defeated the Armada.

PURITAN ATTACKS ON THE THEATRE

While Elizabeth's freebooters were confronting the external threat from the old religion, the new religion of Puritanism was threatening from within. The Puritans had no time for the compromises of the dominant pragmatic religion. Relying on Scriptural authority for their actions, they rejected bishops and prelates: being assured they were of the elect, they preferred their own consciences as their guide. The Puritans were also the fiercest opponents of the theatre, especially after the first permanent playhouses were built. John Northbrooke probably led the way, airing his moral objections in *A Treatise against Dicing, Dancing, Plays and Interludes with Other Idle Pastimes* (1579), and he was followed by the former actor and playwright, Stephen Gosson's *School of Abuse* (1579). Gosson denounced theatre's power to seduce spectators to vice and warned women especially that its attraction hid moral ugliness and endangered their chastity.

Thomas Lodge opposed this attack. In his *Reply to Stephen Gosson's School of Abuse* (1580), he stated his belief that immorality in the drama was visible only to those who sought it and that plays taught morally wholesome lessons. This provoked Anthony Munday, another playwright whose dramatic career was to continue well into the seventeenth century, to publish in 1580 *A Second and Third Blast of Retreat from Plays and Theatres* (1580). Munday may have been feeling particularly disillusioned at this time: his attempts to become an *improvisator* in the style of Dick Tarlton seem to have been singularly unsuccessful, and he had been hissed off the stage in 1579. But his attack was reinforced by Philip Stubbs in the latter's best-selling *Anatomy of Abuses* (1583), in which he reiterated, without evidence, that plays taught lust and sin. A later book by Thomas Beard was the tellingly named *The Theatre of God's Judgement* (1597). Of course, Puritan preaching was hardly as dangerous as Catholic insurrection, but the campaign rumbled on, with the theatres obtaining partial revenge in a long series of satirical portraits of Puritans in their plays, like Thomas Middleton's sex-mad Penitent Brothel in *A Mad World, My Masters* (c.1606), or Cyril Tourneur's platitudinous and hypocritical Langebeau Snuffe in *The Atheist's Tragedy* (1608), or Ben Jonson's furiously self-centred Zeal-of-the-Land Busy in *Bartholomew Fair* (1614).

THE WILTON HOUSE CIRCLE

Gosson, perhaps impertinently, dedicated his work to Sir Philip Sidney, courtier and poet, whose reply, *The Defence of Poesy*, also defended the drama. But he was scornful of the 'gross absurdities' of

English playwrights and suggested their plays 'be neither right tragedies nor right comedies' because they failed to follow classical models. After his death, his sister Mary, Countess of Pembroke, took up his agenda, and her home, Wilton House, became a centre of intellectual and creative life in the last fifteen years of the sixteenth century. Kyd, Nashe, John Donne and Ben Jonson all spent time here, and she herself became a literary figure in her own right, writing, translating and editing extensively. Her aim was to reclaim the stage for classicism, and her translation and adaptation of Robert Garnier's Senecan tragedy, *Antonie*, was published in 1595. Her version uses the story of Antony and Cleopatra to discuss urgent political issues and she rescues Cleopatra from some of the more scurrilous or sexist contemporary writings. Her play was probably never performed, but it was reprinted five times in fifteen years and is an interesting counterbalance to contemporaneous professional drama.

THE LORD MAYOR OF LONDON AND THE THEATRE

The Puritans had supporters in Parliament, and they also controlled the government of London, whose Lord Mayor had jurisdiction over the whole city except the 'liberties' like St Paul's precinct and Blackfriars. In these enclaves, children's theatre companies operated on a part-time basis. The adult companies were kept out, partly because of the crowds that might be stirred to insurrection, partly because the discourse of theatre might prove more popular than the sermons of the preachers, partly because they believed the theatre encouraged immorality and licentiousness and partly for fear of the plague.

THE PLAGUE AND THE THEATRE

This last reason depended on the idea that the plague was spread by crowds, and when there were over a certain number of deaths per week – thirty or forty at different times – the theatres were ordered to close. This applied in the autumn of 1577, from April to October 1580, in the summer and autumn of 1582, the summer of the following year and then in 1592 from June to December, in 1593 from February to December, in 1594 from February to April and in 1596 from July to October. It is a devastating record, which would have killed a less thriving culture, which is why it is strange that so little attention is paid to it in Elizabethan drama. The few references include Mercutio curse of 'a plague' on Capulets and Montagues alike, and Friar Laurence's letter to Romeo held up by plague, in *Romeo and Juliet* (1595); the plague said to be about by Horace to get rid of Crispinus in Ben Jonson's *The Poetaster* (1601); and the plot of the same author's *The Alchemist* (1610) which can only work because the owner of the house in Blackfriars has vacated it while the plague rages in London. There are few other references to it.

THE PRIVY COUNCIL

The queen's government which provided something of a counterweight to the Puritan-dominated city of London, was headed by the Privy Council, about a dozen members functioning somewhat like a modern cabinet. Its chief was the Queen's secretary, William Cecil, later Lord Burghley, a wily politician staunchly loyal to Elizabeth. The Council was supported by a new aristocratic elite, families like the Herberts and the Sidneys, whose members might be in Parliament. Parliament existed to vote taxes, to pass legislation submitted by the Privy Council and to advise the queen on matters such as the desirability of marriage.

RURAL ENGLAND

If there was a precarious balance of power, perhaps an equality, in the city of London between the Privy Council and the city Fathers, in the countryside, things were less easy, as is clear from the anonymous history play, *The Life and Death of Jack Straw* (c.1590) in which the rebel hero does battle for the peasants' cause. The differences between court and country are illustrated rather differently by Margaret in Robert Greene's *Friar Bacon and Friar Bungay* (c.1589), when she notices of the disguised Earl of Lincoln:

> How different is this farmer from the rest . . .
> His words are witty, quickened with a smile,
> His courtesy gentle, smelling of the court,
> Facile and debonair in all his deeds . . .

Differences between rich and poor, the landed and the landless were clearer in the country. There were vast estates belonging to lords, and there were yeomen farmers able to make a reasonable living, but there was also much poverty and in bad years extreme hunger. In *The Pedlar's Prophecy* (c.1583), probably by Robert Wilson, the Artificer cries as the Landlord evicts him, 'O, what a wretched world is this for poor men!' Yet the peasantry remained more or less quiescent throughout Elizabeth's reign until the late 1590s when famine stirred riots.

PATRIOTISM IN PLAYS

Many English people sensed a sort of nationhood for the first time in Elizabeth's reign, and this was nurtured by the history plays which were performed, like Shakespeare's *Edward III* (c.1591) in which Warwick speaks of 'the mighty King of England' and the Black Prince fights 'for the benefits of England's peace'. The use of the name, 'England', is deliberate, and becomes more marked in later works, most notably *Henry V* (1599). Other popular plays reinforce the status of England, like the anonymous *George-a-Green, the Pinner of Wakefield* (c.1590) which one critic has called 'good-natured jingoism', or Kyd's *The Spanish Tragedy* (c.1587), in which, perhaps to further its anti-Spanish standpoint, three historical English knights unexpectedly appear in Hieronimo's masque and hang up their victorious shields, first Robert, Earl of Gloucester; then Edmund, Earl of Kent 'in Albion'; and finally 'brave John of Gaunt', 'a valiant Englishman'.

THE CULT OF ELIZABETH

One of the most telling transformations Elizabeth's propagandists managed to achieve may have been the way the Cult of the Virgin Mary was effectively replaced by the Cult of the Virgin Queen, and it is important to notice how the drama helped effect this transformation. *The Pedlar's Prophecy* ends with a heartfelt prayer 'for the Queen's Majesty'. In John Lyly's *Endymion* (1588), Cynthia, the Virgin Queen, unravels all with her benevolent wisdom. George Peele's hero in *The Arraignment of Paris* (1584)

Figure 2.2
The Sieve portrait of Queen Elizabeth I by Quentin Metsys the Younger: she is depicted as a Vestal Virgin, with her regal symbols – the columns, the globe – in the background

Source: Pinacoteca Nazionale di Siena

pacifies the warring goddesses by awarding the golden apple to Elizabeth. And in Peele's later *Battle of Alcazar* (c.1588), a completely irrelevant encomium to Elizabeth is suddenly introduced by Sebastian:

> . . . heavens and destinies
> Attend and wait upon her majesty.
> Sacred, imperial and holy is her seat
> Shining with wisdom, love and mightiness . . .

And even late in her reign, when she hobbled with a stick and might give way under the weight of her regal clothes, Thomas Dekker could hail her at the end of *Old Fortunatus* (1599) while in *The Shoemaker's Holiday* (c.1600) he goes even further in his special Prologue 'as it was pronounced before the Queen's Majesty':

> Oh grant, bright mirror of true chastity,
> From those life-breathing stars, your sun-like eyes,
> One gracious smile; for your celestial breath
> Must send us life, or sentence us to death.

NOTES

1 Speech at Tilbury, 9 August (old style) 1588, recorded by Leonel Sharp in a letter to Duke of Buckingham, c.1624.
2 Speech on 12 November 1586; see Leah S.Marcus, Janelle Mueller and Mary Beth Rose (eds), *Queen Elizabeth I: Collected Works*, Chicago: University of Chicago Press, 2000, p.194.

Chapter 15: The first permanent theatres

The establishment of permanent theatre buildings for the performance of plays is the outstanding fact of Elizabethan theatre history. By the end of the reign at least half a dozen theatres were in existence, and no two were precisely alike. But once plays could be performed inside permanent buildings, the theatre could become a business.

THE STAGE AND THE SCAFFOLD

Almost all the early playhouses were circular, or polygonal, so that the term 'amphitheatre' is sometimes preferred today. The contemporary term for these buildings was 'playhouse', which may still seem the best. The stage was the focus of the architectural configuration, and the audience almost surrounded it. It reminded of nothing so much as the platform or scaffold surrounded by spectators, which was the place of execution, and contemporary executions had indeed an undeniable theatricality. The victim made his or her 'last dying speech' while the axeman in his black mask stood by. A contemporary report tells of Mary, Queen of Scots,

> her prayers being ended, the executioners, kneeling, desired her grace to forgive them: who answered: 'I forgive you with all my heart, for now, I hope, you shall make an end of all my troubles'. Then they, with her two women, helping her up, began to disrobe her of her apparel: then she, laying her crucifix upon the stool, one of the executioners took from her neck the Agnus Dei, which she, laying hands off it, gave to one of her women.[1]

After some ceremony, the actual execution took place. 'The executioner cut off her head, saving one little gristle, which being cut asunder, he lift up her head to the view of all the assembly, and bade *God save the Queen*'.[2] A little over half a century later, Charles I, King of England, was also executed, and Andrew Marvell described the event in suitably theatrical terms:

> . . . thence the Royal Actor born
> The tragic scaffold might adorn:
> While round the armed bands
> Did clap their bloody hands.
> He nothing common did or mean

Figure 2.3
The execution of Charles I in 1649 took place on a scaffold much like the early open air theatres
Source: British Library, London

> Upon that memorable scene:
> But with his keener eye,
> The axe's edge did try.[3]

As Dr Johnson was to remark nearly two hundred years later: 'Executions are intended to draw spectators. If they do not draw spectators they do not answer their purpose'.[4]

PUBLIC PUNISHMENTS

Lesser punishments were also often done in public before spectators, like public whippings or placing offenders in the stocks, so that humans became almost animal. And indeed the new playhouses were to some degree modelled on bear-baiting rings. A German visitor at the end of Elizabeth's reign noticed the similarity:

> There is still another place, built in the form of a theatre, which serves for the baiting of bulls and bears; they are fastened behind, and then worried by great English bull-dogs. . . . To this entertainment there often follows that of whipping a blinded bear, which is performed by five or six men, standing circularly with whips, which they exercise upon him without any mercy, as he cannot escape from them because of his chain.[5]

Bear-baiting resembled human punishment, and people laughed and applauded as the victim screamed and kicked out. The spectacle was utterly compelling.

PUNISHMENT DRAMATISED

It reappears many times on the Elizabethan and Jacobean stage. In Peele's *Edward I*, while Edward is away, Queen Elinor captures the Mayor of London's wife, ties her to a chair and sets a snake to her breast. She dies in agony. In Wilson's *Three Lords and Three Ladies of London*, Fraud is captured and tied to a stake, but here Dissimulation 'standing behind Fraud, unbinds him, and while all the rest behold Simplicity, they two slip away'. The central image in Lyly's *Galatea* is of a maiden tied to a tree awaiting a dragon-like avenger to come and take her. Shakespeare has several such references. Macbeth protests at the end of his play: 'They have tied me to the stake: I cannot fly, but, bear-like, I must fight the course'. Gloucester is tied to a chair in *King Lear*, tormented and his eyes put out. In *Henry VI* Part 3, Richard of Gloucester seeks his father, the Duke of York in the battle, where he was defying the enemy:

> . . . as a bear, encompass'd round with dogs,
> Who having pinch'd a few and made them cry,
> The rest stand all aloof and bark at him.

But Richard has not seen the end of the event: the Duke of York has been captured and tied to a stake, where Queen Margaret has tormented him, placing a paper crown on his head, wiping his face with a bloody napkin and finally killing him. Chapman's *The Tragedy of Byron* ends with the hero kneeling down and placing his head on the block. In Lording Barry's *Ram Alley* (c.1607), Boutcher tries but fails to hang himself.

THE RED LION PLAYHOUSE

The first bear pit-like theatre to be built in London was at Mile End in the grounds of Red Lion Farm in 1567. The idea for it was conceived by John Brayne, a grocer whose sister married James Burbage, a player with Leicester's Men. He had constructed a large platform on legs, five feet off the ground and approximately forty feet by thirty with a tall turret, rising thirty feet from the back of this stage. There is no mention of a tiring-house or a roof over the stage. A curtain concealed the backstage area, and there was a scaffold grandstand to which entrance was controlled. Further space for the audience to stand was made in front of this stand. The first builder employed,

William Sylvester, did not finish the job: this was left to John Reynolds, whose work Brayne also found unsatisfactory. He sued both builders variously. However, in July 1567 his theatre opened with a performance of *The Story of Samson*.

THE THEATRE

The Red Lion probably only stood for a matter of months. But it was successful enough to tempt Brayne and Burbage to a new venture a few years later. This was the Theatre, which opened in 1576 and continued until it was pulled down in 1599 to provide the materials for the more famous Globe. The Theatre – its name was designedly classical – was built in Finsbury Fields, about a mile north of the east end of the city. It was a pleasant open space with grass and flowers where people picnicked or practiced archery on sunny days. But in the evening it came alive in other ways: brothels, pubs, gaming houses and bowling alleys beckoned the pleasure-seeker. Not far from the royal palace, it was still a place belonging to the citizen, a 'liberty' beyond the reach of the city authorities. It was between court and city, a place betwixt and between the jurisdictions of either, a liminal space, one associated with holidaying or time out of work, beyond the everyday. This factor is one of the crucial strengths of the Elizabethan open air theatre.

Like most later playhouses, the first Theatre was a circular or polygonal building, perhaps as much as a hundred feet in diameter. Made mostly of timber with plaster filling and a tiled roof over the galleries, it contained a yard surrounded by three tiers of galleries. Entrance to these was via a door where money was collected and upstairs. One gallery had special rooms for gentlemen, and entrance here cost more again. The stage jutted out into the yard, but there seems to have been no canopy over it, and hence there were no pillars on the stage as later playhouses had. At the back of the stage was a tiring-house where the actors dressed and waited for their cues, and where there was some kind of balcony. A trapdoor was cut into the stage floor. It was beautifully appointed – a 'gorgeous playing place' according to one witness writing in 1578 – and provided the actors with an extraordinarily versatile space. Huge, self-contained, yet strangely intimate, it was an ineradicably democratic place where, for instance, 'asides' and soliloquies, those bugbears of the proscenium arch theatre, were utterly natural and where a battle, a love scene, a formal procession or a clown's slapstick could equally appeal to any spectator.

The moving spirit behind the building was James Burbage, carpenter turned actor and now the leader of Leicester's Men, already the foremost company in the country. His motives were almost entirely financial. Here would be a place for Leicester's Men to play when they were in London, but more importantly, perhaps, here was a purpose-built place to hire out to other touring companies when they were in London.

In 1576 he had signed a twenty-one-year lease for a large property belonging to Giles Allen and agreed to spend £200 improving the estate. At a cost of £700 he built the theatre here. But he found himself unable to meet the full amount, and enlisted help from his brother-in-law, John Brayne, builder of the Red Lion playhouse. However, Burbage was something of a slippery customer. He used the lease to raise further loans and did what he could to avoid paying what he should. Even actors at the Theatre sometimes went unpaid, and it was reported that Burbage was known to have hidden the takings under his shirt on occasions. When he was supposed to renegotiate the lease with Allen in 1585, as per their agreement, the two fell out, and the dispute ended in the courts. In fact, the litigation dragged on till 1602, by which time Burbage was dead and his case was being conducted by his brother Cuthbert. There were also problems between Burbage and Brayne, and these too led to litigation lasting many years. Brayne died in 1586, whereupon his widow married again and her new husband fought on till 1597.

THE CURTAIN

Within a year of the Theatre's completion, a second playhouse appeared in Shoreditch, the Curtain in Holywell Lane, named after the nearby curtain wall. No doubt the Curtain had distinctive features, but not much detail is known of it. It was round or polygonal, had three galleries with a thatched roof, and opened in the autumn of 1577. It functioned for over fifty years, always as a theatre for hire, never with a permanent company, and staged other attractions besides plays, such as fencing and wrestling matches. It gained fame for its bawdy jigs and for the prostitutes who infested it. One writer described an aged playgoer 'who coming from the Curtain, sneaketh in to some odd garden, noted house of sin'.[6] It was owned in the 1590s by Henry Lanman and seems to have amalgamated with the Theatre when the Queen's Men, as two companies, appeared at both houses simultaneously. Later its ownership seems to have passed to actors: Thomas Greene the clown owned it entirely in the early 1610s; at other times its ownership was shared among groups of actors. Though it was said to be 'in decay' in 1611, it continued well into the 1620s when Prince Charles's Men played there between 1620 and 1623.

THE PLAYHOUSE AT NEWINGTON BUTTS

Meanwhile another theatre appeared at this time (c.1576–7) at Newington Butts, a mile south of London Bridge. It was built on land owned by Richard Hickes who leased it to the actor, Jerome Savage, leader of Warwick's Men. Perhaps he intended it as a base for his company, but he was beset with problems: the authorities pursued him for repeatedly failing to keep the sewer which ran alongside the building clear, and he was continually harassed by Hickes. By 1580 Savage had disappeared and Warwick's Men had disbanded. The theatre was continued as a venue for hire for another fifteen years, however, first by Hickes's son-in-law, Peter Hunningborne, and later by Paul Buck, who dismantled it about 1595. It acquired something of a reputation for banality, however: in Field's *A Woman Is a Weathercock* (1609), a particularly obvious rhyme is called a 'Newington conceit'.

THEATRES ATTACHED TO INNS

At the same time, a number of inns scattered in and around London were cashing in on the popularity of theatre, and building stages in their yards. Foremost among these probably was the Bel Savage on Ludgate Hill near the Old Bailey. With a stage probably over five feet off the ground, a spacious yard and three galleries, the Bel Savage charged one penny to enter and a further penny for 'quiet standing'. It staged prize fights and other spectacles, besides plays, especially on public holidays, between the 1570s and the 1590s. According to George Gascoigne in 1575, it was 'full of pleasant sport', and Stephen Gosson, who railed against the theatre, had to admit in 1579 that 'at the Bel Savage . . . you shall find never a word without wit, never a line without pith, never a letter placed in vain'.[7] Tarlton made his last appearance before his death here in 1588, and according to William

Prynne, a notorious anti-theatre Puritan, writing much later in the 1630s, during a performance of *Dr Faustus* at the Bel Savage, the devil himself appeared on the stage 'to the great amazement both of the actors and spectators'.

The smaller Bull stage on Bishopsgate Street was in use from at least as early as 1577. Equally known for fencing displays, two plays known to have been staged here were *The Jew*, about the evils of greed and usury, and *Ptolemy*, about the defeat of treason, both in 1579. There was nothing here for Stephen Gosson to object to, 'neither amorous gesture wounding the eye nor slovenly talk hurting the ears of the chaste hearers'.[8] The implicit anti-Semitism of the first play obviously did not upset his self-righteousness. The scene of Tarlton playing the Judge in *The Famous Victories of Henry V* apparently occurred at the Bull, perhaps when the Queen's Men played here in 1583, and on another occasion a spectator hurled a 'pippin' at Tarlton during a performance. Later Robert Greene watched a pickpocket at work here. The Bull was the longest surviving Elizabethan playhouse, standing until 1866.

Other inns with playhouses were the Cross Keys in Gracechurch Street, which was presenting plays in the late 1570s, and the Bell, next door to the Cross Keys, which staged 'the play of Cutwell' in 1577 and others later. The bear-baiting amphitheatre at Paris Gardens also occasionally presented plays. There was a terrible accident here in 1583, when a gallery collapsed, killing at least seven people and injuring many more. But still the theatrical scene of the 1570s and 1580s is extraordinarily dynamic and engaging.

ADVANTAGES OF A PERMANENT PLAYHOUSE

From the playing company's point of view, a permanent theatre had certain clear advantages over other venues. On tour admission could be controlled in halls or country houses, but audiences were limited; outdoors, where large crowds could be gathered, there was no sure way of making everyone pay. But admission to the playhouse yard could be controlled. Every entrant had to pay

Figure 2.4
A view of London, c.1588

Source: British Library, London/© British Library Board. All Rights Reserved/Bridgeman Images

one penny to get in, with a further penny to enter the gallery. Samuel Kiechel, a German visitor to London in 1584, calculated that a single performance would probably net about £10 and more for a premiere when prices were doubled.

THE AUDIENCE IN THE ELIZABETHAN PUBLIC PLAYHOUSE

Once inside the theatre, the spectator joined a buzzing crowd who expected to be entertained. Because the audience and the performers were not split apart by something like a proscenium arch the experience in such a large theatre was stimulatingly intimate. The play began at two or three o'clock in the afternoon, there were no intervals, and it was followed by a short 'jig', or song and dance medley usually featuring the company clown.

The spectator rubbed shoulders with vendors of oranges and apples, boys selling beer and others bread or sandwiches, and perhaps ballad sellers, prostitutes and pickpockets, all plying their trades. He or she might expect at least a flirtation. On public holidays especially, people came 'flocking and running' to the Theatre and the Curtain, whose yard and galleries would be packed especially with apprentices and artisans not at work. The capacity of most of the theatres might be about two and a half thousand, and there was plenty of give-and-take between audience and performers. In Wilson's *Three Lords and Three Ladies of London*, Simplicity and Wit compete to see who is the best singer. Like any modern television show, Simplicity turns to 'the auditory': 'Friends, what say you? Which of us sings best?' At the end of *Summer's Last Will and Testament*, Will asks the audience to 'warm your hands with clapping'. But things were not always pleasant. In April 1580 there was a 'great disorder' at the Theatre; in June 1584, a servant called Brown, 'a shifting fellow having a perilous wit of his own', caused a fight at the entrance to the Theatre which erupted in something of a mêlée, during which Brown ran off. In 1600 a pickpocket was convicted of stealing purses at the Curtain during a performance. At other times the spectators took the law into their own hands if they found a pickpocket, as with the 'noted cutpurse' Will Kemp recalled: 'Such a one as we tie to a post on our stage'.[9]

The actor had no easy passage on this stage, but had to grab the spectators' attention, though Gosson recorded that 'in public theatres, when any notable show passeth over the stage, the people arise out of their seats, and stand upright with delight and eagerness to view it'.[10] What Gosson and his like did not approve of was the presence in the audience of as many women as men. The drama was a threat to their chastity, he railed, though perhaps the threat was really to the patriarchy. Who was the woman in the audience? She was not a whore, but she was not a lady – and she was not at home! Who was she? And why had she no male protector? What was more, Gosson could dimly sense that she was 'gazing' at the men on the stage, reversing the accepted way of things, and putting herself in danger of arousing herself. It was an interesting paradox of the time.

In fact, a series of sophisticated exchanges were proceeding, as the audience members were aware of themselves and of each other in the afternoon sunshine, as well as of the players, who in turn were aware of them and of each other. The audience was unconsciously working on several levels at once, their imagination freed to watch the story, the actors, the other spectators and respond to words, music, audience laughter, interruptions, and all in holiday mood, with an apple or a bottle of beer to accompany it. The experience encouraged speculation, fantasy, aspiration and play.

A POPULAR THEATRE

Partly this was possible because it was a genuinely popular theatre – that is to say, anyone could come along and join in, aristocrat or apprentice. No-one was barred, everyone was welcome, and at a penny there were few who could never attend. So in these theatres on the edge of the city, a democratic mingling freed ordinary people's wit and fancy. Once theatre was privatised and moved indoors, it inevitably became less democratic, less open to the wind and therefore less powerful. The greatness of the Elizabethan theatre depended on this liminality, its democratic involvement with anyone who wanted to be there.

NOTES

1 Andreas Höfele, *Stage, Stake and Scaffold*, Oxford: Oxford University Press, 2011, p. 11.
2 *Ibid.*
3 Andrew Marvell, *An Horatian Ode Upon Cromwel's Return from Ireland*.
4 James Boswell, *The Life of Samuel Johnson LLD*, Oxford: World's Classics, 1961, p.1211.
5 Jonathan Bate and Dora Thornton, *Shakespeare, Staging the World*, London: The British Museum Press, 2012.
6 Everard Guilpin, *Skialetheia*, 1598.
7 Stephen Gosson, *Schoole of Abuse*, 1579.
8 *Ibid.*
9 William Kemp, *Nine Daies Wonder*, 1600.
10 Stephen Gosson, *op.cit.*

Chapter 16: Plays and players in the 1570s and 1580s

The first permanent theatres were built in the outskirts of London not to house permanent theatre companies, but to provide state-of-the-art touring venues. Probably no companies of the 1570s and 1580s thought of themselves as 'London companies' – they were touring companies, whose best and most lucrative venues, however, were in London. This was their key market, but it was not an exclusive market.

TOURING

Touring the country was the actors' way of life, not the snug security of playing permanently in a particular theatre. Such a theatrical lifestyle was undreamt of. There were customary circuits which most companies followed for two or three month periods – Kent, Canterbury and the Cinque Ports, perhaps, or the west midlands and the Welsh borders, or Lancaster, Kendal and the north west coast. When they returned to London, they were no doubt glad to perform in the newly constructed amphitheatres. But soon they were up and off again. And it should be noted that touring formed a major part of most companies' lives right until the closing of the theatres in 1642. So the provinces did not lack for theatrical entertainment. Leicester, for instance, averaged over three visits by touring theatre companies every year between 1576 and 1642. In 1587, when the young Shakespeare was just twenty-three years old, at least five different companies visited Stratford-upon-Avon.

For the actors touring was no doubt heavy work. They probably walked between their various performing venues. A horse-drawn wagon carried their props, costumes, playbooks and other paraphernalia, but they rarely covered more than ten miles in a day. At the towns or villages where they paused to perform, the players seem sometimes to have received free food and lodging from their hosts, even though it seems they rarely booked their appearances in advance. And sometimes they fell in with other groups, or itinerant entertainers, with whom they might combine temporarily to present plays together, as the Queen's Men did with Sussex's Men and later with Essex's Men in 1590. Even so, competition between companies was often intense: there were probably too many of them for an easy life, no matter how buoyant their market.

Besides, travel could be dangerous, not least because actors not in livery or without the appropriate authorisation papers were liable to summary arrest. In 1583 Worcester's Men had their papers stolen by another group who then presented themselves in Leicester as a licensed troupe. In 1593 Pembroke's Men became insolvent while on the road and had somehow to make the best of their own ways home. In 1597 vandals attacked Lord Bartlett's Men's wagon.

A statute of 1572 required all companies to be attached to a lord. For the lord, such patronage gave kudos and status; for the players it was absolutely necessary. Without it, not only were they not protected from arrest, but they had no chance of obtaining the necessary licence to perform in any place they came to. Such patronage did not provide them with a guarantee of permission to perform, but if the lord was of any consequence it was clearly extremely helpful. Few municipalities would have dared to refuse the Queen's Men a playing space. And actors could expect their aristocratic patron to provide them with money, occasional lodging, including probably for their wives and families, food, candles and a suit of livery.

THE ACTING COMPANIES

A dozen or so men made up a company – in 1577 Leicester's Men numbered twelve, Bath's Men eleven and Worcester's ten. Actors sometimes moved between companies, as the Dutton brothers did in 1580, leaving Warwick's Men and joining Oxford's. In 1585 Will Kemp joined Leicester's Men. The Queen's Men cherry-picked the best from any company.

PLAYING A TOWN

When the players arrived in any town, they would first present themselves and their patent or other authority to the local mayor. Occasionally the mayor might refuse them permission to perform, for their appearance was almost always unannounced, and they might disrupt the peace of the town and damage to the civic building or other place of performance. But more likely he would invite them to perform for him and his invited guests. This was the 'Mayor's Play', a bespoke performance for which the company would, they hoped, receive a fee. Then the mayor was likely to grant permission for the performance to take place in a specific place – indoors if the players were lucky, for then the weather was no problem, and they would be able to charge admission on the door; but otherwise in a suitable space outdoors, when they would probably 'bottle', that is, collect money by passing round the hat. Before any such public performance, the actors would probably parade the streets, perhaps in costume, probably playing their musical instruments and at strategic points in their progress they would announce the performance, no doubt with suitable flourishes.

VENUES

The actors might perform each of the plays in their repertoire in one town and also hope to present one or more performances at the country houses of any landed gentry nearby, before they moved on. The local guildhall was probably the best place for them – the guildhalls at York, Leicester and Norwich could all hold over two thousand spectators, but town or civic halls, church buildings, schools, inns and other places were all possible.

For performances in Trinity College Hall, Cambridge, in 1629, the college authorities warned student spectators:

> At the comedy, no scholar under a Master of Arts do presume to take any place above the lower rail or bar . . .
> No tobacco to be taken in the hall . . .

Figure 2.5
View into Leicester Guildhall, built before 1400 and still in use: the kind of venue touring theatre companies appreciated
Source: Photo Alex Liivet

> Before the comedy begin, nor all the time thereof, any rude and immodest exclamations be made, nor any humming, hacking, whistling, hissing or laughing be used, nor any stamping or knocking, nor any other such uncivil or unscholar like and boyish demeanour . . .
> Nor any clapping of hands be had until the plaudite at the end of the comedy.[1]

And outdoors there were playing fields, market places, churchyards and inn yards: thus, Essex's Men performed in Shrewsbury market place in 1583, and the Queen's Men in Gloucester churchyard in 1589. Country houses were another kind of venue, perhaps more welcoming than many. None of these spaces were necessarily easy for the performers. They were unlikely to be able to use a scaffold stage, or have the luxury of a canopy for the 'heavens' or even perhaps a trapdoor for the devil. They had to adapt, and several playscripts contain stage directions like that in Robert Greene's *The Comical History of Alphonsus, King of Aragon* (c.1587):

> Exit Venus; or, if you can conveniently, let a chair come down from the top of the stage, and draw her up.

REGULATING THE THEATRE

The picture is one of expansion, of a lively popular art form being commercially sold. The theatre was part of the developing market economy, in which customers paid for what they received, which of course rendered ironic the many citizen comedies, especially of the Jacobean period, which satirised money-making, usury and the commodification of, for instance, sex. Nevertheless, to the authorities, it must have seemed chaotic, and through the 1570s and 1580s a series of attempts to regulate the burgeoning but elusive theatre business were made. In 1572 two Acts were passed, one against 'Retainers', limiting the number of men who could wear a lord's livery, and one for the Punishment of Vagabonds, which threatened any players not wearing the livery of a lord above the rank of a baron. In 1574, a patent granted to Leicester's Men, but to no other company, permitted them to perform throughout the country. But the implication, that other companies were not so permitted, seems never to have been followed up.

In 1579 the Privy Council banned performances in Lent. After a serious accident at the Bear Garden, when a stand collapsed and a number of people were killed, playing on Sundays was also banned in 1583. Meanwhile London's city Fathers prohibited the performance of plays within the city.

THE REVELS OFFICE

In 1581 a crown patent was granted to Edmund Tilney, Master of the Revels, to licence all plays: he was awarded extensive powers to insist on changes to playscripts, or even to ban plays which offended. The offences he looked for included sedition, irreligion, libel and scurrility. No living person was permitted to be represented. Religious ceremonies were not to be enacted. Satire of – or even comment about – the government was not allowed: indeed political matters of any sort were to be strongly discouraged. Lewdness and bawdry were frowned on, but not necessarily banned, but from 1606 sacrilegious oaths were prohibited.

The Revels Office which oversaw all this was under the jurisdiction of the Lord Chamberlain and his assistant, the Master of the Revels, who was initially responsible for the court entertainments wherever the court happened to be. Performers were supposed to perform before him before they could present their work to the queen, but it quickly became clear that there were far too many plays for this to be a realistic proposition. So companies had to submit their scripts to him in order to obtain permission to perform them, and his response was to be taken seriously. He could shut a playhouse or send a manager or author who disobeyed him to gaol. And though it is true that the court was not always efficient in overseeing the censorship, and that Edmund Tilney was not necessarily consistent in his demands, yet his writ was feared, and there is no doubt that it ran among the members of the theatrical profession. Conversely, of course, the companies benefited from the licensing of their work, especially if they faced objection-making local authorities. Later in Elizabeth's reign the Master of the Revels task was extended to cover the licensing of playhouses themselves and early in James's reign to the printing of play texts.

THEATRE COMPANIES OF THE 1570S AND 1580S

But still, the touring companies of the 1570s and 1580s flourished. They were commercial organisations, and there were enough of them to generate serious and sometimes bitter competition. Warwick's Men, for instance, existed before 1580 when they were appearing in London at Newington

Butts. But in 1580 their main stalwarts, John and Lawrence Dutton, left to join Oxford's Men and Warwick's Men seem to have collapsed. Oxford's Men, who continued into the next century despite later losing the Duttons to the Queen's Men, were involved in an affray in 1580 when three of their actors were reported fighting with students from the Inns of Court. Sussex's Men, first heard of in 1569, boasted Richard Tarlton among their number till he was head-hunted by the Queen's Men. Their repertoire seems to have included *George-a-Green the Pinner of Wakefield* and later both *The Jew of Malta* and *Titus Andronicus*. They continued to tour till after 1615.

Hertford's Men were similarly long lived: they were active between 1582 and about 1606, while Worcester's Men, with the great Edward Alleyn among their number in the late 1580s, had a similarly long life. The greatest of these troupes was probably the Earl of Leicester's Men, who were granted a Royal Patent in 1574. Their shareholders at that time included James Burbage, John Perkin, John Lanham, William Johnson and Robert Wilson, three of whom were to become Queen's Men. Shortly before their defection, Leicester's Men were performing at the Theatre in Finsbury Fields, but after it they lost prominence, only to re-emerge in 1585 when the clown Will Kemp joined them. The following year George Bryan and Thomas Pope, both later Lord Chamberlain's Men, also joined to make them again a power in the theatrical landscape. But Leicester, who had wanted an active troupe to spread his name, and perhaps spy for him, died in 1588, and his troupe faded thereafter.

REPERTOIRES

The plays these companies presented on their travels were often made by the actors themselves. The profession of playwright was effectively unknown, though by the 1580s a number of poets began to write for the stage. Most plays were popular, energetic and imbued with a holiday feeling. They dealt with traditional subjects, telling in dramatic form old stories, classical legends, Biblical or romantic tales and half-imagined stories from history. Like all popular literature, they employed devices like repetition, catch phrases, anachronisms and riddles and proverbial sayings in stock situations peopled by stereotypical characters. They rarely began with 'once upon a time', but that was their *genre*. Fairies, monsters and magicians met honest peasants and ploughmen. The confrontations often employed a Presenter, as in Peele's *The Battle of Alcazar* (1588), and their values were the traditional ones of friendliness and solidarity, spiked however with xenophobia and anti-Catholicism.

GEORGE PEELE

Among poet-playwrights, George Peele, a University graduate who also created Lord Mayor's shows, wrote plays which were charming, episodic and often spectacular. His earliest surviving play is *The Arraignment of Paris* (1584), an original pastoral drama, whose ingenuity is contained in a series of set pieces featuring peasants, love songs and excellent verse. Later plays – *David and Bathsabe* (1587), *The Battle of Alcazar*, *Edward I* (1591) and *The Old Wives Tale* (1591) – show a compelling familiarity with popular culture, and an imaginative theatricality.

ROBERT WILSON

Robert Wilson, an actor with Leicester's Men and then the Queen's Men, wrote a number of plays focusing on London, including *Three Ladies of London* (c.1581) and a sequel, *Three Lords and*

Three Ladies of London (1588). Wilson's central characters are the medieval-sounding Lady Lucre, who leads astray Lady Love and Lady Conscience. The plays, sometimes described as 'medleys', are a jumble of scenes, serious, comical and fantastical, which make up an entertainment more like a variety show than a traditional play. Most interesting is Wilson's treatment of London itself: we discover that Will cannot read, and Simplicity says in surprise: 'Not read and brought up in London?'

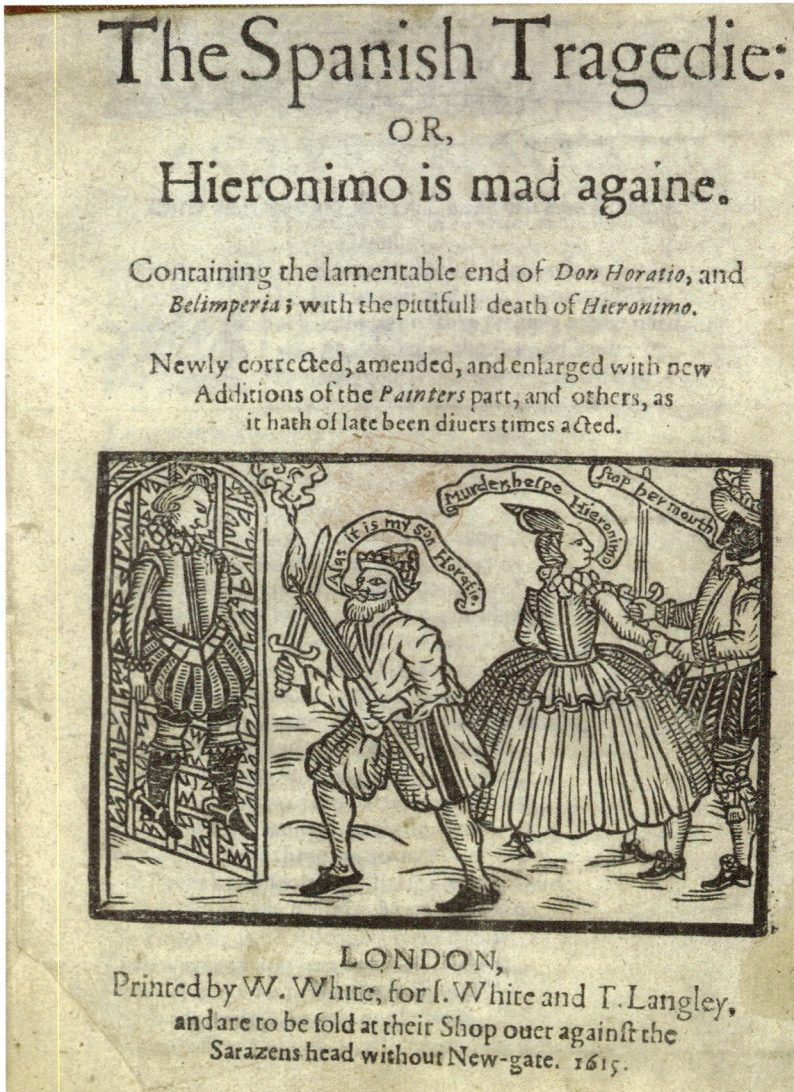

Figure 2.6

Title page of the 1615 edition of Thomas Kyd's *The Spanish Tragedy*. The illustration may give some idea of the staging: Horatio is hanged in the arbour where his parents, Hieronimo and Isabella, discover him

Source: British Library, London

ROBERT GREENE AND THE 'UNIVERSITY WITS'

Robert Greene is better known than Wilson, if only for the reference to Shakespeare in his *Groats-worth of Wit* (which may however have been written by Henry Chettle). He caused scandal by leaving his wife for a woman who may have been a prostitute. His plays, discussed earlier, are often set in an idyllic, impossible past and mingle magic with realism in a genuinely original way. His tragedies are always shot through with romance and comedy, and, interestingly for a University graduate of the period, his plays are the antithesis of classically disciplined. In this his work resembles the anonymous *Arden of Feversham* (c.1591), a sensational domestic tragedy which is chiefly memorable for the guffaw-provoking murderers, who make no fewer than seven attempts to finish their victim, and fail every time. Their stalking of their prey though the fogs of the Kentish countryside provided one of the great acting challenges of the Elizabethan stage.

Greene and Peele were two of the so-called 'University Wits'. Thomas Nashe and Thomas Lodge, later a surgeon, were two more University men turned playwrights, though not many writings have survived from either of them. Nashe's *Summer's Last Will and Testament* (1592) is a subtle and sometimes melancholy meditation on time, while Lodge's *Wounds of Civil War* is very different, centring on Scilla, a sort of jolly tyrant not unlike Shakespeare's Richard III.

THOMAS KYD

The best of these writers was probably Thomas Kyd, author of a number of lost plays as well as *The Spanish Comedy* (c.1575) and its sequel, *The Spanish Tragedy* (c.1587). Kyd's private life, like so many of these writers, was murky. He may have been gay, and at one point he and Marlowe lodged together. Their shared atheism brought them both into disrepute. In 1593 Kyd found himself in prison, and in 1594 he died in disgrace. But his greatest work, *The Spanish Tragedy*, lived on, and for the next fifty years was never out of the repertoire. It is dark, brooding and filled with strange and ghastly events. The action is 'framed' by the presence as Chorus, or Presenters, of Revenge and the Ghost of Andrea, the murdered hero of *The Spanish Comedy*. The play portrays the political corruption of state Catholicism, but it also blazes with a portrait of perhaps the first of the Elizabethan and Jacobean revengers, Hieronimo. Hieronimo goes mad during the course of the play, and he stages an extraordinary play within the play during the workings of which dangerous and innocent characters alike perish. Only the Ghost and Revenge are left to mull over the horrors of the tale.

It provides a fitting finale to this extravagant and energetic period of British drama.

NOTE

1 Alan H. Nelson, *Early Cambridge Theatres*, Cambridge: Cambridge University Press, 1994, p. 40.

Chapter 17: Jigs and jig-makers

JIGS: EARLY REFERENCES

Shakespeare's Hamlet, a somewhat snobbish critic of the drama, deplored Polonius's taste: 'He's for a jig or a tale of bawdry', he scoffs, and later, accused of obscenity, he deprecates himself ironically as 'your only jig-maker'. A jig was an afterpiece, not a real play at all, and contained smut, or worse. And Hamlet was not the only one who claimed superiority: Christopher Marlowe promised to lead his audiences away from

> . . . jigging veins of rhyming mother wits
> And such conceits as clownage keeps in pay.

Lewdness, rhymes and clownage. But one German visitor to England, Thomas Platter, having seen a performance of *Julius Caesar* at the Globe Theatre in 1599, wrote of the jig which followed with notable warmth: 'They danced, according to their custom, exceedingly gracefully: two attired in men's clothes and two in women's performed wonderfully with one another'.

But admired or despised, jigs were always performed in the open air playhouses. Ben Jonson, in *Every Man in His Humour*, speaks of a thing happening 'as ordinarily . . . as a jig after a play', and Sir John Davies records that 'when ended is the play', then comes 'the dance and song'.

THE FORMS OF THE JIG

The jig was a unique form, combining drama, dance and song but the fact that Richard Tarlton and Will Kemp, the two most celebrated Elizabethan clowns, were particularly associated with jigs suggest that it was also comic. Some jigs were little more than a flamboyant hornpipe danced by a specialist, or a simple song between two characters, but more often they were short farcical dramas with plenty of slapstick, plenty of music and plenty of dance for up to five characters. Many jigs were made, but sadly very few remain. It was a performance, not a literary form, and hence ephemeral. But it was also part of the Elizabethan and Jacobean theatrical experience, forming a kind of challenge to more apparently respectable forms of drama.

The jig owes something to medieval sports, carnivals and festivals of misrule, which mixed dance and song with knockabout humour and topsy-turvy games. Carols, rounds and ballads were similarly danced as well as sung. Nicholas Udall recorded in 1542 how a singer 'began to sing such another foolish song (as "Robin in Barnesdale stood") and seemed as though he would dance withal'. The significant point is that the subject of the song, Robin Hood in Barnesdale, is a narrative which the man is to sing *and* dance.

One can detect the jig in embryonic form in earlier Tudor drama: in *Roister Doister* when Ralph and his followers go courting, and there is the clowning of Merrygreek hitting him, as well as the singing and dancing of Harpax and Dobinet; in *Nice Wanton* when Ismael, Iniquity and Delilah enter singing, march about the stage, play dice and flirt; in *Like Will to Like* when the devil dressed as a bear, Nichol Newfangle and Tom Collier play music, stamp and sing; and in Robert Greene's *James IV* when Slipper and Nano '*dance a jig devised for the nonce*' and later when '*Enter Slipper with a companion, boy or wench, dancing a hornpipe, and dance out again*'. The Elizabethan *Wooing of Nan* seems to combine typical folk drama features with jig-like dancing, as it stages a competition for Nan's hand between a series of rustic dancers.

SATIRE

Jigs were often more than mere jollities, however. In the Marprelate controversy, Martin was threatened with a jig in one pamphlet, *A Countercuff*, and it appears that soon a jig by John Laneham was indeed being performed by the Queen's Men and was 'lashing' Martin, so that he was 'nipped in the head and killed clean', having been 'overtaken in his own foolery'. Thomas Nashe positively feared such politically motivated 'news' jigs: 'Look to it, you booksellers and stationers, and let not your shops be infested with such goose giblets or stinking garbage as the jigs of newsmongers'. Jigs used for political purposes can be glimpsed in some Elizabethan plays. In *Edward III*, perhaps by Shakespeare, the Countess fears

> How much they will deride us in the North,
> And in their vile uncivil skipping jigs
> Bray forth their conquest and our overthrow,

while in Marlowe's *Edward II*, Lancaster reflects bitterly:

> And thereof came it that the fleering Scots,
> To England's high disgrace, have made this jig:
>> Maids of England, sore may ye mourn,
>> For your lemans you have lost at Bannockburn, –
>> With a heave and a ho!
>> What weaneth the King of England
>> So soon to have won Scotland!
>> With a rombelow!

In Thomas Heywood's *Edward IV* Part 2, Scales reports of the doings of a French count from whom the English had been expecting help:

> My lord, he lies and revels at St Quentins,
> And laughs at Edward's coming into France.

> There, domineering with his drunken crew,
> Make jigs of us, and in their slavering jests
> Tell how like rogues we lie here in the field.
> Then comes a slave, one of those drunken sots,
> In with a tavern reckoning for a supplication,
> Disguised with a cushion on his head,
> A drawer's apron for a herald's coat,
> And tells the count, the King of France craves
> One of his worthy honour's dog kennels
> To be his lodging for a day or two,
> With such other tavern foolery:
> With that, this filthy rascal greasy rout
> Burst out in laughter at this worthy jest,
> Neighing like horses.

It is a brilliant description not only of the jig's unpretentiousness ('a cushion on his head') but also its unbuttoned auditory, laughing like horses.

In 1641 the political jig was still giving offence. Baskervill quotes an anti-Covenanter pamphlet, *Vox Borealis, or the Northern Discoveries*, which recounts how the Governor of Edinburgh Castle

> keeps a couple of false knaves, to laugh at the lords (a fool and a fiddler) and when he and they are almost drunk, then they go to singing of Scots' jigs, in a jeering manner, at the Covenanters, for surrendering up their castles. The fiddler he flings out his heels and dances and sings:

> > Put up thy dagger, Jamie,
> >   And all things shall be mended,
> > Bishops shall fall, no, not at all,
> >   When the Parliament is ended.

> Then the fool he flirts out his folly and whilst the fiddler plays, he sings

> > Which never was intended,
> >   But only for to flame thee:
> > We have gotten the game,
> >   We'll keep the same,
> > Put up thy dagger, Jamie.

RICHARD TARLTON

It is no wonder to find this spirited form appealing to professional performers, especially the professional clowns. Prince among these was Richard Tarlton, the 'wonder of the world', according to one writer. Tarlton may have begun his adult career as a publican – his style certainly had something of the later music hall chairman's brashness about it – but he was first discovered on the stage with Sussex's Men and then became a founder member of the Queen's Men. Politically, hardly surprisingly, he opposed the Puritans, supporting 'maypoles and merriments', and his stage persona was that of a countryman, a peasant or ploughman. He was sly, witty and always mocked pretension: when one Richard Harvey used esoteric astrological obfuscations to predict wild weather, which never arrived, Tarlton mocked him mercilessly from the stage. He was a smallish, squarish man, with curly hair, a flat nose and a squint.

On stage, he wore a buttoned cap and a russet coat, and he carried a kind of satchel and a slapstick. As he approached, he often beat a drum so the audience knew he was coming. His was 'a wondrous plentiful pleasant extemporal wit', according to Edmund Howes remembering him a quarter of a century after his death, though it was probably salacious, scatological and laced with *double entendres*.

Tarlton's comic turns included playing 'the God Luz with a flitch of bacon at his back'; fighting the Queen's little dog, Perrico, with his sword and a staff, and begging her to call off her mastiff; standing on one toe; and peeping through the curtains, like Eric Morecombe on television four hundred years later. Tarlton used to invite his audience to suggest a theme to him, and would improvise rhymes, or even songs, on it *extempore*. Henry Peachum recorded a time when he played the third son, a scapegrace, of a rich father who lay dying. The old man called his sons to his bedside, and promised the two elder ones riches and finery: 'Oh no', they each protested, 'we want *you* to live to enjoy these'. Then he called the third son, Tarlton, and recalled how he had had to rescue him from prison many times. He promised to leave him nothing but a rope and the gallows. 'Oh no', protested Tarlton's character, 'I want *you* to enjoy those things!' Perhaps the finest tribute to Tarlton comes in Wilson's *The Three Lords and Three Ladies of London*, written shortly after the great comic's death. Simplicity shows Will a picture:

SIMPLICITY: This is Tarlton's picture. Didst thou never know Tarlton?

WILL: No. What was that Tarlton? I never knew him.

SIMPLICITY: What was he? A prentice in his youth of this honourable city, God be with him. When he was young he was leaning to the trade that my wife useth now, and I have used, vide lice shirt, water bearing. I wis, he hath tossed a tankard in Cornhill now. If thou knewest him not, I will not call thee ingram; but if thou knewest him not, thou knewest nobody. I warrant here's two crackropes knew him.

WIT: I dwelt with him.

SIMPLICITY: Didst thou? Now, give me thy hand. I love thee the better.

WILL: And I too, sometime.

SIMPLICITY: You, child? Did you dwell with him sometime?

Wit dwelt with him indeed, as appeared by his rhyme,

And served him well; and Will was with him now and then.

But soft, thy name is Wealth: I think

In earnest he was little acquainted with thee.

O, it was a fine fellow as e'er was born:

There will never come his like while the earth can corn.

O, passing fine Tarlton! I would thou hadst lived yet.

WEALTH: He might have some, but thou showest small wit.

There is no such fineness in the picture that I see.

SIMPLICITY: Thou art no Cinque Port man; thou art not wit free.

The fineness was within, for without he was plain;

But it was the merriest fellow, and had such jests in store,

That, if thou hadst seen him, thou wouldst have laughed thy heart sore.

Tarlton was also a playwright: unfortunately, his *Seven Deadly Sins*, which was extremely popular, has not survived. Nor have any of his jigs, though there are records of *Tarlton's Toys*, registered in 1576, and two later jigs, *Tarlton's News Out of Purgatory* and *The Cobbler of Canterbury*.

WILL KEMP

After Tarlton's death, his place in the people's affections seems to have been taken by Will Kemp, a stout man but evidently quick on his feet. Nashe described him as 'that most comical and conceited Cavalier Monsieur du Kemp, jest-monger and vice-regent general to the ghost of Dick Tarlton'.[1] In the 1580s Kemp spent time in Europe, especially in Germany and Netherlands, but in 1588 he joined Strange's Men. In 1594 he was a founder member of the Lord Chamberlain's Men, but he left them abruptly in 1599, and in 1600 he famously danced from London to Norwich, writing his own brief but amusing account of the feat in *Kemp's Nine Days Wonder*. After this he toured Europe again, then joined Worcester's Men in 1602, but he died in 1603.

Kemp and Robert Wilson may have formed a double act with Leicester's Men in the Netherlands in 1585–6, and when he was with the Lord Chamberlain's Men he forged another double act with Richard Cowley: they were Dogberry and Verges in *Much Ado about Nothing*. Other parts Kemp may have created include Cob in *Every Man in His Humour*, Launcelot Gobbo in *The Merchant of Venice*,

Figure 2.7
The star of many Elizabethan jigs, Will Kempe, dancing, accompanied by a solo musician

Bottom in *A Midsummer Night's Dream*, and Falstaff in both parts of *Henry IV* and *The Merry Wives of Windsor*. He also appeared in *A Knack to Know a Knave* with Strange's Men in 1592; when the script of this play was published, it was with 'Kemp's applauded merriments of the Men of Gotham on receiving the King into Gotham', which sounds almost like a jig itself. We get a flavour of his comedian's patter in his *Nine Days Wonder*: he describes how the spectators pressed him to drink with them:

> But I warrant you Will Kemp was wise enough: to their full cups, kind thanks was my return, with
> gentlemanlike protestations: as, truly sir, I dare not, it stands not with the congruity of my health. Congruity,
> said I? How came that strange language in my mouth?
> I think scarcely that it is any Christian word, and yet it may be a good word for ought I know, though I never
> made it, nor do very well understand it. Yet I am sure I have bought it at the wordmongers, at as dear a rate as
> I could have had a whole hundred of bavins at the woodmongers. (A 'bavin' is a bundle of brushwood.)

Kemp declared that he had 'spent his life in mad jigs and merry jests', and at least three jigs are known as 'Kemp's Jig'. One of these is also known as *Singing Simpkin* and is discussed below, and then there is 'Kemp's New Jig of the Kitchen Stuff Woman'. Kemp seems to have put more emphasis on dancing than did Tarlton, but essentially his humour was as broad as were his tendencies to ad-lib when on stage, to challenge or respond to his audience and to employ physical humour.

POPULAR PERFORMERS IN JIGS

And so indeed, more or less, were the later stars of the jig. Like twentieth-century pantomimes, Elizabethan and seventeenth-century jigs relied heavily on the star: of the first eleven jigs registered for licences in the 1590s, six – more than half – were known by the name of the star. Kemp's jigs have already been mentioned. *Attewell's Jig* was performed by George Attewell, an actor with Strange's Men and then Admiral's, and known for his physical agility. *Phillips' Jig of the Slippers* points to Shakespeare's colleague, Augustine Phillips, performing at least one jig, and *Shank's Ordinary* is a jig performed by John Shank early in the new century, before Shank joined the King's Men. A rhyme of the time indicates not only Shank's move of company but refers also to the clowns then (1613) best known for jigs, William Rowley, a fat man, and Thomas Greene, thin:

> That's the fat fool of the Curtain,
> And the lean fool of the Bull:
> Since Shank did leave to sing his rhymes,
> He is counted but a gull.[2]

Later stars included Andrew Cane, who worked at the Red Bull and the Fortune in the 1630s, and his contemporary, Robert Cox, perhaps the last star of the jig, who continued performing them for years after Parliament had banned them in 1642.

THE POPULARITY OF JIGS

The popularity of jigs is hard to overestimate. Philip Hentzner, who visited London at the end of the sixteenth century, noted how jigs were greatly applauded in the theatre, and Sir John Davies wrote:

> For as we see at all the playhouse doors,
> When ended is the play, the dance and song,
> A thousand townsmen, gentlemen and whores,
> Porters and serving-men together throng.[3]

It appears jigs were loved by all classes. In 1612 an attempt was made to ban jigs, partly because 'divers cutpurses and other lewd and ill-disposed persons in great multitudes do resort thither at the end of every play, many times causing tumults and outrages'.[4] It was during the jig that spectators were so absorbed that they failed to notice when their pocket was being picked. Their absorption stemmed at least partly from the way the jig engaged with the audience. Tarlton challenging them to give him suggestions for improvised comic song-making was one example of this. Presumably the use of known popular tunes enabled the spectators to join in the choruses, and there were, for example, riddles asked, which also inevitably included audience response. And people laughed both at Tarlton the clown and also at the fictional story in which Tarlton played a part. There was pleasure on more than one level.

SIMPLE JIGS

Examples of jigs include a number of pair jigs, always with plenty of sexual content. *A Merry New Jig between Jenkin the Collier and Nancy* (1592) is one such, *A Mad Kind of Wooing, or, A Dialogue between Will the Simple and Nan the Subtle* is another. Then there is a Scottish jig, *The Wooing of Jock and Jenny* in which Jock offers Jenny a cow, fifteen pigs and a wheelbarrow, and boasts of his ability with the flail, and in the dance; and *The Merry Wooing of Robin and Joan* in which the main attraction may be the beautiful folk music.

COMPLEX JIGS

More complex jigs include more than two characters. In *Rowland's Godson* (c.1590), Bessie and her servant, John, completely befuddle Bessie's husband so that they might continue their amorous liaison. In *Attewell's Jig* (c.1595), another Bessie, again married, apparently agrees to the passionate advances of a gentleman. She arranges an assignation, but then gets her husband to ask the gentleman's wife to keep the tryst. *Singing Simpkin* (c.1595) is one of the best-known jigs: apparently Will Kemp played the part of Simpkin. The plot concerns his wooing of another married woman, who this time is pregnant. They are disturbed by another lover, a blustering roarer. Simpkin hides in a trunk when he appears, but soon the husband knocks on the door. The wife convinces the roarer to pretend he has come into the house chasing a malefactor, and when he has gone Simpkin appears, pretending to be the malefactor. In the original version the husband goes to fetch them wine, leaving Simpkin and his wife to continue their lovemaking. But in a later version, Simpkin is beaten by the husband. The question of the unborn baby's paternity is left unanswered.

Somewhat more complicated than these is *The Blackman* (early seventeenth century), in which Thumpkin and Susan's idyllic courtship is interrupted by two bullies, who ambush them and kidnap Susan. Thumpkin returns disguised as an old man, and while the two bullies fight over Susan, he carries her away. Not far, however, for the bullies catch them and force Thumpkin to sit on a stool covered with a sheet and shout 'Mum' from time to time so they know he is still there. A passing broom-seller takes Thumpkin for a ghost and flees. Thumpkin decides to change his 'Mum' to 'Ho ho ho'. The blackman (seller of lamp black) is scared but when he discovers who is under the sheet he agrees to exchange places with Thumpkin. When the bullies return, they think there must be a ghost under the sheet. Already scared, they see Thumpkin, his face now smeared with lamp black, and take him for the devil. Thumpkin and the blackman chase them away.

MUSIC

Even from these brief descriptions it is possible to isolate the chief features of the jig. The music is always in a popular idiom and frequently existing tunes are reworked so that new words can be fitted to them. Changes of metre in the printed texts are one way in which changes of tune are indicated. The audience probably enjoyed the music as music, but it seems that it fulfilled an important distancing function: in this sort of comedy, empathy is not desirable. The popular tunes are used to guide the action and to help the caricature. Thus, in *The Blackman*, the broom-seller sings a jaunty song when he appears. At the end of the verse Thumpkin moans, shocking the Brush Seller, who changes the tempo and becomes exaggeratedly frightened, but sings still to the same tune. This music, in other words, is immensely versatile.

MOVEMENT AND DANCE

It is useful in the dance, too. Charles Read Baskervill insisted that it was the dance which the spectators really loved in the jigs, but they probably equally enjoyed the tumbling, slapstick, pratfalls and so on. The way Thumpkin and Susan run off while the bullies are fighting in *The Blackman* is a traditional *lazzo* frequently found in Italian *commedia dell'arte*, for example, as is Thumpkin's position under a sheet in a parody of the stage ghost. The jig is intensely physical, and many must have lasted longer than the texts suggest because much was inserted which is not recorded. When Thumpkin and Susan enter singing, 'Jog on, jog on', it is easy to see that music and movement go together. At other times action and song may have been more separated.

The steps available to jig performers were very varied, from the *galiard*, a strong, muscular dance with leaps and turns, and the somewhat similar *volta*, to the more stately *branle*, though this too could involve jumping and pirouetting. Then there were sword dances: Tarlton was a Master of Fence and there was almost certainly some sort of sword dance in *The Blackman* when the bullies draw their swords to capture Susan and drive Thumpkin away. Morris dances, too, were popular, and the morris seems to have been a favourite of Will Kemp, who morrised from London to Norwich in 1600. Cuddy in *The Witch of Edmonton* is another compulsive morris dancer. The hornpipe, a sailor's dance, was common, and indeed the jig, when the performer presumably whirled like a child's spinning top, or whirligig, was a dance in its own right.

TRADITIONAL CHARACTERS

Within this format, however, jigs employed thoroughly traditional characters: the clown himself, braggart soldiers, old and cuckolded husbands, saucy and resourceful wives, simple tradesmen and comic servants. The clown was usually central. The story frequently concerned a clown who finds

Figure 2.8
A ball at the Valois court, early sixteenth century. Notice the energy of the dancers

Source: Musée des Beaux-Arts, Rennes, France/Bridgeman Images

himself in a more or less dire predicament, only to extricate himself from it either by his own enterprise or his good fortune. And, significantly, he emerges from his adventure still dancing.

JIGS AND BAWDRY

Jigs were also notably bawdy. The Wife, wishing to hide Simpkin, sings: 'I have a place behind here Which yet is known to no man', to which Simpkin replies in an aside to the audience: 'She has a place before, too, But that is all too common!' Dekker deplored a 'nasty bawdy jig', and the term is of course slang for sexual intercourse. One modern critic has gone so far as to call the jig 'a form of soft commercial pornography'.

Indeed it was probably the lewdness of a lost jig, called *Garlic*, which led to the order to suppress jigs in 1612, an order which seems to have been ignored, however, for a few years later one spectator decided against going to one of the private indoor playhouses because it was too expensive:

> I'll go to the Bull or the Fortune, and there see
> A play for two pence with a jig to boot.[5]

LATER JIGS

In 1632 a commentator noted that 'most commonly when the play is done, you shall have a jig or dance of all trades',[6] though in the theatres of the later Caroline period, they often became scurrilous and politically motivated. However, jigs continued to be performed into the period of the commonwealth in taverns and at fairs, partly because they were not regarded as straight dramas. The inclusion of music to some extent saved them. One of the last jigs to be created, *The Cheaters Cheated*, in which a countryman has his pocket picked by two city spivs, only to get his own back by a clever trick involving a baby, which they also steal believing it to be treasure, was composed in about 1660. The form at this time, however, seems gradually to have given way, partly to the largely spoken afterpiece, or 'droll', and partly to the new-fangled opera.

NOTES

1 Thomas Nashe, *An Almond for a Parrot*.
2 William Turner, *Dish of Lenten Stuffe*, c.1613.
3 Sir John Davies, *Epigram XVII*, c.1595.
4 Charles Read Baskervill, *The Elizabethan Jig and Related Song Drama*, New York: Dover, 1965, p. 116.
5 Thomas Goffe, *The Careless Shepherdess*, 1619.
6 Donald Lupton, *London and the Countrey Carbonadoed and Quartred*, 1632.

Chapter 18: 1587–94: The making of 'Elizabethan' theatre

THE ROSE THEATRE

In 1587, in a move which was both risky and significant, Philip Henslowe, speculator and entrepreneur, opened a theatre on the south bank of the Thames. It was a deliberate move away from the other amphitheatres to the north of the city and considerably closer to the metropolis than the old Newington Butts playhouse. With financial backing from John Cholmley, Henslowe erected the new Rose Theatre on Rose Alley at the corner with Maiden Lane, beyond the reach of the Lord Mayor of London. This was the 'Liberty' of the Clink (a 'clink' being a prison), nominally though distinctly not actively controlled by the Bishop of Winchester. It was a notorious and even dangerous area. Bull- and bear-baiting were already favourite pastimes here, but its real disrepute stemmed from its long line of brothels which faced the Thames waterfront, for it was London's main red light district.

The Rose was somewhat different from the earlier playhouses, being smaller and more ornate. Henslowe was probably hoping for a better class of clientele. The building had an outside diameter of approximately seventy-two feet, and an irregular polygon shape with probably fourteen sides. The walls were of brick at the foot supporting a timber frame, and it had a thatched roof. The yard was just less than fifty feet across, with a mortar floor unexpectedly raked towards the stage. There were three galleries. The stage itself was probably five feet high and was also irregular, being in the form of a tapering hexagon which jutted into the yard sixteen feet six inches, much less than in other playhouses. It was consequently rather small, even though it measured about thirty-six feet nine inches at the back and twenty-six feet ten inches at the front. It was somewhat enlarged a few years later. Because the stage was oddly shaped, or perhaps dictating this shape, the tiring-house wall at the back of the stage was at something of an angle. There seem to have been no pillars on the stage and therefore probably no covering for it either.

The theatre held approximately five hundred people in its yard and probably eleven hundred in its galleries (though the average attendance through the 1590s was no more than six hundred per performance). Its lavish décor was slightly undermined by the fact that spectators, to reach the entrance, had to cross a footbridge over a drain, used as an open urinal. 'Plucking a rose' was a euphemism for urinating, and next to the theatre was the Little Rose, a notorious brothel operated by Henslowe himself.

The size of the theatre made for a dynamic proximity of the actor to the spectator. The Rose was the most intimate of all the open air playhouses, yet some of the 'biggest' Elizabethan plays, including *Tamburlaine*, *The Jew of Malta* and *Titus Andronicus*, were seen here. In 1592 the theatre was extended, adding four hundred to its capacity, flattening the rake in the yard, and enlarging the stage, the galleries and the backstage area, thereby making its overall shape ovoid. But it was still much smaller than the Theatre or the later Globe, even after a roof over the stage was added. Through the 1590s it was one of two extraordinarily successful playhouses. Yet it was pulled down in 1605, only for its archaeological remnants to be surprisingly uncovered in 1989 to international fascination.

MOVES TOWARDS BUILDING-BASED THEATRES

The year the Rose opened marks perhaps the beginning of the transition from a theatre organised around touring to one which was building-based. It may be no more than coincidence that these years also saw the first of the plays which are still revived regularly over four hundred years later, such as Kyd's *The Spanish Tragedy* and Marlowe's *Tamburlaine the Great*, both of which were probably first performed in 1587. It also saw one of those horrible accidents which dot the history of the theatre: an actor of the Admiral's Men, in a spectacular scene, was tied to a post like a baited bear. There, he was required to be shot at by another actor. The gun was fired, and the shot accidentally hit and killed a pregnant woman and a child in the audience.

LEICESTER'S MEN AND STRANGE'S MEN

A year later, in September 1588, the same month that Dick Tarlton died, Robert Dudley, Earl of Leicester, also died. He had been in overall command of the forces facing the Armada months earlier, but he was also a notable supporter of the theatre. His Men had been a leading force in the 1570s and 1580s, but now they were disbanded, and many of their members joined Lord Strange's Men. It was a move which marked the beginning of the rise to supremacy of this company.

Led by Edward Alleyn, a brilliant actor who had bought plays by Peele, Munday, Marlowe and others, it now included George Bryan, Thomas Pope, Richard Cowley, Augustine Phillips, George Attewell, John Tunstall, Will Sly and probably Richard Burbage. Soon Will Kemp, leading comic actor, would join them. In London they played at James Burbage's Theatre. But in May 1591, the company and the elder Burbage became seriously at odds over Box Office receipts. It seemed that James Burbage was failing to pay the actors appropriately, and Strange's Company walked out in dudgeon, probably leaving the young Richard Burbage with his father. They moved to Henslowe's Rose Theatre, where they played from February to June 1592, probably the longest stay by any company in a single venue till now.

LONDON THEATRES DISRUPTED

But in June 1592 everything suddenly changed. After considerable unrest in Southwark, the Lord Mayor petitioned Lord Burghley to close the theatres down, and he partially acceded with a ban till Michaelmas in September. But in any case the plague was raging in London, the deaths per week had reached thirty and the theatres had to close. In September, the playwright Robert Greene died. By then Strange's Men had embarked on a seemingly endless tour of the provinces, taking in Cambridge, Rye, Canterbury, Bristol, Shrewsbury, Chester, York, Ipswich, Bath, Oxford and

Figure 2.9
Edward Alleyn, the brilliant actor who led Lord Strange's Men from 1587

more. Pembroke's Men were also touring, waiting for the plague to die down, and Henslowe, who had begun his famous 'Diary' (really an account book) earlier in this year, took the opportunity to remodel and enlarge the Rose Theatre in hopes of better times to come. In October, his stepdaughter married Edward Alleyn, thus uniting the leading actor with the theatre's manager.

At last, in December 1592, the plague had abated enough to allow Strange's Men to return to the Rose. With a company that now included John Hemminges and Thomas Downton, they presented a spirited repertory, the most popular play in which, judging by audience figures, was *The Jew of Malta*, though they performed *A Knack to Know a Knave* (with Kemp's 'merriments') most frequently. But in February 1593, the plague struck again, and for the rest of that year the theatres in London were once more shut. Strange's Men, probably reluctantly, again took their repertoire on tour: *Friar Bacon and Friar Bungay*, *The Jew of Malta*, *A Knack to Know a Knave*, *The Massacre at Paris*, *Orlando Furioso*, *The Spanish Tragedy*, *Titus Andronicus*.

Other companies were touring too. Sussex's Men were one group fighting to survive, Pembroke's were another. Their company was led by John Holland, John Sinclair and Gabriel Spencer, and there is some suggestion that William Shakespeare was a member. Their repertoire certainly included plays by Shakespeare: *Henry VI* Parts 2 and 3, *Richard III* and *The Taming of the Shrew*, as well as Marlowe's *Edward II*. For Pembroke's Men, however, this tour became unviable. In dire financial straits, they were forced to sell their costumes and their playbooks, and at least for a time they disappeared from view, though they resurfaced in 1597 at the Swan Theatre. Meanwhile in September 1593 Lord Strange became Earl of Derby, but his theatre company was by now weakened by touring, as well as, perhaps, by the death of their most popular playwright, Christopher Marlowe.

NEW THEATRE COMPANIES

In 1594 the plague was less severe, only disrupting the theatres for three months from February to April. But this was enough to allow a new configuration of the theatre companies and playhouses to emerge from all the trials of shut theatres and endless provincial touring, one which was to last for some years. From December 1593 to the closure of the theatres in February 1594, Sussex's Men were playing at Henslowe's Rose Theatre. Strange's Men (now Derby's Men) seem to have been at Newington Butts and the Cross Keys Inn. When the theatres reopened in April, Sussex's shared the Rose for the first week with the Queen's Men. But that same month the Earl of Derby died, and his troupe was disbanded. Meanwhile Lord Hunsden, the Lord Chamberlain and father-in-law of the Lord Admiral, decided to reinstate the sort of monopoly designed for the Queen's Men in 1583, but now to include two companies, both to be based in London rather than on touring. Other companies, including the Queen's Men, could continue to play in London occasionally, but were to be mainly provincial touring companies.

THE DUOPOLY ESTABLISHED

It was decided that the patrons of the two London companies would have to be Privy Councillors, and it so happened that Hunsden himself and the Lord Admiral, his son-in-law, were both members of the Council. So the two companies were to take them for patrons: the Lord Chamberlain's Men and the Lord Admiral's Men. These two companies drew their members from existing companies. Most of Derby's, for instance, immediately joined the Lord Chamberlain's, though it was notable that Edward Alleyn did not. Had he been too dominant in Derby's Men? Or was the fact that Richard Burbage (brought in from Pembroke's Men) was a prominent member of the Lord Chamberlain's new group significant, considering how Alleyn and Burbage Senior had quarrelled the year before? Play texts were also shared out: Marlowe's and Kyd's plays went to the Admiral's company, the old Queen's Men's repertoire went to the Lord Chamberlain's (where several of them were rewritten by William Shakespeare).

Much was once made of the apparent rivalry between these two new London-based companies, but it is now thought more probable that it was in both their interests to preserve their duopoly, and that they were more comparable to friendly but competing members of a trade guild. In May and June they appeared on alternate days, first at Newington Butts, then at the Rose, but then the Lord Chamberlain's Men departed for James Burbage's Theatre, while the Admiral's Men stayed at the Rose.

With the death of Thomas Kyd in August, following the deaths of Greene and Marlowe (Peele was to follow them to the grave in 1596) and the demise of the old leading companies, Lord Strange's Men, and the Earl of Leicester's and the virtual banishment of the Queen's Men, suddenly there was something new in the theatrical air. There was space now for these two companies each to develop a distinct identity and to attract their own sort of audience.

THE SWAN THEATRE

The feeling of a new beginning was reinforced by the decision of Francis Langley, a goldsmith and well-known speculator, to build a new theatre on the Bankside. Presumably noting Henslowe's success, he used the Paris Garden Manor, which he had bought in 1589, for this new theatre which he called the Swan. It may not have been a particularly good decision, because it was much further west than the Rose: theatre-seeking pedestrians who crossed the Thames by London Bridge would come to the Rose well before they saw the Swan. Besides, he had no theatrical experience as far as is known with which to compete against such a wily operator as Henslowe. Hardly surprisingly, the Lord Mayor objected, and wrote to the Lord High Treasurer:

> Forasmuch as we find by daily experience the great inconvenience which groweth to this city and the government thereof by the said plays, I have emboldened myself to bean humble suitor to your good lord to be a means for us rather to suppress all such places built for that kind of exercise than to erect any more of the same sort.[1]

Equally unsurprisingly, the objection was not sustained, and the new building, of stone, timber-framed, and using flint infill, opened in 1595. It was about one hundred feet in diameter, with three galleries divided into sections, or 'rooms'. The rectangular stage reached virtually to the middle of the yard, with two pillars on the stage supporting a roof which, however, only covered the rear half of the stage. The back wall, the tiring-house frontage, contained at least two doors and a gallery above, though whether this was for actors or musicians or spectators is not clear. Above the stage roof was a hut from which a trumpeter emerged to blow his instrument before a play began. The Swan could hold at least three thousand people, and Langley obviously spent much on decoration, for it was more splendid even than the Rose.

The Swan is the only Elizabethan theatre of which there is a picture, albeit a rather skimpy sketch which has caused more disagreement than almost any other contemporary theatre document. Actually a copy made by Arend van Buchell from the original by Johannes de Witt, this sketch raises a number of awkward questions: why are the galleries empty? Why are there only two doors at the back, and no 'discovery' space, when one of the only two plays known to have been performed there, Thomas Middleton's *A Chaste Maid in Cheapside*, performed by Lady Elizabeth's

Figure 2.10
The only contemporary drawing of an open air Elizabethan playhouse, copied from an original sketch by Johannes de Witt. Atmospheric and intriguing, it seems to raise more questions than it answers.

Source: University Library, Utrecht

Men, probably in 1611, requires a 'discovery' space in its very first scene? (The other play known to have been presented there was also by Middleton, with William Rowley, *The World Tossed at Tennis*, presented by Prince Charles's Men in 1620.) Other questions include: what is beneath the stage? Why is the trumpeter blowing his trumpet when the play is proceeding? Who are the people above and behind the stage? But still the drawing's charm is undeniable, and it is also useful even if tantalisingly difficult to interpret.

De Witt's written description accompanies the drawing:

> Of all the theatres . . . the largest and most magnificent is that one of which the sign is a swan, called in the vernacular the Swan Theatre; for it accommodates in its seats three thousand persons, and is built of a mass of flint stones . . . and supported by wooden columns painted in such excellent imitation of marble that it is able to deceive even the most cunning.[2]

In spite of this, the Swan's history shows it did not fulfil its promise. It remained a touring venue into the 1620s, and in 1637, though it was still standing, apparently it had not been used for years.

NOTES

1 Edmund K. Chambers, *The Elizabethan Stage*, Oxford: Clarendon Press, 1923, IV, p. 316.
2 A.M. Nagler, *A Source Book in Theatrical History*, New York: Dover Publications, 1952, p. 117.

Chapter 19: Shakespeare and the Lord Chamberlain's Men

THE LORD CHAMBERLAIN'S MEN: THE EARLY YEARS

The Lord Chamberlain's Men settled at the Theatre, Finsbury Fields, in 1594. Probably content with the duopoly they formed with the Admiral's Men on the south bank, they operated as a kind of cartel, combining to keep other companies out of the capital.

For two years this arrangement seemed to operate smoothly enough, but James Burbage knew that his lease on the Theatre would expire in 1597, and he knew also that the owner did not look favourably upon the players. Consequently in 1596, while the players left the Theatre and based themselves at the Cross Keys Inn, Burbage bought an upstairs hall in the Blackfriars precinct, and at some expense had it refurbished and remodelled as a theatre. However, when the new theatre was ready, the wealthy residents of the precinct, including Lord Hunsdon, the Lord Chamberlain himself, petitioned the Privy Council against this intrusion on their privatised haven. The Privy Council upheld their objections. The actors were stumped. Burbage was confounded, having spent considerably on what was now seen to be a white elephant. And things went from bad to worse in July when Lord Hunsdon died, and was succeeded in his post by Lord Brooke, a known opponent of the theatre. The Lord Chamberlain's Men, with neither financial reserves nor a proper home, were now in danger of losing their privileged London status and open to the Lord Mayor's harassment. And in February 1597, perhaps tired with these turbulent fortunes, James Burbage died.

However, the following month, Lord Brooke, too, died, and he was succeeded by Lord Hunsdon's son, Sir George Carey, as Lord Chamberlain. Carey, a supporter of the theatre, also assumed the patronage of Burbage's Company, leaving Brooke as no more than a bitter memory recreated in the caricature, Brook, Ford's absurd *alter ego* in *The Merry Wives of Windsor*. However, the Lord Chamberlain's Men were still forced into an unsatisfactory compromise in moving to the Curtain, disdainfully referred to by Shakespeare as 'this unworthy scaffold' and 'this wooden O'. By late 1598 their position had become so frustrating that the players, having acquired a plot of land near Henslowe's Rose Theatre on the south bank, but still impoverished from James Burbage's excesses, raided the old Theatre, pulling it down and making off with its timbers. These they reassembled and refashioned to make the Globe Theatre which opened in 1599.

THE BUSINESS

Despite James Burbage's financial unreliability, the Lord Chamberlain's Men were economically a thoroughly viable business. With an enclosed playhouse, they could ensure that all patrons paid in advance, and at a penny for entry to the yard, another penny to watch from the more comfortable gallery and a further penny for a private room, annual Box Office income might be at least £2500. Annual expenditure was certainly less than that. The major outgoings were production costs, which might reach £1200 per year. Wages might amount to £400, licensing £100, building maintenance £100, purchase of plays from playwrights £100. Shareholders had to be paid out of the remainder, and some money kept for future investment and as a financial reserve. But still, it is easy to see that a London-based theatre company at the end of Elizabeth I's reign was a sustainable – and potentially profitable – enterprise.

COMPANY ORGANISATION

The company members were organised on three levels: first, the sharers, then the hired men, and finally the apprentice boys. The original sharers in the Lord Chamberlain's Men were Richard and Cuthbert Burbage with a 25% stake each, and Thomas Pope, Augustine Phillips, William Shake-speare, Will Kemp and John Hemminges, who each held 10%. When Kemp left in 1599, Pope, Phil-lips, Shakespeare and Hemminges each increased their share to 12.5%, though later Henry Condell and William Sly became sharers so that these six then owned 8.33% each. The sharers controlled policy and, on stage, probably took most of the main parts. They were responsible for the upkeep of the building, they bought the plays to be presented, they hired needed personnel and paid the licensing fees. In this company at least, all seemed to share responsibility in all these areas, no-one specialised, so that the company operated as a kind of co-operative. Their reward was half the money collected at the galleries' door.

The people the company needed to hire included extra actors, musicians, property men, ward-robe supervisors, doorman and stage keepers (stage hands) who could be drafted in as extras in crowd scenes. The boy members, who played the women's parts, were apprenticed to specific members of the company and might live in their houses as apprentices in any other trade did.

PLAYING CONDITIONS

The season opened in September, and the company played through till Christmas, when they hoped to appear at court. They played on till Lent when there was a break until playing resumed on Easter Monday, continuing till June. July and August were often spent in touring the provinces, but by September the company was ready to start a new season. They presented a different play every afternoon, announcing the next day's play at the end of this day's, though sometimes being guided by an audience's vocal demand. A new play would enter the repertory and be performed perhaps two or three times in ten days. Performances would usually become less frequent with time – per-haps once a fortnight, then once a month and finally the play would fade from the repertoire. But it might be revived two or three years later, and if it was extremely popular it would receive many more performances than this implies.

WILLIAM SHAKESPEARE: COMPANY PLAYWRIGHT

It is easy to see therefore that the company's survival depended in no small measure on a good sup-ply of new plays. Indeed the play became a commodity in its own right in this period. The playwright sold it to the company, and the company sold it to the paying public. In these circumstances it is astonishing that before they moved to the Globe in 1599 and except for two plays by Ben Jonson at the end of this period, Shakespeare is the only author known to have supplied new plays to the Lord Chamberlain's Men. A few plays from the company do survive by the ubiquitous 'Anon', but the fact is still remarkable, no less remarkable than Shakespeare's productivity in the same period. He generally supplied the company with at least two plays per year, usually one serious and one more light-hearted. The fact that almost all Shakespeare's plays were authored by him alone is also unusual in an age when script production was very frequently collaborative. Furthermore, Shake-speare, unlike almost all his contemporaries, worked extremely closely with his actors at all times – indeed he was one of his actors himself.

Figure 2.11
Portrait of William Shakespeare, attributed to John Taylor, c.1610

Source: Universal Art Archive/Alamy Stock Photo

All these factors help to explain the extraordinary quality of Shakespeare's drama, and in themselves fatally undermine the absurd theories of those who say someone else wrote these plays. In them, Shakespeare combined irony with the ability to carry us away; he made the action and the actors both familiar and strange, and if he presented something not quite exotic, nor was it everyday or commonplace. The key perhaps lay in the way Shakespeare thought in a uniquely theatrical way. The fulcrum of very many of his plays is theatrical in itself: in *Henry IV* Part 1, for example, the play's movement turns on the scene in the Eastcheap tavern when Falstaff and Hal act out the scene between the King and the Prince, taking turns to play each part; in *King Lear* it is the moment on the heath when Lear sets up the play courtroom and acts the trial of his daughters; in *As You Like It* it is when Rosalind, playing Ganymede, playing Rosalind, acts out her marriage to Orlando. These theatricalisations are at the heart of Shakespeare's plays.

HISTORY PLAYS

Notable in this period of Shakespeare's career, as he settled into the role of company sharer and company dramatist, is the fact that apart from *Romeo and Juliet*, all the plays he wrote were either comedies or histories. Shakespeare did not invent the history play, but after him few history plays were written. Besides the disputed *Edward III* and *King John*, his major sequence of history plays traced the fortunes of England over a stormy century before the advent of the Tudors. Politics makes theatre and theatre makes politics, as so often in history. Shakespeare wrote eight plays in two cohesive tetralogies, and his work has probably influenced to some degree everyone who has thought about the late middle ages in England since.

Though his work derives from that of John Bale, and then from the plays of the Queen's Men and the playwrights of the late 1580s and early 1590s, Shakespeare's canvas is much wider than their simple chronicles. He sees the interdependency of one part of society and another; he demonstrates how if one element is out of step with the rest, the whole commonwealth shakes. He understands how much in these feudal or post-feudal societies depends on the king, and he probes questions such as: what makes a good king? Do kings have a divine right to rule? What if the king mismanages his kingdom? When is disobedience or even rebellion justified? What about the killing of a king, as would happen in England just a generation after Shakespeare's death? He added to these reflections, others about the problems of succession and inheritance, especially apposite in Elizabethan England, and the problem of factionalism in government at a time of dangerous competition between the Essex and Dudley factions in Elizabeth's court. Shakespeare's history plays embody questions of authority, and the derivation of authority and articulate urgent questions concerning order and disorder in the state.

Tudor England seemed to have achieved the status of an independent nation state in which peace largely prevailed. How had this come about? To find the answer to this question, people turned to history, to the chronicles written by Ralph Holinshed and Edward Hall, to poems like Samuel Daniels' *The Civil War between the Two Houses of Lancaster and York* and Michael Drayton's *Piers Gaveston*, or to the plays already mentioned. Drama had a special immediacy, of course, and Shakespeare deploys with increasing assurance the techniques of epic first employed in the medieval mystery cycles. His picture stretches from the countryside in Gloucestershire to the tavern in Eastcheap, and from the wilds of Wales to the battlefields of France. But beside this portrayal of mighty forces locked in massive combat, details appear in vivid close-up, as when the Duchess of York and the Queen, awaiting the boy king, Edward V, chatter with the king's younger brother. The Queen scolds him: 'A parlous boy! Go to, you are too shrewd!' The Duchess of York says: 'Good madame, be not angry with the child', but the Queen flashes back: 'Pitchers have ears'. It is a terrifying moment, subsumed just seconds later when Edward arrives with a train of courtiers processing in gorgeous apparel to the brazen flourishes of the trumpets. The effect is further enhanced by Shakespeare's use of emblematic devices, such as the blue and tawny coats of the followers of the Duke of Gloucester and the Bishop of Winchester, the red blood of the napkin Margaret wipes in York's face, or the scene in the garden when the Yorkists and the Lancastrians each pluck white or red roses. Such moments are stylised and conventional, but they cut unerringly to the heart of history.

Fitzdottrel, the country squire in Jonson's *The Devil Is an Ass*, believes 'playbooks' are more 'authentic' than chronicles, and in a sense he is correct. In plays the past becomes present, history attains a new reality, and what emerges from Shakespeare's extraordinary epic is an idea of England. The performance has opened up the core of England, a notion of community and shared identity. The paradox at the centre of this is the paradox of theatre itself: acting is pretending, but through acting emerges truth. Thomas Nashe, after seeing perhaps the first performance of *Henry VI* Part 1, wrote:

> How it would have joyed brave Talbot (the terror of the French) to think that after he had lain two hundred
> year in his tomb, he should triumph again on the stage, and have his bones new embalmed with the tears of
> ten thousand spectators at least (at several times) who, in the tragedian that represents his person, imagine
> they behold him fresh bleeding.[1]

COMEDIES

If history plays are about community, comedies (and tragedies) are about individual identity. Shakespeare's comedies are subversive, funny and disturbing. They are subversive not so much of the social order, though that is sometimes seen as less solid than it might appear, but of individual equilibrium. The spectator who attends *Much Ado about Nothing* or who surrenders to *As You Like It*, experiences what it feels like to fall in love. It is a woozy and destabilising sensation, the best possible example of that dangerous imitation of life of which the theatre is capable, and it explains why people return to these comedies time after time.

The comedies are also funny. Not many writers can convulse an audience in genuine laughter four hundred years after their death, but anyone attending a good production of *Twelfth Night* today will witness this. The most obvious form of humour in Shakespeare's comedies was probably more appreciated in his own day than in ours: wit and wordplay. In *As You Like It*, Rosalind and Celia play on the words 'Nature' and 'Fortune' extensively till Touchstone the clown enters:

CELIA: When Nature hath made a fair creature, may she not by Fortune fall into the fire?
  Though Nature hath given us wit to flout at Fortune, hath not Fortune sent in this fool to cut off the argument?
ROSALIND: Indeed, there is Fortune too hard for Nature, when Fortune makes Nature's natural the cutter-off of
  Nature's wit.
CELIA: Peradventure this is not Fortune's work, neither, but Nature's, who perceiveth our natural wits too dull to reason of
  such goddesses, and hath sent this natural for our whetstone; for always the dullness of the fool is the whetstone of
  the wits. How now, wit: whither wander you?

Such profusions of humour often expand to whole scenes, as in the final performance of the *Pyramus and Thisbe* play in *A Midsummer Nights Dream* when Bottom's galloping extravagance demonstrates at least one kind of prodigal theatricality.

CROSS-DRESSING AND SEXUALITY

One characteristic of Shakespeare's comedies (and those of many his contemporaries) is the cross-dressing he so frequently employs, and the disturbing questions of gendering which result. In the whole Elizabethan-Jacobean period, it has been calculated that in at least seventy-four plays, female characters dress as boys. In Shakespeare's canon, that includes *The Two Gentlemen of Verona*, *The Merchant of Venice*, *As You Like It*, *Twelfth Night* and *Cymbeline*. The complications can be almost dizzying, as in *As You Like It*, when not only does Rosalind disguise herself as Ganymede who then 'acts' Rosalind in scenes with Rosalind's beloved Orlando, but Phoebe falls for Ganymede in an unexpected complication of gender uncertainty. Rosalind's quadrupled gender identity is not unique to Shakespeare: in *The Wise Woman of Hogsdon* by Thomas Heywood (c.1604), the character called 'Second Luce' is played by a boy who plays a girl (Second Luce) who plays a boy (Jack) who plays a girl (Young Chartley's bride).

The cross-dressing of young men (some 'boy' actors were well into their twenties) was merely a convention, it has been argued, and as such audiences were blind to it. Thomas Nashe was positively proud of it:

> Our players are not as the players beyond the sea, a sort of squirting bawdy comedians that have whores and common courtesans to play women's parts, and forbears no immodest speech or unchaste action that may provoke laughter.[2]

Yet it is still hard to know why no women at all were on stage, since no law forbade it and there were plenty of women in the audience. Nashe makes the mistake of imagining that actions performed by an actor ('pretend' actions) are done for real. It is true that theatre is a voyeur's art which releases the spectator's imagination, and Rosalind herself, in the Epilogue to *As You Like It*, undermines the pretence: 'It is not the fashion to see the lady the epilogue', she begins, but continues: 'If I were a woman I would kiss as many of you as had beards that pleased me, complexions that liked me, and breaths that I defied not'. The convention is thus fractured, the reality dangerous. One Puritan, John Rainoldes, railed in the same year *As You Like It* was written: 'Beautiful boys transformed into women are an occasion of drawing and provoking corruptly minded men to most heinous wickedness' and 'beautiful boys by kissing do sting and power secretly in a kind of poison, the poison of incontinency'.

Many Puritans believed that boys who played women would become gay. Middleton, in *Father Hubbard's Tale* (1604), suggested that if a man 'call in at the Blackfriars (the boy's company's theatre) . . . he should see a nest of boys able to ravish a man', and it is easy to see the potential for sodomy in any of these stage relationships, though it should be added that sodomy was less a sin in the eyes of the Elizabethans than it has been for some later generations. However, it is also true that many men through the ages have enjoyed gazing at boys dressed as women: they can experience the thrill of sexual ambivalence in doing so, and there is a *frisson* of pleasure to be had from setting free transgressive sexual fantasies, or from allowing androgyny to provoke. The wedding night undressing of Evadne by her ladies (all played by boys) in Beaumont and Fletcher's *The Maid's Tragedy* is inherently titillating, and it is impossible to deny a strand of homoeroticism in Orlando and Ganymede's love play in *As You Like It*. The relationship between Achilles and Patroclus in *Troilus and Cressida* is overtly homosexual. The fact is that transvestism contains both masculine and feminine. In many old ballads and folk tales, young women dress as soldiers or sailors and follow their beloveds to the wars: see, for instance, songs number 6, 7 and 72 in *The New Penguin Book of English Folk Songs* (2014). Bess Bridges, the heroine of Thomas Heywood's *The Fair Maid of the West* (c.1610) does the same. These women are both heroically masculine and still seductively feminine.

Whatever the male custodians of culture may have intended – and it is likely that it was thought 'safe' to keep women off the stage – casting boys as women sows seeds which may at any moment undermine masculinist ideologies. It undermines the social order which depends on a binary system of fixed gender and sexual relations, it challenges those basic categories by which identity can be controlled, and it suggests that sexual energy can be profitably or entertainingly diverted from acceptable channels. The gender system has perhaps always been a site of major anxiety for men, which is why in real life women were forbidden to dress as men. But of course, any system which depends on what people wear is an extremely flimsy one and presumably may easily be blown away.

Shakespeare's work (and the work of many of his contemporaries) suggests an altogether healthier and more expansive way of approaching these problems. As a bisexual man, one who seems to have worked his own way through this sexual jungle if his sonnets are anywhere near truthful, Shakespeare seems happy to allow us space for confused desires. For him, the blurring of gender distinctions seems to induce harmony and friendliness. He saw and revelled in the contradictions of the theatre itself – play as truth, for instance, or the platform stage as any place, and the convention of boy as woman seems to have been for him equally striking and equally playful. Such contradictions might be dangerous on one level, but they set the imagination free, enabling anyone to accept identity as fluid, gender as a construct and to accommodate others as individuals, not as gendered stereotypes.

Importantly, it was not only Shakespeare who was able to play with these conventions. He was preceded by John Lyly, for example, whose *Galatea* (1584) contains an overtly erotic relationship between Galatea and Phillida, both women dressed as boys, and provides a simple solution to their homoerotic desires: the goddess Venus will change one of them into a man. In Robert Greene's *James IV*, Queen Dorothea dons male disguise and spends time learning to perform her new gender role. She is successful enough to find Lady Anderson falling in love with her. Marlowe's Edward II and Piers Gaveston have a close homosexual bond which is unobjectionable until Edward begins to shower favours on Gaveston; then the peers decide Gaveston must be gotten rid of. In Ben Jonson's *Epicoene, or The Silent Woman*, Morose is frightened of a nagging wife and marries someone he believes is a silent woman, only to find 'she' is a man, while in *The New Inn* Frank, the Host's 'son', is actually Lady Frampul's younger sister in disguise. 'She' marries Beaufort. Middleton, apart from creating the masculine female figure of Moll, the Roaring Girl, has some notably homoerotic relationships. In *Michaelmas Term*, for instance, Shortyard and Easy are 'bedfellows' – 'in a word, we're man and wife; they can but lie together, and so do we'. And in *No Wit/Help Like a Woman's*, Lady Golden fleece falls for the intelligent and resourceful Mistress Low-water, who makes her face the truth of how she benefitted from her dead husband's exploitative behaviour.

The Roaring Girle.

OR

Moll Cut-Purse.

As it hath lately beene Acted on the Fortune-stage by
the Prince his Players.

Written by T. Middleton and T. Dekkar.

My cafe is alter'd, I muft worke for my liuing.

Printed at London for Thomas Archer, and are to be fold at his
shop in Popes head-pallace, neere the Royall
Exchange. 1611.

Figure 2.12
Title page of Thomas Middleton and Thomas Dekker's *The Roaring Girl*, 1611, in which the central character, the pipe-smoking Moll Cutpurse, was played by a man

THE PRESENTATION OF WOMEN

Shakespeare's reverberative treatment of 'gender trouble' is matched by his presentation of women, a number of whom are strong and admirable. The Victorian actress, Ellen Terry, suggested that the women in Shakespeare's plays have more moral courage than the men. Titania stands up to Oberon's bullying in *A Midsummer Night's Dream*, and Portia rescues Bassanio in *The Merchant of Venice*. Later he created Beatrice and Rosalind, not to mention Lady Macbeth, Goneril and Regan, Cleopatra and Miranda. He is, of course, not the only Elizabethan playwright to present estimable women. In Dekker's *The Shoemaker's Holiday*, for example, Margery is assertive and clever (though some of her menfolk think she is therefore shrewish), who remains loyal but not blinkered and who knows herself well enough to realise that the enjoyment she derives from dressing in finery is pure vanity, but she is strong enough to continue to enjoy it.

The real danger in many male minds was that women might have a sexual drive of their own. This helps to explain why in too many plays there are too many generalisations about women, and too many cuckolding jokes, which seem to reflect nothing so much as male insecurity. Isabella, the heroine of Barksted and Machin's *The Insatiate Countess* (c.1610, after Marston), is probably the Jacobean female whose sexuality is most clearly shown, especially after the incomparable stage direction, '*Isabella falls in love*'! But it is notable that whereas she is executed for her promiscuity, Don Sago, murderer of one of her lovers, Rogero, is pardoned. In *The Duchess of Malfi* (1614) by John Webster, the Duchess's sexuality terrifies the men who take it upon themselves to control her. Conversely, in the same playwright's *The Devil's Law Case*, Romelio tries to force his sister to marry against her will.

The danger women pose to men is everywhere evident in Elizabethan and Jacobean drama. In a telling moment in Jonson's *The Devil Is an Ass*, Fitzdottrel, wishing to discuss business, dismisses his wife extraordinarily patronisingly:

> I see thou hast no talent
> This way, wife. Up to the gallery; do, chuck,
> Leave us to talk of it who understand it.

Middleton and Rowley's *A Fair Quarrel* (c.1616) is shot through with the idea of women's untrustworthiness, as when Anne tells Jane

> I will revive a reputation
> That woman long has lost: I'll keep council,

and Captain Ager (not unlike Hamlet in this) feels himself contaminated by his mother's sin. Women are frequently regarded as either whore or angel. The title of Dekker and Middleton's *The Honest Whore* is meant to point to an impossibility; in it, Hippolito tells Infelice:

> O, women,
> You were created angels, pure and fair;
> But since the first fell, tempting devils you are.
> You should be men's bliss, but you prove their rods:
> Were there no women, men might live like gods,

THE
SHOMAKERS
Holiday.
OR
The Gentle Craft.

With the humorous life of Simon
Eyre, ſhoomaker, and Lord Maior
of London.

As it was acted before the Queenes moſt excellent Ma-
ieſtie on New-yeares day at night laſt, by the right
honourable the Earle of Notingham, Lord high Ad-
mirall of England, his ſeruants.

Printed by Valentine Sims dwelling at the foote of Adling
hill, neere Bainards Caſtle, at the ſigne of the White
Swanne, and are there to be ſold.
1 6 0 0.

Figure 2.13
Title page of Thomas Dekker's *The Shoemaker's Holiday*, 1599, which presents an unusually strong woman, Margery Eyre

To which Infelice replies ironically:

> O, men,
> You were created angels, pure and fair,
> But since the first fell, worse than devils you are.
> You should our shields be, but you prove our rods:
> Were there no men, women might live like gods.

In *The Witch of Edmonton* (c.1623) by Dekker, Rowley and Ford, Mother Sawyer suffers from another cliché, that all old women must be either bawds or witches.

Finally, in more than one play – Middleton's *The Lady's Tragedy*, for example, or Nathan Field's *Amends for Ladies* (1611) – women's fidelity is shown being tested in a callous man's world: thus, in a typical trope of male anxiety, Field's Sir John Loveall persuades his friend Subtle to 'try' his wife's fidelity, while at the same time he is planning his own adultery. More comically, in this play, young Bold disguises himself as a waiting woman to try – unsuccessfully, as it transpires – to steal into his beloved's bed, though this creates some excellent comedy when Bold's clumsiness cannot perform simple women's tasks like threading a needle, and when he is thrown out of the house he finds himself in the street with next to nothing on. Field's attitude may be ambivalent: Shakespeare's is not. In *The Merry Wives of Windsor*, the women are sensible, sure of themselves and clever, as Master Ford (alias Brook)'s jealousy and Falstaff's self-congratulatory scheming are equally exposed as ridiculous. *The Merry Wives of Windsor* is a good example of the best of Elizabethan drama's ability to treat of women: it is comic, certainly, but also level-headed and – typically for Shakespeare – expansive and honest.

NOTES

1 Thomas Nashe, *Pierce Penilesse His Supplication to the Divell*, 1592.
2 *Ibid.*

Chapter 20: The Admiral's Men at the Rose Theatre

When the Admiral's Men settled at Henslowe's Rose Theatre in 1594, they had two principal assets: the acting of Edward Alleyn and the plays of Christopher Marlowe. In that first season, *Tamburlaine* Part 1 was performed fourteen times and Part 2 six times; *Dr Faustus* was given twelve times, *The Massacre at Paris* ten times and *The Jew of Malta* nine times.

CHRISTOPHER MARLOWE

Marlowe brought something new to the theatre, but there would be no more plays from his pen now, for he had died in 1593. Born in 1564, the son of a Canterbury shoemaker, Marlowe went to King's School, Canterbury, and at the age of sixteen to Corpus Christi College, Cambridge, where he took his BA in 1584. Within a few years he seems to have been involved in the government's secret service, who bailed him out when he was in trouble with the University authorities for too many absences in 1587. By then he had started writing plays, but his life was a turbulent one. In 1589 he was involved in a serious fight, the culmination of a long-standing feud between one William Bradley and his friends, and the poet Thomas Watson, John Alleyn, the actor's brother, and Marlowe himself. All accounts of such incidents are to be treated with scepticism, but in this case it seems that Bradley attacked Marlowe in the street, Watson tried to intervene and Bradley turned on him, wounding him so he bled. Watson fought back, and stabbed Bradley to death. Marlowe and Watson were both sent to prison, but within two weeks Marlowe was free, though Watson languished for another two months or more.

Soon after this, if we are to believe the dramatist Thomas Kyd, Marlowe and Kyd were sharing rooms, and papers found here, which Kyd said were Marlowe's, contained atheistic matter, jesting at the divine scriptures and suggesting Christ was homosexual. This only came to light in 1593, when it was too late for Marlowe to present his side of the story, but in 1592 he was again in trouble. That year he was in a fight with a tailor named William Corkine. Later he was found in Flushing, perhaps on clandestine government business, but where he and two friends began making counterfeit Dutch currency. He was arrested again, but released without charge.

Ten days after this release, he went to the house – a boarding house or inn – of one Eleanor Bull in Deptford with three other men, Nicholas Skeres, Robert Poley and Ingram Frizer. They ate lunch, talked confidentially, walked in the garden and then had supper. It seemed an argument about the bill flared up; Marlowe grabbed Frizer's dagger and wounded him with it. Frizer wrenched it away,

Figure 2.14
The playwright Christopher Marlowe
Source: GL Archive/Alamy Stock Photo

and launched out at Marlowe, killing him. Frizer was to claim his action was in self-defence, though it has been suggested that there may have been some secret conspiracy at work; at any rate, Frizer was pardoned, and the Admiral's Men were left with his plays.

MARLOWE'S PLAYS

Marlowe created a new kind of drama, highly theatrical but most widely acclaimed for his development of blank verse as a medium for dramatic speech. He showed the true versatility of this form,

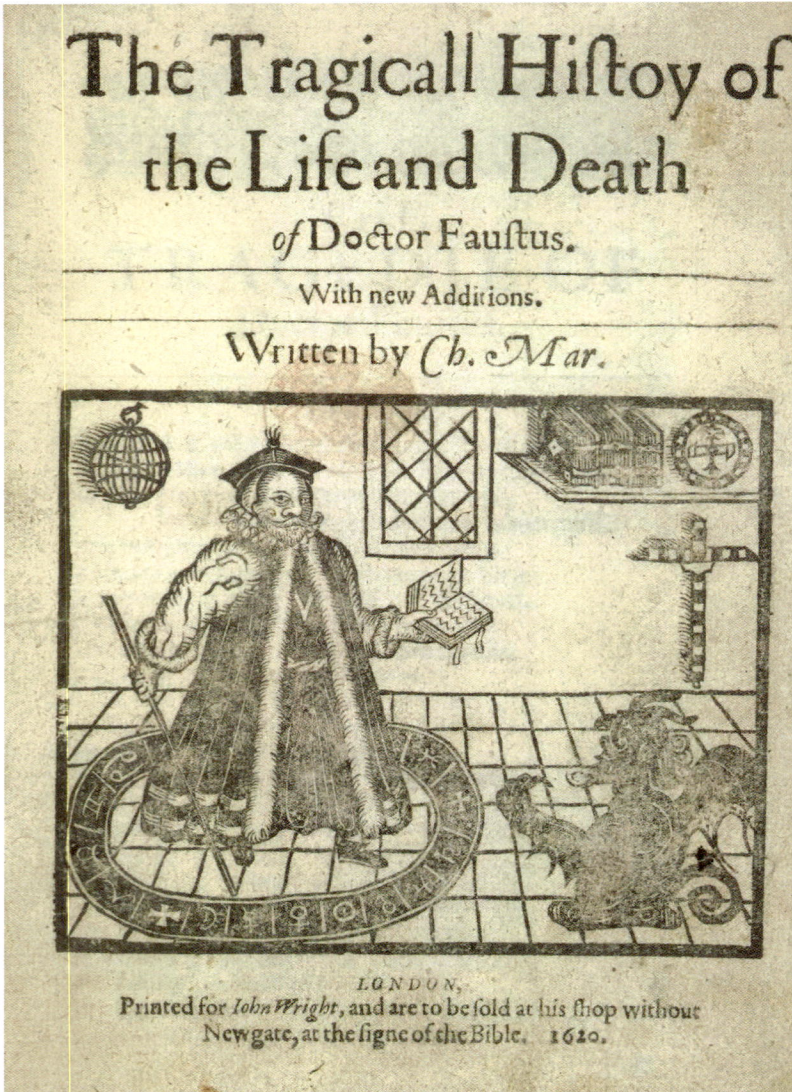

Figure 2.15
Title page of the 1620 edition of Christopher Marlowe's *Doctor Faustus*, which gives some idea of the staging of the hero's conjuring of Mephistophilis

and if he lacked Shakespeare's extraordinary control and agility with it, he led the way. To begin with, in *Tamburlaine*, he tended to write 'great and thundering speeches', such as Tamburlaine's

> I hold the Fates bound fast in iron chains,
> And with my hand turn Fortune's wheel about;
> And sooner shall the sun fall from his sphere
> Than Tamburlaine be slain or overcome.

The poet evident here is to be seen in all his later plays, even if his use of the medium became more flexible with time. But Marlowe is more than great speeches. He is a dramatist who brings something of his life's extravagance to his plays. He is capable of enormously popular scenes of gore and horror, from the opening of *Tamburlaine* –

> I long to see thee back return from thence,
> That I may view these milk-white steeds of mine
> All loaden with the heads of killed men,
> And from their knees even to their hooves below,
> Besmear'd with blood that makes a dainty show

– to the end of his last play, *The Massacre at Paris*, when, in a weirdly prophetic action, the Friar *'stabs the king with a knife, as he reads the letter; and then the king gets the knife, and kills him'*. Marlowe also brought extraordinary spectacle to the Elizabethan stage: the conquered Bajazeth in a cage which Tamburlaine uses as a footstool, or the kings who drag his chariot with bits between their teeth while Tamburlaine whips them. There is the conjuring of Mephistophilis and the vision of the Seven Deadly Sins in *Doctor Faustus*, Barabas falling into the cauldron in *The Jew of Malta*, and many more such scenes. Barabas is the horrifically fascinating anti-hero of *The Jew of Malta*, which bubbles over with cynicism, murder and Gothic fantasy. In the same vein, the Duke of Guise is frighteningly destructive yet compelling in *The Massacre at Paris*. Even the almost idyllic early play, *Dido, Queen of Carthage* ends with the triple suicide of Dido throwing herself into a fire, Iarbus stabbing himself and Anna doing the same to herself. *Dido, Queen of Carthage* also contained Marlowe's first presentation of homoeroticism in the scenes between Jupiter and Ganymede, a theme most intensely developed in his *Edward II*.

EDWARD ALLEYN AND THE ADMIRAL'S MEN

The Admiral's Men's other valuable asset was Edward Alleyn, the leading actor in England. Born in 1566, Alleyn had joined Worcester's Men in 1582 at the age of sixteen and rose steadily. Towards the end of the 1580s he joined the Lord Admiral's Men for whom he was cast in starring roles in Marlowe's plays. With an eye to his own future perhaps, he began buying up playscripts by writers such as Peele and Munday, and in 1594 he formed the new company under the Lord Admiral's patronage to be based at the Rose Theatre. The sharers, besides himself, were Richard Jones, who had been with Worcester's Men, but had also spent some considerable time performing on the continent of Europe; Thomas Downton, who joined from Strange's Men; John Singer, from the Queen's Men; Edward Juby, an Admiral's Man till his death in 1618; Thomas Towne, who was perhaps related to the Queen's Man, John Towne; James Tunstall, also from Worcester's Men, though he had joined the Admiral's Men in 1591; and Martin Slater, who later managed children's companies, including the Children of the King's Revels and a children's company in Bristol in 1618. The hired men included Richard Alleyn, Charles Massey and Sam Rowley.

In their first three years, the company performed well over a hundred different plays to daily audiences of a thousand or more spectators. In the first season, they presented thirty-eight plays, twenty-one of which were new. In those three years, Alleyn alone played over seventy different roles. Moreover, though they broke for Lent, they took to the road every summer and presented their productions across the country. In 1595, Henslowe further modernised the Rose Theatre. In 1596, a small group of actors tried to break away and join Pembroke's Men at the Swan Theatre; the Privy Council ordered them back to the Rose, where Henslowe made them sign loyalty agreements. Despite this, the picture is one of surprising stability, with the company producing a two- or three-hour play every afternoon, including a brand new piece about every fifteen to twenty days.

In 1597, Alleyn retired, though he remained connected to the company, and indeed enjoyed a 'comeback' in 1601, only to retire finally in 1603. He was very much involved with the building of and move to the Fortune Theatre in 1600 and went on to become a highly successful entrepreneur, not only in the theatre, but in bear-baiting and other 'sports', too. He was able to endow a number of charitable institutions, such as the school which still bears his name, before he died a wealthy man in 1626. Meanwhile, in 1597 and 1598, the Admiral's Men, having lost Juby, Tunstall and Slater, admitted as new shareholders Robert Shaw, William Bird, Gabriel Spencer, Humphrey and Anthony Jeffes, and the former hired men, Sam Rowley and Charles Massey.

PHILIP HENSLOWE

A good part of the reason this company was so stable and successful was due to the skill and diligence of the owner of the Rose Theatre, Philip Henslowe. Born in the 1550s, Henslowe was apprenticed to Henry Woodward, a dyer, who died in December 1578. Two months later Henslowe married Woodward's daughter and came into the money which enabled him to pursue a career beyond dyeing. His erection of the Rose Theatre was a not untypical speculation, but it paid off handsomely. As the Rose's landlord, he took 50% of the gallery receipts of every performance. He was not the manager of the Admiral's Men, as is sometimes suggested, but he involved himself heavily in the

Figure 2.16
Excavation at the Rose Theatre on the Bankside of the theatre's ruins, which were uncovered in 1989
Source: Terry Smith/The LIFE Images Collection/Getty Images

daily running of the building and its occupants, and he gradually assumed the role of their treasurer on an unofficial basis. His so-called 'Diary' is really a theatrical accounts book with occasional notes about plays and people, and contains legal agreements and other documents. When Edward Alleyn married Henslowe's stepdaughter, they combined to create a powerful and profitable business partnership which continued until Henslowe's death in 1616.

NEW PLAYS

Henslowe's Diary offers a unique insight into the running of a late Elizabethan theatre. For example, he is clear about obtaining plays for performance. The demand for new playscripts was relentless, with a new play mounted at least every three weeks. Well over half the plays presented were multi-authored, including old scripts revised by young playwrights. In 1598 Henslowe purchased eighty-nine plays and only thirty-four of them were not the result of authorial collaborations. In this

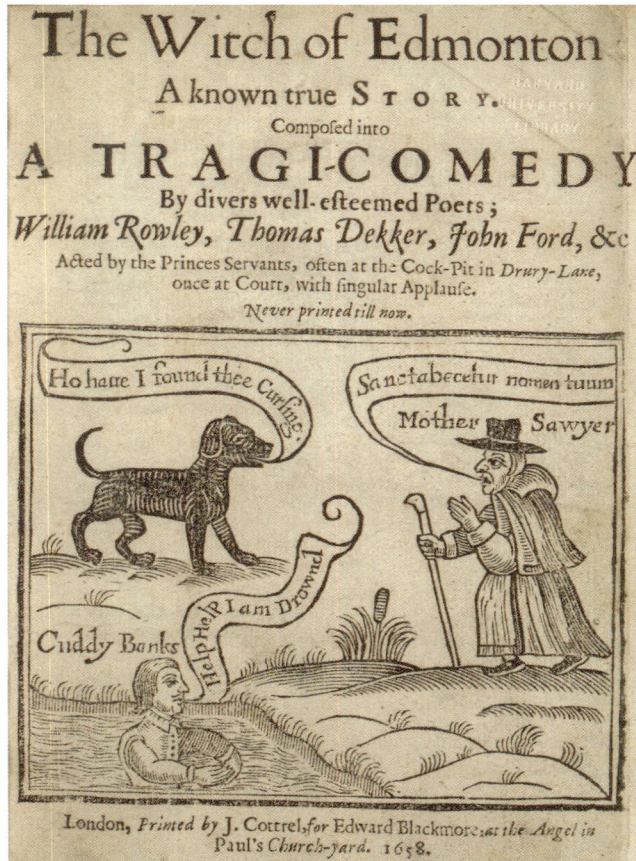

Figure 2.17
Title page of John Ford, William Rowley and Thomas Dekker's topical *The Witch of Edmonton*, 1621

atmosphere it is important to realise that the playwrights were not much in competition with each other: they all wanted the theatre to continue to expand so that their income could be guaranteed or even rise, and they co-operated to see that this happened.

Plays were written and produced quickly. Often a script was on stage within three weeks of its delivery to the theatre. The playwrights were extraordinarily prolific, though what they produced was rarely perhaps 'literature'. Fewer than 20% of the plays staged between 1576 and 1642 have survived, and they are probably the best of them. A play could be cobbled together in less than a month, and any item of topical news could be dramatised within weeks of its happening, often satirically. Shakespeare's Cleopatra fears that

> The quick comedians
> Extemporally will stage us, and present
> Our Alexandrian revels: Antony
> Shall be brought drunken forth, and I shall see
> Some squeaking Cleopatra boy my greatness
> I' the posture of a whore.

The Witch of Edmonton (1621), written collaboratively by John Ford, William Rowley and Thomas Dekker, was on the stage just months after its source, *The Wonderful Discovery of Elizabeth Sawyer a Witch Late of Edmonton*, was published, and it remains an excellent play. Sequels, spin-offs and second parts of successful plays were also common.

A PLAYWRIGHT'S LIFE

A playwright was paid a flat fee of between £5 and £10 for a script, which was then the property of the theatre company. Lesser sums were paid for revisions, or for new Prologues or Epilogues. It was not much. Henslowe paid more for the dress worn by the boy who played Anne Frankford in *A Woman Killed with Kindness* than he did to the author, Thomas Heywood, for the script. It is hardly surprising that some of these lower-middle-class writers, including Ben Jonson, Thomas Dekker, Nathan Field and Philip Massinger, were imprisoned for debt at one time or another. In the later Jacobean and Caroline period, a few playwrights were successful in obtaining longer-term contracts which paid them a certain amount per year in return for two or three plays.

PLAYWRIGHTS AND COLLABORATION

Collaborations usually had a 'lead' writer, who was in overall charge, and allocated an act or two, or a strand or two of the plot, to his fellow or fellows, and he was responsible for delivery of the finished piece to the theatre. The permutations of playwrights collaborating were fascinating. Chettle worked with eleven other writers; Dekker with eight others. *Sir Thomas More* was created by Anthony Munday, Thomas Dekker and Henry Chettle, with some revisions by William Shakespeare and others by Thomas Heywood. The theatre scribe may have added some lines, too. Shakespeare collaborated on several of his plays, including *Henry VI* Part 1, *Titus Andronicus*, *Edward III*, *All's Well That Ends Well*, *Timon of Athens*, *Pericles*, *Henry VIII* and *The Two Noble Kinsmen*, and the versions of both *Measure for Measure* and *Macbeth* which survive are revisions by Thomas Middleton.

It is also worth noting that once a script had been bought, it was copied into parts for the actors by the theatre scribe, who might emend it, and when it came to be acted, the actors were likely to hone the script to their own liking and to add at least exclamations, greetings and so on, and in the case of the clowns, probably much more than that.

THE REPERTOIRE

Plays mounted by the Admiral's Men include *The Life of Sir John Oldcastle* (1599), a two-part pseudo-history play by Michael Drayton, Richard Hathaway, Anthony Munday and Robert Wilson, which opens with a street brawl interrupted by the appearance of the sheriff. But he is only partially able to stop it: '*Helter skelter again*', says the stage direction after his intervention. *Captain Thomas Stukeley*, another play from the company's repertoire, a picaresque yarn about a more or less contemporary swashbuckling adventurer, also seems to be by a group of authors, but their names are not recorded. But these plays were popular and achieved their purpose, enabling the theatre to grow and prosper.

Admiral's authors included John Day, who was expelled from Cambridge University in 1593, and who five years later was collaborating with or revising plays by Chettle, Haughton, Dekker and others. After the turn of the century he wrote some plays alone, for Worcester's Men as well as Admiral's and later for children's companies, including *Humour Out of Breath* (1608), a sort of triple Romeo and Juliet story, in which the usurping Duke has two sons and a daughter, and his enemy two daughters and a son. The triple wedding reconciles the warring families. Henry Chettle was a stationer and printer before falling in with Robert Greene and his circle and becoming a jobbing writer. He was a prolific collaborator, but sometimes wrote alone, as with *The Tragedy of Hoffman* (1602) for the Admiral's Men, a revenge drama in the tradition of *The Spanish Tragedy* and *The Massacre at Paris*. William Haughton, too, is remembered for one play, *Englishmen for My Money* (1598), which has been claimed as the first 'citizen comedy'. And Henry Porter also wrote at least one extremely successful comedy, *The Two Angry Women of Abingdon* (1598).

Anthony Munday's *The Downfall of Robert, Earl of Huntington* (1597) and *The Death of Robert, Earl of Huntington* (1598) were probably the most successful of a number of plays about Robin Hood staged during these years. Others included the anonymous *George-a-Green, the Pinner of Wakefield* (c.1591), Peele's *Edward I* (c.1592) and two more anonymous plays, *A Pleasant Pastoral Comedy of Robin Hood and Little John* (1594) and *Look about You* (1598). Ben Jonson's final unfinished work was a Robin Hood play, *The Sad Shepherd* (1636), in which Robin, Marian and the merry men are beset by Maudlin, the witch of Papplewick, and her daughter. Besides Munday's Robin Hood plays, others with second parts included *Tamburlaine*, the anonymous *Hercules* (1596 and 1597) and *The Life of Sir John Oldcastle*.

GEORGE CHAPMAN

George Chapman and Thomas Dekker were among the company's leading writers. Chapman's career began with the Admiral's Men who performed *The Blind Beggar of Alexandria* (1596) and *A Humorous Day's Mirth* (1597). The blind beggar is a man of multiple disguises who confides in and boasts to the audience rather as Shakespeare's Richard III does. It offered a virtuoso role to Edward Alleyn as the beggar assumes a multiplicity of different roles. He even cuckolds himself at one point. *An Humorous Day's Mirth* includes Florilla, the seductive and much-courted Puritan wife of Count Labervele: 'Every man for her sake is a Puritan, the devil I think will shortly turn Puritan, or the Puritan will turn devil'. But the play may also be seen as a precursor to Jonson's comedies of 'humours', making fun of the vapidity of the court and affected social climbers. Most of Chapman's later extensive dramatic output was performed by the children's companies. After a series of comedies he extended his range to tragedy, notably in two paired works, *Bussy D'Ambois* (1604), a slow-burning melodrama with a faint odour of decay, and *The Revenge of Bussy D'Ambois* (1610), in which Bussy's ghost returns to orchestrate revenge for his murder; and the more controversial *The Downfall of Charles, Duke of Byron* and *The Death of Charles, Duke of Byron*, set in contemporary France. These depicted a somewhat Tamburlaine-like hero whose high self-regard leads to the play's catastrophe.

THOMAS DEKKER

Thomas Dekker was one of Henslowe's most prolific writers: in 1598 he had a hand in no fewer than sixteen plays Henslowe bought. His best solo plays were performed at the Rose, even though he complained of the theatre's 'small circumference' in *Old Fortunatus* (1599). This play depicts the magic, thievery and mayhem which follow the adventures of a magic purse which never runs out of money and a magic hat which can transport its wearer wherever he wants to go. 'Your quick imaginations we must charm', he urges, and in this he surely succeeds. *The Shoemaker's Holiday* (1600) is a high-spirited, optimistic comedy which has been frequently revived, probably for its unquenchable good humour. Two of Dekker's later collaborations with Thomas Middleton were also markedly successful: *The Roaring Girl* (c.1610) and *The Honest Whore* (1611), both produced at the Fortune for Prince Henry's Men, into which the Admiral's Men had metamorphosed.

SCANDALS AND PROBLEMS

But not everything was straightforward for the theatres in the late 1590s. In July 1597, *The Isle of Dogs* by Thomas Nashe and Ben Jonson was presented by Pembroke's Men at the Swan Theatre. A complaint was made which found its way to the Privy Council who accused the theatre of sedition. While Nashe fled to Great Yarmouth, Ben Jonson and two of the actors, Gabriel Spencer and Robert Shaw, were thrown into the Marshalsea Prison, the theatres were closed and the buildings ordered to be immediately pulled down. It is impossible to judge what was seditious in this play, partly because it seems the actors sensibly but surreptitiously destroyed all copies of it. Without the evidence the script might have provided, the draconian punishments were quietly forgotten. No theatre buildings were pulled down. Jonson and the two actors were released in October, and the Lord Chamberlain's Men and the Admiral's Men, not without anxiety, began to perform again. But for the Admiral's Men, the imbroglio brought significant changes. Alleyn, already under strain from carrying so many leading parts, abruptly retired. Henslowe became officially the company's financial manager. And Spencer and Shaw, newly released, joined the Admiral's Men.

It was an unpleasant episode and was the prelude to others. A year later, Jonson and Spencer met at Hoxton, a known duelling venue, and after a fight (probably not a regular duel), Jonson killed Spencer with his rapier. He admitted guilt, but pleaded benefit of clergy, an anomalous loophole which enabled him to avoid the death penalty, though he was branded on the thumb. In June the following year, two of Henslowe's young playwrights were involved in another fracas, and John Day killed Henry Porter. In 1600, Ben Jonson was imprisoned for debt.

THE 'WAR OF THE THEATRES'

Jonson's irascibility and *amour proper* were becoming known. He had already mocked the pomposity and affectation of a fellow playwright, widely deemed to be Anthony Munday, as Antonio Balladino, 'a pageant poet' (which Munday was) in *The Case Is Altered*. And in Juniper in the same play might be detected a lampoon of the playwright, John Marston. Now Marston penned an irreverent response, a caricature of Jonson in his play *Jack Drum's Entertainment* (c.1599), and followed this up with another in *Histriomastix* (1600). Jonson turned all his guns on Marston and Dekker in his next play, *The Poetaster*, which drew a clear distinction between true poets, such as Virgil, Horace and (by implication) Jonson, and mere 'poetasters' like Marston and Dekker. Satirised as Crispinus and Demetrius, they were arraigned and found wanting at the climax of the play. Crispinus (Marston) was forced to vomit up his pedantic and high-falutin words: 'turgious', 'ventosity', 'oblatrant', he heaves, 'fatuate', 'prorumped', 'anagogical'. This hilarious travesty was answered by Dekker and Marston in a further play, *Satiromastix*, which in turn mocked Jonson's pretensions and pretentiousness. Probably this 'war of the theatres' was not very serious. Jonson worked with both Dekker and Marston again in the next few years, apparently amicably enough. Almost certainly, despite the long faces of some commentators, this was high spirits and – more importantly – the kind of storm in a teacup made to whip up interest in the theatre and give the punters something to gossip about.

BEN JONSON AND THE PRINTING OF PLAY TEXTS

Nevertheless, Jonson did take himself and his work seriously. This can be seen from the way he steered his plays into print. Plays were, of course, the property of the theatre companies, and there were two notable periods of play publication towards the end of Elizabeth's reign – around 1593, a time of plague when companies hoped to make a little money from the sale of their playbooks, and around 1599–1600, when publication became comparatively lucrative and a play with the company's name prominently displayed might be useful publicity.

These published texts give a unique insight into the Elizabethan and Jacobean theatre, but they need to be treated circumspectly. Who were they published for? Readers? Future performers? And what exactly were they? Records of what happened in a theatre on a particular day or books to be enjoyed privately? The printers wanted the book-buying public to buy them and probably did not see as important the writer's opinion, or indeed the needs of theatre historians four hundred years later. Thus, stage directions are problematic. Who suggested the references to curtains or discoveries, costumes or props or trapdoors or balconies? If the writer wanted these, were they practicable on the stage? Perhaps they were the inventions of the scribe? Or reminders to the prompter or actor? The problem is to assess the relationship between these printed texts and what actually occurred on any Elizabethan stage. The printer of Marlowe's *Tamburlaine* wrote:

> Gentlemen, and courteous readers whosoever: I have here published in print for your sakes the two tragical discourses of the Scythian shepherd, Tamburlaine, that became so great a conqueror and so mighty a monarch. My hope is that they will be now no less acceptable unto you to read after your serious affairs and

studies than they have been (lately) delightful for many of you to see, when the same were showed in London upon stages. I have (purposely) omitted and left out some fond and frivolous gestures, digressing, and (in my poor opinion) far unmeet for the matter, which I thought might seem more tedious unto the wise than any way else to be regarded, though (haply) they have been of some vain conceited fondlings greatly gaped at, what times they were showed upon the stage in their graced deformities. Nevertheless, now, to be mixtured in print with such matter of worth, it would prove a great disgrace to so honourable and stately a history.[1]

A play text may be a beginning for actors to work from; but it is also, arguably, a piece of literature, and these conflicting purposes must somehow be reconciled.

It was Jonson whose career introduced the notion of published plays as respectable literary artefacts. The quarto edition of his *Sejanus* was a warren of footnotes and learned references, and in 1616 he published a fat folio of his *Works* which included many of his playscripts. Seeing this, some unscrupulous printer published ten of Shakespeare's plays in 1619, which in turn probably fired Shakespeare's former colleagues to collect his plays, or 'works', into a large folio edition, which was published in 1623. From that moment, Shakespeare was no longer a player who composed scripts for his fellows to work from. Shakespeare was now an 'author'! It must still be asked, of course: who was Jaggard, the publisher, trying to please? Shakespeare's posterity? Hemminges and Condell, the editors? Prospective purchasers? All of which calls into question the precise status of the great book.

Nevertheless, it is important that these texts were published, and whatever our answers to such troubling questions, at least Jaggard, Hemminges and Condell ensured that we, their posterity, have Shakespeare's plays.

NOTE

1 Robert Weimann, *Author's Pen and Actor's Voice*, Cambridge: Cambridge University Press, 2000.

Chapter 21: Staging in the open air playhouse

The Elizabethan playhouse, with its open-to-the-sky space and its democratic assembly, created opportunities for staging and instituted conventions powerful enough to be adopted by the indoor private theatres of the seventeenth century. Only gradually were these dropped from general theatre practice.

PLACE ON THE ELIZABETHAN STAGE

There was no interval in the performance, and actors spoke rapidly so that the play and jig lasted less than three hours together. The stage space, as in earlier times, was basically an unlocalised *platea* with occasional specified *loci* often at the rear or in the balcony. This stage was neither symbolic, as the ancient Greek stage was, nor realistic, like the Naturalist stage: it was functional and conventional, and the audience on at least three sides understood its workings as largely citational. The supposed settings often seemed either far away and generalised – Rome, a lost island, Scotland – or very specific and close – a friar's cell or a hovel on a heath. In the first case, identification of place was thoroughly perfunctory: 'Welcome, sweet prince, to London', not to St Paul's Cathedral or Bishopsgate Street. Or 'this is the Forest of Arden', and in our imaginations, it is. More significantly, the space is fluid: Act IV Scene iii in *Othello* begins in some public room but soon melts into Desdemona's dressing room. Marlowe's *Edward II* opens in France but returns to England with no comment to help the audience. In *The Fair Maid of the West* by Thomas Heywood, Spencer and Captain Goodlack arrive in front of the tavern, but after a minute or two, without actually moving, they are inside it.

THE 'HEAVENS'

Above the stage, the ceiling was painted to resemble the sky and called the 'heavens'. Machinery housed here allowed various flying effects. An early example occurs in Thomas Lodge and Robert Greens's *A Looking Glass for London and England* (c.1590), in which Oseas the prophet is '*brought in by an Angel . . . and let down over the stage in a throne*', while in the Jacobean *Valentinian* (1614) by John Fletcher, the same effect was employed: '*Enter a Chorus of Singers. A boy, in the costume of a Grace, descends, carrying a wreath*'.

DISCOVERIES

On the stage itself, the inner room at the rear was particularly useful for discoveries of various kinds. Ben Jonson was especially addicted to this effect: in *The Case Is Altered*, Juniper is discovered in his shop there; in *The Poetaster*, Ovid is discovered in his study; and in *Volpone*, Mosca draws the curtain to reveal Volpone's gold. This is also the curtain which is not drawn when Hamlet stabs through it and kills Polonius. But it is drawn back to reveal the hero's father's body in *The Tragedy of Hoffman* by Henry Chettle and in Beaumont and Fletcher's *The Maid's Tragedy*, when Evadne reveals the sleeping king before she ties him up and stabs him.

THE BALCONY

Above the inner room was the balcony, most famously the place where Juliet appears after she has met Romeo – 'the balcony scene'. But it is also from here that Prince Arthur falls to his death in *The Troublesome Reign of King John* – presumably the actor was cushioned somehow – and where the Duke surprises and seduces Bianca in Thomas Middleton's *Women Beware Women* (c.1621), while her mother-in-law plays chess below, oblivious to the betrayal 'above'.

TRAPDOORS

The trapdoor cut into the stage floor was similarly versatile. In Peele's *Edward I*, Queen Elinor protests her innocence: if what she said was not true, she wished the earth might 'gape and swallow' her, whereupon the earth (the trapdoor) opens and she falls down. In the same author's *The Old Wives' Tale*, the trapdoor forms the grave into which Jack jumps, just as Laertes and Hamlet jump into Ophelia's grave; while in *A Looking Glass for London and England*, '*the Magi with their rods beat the ground and from under the same rises a brave arbour*', and later '*a flame of fire appeareth from beneath and Radogon is swallowed*'. In Fletcher's *The Faithful Shepherdess*, the Sullen Shepherd lets Amarillis down into the well to change her shape into that of Amoret, and later Amoret is flung into the well, only for the God of the River to appear from below with her in his arms. Devils were especially wont to appear through the trapdoor, as at the very beginning of Jonson's *The Poetaster*, after the trumpets have sounded announcing the play for the second (not yet the third) time, Livor, the personification of Envy, arises from '*below*'. And there must have been a huge trapdoor on the stage of the Globe in 1624 when it was used in Middleton's *A Game at Chess* as the 'bag' into which were put the taken chess pieces, including the Fat Bishop played by the overweight William Rowley.

STAGE FURNITURE

Furniture – a throne, a bed, an altar – might swiftly define a location. Most such items were brought on, probably by stage hands, and were not pre-set. '*A bed thrust out upon the stage, Allwit's Wife in it*' from Middleton's *A Chaste Maid in Cheapside* probably required more than one stage hand. And a huge throne was required for *Edward II* in order to seat Gaveston and the king side by side. But perhaps the actors themselves brought on the 'low stools' in *Coriolanus*: '*Enter Volumnia and Virgilia. . . . They set them down on two low stools and sew*'. Larger scenic pieces placed by stage hands might include the 'arbour' in which the conspirators hang Horatio in *The Spanish Tragedy*, which seems to have been a kind of trellis.

Figure 2.18
The Red Bull Playhouse in 1662, showing the open stage, the curtain drawn across the inner room at the back of the stage and the balcony above

Source: Antiqua Print Gallery/Alamy Stock Photo

STAGE PROPS

Hand props were also various and perhaps defining. A property list in Henslowe's *Diary* for the Admiral's Men at the Rose includes everything from a wooden leg to Cupid's bow and arrow, and from the Pope's mitre to fans of feathers. Some of these were general and presumably used in more than one play; but some were specific, especially those with horrific connections, such as de

Piracquo's finger brought by De Flores to Beatrice-Joanna in *The Changeling* by Thomas Middleton and William Rowley, or Annabella's heart, which Giovanni brings in spiked on his dagger in Ford's *'Tis Pity She's a Whore*. Blood, a common requirement of the Elizabethan and Jacobean drama, was sometimes held in a bladder tied to the actor's chest or stomach ready to spill out when he was stabbed, but might also be vermilion, red ink or paint.

LIGHT AND DARK

However, daylight usually inhibited illusionistic effects. Especially after 1595, when plays were required to start at two PM, the actors never had special lighting. Night was indicated by night shirts and torches, as in the early scene in *Othello*, when candles burning on the table also convey the hour. Hieronimo carries a torch in *The Spanish Tragedy* to indicate night, and there are candles and 'dark lanterns' in Webster's *The Duchess of Malfi*, performed at Blackfriars indoor theatre as well as at the Globe. Several plays create plenty of fun by setting scenes at night, as in the anonymous *Arden of Feversham*, when the murderers stalk their prey with hopeless ineptitude, or Porter's *The Two Angry Women of Abingdon* (1598), when Hodge '*stumbles on*' Dick Coombes, and there are passages of dialogue such as:

(Enter Sir Ralph Smith.)
SIR RALPH: So ho!
MASTER GOURSEY: So ho!
SIR RALPH: Who there?
MASTER BARNES: Here's one or two.
SIR RALPH: Is Will there?
MASTER BARNES: No, Philip.
MASTER GOURSEY: Frank?
SIR RALPH: No, no. Was ever man deluded thus like me?

The anonymous *Merry Devil of Edmonton* presents a similar, perhaps even more extravagant and hilarious scene of mistaken identities, characters pursuing the wrong characters, others dressing in the wrong clothes and harmless people mistaken for ghosts.

SOUND

The performance was heralded by three blasts of the trumpet blown from the roof of the 'heavens', and music was a constant support for the drama. Drums and trumpets accompany warlike movements, and banquets and processions rarely occur without the sound of the 'hautboy', a larger and louder instrument than today's oboe. But music could also be more pervasive, and, especially in fairy plays or other fantasies, the stage, like Caliban's island, could be 'full of noises,/Sounds and sweet airs'. Against this was the frequently called-for 'thunder', usually made by rolling a heavy canon ball down a rough trough situated in the 'heavens'. The trough might be set on a seesaw-like fulcrum, so it could roll backwards and forwards continually.

STAGE BATTLES

Other 'noises off' were made more simply, such as the knocking on Macbeth's gate, but offstage shouts and clashes of swords often indicated a battle, which might then erupt onto the stage. Shakespeare's history plays probably exhibit the best-known stage battles of the period, but the stage directions for the battle in *Cymbeline* perhaps tell us more about how they were staged:

> Enter Lucius, Iachimo and the Roman Army at one door: and the Briton army at another. . . . They march over, and go out. Then enter again, in skirmish, Iachimo and Posthumus: he vanquisheth and disarmeth Iachimo, and then leaves him. . . . The battle continues, the Britons fly, Cymbeline is taken: then enter, to his rescue, Belarius, Guiderius and Arviragus. . . . Re-enter Posthumus, and seconds the Britons. They rescue Cymbeline. Then re-enter Lucius, Iachimo and Imagen.

The battle alternates between general fighting, and close-ups of specific moments which the audience needs to appreciate. Single combats were also common, and among the audience were those enthusiastic for fencing who had to be entertained. Richard Tarlton was himself a 'Master of Fence', and several plays, including Peele's *Edward I*, Greene's *Orlando Furioso* and Webster's *The Devil's Law Case*, ask for 'long' sword fights, presumably for this reason. Other plays where the fencing is specifically a spectacle include Middleton and Rowley's *A Fair Quarrel* and Rowley, Middleton and Heywood's *The Old Law*.

DANCE

Dancing was an extremely popular pastime with Elizabethan and Jacobean people, and the stage reflects this: devils dance frantically in *Dr Faustus*, witches dance ominously in *Macbeth*, and lovers dance romantically in *Love's Labours Lost* and *Romeo and Juliet*. In *The Duchess of Malfi* and *The Changeling* madmen dance and sing, and in *The Insatiate Countess*, in the wedding scene, the company dances three 'changes', '*after which the Ladies fall off*'. Then '*Rogero dances a lavolta, or a galliard, and in the midst of it, falleth into the bride's lap, but straight leaps up, and danceth it out*'.

NON-HUMAN CHARACTERS

Probably more spectacular were the ghosts, witches, fairies, gods and devils who thronged these stages. The devils in *Dr Faustus* were especially notable:

> Shag-haired devils run roaring over the stage with squibs in their mouths, while drummers make thunder in the tiring-house, and the twelve-penny hirelings make artificial lightening in their Heavens.[1]

Halfway between devil and human were some of the fairy figures, such as Robin Goodfellow, 'Puck-hairy' in Jonson's unfinished *The Sad Shepherd* (1636), with his horns and goat's legs. Less ambivalent were the fairies in *The Merry Wives of Windsor*, when those dancing in the ring near Herne's Oak in Windsor Park were really schoolchildren, and it was human folly, not other worldly witchcraft, which was being castigated. There are also innumerable ghosts, from Hamlet's stately father to the busy and active Bussy in Chapman's *The Revenge of Bussy D'Ambois*. Worth mentioning, too, are the freaks who entertain Volpone in Jonson's play – a dwarf, a hermaphrodite and a eunuch.

CEREMONY

The procession or other ceremonial event was another favourite motif: the large stage and the expansive context could make moments of ceremony key in the unfolding of the drama. Processions were also, of course, exciting or amazing spectacles in themselves, an opportunity for the theatre company to show off its splendid costumes, glittering props and grand music. Thus Shakespeare and Fletcher staged Anne Boleyn's coronation in *Henry VIII* by numbers:

1 A lively flourish of trumpets.
2 Then, two judges.
3 Lord Chancellor, with purse and mace before him.
4 Choristers singing. Music.
5 Mayor of London, bearing the mace. Then Garter, in his coat of arms, and on his head he wore a gilt copper crown.
6 Marquess Dorset, bearing a sceptre of gold, on his head a demi-coronal of gold. With him, the Earl of Surrey, bearing the rod of silver with the dove, crowned with an earl's coronet. Collars of Esses.
7 Duke of Suffolk, in his robe of estate, his coronet on his head, bearing a long white wand, as High Steward. With him, the Duke of Norfolk, with the rod of marshalship, acoronet on his head. Collars of Esses.
8 A canopy, born by four of the Cinque-ports, under it the Queen, in her robe; in her hair, richly adorned with pearl, crowned. On each side her, the Bishops of London and Winchester.
9 The old Duchess of Norfolk, in a coronal of gold, wrought with flowers, bearing the queen's train.
10 Certain ladies or countesses, with plain circlets of gold without flowers. Exeunt, first passing over the stage in order and state, and then, a great flourish of trumpets.

In *Troilus and Cressida*, a turning point is the procession of warriors from the field of battle when the watching Cressida spies the heroic Troilus, and in *Pericles*, the knights process to the lists in great solemnity, each presenting his shield to Simonides, the King of Pentapolis, until the eighth and last knight appears, Pericles, '*in rusty armour without shield, and unaccompanied*'.

Weddings also provide an excuse for a procession. In *The Two Noble Kinsmen* by Shakespeare and Fletcher, the marriage begins with music:

Enter Hymen with a torch burning; a Boy, in a white robe, before, singing and strewing flowers; after Hymen, a Nymph encompassed in her tresses, bearing a wheaten garland.
Then Theseus between two other nymphs with wheaten chaplets on their heads. Then Hippolyta, the bride, led by Pirithous and another holding a garland over her head (her tresses likewise hanging). After her, Emilia, holding up her train.

The wedding in *A Chaste Maid in Cheapside* emerges from what appears to be the double funeral of the persecuted lovers; but the symmetry and solemnity are notable:

> Recorders dolefully playing; enter at one door the coffin of the gentleman, solemnly decked, his sword upon it, attended by many in black, his brother being the chief mourner; at the other door, the coffin of the virgin, with a garland of flowers, with epitaphs pinned on't, attended by maids and women. Then set them down, one right over-against the other. While all the company seem to weep and mourn, there is a sad song in the music-room.

But after a few moments, '*Moll and Touchwood Junior rise out of their coffins*'.

DUMB SHOWS

The theatrically conscious theatre of the open air was also noted for consciously theatricalising its material in dumb shows, masques and plays within plays. The dumb show, of course, had a history going back to the medieval period, but was still used creatively in the Elizabethan and Jacobean theatre. Apart from being an attraction in its own right, the dumb show could condense the action or move it forward, warn the audience of what was to come – perhaps allegorically – and give a perspective on it, or it could tighten the tension or provide an extra *frisson* of fear or horror. The best-known dumb show is in *Hamlet* and is described by the Prince of Denmark as 'miching malleco' ('skulking mischief'). The dumb show in *The Fair Maid of the West* purports to show the Earl of Essex setting out with his fleet from Plymouth, while that in Peele's *The Battler of Alcazar* has a certain dream-like quality:

> Sound sennet. Enter Muly Mahamet the Moor, his son, three Moors attendant and two pages to attend the Moor. To them the Moor's two young Brethren. The Moor showeth them the bed, and then takes his leave of them, and they betake them to their rest. And then the Presenter speaketh.

The dumb show at the end of *The Spanish Comedy*, on the other hand, has dreadful import:

> Enter two, dragging of ensigns; then the funeral of Andrea; next Horatio and Lorenzo, leading Prince Balthazar captive; then the Lord General with others mourning. A great cry within, 'Charon, a boat, a boat'. Then enter Charon and the ghost of Andrea, and Revenge.

MASQUES AND PLAYS WITHIN PLAYS

The masque, copied from court entertainments, is usually much lighter than these dumb shows and often symbolic. If it explores human emotions it does so often out of the human world. Perhaps the most complete masque in a play is in Beaumont and Fletcher's *The Maid's Tragedy*, though the best known is probably that in Shakespeare's *The Tempest*. In Chapman's *May Day*, the masque ends with the performers inviting the privileged spectators to join them, as often occurred at court.

As for plays within the plays, Shakespeare again provided some of the best and most amusing, notably in *Love's Labours Lost* and *A Midsummer Night's Dream*. In *Hamlet*, things are much more serious: the play is performed in order to uncover the king's guilt. And in *The Spanish Tragedy*, the play spills over into 'reality' when Bel-Imperia actually does stab first Balthazar and then herself, before Hieronimo interrupts the illusion to bring the attention of the court to his terrible grievance. In Middleton's *A Mad World, My Masters*, the Constable from the real world – or rather, from the play's 'real' world – enters to arrest the players, but they pretend he is part of the play, to the amusement of the spectators, who refuse to help him, thinking he is an actor. The imposters tie the Constable up, gag him and make their getaway before the truth about them can come out.

In Jonson's *Bartholomew Fair* (1614), the play within the play takes the form of a puppet show, which tells the ancient story of Hero and Leander, but in a decidedly modern and low-class version: Leander is a dyer from Puddle Wharf, while Hero is from the Bankside. She is on an outing to eat herrings, but soon gets drunk on three pints of sherry. But this amusing fable is interrupted by the fanatical Puritan, Zeal-of-the-Land Busy, who tries to throw down the puppet booth as a heathen idol. Instead he is persuaded to engage with one of the puppets in an argument about the morality of drama as a whole. 'It is your old stale argument against the players', the puppet answers, 'but it will not hold against the puppets'. Busy is forced to retire: 'I am confuted, the cause has failed me . . . let the play go on!'

The Downfall of Robert, Earl of Huntingdon (1597) by Anthony Munday actually is a play within a play, or rather a rehearsal within a play. Sir John Eltham knocks on Skelton's door. Skelton assures him the players are ready, and '*at every door all the players run out, some crying "Where? Where?", others, "Welcome, Sir John"'*. As the piece proceeds, Sir John and Skelton interrupt it to discuss the play. Eltham worries that Henry VIII will dislike it, but Skelton tries to calm him. At one point Eltham's scepticism turns on Skelton himself:

> One thing besides, you fall into your vein
> Of ribble rabble rhymes, Skeltonical,
> So oft, and stand so long, that you offend.

Skelton, in some dudgeon, demurs. The play within the play was a significant authorial device for endistancing or objectifying the play's content.

SPECTACULAR EFFECTS

The Elizabethan stage was also capable of all sorts of other spectacular effects. In Greene's *Friar Bacon and Friar Bungay*, '*Bungay conjures, and the tree appears with the dragon shooting fire*', and later a 'Brazen Head', set on a table, speaks, and then '*a lightening flasheth forth, and a hand appears that breaketh down the Head with a hammer*'. In Peele's *David and Bathsabe*, after the battle, Absolon is found hanging by the hair: Henslowe records paying fourteen pence for 'poles and workmanship for to hang Absolon'. Middleton was paid to add some spectacular moments to *Macbeth*. These include scenes with Hecate, Queen of the Witches, with songs and dances, and the apparition of '*a cloud . . . carrying a spirit like a cat*'. Hecate cries:

> Hark, I am called, my little spirit, see,
> Sits in a foggy cloud and stays for me.

A little later, the cat-spirit descends, while three more witches are seen 'above', and the cat mews:

FOURTH WITCH: Here comes down one to fetch his dues:
    A kiss, a coll, a sip of blood,
    And why thou stay'st so long.
CAT: I muse, I muse.
FOURTH WITCH: Since the air's so sweet and good.
HECATE: O, thou art come.
CAT: What news? What news?
FIFTH WITCH: All goes still to our delight.
    Either come or else –
CAT: Refuse, refuse.
HECATE: Now I am furnished for the flight.
(Hecate and the cat go up.)

This last direction suggests they are suspended from the roof, because a few lines later, '*exeunt Hecate and the cat into the heavens*'.

In *The Lady's Tragedy* (1611) by Middleton, Govianus goes to the lady's tomb and there experiences a vision:

> On a sudden in a kind of noise like a wind, the doors clattering, the tombstone flies open, and a great light appears in the midst of the tomb; his Lady . . . standing just before him allin white, stuck with jewels and a great crucifix on her breast.

Finally, in an echo of the scaffold upon which the Elizabethan stage was partly modelled, Isabella, in *The Insatiate Countess*, is actually beheaded. Presumably the boy actor playing the part set his head on the block upstage, away from the audience. Perhaps a false head was rolled out. Then, as the stage direction indicates, '*the traverse curtain is drawn over the scaffold*'.

NOTE

1 Farah Karin-Cooper and Tiffany Stern (eds), *Shakespeare's Theatres and the Effects of Performance*, London: Bloomsbury, 2013.

Chapter 22: Acting in the open air playhouse

CONVENTIONAL ACTING

Acting in the open air playhouse, like the staging, was largely conventional. Several factors contributed to this: lack of rehearsal time, a repertory system which made huge demands on the actor, the need for doubling – not just the need for one player to play several parts, but also occasionally the need for different players to play the same part – and also for type casting, which (as the Italian actors in *commedia dell'arte* discovered) made for smoother, quicker role-creation. Almost all Elizabethan and Jacobean plays had casts which required every member of the company to be fully employed. Once a play had been accepted, each character's part was copied by a scribe onto a long roll, so that the actor received the lines of his speeches preceded by two or three cue words, but not a full text. In performance, he was expected to listen for the cue words and speak his own lines immediately when he heard them. If this meant that what we might consider the nuances of interpretation were lacking in any speech, it also meant that every actor on the stage was extremely alert, listening, concentrating, involved. The Elizabethan actor spent little time finding subtext or psychology, and the play was able to rattle through.

Stage 'business' was largely traditional and expected: the skill of the performer was to make such business – the drawing of a circle with a wand by a magician, or the gazing at the whitened skull by a revenger – happen *in the present*. To this end he cultivated a personal repertoire of antics appropriate to the theatre, songs, walks, poses, pratfalls, hand gestures, which could be regularly modified and endlessly employed. He was intellectually nimble and extremely versatile. *The Rich Cabinet Furnished with Variety of Excellent Descriptions* (1616) lists some of the qualities which might be expected of the actor: 'dancing, activity, music, song, elocution, ability of body, memory, skill of weapon, pregnancy of wit'.[1]

REPRESENTATIONAL TRUTH

The actor strove for a representational rather than a psychological truth, a gestic rather than an emotional style, a presentation that was relaxed and open (necessary in any case in the daylight shared with the audience), rather than intense or driven. This should not be taken to imply that the actor's performance was passionless, or that he was unable to rise to moments of extreme agony or desire. On the contrary, his skills were multifarious. Sir Thomas Overbury contended in 1615 that 'by a full and significant action of body (the actor) charms our attention'.[2]

Unlike the nineteenth-century actor and his descendants, the Elizabethan actor did not perform *in* a set, he acted on a bare stage. This gave added prominence to stage groupings as abstractions of the scene being played and an unusual significance to the tableau. This in turn required actors to stand still and be attentive. Thomas Nashe urged that 'none of you stroke your beards to make action, play with your codpiece points, or stand fumbling on your buttons, when you know not how to bestow your fingers. Serve God, and act cleanly', he inveighed.[3] Groups on stage were conventionally formalised (novelty of grouping is a feature of director's theatre), so that the king or other central figure stood upstage and in the centre, flanked by his courtiers in descending order of importance. In *Antonio and Mellida*, Marston directs that the main procession '*being enter'd, they make a stand in divided files*'. When scenes had no such formal focus, and sometimes when they did, they tended to centre either on a specific activity such as a combat or a political speech, or on an item of furniture, a bed or a throne. Greetings and partings supplied another form of conventionalised hub, involving kneeling, or doffing the hat, or shaking hands, bowing or simply inclining the head. Only a single picture of a group of actors on an Elizabethan stage survives, a highly contentious sketch, purportedly of a scene from *Titus Andronicus*. This shows Titus as a Roman, his enemies with Tudor weapons and Tamora in a typical Elizabethan *haute-bourgeoise* lady's gown. Apart from what this might tell of costuming in the Elizabethan theatre, there is a possibility that it does not show a production of the play by Shakespeare at all, and it may even be of a German, not an English, company. Furthermore, there is some doubt that it represents a 'snapshot' of a specific moment on stage: it may be a symbolic *genre* drawing, or simply an idle – and therefore not very accurate – sketch.

The actor's approach to his role was through the physical and the external. First he needed to know what might be called a grammar of gesture: people scratch their head when they are thinking, roll up their sleeves or rub their hands together when preparing for work, shake their fist when threatening. Voice betrays character similarly: it becomes squeaky when the speaker is afraid, or

Figure 2.19
Image from 1595 purporting to show a performance of *Titus Andronicus*

Source: Reproduced by permission of the Marquess of Bath, Longleat House, Warminster, Wiltshire

goes deeper to utter a threat. Then, social position also affects external behaviour: we may say that a cardinal acts like this, a grocer like that. Heywood wrote that he wanted 'to see a soldier shaped like a soldier, walk, speak, act like a soldier'.[4] Again, an old man moves like this, a young man like that. And so on. The actor tried to combine elements like these in order to create his 'character'. Thus a young, frightened grocer would act differently from an old frightened cardinal, but not so differently from an old frightened grocer, or a young, self-confident grocer.

Figure 2.20
Title page of Francis Beaumont and John Fletcher's *A King and No King*, 1619, illustrating the actor's physical and external performance

TEMPERAMENT AND 'HUMOURS'

These calculations were not so simple, however. For example, the actor needed to consider temperament. Temperament is the basis of the 'humours' play – that one person is predisposed towards anger, say, while another is more passive. One may be disputatious, another nervous, one may be a sycophant, another a braggart. This is further complicated by the fact, which the social psychologist Erving Goffman noted in the mid-twentieth century, that people act differently in different contexts. Thus, with one's parents, one tends to behave as a child whatever one's age; with the bank manager one might act as a supplicant; whereas with one's friends one might be a 'good fellow'. And so on. Thus, the actor of Gertrude in *Hamlet* might consider in which scenes she was behaving as a Queen, in which she was a mother, and in which she was simply a woman; the actor of Hamlet would think about when Hamlet was Rosencrantz's fellow student, when he was Ophelia's lover, or when he was the Ghost's son. Of course, as described here, the acting process seems overly mechanical, and it is in no way suggested that any actor ever sat down to compile some kind of automated, impersonal chart for his character. However, these ideas were certainly applied by the Elizabethan actor to his role, and this in turn suggests that the performance was structured as a series of scenes, rather than a homogenous play, or even as a series of gestures, rather than a series of scenes.

THE REPRESENTATION OF EMOTION

As for the creation of authentic emotion, the Elizabethan actor sought representation, not feeling. The picture presented was the key. 'Your face, my thane', says Lady Macbeth, 'is as a book where men may read strange matters'. Rosalind scoffs at Orlando's protestations that he is in love by pointing out that he does not *appear* like a lover. A lover, she protests, has

> a lean cheek, which you have not; a blue eye and sunken, which you have not; an unquestionable spirit, which you have not; a beard neglected, which you have not. . . . Then your hose should be ungartered, your bonnet unbanded, your sleeve unbuttoned, your shoe untied, and everything about you demonstrating a careless desolation.

Arden of Feversham, a somewhat meek individual, demonstrates jealousy thus:

> Now will he shake his care-oppresséd head,
> The fix his sad eyes on the sullen earth,
> Ashamed to gaze upon the open world;
> Now will he cast his eyes up towards the heavens,
> Looking that ways for redress of wrong;

Fabell in *The Merry Devil of Edmonton* expresses fear early in the play: '*The chime goes, in which time Fabell is oft seen to stare about him, and hold up his hands*'. Richard III remarks that 'the deep tragedian', that is the actor in a tragedy, can

> Speak, and look back, and pry on every side,
> Tremble and start at wagging of a straw,
> Intending deep suspicion.

FALSIFYING EMOTION

Such examples could easily be multiplied, but it is worth noting that the outward sign can also be manipulated or even falsified. 'A man may smile and smile and be a villain', Hamlet notes, and Duncan in *Macbeth* remarks, 'There's no art to find the mind's construction in the face'. Antonio, in *The Duchess of Malfi*, complains of the Cardinal that 'the spring in his face is nothing but the engend'ring of toads', and 'what appears in him mirth, is merely outside'. And sometimes, the actor's representation of emotion is extraordinarily authentic. Hamlet marvels that the Player King, during his recitation, had 'tears in his eyes, distraction in's aspect' – and 'all for nothing'. The boy player of Desdemona, whose death scene was described in Latin, translated here by Anthony B. Dawson, achieved a similar authenticity:

> Desdemona, killed in front of us by her husband, although she acted her part excellently throughout, in her death moved us especially when, as she lay in her bed, with her face alone she implored the pity of the audience.[5]

STAGE DIRECTIONS

Gestic and representational acting is also apparent in many stage directions in printed play texts, which seem to be either descriptions of actual actor's actions, or else demands from the playwright for such actions. It is worth noting that most of these expressive stage directions come from the early Jacobean period, when the whole method had become more codified and to some degree more moderate, so that it may be the authors are actually asking for restraint. In George Chapman's *May Day* (c.1602), for instance, Temperance enters, '*stealing along the stage*'; in the same writer's *The Widow's Tears* (1605), Lysander '*stamps and goes out vexed*', while towards the end of the same play, the gentleman usher receives the laconic direction: '*Argus stalks*'. In Middleton's *The Revenger's Tragedy* (1606), the Duchess enters '*arm in arm with the Bastard Spurio; he seemeth lasciviously to her*' while in Cyril Tourneur's *The Atheist's Tragedy* (1608), Borachio enters '*warily and hastily over the stage*' and later '*Fresco peeps fearfully forth from behind the arras*'. Webster includes a fascinating stage direction in *The White Devil* (1612). Brachiano is brought in, ill in bed:

FRANCISCO: There's death in's face already.
VITTORIA: O my good lord!
(These speeches are several kinds of distractions and in the action should appear so.)

The famous stage direction in *The Insatiate Countess* (1610) would have been rather less easy for most actors to follow: '*Isabella falls in love*'. Presumably Isabella was supposed to gaze at her new beloved longingly and perhaps make some gesture.

REALISM ON THE OPEN AIR STAGE

The kind of in-the-present, expressive, scenic acting all this indicates was certainly capable of what we might call 'realism'. One anonymous commentator described a 'jesting-player (who) so truly counterfeited every thing, that it seemed to be the very person whom he acted', and an elegy written after Richard Burbage's death remembered the famous actor as Hamlet:

> Oft have I seen him leap into the grave,
> Suiting the person, which he seemed to have
> Of a sad lover, with so true an eye
> That there I would have sworn he meant to die.[6]

What this spectator is recalling is a specific moment, a single emotion-charged action, which gives the spectator a vivid image of truth to life. But it is only one moment, and is actually one of a series of such vivid moments, a montage, which may not, however, add up to what a modern actor might call a 'through line', or a rounded or consistent character.

DISGUISE AND IDENTITY

The Elizabethan actor had also to be a master of disguise. Not only did boys frequently play women disguised as men, but vast numbers of Elizabethan and Jacobean dramas play on disguise. Apart from Shakespeare, who employed disguise in plays from *The Two Gentlemen of Verona* through *Measure for Measure* to *King Lear*, other playwrights were equally fond of the device. Thus, Munday in *The Downfall of Robert Earl of Huntingdon* makes the Bishop dress first as a woman, '*with a yard in his hand, and linen cloth*', and later '*like a country man with a basket*', to escape Robin Hood; in John Day's *Humour out of Breath* (1608), Octavio disguises himself to spy on his two sons; George Chapman creates probably the most extravagant use of disguise in *The Blind Beggar of Alexandria* when the hero assumes so many different characters that one is able actually to cuckold another; while in Middleton's *The Revenger's Tragedy*, Lussurioso bribes Vindice to murder Piato, without realising that Piato is Vindice in disguise. The most spectacular denouement in Jacobean drama perhaps comes at the end of Jonson's *Epicoene*, when Sir Dauphine has reduced his uncle to utter misery. 'Here is your release', cries Dauphine, and '*takes off Epicoene's peruke and other disguises*'. 'You have married a boy', he crows.

The near-obsession with disguise relates to the kind of identity problems we have already seen besetting the Elizabethans and Jacobeans. It suggests that they were at least as aware of the instability of identity as we are in the twenty-first century. Disguise in these plays, may be active, to achieve some end, or passive, to conceal or even lose the self, but it always contains an unspoken question about individuality and selfhood.

COSTUME

Another way of exploring identity was through the use of costume. The sumptuary laws, which dictated what clothes people of differing social ranks might wear, were fading by the end of the sixteenth century, but clothes were still important. In *The Honest Whore*, Candido has to go to the Senate House but has mislaid the key to his wardrobe. He must wear a gown so he decides to use the carpet. He cuts a hole for his head and slips that on for his visit! For *A Woman Killed with Kindness*, notoriously, Henslowe paid more for the gown for Mistress Frankford than he did to Heywood for the actual playscript. Mistress Frankford's gown is a stark contrast to Sir Charles's costume when he is in gaol, '*with irons, his feet bare, his garments all ragged and torn*', and it is notable that when he is released he reappears '*well dressed*'. Shakespeare has something of the same contrast, expressed with extreme intensity, in *King Lear*: 'Nature needs not what thou, gorgeous, wearest', Lear rails at Regan. Later, he tears off his own clothes in a symbolic gesture. 'Robes and furred gowns hide all'.

Symbolism can appear in the costumes themselves. *Henry IV* Part 2 is introduced by Rumour, '*painted full of tongues*', Galatea, the eponymous heroine of Lyly's play, wears virgin white, while Hamlet is dressed in solemn black. Tamburlaine appears '*all in scarlet*' in his moment of triumph, only to appear '*all in black*' a few minutes later. Less grandly, wearing yellow hose denoted the wearer's sexual availability. This explains Malvolio's costume in *Twelfth Night*, but also Security's Wife's comment in Chapman, Jonson and Marston's *Eastward Ho!* When her husband sighs, 'Would I were a cuckold', she replies: 'Cuckold, husband? Why, I think this wearing of yellow has infected you'. And in *The Honest Whore*, Part 2, Lodovico asks Infelice urgently: 'What stockings have you put on this morning, madam? If they be not yellow, change them'.

Clothes make the man, or woman. *The Staple of News* opens with Penny boy Junior attended by his shoemaker and his tailor, making himself new. Thomas the barber tells him:

> Master Fashioner
> Has hit your measure, sir. H'has moulded you
> And made you, as they say.

Charles, the scholar in Fletcher's *The Elder Brother*, compares his clothes with his brother's finery, but it takes Angelina to point out that not all may be as it seems:

CHARLES: You look upon my clothes, and laugh at me, My scurvy clothes!
ANGELINA: They have rich linings, sir.
   I would your brother –
CHARLES: His are gold and gawdy.
ANGELINA: But touch 'em inwardly, they smell of copper.

Costume was the accessory upon which probably most money and imagination were spent. It was an indicator of gender (when Moll, in *The Roaring Girl* dresses as a man, she behaves like one), and the very point of some satire. When the King's Men staged Middleton's controversial *A Game at Chess*, they went so far as to obtain a cast-off suit of clothes which had belonged to Gondomar, Spain's ambassador to London, for the Black Knight, to help the audience recognise the chief villain, a biting caricature of Gondomar.

FULL-BLOODED ACTING ON THE OPEN AIR STAGE

It is sometimes supposed that seventeenth-century acting was subtler than that of the Elizabethans, but this may be a reflection of the fact that as the seventeenth century progressed, more and more of the new plays were presented in the private enclosed theatres. In the open air playhouses, acting continued to be thoroughly full-blooded. In 1622 at the Red Bull, the actor Richard Baxter so swung his sword that he wounded a citizen sitting on the stage. Middleton wrote disparagingly in

The Puritan (1607) of the 'stalking-stamping player, that will raise a tempest with his tongue and thunder with his heels', but there is no reason to suppose that the popular audiences of the open air theatres disliked either swashbuckling or grandiloquence.

THE JOB OF THE ACTOR

As to the practicalities of the actor's working life, when a play was accepted by the company, the first 'rehearsal' seems to have consisted of the author reading his text to the assembled actors, and perhaps discussing aspects of the work with them. The actors might then read it through together, though this was by no means certain. What was important for each of them was to receive his part from the theatre's scribe and then go away and learn the lines and the cues. This might take up to three weeks, during which time many other plays were performed. Rehearsals were a luxury and perhaps not needed since the conventions always operated and all the actors understood them. In any case they knew they could rely on each other. Consequently, there might be one general rehearsal towards the end of the three weeks, perhaps in a morning when a well-known play that needed no rehearsal was to be performed that afternoon, and a final rehearsal on the morning of the premiere. Specific problems an actor had with his part seem to have been addressed by his fellows or the author more or less in their spare time. In the Caroline period, and perhaps earlier, if the play was liked the second night was a 'benefit' for the author.

EDWARD ALLEYN

Among the actors who gained fame in the open air playhouses the greatest stars were Edward Alleyn and Richard Burbage. Alleyn was a great heroic actor, who could also turn his hand to full-blooded melodrama. His finest parts, as mentioned earlier, were Marlowe's heroes, especially Tamburlaine, Barabas and the Duke of Guise, and Orlando Furioso and the Blind Beggar of Alexandria. He seems to have had an intensity in his performing, as well as an understanding of what Stanislavsky centuries later was to call the actor's 'objective', for it is only through understanding the objective that the actor can perform the appropriate 'action'. Thomas Nashe, having noted that Alleyn was able to 'make an ill matter good', suggested that 'not Roscius nor Aesop, those admired tragedians that have lived ever since Christ was born, could ever perform more in action than famous Ned Alleyn'.[7]

RICHARD BURBAGE

Alleyn retired early, leaving the firmament to support only one true star, Richard Burbage, who created all Shakespeare's greatest parts – Hamlet, Lear, Prospero and the others. His versatility is evident here: Hamlet is young and active, Lear old and crotchety. His moment as Hamlet has already been referred to; another such moment seems to have been when, as Macbeth, he turned to see the ghost of Banquo and poured out a stream of uncontrolled passion and fear. But there was more to Burbage's acting than this. Flecknoe, more than forty years after Burbage's death, remembered his vivid, in-the-moment performances: he was a 'delightful Proteus, so wholly transforming himself into his part, and putting off himself with his clothes, as he never (not so much as in the tiring-house) assumed himself again until the play was done'. Flecknoe went on to note that 'he was

Figure 2.21
Richard Burbage, leading actor with the King's Men, who created most of Shakespeare's greatest roles
Source: Archivart/Alamy Stock Photo

an excellent actor . . . never failing in his part when he had done speaking: but with his looks and gesture, maintaining it still'.[8] There is no doubt that Burbage's consistent brilliance helped Shakespeare to write as he did: he knew that here was an actor who could make his most extraordinary creations live. He died in harness in 1619.

OTHER ACTORS ON THE OPEN AIR STAGE

There were other brilliant actors in this theatre who are sometimes nearly forgotten. Nathan Field, for example, who was also a good playwright, who had begun his career as a boy actor with the Children of the Queen's Revels, but later joined the King's Men and was regarded after about 1615 as Burbage's equal. Sadly he died young in 1620. Still, when Chapman's *Bussy D'Ambois* was revived in 1634, a new Prologue recalled his contribution, with the hint that no-one could play the part as well: 'Field is gone/Whose action first did give it (the play) name'. Other leading actors in the King's Men were Richard Cowley, a thin man who created parts such as Verges, Sir Andrew Aguecheek and Trinculo, and John Hemminges, the original Corbaccio in *Volpone*, who gradually retired after 1610 to become the company's business manager. And among the Admiral's, William

Cartwright and Sam Rowley might be picked out, the former a strong actor who created among other parts Pisano in *The Battle of Alcazar*, while Sam Rowley was an outstanding actor who, like Field, was also a successful playwright.

FAMOUS CLOWNS

Finally, the clowns in the open air playhouses retained their popularity, even while their roles in the private indoor theatres diminished. For the King's Men, Robert Armin was a Pierrot-style comic actor who was reputed to have been 'spotted' by Dick Tarlton, though there is no record of him performing before 1594. His creations included Feste in *Twelfth Night* and the Fool in *King Lear*, and he too was a successful playwright. When he died in 1615, his place in the King's Men was taken by John Shank, who may actually have worked with Tarlton. His career began before Armin's, and it continued long after. He was in charge of the company's apprentices until his death in 1635.

Outside the King's Men, the most notable clown of the Jacobean period was probably Thomas Greene of Queen Anne's Company at the Red Bull Theatre. Greene was a notable *improvisator*, and often bawdy, as suggested by the erect codpiece in his portrait. Cooke's *Greene's Tu Quoque* (1611), performed at the Red Bull, gained its name from the clown's catch phrase: 'Tu quoque', meaning 'Same to you'. Other clowns of the Jacobean and Caroline period included Thomas Pollard, a protégé of John Shank, and Timothy Read, but probably the leading clown of the Caroline period was Andrew Cane. He was quick-witted and a notable performer in jigs. Apprenticed as a goldsmith, and apparently keeping his hand in at this trade all his life, he was nevertheless the leading comic man at the Fortune in the 1620s and later led Prince Charles's Men at the Red Bull and the Fortune. After the theatres closed in 1642, Cane continued to clown and was popular until his death in 1659.

NOTES

1 Thomas Gainsford, *The Rich Cabinet Furnished with Variety of Excellent Descriptions*, 1616.
2 Glynne Wickham, Herbert Berry and William Ingram, *English Professional Theatre, 1530–1660*, Cambridge: Cambridge University Press, 2000, p. 181.
3 Thomas Nashe, *Summer's Last Will and Testament*.
4 Thomas Heywood, *An Apologie for Actors*, 1612.
5 Henry Jackson, translated from the Latin by Anthony B. Dawson; see Anthony B. Dawson and Paul Yachnin, *The Culture of Playgoing in Shakespeare's England*, Cambridge: Cambridge University Press, 2001.
6 'A Funeral Elegy, on the Death of the Famous Actor, Richard Burbage'. Note: it is suspected that some parts of this poem may have been forged by John Payne Collier in the early nineteenth century. The lines quoted, however, are probably not forged.
7 Thomas Nashe, *Pierce Penilesse His Supplication to the Divell*, 1592.
8 Edmund K. Chambers, *The Elizabethan Stage*, Oxford: Clarendon Press, 1923, IV, p. 370.

Chapter 23: Elizabethan and Jacobean

THE EARL OF ESSEX

The last sad act of Elizabeth's long reign was the rebellion of the Earl of Essex. Essex was a handsome and ambitious soldier-courtier whom the queen found charming, if not fascinating. But he was neither a lucky nor an intelligent commander, and his attempts to draw Spain's teeth, and then to subdue Ireland, were both pathetically unsuccessful. Undaunted, Essex lobbied hard for Lord Burghley's position as Secretary of State and Lord Privy Seal when the latter died in August 1598. But he was not appointed: instead, Burghley's son, the hunchbacked Robert Cecil took his father's place, indicating Essex's virtual defeat in the feud between these two ambitious courtiers.

ESSEX AND THE THEATRE

But Essex mounted a final challenge which brushed the theatre alarmingly closely. He and his leading supporter, the Earl of Southampton, had always loved the theatre – Southampton, indeed, was well known as Shakespeare's patron and was perhaps the loved boy of the sonnets. There were a number of 'Essex plays', before and after his rebellion, including Fulke Greville's *Antony and Cleopatra* (1601) and Samuel Daniel's *Philotas* (1604), but most famously, Shakespeare's *Henry V* (1599). In this, Essex was supposed to return from Ireland triumphant, just as Henry V had returned from France after the Battle of Agincourt:

> The mayor and all his brethren in best sort,
> . . .
> Go forth and fetch their conqu'ring Caesar in:
> As, by a lower but by loving likelihood,
> Were now the general of our gracious empress,
> As in good time he may, from Ireland coming,
> Bringing rebellion broached on his sword,
> How many would the peaceful city quit
> To welcome him!

This seems to be Shakespeare's most explicit reference to contemporary politics.

Figure 2.22
Robert Devereux, second Earl of Essex

Source: Heritage Images/Fine Art Images/Diomedia

ESSEX AND ELIZABETH

On 28 September, Essex did return from Ireland and presented himself dramatically, even theatrically, in the Queen's private chamber when she was half dressed. She was confused, amazed, perhaps flattered. She and he spent the rest of the day huddled in conversation, but at the end of it, he found himself returned to York House and put under house arrest. His importunity had led to nothing, and he was left to kick his heels in confinement for the best part of a year.

THE ESSEX REBELLION

In August 1600 Essex was freed, but he was out of favour and impoverished. The following January, Ben Jonson's *Cynthia's Revels* was presented by the Children of the Chapel Royal at court. The play, besides praising her Majesty lavishly, refers to Actaeon, who in classical mythology glimpsed Cynthia bathing naked in a pool and was turned into a stag and devoured by his own hounds, and to whom Essex was often compared. The comparison with Essex's appearance in Elizabeth's private apartment was unmistakeable now, but Jonson's plea for clemency was premature. A month later, one of Essex's followers, Sir Gilly Merrick, appeared to the Lord Chamberlain's Men and paid them 'forty pieces of silver' to perform *Richard II*, the story of the overthrow of a king. Augustine Phillips was to say later that the company objected to the request, because the play was 'so old and so long out of use', but they did perform it, though to what reception is unrecorded. The following day Essex led three hundred armed men into the city. But the city remained barred, the populace failed to rise, and Essex fled, only to be quickly apprehended. He was tried for treason, and executed on 25 February 1601. The whole affair was surely more theatrical than realistic.

POLITICAL PROBLEMS TOWARDS THE END OF ELIZABETH I'S REIGN

If the Essex rebellion poisoned the last years of Elizabeth's reign, other things were going wrong, too. In 1595 there were violent riots over the price of butter. The theatres were closed as a precaution, and the rioters executed. Problems from bad harvests, inflation and an influx of jobless vagrants into London were further compounded by the ongoing war with Spain. A second Armada of seventy-five hundred soldiers in the autumn of 1598 was only turned back by bad weather. Even the theatres came under new regulation in an Act of February 1598, which repealed all existing regulation concerning actors and instituted harsher penalties for unlicensed entertainers: they were to be 'stripped naked from the middle upwards and . . . openly whipped until his or her body be bloody'. It also reinforced the order in favour of the theatrical duopoly of the Lord Chamberlain's Men and the Lord Admiral's Men, leaving the Swan Theatre, the Curtain as well as any ambitious inns, to cope as best they could.

THE ACCESSION OF JAMES I

But the major problem remained the succession to the throne. Public discussion of this was banned and construed as treason. James VI of Scotland was the obvious and dynastic candidate for the English throne, but he was not the only one, and the Catholics in particular had high hopes of a Catholic sympathiser being installed. In March 1603 the old queen finally died. In the circumstances, the swift and smooth succession by James – now James I – was a triumph and for the rest of that spring and through the summer excitement at the prospect of a new regime, a male king with two male heirs, ran high, while he made his way south with stately slowness and an outbreak of plague flared in London.

JAMES, THE SCOTS AND THE ENGLISH CATHOLICS

James's first ambition was not simply a union of two crowns, but the creation of a single country, 'Great Britain'. This rapidly ran into trouble, however, when it was seen to involve a high level of participation of Scotsmen in the English – or Great British – government. Noses were put out of joint, including the noses of Catholics to whom James, though a Protestant himself, was not especially hostile. And the Catholics did nothing to help themselves. Before James had set eyes on his new palace in London, they attempted to kidnap his elder son, Henry, in what came to be known as the 'Bye' plot. James was furious, and ordered the Jesuits to leave Britain. The Catholics responded with a further plot, this time to blow up the Houses of Parliament. They were foiled, and by May 1606, when Henry Garnet, the head of the Jesuits in England, was hanged, drawn and quartered, the Catholics' chances of ever becoming again an official religion in Britain were over.

JAMES IN EARLY JACOBEAN DRAMA

Guy Fawkes, in Spain to rally support for the Gunpowder Plot, complained to his hosts: 'There is a natural hostility between the English and the Scots', and though his assertion was both inaccurate and politically motivated, it did reflect a real affront which many English felt. The resentment found its way into Marston, Jonson and Chapman's *Eastward Ho!*, performed at Blackfriars by the Children of the Queen's Revels. The play's protagonist, Sir Petronel Flash has paid for his knighthood, like others whose self-admiration helped to finance James, and he sets out on a voyage to recoup his fortune. But he is shipwrecked on the Isle of Dogs, opposite the royal palace, where he encounters two 'gentlemen' and converses with them briefly. On the way out, one of the gentlemen mutters

Figure 2.23
Macbeth and Banquo encounter the three Weird Sisters: an illustration from Raphael Holinshed's *Chronicle*, 1587
Source: British Library, London

in a Scottish accent the authors clearly indicate: 'I ken the man weel: he's one of my thirty pound knights'. In other words, Sir Petronel has met James himself!

The repercussions of this illegal representation of the monarch, and other satirical references in the play, were serious. Jonson and Chapman were gaoled, though Marston, whom they both protested had written the offending passage, seems to have escaped. Equally seriously, John Day's anti-Cecil play (though not overtly anti-Scots), *The Isle of Gulls*, produced in 1606, was stopped and two of the actors from the Queen's Revels company were this time sent to gaol. A breach between the drama-loving Scottish king and the theatre community was in danger of opening up. Jonson's masque, *Hymenaei*, celebrating the marriage of Robert Devereux and Frances Howard, was perhaps one step towards reconciliation, associating as it did the happy marriage with the union of the English and Scottish crowns, and Shakespeare's *Macbeth* (1606) may have attempted to reinforce the mood of reconciliation. The play explored some of Scotland's wilder history while paying James a compliment in references to the descendants of Banquo and Fleance.

THE REPRESENTATION OF FOREIGNERS ON THE STAGE

This is notable partly because the English never tired of ridiculing funny not-English 'others', including Scots. *Henry V* includes a funny Scotsman, Jamy, as well as a Welshman, Fluellen and an Irishman, Macmorris. Middleton's *A Chaste Maid in Cheapside* has a funny Welsh woman, and *The Honest Whore* Part 2, by Dekker, has perhaps the first of an almost endless stream of comic stage Irishmen. In Greene's *James IV* there is even a funny Frenchman.

THE REPRESENTATION OF BLACK PEOPLE ON THE STAGE

But the most virulent prejudice, then as now, was against black people. Though there were probably well under a thousand black people among London's population of two hundred thousand, three orders were issued for the deportation of 'blackamoors' between 1596 and 1601, and some were actually sold into slavery. The drama furnishes plenty of examples of prejudice: Muly Mahomet is the remorseless villain in *The Battle of Alcazar*; Marlowe's anti-semitic portrait of the Jew of Malta is complemented by the Jew's chief supporter, the black slave, Ithamore, while in *Dido, Queen of Carthage* he depicts a white adventurer tempted by a seductive black woman; in Middleton and Rowley's *A Fair Quarrel*, Jane, assailed by the lustful Physician, repulses him with the words: 'Y'are a blackamoor'; in Webster's *The White Devil*, Vittoria Corombona, the white devil, is served by the Moor, Zanche, 'the black devil'; and in the Caroline period, in Berkeley's *The Lost Lady* (1637), Milesia is presumed dead, but in reality lives disguised as a Moor, that is, with blacked face. As a black, she seems either mischievous or wicked, but when, having taken poison supplied by her former lover, she lies in agony on her bed and her friends apply water to her face, the blackness 'falls away'. Now she is

> White as lilies, as the snow
> That falls upon Parnassus.

And of course her virtues shine out again. The list could be considerably lengthened.

Figure 2.24
Portrait of an African man by the Dutch painter, Jan Mostaert, c.1530
Source: Rijksmuseum, Amsterdam

The most interesting playwright in this, as in so many other things, is Shakespeare, whose own desire for a 'dark lady' he wrestled with in his sonnets. His blood-boltered early tragedy, *Titus Andronicus*, is a work increasingly admired in the post-Holocaust era, when there have been such grim events in Bosnia, Rwanda, Syria and elsewhere, and dramas like Sarah Kane's *Blasted* have made such an impression. At its heart stands Aaron, the black lover of Queen Tamora. He is a 'swart Cimmerian' who cherishes his 'fleece of woolly hair' and exults:

> Coal-black is better than another hue,
> In that it scorns to bear another hue,
> For all the water in the ocean
> Can never turn the swan's black legs to white,
> Although she lave them hourly in the flood.

'Aaron will have his soul black like his face', he chuckles after cutting off Titus's hand. Is his blackness merely an exotic coating for his villainy? Or are we to understand that all black people are villainous? Perhaps his villainy is the result of oppression? Shakespeare refuses to solve this problem for us.

Against Aaron must be set Othello, whose transparent goodness is traduced by Iago, but whose blackness is pointed up. Iago welcomes 'a brace of Cyprus gallants, that would fain have a measure to the health of the black Othello', and Emilia exclaims, when Othello admits he has killed Desdemona: 'O, the more angel she,/And you the blacker devil!' Yet he is also the 'noble Moor' who has won the trust and admiration of the Venetian Senate. Othello is probably the first black character presented on the British stage as anything but a buffoon or a villain.

Perhaps Shakespeare's most arresting black character is Cleopatra in *Antony and Cleopatra*, who as a black woman and a queen desperately threatens the empire. Her exotic sexuality holds the secret fear and fascination the black body always holds in the white imagination: the Rome of Antony and Octavius may represent civilisation, but Cleopatra's Egypt is dangerous, alluring, strange and irresistible.

IMPERIALISM

Rome's attitude to Egypt in this play is fundamentally that of an imperialist power, and the late sixteenth and early seventeenth centuries marked the very beginning of western imperialist expansion. The East India Company was founded in 1600; the Pilgrim Fathers set sail for a new home in America in 1620; Sir Walter Raleigh was in search of El Dorado at this time; and the slave trade was bringing increasing riches into British coffers.

THE TEMPEST

Shakespeare struggles with all this most fiercely in *The Tempest*. The play presented its popular audiences with something exotic, something 'oriental', demonstrating the wonder of travel and the strange world beyond the sea. And it would have excited spectators at least for this reason. But the play is more of a tangle than this implies. It is set on a far away island, which is not quite as deserted as it seems. There is a family here, whom Prospero, an archetypal imperialist, divides and rules. He demonises the mother, Sycorax, as a witch, and 'buys' her son, Caliban: 'When thou cam'st first,/ Thou strok'st me, and made much of me', Caliban remembers. But Caliban, whose name is an anagram of 'cannibal', is not to be regarded as an equal. His sexual desire for Prospero's daughter, for example, is not acceptable: Prospero shares Sebastian's racist attitude voiced when Alonso is bewailing the loss of his son in the shipwreck:

> Sir, you may thank yourself for this great loss,
> That would not bless our Europe with your daughter,
> But rather loose her to an African.

But Prospero's colonial perspective is not necessarily Shakespeare's, nor should it be ours. He uses his magic to enforce his will as the British red coats were to use the Gatling gun to enforce British imperialism on unarmed 'natives'. Caliban's attempt at insurrection, with Stephano and Trinculo, the lower class Europeans, is mere foolery, partly because Stephano and Trinculo share too many of the colonialists' attitudes. For instance, Trinculo, faced with Caliban, is unable to decide what or who he is: 'I do now let loose my opinion, hold it no longer: this is no fish, but an islander'. And having decided that, he and Stephano ply him with drink, as the settlers in America plied the native Americans with drink, and thus they subdue him. Yet Caliban is vividly aware of the finer things in life. He is generous:

> I prithee, let me bring thee where crabs grow;
> And I with my long nails will dig thee pig-nuts;
> Show thee a jay's nest, and instruct thee how
> To snare the nimble marmoset; I'll bring thee
> To clustering filberts, and sometimes I'll get thee
> Young scamels from the rock.

And he appreciates beauty, physical and spiritual:

> Be not afeard; the isle is full of noises,
> Sounds and sweet airs, that give delight and hurt not.
> Sometimes a thousand twangling instruments
> Will hum about mine ears; and sometimes voices,
> That if I then had wak'd from long sleep,
> Will make me sleep again: and then, in dreaming,
> The clouds methought would open, and show riches
> Ready to drop upon me; that, when I wak'd,
> I cried to dream again.

Ariel, Prospero's other native slave, wants his freedom, too, but he agrees to collaborate with the coloniser to attain it. This prefigures many colonial people who collaborated with the British in the twentieth-century's world wars in exchange for a similar promise of postwar freedom, though Britain was not always as true to its word as Prospero is to his.

COMMERCIAL LONDON

Imperialism exploits the idea of commerce and profit, and international commerce was following the explorers and opening up in the late sixteenth and seventeenth centuries as never before. London became a major hub for this new international trade, its strength and self-confidence epitomised in the Royal Exchange, the centre of the City of London, and the New Exchange, opened in 1608 in the Strand midway between the city and Westminster. Effectively a shopping mall with financial dealing attached, it prompted a new consumerism and its attendant conspicuous consumption which was to continue until the 1640s.

KING JAMES AND THE PATRONAGE OF THE THEATRE

At the head of the new fashionable society was the royal family, and one of their pet hobbies was theatre. James and his wife, Anne, both indulged their love of theatricals in the magnificent and

Figure 2.25
The Royal Exchange, the heart of the City of London's expanding international trade in the Jacobean period and after

hugely costly masques mounted in their court and discussed next, but before ever this had time to be noticed, they had intervened in the London theatre scene. Ten days after arriving in London, the Lord Chamberlain's Men became the King's Men, a title they retained till the 1640s; the Admiral's Men became Prince Henry's Men, and Worcester's Men, the third company precariously surviving in London, became Queen Anne's Men and took on a new lease of life at the Curtain Theatre. James seems to have decided to incorporate the theatre into his wider project, not just because he and his family were excited aficionados of all things theatrical, but also because the theatre, with its rituals, its splendour and its mystery, seemed implicitly to endorse his regalist philosophy.

The consequences were several. The 1606 Act to Restrain the Abuses of Players stopped authors from including oaths in their texts. On the other hand, seeing the king's enthusiasm, the city of London became noticeably less hostile to the players. And the court gave many more opportunities to perform for the royal family than Elizabeth ever had: in 1613, for instance, when James's daughter Elizabeth married Frederick V, Elector of the Palatinate of Germany, over twenty plays were performed at court during the celebrations. But against this, the theatre began to lose that dangerous indeterminate position, the liminality which had given it such artistic freedom and intellectual and emotional power. As time went on, and especially as the most innovative theatre work shifted more and more to the private theatres – Blackfriars, Whitefriars, and later the Cockpit and Salisbury Court – so the theatre lost that *brio* and special power which it had had almost accidentally in the late years of the Elizabethan period. Perhaps Thomas Middleton's 1624 *A Game at Chess* was the last time theatre could truly be said to inhabit that threshold position where imagination liberates perception and soars.

Chapter 24: Life of the Globe

THE GLOBE THEATRE, 1599

After the death of their father in 1597, Cuthbert and Richard Burbage tried to renegotiate a lease on the Theatre in Finsbury Fields. But their efforts led to stalemate. Simultaneously, they leased a piece of land near the Rose Theatre in the Liberty of the Clink, and in December 1598, they took matters into their own hands. During the Christmas holiday, they led a team of sixteen men, including the master carpenter Peter Street and their friend William Smith, with twelve workmen, and tore down the Theatre building their father had built over twenty years earlier. It took them nearly three days to remove what they regarded as their timbers, which they then transported across the Thames to their new site. Here they re-erected the theatre presumably more or less as it had been in Finsbury Fields, though perhaps with some added refinements. And they named it the 'Globe'.

The new theatre, like the old one, had an outer diameter of just under a hundred feet, and its stage was nearly fifty feet wide, jutting out into the yard and covered with a thatched roof. A Swiss visitor described how the play was performed 'on a raised scaffold', and people paid one penny to stand and watch. But one could pay an extra penny to enter one of the galleries and 'sit more pleasantly and better'; and for a further penny, one could sit on a cushion, and not only see but be seen too. The Globe was, said Ben Jonson, 'the glory of the Bank'.

THE GLOBE AND THE WORLD: LIVING AND ACTING

The Globe's name was probably intended to be symbolic, and indeed over the next fourteen years it seemed to stage the world. In one of the early plays to receive its premiere there, *As You Like It*, Shakespeare gave voice to this:

> All the world's a stage, and all the men and women
> Merely players.

Another name for the player, or actor, was 'shadow', as Shakespeare also noted:

> Life's but a walking shadow, a poor player,
> That struts and frets his hour upon the stage.

The conflation of life with acting, the world with the stage, was one which is reiterated in many of the Globe's plays. Ben Jonson, in *Volpone* (1606), presents Sir Politick Would-be as worthy of the stage, except it would be thought the author 'feigned', as Shakespeare in *Twelfth Night* presents Malvolio: 'If this were played upon a stage now, I could condemn it as an improbable fiction'. In *The Alchemist* (1610), a success at the Globe, though originally staged at Blackfriars, Jonson plays with illusion and reality even more disconcertingly, setting the action in Blackfriars in October 1610 – where and when the play was actually set. (Face admits regretfully in his Epilogue, that his part 'fell a little at the end'.) And in *The Devil Is an Ass* (1616), Fitzdottrel spends the whole play dashing about because he has to get to the premiere of the new play at the Globe – which is *The Devil Is an Ass*.

In Middleton's *The Lady's Tragedy* (1611), played at the Globe and the Blackfriars in 1611, Leonella sets up the denouement for Bellarius to watch:

> Thou mayst sit
> Like a most private gallant in yon corner,
> See all the play, and ne'er be seen thyself.

Presumably the actor playing Bellarius was put among the 'gallants' in the audience, as the play within the play turns into a kind of acted reality. In *The Duchess of Malfi*, performed in 1614, Webster keeps up an almost tormented argument about the interpenetration of stage and life, illusion and reality: 'in tragedies, a good actor is cursed', he says, and the Duchess, in her despair, remarks:

> I account this world a tedious theatre,
> For I do play a part in't 'gainst my will.

The White Queen's Pawn in *A Game at Chess* (1624) by Thomas Middleton, decries the Black Bishop's Pawn's refusal to treat life as drama:

> The world's a stage, on which all parts are played.
> You'd count it strange to have a devil
> Presented there not in a devil's shape,
> Or – wanting one – to send him out in yours.
> You'd rail at that for an absurdity
> No college e'er committed. For decorum's sake, then,
> For pity's cause, for sacred virtue's honour,
> If you'll persist still in your dev'lish part,
> Present him as you should do, and let one
> That carries up the goodness of the play
> Come in that habit, and I'll speak with him.
> Then will the parts be fitted, and the spectators
> Know which is which.

There are many more examples. For Nashe, 'Heaven is our heritage,/Earth but a player's stage'. In Chettle's *The Tragedy of Hoffman* (1602), Hoffman urges Lorrique, 'Now or never play thy part', while in Heywood's *The Wise Woman of Hogsdon* (1604), when the characters, masked or vizarded, have changed clothes and married they know not who, one of them chuckles, 'Here were even a plot to make a play on!' When *The Roaring Girl* (1611) was presented on stage, Moll Frith, the real-life model for the play's central character, came on stage and entertained the audience as herself. And when Baligny, in Chapman's *The Revenge of Bussy D'Ambois* (1610), asks, 'is not all the world esteem'd a stage?' Clermont replies:

Yes, and right worthily; and stages too
Have a respect due to them, if but only
For what the good Greek moralist says of them:

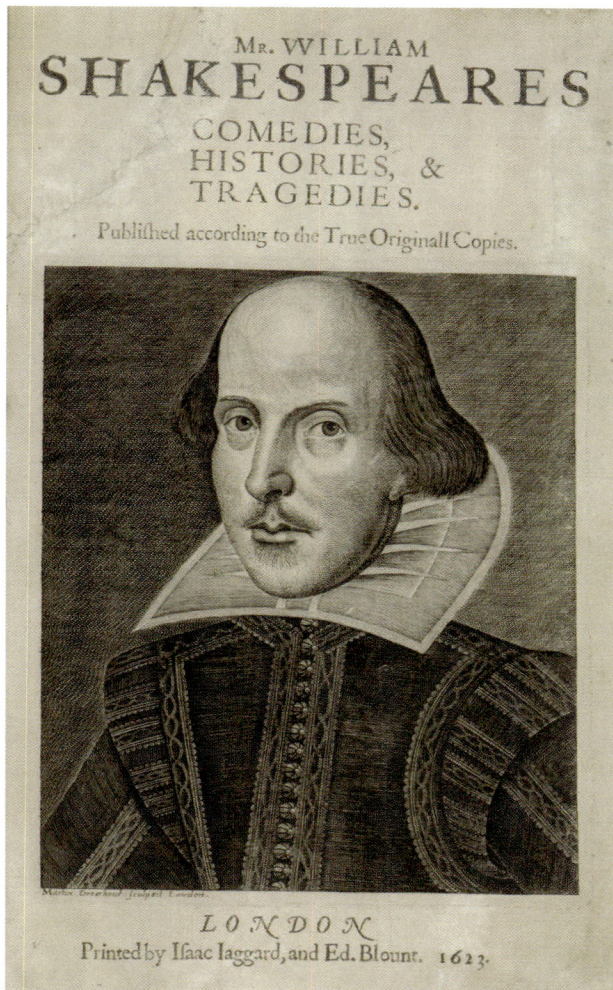

Figure 2.26
Title page of the First Folio of William Shakespeare's plays
Source: British Library, London

'Is a man proud of greatness, or of riches?
Give me an expert actor, I'll show all
That can within his greatest glory fall.
Is a man fray'd with poverty and lowness?
Give me an actor, I'll show every eye
What he laments so, and so much doth fly,
The best and worst of both'.

But Shakespeare himself is the most persistent player on this particular instrument. At the end of *Love's Labour's Lost* (c.1595), Berowne complains: 'Our wooing doth not end like an old play'; and Coriolanus is pursued by the image. Early on, urged to present himself for election to the people, he responds: 'It is a part/That I shall blush in acting'. And when he does go to the people, he comments:

You have put me now to such a part which never
I shall discharge to th' life.

Cominius encourages him: 'Come, come, we'll prompt you', and Volumnia adds, 'Perform a part/ Thou hast not done before'. And at the end, he recognises his failure: 'Like a dull actor now,/I have forgot my part'. This theatre interrogates life, as life interrogates the theatre.

THE KING'S MEN

Shakespeare's work continued to dominate the repertoire of his company, who had now become the King's Men. His career at the Globe Theatre moved from troubled comedies, *All's Well That Ends Well* (1602), *Troilus and Cressida* (c.1603) and *Measure for Measure* (1604), to full-blown tragedies, *Hamlet* (1601) and then *Othello* (1604), *King Lear* (1605), *Macbeth* (1606) and *Antony and Cleopatra* (1607). By 1608 his major tragedies were written, and it was in this year that at last Burbage obtained back the lease of the Blackfriars indoor theatre and was able to open it to the King's Men. From this year, the company operated two theatres, though not necessarily in so simple a way as performing at the Globe in the summer and Blackfriars in the winter, as has sometimes been suggested. Gradually, over years, most plays seemed to open at Blackfriars, and went on to the Globe only later. However, it may be that the increasing emphasis on the Blackfriars where after all more money could be made per performance, compromised the company's 'artistic freedom' to some degree. Commercial advantage was taking the company's centre of operations away from the 'Liberty' of the Clink and the old liminality was subtly eroded.

FLETCHER AND TRAGICOMEDY

1608 was also the year when John Fletcher wrote *The Faithful Shepherdess*, and although this was staged by the Children of the Queen's Revels, not by the King's Men, it was to have a profound effect on the development of England's leading company. *The Faithful Shepherdess* was loosely adapted from *Il Pastor Fido* by Giovanni Battista Guarini, who justified his apparently nebulous work by describing it as a 'tragicomedy'. In 1601 his essay justifying the form was published in English. Fletcher paraphrased Guarini:

> A tragi-comedy is not so called in respect of mirth and killing, but in respect it wants deaths, which is enough to make it no tragedy, yet it brings some near it, which is enough to make it no comedy.[1]

Its other characteristics, according to Fletcher, were a certain naturalism, and a cast in which gods, aristocrats and 'mean people' could be mixed. *The Faithful Shepherdess* sometimes seems like a cross between a stately dance and a game of chess, in either of which emotions may run high without leading to fatal consequences. Though the play was not popular, it sparked a series of tragicomedies – indeed tragicomedy became perhaps the form *par excellence* of the 1610s, as Shakespeare, Middleton, Beaumont, Massinger, Field and others all tried their hand at the *genre*. Apart from its apparent elegance, in tune perhaps with new fashions, tragicomedy offered a sequence of almost self-contained scenes, some formal, some informal, some emotional, others plot-filled, some dangerous, others pathetic, in a delightfully unexpected procession.

THE GLOBE BURNS DOWN

The move to Blackfriars, an indoor 'private' theatre, helped the King's Men to make this kind of drama *chic*. But five years after Fletcher had introduced it, and after their acquisition of the Black-friars Theatre, disaster struck the Globe. On 29 June 1613, during a staging of Shakespeare and Fletcher's *Henry VIII* (1613), 'chambers' were 'discharged' in accordance with a stage direction, and, according to Sir Henry Wotton, an eye-witness,

> some of the paper or other stuff wherewith one of (the canons) was stopped, did light on the thatch, where being thought at first but an idle smoke, and their eyes more attentive to the show, it kindled inwardly, and ran round like a train, consuming within less than an hour the whole house to the very ground. This was the fatal period of that virtuous fabric; wherein nothing did perish but wood and straw, and a few forsaken cloaks; only one man had his breeches set on fire, that would perhaps have broiled him, if he had not, by the benefit of a provident wit, put it out with bottle ale.[2]

The events were further recorded in a ballad of the time:

> This fearful fire began above,
>   A wonder strange and true,
> And to the stage-house did remove,
>   As round as tailor's clew;
> And burned down both beam and snag,
> And did not spare the silken flag,
>   O sorrow, pitiful sorrow,
>   And yet all this is true.
>
> Out run the knights, out run the lords,
>   And there was great ado;

> Some lost their hats and some their swords;
>> And out run Burbage too;
> The reprobates, though drunk on Monday,
> Prayed for the Fool and Henry Condy,
>> O sorrow, pitiful sorrow,
>> And yet all this is true.[3]

THE SECOND GLOBE AND THE KING'S MEN

The King's Men, however, set to work to build their theatre again, and within a few months it was ready to open. The new Globe was probably the same size and shape as its predecessor (and therefore as the original Theatre, too), but this time it had a tiled roof. Its interior was probably even more splendid than its predecessor's. John Chamberlain wrote in 1614: 'I hear such speech of this new playhouse, which is said to be the fairest that ever was in England',[4] and an anonymous poet called it 'our world's best stage'. It may be added that in 1989, archaeologists found the trace of a corner of the second Globe, causing much excitement in the theatre world, though actually and sadly not much could be deduced from it.

It enabled the King's Men to continue their ever more successful progress. That can be measured by the fact that from now certainly until the end of James's reign, the company gave a dozen or more performances at court every year – more than all the other companies put together. In 1619 they were granted a new Royal Patent to continue at the Globe and Blackfriars, and in 1624, despite

Figure 2.27
Detail from Claes Visscher's Panorama of London, 1616, showing the second Globe Theatre on the south bank of the Thames
Source: Library of Congress, Washington, D.C.

the furore over *A Game at Chess*, their company had swelled to at least thirty-five full-time members, including eighteen actors, musicians, attendants and so on. Further prestige accrued from the publication in 1623 of the First Folio of Shakespeare's plays, in which were listed twenty-six 'principal actors', many of whom were now dead. In 1629 Ben Jonson complained of the company that his comedy, *The New Inn* (1629), 'was never acted, but most negligently played', but such grumbling may owe more to Jonson's temperament than the skill of the actors. Five years later, another play, *The Late Lancashire Witches* by Thomas Heywood and Richard Brome (1634), was hugely successful, running for three days in succession and attracting 'a great concourse of people'. Unlike Jonson's play, however, it was crammed with magic, songs and dances, spectacular events and plenty of buffoonery.

ACTORS AT THE GLOBE

The acting traditions the company developed were long-lasting and clear, and the part of Henry VIII, for instance, was handed down from John Lowin, the original performer of the part, who 'had his instructions from Mr Shakespeare himself' to William Davenant, who in turn handed it on to Thomas Betterton, the greatest star of the 1680s and 1690s. Several of the company's actors were also playwrights, too. Robert Armin, the clown, wrote *The History of Two Maids of More-Clacke* (1608) and several comic pamphlets. William Rowley, another clown who joined the company in 1623, having worked with Prince Charles's Men mostly before this at the Hope, the Red Bull and elsewhere, was a very different sort of performer – a fat man, though light on his feet. Before he died in 1626, he had contributed to no fewer than seventeen plays, the best of which – *A Fair Quarrel* (c.1616), for instance, and *The Changeling* (c.1622), both in collaboration with Middleton – were among the best plays of the period. Nathan Field, a very fine serious actor, wrote at least two excellent plays, *A Woman Is a Weathercock* (1609) and *Amends for Ladies* (1611), in his early twenties, and collaborated on several more plays before his early death in1620.

BEN JONSON'S LATER PLAYS

By the second decade of the seventeenth century the King's Men were staging a wide range of plays by a variety of authors. Ben Jonson, for instance, had become a King's Men's author. In his early life he had been a bricklayer, a soldier and an actor, and he had been a confessing Catholic for a while, even peripherally mixed up in the Gunpowder Plot. His first play for the King's Men was *Volpone* (1606) and his second *The Alchemist* (1610), and these are surely two of the finest comedies in English. His aim, he said, was to 'imitate justice and instruct to life', and here he succeeded through a wonderfully rich array of comic eventualities. His tragedy, *Cataline* (1611), was distinctly less successful, and none of the other comedies he wrote for the King's Men – *The Devil Is an Ass* (1616), *The Staple of News* (1626), *The New Inn* (1629) and *The Magnetic Lady* (1632) – were anything like as successful as the two earlier plays, for all that each of these has something to commend it and to enjoy in it. More of Jonson's energy by the 1620s was going into the creation of court masques, and when he was not working on these, he was being convivial with his disciples, the 'Tribe of Ben', in the Apollo Rooms at the Devil and St Dunstan Tavern in Fleet Street.

JOHN FLETCHER AND THE KING'S MEN'S PLAYS

The anonymous *Merry Devil of Edmonton* (1602), Wilkins's *The Miseries of Enforced Marriage* (1606) and Dekker, Rowley and Ford's *The Witch of Edmonton* (1621) were other King's Men's successes, but after Shakespeare's retirement, it was Fletcher who took over as the leading dramatist for the company. Fletcher was a bachelor interested in alternative lifestyles. In *The Night Walker* (1611), he even depicts male sexual intercourse between Wildbrain and the coachman, Tobie. Wildbrain puts out the candle and penetrates Tobie: 'In, in, presently', he says and Tobie comments, 'I feel his talents through me, 'tis an old haggard devil, what will he do with me?' 'Let me kiss thee first', says Wildbrain, 'quick, quick' and then 'what a hairy whore 'tis'. A similar relationship is depicted, though less graphically, in Fletcher, Field and Massinger's *The Honest Man's Fortune* (1613), between Veramour and the page Montaigne. In *A King and No King* (1611), Fletcher, this time working with Francis Beaumont, explores incest, though the supposed pair are in fact not siblings. Fletcher was extremely prolific and besides writing at least one play a year by himself, he seems to have been the centre of something like a playwriting circle. His most famous collaboration was with Beaumont, with whom he also wrote *Philaster* (1609) and *The Maid's Tragedy* (1610), but he also worked with Shakespeare on *Henry VIII* (1613) and *The Two Noble Kinsmen* (also 1613), and with Massinger, Field and others on a string of plays. His tragicomedies especially are notable for their smooth stylishness which is less accessible to audiences in the twenty-first century than the rougher plays of some of his contemporaries, but he had a facility and elegance which are very rare.

REVENGE TRAGEDY

The other form developed conspicuously by the King's Men was the revenge tragedy. In a society where there was no police force, the obtaining of justice even for the murder of a loved one was no easy matter. Despite the convenient label, justice in these plays is not so much revenge as a way of enabling the wronged protagonist to reintegrate their own identity which has been fractured by the wrong they have suffered. Philosophically the plays may be seen as searches for identity, therefore, or even searches for happiness or contentedness in a nightmarish world rotten with corruption, horror and malice. Revenge is therefore more than a social dilemma; it is also psychological and religious as well. These considerations inform *Hamlet*, the archetypal revenge play, but also others, including Middleton's *The Revenger's Tragedy* (c.1607), Tourneur's *The Atheist's Tragedy* (c.1609) and Webster's *The Duchess of Malfi* (1614), in which the central figures are driven to self-torturing distraction. Indeed these agonies are sometimes so great that they become virtually self-parodies. With typically laconic coolness, Middleton presents his audience with a human skull in *The Revenger's Tragedy*, not as a prompt for philosophical speculation but as a trick prop to poison yet another villain. 'When the bad bleed, then is the tragedy good', Vindice observes self-reflexively.

In Webster's *The Duchess of Malfi*, Antonio, the Duchess's lover or husband, dies by 'such a mistake as I have often seen/In a play', and the sombre doom seems even more relentless than in the same author's earlier *The White Devil* (staged at the Red Bull, 1612). Cyril Tourneur's *The Atheist's Tragedy* is considerably less powerful, but has a kind of neatness in which each self-contained scene deepens the anguish.

THOMAS MIDDLETON

Tourneur was for long thought to be the author of *The Revenger's Tragedy*, but this is now recognised as the work of Thomas Middleton. Middleton is a wholly London writer who dissects, exposes and grins a ghastly grin at the money drives and sexual allures of the capital. His anger is only somewhat appeased by the women characters he creates who have both good humour and energy. Besides *The Revenger's Tragedy*, the alarmingly brief *Yorkshire Tragedy* (1606) is a searing study of affliction and obsession, and several of his other tragedies, first performed by the King's Men, have a not dissimilar harrowing quality which makes them resonate particularly with our time: *The Lady's Tragedy* (1611), *The Bloody Banquet* (c.1619) which only survives in a much adapted form, and *Women Beware Women* (c.1621), the first performance of which is actually unrecorded. The irony, parody and detachment of the final scene of *Women Beware Women* make it particularly difficult to stage, but it still seems a shame that several modern productions have dodged the challenge. Yet this play and *The Changeling* (staged at the Cockpit in 1622) are exceptional.

Middleton also wrote a large number of comedies and tragicomedies, most of which after about 1610 were presented by the King's Men. His earlier comedies for the children's companies earned him the reputation as the most consistently successful writer of so-called 'citizen comedies'. The local colour and the accurate topography of these make his teeming London a city of spivs, blackmailers, decayed country gents, sexual predators and social parasites almost Dickensian in its variety and vitality, though Middleton never succumbs to Dickens's sentimentality. Social ambition, the power of money, greed and personal manipulation are what galvanise and invigorate this astonishing array of tricksters, rogues and lechers, and Middleton's language is as economical and poetic as Harold Pinter's. *More Dissemblers Besides Women* (c.1614) and *Anything for a Quiet Life* (c.1621) are the best comedies he did for the King's Men, but those he wrote for the children's companies, as well as others such as *A Chaste Maid in Cheapside* (1613), demonstrate his extraordinary versatility. His world made the Globe smaller, but fiercer, less relaxed but more material.

COLLABORATION

Middleton's *oeuvre* also raises acutely the question of collaboration. Probably well over half the plays created in the Elizabethan and Jacobean period were the result of writers working together, and Middleton joined at different times with virtually every major playwright of the period except Marlowe and Chapman. His partnerships with Dekker (*The Honest Whore*, *The Bloody Banquet* and *The Roaring Girl*), Rowley (*Wit at Several Weapons*, *A Fair Quarrel*, *The World Tossed at Tennis* and *The Changeling*) and Shakespeare (*A Yorkshire Tragedy*, *Timon of Athens*, *Macbeth* and *Measure for Measure*) were particularly fruitful, and his varied practice raises vital questions of 'author'-ship and 'author'-ised versions. For example, it is likely that Middleton and Dekker worked very closely together on *The Roaring Girl*. Middleton's relationship with Rowley on *The Changeling* may have been more business-like, with Rowley responsible for the subplot and the opening and final scenes, while Middleton developed the main plot. As for Shakespeare, while Middleton probably reworked *Macbeth* without input from Shakespeare, Shakespeare seems to have retouched Middleton's original *A Yorkshire Tragedy*.

All this occurred in what was inevitably a collaborative art form – theatre. It begs questions not only of how playwrights co-operated, but of how others, too, contributed to surviving texts: scripts were sold to companies who were at liberty to change and adapt them, and then sold by the companies to printers who might also revise or clarify them. It is therefore important to recognise that playscripts from this time are never the sacred texts demanded by later, more romantic ages.

NOTES

1 John Fletcher, 'To the Reader', in *The Faithful Shepherdess*, 1608.
2 Sir Henry Wotton, letter to Edmund Bacon, 2 July 1613, *Reliquiae Wottonianae*, 1672.
3 *A Sonnet upon the pitiful burning of the Globe playhouse in London*, c.1613.
4 Letter, 30 June 1614, in Elizabeth Thomson (ed), *The Chamberlain Letters*, New York: Capricorn, 1966, p. 157.

Chapter 25: Popular theatres, 1600–42

THE FORTUNE THEATRE

When the Lord Chamberlain's Men moved south of the river and opened the Globe Theatre virtually next door to the Rose, it seemed as if Henslowe and Alleyn felt the competition might be too much. Immediately they began to negotiate for a plot of land north of the city, but further west than the Theatre and the Curtain, on Golden Lane. In December 1599, Alleyn paid to lease the plot for twenty-five years, and he and Henslowe turned to Peter Street, builder of the Globe, to construct a new theatre for them. Interestingly, when the Privy Council objected to the plan for the new theatre, the local residents opposed them, and begged for the theatre to be built. Apart from anything else, they knew the acting companies paid good poor relief.

Though specifying it should be like the Globe, actually the new theatre was in many ways different. It was a square building, not circular or polygonal, with the sides measuring eighty feet on the outside. The stage was very similar to the Globe's, being forty-three feet wide and jutting out twenty-seven feet six inches into the yard. Behind it was the tiring-house which contained glass windows at the back. The roof was tiled. The yard itself was fifty-five feet across, with the stage probably on the north side. The timber-framed building had three galleries, all containing seats and divided into 'two penny rooms' and 'gentlemen's rooms', access to which was by staircase. It seems that the gallery was also occasionally used for acting. The interior was painted throughout, and the tops of the square pillars were carved with satyrs. The theatre would hold up to two and a half thousand spectators ('our vast theatre', Middleton calls it in the Prologue to *The Roaring Girl*.) Its sign showed Dame Fortune: it was named 'Fortune'.

It the autumn of 1600 the Fortune was ready, and the Admiral's Men moved over, leaving the Rose empty. Though it was used occasionally after the Admiral's Men had left, the old theatre was now really surplus to London's needs and was pulled down in 1605.

JIGS AT THE FORTUNE

Alleyn was excited enough by the new building to return to the stage himself. But how well his grand style was suited to the new Fortune may be questioned, and he retired for good two or three years later. More popular were the jigs at the Fortune, and it appears that large numbers of spectators waited until the play was over before entering to enjoy the post-play jig. In 1612, a jig called *Garlic*, which unfortunately has not survived, excited the spectators to extreme rowdiness. One commentator spoke of the

> Fortune-fatted fools . . . whose garb is the toothache of wit, the plague-sore of judgment . . . who are fain to produce blind Impudence to personate himself upon their stage, be hung with chains of garlic, as an antidote against their own infectious breaths, lest it should kill their oyster-crying audience.[1]

The result was serious: the Justices were called in and stated their conclusion:

> Whereas complaints have been made at this last general sessions that by reason of certain lewd jigs, songs and dances used and accustomed at the playhouse called the Fortune in Golden Lane, divers cutpurses and other lewd and ill-disposed persons in great multitudes do resort thither at the end of every play, many times causing tumults and outrages whereby his Majesty's peace is often broke and much mischief like to ensure thereby: it was hereupon expressly commanded and ordered by the justice of the said bench that all actors of every playhouse . . . utterly abolish all jigs, rhymes and dances after their plays . . . upon pain of imprisonment and putting down and suppressing of their plays, and such further punishment to be inflicted upon them as their offences shall deserve.[2]

The law's affront, however, seems to have had little lasting impact, and jigs continued at the Fortune and the other popular playhouses apparently unmolested.

THE FORTUNE BURNS DOWN

However, on 9 December 1621, the Fortune burned down. Immediately Alleyn (without Henslowe, who had died in 1616) set about rebuilding it on the same Golden Lane site at a cost of over £1,000. The new theatre opened in early 1624. Few details of it survive, but it was brick-built, and probably polygonal, the experiment of a square theatre being now rejected. It was, according to Edmund Howe in 1631, 'far fairer' than its predecessor. Nevertheless, the fire ruined the company which had been resident there since its foundation, first as the Admiral's Men, then as Queen Anne's and after her death as Lord Palsgrave's, and the new theatre never acquired the same stability of performing company that it had enjoyed through its first incarnation.

THE RED BULL

In late March 1606, another new theatre, the Red Bull, was opened. It was to the north and west of the Fortune in Clerkenwell and was adapted from an inn and its stables under the direction of Martin Slatiar, an actor with Queen Anne's Men who came to occupy it, and Aaron Holland. It was the third successful theatre, along with the Globe and the Fortune, in the period from now until 1642, and it was the largest of the three.

The Red Bull was a four-sided building, one hundred seventy feet by about one hundred fifty feet; its yard was fifty-seven feet by sixty-seven, with a tiring-house sixteen feet by thirty-three feet. Pillars held up the roof over the stage, where there was machinery for 'flying', and the stage had at least one large trapdoor, probably two, and three doors at the back. It also had a low rail running round the edge of the stage. There was a notably small balcony for actors, though the building did have a music room above stage level, and a much-used 'discovery' space below, besides some kind of moveable rostrum. Though the theatre acquired a reputation for 'popular' drama (and indeed other entertainments, such as fencing displays, wrestling and more), which would usually imply trouble with the local residents, it seems that the socially mixed population of Clerkenwell was happy with the actors, who contributed to the welfare of the district, for instance by paying for handrails to be placed on the pavements near the theatre.

THE BOAR'S HEAD

Two other popular open air theatres of the seventeenth century need to be noted, neither of them long lived. The Boar's Head, like the Red Bull constructed out of an inn, was situated in Whitechapel near the east gate of the city. Its owner was Oliver Woodliffe, and his prospective manager, Richard Samwell. However much the Lord Chamberlain's Men and the Admiral's Men may have objected to another invasion of their duopoly, they had no actual power to stop another playhouse being opened, and the Privy Council seemed uninterested, perhaps because one prospective tenant of the new theatre were Worcester's Men and the Earl of Worcester was a member of the Council. At any rate, in 1598 the Boar's Head stopped being a tavern and Woodliffe and Samwell put a stage in the fifty-five feet square innyard, with a two-storey gallery facing the stage, single storey galleries on either side and a tiring-house at the back. Unusually, however, it seems that they sited the stage away from the tiring-house and had it freestanding in the yard, with spectators on all four sides and actors having to push through them to get to it. But this configuration did not last long. The following year, the stage was extended back to the tiring-house, a roof was added over it and the galleries were enlarged, though the capacity remained lower than at the other playhouses. The stage itself was now only a little smaller than the Fortune's, and it had two doors at the back as well as a balcony. At the back of the auditorium was the first indoor toilet at any theatre.

But trouble was almost inevitable when Woodliffe sold the site to Francis Langley, who already had the failing Swan Theatre in his portfolio. No sooner was the new theatre opened, than Langley tried to capture it by main force. Four times before the end of the year he and a gang of supporters armed with cudgels, billhooks and even daggers and swords, attacked the place, and four times they were repulsed. Soon the controversy had found its way into the courts. Meanwhile Oxford's Men appeared at the theatre briefly and in 1602, at last Worcester's Men took over. Their leader, Robert Browne, had by now superseded Samwell as business manager, but both he and Woodliffe died of the plague in 1603, leaving their suit against Langley hanging. Worcester's Men, now Queen Anne's Men, soldiered on here for a year or two, but then transferred to the bigger and more congenial Red Bull, and the Boar's Head faded away as a theatre.

THE HOPE THEATRE

The other short-lived theatre was the Hope which opened in the spring of 1614 on the Bankside on the site of the old Bear Garden. This seems to have been the brainchild of Henslowe, Jacob Meade and perhaps Edward Alleyn, intended perhaps to replace both the demolished Rose Theatre and the old Bear Garden. Modelled to some extent on the Swan Theatre, the Hope had a brick foundation and a diameter of ninety-nine feet. There were no pillars on the stage, and the roof was cantilevered to allow the trestle stage to be removed for bear-baiting. There were three galleries round the yard, with separate rooms for the better-off patrons, and a tiring house with a tile roof. The fact that it was supposed to produce both plays and animal sports seems however to have been misjudged. Though plays were staged on three out of every four days, the two forms of entertainment did not cohabit easily, and the players were bitter in their criticism of everything from the stink of bears to the management's priorities. Two companies, first Lady Elizabeth's Men and then Prince Charles's Men, tried to make the arrangement work, but both failed and by 1620 theatre production here was virtually over. By the 1630s, even the name seems to have reverted to Bear Garden.

THEATRES OUTSIDE LONDON

The seventeenth century also saw the tentative beginnings of theatrical performances in purpose-built buildings outside London. The records are scanty, or not much researched, but Bristol, for instance, may have had two playhouses in the first half of the century, one in Wine Street operating from the very end of Elizabeth's reign until about 1625, and the other on Redcliffe Hill which may have continued into the 1630s. The Wine Street playhouse was probably built and owned by Nicholas Wolfe, though the business was managed by Richard Cooke, who leased it from him in 1604. Wolfe took a share of the Box Office receipts and also let rooms to touring actors. He died in 1614, but the theatre business had been lucrative enough for him to leave specific bequests in his will from the playhouse profits. The playhouse continued to make payments to Bristol Corporation until about 1630, though the theatre may actually have closed five years before that. Even less information about the Redcliffe Hill playhouse has been found. It may have been operating before 1614 when its builder, one Barker, died, according to his widow Sarah, whose 1637 will refers to it as the 'playhouse' which 'my late husband built'.

Wolfe's Wine Street playhouse was almost certainly a venue for touring companies, for whom it no doubt made a welcome relief from guildhalls, market squares and inconvenient stately homes. Bristol Corporation was not a welcoming authority, and Wolfe may have provided an agreeable alternative to their halls. But his theatre may also have provided a stage for a children's company which was based in the city for some years from about 1615 under the direction of John Daniel, brother of the poet and playwright, Samuel Daniel, and later Martin Slater, formerly of the Admiral's Men in London.

Probably earlier than these, and perhaps flourishing at the end of Elizabeth's reign, was a small playhouse in Prescot in Lancashire. Established by Richard Harrington, it was still operating when he died in 1603, and may have continued till at least 1609. There is also a record of permission granted for a playhouse in York in September 1609, permission which was then rescinded in December of the same year, which suggests it was never operational if it was ever built.

JACOBEAN AND CAROLINE THEATRE COMPANIES

During the forty years from James I's accession to the closing of the theatres, there were effectively seven companies operating in London, but their changes of name and changes of theatre, their moving to indoor private theatres and then back to outdoor theatres, and the fact that some companies sometimes spent whole years touring the provinces, complicates their story. Outbreaks of the plague, which closed the theatres in 1625, 1630, 1636–7 and 1640, and thereby sometimes ruined companies, further confuses the tale.

The first company, which in the 1590s was known as the Admiral's Men, became Prince Henry's Men in 1603, and when Prince Henry died in 1612 they became Lord Palsgrave's Men. Lord Palsgrave, the Count Palatine of the Rhine, was the husband of James's daughter Elizabeth. They performed at the Fortune until 1625 when they disbanded.

Table 2.1

Jacobean theatres and theatre companies

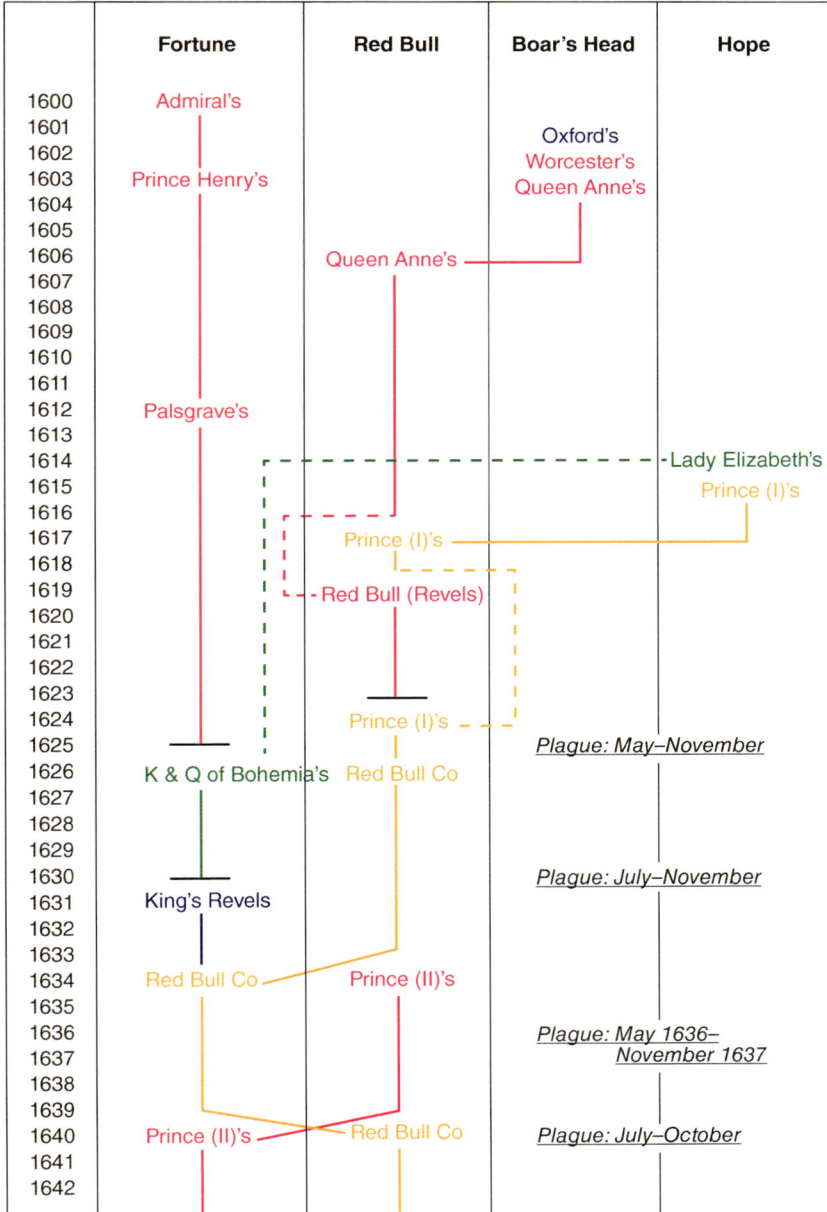

The second company began life as Worcester's Men and became Queen Anne's Men in 1603. When she died in 1619 they took the name Red Bull (Revels) Company, but did not last long, disappearing in 1623. They performed at the Boar's Head but mostly at the Red Bull. Lady Elizabeth's Men had a chequered existence, based mostly at the Hope and the Fortune, and, after the demise of Palsgrave's Men, they became known as the King and Queen of Bohemia's Men. Prince Charles's Men, whose patron became King Charles I, existed before Prince Henry died, but only after that did they became a significant company. They metamorphosed into the Red Bull Company after Charles ascended the throne and became the King's Men's patron; they performed at various times at the Hope, the Red Bull and the Fortune.

The only other companies of note were formed in the 1630s: the Prince's Men whose patron was the future King Charles II and who used both the Fortune and the Red Bull at different times; and the King's Revels Company who were at the Fortune for a while. The accompanying diagram attempts to unravel the companies and their various tenancies, but needs to be read with caution: not all companies existed continuously through their apparent careers; some spent years touring without a London base; and any company might move for a time to one of the indoor theatres, the Cockpit or the Salisbury Court.

What had been the Admiral's Men and became first Prince Henry's Men and then Lord Palsgrave's, was a remarkably stable company, based at the Fortune Theatre. In 1616 its leading members were Thomas Downton, Edward Jubey, William Bird, Sam Rowley, Charles Massey and Humphrey Jeffes, all of whom had been with the company for twenty years, supported by Frank Grace, William Cartwright, Edward Colebrander, William Parry and William Stratford. Most of these were still there in 1624 just before the company disbanded, with the addition of Richard Fowler and Andrew Cane. But they were also conservative. Unlike the King's Men, they never showed an interest in developing a second indoor theatre, and they became increasingly old fashioned, which is not to say their artistic standards slipped. But it seems they never completely recovered from the fire at their theatre in 1621 and when the plague struck in 1625 and forced the theatres to shut, the company collapsed.

The company mostly associated with the Red Bull also collapsed in the 1620s. They were Worcester's Men, a company existing since at least the 1580s. They may have amalgamated with Oxford's Men in 1602 when they were licensed as the third London company based at the Boar's Head. They included some important names: Will Kemp, John Duke, Christopher Beeston, Robert Pallant from the Admiral's Men, John Lowin, later a leading actor with the King's Men, Richard Perkins and Thomas Heywood, better known as a playwright. Kemp died in 1603 and was replaced by Thomas Greene, a forceful character as well as a clown. Greene gradually became the *de facto* leader of the company, and his name appears first in the list of those granted a licence to perform in 1609, along with Beeston, Heywood, Perkins, Pallant, Duke, Thomas Swinnerton, Robert Lees, James Hault and Robert Beeston.

THOMAS GREENE

Thomas Greene was born in 1573 and acquired a leading share in the Boar's Head when he married Robert Browne's widow in 1604. He collected such stakes in theatrical property. He owned some part in the Curtain Theatre as well as half the tiring-house and yard at the Red Bull. He was also a highly acclaimed comic actor, probably best known for his part in John Cooke's *Greene's Tu Quoque* (1611) (meaning 'same to you!'). Here he wore a modified Harlequin costume and, as a servant like Harlequin, he changed places with his master and caused delicious mayhem. At one point his character, Bubble, and his friends decide to go to the theatre:

SCATT: Let's go see a play at the Globe.

BUBBLE: I care not; any whither, so the clown have a part; for i'faith I am nobody without a fool.

GERALDINE: Then we'll go to the Red Bull; they say Greene's a good clown.

BUBBLE: Greene? Greene's an ass!

SCATT: Wherefore do you say so?

BUBBLE: Indeed I have no reason: for they say he is as like me as ever he can look.

As leader of the troupe, it seems his financial dealings were not perhaps as honest as they might have been, but he died in 1612. His widow tried to obtain her inherited rights in the company, but without much success, despite litigation which dragged on for years.

CHRISTOPHER BEESTON

Meanwhile, Christopher Beeston gradually assumed managerial control of the company, and it must be added that his financial dealings, too, seem to have been less than above board. His aim seems to have been to combine the open air, public playhouse business with a private theatre, as the King's Men did, and he soon acquired the royal cockpit which he was to turn into just such an indoor theatre. The plan turned out to be more fraught than he imagined. When he brought Queen Anne's company to the newly finished Cockpit in 1617, there was a riot, considerable damage was caused and lives were lost. But Beeston, with whom Edward Alleyn was now also connected, persisted in placing Queen Anne's Men at the Cockpit, and brought in the Prince's Men to fill the gap at the Red Bull. The arrangement was perhaps not very satisfactory, Queen Anne's Men being more used to the open air democratic theatre, and when Queen Anne herself died two years later, he took the opportunity for a further reshuffle and returned that company, or what was left of it, to the Red Bull and brought the Prince's Men to the Cockpit. But Queen Anne's Men, now the Red Bull (Revels) Company, did not last long and disbanded around 1624.

LADY ELIZABETH'S MEN

Lady Elizabeth's Men, who opened the Hope in 1614 and had a company of eighteen in 1618, were nevertheless out of sight for much of the time till the mid-1620s, when they surfaced at the Fortune after Palsgrave's Men had foundered. They were now known as the King and Queen of Bohemia's Men, the King having previously been Lord Palsgrave and the Queen Lady Elizabeth. Elizabeth was the sister of the future Charles I, whose company became the Red Bull Company when he acceded to the throne. This company confusingly moved to the Fortune in 1634, so that now the Red Bull Company was at the Fortune, while Prince (Charles II)'s Men were at the Red Bull. However, they changed places in 1640 when, the Red Bull actors claimed, they were forced out of the Fortune. This happened perhaps because of their production in 1639 of *The Cardinal's Conspiracy*, which satirised the bishops and church ritual. It led to the arrest of several of the actors. The company was also reprimanded for mocking the London aldermen and proctors.

POPULAR PLAYS IN THE JACOBEAN AND CAROLINE OPEN AIR THEATRES

For most playgoers the theatre, not the company, was probably the chief attraction. The huge Red Bull asked for a certain sort of play, and a certain sort of acting, no matter which company happened to be in residence. Thus it is perhaps significant that we do not know which company premiered the anonymous *Nero* in 1624: it could presumably have been created by any of the companies who would have given full rein to the actor playing Nero – a marvellous portrait of a manic, paranoid, cowardly, narcissistic, spoiled brat of an emperor. All the companies had large repertoires of such spectacular epic-style plays, whose strength lay in their ability to make an effect in an instant, their potential for moment-by-moment intensity.

The Fortune continued to rely on Marlowe's drawing power almost to the 1640s, but after Alleyn retired the repertoire undoubtedly became more 'popular' as playwrights seeking inspiration reputedly visited local taverns to hear not only the latest vernacular but also the most up-to-date gossip and most exciting tall stories for their plays, An underestimated writer whose works were performed here for years was William Haughton, whose *Englishmen for My Money* (1598) is an excellent 'citizen comedy' while *Grim the Collier of Croydon* (1600) is a farce featuring a picturesque devil. Middleton, too, had several plays performed at the Fortune, and showed that popular appeal does not have to mean a loss of radicalism. His *No Wit/Help Like a Woman's* (1611) uses a ballad-like story to question gender roles and women's economic exclusion, while his much-liked *The Roaring Girl*, written with Thomas Dekker, is fast-moving, dynamic and blowsy, like its heroine, Moll Frith, a real-life cross-dressing woman, charismatic, dangerous and a natural enemy of propriety and Puritanism.

The plays associated with the Red Bull were usually more extreme than these, in the sense that they were much more likely to indulge in swordplay and battles, high adventure, low comedy and all manner of spectacle. *Swetnam the Woman-Hater Arraigned by Women* (1618) was a comedy which climaxed when Swetnam was bound to a post by the women who pricked him with pins. *Two Merry Milkmaids* (1619) included a conjuror, a devil and a clown, while *The Late Murder in Whitechapel, or Keep the Widow Waking* (1624) by Dekker, Webster, Ford and Rowley dramatised a recent terrifying murder in Whitechapel, as well as an unappetising incident involving an attempt to rob an old woman by tricking her into marriage – a scandalous episode in which Dekker himself may have been implicated. The title derived from a topical ballad:

> And you who fain would hear the full
> Discourse of this matchmaking,
> The play will teach you at the Red Bull
> To keep the widow waking.[3]

The best-known failure at the Red Bull was John Webster's *The White Devil* (1612), usually regarded as one of the age's finest tragedies but a dismal failure when presented here. According to Webster this was partly because 'it was acted in so dull a time of winter', but also because it was 'presented in so open and black a theatre', where the audience 'resemble those ignorant asses who visiting stationers' shops (do not) inquire for good books, but new books'.[4]

THOMAS HEYWOOD

The most successful Red Bull author was Thomas Heywood, a long-lived actor-turned-jobbing-playwright, collaborator, reviser and pamphleteer. Easy-going and friendly, Heywood remained on close and sociable terms with such 'difficult' characters as his bosses, Thomas Greene and Christopher Beeston. His *Apologie for Actors* (1612) is really a sensible defence of the morality of theatre, and he claimed to have had a hand in at least two hundred and twenty plays. His best was probably *A Woman Killed with Kindness* (1603), a real tear-jerker, but other plays were also noteworthy. *The Wise Woman of Hogsdon*, for instance, includes wizardry, gender-shifting comedy and a neat denouement. This wise woman may be a fraud, but she stage manages the enormously complicated happy ending with brilliant aplomb. *The Rape of Lucrece* (1607) may be the closest Heywood ever came to subversion: it was watched privately by Queen Anne and Prince Henry without King James being present. *The Fair Maid of the West* (1610) is probably the most typical Red Bull play of these, with fencing bouts and derring-do on the high seas.

Heywood was too prodigal of his talents, and too busy a writer, to confine his efforts to one theatre. He supplied the two parts of *If You Know Not Me You Know Nobody* (1604, 1605) to the Boar's Head, as well perhaps as *The Fair Maid of the Exchange* (1602). Other Boar's Head plays were Dekker and Webster's *The Famous History of Sir Thomas Wyat* (1604) and the anonymous *Nobody and Somebody* (1605). Beside this list, the Hope's solitary recorded premiere, Ben Jonson's *Bartholomew Fair* (1614), seems paltry, but the theatre lasted for a very short time.

These theatres, however, did keep alive the spirit of the Elizabethan theatre until 1642, when they were 'temporarily' closed.

NOTES

1 'I.H.', This World's Folly, 1615, in Edmund K. Chambers, *The Elizabethan Stage*, Oxford: Clarendon Press, 1923, IV, p. 254.
2 Charles Read Baskervill, *The Elizabethan Jig and Related Song Drama*, New York: Dover Publications, 1965, p. 116.
3 Charles J. Sisson, 'Keep the Widow Waking: A Lost Play by Dekker', *The Library*, 1927–8, pp. 238–240.
4 John Webster, 'To the Reader', in *The White Devil*, 1612.

Chapter 26: Popular audiences in the open air theatres

Generalisations about audience responses to plays are neither sensible nor possible. Audiences are composed of individuals, and each individual has unique prejudices, desires and interests. But it is possible to open a discussion of the popular audience in the open air theatres by taking note that this was a theatre of conventions. Implicitly, actors and audience accepted these conventions. Without that agreement, the theatre practice would have broken down.

PLAYS ARE CITATIONAL

Playgoing was citational. Any new play was apprehended because of other plays that had been given here. Each single play spoke to all the other plays which had been on this (or any other) stage: the Good and Bad Angels in Marlowe's *Dr Faustus* referred to medieval dramas; Vindice, the revenger looking on the skull, referred to Hamlet, another revenger who looked at a skull. Hamlet referred to *The Spanish Tragedy's* Hieronimo. And so on. The spectator's previous experience of playgoing gave access to the whole theatre experience from where to stand in the yard to how to control the tears – or let them flow – at the climax of the play.

The lack of scenery on this stage did not mean the spectator would not need to suspend disbelief. And if the actor came to the edge of the stage and spoke confidentially, the spectator immediately understood the import of the action. Each single play conformed to or disrupted these understandings, and in doing so provoked in each single spectator their particular response.

'LEVELS' OF PERFORMANCE

It is especially true of popular audiences that they are awake to a performance on several levels. They follow the story; they empathise or disdain the character as a character; they appreciate the skill of the actor; and they are aware of the theatre building, their fellow spectators, the 'real' context of the experience. For example, in Act Five of *Macbeth*, the spectator sees the invasion of Scotland proceeding; feels a certain sympathy creeping in for the murderer-hero; notices the actor playing Macbeth using new gestures and tones of voice; and feels the atmosphere in the auditorium tightening. But this theatre's special distinction is that all this happens without any recourse to illusionism. This combination of multiple levels of consciousness and the simultaneous lack of illusion, seems to be what especially liberates the imagination, and encourages fantasy and speculation.

'Let us', says the Chorus in *Henry V* 'on your imaginary forces work', and Dekker echoes this in *Old Fortunatus* (1599), 'Your quick imaginations we must charm'.

THE POPULARITY OF PLAYGOING

The suggestion is that this happens especially powerfully with a popular audience, 'folk making merry together', as Platter described theatre spectators in 1599, implying that they were both enjoying themselves communally and that they were engaged at an individual level with the entertainment. The two, communal enjoyment and individual engagement, are merged in the theatre. It has been estimated that at least fifteen thousand people visited the theatre each week in the late Elizabethan period and that this number may have risen to twenty-five thousand by the mid-1620s. The theatre was open to anyone, and the price of entry low enough to make it available to almost anyone. So, one commentator noted in 1602 that in the theatre audience were not only 'gentlemen, and serving-men, but lawyers, clerks, countrymen that had law cases, aye, the Queen's men, knights, and as it was credibly reported, one earl', and Sir John Davies, in an epigram, recorded:

> For as we see at all the playhouse doors,
> When ended is the play, the dance and song,
> A thousand townsmen, gentlemen and whores,
> Porters and serving-men together throng.[1]

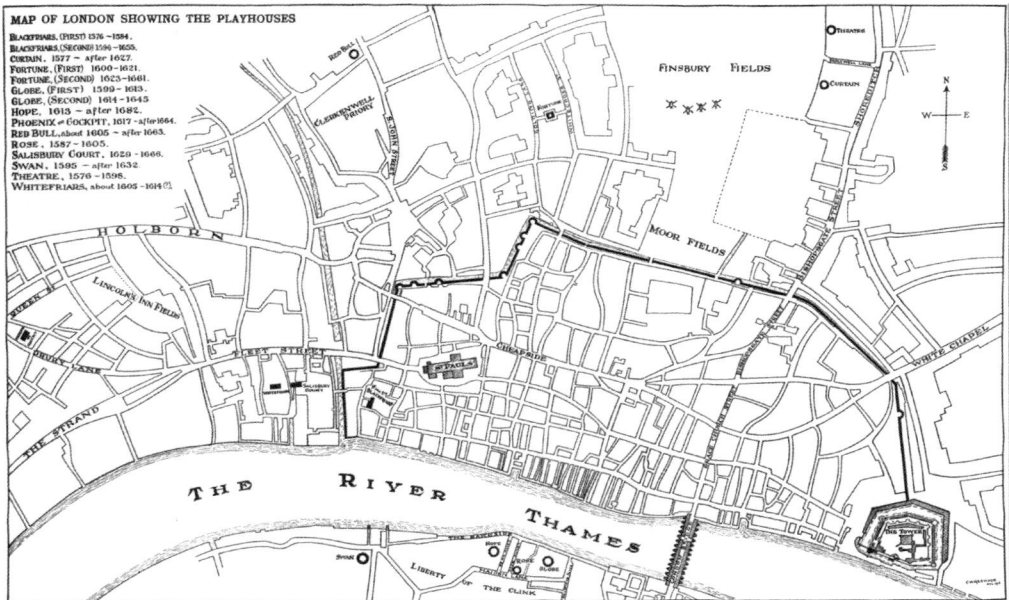

Figure 2.28
Map of London showing the playhouses from 1576 to the Restoration period

And *A Game at Chess* at the Globe was attended by an 'extraordinary concourse', including 'all sorts of people, rich and poor, masters and servants, papists and puritans, wise men, churchmen and statesmen'. John Fletcher seems to have spoken for many when he asserted that the theatre offered good value for money:

> We have your money, and you have our ware,
> And, to our understanding, good and fair,

he wrote in the Epilogue to *Valentinian* (1614), and:

> The price is easy, and so light the play,
> That ye may new-digest it every day.

THE DEMOCRATIC THEATRE

The fact that anyone could (and did) come inevitably meant a levelling of class and other social distinctions so that the theatre provided a genuinely democratic forum. This was true even after allowance is made for the distinctions the theatre did make, like the existence of 'gentlemen's rooms' and the fact that a certain kind of gallant-about-town liked to sit on the stage and preen himself there. And the effect was extraordinary, and perhaps as fascinating to the actors on the stage as the stage action was to the spectators in the yard and the galleries. Middleton or Dekker described the overall effect of the audience from the actors' point of view in *The Roaring Girl*:

> Stories of men and women, mixed together
> Fair ones with foul, like sunshine in wet weather;
> Within one square a thousand heads are laid
> So close that all of heads the room seems made;
> As many faces there, filled with blithe looks,
> Show like the promising titles of new books
> Writ merrily, the readers being their own eyes,
> Which seem to move and give plaudities;
> And here and there, whilst with obsequious ears
> Thronged heaps do listen, a cutpurse thrusts and leers
> With hawk's eyes for his prey: I need not show him,
> By a hanging villainous look yourselves may know him,
> The face is drawn so rarely. Then, sir, below,
> The very floor, as 'twere, waves to and fro,
> And like a floating island seems to move,
> Upon a sea bound in with shores above.

This description also suggests vividly how the audience was an active part of the performance. In a sense they 'own' the performance. This idea is reinforced by what happened in the Cockpit riots of 1617. It seems that the 'popular' audience, or at least the younger part of it, was so infuriated by the 'theft' of 'their' plays from the Red Bull by the indoor, expensive Cockpit Theatre that they came almost as an avenging army to take them back. That the audience *engaged* with the play, virtually participated in its making, is clear also from Jonson's faintly disdainful description in *The Case Is Altered*:

> The sport is at a new play, to observe the sway and variety of opinion that passeth it. A man shall have such a confused mixture of judgment, poured out in the throng there, as ridiculous as laughter itself. One says he likes not the writing, another likes not the plot, another not the playing; and sometimes a fellow, that comes not there not once in five years, . . . will be as deep mired in censuring as the best, and swear by god's foot he would never stir his foot such as that is.

Dekker's attitude seems to be similar to Jonson's:

> Your stinkard has the self-same liberty to be there in his tobacco fumes, which your sweet courtier hath; . . . your carman and tinker claim as strong a voice in their suffrage, and sit to give judgment on the play's life and death, as well as the proudest Momus among the tribe of Critic.[2]

Dekker is also capable, however, of noticing the 'rare silence' among the spectators at a telling passage in a play, after which they will 'clap their brawny hands'. It may be significant that when the Globe burned down in 1613, at first the audience paid no attention because 'their eyes (were) more attentive to the show', as Sir Henry Wotton reported.

AUDIENCE BEHAVIOUR

But part of the experience of playgoing was what else went on in the auditorium during the performance, which of course ran without an interval. Food and drink were sold and consumed, people came dressed in their best finery, sometimes chatted to their neighbours, kept a watch for pickpockets and perhaps avoided (or perhaps made assignations with) the prostitutes at work there. The impression given by all the accounts taken together, even granted that many are written by commentators hostile to the stage, is of a busy, energetic, engaged crowd, mostly good humoured, whether throwing an apple at the stage, munching nuts, seeking out sexual gratification or watching the exciting action being performed by the actors.

The gallants liked to sit on the stage in full view of the audience, as Fitzdotterel intends to do in *The Devil Is an Ass*. But this was not always a good idea: in 1622, Richard Baxter of the Red Bull (Revels) company accidentally slashed a young man seated on a stage stool with his sword during a performance. As for the pickpockets, one ballad tells how

> Most of my money being spent,
> To St John Street to the Red Bull I went,
> Where I the roaring rhymer saw,
> And to my face was made a daw;
> And pressing forth among the folk,
> I lost my purse, my hat and cloak.[3]

WOMEN AND THE OPEN AIR PLAYHOUSES

The theatre yard and galleries were also an arena where women had a freedom and legitimacy often denied them elsewhere. Some were simply fans, as those Sue Turnup describes in Field's *Amends for Ladies*: 'She swears all the gentlewomen went to see a play at the Fortune, and they are not come in yet, and she believes they sup with the players'. Other women found naughtier amusements, as the woman reported by Henry Peachum, who returned from the theatre and told her husband she had lost her purse. When he asked where she had kept it before it was stolen, she told him she had concealed it 'under my petticoat'. He could hardly believe her. 'Did you feel nobody's hand there?' he asked. ' "Yes", quoth she, "I felt one's hand there; but I did not think he'd come for that" '.[4]

Moll Frith, the cross-dressing model for Dekker and Middleton's 'roaring girl', was a popular figure in the audience often at the Fortune. She dabbled in various shady businesses, was known as a fence and even a highwaywoman: she reputedly robbed General Fairfax on Hounslow Heath. She was always a centre of attention in the Fortune audience, flaunting her fancy male clothes and ribbing her neighbours. However, it should be added that at least one modern critic has questioned Moll's exceptional status as 'player, cutpurse and roaring girl', and depicted her rather as 'a worker within the networks of commerce surrounding early modern London's public theatres'.[5] Of course this view begs the question: why in that case did Dekker and Middleton feel she was exceptional enough to make her the centre of their comedy?

AUDIENCE-ACTOR RELATIONSHIP

The success of the open air theatres depended to a significant extent on the ability of the audience to participate in the creation of the event. Meaningful elements in the performance which contributed to the relationship included the daylight, the fact that audience and players were all equally visible to one another, creating a democratic feel to proceedings which few theatres before or since have achieved; and the lack of illusion, which is not the same as the suspension of disbelief. It meant that the actor performed for the audience, he never attempted to keep what he was doing behind the footlights. There were no footlights: that is the point. And the relationship often involved the actor taking the audience into his confidence, something that could never happen in a proscenium arch theatre. Shakespeare's Richard III is a prime example of a character who confides in, argues with, teases the audience. Chapman's Blind Beggar, Irus, is another:

> I am Cleanthes and blind Irus too,
> And more than these, as you shall soon perceive.

Throughout the play he boasts to the spectators, almost daring them to give away his plots and machinations. The same impulse of confiding in the audience, making them confederate with the action, is seen in a different key, this time thoroughly domestic, in Heywood's *A Woman Killed with Kindness* when Jenkin the servant says: 'You may see, my masters, though it be afternoon with you, 'tis but early days with us'. And because of this relationship, it must have seemed only sensible for the actors to ask the audience at the end of the play what they would like to see the following day – even if they did not always receive the answer they desired. The old plays were liked the best: even in the 1630s, figures like Marlowe's ranting heroes were what they enjoyed most, no matter whether the players were bored with them. And then handbills were rapidly got up and nailed on posts across the town ('posters') to proclaim what would be presented the next afternoon.

But what happened when the audience threw aside convention, and used their powers to too great an effect? This account is by Edmund Gayton, admittedly an opponent of the theatre, and written in 1654, when the theatres had been closed officially for over a decade. Nevertheless, even if it is only a nightmare (and it is surely more than that), it points clearly to the difficulty of maintaining the balance between audience involvement and an audience out of control:

> Men come not to study at a playhouse, but love such expressions and passages which with ease insinuate themselves into their capacities . . . to them bring Jack Drum's Entertainment, Greene's Tu Quoque, The Devil of Edmonton, and the like; or if it be on holy days, when sailors, watermen, shoemakers, butchers and apprentices are at leisure, then it is good policy to amaze those violent spirits with some tearing tragedy full of fights and skirmishes, as the Guelphs and Gibbelines, Greeks and Trojans, or the three London Apprentices, which commonly ends in six acts, the spectators frequently mounting the stage, and making a more bloody catastrophe amongst themselves, than the players did. I have known upon one of these festivals, but especially at Shrovetide, where the players have been appointed, notwithstanding their bills to the contrary, to act what the major part of the company had a mind to: sometimes Tamburlaine, sometimes Jugurth (a tragedy by William Boyd, first performed by the Admiral's Men in1600), sometimes The Jew of Malta, and sometimes parts of all these, and at last, none of the three taking, they were forced to undress and put off their tragic habits, and conclude the day with The Merry Milkmaids. And unless this were done, and the popular humour satisfied, as sometimes it so fortuned that the players were refractory, the benches, the tiles, the laths, the stones, oranges, apples, nuts flew about most liberally, and as there were mechanics of all professions, who fell everyone to his own trade, and dissolved a house in an instant, and made a ruin of a stately fabric. It was not then the most mimical or fighting man, Fowler nor Andrew Cane, could pacify; Prologues and Epilogues would prevail; the devil and the fool were quite out of favour. Nothing but noise and tumult fills the house, until a cog take 'em, and then to the bawdy houses, and reform them; and instantly to the Bankside, where the poor bears must conclude the riot, and fight twenty dogs at a time beside the butchers, which sometimes fell into the service; this performed, and The Horse and Jack-an-Apes for a jig, they had sport enough that day for nothing.[6]

NOTES

1 Sir John Davies, *Epigram XVII*, c.1595.
2 Thomas Dekker, *Gull's Hornbook*, 1609.
3 Glynne Wickham, Herbert Berry, William Ingram, *English Professional Theatre*, Cambridge: Cambridge University Press, 2000, p. 570.
4 Henry Peachum, *Thalia's Banquet Furnished with an Hundred and Odde Dishes of Newly Devised Epigrammes*, 1620.
5 Pamela Allen Brown and Peter Parolin (eds), *Women Players in England: Beyond the All-Male Stage*, Aldershot: Ashgate, 2005, p. 71.
6 Edmund Gayton, *Pleasant Notes Upon Don Quichote*, 1654.

Select bibliography

Astington, John H., *Actors and Acting in Shakespeare's Time*, Cambridge: Cambridge University Press, 2010

Berry, Herbert, *The Boar's Head Playhouse*, London: Associated University Press, 1986

Berry, Herbert (ed), *The First Public Playhouse: The Theatre in Shoreditch, 1576–1598*, Montreal: McGill-Queen's University Press, 1979

Brown, Pamela Allen, and Parolin, Peter (eds), *Women Players in England 1500–1660*, Aldershot: Ashgate Publishing, 2005

Eccles, Christine, *The Rose Theatre*, London: National Housing Bank, 1990

Griffith, Eva, *A Jacobean Company and Its Playhouse: The Queen's Servants at the Red Bull Theatre (c.1605–1619)*, Cambridge: Cambridge University Press, 2013

Gurr, Andrew, *Shakespeare's Opposites: The Admiral's Company, 1594–1625*, Cambridge: Cambridge University Press, 2009

Gurr, Andrew, *The Shakespeare Playing Companies*, Oxford: Oxford University Press, 1996

Hunter, G.K., *English Drama 1586–1642: The Age of Shakespeare*, Oxford: Clarendon Press,1997

Karin-Cooper, Farah, and Stern, Tiffany (eds), *Shakespeare's Theatres and the Effects of Performance*, London: Bloomsbury, 2013

Keenan, Siobhan, *Acting Companies and Their Plays in Shakespeare's London*, London: Bloomsbury, 2014

Keenan, Siobhan, *Travelling Players in Shakespeare's England*, Basingstoke: Palgrave Macmillan, 2002

Leggatt, Alexander, *Jacobean Public Theatre*, London: Routledge, 1992

Milling, Jane, and Thomson, Peter (eds), *The Cambridge History of British Theatre*, vol 1, Cambridge: Cambridge University Press, 2004

Schoone-Jongen, Terence G., *Shakespeare's Companies: William Shakespeare's Early Career and the Acting Companies, 1577–1594*, Farnham: Ashgate, 2006

Shapiro, James, *1599: A Year in the Life of William Shakespeare*, London: Faber and Faber, 2005

Shaughnessy, Robert, *The Routledge Guide to Shakespeare*, London: Routledge, 2011

Wells, Stanley, *Shakespeare and Co*, London: Penguin, 2006

Wickham, Glynne, Berry, Herbert, and Ingram, William (eds), *English Professional Theatre, 1530–1660*, Cambridge: Cambridge University Press, 2000

Interlude: The boy companies of St Paul's and the Chapel Royal

A curious anomaly on the Elizabethan and Jacobean theatrical scene was the existence of two apparently professional companies of boy players. Known now for little more than some acid remarks about them in Shakespeare's *Hamlet*, they grew from the grammar schools and choir schools of the previous century, where an important part of the curriculum concerned rhetoric and public speaking, besides, for the choirboys, training their singing voices. The boys were invited to practise in public, at great houses and even at court. Though these were essentially academic exercises, they grew into full-scale productions of some of the more significant plays of the period: the Chapel Royal boys publicly presented Cornwall's *Troilus and Pandar* in 1516, Rastell's *Love and Riches* in 1527 and Edwards's *Damon and Pythias* in 1564, and the St Paul's boys had a similar record: they presented Heywood's *Play of the Weather* around 1530, Redford's *Wit and Science* ten years later and *Patient Grissell* in about 1560.

ST PAUL'S CATHEDRAL CHOIR SCHOOL

In 1575, Sebastian Westcott, Master of St Paul's Cathedral choir school, adapted a hall in the St Paul's precinct (that is, beyond the jurisdiction of the Lord Mayor of London) by erecting a platform in front of the screen. Rows of benches or chairs were set facing the platform. He thus created an intimate performing space for seventy or eighty spectators.

THE CHAPEL ROYAL BOYS

Westcott was perhaps following the example of the Chapel Royal, where the Master, William Hunnis, had occasionally presented plays to public audiences. In 1576, Richard Farrant, Master of the Children at Windsor Chapel since 1564, joined his boys with Hunnis's, and leased the Old Buttery in the former priory of Blackfriars, which was also beyond the Lord Mayor's reach and which he now turned into a theatre. The Buttery was forty-six feet wide and sixty-six feet long, with a paved floor, and here Farrant installed a twenty-six feet wide raised platform stage in an attempt to replicate the conditions of a court performance. Then, using children of the two chapels, he 'rehearsed' the plays he hoped would be chosen for performance before the Queen, before a paying audience. The boys ranged in age from eight to sixteen, and their biggest success was probably George Peele's earliest play, *The Arraignment of Paris* (1581).

OXFORD'S BOYS

But in 1580 Farrant died, and William Hunnis resumed control of the troupe. He co-opted Henry Evans and John Lyly to try to keep the play productions going. But meanwhile, in 1582 Sebastian Westcott also died. Had it not been for the ambition of Edward de Vere, Earl of Oxford, the idea of boys performing publicly and professionally might have died, too. But Oxford was desperate to ingratiate himself with the Queen, and performances by boys under his auspices might be the way to do it. He had already appointed as his secretary John Lyly, who since the publication of his novel, *Euphues: The Anatomy of Wit* had been recognised as a most significant author, and now he thought the boys could present plays by Lyly for his (Oxford's) greater glory. The boys of St Paul's and the Chapel Royal were brought together at Blackfriars under Lyly and Evans's management in 1583, and their public performances resumed. They were known as 'Oxford's Boys', and probably gave both Lyly's *Campaspe* (1584) and his *Sappho and Phao* (1584) during this time. But for Sir William More, landlord of Blackfriars, this was not acceptable, and at Easter 1584 he called in the lease. The project collapsed. The Chapel Royal choristers left the company, and Lyly and the St Paul's boys returned to Westcott's tiny theatre.

JOHN LYLY

Here for the next six years they continued to perform publicly. Lyly was joined in the management of the company by the master of St Paul's, Thomas Giles. They charged fourpence or sixpence entry, and their project was successful enough for repeated invitations to appear at court through the 1580s and for Giles as royal choirmaster to be given enhanced powers to 'impress' boys into the Queen's service – effectively to kidnap them and make them members of his troupe. The tiny theatre, lit by mutton fat candles and oil in cressets, must have had an unworldly, perhaps erotic, atmosphere most unlike the raucous life of the open air theatres. And their plays showed this. Marlowe's *Dido, Queen of Carthage*, for instance, presented about 1587, shows Cupid dandling on Dido's knee in an inevitably homoerotic sequence.

But it was Lyly's plays which formed the backbone of the Paul's boys' repertoire. Fanciful, playful and extravagant, his pastoral idealises the past and the countryside in order to expose the hollowness of the present and the urban, as well as to dramatise the conflict between desire and chastity. The balanced cadences of Lyly's Euphuistic prose was adapted for the stage, as in *Galatea* (1585):

CUPID: What is Diana, a goddess? What her nymphs, virgins? What her pastimes, hunting?
NYMPH: A goddess? Who knows it not? Virgins? Who thinks it not? Hunting? Who loves it not?

Lyly presented comedy for the educated, who could hug themselves when they saw, in *Campaspe*, Alexander the Great meeting Plato and Aristotle or Diogenes in his tub. But the erudition was tempered by an ongoing engagement with the popular, as in the *commedia dell' arte*-style resourceful servants and foolish masters in *Mother Bombie* (1589) and the stock types like Sir Tophas, the braggart in *Endymion* (1588). It made for a charming and highly original mix, a rarefied pleasure enhanced by the long speeches which were poetic but not emotionally demanding, the Latin tags and the occasional choric effects.

In 1589 Lyly became embroiled in the Marprelate controversy, and when he involved the boys of St Paul's, support for their public performances collapsed. Lyly withdrew from the theatre and became an MP in the 1590s. He set his sights on the office of Master of the Revels, but in vain, and he died in 1606 a disappointed if not a bitter man.

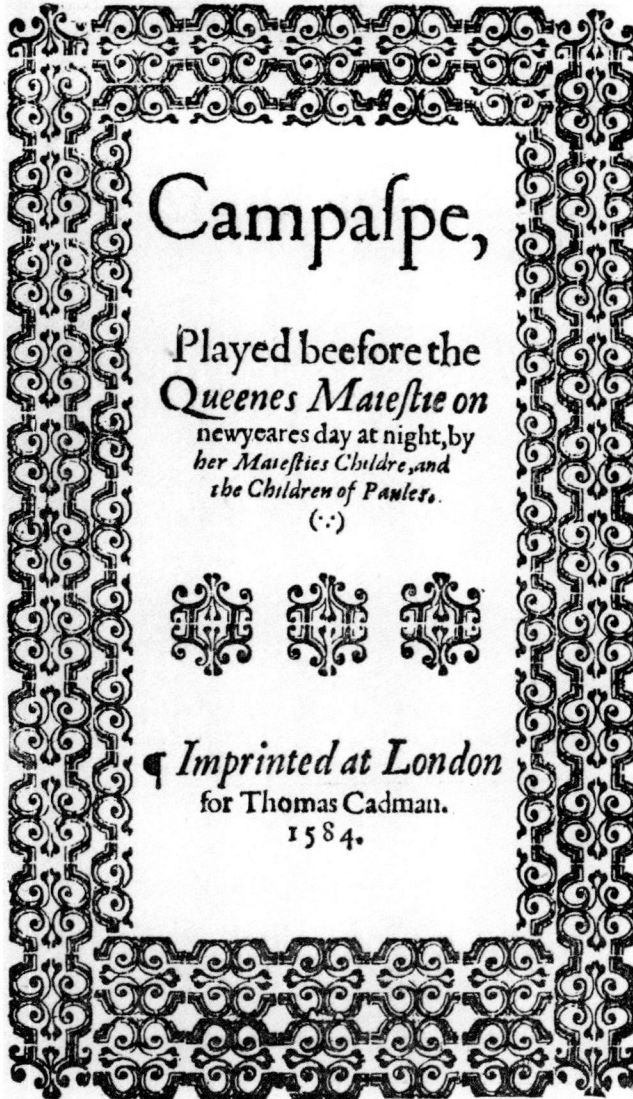

Figure 2.29
Title page of John Lyly's *Campaspe*, 1584

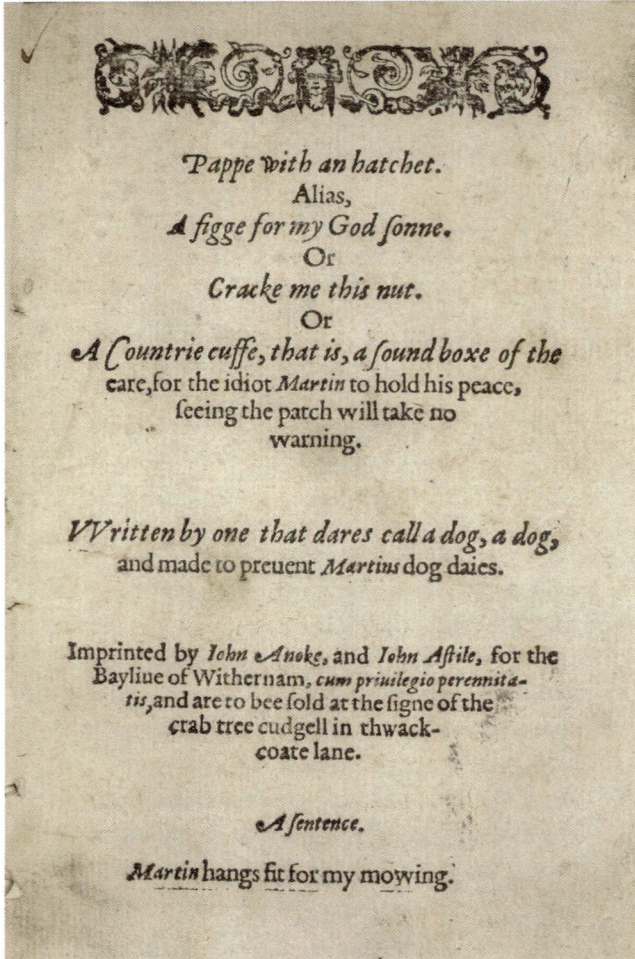

Figure 2.30
John Lyly's *Pappe with an Hatchet, alias a Fig for My Godson, or Crack Me This Nut, or A Country Cuff*, his contribution to the Marprelate controversy, 1589

Source: By permission of the Folger Shakespeare Library

THE BOYS' COMPANIES REVIVED: ST PAUL'S

But both boys' companies were to obtain a second lease of life. In 1599, Thomas Giles retired from St Paul's, and his place was taken by Edward Pearce. The new master immediately prepared to re-open the little theatre and employed John Marston, a satirical poet with dramatic pretensions, to manage it. Performances were held on Sunday and Monday afternoons from four PM to six PM, and the entry charge was initially two pence, though it rose to fourpence and sixpence later. The new venture probably opened with Marston's *Antonio and Mellida* (1599) which begins wittily with the young actors entering '*with parts in their hands*' and discussing who will do what in the play to come:

GALEATZO: Come sirs, come! The music will sound straight for entrance. Are ye ready? Are ye perfect?

PIERO: Faith, we can say our parts; but we are ignorant in what mould we must cast our actors.

ALBERTO: Whom do you personate?

PIERO: Piero, Duke of Venice.

ALBERTO: O, ho; then thus frame your exterior shape

    To haughty form of elate majesty

    As if you held the palsy-shaking head

    Of reeling chance under your fortune's belt

    In strictest vassalage; grow big in thought

    As swoll'n with glory of successful arms.

The passage illustrates with remarkable clarity the *external* approach to acting, not only of this boys' company, but of Elizabethan and Jacobean acting in general.

Marston provided three other plays, his updated version of *Histriomastix* (1599), *Antonio's Revenge* (1600) and *Jack Drum's Entertainment* (1600) before defecting to the newly revived Chapel Royal boys' company. His place at St Paul's was taken by Edward Woodford, who however soon fell out with Pearce. He was succeeded by Edward Kirkham, Yeoman of the Revels, who already had a finger in the Chapel Royal pie, but who seems to have installed Thomas Middleton as the company dramatist. Middleton had already provided Paul's boys with *The Phoenix* (1604), but now he created an extraordinary series of scabrous and bawdy comedies, including *The Puritan Widow* (c.1604), *Michaelmas Term* (c.1605), *A Trick to Catch the Old One* (c.1605), *A Mad World, My Masters* (c.1605) and *Your Five Gallants* (c.1607), a brilliant and *avant-garde* sequence, but not enough to save St Paul's boys. Kirkham soon left, and though Pearce tried to manage the business himself for a while, by 1608 when the plague closed the theatres, he found it impossible to continue.

THE BOYS' COMPANIES REVIVED: CHILDREN OF THE CHAPEL ROYAL

But by then the Children of the Chapel Royal had resurfaced successfully. In 1600 Henry Evans had leased from Richard Burbage that part of the Blackfriars Priory which had been redesigned as a theatre by Burbage's father in the late 1590s. This was the old Parliament Chamber or dining hall, a large space with a stage jutting into the auditorium as in the open air playhouses. It had seating for seven hundred people including side boxes at stage level. At the back of the stage were three doors, a space above for acting and another special room which could be curtained off for musicians. Music was a prominent feature of the performances in the indoor 'private' theatres, and soon some of the best concerts in London were to be heard here. The theatres had to be lit by candles which required trimming at regular intervals: the play's division into 'acts' had more to do with this necessity than with the dramatic structure of the play, and during the intervals, music would be played. Performances took place no more than twice a week, and admission was sixpence or even twice that, a shilling.

Evans was assisted in his enterprise by Edward Kirkham and Nathaniel Giles, master of the children of Windsor Chapel, and no relation of Thomas Giles. By an order of 1597, Giles's permission to impress boys had been strengthened, but in 1601 the father of one impressed boy vigorously contested this. He won his case, and Giles left the company. Interestingly, a 1606 Royal Patent finally outlawed the practice of impressing boys for the purposes of performing.

CHILDREN OF THE QUEEN'S REVELS

Evans himself departed soon after Giles and a series of management reshuffles followed, culminating in the temporary closure of the company following Queen Elizabeth's death and a bad outbreak of plague in 1603. But in 1604 the company resumed under the patronage of the new Queen, Anne of Denmark, and became known as the Children of the Queen's Revels. With Samuel Daniel installed as licensee, the company presented an extraordinarily exciting repertoire, including plays by Ben Jonson, George Chapman and John Marston. They interspersed these with other more daring and iconoclastic plays. Daniel's *Philotas* (1604), for instance, seemed to offer a favourable view of the Essex rebellion of a few years earlier. In 1605 came *Eastward Ho!* by Marston, Jonson and Chapman, which led to the imprisonment of the latter two authors and the resignation of Daniel, who was succeeded by John Gerrard.

Day's 1606 comedy, *The Isle of Gulls* led to more imprisonments, probably including some of the boy actors, for its satire of the Scottish element at James I's court. The Queen's patronage was withdrawn and the company became simply the Children of Blackfriars. Then in 1608 came two more scandalous productions. The first was *The Silver Mine* (1608) by an unknown playwright, poking fun at the king's involvement in a supposed silver mine in Scotland. The second was Chapman's *Tragedy of Byron* (1608) which provoked the French ambassador into complaining to James about the depiction of the French court and – he hinted – at the presentation of James himself as a drunk! The consequences were severe. Marston, who had joined the company in some sort of managerial role in 1604, was imprisoned, though Chapman this time was not. (After his release, Marston left the theatre to become a country clergyman.) All the theatres were shut for several days, the Children of Blackfriars company was dissolved and the King's Men moved into their theatre.

However, several members of the company came together to perform, surprisingly enough, at court during the 1608–9 Christmas season and then went on tour. They reappeared in London that winter under their old title, the Children of the Queen's Revels, even though they were by now mostly young men in their early twenties. Their managers were Robert Keysar and Philip Roseter and they went on to open a new theatre at the old monastery at Whitefriars. The performance space was a long thin hall, ninety feet by seventeen feet, with a thin deep stage and a large discovery space. They obtained a Royal Patent in January 1610 and performed six days a week. The company lasted just over three years until 1613, when Roseter went into partnership with Philip Henslowe, and the Children of the Queen's Revels were dissolved into Lady Elizabeth's Men.

THE WHITEFRIARS THEATRE REPERTOIRE

At Whitefriars, the repertoire was again enormously impressive, eclectic and dynamic. It included *Ram Alley* by Lording Barry (1608), a member of the management until his debts caught up with him and he fled to become a pirate! Fletcher and Beaumont were both well represented, Fletcher with *The Faithful Shepherdess* (1608), Beaumont with *The Knight of the Burning Pestle* (c.1607), and together with *Cupid's Revenge* (1608) and *The Scornful Lady* (1613). Other plays presented were Day's *Humour out of Breath* (1608), Nathan Field's *Amends for Ladies* and *A Woman Is a Weathercock*, Ben Jonson's *Epicoene* (1609), and Barksted and Machin's completed version of Marston's *The Insatiate Countess* (1610).

Many of these plays were remarkably audacious either politically or sexually (or both), prompting the speculation that perhaps a company of boys encouraged a playwright to dare more. Most of the plays were satirical comedies, often employing stock characters like Quintiliano, the braggart, in *May Day* (1602), or stock situations, like the chase after the eloping couple in *Ram Alley*. But the combination of this stock theatricality with a new kind of realism was what really gives these and the earlier boys' company plays their overt power.

The plays are also concerned with children, and on several levels. *Cynthia's Revels* (1601) opens with the children performers quarrelling over who should speak the Prologue, and there are also versions of children's games in several of them – Drop Handkerchief in *Ram Alley*, a game of tease in Marston's *Antonio and Mellida* and snatching the ring in *The Dutch Courtesan* (1604). But against this, or perhaps complementing it, there is what gave the audience a particular kind of *frisson* – children mouthing filthy puns, and enacting fierce, perhaps adulterous, passions or forbidden lusts. There may be no clowns in these plays for the private playhouses, but there was perhaps the beginnings of a 'west end' concept of theatre.

AUDIENCES AT THE PRIVATE THEATRES

The audiences at Blackfriars, Whitefriars and Paul's were men-about-town, Inns of Court men, with a leavening of aristocrats and gentry, as well as some citizens and their wives like those who interrupt *The Knight of the Burning Pestle*. For these people to watch boys mimicking adults – children as kings, lovers, warriors, beautiful young women, seductive courtesans, frantic old men and so on – was both self-conscious and sexy. It was a kind of parody and undeniably subversive, perhaps enhanced by the presence of gallants on stage beside the boys. Ben Jonson described the audience at Whitefriars as being

> Composed of gamester, captain, knight, knight's man,
> Lady or pusil, that wears mask or fan,
> Velvet or taffeta cap, cauked in the dark
> With the shop's foreman, or some such brave spark.[1]

Jonson condemns the power of such an audience to damn a play, and it is true that *The Knight of the Burning Pestle* for instance, was a failure at first, though its metatheatrical elements and its juxtaposing of city comedy, romantic adventure and domestic gossip made it exceptionally popular in later centuries. But it is also the case that such a progressive repertoire could only have been presented to this type of exclusive audience, intellectual and insouciant.

ACTORS

It is also true that such a repertoire could only have been sustained by an excellent group of actors, and by 1611 one writer called the Whitefriars boys 'the best company in London', at a time when the King's Men were at the height of their powers. Nathan Field has already been mentioned. Born in 1587, the son of a well-known Puritan preacher, it seems he was impressed in 1600 into the Children of the Chapel Royal and appeared in Jonson's *Cynthia's Revels* and *The Poetaster* as well as in Chapman's *Bussy D'Ambois*. In 1613 he joined Lady Elizabeth's Men, and two or three years later may have bought Shakespeare's share in the King's Men, for whom he became a star. He was especially popular with women playgoers, and is even said to have had a child with the wife of the Earl of Argyll: this may not be verifiable, but it perhaps indicates something of his character. He is associated with Salomon Pavey who joined – or perhaps was impressed – into the company at the same time, and played old men in *Cynthia's Revels* and *The Poetaster* so well that, according to Jonson, Death mistook him for an old man and carried him off even though he was still a boy.

Other actors from the boys' companies who went on to adult companies after 1613 included John Underwood and William Ostler, both of whom acted in the early Jonson plays and both of whom went on to successful careers with the King's Men. Robert Benfield joined Lady Elizabeth's Men in 1613 and then went on to the King's Men in 1615, perhaps replacing Ostler there. His career lasted well into the 1630s: he played Ladislas in Massinger's *The Picture* (1629), the King in Carlell's *The Deserving Favourite* (1629) and Marcellus in Massinger's *Believe as You List* (1631). William Barksted, final author of *The Insatiate Countess*, was Morose in the original production of *Epicoene* by Ben Jonson, and was arrested in a bawdy house in Field Lane in 1610. He joined Lady Elizabeth's Men in 1613 and went on to Prince Charles's Men in about 1615. Like Field, he seems to have died young. Emanuel Reade, a friend of Christopher Beeston, also joined Lady Elizabeth's Men in 1613, but two or three years later was attached to Queen Anne's Men. Hugh Attewell, probably the son of George Attewell of *Attewell's Jig*, was La Foole in the first production of *Epicoene*, after which he joined Prince Charles's Men. A small man, nevertheless William Rowley called 'his tongue a silver bell'.

These were clearly highly talented actors, but a major strength of the boys' companies also lay in their ensemble playing. The broadly presentational style of the Elizabethan period modulated in the work of these companies into something more studied, less rough, though in no sense 'naturalistic'. They set the pattern for future theatrical developments in the Jacobean and Caroline theatres, and to some extent left the open air playhouse practices behind.

NOTE

1 Ben Jonson, 'Lines Addressed to the Author of the Faithful Shepherdess'; see J. St, Loe Strachey (ed), *Beaumont and Fletcher*, vol II, London: Ernest Benn, 1950, p. 316.

SELECT BIBLIOGRAPHY

Gair, Reavley, *The Children of Paul's: The Story of a Theatre Company, 1553–1608*, Cambridge: Cambridge University Press, 1982
Munro, Lucy, *Children of the Queen's Revels*, Cambridge: Cambridge University Press, 2005
Shapiro, Michael, *Children of the Revels*, New York: Columbia University Press, 1977

PART THREE

CAVALIER THEATRE

Timeline

	Society and politics	Theatre
1603	Accession of James I	
1605	Gunpowder Plot	Jonson, *The Masque of Blackness*
1607		Beaumont, *The Knight of the Burning Pestle*
1608	New Exchange, The Strand, opened	King's Men take over Blackfriars Theatre Fletcher, *The Faithful Shepherdess*
1609		Children of the Queen's Revels open Whitefriars Theatre Jonson, *The Masque of Queens*
1611		Middleton, *A Chaste Maid in Cheapside*
1612	Death of Henry, Prince of Wales	Shakespeare, *The Tempest*
1614		Webster, *The Duchess of Malfi*
1616	Investiture of Charles as Prince of Wales	Death of William Shakespeare Jonson, *Works* published
1617		Cockpit Theatre opened and damaged by rioters *Cupid's Banishment* performed before Queen Anne: Anne Watkins becomes the first woman to speak on the British stage
1619	Death of Queen Anne	
1620	Pilgrim Fathers land in America	Middleton and Rowley, *The World Tossed at Tennis*
1621		Jonson, *The Gypsies Metamorphosed*
1622		Banqueting House, Whitehall, opened
1623		Shakespeare, *Comedies, Histories & Tragedies* published Sir Henry Herbert becomes Master of the Revels

1624	Prince Charles and Duke of Buckingham leave London disguised, to woo Infanta of Spain	Middleton, *A Game at Chess*
1625	Death of James I: accession of Charles I	
1626		Massinger, *The Roman Actor*
1627		Death of Thomas Middleton
1628	Murder of Duke of Buckingham	
1629	Charles I dissolves Parliament, rules without Parliament till 1640	Salisbury Court Theatre opened
1630		Cockpit-in-Court opened
1632		Montague, *The Shepherd's Paradise* produced at court Ford, *'Tis Pity She's a Whore* Shirley, *The Lady of Pleasure*
1633		Somerset House theatre opened
1634	William Laud becomes Archbishop of Canterbury	Prynne, *Histrio-Mastix* published Davenant, *The Wits*
1637		Death of Ben Jonson Beeston's Boys established Masquing House, Whitehall, opened
1638		Death of Christopher Beeston
1640	Rebellions in Scotland and Ireland	Davenant, *Salmacida Spolia*
1641	Execution of king's chief minister, Thomas Wentworth, Earl of Strafford	Brome, *A Jovial Crew*
1642	English Civil War begins	All theatres officially closed
1644	Battle of Marston Moor	Globe Theatre demolished
1645	Cromwell's New Model Army Battle of Naseby End of First Civil War	Cavendish and Brackley, *The Concealed Fancies*
1647	The Putney Debates Second Civil War begins	Plays by 'Beaumont & Fletcher' published
1649	Execution of Charles I; Commonwealth declared	
1651	Battle of Worcester	
1652		Death of Richard Brome
1653	Protectorate declared: Cromwell named Lord Protector	Shirley, *Cupid and Death*
1656		Davenant, *The Siege of Rhodes*

1658	Death of Oliver Cromwell: Richard Cromwell named Lord Protector	
1660	Restoration of Charles II	Reopening of the theatres: King's Company at Tennis Court, Vere Street, Duke's Company at Salisbury Court First professional actresses on British stage
1661		Duke's Company at Lisle's Tennis Court
1662	Act of Uniformity	Tuke, *The Adventures of Five Hours*
1663		King's Company at Bridges Street Theatre
1665	Great plague in London	
1666	Great Fire of London	
1667	Milton, *Paradise Lost*	Dryden, *Sir Martin Mar-all* Davenant and Dryden, *The Enchanted Island*
1668		Death of Sir William Davenant Dryden, *An Essay of Dramatic Poesy*
1671		Duke's Company at Dorset Gardens Buckingham, *The Rehearsal*
1672		Bridges Street Theatre burns down
1673	Duke of York marries Mary of Modena, a Catholic	Settle, *The Empress of Morocco*
1674		King's Company at Drury Lane Theatre
1675		Wycherley, *The Country Wife*
1676		Etherege, *The Man of Mode* Shadwell, *The Virtuoso*
1677		Charles Killigrew takes control of King's Company Behn, *The Rover* Dryden, *All for Love*
1678	Popish Plot	
1679		Behn, *The Feigned Courtesans*
1680	Exclusion Crisis Duke of York in exile	Lee, *Lucius Junius Brutus*
1681		Tate, *The History of King Lear*
1682	Duke of York returns from exile	King's Company taken over by Duke's Company to form United Company Otway, *Venice Preserv'd*

1683	Rye House Plot
1685	Death of Charles II: accession of Duke of York as James II Monmouth rebellion
1688	Glorious Revolution: James II flees the country
1689	Accession of William III and Mary II

Chapter 27: The Stuart monarchy and the theatre

The four Stuart kings who reigned in Britain for most of the seventeenth century were perhaps the most enthusiastic theatre buffs who have ever occupied the throne. It seemed that only a royal death or a severe outbreak of plague (and there were very severe outbreaks from February to November 1625, and from May 1636 to October 1637) could stop the tide of continual playmaking, until the Civil War and the Interregnum of Cromwellian rule dammed its flow. But despite this notable interruption, the spate gathered new force with the Restoration of the monarchy in 1660 and only diminished twenty-five or thirty years later. During the seventeenth century, it may be that the theatre evolved more rapidly than over any equivalent period since.

INNOVATIONS OF CAVALIER THEATRE

The most obvious change saw the appearance of women in every department of the theatre, from taking money at the door, to sharing in theatrical enterprises, as Marie Bryant did when she bought a one-twelfth share in the Fortune Theatre in 1623. By 1689 women could not only act in public, they could lead a major London company, and they were writers, managers, agents and critics.

Theatre came indoors. The huge open air amphitheatres of the Elizabethans were all closed in the mid-century by which time indoor, candle-lit auditoria and stages had totally replaced them. Indoor theatres encouraged revolutionary developments in staging: by the end of the period, every regular theatre boasted moveable scenery, and the search for scenic realism had begun.

Written play texts became recognised as literature and many more were printed and published, giving a new status to drama. Consequently, we know pretty well what audiences at the theatre of the seventeenth century came to see.

Besides these developments, however, there were other, less obvious changes. The fact that the Stuart kings were such avid theatregoers meant that theatre itself was incorporated into their project to assert the right of the monarch to rule with or without the help or counsel of Parliament or secretaries or any specially chosen advisers. The stage became a prime site for any debate about political philosophy or its practical consequences for the kingdom. These arguments were often conducted through the subtexts of the plays and masques, through symbolism, nuances or fantasy, so the ideas scrutinised often passed the average spectator by, as they have passed many later critics by, too. But twenty-first-century scholarship has uncovered to an often-astonishing degree how this subtext operated.

THE COURTS OF JAMES VI AND I

James VI of Scotland arrived in London to assume the additional title of James I of England in 1603. He was a Protestant. He had married Anne of Denmark in 1589, and they had two sons. All this was enormously reassuring to the English aristocracy, which had fretted for years over the succession to the throne. But the fact of a monarch with a consort also brought problems: where Elizabeth had been a sole ruler and had had one court, James and Anne each had their own court, an arrangement amplified by Charles I and his queen, Henrietta Maria.

Figure 3.1
James VI of Scotland and I of England, attributed to John de Critz, c.1605
Source: Museo del Prado, Madrid

Perhaps this unaccustomed arrangement led to James's rapid falling out with the aristocracy and their descent into factionalism. The main factions clustered round the families of Essex, Howard and Sidney, and the mix was further stirred by James's *penchant* for favourites – usually attractive young men such as Robert Carr, who was allied to the Howard family, and whom James made Duke of Somerset, and, after Carr's fall from grace, George Villiers, whom James created Duke of Buckingham. Charles took over Buckingham as a special favourite when he succeeded to the throne in 1625. Indeed, it is reported that Charles slept with Buckingham on the night of his coronation. Furthermore, Henrietta Maria, Charles's queen, soon involved herself in political intrigues both in her native France and Europe, and in England.

THE SIGNIFICANCE OF THEATRE DURING THE REIGNS OF JAMES I AND CHARLES I

The theatre became a site for the airing of factional positions because the king, whether James or Charles, took note of it. The records of performances at court are incomplete, but it seems that throughout these two reigns approximately twenty different plays were performed at court each year. This is a staggering number. Moreover, every major theatre company in London acquired a royal patron, and Queen Henrietta Maria was to break all conventions by visiting a public theatre, the Black-friars, on more than one occasion. Royal progresses through the country were almost always marked by theatrical presentations, such as the entertainment created by Thomas Campion when the Queen stayed at Caversham House near Reading in 1613; or the plays enacted by the members of Trinity College and Clare Hall at Cambridge when James and Charles stayed there in 1615; or the series of masque-like pageants given in Edinburgh (Bacchus toasting him at Market Cross, 'nine pretty boys representing the nine nymphs or muses' further down the Royal Mile, and so on) when Charles visited the city in 1633; or, almost the last work of Ben Jonson to receive a performance, his masque, *Love's Welcome*, presented to the king and queen at Bolsover Castle in 1634.

Perhaps because of this acknowledged infatuation with theatre, in the 1630s courtiers, like Sir John Suckling, William Cartwright and the Duke of Newcastle, took to writing plays. Cartwright's *The Royal Slave*, portraying a slave adopting kingly attributes, and so being permitted to reign, was presented at Christ Church, Oxford in 1636. The political implications of this play's content are intriguing, and similar content found its way onto the professional stage, too. Thus, John Ford urged in *Perkin Warbeck* (1633):

> Public states,
> As our particular bodies, taste most good
> In health, when purged of corrupted blood,

And Henry Glapthorne wrote in *The Tragedy of Albertus Wallenstein* (1634) that

> It is
> No such strange crime to disobey a Prince
> In things unjust.

These quotations, implicitly challenging the Stuart political *credo* and hence, if not subversive, at least dangerous, give a flavour of the political discourse of the drama of the Caroline period. They could be multiplied. Philip Massinger, for example, wrote a series of plays which among other things examine the place and powers of royal favourites and advisers: Fulgentio is the king's 'catamite' in *The Maid of Honour* (1621), in which Roberto's peaceable intentions offer a reflection of James's pacific foreign policy; the Duke's favourite, Francisco, in *The Duke of Milan* (1621), reminds the spectator irresistibly of Robert Carr; and Sanazarro's relationship with his lord, in *The Great Duke of Florence* (1627) is discussed by Charmonte:

> For princes never more make known their wisdom
> Than where they cherish goodness where they find it;
> They being men, and not gods, Contarino,
> They can give wealth and titles, but no virtues:
> That is without their power. When they advance,
> Not out of judgment, but deceiving fancy,
> An undeserving man, howe'er set off
> With all the trim of greatness, state, and power,
> And of a creature even grown terrible
> To him from whom he took his giant form,
> This thing is still a comet, no true star;
> And when the bounties feeding his false fire
> Begin to fail, will of itself go out,
> And what was dreadful proves ridiculous.

In the same play, Cozimo, the Duke, puts the case for the ruler's divine right, the position the Stuart kings held so steadfastly:

> You press us
> With solid arguments, we grant; and, though
> We stand not bound to yield account to any
> Why we do this or that, (the full consent
> Of our subjects being included in our will,)
> We, out of our free bounties, will deliver
> The motives that divert us.

The political ideas and problems of the time were energised on the stage, partly because politics happened in the court, and not beyond it. Parliament may have tried to rein in the king in the 1620s, but it was to no avail. Parliamentarians may have thought their mission was to hold onto the achievements of Queen Elizabeth and to uphold the Magna Carta but their essentially conservative position, and their resistance to Charles I's innovations, merely meant they were ignored. The situation was aggravated by Charles's lack of flexibility: he could not conceive that he might have a duty to respond to dissent.

STUART POLITICS AND RELIGION

The political deadlock was exacerbated by religious difficulties, struggles and suspicions. Politics and religion are not a productive mix because where successful politics requires flexibility and imagination, those with a strong faith inevitably dismiss compromise: they seek power for their own religious principles to the disadvantage of those of another religion. A believer wishes to convert opponents, not negotiate with them. In England in the seventeenth century, there were three versions of more or less uncompromising Christianity vying for the power to crush the others. At one extreme, Catholics believed in hierarchy, authority and the Pope in Rome. Against them were the Puritans, not a monolithic group as has been sometimes implied, but a disparate number of sects each with their own priorities: Baptists, Anabaptists, Seekers, Quakers, Presbyterians and others. Though they were almost all against the institution of bishops, and all believed in personal salvation, they were not as hostile to the theatre as many had been in Elizabethan days. This was partly because the new indoor playhouses were more respectable than the old open air amphitheatres, and partly because plays were no longer performed on Sundays. Somewhere in the middle of the religious debate were the less fanatical Protestants.

But Protestants and Puritans alike were strongly opposed to Catholicism. Thus, the crises of 1624 and 1625 began with Charles and the Duke of Buckingham leaving London disguised in false beards, to woo the Infanta of Spain, a Catholic. When Charles's suit to her failed, and the threat of a Catholic queen was apparently done with, there was great rejoicing and Charles's popularity soared. Jonson's masque, *Neptune's Triumph for the Return of Albion*, celebrates precisely this. The operation seems to have heated the desire for war against the Spanish and against Catholicism in general, as voiced in plays such as Massinger's *The Bondman* (1623), Dekker and Ford's *The Sun's Darling* (1624) and most controversially, Middleton's *A Game at Chess* (1624). But in 1625 James I died, and Charles succeeded him. Soon after he married a French princess, Henrietta Maria. But she, too, was a Catholic, and when Charles rescinded the laws against Catholics, freed those who were imprisoned, and even aided the King of France to crush the French Huguenots, his popularity slumped.

For a time he ruled without Parliament, relying on his trick of 'ship money' for revenue, and on a few advisers like Archbishop William Laud and Thomas Wentworth, first Earl of Strafford, for support. By 1640 there were rebellions in Scotland and Ireland. He was forced to recall Parliament, who promptly impeached and then executed Strafford. Charles tried to have the leading Parliamentarians arrested. When this failed, he left London, and in August 1642 he raised his standard in Nottingham, and prepared to fight for his kingdom. A consequence of his action was that Parliament closed the theatres, ostensibly while these troubles continued.

SOCIAL LIFE IN THE 1630S

It was a brutal end to what had seemed to many an almost idyllic time. The illusion among the better off in the 1630s was that England was a haven of peace while Europe was ravaged by war. In fact, London during this period became a centre for self-indulgence and conspicuous consumption, as the spectators at James Shirley's comedy, *The Lady of Pleasure* (1632), could observe. London's centre of gravity was shifting west, and the more fashionable theatres were situated there – Blackfriars, the Salisbury Court opposite the old Whitefriars and the Cockpit even further west in Drury Lane. This was where the gentry lived and gossiped – Hyde Park, the Royal Exchange and Covent Garden, the newly built suburb designed largely by Inigo Jones. Well-off families came from the country to town for its social activities and enjoyed pageants, executions, wrestling, gambling and theatre performances. A visit to one of the indoor 'private' theatres in the 1630s was a social event:

Figure 3.2
Covent Garden, c.1647, by Wenceslaus Hollar

thus, in Davenant's *The Wits* (1634), fashionable young Pallatine suggests to his companions that they should 'meet me at the play fair and perfumed' before an evening's excitement. Plays catered for the rising class of professional men and merchants, but perhaps even more for the socially superior country gentry who had no need to work for a living, and whom Charles tried to keep at home to ensure his writ was followed there. But the magnet which was London was powerful.

Not everybody shared London's carefree delights, however: there were plenty of usurious money lenders on the prowl, plenty of quacks and monopolists to take advantage of the naïve and the less well off. Life for the lowest classes was exceptionally hard. Between 1620 and 1650, there grew a disproportionate gap between the rich and the poor. For the poor, poverty was a brutal reality, with substantial food shortages and prices even of necessities soaring. The poet in Richard Brome's *A Jovial Crew* (1641) is not the only person in those days who had fallen into poverty. Indeed, several of the angry comedies of Brome fittingly expose the disparity between pretension and reality in Charles I's England.

IDEAS AND ARGUMENTS IN THE 1630S AND 1640S

However, it was the Levellers in the later 1640s who tried to create a different inclusive kind of politics, based in ideology and involving popular participation, which would change people's lives. Only then was it possible for a Thomas Rainsborough to argue: 'I think that the poorest he in England hath a life to live as the greatest he', a sentiment entirely at odds with the politics of faction, intrigue and patronage which characterised the reigns of James and Charles.

Brome's work exemplifies how the mid-century theatre struggled to articulate an alternative politics. Of course, not every play engaged in political argument: in the first half of the century the old amphitheatres continued to attract the mass of the theatregoing public, while the Cavalier project was to be found almost exclusively in the 'private', enclosed theatres, and in the theatres of the courts. But by the 1630s, almost all the original and challenging drama was being premiered at the private theatres, and most of this did have a political import.

CAVALIER THEATRE AFTER THE RESTORATION

After the disruptions of the Civil War and the Commonwealth, the Cavalier theatre returned, rejuvenated and refreshed. Restoration drama has a kind of triumphalism which is related to the return of Charles II. This does not mean that the drama of the private theatres of the 1630s was simply restored in the patent houses of the 1660s. Much was completely changed.

The ascendancy of the Cavalier theatre lasted for less than thirty years after 1660. By the end of Charles II's reign, the flowering had turned to fall, the two London companies merged, and the rise of the *bourgeoisie* meant the beginnings of a new sort of theatre.

Chapter 28: *A Game at Chess*

THOMAS MIDDLETON AND POLITICAL PAGEANTRY

The most egregious intertangling of politics and theatre in the seventeenth century came with the production in August 1624 by the King's Men at the Globe Theatre of Thomas Middleton's *A Game at Chess*. Middleton's earlier work has been noted above, but there was little in it to suggest he would produce this extraordinary *success du scandale*. However, beside his conventional theatre work, Middleton had by 1624 become London's most successful creator of pageantry, an inevitably political line of work, and he had also been appointed to the post of City Chronologer. There were plenty of civic pageants to be created in the Jacobean period – both outdoors and indoors, as well as for the court, the aristocracy, the Inns of Court and so on. And each 29 October came the Lord Mayor's Show when the newly elected Lord Mayor of London travelled from Guildhall to Westminster partly by boat on the Thames, to take his oath of office, and then return to Guildhall. Along the way, the Guild which sponsored him provided a lavish show of pageantry and entertainment: the 1613 show, for instance, cost no less than £1300, enough to rebuild the burned-down Globe Theatre.

For the creators of these shows, remuneration was considerable, and writers vied with one another to devise them. Thus in 1619, Middleton, Munday and Grimston all submitted bids for the position; and in 1617 Middleton received the huge fee of £282 for his work, though from this he had to pay for props, costumes, carpenter's wages and more. Moreover, the city was pleased for the scripts written for these shows to be published, and this generated further income for the writer. They proclaimed the civic virtues of prosperity, good citizenship, international trade, and the city as the mother of her people. Drayton, Jonson and Dekker all worked on early Lord Mayor's shows, but Munday was perhaps the favourite before about 1615. After that date, Middleton was the preferred writer, and after his death, Dekker and then Thomas Heywood made most of the entertainments until 1639.

Of course, the very existence of the Lord Mayor, who was elected but who governed the city for a strictly limited period by the consent of his peers, was an implicit criticism, or even threat, to a hereditary monarchy governing by whim or personal belief. From Elizabethan times, the city's civic government had come into conflict with the Privy Council, not least over the matter of the theatre's continuance: these theatricalised festivals deepened this political paradox.

JAMES I'S CORONATION, 1604

Equally paradoxically, James I and VI's coronation entry to London in 1604 provided something of a pattern for future Lord Mayor's Shows. It involved hundreds of participants, aristocrats, courtiers,

Figure 3.3
The Royal and Magnificent Entertainment, with the Arches of Triumph, 1604, was a pageant to mark the coronation of James I of England, when a series of spectacular triumphal arches was erected in the capital

Source: British Library, London

city Fathers and other prominent people processing past many thousands of spectators in a show which cost more than £35,000 – probably much more. The whole centred on eight pageants which together constructed an image of monarchy and popular happiness at this king's accession in speeches or sequences composed by poets including Dekker, Ben Jonson, Middleton and others.

The procession passed through huge, decorated arches erected along the route to the designs of Stephen Harrison. The fourth arch, for example, was eighteen feet tall and twelve feet wide. The decorative panels contained gold writing on an azure background. As the king approached, the curtains above the central arch were drawn apart to reveal seventeen damsels 'sumptuously adorned' and then a boy, dressed in white silk and crowned with a laurel wreath, addressed the king in Latin. Meanwhile, the crowd's raucous cheering often drowned the poet's words, as they enjoyed the brilliant banners, the flamboyant horse cloths, richly decorated canopies and the tapestries on the outside walls of the buildings. Free wine flowed in the water conduits of the city, and the bells from one hundred twenty-three churches rang out.

STREET ENTERTAINMENTS

This set the tone for other pageants and street exhibitions, most notably the annual Lord Mayor's shows. The Russian ambassador described the 1613 show, when the Mayor was accompanied by a hundred and fifty brightly uniformed soldiers, trumpeters, drummers, all sorts of dignitaries in their robes, floats with tableaux, banners, flags and so on. The crowds in 1617 were described by an Italian visitor:

> Looking below us onto the street we saw a huge mass of people, surging like the sea, moving here and there in search of places to watch or rest – which proved impossible because of the constant press of newcomers. It was a chaotic mixture: dotards; insolent youths and children . . . beribboned serving wenches; lower class women with their children in their arms; all were there to see the beautiful show.[1]

Directed largely by the writers, the shows relied heavily on the stage managers, architects and carpenters: the published descriptions frequently make a point of acknowledging these. 'The firework being made by master Humphrey Nichols, a man excellent in his art', noted Middleton at the end of the book of the 1613 procession; 'and the whole work and body of the triumph, with all the proper beauties of the workmanship, most artfully and faithfully performed by John Grinkin'.[2] Later shows were designed and built by Garret Christmas, working sometimes with Robert Norman and consistently until 1639 with his own sons. Christmas thus contributed significantly to the development of stage scenery, though that contribution has yet to be fully acknowledged and evaluated.

LONDON IN MIDDLETON'S PAGEANTS

The city's international importance as a centre of world trade led to several shows with global themes. For instance, Middleton's 1617 show, *The Triumphs of Honour and Industry*, introduces the Island of Spice, where 'a company of Indians, attired according to the true nature of their country, seeming for the most part naked' are seen planting nutmeg trees, bagging up pepper and, after their work is done, 'dancing about the trees'. Five years later, in *The Triumphs of Honour and Virtue*, Middleton created 'a black personage representing India, called, for her odours and riches, the Queen of Merchandise'. In the show, 'the riches and sweetness of the east' are traded for 'celestial knowledge', that is, Christianity, and the black and brown emperors and queens praise Britain and British trade. This was, of course, the period of the initial growth of the East India Company, as well as the beginnings of the slave trade as a serious business. These performances were crudely clear examples of orientalist objectification of the exotic. They were, however, part of the picture which the city wished to paint of itself, especially as a centre of the busy and varied world.

THE WORLD TOSSED AT TENNIS

Middleton's further involvement in the politics of the time may be seen in his adherence to the young Charles, Prince of Wales, especially when he opposed his father, the king. He wrote *Civitatis Amor* in celebration of Charles's investiture as Prince of Wales in 1616, and four years later the Prince commissioned William Rowley to make a masque for performance at his residence of Denmark House. Rowley enlisted his frequent collaborator, Thomas Middleton's help and the two created the highly experimental *The World Tossed at Tennis*, a political squib, which proved impossible as a royal masque but was performed successfully at the Swan Theatre by the Prince's Men, whom Rowley led.

The World Tossed at Tennis contrasts King James's pacific foreign policy with Charles's faction's more interventionist tendencies in favour of Europe's Protestants in what was to become the Thirty Years War. The drama was intended as part of Charles's attempts to change James's stubborn mind: at the end, the Soldier requests agreement for his desire for war from the chief spectator, to be signalled by his applause. This was too audacious for the court, but the popular audience was highly enthusiastic. *The World Tossed at Tennis*, however, is more ambivalent than this implies, for the authors are careful to endorse also the Scholar's non-belligerence, so that the final message is less one of partisanship than of harmony and the need for collaboration and inclusiveness. While it valorises Charles's political stance, it also asserts that good government depends on the co-operation of the natural rulers with the armed forces, the intelligentsia and the professions, each of whom has a significant place in the commonweal.

As drama, *The World Tossed at Tennis* is a notable achievement. It includes some of Middleton's most robust language:

SOLDIER (to Scholar): Very well, sir, and I'll warrant thee thou shalt never want subject to write of: one hangs himself today, another drowns himself tomorrow, as ergeant stabbed next day, here a pettifogger a' the pillory, a bawd in the cart's nose, and a pandar in the tail. *Hic Mulier, Haec Vir,* fashions, fictions, felonies, fooleries – a hundred havens has the balladmonger to traffic at, and new ones still daily discovered.

It employs a range of stage effects, from the 'flying in' of gods on platforms concealed behind painted clouds, to the 'discovery' of the Nine Worthies in their individualised costumes on the upper stage, from where they are each led down by one of the Muses. There is plenty of stage action – songs, dances, the Starches who jostle each other to make their dance 'ridiculous', the raucous sailors' entry, and the amazing finale, when the world itself, represented by a tennis ball, is tossed between the actors as if they were playing Pig in the Middle. Throughout the play, whoever holds the world, the tennis ball which is passed, or batted, from one character to another, there is always Deceit trying to traduce him; and the whole is watched, first by Jupiter and Pallas Athene, and then by the Soldier and the Scholar, so that we see that all is a performance, and all the actions are mediated for us by these overseers.

A GAME AT CHESS AT THE GLOBE THEATRE

Middleton's most sensational political intervention came four years later in August 1624, when his play *A Game at Chess* ran for nine consecutive days, a record at that time, at the Globe Theatre: 'So many people come to see [it]', wrote the Spanish ambassador in alarm,

> that there were more than 3000 persons there on the day that the audience was the smallest. There was such merriment, hubbub and applause that even if I had been many leagues away it would not have been possible for me not to have taken notice of it.[3]

Figure 3.4
Title page of Thomas Middleton's *A Game at Chess*, c.1624

Every day for over a week, the actors and the public expected the authorities to stop the production, but for those glorious nine days this abusive attack on Spain and Catholicism shone in London's firmament. The King's Men made more money than ever before.

Taking as its starting-point the visit of Prince Charles and the Duke of Buckingham to Spain to seek the Infanta Maria as bride for the Prince of Wales (though in the play their visit is to confound Spanish plans for conquest), this epic play, which still has the power to make the nerve ends tingle, becomes a polemical satire not irrelevant today, when priests are found sexually abusing their followers, hierarchies cover up for them and the only punishment is handed out to the abused. It does not attempt to be a detailed or factual history, but catches a moment of antagonism between the British people and Spain and dramatises it with full force. The Black Knight in the chess game is the hated Gondomar, the Spanish ambassador, whom it was believed had too much influence with King James. As a character he is in the line of Marlowe's Barabas and Shakespeare's Richard III, a villain who relishes his own villainy, and who involves the audience in his machinations. He was portrayed to the life: the actors even acquired his clothes and his litter with its chair like a lavatory seat to ease his anal fistula, and the actor playing the Black Knight mimicked his every mannerism, to the delight of the spectators. Other obvious personations included Charles as the White Knight, Buckingham as the White Rook and James as the White King. This last was particularly dangerous: the representation of any living Christian monarch on the stage was strictly forbidden, and the king's weakness in chess could be taken as a reflection of James's weakness, though of course the presentation of the Spanish monarch as the Black King might have been intended to mitigate the implication. Less equivocally, the Fat Bishop, played by Rowley, was a representation of Marco Antonio de Dominis who had left the Catholic Church to become an Anglican, only to be re-converted to Catholicism. Other resemblances were more generic than particular – the White King's Pawn, for instance, connoted a rapacious courtier rather than anyone specific.

The chess motif provided the drama with a defamiliarising agent of a singularly effective kind. The play showed a game of chess, which however kept going wrong. The rules were unexpectedly broken, pieces behaved in ways not allowed in chess, and what seemed white suddenly seemed more like black, as with the treacherous White King's Pawn and the Fat Bishop himself. Black is on the offensive for most of the game, but White's defences hold and in the end Black is checkmated by discovered check, a particularly humiliating way to lose a chess game. The Black Bishop's Pawn, a Jesuit, has meanwhile tried and failed to seduce the White Queen's Pawn, who is a typical English rose, and the bad have been chucked into a bag, which takes the place of the traditional hell's mouth. Finally, a reader may forget what a spectator does not, that the whole is further endistanced by being a play within a play, Envy's dream told to Ignatius Loyola.

It was not so much the specific satire against the king that gave offence in *A Game at Chess*, as the simple fact of questioning the king's policy in public. James was on a progress through the country when the play was produced. The new Spanish ambassador (who had just replaced Gondomar) complained, and James scurried to try to find out what was going on. Suddenly there was official fury: the play was stopped, and the King's Men banned from performing at all. The Privy Council called Sir Henry Herbert, the Master of the Revels, and Middleton himself, before them. Herbert was in trouble because he had passed the play for performance. Middleton was nowhere to be found, though his son was dragged before the authorities. Later Middleton was found and may have been imprisoned. But the scandal fizzled out, the only consequence of note being that Thomas Middleton, probably England's greatest dramatist after Shakespeare, never wrote another play. It is small consolation that three quarto editions were published in the following eighteen months, which however must have brought some financial reward to the author.

STAGE CENSORSHIP

The most puzzling feature of the furore over *A Game at Chess* may be the part played in it by Sir Henry Herbert, the Master of the Revels. It could not be denied that he had passed the play for public performance in June 1624. But in fact it seems that the whole censorship administration was unexpectedly feeble.

Herbert was the fourth Master after Edmund Tilney (Master of the Revels 1578–1610), Sir George Buck (1610–22), Sir John Astley (1622–3), from whom Herbert purchased the office when Ben Jonson was actually next in line for it. He retained the office until August 1642, when the theatres were closed, but he regained it at the Restoration in 1660. The Master of the Revels's original job, which to some extent still held good, was to choose plays for performance at court, to scrutinise the text and to supervise rehearsals, lighting and so on. Given the fiction that all public performances were merely rehearsals for court performance, this gave him executive power under the Lord Chamberlain over all performances, and he was also responsible for relicensing old plays and licensing jugglers, conjurors, tumblers, rope-dancers, puppet shows, waxworks, freak shows, menageries, musical performances and more. He had the right, established in 1581 and renewed in 1603, to censure any play or any part of a play on political, religious or moral grounds; he was also to ban comments on Britain's or foreign governments, or any personation of powerful people – especially the reigning monarch. He licensed the publication of plays, until 1637 when the Star Chamber refused to recognise his right to do this. Any individual could ask him to suppress any play for what seemed to them a good reason, such as libel, but he dealt with the producing company, not the writer, when negotiating about any specific play.

Herbert was a conscientious censor, marking every script he received with brackets and underlinings and crossings-out, and his stamp at the end of the script was his sign that the play had passed for performance. There was no denying his stamp at the end of the script of *A Game at Chess*, but he seems not to have even received a reprimand over it. Actually the system seems to have been strikingly inefficient. Under Sir George Buck, another politically dubious play, Fletcher and Massinger's *Sir John van Olden Barnavelt* (1619), was attacked by the Bishop of London and banned even after Sir George had licensed it. But Herbert, though he often demanded – and got – changes to scripts, seems to have rarely been particularly effective. He protested against the anonymous *The Plantation of Virginia* (1623) for profaneness, and Thomas Drue's *The Duchess of Suffolk* (1624), which was, he said, 'full of dangerous matter'. But both continued with only minor alterations to the scripts. As far as personal slander was concerned, he was perhaps more effective. In 1632, after complaints, he censored Shirley's *The Ball*, insisting the caricatures of real people be altered, and the following year did the same with the anonymous *The City Shuffler* (1633) after an objection by a Mr Sewster, the object of the play's satire. In the same year he required changes to Jonson's *Tale of a Tub* (1633), because the character of Vitruvius Hoop was based on the indignant Inigo Jones.

Strong oaths were also forbidden. In 1633 Herbert insisted that for a production of Walter Mountford's *The Launching of the Mary* (1633) 'all the oaths must be left out'; but when he objected to Davenant's oaths in *The Wits* (1634), the author complained to the king, who overruled Herbert, and the oaths stayed in the text. By the end of the decade, he again faced political challenges. In

1638, it was Charles I who found Massinger's *The King and the Subject* 'too insolent' whereupon Herbert asked for it to be changed. Then the following year at the Red Bull Theatre, Prince Charles's Men were found performing the anonymous *The Whore New Vamped* (1639), which satirised official peculation and contained slanderous material about a City Alderman. Herbert had not even licensed this play. It was the Attorney General who decided that the author and the actors were to be punished. But there is no record of this happening. The same year Archbishop Laud prosecuted the Fortune Theatre for 'contempt for the ceremonies of the church' in the revived version of *The Cardinal's Conspiracy* (1639), and the actors were gaoled for a few days.

In early 1640 William Beeston mounted a production of another unlicensed play at the Cockpit Theatre which commented unfavourably on the king's unsuccessful expedition north to subdue the Scottish Covenanters. When the king heard of this, he drew Herbert's attention forcibly to it, and the Lord Chamberlain (Herbert's immediate superior) issued a warrant to have the theatre closed down and three members of the company, including Beeston, gaoled. But the actors petitioned Herbert for their release, which he granted after three days. Beeston was not re-employed, and the theatre was passed to the loyal William Davenant. But when Davenant returned to fight King Charles's wars, Beeston seems to have quietly resumed control of the theatre and the company.

NOTES

1 Gary Taylor and John Lavagnino, *Thomas Middleton: The Collected Works*, Oxford: Clarendon Press, 2007, p. 1266.
2 Thomas Middleton, *The Triumphs of Truth*, 1613; see Gary Taylor and John Lavagnino, *op.cit.*, p. 976.
3 Letter from Don Carlos de Coloma to the Conde-Duque Olivares, 10 August 1624, in Edward M. Wilson and Olga Turner, 'The Spanish Protest Against a Game at Chesse', *Modern Languages Review*, 44 (1949), p. 480.

Chapter 29: The King's Men at the Blackfriars Theatre

THE SECOND BLACKFRIARS THEATRE

A Game at Chess was probably the last time a significantly innovative play would be premiered at one of London's open air playhouses: after this, theatrical originality was found more and more in the private, indoor theatres. The first of these, and the dominant indoor theatre right through to 1642, was the Blackfriars, in the fashionable area just within the city walls. James Burbage had purchased this building for £600 as long ago as 1596, but he was unable to use the premises because leading residents of the neighbourhood petitioned the Privy Council against it. For a while, Burbage let the new space to the Children of the Chapel Royal. But in 1608, with a little help perhaps from suitable bribes, the King's Men took it over.

As a theatrical space, it was intense, focused and, of course, not subject to the weather. The Globe could accommodate six times as many spectators, but since at Blackfriars patrons were charged at least six times as much, often more, the smaller venue soon became much the more profitable of the two. Though it has been widely assumed that the company played at the Blackfriars between October and May each year, and then at the Globe in the summer, this seems unlikely: would the company have left the Globe empty through the whole of each winter? Whatever the answer to that question, they soon found that the smaller theatre was best for the first performance of a new play.

THE LEADING THEATRE COMPANY

Throughout the Jacobean and Caroline periods, the King's Men were the dominant theatre company in London, and their title – the *King's* Men – was no idle one. Far more than any other company they were invited to perform at court. Though royal favour gave them protection and status, and allowed the actors to wear the royal livery, court performances were not particularly profitable: the fees received for up to twenty performances never amounted to even ten per cent of the company's annual income. In the 1630s, Queen Henrietta Maria scandalised many by visiting the Blackfriars Theatre at least three times, and she invited the leading actor, Joseph Taylor, to coach her ladies and herself in acting. After her presentation of Walter Montague's *The Shepherds Paradise* (1633) at court, she donated all the costumes to the King's Men's wardrobe. She also encouraged her courtiers to write plays for them, which several did. One of those was Sir John Suckling, and when they performed his drama, *Aglaura* (1637), he followed her lead and gave them £400 for costumes – 'an unheard of prodigality', according to his contemporary, George Gerrard.

REPERTOIRE

Plays by courtiers like Suckling had not always been the fare at the Blackfriars. It had been the chosen playhouse for the first performances of plays by professionals – Shakespeare, Jonson, Beaumont and Fletcher and Middleton. Fletcher, the King's Men's house dramatist after the retirement of Shakespeare, honed a style particularly suited to the more fervid atmosphere of the candle-lit Blackfriars. His plays for this theatre, like *The Mad Lover* (1617), *The Loyal Subject* (1618) and *The Island Princess* (1621), are marked by clever plotting and issues of love and honour. There is danger

Figure 3.5
John Fletcher's *The Island Princess*, 1621, was a typical Jacobean tragicomedy: it climaxed with a ferocious assault on the island of Tidore in India, the outcome of which was not disaster but reconciliation. This illustration dates from 1710.

Source: British Library, London

which faces the protagonists, sometimes extreme danger – but not death, as Fletcher's Italian mentor, Giovanni Battista Guarini taught. The style was perfect for the theatre, but the involvement by the 1630s of amateur playwrights may suggest that it was too easily imitated.

PHILIP MASSINGER

Fletcher died of the plague in 1625, and his place as the company's contracted writer was taken by his close friend, Philip Massinger. He had already shown his talent with plays such as *The Duke of Milan* (1621), whose excellence is not negated by its somewhat melodramatic ending, and *A New Way to Pay Old Debts* (1624), which has some affinities with Middleton's *A Trick to Catch the Old*

Figure 3.6
The playwright Philip Massinger
Source: British Library, London

One, but is more leisurely, and is set among a higher social class. It stayed in the repertoire for two centuries. Its comedy is brilliantly apt, as when the glutton, Greedy, has to miss the banquet because too many people arrive at Overreach's. And in Overreach it presents a compelling example of the newly rich, grasping and too clever by half.

As the King's Men's new contracted playwright, Massinger set about writing plays at the rate of two per year for the next fifteen years – too many, of course, but his *oeuvre* contains some remarkable dramas. *The Roman Actor* (1626) explores the relationship of a theatre company to a tyrant, grimly, but also upliftingly; *The Great Duke of Florence* (1627) has an excellent ending of reconciliation, which even brings together the comic couple so that fools, too, will not die out; *The City Madam* (1632) is a complex and bitter satire on greed and official corruption; and *The Guardian* (1633) offers a sort of alternative society, implicitly critiquing the society Massinger lives in. It seems that he became more radical as he grew older. Several of his plays of the 1630s have an unexpected political bite, including *Believe as You List* (1631) and *The King and the Subject* (1638). Massinger, perhaps because of the nature of the enclosed theatre and the candlelight, created a nearer equality in interest in female concerns to those of the male. Often the drama became female-centred, not in a melodramatic or sensationalist way, but seriously and intelligently.

WOMEN PLAYWRIGHTS

A number of women were writing plays in the Stuart age, though it was difficult for them to be produced, unless perhaps as a private performance at the author's dwelling. One of these plays is the Senecan *Tragedy of Mariam* by Elizabeth Cary (c.1603). Cary bore eleven children, though her marriage seems not to have been a happy one, and she and her husband separated. She found consolation in Catholicism and became a member of Queen Henrietta Maria's circle in the Caroline period. *The Tragedy of Mariam* belongs to an earlier time in her life. It is the first original British tragedy written by a woman, and it centres on Herod, his second wife, Mariam, and his sister Salomé. It takes a few scenes for the drama to warm up, but eventually we are drawn irresistibly into the contention between two strong women. The play asks the question: unhappy in marriage, how can a woman be free? Its insight into the heroine's plight is unique because it is a woman's, and the play ends with a strong affirmation of female independence in the face of tyranny.

A second play by a female author is *Love's Victory* (c.1620) by Lady Mary Wroth. Wroth had performed in court masques with Queen Anne, and after the death of her husband she conducted an affair with her cousin, the already-married William Herbert, with whom she had two children. *Love's Victory* is an accomplished and rewarding tragicomedy which can certainly be set beside some of Fletcher's better-known plays. Here too it seems the central characters approach death, but the potion they have drunk turns out not to be poison, so that from the direst danger is drawn relief and perhaps purgation.

AMATEUR PLAYWRIGHTS

These women writers were amateurs, like Suckling, though their plays were never performed professionally. But they too were well acquainted with court circles, especially those around Charles I's wife, Henrietta Maria, who encouraged her male courtiers – Suckling, Davenant, the Duke of

Newcastle and others – to write plays, to Ben Jonson's disgust. He wrote to his former apprentice, Richard Brome:

> You . . . served your time
> Apprenticeship; which few do nowadays.
> Now each court hobby-horse will wince in rhyme;
> Both learned and unlearned, all write plays.
> It was not so of old.[1]

Brome's own bitterness at these vanity productions was to be made clear in *The Court Beggar* (c.1640):

> My project is that no play may be admitted to the stage, but of their making who professor endeavour to live
> by the quality, that no courtiers, divines, students-at-law, lawyers' clerks, tradesmen or prentices be allowed
> to write 'em, nor the works of any lay-poet whatsoever to be received to the stage, nay though any such poet
> should give a sum of money with his play.

Brome does not even mention women playwrights, and neither he nor Jonson could stop the male courtiers' pens. The most accomplished of them was undoubtedly William Davenant. He was an energetic acolyte of the queen, a fanatical royalist who sometimes claimed to be Shakespeare's illegitimate son. He began his social climb by purchasing an outlandish silk suit, which served its purpose of getting him noticed. His plays (after a false start writing highly charged but uncontrolled tragedies) tended to be emotional tragicomedies after the fashion of the day, the best usually being thought to be the comic, mildly satirical *The Wits* (1634). His *News from Plymouth* (1635) is also brisk and amusing. Through the Commonwealth period, and on past the Restoration, Davenant was to become the most dynamic force in English theatre.

Lodowick Carlell was in some ways a more interesting playwright, seemingly more resourceful and able to conjure arresting dramatic moments in plays such as *The Deserving Favourite* (1629) and *Arviragus and Philicia* (1636). Thomas Killigrew, who was first a page and then a member of the royal household, wrote a cynical, not unamusing, class-conscious comedy, *The Parson's Wedding* (1641) and, like Davenant, was to go on to greater theatrical heights after the Restoration. The prodigal Sir John Suckling, who made the production of his comedy *Aglaura* into something of a vanity project, wrote several other plays, including the unperformed tragedy, *Brennoralt* (1640), which implicitly – and surprisingly – criticised Charles I for his tardy response to the threat of the Scottish Covenanters. His comedy, *The Goblins* (1638), is set in a sort of fairyland, intended probably to be a Utopian alternative society, and is notable because the production was one of the earliest to use scenery on public stage. But it is also notorious for its caricaturing of Ben Jonson, even though Jonson had died the year before the play was performed. Perhaps in revenge, Richard Brome, a far superior playwright, and Jonson's former apprentice, caricatured Suckling as the ridiculous Sir Ferdinand in his comedy, *The Court Beggar* (1640).

ACTORS

It was not these amateur dramatists, however, who were responsible for the reputation of the King's Men. That fell to the actors. It was they whom the passengers in the 'multitude of coaches' which were the subject of a petition to close the theatre in 1619 came to see. The petition was dismissed with contempt by the Lord Chamberlain, and a new Royal Patent was issued instead. In 1633 there were again complaints about the traffic outside Blackfriars, and again the complaints were dismissed, this time with some adjustment to the parking regulations.

By this date, John Heminges and Henry Condell, who had led the company before King Charles came to the throne, had both died, and the management was in the hands of John Lowin and Joseph Taylor. Lowin, whose acting career began at the very end of Elizabeth's reign, and who lived to see Cromwell rule Britain, was a large man with a big beard. He seems usually to have played bluff no-nonsense characters – honest friends, foursquare villains, outspoken politicians, including Bosola in *The Duchess of Malfi*, Domitian in *The Roman Actor* and Titus Flaminius in *Believe as You List*. He also appeared in revivals as Falstaff and Henry VIII, Volpone, Sir Epicure Mammon and Morose. He is reputed to have retired when the theatres closed in 1642, not to fight in the Civil War, like many of his fellows, but to open a public house, The Three Pigeons, in Brentford. He died in 1653 aged 77.

Joseph Taylor may have been the most compelling actor of his age. He was with the Lady Elizabeth's Company from 1611 till 1616, and then with Prince Charles's Men till 1619, when he joined the King's Men. He soon made his mark, and after a short time he was performing almost all Burbage's great roles. He played Hamlet, for instance, 'incomparably well', and also appeared as Iago, Truewit in Jonson's *Epicoene* and Face in *The Alchemist*. He seems to have been particularly admired at court, and Henrietta Maria persuaded him to coach her and her ladies for their court performance of *The Shepherds' Paradise*.

But the King's Men was no two-man band. There was John Shank, a jig-maker and dancer, who became the company's chief clown after Robert Armin's death. His apprentice was Thomas Pollard, who also became a fine clown. Eyllaerdt Swanston was a popular actor entrusted with roles like Othello and Bussy D'Ambois, but also with a string of villains. Robert Benfield played less eye-catching but still important parts like Junius Rusticus in *The Roman Actor* and Marcellus in *Believe as You List* and Anthony Smith was another versatile and reliable performer.

BOY ACTORS

Boy actors who took the women's parts were not expected to last as long as some of these, but the King's Men had several outstanding boys. Dick Robinson was Richard Burbage's apprentice, and indeed married Burbage's widow after the great man died. His skill is well captured by Engine in Ben Jonson's *The Devil Is an Ass*:

> There be some of 'em (actors)
> Are very honest lads. There's Dick Robinson,
> A very pretty fellow, and comes often
> To a gentleman's chamber, a friend's of mine. We had
> The merriest supper of it there one night –
> The gentleman's landlady invited him
> To a gossip's feast. Now he, sir, brought Dick Robinson
> Dressed like a lawyer's wife amongst 'em all
> (I lent him clothes), but to see him behave it,

> And lay the law, and carve, and drink unto 'em,
> And then talk bawdy, and send frolics! Oh,
> It would have burst your buttons, or not left you
> A seam.

Robinson was followed by John Thompson, the company's leading boy actor in the 1620s, who was famed for his regal ladies, his proud queens and haughty villainesses. He was the Cardinal's Mistress in *The Duchess of Malfi* and Domitia in *The Roman Actor*. Thompson was also an excellent singer, and he moved on to adult roles later, playing them till he died in 1634. He was often partnered, and later followed, by the younger John Honeyman, who played, for instance, Domitilla in *The Roman Actor*. Honeyman was, according to the playwright John Ford, 'a man . . . sweetly good'. In the early 1630s he began playing adult roles, too, and he wrote at least one play which unfortunately is now lost. His brother acted with the Prince's Players. John Honeyman died in 1636.

STEPHEN HAMMERTON

Stephen Hammerton who started as a boy actor in the early 1630s, became probably the most popular star in England in the last years before the closing of the theatres. Hammerton was the idol especially of the female theatregoers at the Blackfriars. At the end of Killigrew's *The Parson's Wedding* (1641) the Captain begs for the audience's applause: 'If you refuse, Stephen misses the wench, and then you cannot justly blame the poet', he says. Though this presumably refers to the character Hammerton was playing in the play, the fact that his real name is used here may suggest that some other assignation awaits him. Suckling's epilogue to *The Goblins* also refers to Hammerton's popularity with the ladies:

> Oh, if Stephen should be killed
> Or miss the lady, how the plot is spilled!

In 1642 his career was summarised thus: 'at first a most noted and beautiful woman actor, but afterwards he acted with equal grace and applause, a young lover's part'.

MUSIC AT THE BLACKFRIARS

One other feature of the Blackfriars' experience must be noticed: the music. When they took over the theatre from the Chapel Children in 1608, the King's Men also took over the theatre orchestra, whose playing was already popular. They started playing a full hour before the play began, and they played between the acts, too. While the candles were being replaced, the audience stood to stretch their legs, and the orchestra played. Viols, cittern, lute, a recorder and flute made up the players, and the band became renowned as the best in London.

It was another facet of the King's Men's domination of the London theatre.

NOTE

1 Ben Jonson, 'To my faithful servant, and (by his virtue) my loving friend, the author of this work, Mr Richard Brome', prefatory verse in Richard Brome, *The Northern Lass*, 1632.

Chapter 30: Beeston's Boys and the Sons of Ben

RIOTS AT THE COCKPIT THEATRE'S OPENING

In August 1616, Christopher Beeston, manager of Queen Anne's Men at the Red Bull, acquired the lease of the Royal Cockpit in Drury Lane which was still administered by John Best, cockmaster to the now-deceased Henry, Prince of Wales. He paid £45 per year for the Cockpit 'and the sheds thereunto adjoining', intending to convert the old building, fashionably situated as it was near the royal residences of Whitehall in the west end of the growing city, into a 'private' theatre. The members of nearby Lincoln's Inn, when they heard of Beeston's plans, objected vociferously; but they were overruled, and when it was discovered that he was erecting not so much a small extension to the original building, more a new building altogether, he also ran into trouble. But he continued, and the new Cockpit opened early in 1617. Then on 4 March there was more trouble. This time a large and rowdy group of apprentices ran amok, causing mayhem from Finsbury to Lincoln's Inn Fields, including attacking the new theatre. The actors defended the premises with guns, and even killed three of the hooligans, but still they

> broke in, wounded divers of the players, broke open their trunks and what apparel, books and other things they
> found, they burned and cut in pieces; and not content herewith, got on the top of the house and untiled it.[1]

Whatever mayhem they caused elsewhere, there is evidence that those who assaulted the Cockpit did not do so by chance but because where they had been able to see the plays and players for one penny at the Red Bull, they would now have to pay up to sixpence for the privilege. But Beeston was not to be thwarted. He set to and repaired the damage, renamed it 'The Phoenix' and re-opened for business in June. But the ruffians who had objected in 1617 planned a second attack, this time on both the Red Bull and the Cockpit-Phoenix. Unfortunately for them, the Privy Council got wind of their plan, and were able to head it off. But the battles show vividly how the drama was being removed from the possession of everybody and becoming the property of a section of the population.

THE COCKPIT THEATRE

There is no certain picture or plan extant of the Cockpit (as the Phoenix continued to be called), but a series of drawings by Inigo Jones have been identified with some confidence as pertaining to it. If

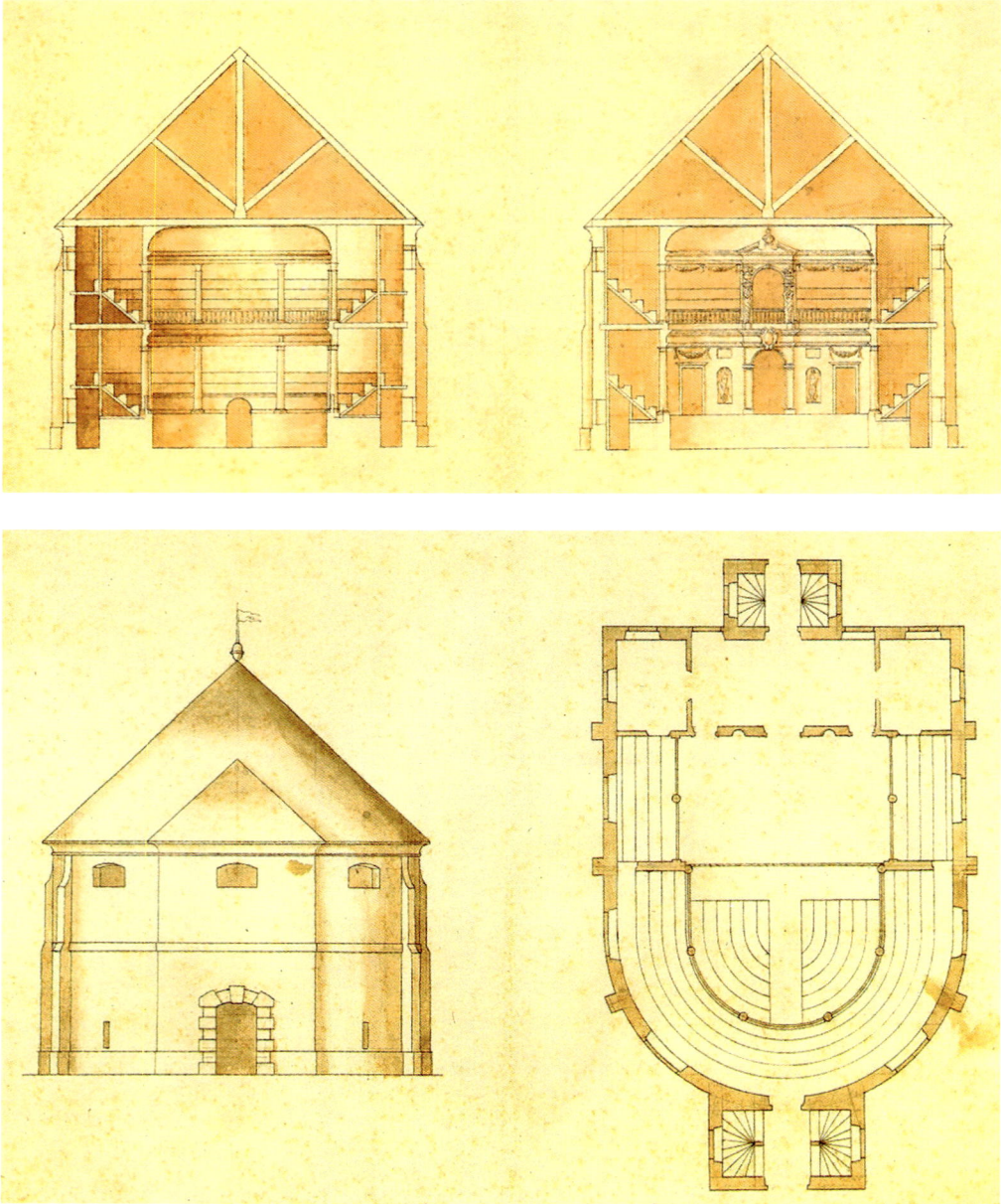

Figure 3.7
Cockpit Theatre, elevation and ground plan

they are correct, then the Cockpit's originally circular shape was remodelled to contain the auditorium and added to, to double the length of the building, by a rectangular extension within which was housed the platform stage, and backstage area. Even so the new theatre was considerably smaller than Blackfriars, and may have held at most five hundred spectators. In the auditorium the most expensive places were the boxes which abutted the sides of the stage, and the pit, where benches replaced the open air amphitheatre's yard for standing spectators. Two or perhaps three U-shaped galleries ran round the back of the auditorium, behind and above the pit, and perhaps continuing behind the stage itself. The stage was backed by two small doors, only five feet six inches high, at either side, and probably a much larger arched entrance in the centre at the back, which entrance was perhaps often curtained off and used for 'discoveries'. The central arch was surmounted by another arch housing a small acting area 'above'. The whole was brick-built, but the interior was painted to look like marbled stone, the wooden seats were covered with rush matting while the pit benches were painted red-brown. The stage floor was covered in green baize, and the ceiling painted azure, overlaid with bubbly clouds and the signs of the zodiac.

This description, based on the Jones plans and John Orrell's reconstruction,[2] does not solve every problem. Where were the musicians, who were certainly a feature here, stationed? There was certainly no scenery on stage, not least because those in the high-priced side boxes would be unable to see it. And the size of the Cockpit obviously precluded battle scenes with armies: thus in John Ford's *Perkin Warbeck*, which was premiered here in 1633, the siege of Norham ends in a parley, and the Scots retreat without a battle. Later, the Cornish uprising remains firmly off stage. The same was true of the Blackfriars, where, for example, in Massinger's *The Maid of Honour* (1621), a stage direction reads: '*Chambers shot off: a flourish as to an Assault*', when the assault was not actually staged; though later in the same play there is '*a long charge: after which, a Flourish for victory*'. This is not, of course, a battle, but the Blackfriars stage was twice the size of the Cockpit's, so presumably could stage even 'a long charge' more easily. Still, all these directions indicate something fundamentally different from, say, the battles in Shakespeare's Wars of the Roses plays. But in the much more intimate, candle-lit surroundings of the Cockpit, other simpler actions might be seen in thrilling close-up. In Thomas Nabbes's *The Bride* (1638), for example, Theophilus '*throws his cloak on the other's point, gets within him, and takes away his sword*'.

CHRISTOPHER BEESTON AND HIS COMPANIES

The Cockpit was controlled by Christopher Beeston from its inception till his death in 1638. He had entered the theatrical profession as a boy player with the Lord Chamberlain's Company, and sometime around 1603 had joined Queen Anne's Men. By 1612 he had risen to the position of business manager, and with the founding of the Cockpit became a significant impresario in his own right. But success did not come easily. Queen Anne's Men never recovered from the devastating attack on the building by the rioting crowds, and in 1619 Beeston dissolved the company and formed a new one, the Prince's Men, who made a fresh start. But they too failed and were soon disbanded. Middleton suggested that the theatre was cursed: he wondered whether 'some quean pissed upon the first brick'.

In 1622 Beeston formed Lady Elizabeth's Men. They were much more successful, and premiered a number of the best plays of the period, including Middleton and Rowley's *The Changeling* and Massinger's *The Bondman* (1623), as well as reviving with notable success the highly popular farce by John Cooke, *Greene's Tu Quoque*. However, in 1625 the death of the king and then a terrible outbreak of the plague closed the theatres for many months, and Lady Elizabeth's Men did not survive.

When the theatres re-opened, Beeston established yet another new company with some excellent actors, Queen Henrietta Maria's Men, and he also contracted the playwright, James Shirley to supply them with new plays. They played with considerable success at the Cockpit for over a decade, and because they were the new queen's company, they were permitted to wear the royal livery. Beeston, no longer acting now, managed the company: he looked after the actors, including being responsible for the training of young actors, he oversaw the wardrobe and properties, he kept the accounts and he was the public face of the company.

He was clearly a powerful personality who did not suffer fools gladly. When his accounts were queried, he replied he was not responsible because he had been ill. In any case the complaints referred to the Queen's Men who had long since disbanded! In 1623, there were rumours of his embezzling moneys paid to the company. But nothing was ever proved. He may have been a Catholic. He was certainly autocratic. But he was also clever enough to see the advantage of retaining the favour of the Master of the Revels: he gave him a book by Sir Walter Raleigh in 1623, and a decade later gave his wife a very fine pair of gloves. Thus when Shirley's play *The Ball* ran into difficulties in 1632, because it guyed certain living people, he was able to draw the sting from the Master of the Revels' censures and smooth matters over successfully.

In 1636 the plague closed the theatres again, this time for fifteen months. Beeston's company, like its predecessors, and unlike the financially robust, democratically controlled King's Men, could not withstand the pressures and was dissolved. When the Cockpit re-opened in 1637, Beeston formed a new company. This time it was called the King and Queen's Young Company, and it was dedicated to the training of young actors. This was a unique enterprise which enjoyed royal approval, but because the company contained an unusual number of boy players, it soon became known as Beeston's Boys. Beeston, however, did not live to see this training project through. He died in 1638, handing on to not only the theatre, but also an enviable property portfolio to his son William.

WILLIAM BEESTON

William Beeston, an admired acting teacher, immediately tempted the best playwright of the time, Richard Brome, to break his contract with the Salisbury Court Theatre and join the Cockpit, and he was soon mounting some of Brome's best plays, *A Mad Couple Well Match'd* (1639), *The Court Beggar* (1640) and *A Jovial Crew* (1641). But in 1640 disaster struck. Beeston presented a play whose title has not been recorded which seemed to attack the king's policy towards the Scots. The king was outraged, and demanded action. Immediately the Lord Chamberlain issued warrants which banned the company from playing and put the leading actors and Beeston himself in the Marshalsea Prison. But in fact the ban was only temporary, and in three days the actors were released. Beeston himself, however, was incarcerated for longer, and William Davenant, courtier playwright and, since the death of Ben Jonson, Poet Laureate, was appointed to head the company at the Cockpit. Strangely enough, he only stayed a few months before hot-footing it out of London when his royalist plotting was uncovered, and Beeston quietly resumed control of the Cockpit.

WILLIAM DAVENANT IN THE 1630S AND 1640S

Davenant may have received the appointment in the first place after the collapse of a notably grand scheme he had been labouring on since early 1639. He had obtained permission to build 'a theatre or playhouse with necessary tiring and retiring rooms and other places convenient' in Fleet Street, just north of Blackfriars and Salisbury Court. He was granted permission 'to gather together, entertain, govern, privilege and keep such and so many players and persons, to exercise action, musical presentments, scenes, dancing and the like . . . for the honest recreation of such as shall desire to see the same'.[3] Davenant wanted to build an indoor playhouse able to utilise the scenic marvels which Inigo Jones had developed for court performances, to make them available in a public (or 'private') theatre. But though the licence to build this splendid new addition to London's theatre world was granted, Davenant's political convictions forced him to postpone any work on the project while he fought with the king in what was called the 'First Bishops' War' in Scotland. By the time he returned, the permission had been revoked, and he was offered the Cockpit directorship for the time being. As we have seen, politics again intervened, and Davenant was further caught up in what was fast becoming a civil war in England. Through many vicissitudes over the next years, which included exile and prison, Davenant never lost his ambition as a theatrical entrepreneur, and his dreams were to an extent finally fulfilled only after the Restoration of the monarchy.

ACTORS AT THE COCKPIT

William Beeston had been an actor, though not a particularly successful one. But the company his father gathered, especially during his final decade at the Cockpit, was almost as strong as the King's Men. The leading actor was Richard Perkins, a versatile performer who was first acknowledged by John Webster after his performance in *The White Devil* in 1612: Webster wrote of 'his well approved industry' and 'the worth of his action [which] did crown both the beginning and the end' of the play. He was notably successful as Barabus in *The Jew of Malta* and as Sir John Belfare in Shirley's *The Wedding* (1626). His performance in Robert Davenport's *King John and Matilda* (1631) 'gave grace to the play', according to one commentator.

The company had two clowns, William Sherlock, who was fat, and William Robbins, who was lean, as in Shirley's *The Wedding*, when Robbins was the skinflint Rawbone, and Sherlock the portly Lodam. At one moment, Rawbone runs on stage, bumps into Lodam and bounces off him. Their duel consists of '*a doublet stuffed with straw advancing on a bullrush*', and Lodam complains that the contest is unfair because he presents so much larger a target for a sword than his skinny opponent.

Anthony Turner played older men such as Justice Landby in *The Wedding* and Piston in Nabbes's *Hannibal and Scipio* (1635) with quiet strength. William Allen was equally compelling in often more energetic roles like Nabbes's Hannibal.

The best of the company's boy actors were probably Theophilus Bird and Ezekial Fenn. Bird was the Queen in the second part of Heywood's *Fair Maid of the West* (1630) and Massanissa in *Hannibal and Scipio*, and graduated to adult parts when he grew up. He was a friend of the playwright John Ford, and married his boss, Christopher Beeston's daughter. Fenn was possibly the better actor, versatile and energetic, Sophonisba in *Hannibal and Scipio*. He, too, became a successful adult actor, an elevation Henry Glapthorne's poem 'For Ezekial Fenn at His First Acting a Man's Part', compares to an 'adventurous man seeking new paths i' th' angry ocean'.

JOHN FORD

Some professional writers, unhappy at the King's Men's employment of courtier playwrights, gravitated to the Cockpit, helping to make that company the equal of their more renowned rivals. The best of them, John Ford and James Shirley, responded to the dream-like intensity of the indoor the-atre, the candlelight, the music and the proximity of the actors to the audience, to create a kind of play which was specific to the Caroline theatre. The plays explored the lives of leisured people, the fashionable West End men and women who formed a good part of their audiences, whose social events – weddings, balls and parading in the park – often provided the pivot of the plays. But there was also often an unexpected eroticism in these works which saw women as not merely objects, but as having their own active sexuality. This often comes from an almost hypnotic intensity which can perhaps best be seen in a play like Ford's *The Broken Heart* (c.1630), as when Orgilus dons his disguise, and his sister and her lover, whom Orgilus hates, enter. '*Prophilus passes by*', reads the stage direction, '*supporting Euphrania and whispering*', and the scene acquires a dream-like quality which renders it impossible for the spectator to question its logic. Later in the same play, there is 'discovered':

> An altar covered with white: two lights of virgin wax upon it. Recorders play, during which enter Attendants bearing Ithocles on a hearse (in a rich robe, with a crown on his head) and place him on one side of the altar. Afterwards, enter Calantha in white, crowned, attended. . . . Calantha kneels before the altar, the Ladies kneeling behind her, the rest standoff. The recorders cease during her devotions. Soft music. Calantha and the rest rise, doing obeisance to the altar.

JAMES SHIRLEY

Shirley, a schoolteacher and minister before he became a playwright, was conscious that the drama of the 1630s was new and different. In *The Doubtful Heir* (1638) he notes what this drama does not contain, as compared with what Elizabethans offered:

> No shows, no dance, and what you most delight in,
> Grave understanders, here's no target fighting
> Upon the stage, all work for cutlers barred,
> No bawdry, nor no ballads; . . .
> No clowns, no squibs, no devil in't . . .

Shirley was also able to create dream-like effects, concentrated in the intensity of the moment. In *The Wedding* (1626), when Beauford has been told Gratiana is unfaithful to him, he does not stop to check the facts, he simply berates her with extreme passion. She cannot stop this tirade, it overwhelms her, and as in a dream, we identify completely with the character. *The Lady of Pleasure* (1632) explores dangerous fantasies and offers its spectators the chance of indulging these, again as in a dream, without the social consequences.

Fashionable places of resort, like Shirley's *Hyde Park* (1632), and Nabbes's *Covent Garden* (1633), which, because of the building work, is ankle-deep in mud, and *Tottenham Court Fair* (c.1634), are seen as alluring spaces where characters flit in and out of the shadows, meet unex-pected potential lovers and find no need for responsible or moral constrictions. Even Glapthorne's melodramatic *Tragedy of Alphonsus Wallenstein* has a seductive fantastical quality quite unlike earlier history plays.

THE SONS OF BEN

Ford's *Perkin Warbeck* (1634) has a not dissimilar unreality about it, though it also valorises the author's political friends in the oppositional Essex faction. This play, however, also questions kingly behaviour in the context of Charles I's wilfulness. These writers, and fringe playwrights like William Cartwright, Thomas Randolph and Shackerley Marmion, called themselves 'The Sons of Ben', often drinking with Jonson in the Devil Tavern near Temple Bar, perhaps as Jonson had himself in earlier years drunk with John Donne, John Fletcher, Francis Beaumont and perhaps even William Shakespeare at the Mermaid Tavern in Cheapside. But the plays of the 'Sons of Ben' were not really like his. The most intriguing member of the group from this point of view was Richard Brome, who had been Jonson's servant, and was most closely associated with the Salisbury Court Theatre in the 1630s.

SALISBURY COURT THEATRE

The Salisbury Court was the third of the 'private' theatres in Caroline London, opened in 1629. It was built on land belonging to Thomas Sackville, fourth Earl of Dorset, who was Chamberlain to Queen Henrietta Maria and a theatre enthusiast. He rented the land for forty-one and a half years for £25 for the first six months of occupancy and for £100 per annum thereafter to William Blagrave, deputy to Sir Henry Herbert as Master of the Revels, and Richard Gunnell, a former actor who had been managing the Fortune Theatre, though not very successfully, since 1623. The Salisbury Court was situated near the new and newly fashionable Covent Garden, just outside the old city walls, and was probably like Blackfriars in its stage space and auditorium configuration. The new King's Revels Company which Gunnell formed to play in this theatre aimed, like the later Beeston's Boys,

> to train and bring up certain boys in the quality of playing not only with intent to be a supply of able actors to his Majesty's servants of Blackfriars . . . but the solace of his Royal Majesty when his Majesty should please to see them, and also for the recreation of his Majesty's loving subjects.[4]

The venture however was not greatly successful and the theatre's finances were always precarious. The King's Revels Company gave way to Prince Charles's Men in 1631, but took back the theatre two years later. Gunnell died in 1634, though not before he had opened negotiations with Richard Brome to become resident playwright, displacing Thomas Randolph who died in 1635. The ambitious Richard Heton took over, though the theatre was hardly more successful under his regime. Though the King's Revels were disbanded at this time, Brome was retained and it was the remnants of Queen Henrietta Maria's Men, still including Richard Perkins, William Sherlock, Anthony Turner, besides others from their Cockpit days, who took over the theatre.

RICHARD BROME

Brome's contract was renewed in 1638, but within a year or two he was persuaded to break it by William Beeston, and, despite a series of court cases, his next plays were written for the Cockpit. Because he served Ben Jonson, he has been called 'Jonsonian', but his comedies are more original

Figure 3.8
Title page of Nathanael Richards's *Messalina*, staged by the King's Revels Company in 1635 at the Salisbury Court Theatre

Source: By permission of the Folger Shakespeare Library

than this implies. It is true his extravagant, freewheeling language can remind us of the older writer, and so too can his energy, but Brome's success actually annoyed Jonson, who himself denied a similarity and quarrelled with his young protégé. Brome's thought was more progressive, too, though he was not an adherent of any identifiable political ideology.

In *The Weeding of Covent Garden* (1633), he is on the side of the young against the whims of authority. In *The Damoiselle* (1638) his disgust at corruption, usury and many of the dealings of the legal profession is clear, and the satire has a political bias. In *The Antipodes* (1638), the lengthy play-within-the-play stands Caroline England on its head in an attempt to exhibit fashionable pessimism for what it is. *A Mad Couple Well Match'd* (1639) and *The Court Beggar* (1640) are also bitter and sardonic about the whole of Caroline society, especially the one-person rule which, for Brome, leads inevitably to corruption. He sees the gap between rich and poor growing wider, and how the poor are preyed on by spivs, swindlers and city sharks. And the good old days which he conjures up in *A Jovial Crew* are soon seen to offer no way forward. This is a 'state of the nation' play in which freedom from the constrictions of society is seen as desirable but illusory. Brome's urgent desire to assert the way of the gypsy or the beggar as leading to freedom foreshadows the work of some

Reader, lo heere thou wilt two faces finde,
One of the body, t'other of the Minde ;
This by the Graver so, that with much strife
Wee thinke Brome dead, hee's drawne so to the life
That by's owne pen's done so ingeinously
That who reads it, must thinke hee nere shall dy.

T. Crosse Sculpsit.

A·B·

Figure 3.9
The playwright Richard Brome
Source: Old Paper Studios/Alamy Stock Photo

later playwrights, such as Gay in *The Beggar's Opera* or Arden in *Live Like Pigs* or Butterworth in *Jerusalem*, and chimes with a deep yearning we all feel sometimes.

Brome's natural sympathy with the outsider also manifests itself in his treatment of women. His attitude is no mere tokenism, but what might be called a full-bodied feminism, as in *The Weeding of Covent Garden* which questions the confining of English women and compares this with what pertains in Italy:

> Our desires
> Are high as theirs; our will as apt and forward;
> Our wits as ripe, our beauties more attractive.

What holds women in England back then?

> Only in bashful coward custom that
> Stoops i' the shoulders, and submits the neck
> To bondage of authority, to these laws
> That men of feeble age and weaker eyesight
> Have framed, to bar their sons from youthful pleasures.

The radicalism in Brome's dramas feeds into the discontents of the time, but where Brome's adherence lay when the English Civil War broke out in 1642 is not clear. Indeed, from the time of the closing of the theatres very little is known of him. In 1650 he was admitted to Charterhouse charity hospital, and he died there in 1652. But his plays remain, fusing features of the Elizabethan drama like the play within the play (more than half his plays employ this device) with the best characteristics of Caroline theatre practice. This includes a bitter political awareness and a carnivalesque energy. At his best, Brome transcends the conventional and joins with gypsies and other outsiders in a celebration of freedom, however time limited or partial that is.

NOTES

1 Edward Sherbourne, quoted in G.E. Bentley, *The Jacobean and Caroline Stage*, vol 6, Oxford: Oxford University Press, 1967, p. 54.
2 John Orrell, *The Theatres of Inigo Jones and John Webb*, Cambridge: Cambridge University Press, 1985, pp. 39–60.
3 Mary Edmond, *Rare Sir William Davenant*, Manchester: Manchester University Press, 1987, p. 75.
4 Philip Edwards, Gerald Eades Bentley, Kathleen McLuskie and Lois Potter, *The Revels History of Drama in English*, vol IV, London: Methuen, 1981, p. 105.

Chapter 31: Playgoing in the private theatres

A SOCIAL EVENT

A visit to a private theatre in the 1620s or 1630s was a social event. The audience included as many females as males, and though there were probably a disproportionate number of better-off people, plenty of ordinary citizens also attended. The crowds coming to Blackfriars of an afternoon were large enough to annoy the local residents. Many in the audience probably knew one another, and in the comparative darkness there was plenty of scope for sexual naughtiness, as well as for laughing and quarrelling. Lord Thurles tried to stab Captain Charles Essex in Blackfriars in 1632. Other quarrels were known to end in duels.

Admission prices to Blackfriars were sixpence, a shilling and one shilling and sixpence, which was expensive. Those who wanted to be seen as well as to see could purchase a seat on a stool on stage for an extra sixpence. Prices were usually double for the first performance of a new play. The second night was usually for the author's benefit. In the private theatres, intervals were necessary to trim or change the candles, and these offered a chance to play music or even present a dance, but also allowed members of the audience to socialise. The spectators were interested in the actors, and gossiped about them, but also about the play:

> O what a monster wit must that man have
> That could please all which now their twelvepence gave:
> High characters (cries one) and he would see
> Things that ne'er were, nor are, nor ne'er will be.
> Romances, cries easy-souls, and then they swear
> The play's well writ, though scarce a good line's there.[1]

So wrote Suckling. Brome preferred to josh his audience, in a manner which suggests the intimacy between stage and auditorium, and between players and spectators:

> Well! Had your mirth enough? Much good may't do you.
> If not, 'tis more than I did promise to you.
> 'Tis your own fault, for it is you, not we,
> Make a play good or bad.[2]

REPERTOIRES TO SUIT AUDIENCES

The fact was that this was a more intimate audience than had been seen in any previous theatre. Private anguish and sociability did not entirely take over from the public consequences of action in the drama, but the plays engaged with issues of relevance to their audiences while absorbing them emotionally in new ways. Issues of religion and politics were raised here, but so too were the differences of living in the country or the town or the court, nuanced sexual relationships, questions of individual responsibility, and more. And the theatre companies tailored what they offered to their patrons' interests: plays were often cut or re-ordered after the first performance, songs might be added, and prologues or epilogues, special to the first performance, dropped. And of course, with a comparatively limited clientele, companies had to have large repertoires: they presented up to five different plays in an average week.

THE ACTOR IN THE SPECTATOR'S GAZE

In these candle-lit theatres, the actors were very close to the spectators and could move swiftly and easily from action to dialogue, from dialogue to soliloquy. An actor entered from the back of the stage and moved forward. He was viewed from the sides and probably from behind, as well as from the front. It was intimate and three-dimensional, and if the arrangement lost some impressiveness in processions or other ostentatious actions as compared to the open air playhouses, it gained much in naturalness. And this encouraged what has come to be known as 'the gaze', that longing stare, part voyeuristic, part devotional which one person trains on another, and seems to objectify them. And of course those on stools on the stage were also choosing to be made the object of the gaze. It emphasises the validity of current thinking which sees the body as the site of cultural, social, psychological and political struggle, and puts an unexpected onus on the body to make meanings. But if the gaze is an unspoken attempt to control the other person, here the relationship was less clear. It was the actor who was active, whose energy, status and fictional predicament controlled the gazer's responses. The actor's position *vis-à-vis* the spectator was not the same as that, say, of the prisoner *vis-à-vis* the guard.

ACTING IN THE PRIVATE THEATRES

Acting in the private theatres became more natural, less bombastic perhaps, than in the old open air playhouses. In Brome's *The Antipodes* Letoy points out some typical failings in actors, for these will be more noticeable in the small indoor theatres:

> Let me not see you act now
> In your scholastic way you brought to town wi' ye,
> With see-saw sack-a-down, like a sawyer;
> Nor in a comic scene play Hercules Furens,
> Tearing your throat to split the audience's ears.

There was no need for the actor to shout in this intimate space:

> And you, sir, that had got a trick of late
> Of holding out your bum in a set speech,

> Your fingers fibulating on your breast,
> As if your buttons or your band-strings were
> Helps to your memory.

Nor could the actor relax on stage:

> And when you have spoke, at end of every speech,
> Not minding the reply, you turn you round
> As tumblers do, when betwixt every feat
> They gather wind by firking up their breeches.

As every good actor knows, not to listen to his partner on stage not only hobbles his own performance, but destroys the credibility the audience needs.

Yet this was not 'naturalism': the actor still had to command conventional attitudes. In Ford's *The Lover's Melancholy* (1628), Cuculus is learning how to court a lady:

(Enter Cuculus and Grilla, the former in a black velvet cap and a white feather, with paper in his hand'.)
CUCULUS: Do not I look freshly, and like a youth of the trim?
GRILLA: As rare an old youth as ever walked cross-gartered.

Then he takes up his stance: 'I must look big, and care little or nothing for her, because she is a creature that stands at livery. Thus I talk wisely and to no purpose'. Of another woman he states, 'I must come at her in whining tune; sigh, wipe mine eyes, fold my arms, and blubber out my speech'. For a third who is 'abominably proud' he has written a speech which he reads. He is standing as the exquisite lover when Pelias enters, and immediately recognises the posture of the lover:

> In amorous contemplation, on my life,
> Courting his page.

In Glapthorne's *The Ladies Privilege*, Adorni and Corimba practice by copying a love scene they have watched in the theatre, while in the same author's *Tragedy of Albertus Wallenstein*, Newman instructs Frederick:

> You must not then accost her with a shrug,
> As you were lousy, with your 'Lady, sweet Lady',
> Or 'most super excellent lady',
> Nor in the Spanish garb, with a state face,
> As you had new been eating of a radish,
> And meant to swallow her for mutton to it.

The concept of character here owes little to psychology. It is the performance of the part which convinces. In *'Tis Pity She's a Whore*, Soranzo *acts* the wronged husband; in *Perkin Warbeck*, Perkin's claim rests partly on the fact that he *plays the part* of king so believably and better than Henry VII.

Every small movement is important in this theatre where the actor is so scrutinised: in Shirley's *The Traitor* (1631), Pisano says:

> Be you
> Comforted, lady; let all griefs repair
> To this, their proper centre. (*Lays his hand on his breast.*)

Sometimes costume makes the character: 'You wear your hat too like a citizen', says the Steward in Shirley's *The Lady of Pleasure*, and the Duke in Massinger's *The Duke of Milan* is advised to 'wear yellow breeches' because he (like Shakespeare's Malvolio) is hot for love. Even a cavalier can be told from his dress. Brome's Wat in *A Mad Couple Well Matched* has 'a stock of rich cloth, and then we will put draymen and wine-porters, Cornish wrestlers and such like into those clothes and make them country cavaliers'.

AN INTIMATE THEATRE

The intimate stage may have inhibited grandiloquent dramatic moments, but there were compensations. From the stage directions in surviving plays, we can grasp something of the effective acting which was possible, even as we heed Killigrew's warning in *The Parson's Wedding*; after a notably complicated instruction he adds, '*if the scene can be so ordered*'. However, his stage directions are still among the most helpful to anyone seeking to discover how the plays of the period were staged. Here are three from *The Parson's Wedding*:

> *Jolly salutes them; then he goes to the Captain to embrace him. The Captain stands in a French posture and slides from his old way of embracing.*

> *Jolly kisses her and she shoves him away with her mouth.*

> *Still as he offers to touch her she starts as if he plucked up her coats.*

From Massinger's *The City Madam*:

> *Enter Stargaze, Lady Frugal, Anne, Mary and Millicent, in several affected postures, with looking-glasses at their girdles.*

And from Davenant's *The Wits*:

> *They step aside, whilst he calls between the hangings.*

This direction refers to the hangings at the back of the stage in front of the main central entrance.

This stage was also powerful in staging rituals, especially those of a hushed or holy kind. The dance and funeral in Ford's *The Broken Heart* may be the best example, but Ford managed something virtually as striking with the masked dance in *'Tis Pity She's a Whore*. In Massinger's *The City Madam* the characters dance a kind of ritualised version of the Orpheus story. Then, to 'sad music' young Goldwire and young Tradewell enter '*as from prison*', followed by other characters, including

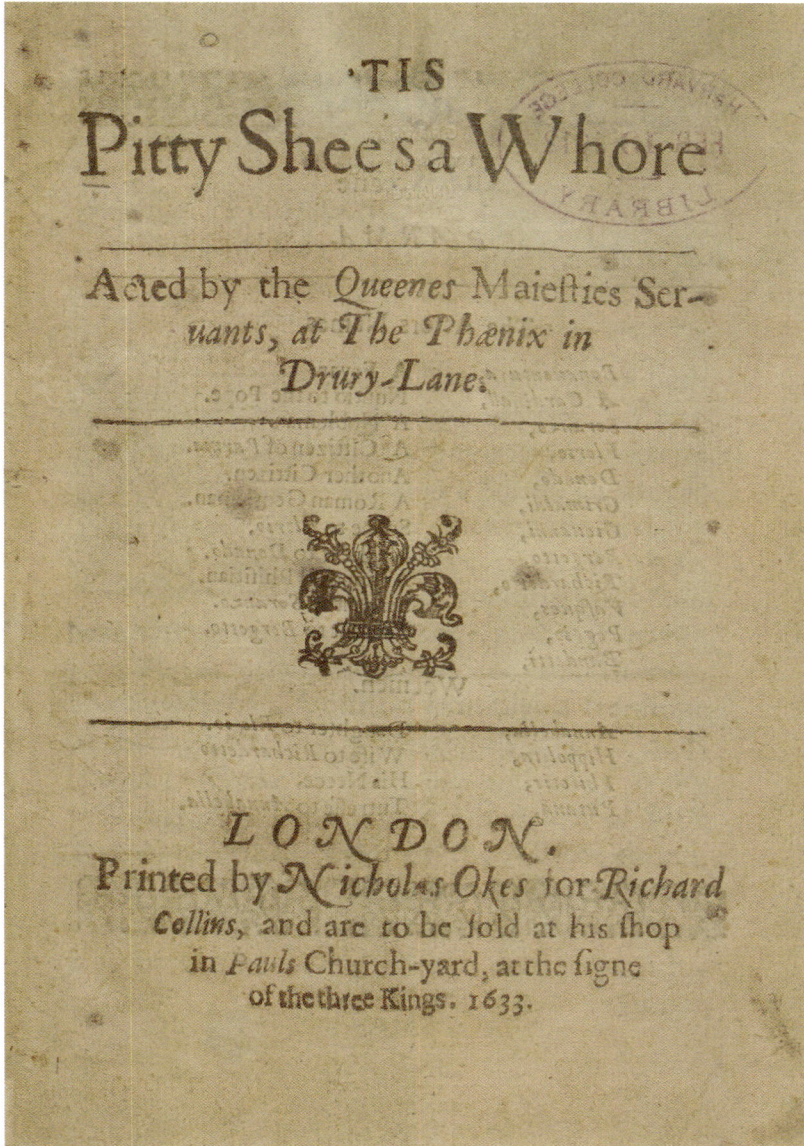

Figure 3.10

Title page of John Ford's *'Tis Pity She's a Whore*, staged in 1632 at the Cockpit (or Phoenix) Theatre

Source: Houghton Library, Harvard University

Shave'em in the livery of Bridewell; they kneel, *'lifting up their hands'*. Finally, Sir John *'burns incense and makes mystical gesticulations'* which seem to bring back to life two characters who were imagined dead. And disguise can further complicate ritual, as when the thieves in Suckling's *The Goblins* dress as devils, or when Decoy, disguised as an old woman, appears to the blindfolded Kickshaw in Shirley's *The Lady of Pleasure*.

This was a theatre of naturalness and intimacy, but also one which could drift into a kind of dream world, or into ritual or delightful or dangerous fantasy.

NOTES

1 Sir John Suckling, *Epilogue to the Goblins*, 1638.
2 Richard Brome, *Epilogue to a Mad Couple Well Matched*, 1639.

Chapter 32: Theatre at the courts of King James and King Charles

The theatre at the courts of James I and VI and Charles I and their queens was elitist, even self-absorbed, but its importance in history can hardly be exaggerated: it was in this theatre that women first acted in Britain, and it was here that scenery was first introduced.

THE MASQUE OF BLACKNESS

The Masque of Blackness written by Ben Jonson was perhaps the first Stuart court masque to make a significant impact. It was presented at Whitehall on Twelfth Night 1605, where in the rectangular great hall a stage was erected about forty feet square, with wing space to the sides and seating for several hundred spectators. The masque's plot, like that of virtually every masque which followed it over nearly forty years, was slight: twelve black nymphs enter, as it were from a great seashell. They seek a 'blesséd isle' whose names ends in – *tannia*. The land is 'Britannia'. They have arrived, and now invite the gentlemen in the audience to dance with them. The first, most obvious aim of all the masques, and certainly this one, was to unravel and celebrate Stuart values and ideals, and here the masquers paid homage to King James, seated in the centre of the audience. Though the main speaking parts were taken by professional actors, the nymphs were played by the Queen and her ladies, who were 'blacked up', and they danced at the end with the king's male courtiers. The whole was a kind of fantasy set in the dazzling locale created by Inigo Jones. A fragment of Jonson's description indicates its splendour:

> The masquers were placed in a great concave shell like mother of pearl, curiously made to move on those waters and rise from the billow: the top thereof was stuck with a chevron of lights, which, indented to the proportion of the shell, struck a glorious beam upon them as they were seated one above another; so that they were all seen, but in an extravagant order.
>
> On the sides of the shell did swim six huge sea monsters, varied in their shapes and dispositions, bearing on their backs the twelve torchbearers, who were planted there in several greces (steps), so that the backs of some were seen, some in profile or side, others in face; and all having their lights burning out of whelks or murex shells.

Even in this early masque, the lavishness of the presentation was extraordinary: it was reputed to have cost £3000 when the average yearly receipts at the Globe Theatre were no more than £2000.

The Masque of Blackness was performed once and not repeated. The text we have is a record of a performance, not a script to work from.

The implicit sense of the masque reflected James's glory (masques are 'tied to rules of flattery', said Fletcher disparagingly): unlike the African sun, James's sun is temperate, and burns no-one. Blackness is as white in James's Britain, though something strange was adrift in this idyll. One spectator described how the women's 'apparel was rich but too light and courtesan-like for such great ones. Instead of vizards, their faces and arms up to the elbows were painted black, which was disguise sufficient, for they were hard to be known'.[1]

The blackness of the beautiful young women's undressed arms and legs should not have titillated. But it did. Jones's costumes, azure and silver, with feathered headdresses, flashing jewellery and diaphanous over-dresses floating in the charged candlelight made them exquisitely erotic and dangerous. The king may have been the still centre of the extravaganza, but the women's untamed elegance suggested forbidden fantasies.

WOMEN IN JACOBEAN SOCIETY

The Masque of Blackness started a rarely articulated or acknowledged debate concerning the place of women in the Jacobean polity. Among the masques which followed, another staged at Whitehall in February 1609, *The Masque of Queens* also by Ben Jonson, most notably developed the theme. In this masque, a fantastical Witches' Sabbath is interrupted, and the witches dispersed, by a character called Heroic Virtue. Once they are gone, Fame brings on stage the twelve queens, the masquers, in spectacular chariots, pulled by both fabulous beasts and the defeated witches. Songs and dance with the chosen courtiers follow. Written to flatter the Queen, who again played one of the masquers, this time there was a distinct sense that it was her brilliance which had tamed the witches. But though the women were triumphant, they still seemed subservient to the king, who sat sedately in his place of honour. *The Masque of Queens* implicitly challenged this. The question was, who is performing what? Here, beautiful women triumph over witches, played by men. The gender hierarchy is effectively disputed. And it is to be noted that Queen Anne danced in more masques than just these two, her actions thereby asserting not just women's right to perform, but also implicitly the beginnings of a different approach to the arts and society. For the next thirty, or perhaps fifty years, this struggle for women's place in the theatre and in the Stuart dispensation would continue.

STRUCTURE OF THE MASQUE

With *The Masque of Queens*, Jonson's form is evident, and the structure he devised reflected the political dialectic the masque embodied. First there was the 'anti-masque', comic or burlesque, and presented by professional actors or dancers, in which alien voices or presences invade the court and question its values. But they are first contained and then expelled by the courtier-masquers, who renew the harmony of the court and kingdom in the final dance or dances. The 'characters' in the masques (if such they can be called) were usually drawn from myth or legend, and the presentation, partly because it was unique and not to be repeated, partook of the nature of ritual. As such it mystified the royal power, and the participants and spectators emerged with renewed faith in the monarchy.

WRITERS OF MASQUES

Jonson probably wrote about half the extant masque texts, and these have often dominated discussion of the form, but there were other writers whose work made significant contributions to it. Francis Beaumont, for instance, made a masque for the Inner Temple and Gray's Inn in which there were two distinct antimasques, first, classical characters, then British folk characters, before a group of 'Olympian knights' reconciled all in the main masque. This masque was also notorious for its near-naked Cupids – four boys '*attired in flame-coloured taffeta close to their bodies like naked boys*'. Thomas Campion, composer as well as poet, created a series of masques which emphasised what might be called the 'psychological' rather than the ritualistic, and Samuel Daniel, whose *Vision of Twelve Goddesses* was the very first Jacobean court masque, was more philosophical and speculative than Jonson.

MASQUES, QUEEN ANNE AND WOMEN ON STAGE

Daniel's *Tethys' Festival*, made for Prince Henry's investiture as Prince of Wales in 1610, was a notable addition to the *genre*. In it, Queen Anna, as Tethys, 'reposed', between dances, 'under the Tree of Victory' where the spectators could gaze on her. Once again she was the ambivalent focus for Stuart culture. And so she remained until the end: in May 1617, she presided over *Cupid's Banishment* as her husband had so often presided over court masques. This was presented to her by the young ladies of Deptford Ladies' Hall, a private finishing school, and depicted Venus, chaste love, ousting Cupid, carnal desire, in what was perhaps an assertion of women's right to be independent of men. But perhaps the most notable feature of this event was that while almost all the speaking parts were, as usual, performed by males, the part of Fortune was played by a female, Anne Watkins, who pronounced what were perhaps the first words ever spoken on the stage by a woman in England:

> We are engaged to Time for this occasion
> That meets our wishes with such good success.
> For this great courtesy I'll create
> Some unexpected joy to crown thy hours,
> Thy minutes, I'll so turn upon this wheel of mine
> That men hereafter shall call happy Time.
> Hymen, Mercury, how welcome you are hither.
> We can no more express than we already have.

MIDDLETON'S MASQUES

A more formidable challenge to Jonson's masque form came from Thomas Middleton. His *Masque of Cupids*, created to celebrate the controversial marriage of the king's favourite, Robert Carr, to the beautiful and amorous divorcée, Frances Howard, was performed at the Merchant Taylor's Hall in January 1613. Most of the text is lost, but its commission by the Lord Mayor of London as part of extensive entertainments is suggestive. Middleton's *Masque of Heroes* for the Inner Temple, performed in 1619, celebrates the New Year by using not Jonson's characters from classical myth, but more homely characters, drawn from British folklore, like Doctor Almanac and Plumporridge (played, by the way, by such formidable actors as Joseph Taylor and William Rowley). Middleton presents three antemasques before Harmony is restored by the Nine Worthies and there is a dance including members of the audience. Though the piece endorses James's support for the traditional Christmas against Puritan strictures, the Worthies propose and achieve social harmony not through royal favour but through communal goodwill. The masque further engages in current arguments about foreign policy, and the advisability or otherwise of Britain joining the European war against the Catholic powers, a subject which Middleton would revert to, not least in *A Game at Chess*. It is the transformation of antimasque ('not-masque') into antemasque ('before the masque'), however, which is Middleton's most notable contribution to the *genre*: the adversarial forces here are not expelled, but rather absorbed, opposites are reconciled and Harmony institutes new 'friendship' which embraces all – a pattern repeated in the masque-like play, or play-like masque, *The World Tossed at Tennis*. The antemasque in *The Masque of Heroes* is thus not the antithesis of the masque proper, it is rather what goes before it, which will be incorporated into it: this is a materialist concept which implicitly rejects the mystery of royal authority. Middleton's New Year is truly auspicious because it is natural, popular fun, not courtly ceremonial flummery.

THE GYPSIES METAMORPHOSED

Nevertheless, Jonson continued to be the court's favourite masque writer, even after the death of Queen Anne, when the king's court became almost suffocatingly masculine. In 1621 Jonson's longest masque, *The Gypsies Metamorphosed* was presented with courtiers, not professional actors, in the grotesque antimasque. It was performed three times, at Burley-on-the-Hill, the Duke of Buckingham's estate, on 3 August, at Belvoir Castle on 5 August and a month later at Windsor Castle. Its plot is simple: a group of gypsies cavort about, telling fortunes, picking pockets, dancing and singing, before revealing themselves as James's favourite courtiers. Their leader was Buckingham himself, whom the king was said to love as Jesus loved John the disciple, and whose attraction here was not without a homoerotic element. He flaunted his long legs and his charismatic dancing gave him an almost irresistible glamour.

This masque was unusual not only because of its three performances, but because it relied little upon scenic splendour. For many, the designs of Inigo Jones were always more important to the success of the masque than the words of Ben Jonson.

THE PLACE OF PERFORMANCE

The venue itself was integral to the spectacle, and often special stages were built in the magnificent chambers where the performances took place. A favourite venue for James was the Banqueting House in Whitehall which however burned down in 1619. It was rebuilt by Inigo Jones as an even more impressive location with ceilings by Peter Paul Rubens and an audience capacity of over a thousand. The much smaller Cockpit-in-Court, which opened in 1630, was an Italianate theatre: it was square, with a stage which jutted out into the auditorium and had at the back six flat walls forming effectively a semi-circle or half a dodecahedron. Between these flats were five entrances, two doorways at each side and a larger central arch. In 1633 a new theatre in Somerset House was opened. Designed by Jones and John Webb, and again based on Italian models, this was the first

Figure 3.11
Whitehall: the Banqueting House, with ceiling by Peter Paul Rubens
Source: Photo Michel Wal

scenic theatre built in England. The stage end of the theatre was twenty-five feet deep and fifty feet wide, the stage floor was raked, with wings, back shutters and borders. Yet another Masquing House was built in 1637 after it was discovered that smoke from the candles needed for performing in the Banqueting House was damaging the Rubens ceilings.

Whatever hall was used for the performance of a masque, the spatial configuration needed three distinct areas – a scenic stage, a dance floor accessible both from the stage and the auditorium, and the auditorium itself. In the exact centre of the audience was placed the king's throne, on a dais so that he could be seen by all. His place was the position where the effect of the perspective scenery was perfect. He saw all and was seen by all.

SCENIC SPECTACLE

The court masque introduced onto the English stage curtains, flats (shutters) running in grooves across the stage, and the proscenium arch. It gave the theatre the framed stage with wings, painted backdrops and hanging borders which were the elements of a perspectival pictorial presentation. It could represent convincingly trees or houses, rocks, cliffs, seashores and mountains, as well as grassy knolls and arbours or bowers for actors to appear in, though of course perspective scenery can really only convince if the actors stay well in front of it on a forestage. This scenery was moveable. It could be raised, slid into the wings or revolved. Wing pieces could have three faces, each with part of a different scene painted on it. When it, and simultaneously three or five other wing pieces, were revolved, a startling transformation occurred virtually in the blink of an eye. Other effects also became possible, such as that described by Campion for *The Lord Hay's Masque* (1607):

> When the trees had sunk a yard, they cleft in three parts, and the masquers appeared out of the tops of them,
> the trees were suddenly conveyed away, and the first three masquers were raised again by the engine.

The machines, or 'engines', used to procure these startling transformations would probably appear intolerably clumsy and noisy to someone familiar with computer-generated effects: to the Jacobeans and their immediate successors, they seemed magical.

Backstage were hemp ropes, capstans, windlasses and weights and counter-weights. For Davenant's *Salmacida Spolia* (1640), there were five sets of wings and shutters, decreasing in height towards upstage on the raked floor, with a moving chair at the rear, raised or lowered by ropes running over pulleys and worked from a machine room below the stage. Above the stage was the fly gallery from where clouds, rainbows and moons were controlled. At first this was fairly crude, as can be judged from Campion's description in *The Lord Hay's Masque*: '*About it (Flora's bower) were placed on wire artificial bats and owls, continually moving*'. Later effects were much more complicated. In Aurelian Townshend's *Tempe Restored* (1632):

> In the midst of the air the eight spheres in rich habits were seated on a cloud, which in a circular form was on
> each side continued unto the highest part of the heaven, and seemed to have let them down as in a chain.

> To the music of these spheres there appeared two other clouds descending, and in them were discovered
> eight stars. These being come to the middle region of the sky, another greater cloud came down above them,
> which by little and little descending, discovered other glistering stars to the number of six. And above all, in a
> chariot of goldsmith's work richly adorned with precious gems, sat Divine Beauty, over whose head appeared
> a brightness full of small stars that environed the top of the chariot, striking a light roundabout it.

Townshend added admiringly: '*This sight altogether was, for the difficulty of the engining and the number of the persons, the greatest that hath been seen here in our time*'.

The references to light 'glistering' and reflecting off shiny surfaces is also important: this was a feature which particularly amazed many spectators. It was achieved by strategically placed groups of candles and beeswax tapers, and by oil lamps or candles behind coloured glass. Because a single candle or oil lamp is dim, huge banks of them were built up to cast an unequalled brilliance over the proceedings. It was, however, these multitudes of lights which caused the ceilings to blacken, and often the more intimate Cockpit-in-Court, which required fewer lights, was preferred for this reason.

INIGO JONES, DESIGNER

Inigo Jones was almost wholly responsible for this theatrical revolution. In *The Masque of Queens* Jonson records how 'the invention and architecture of the whole scene and machine' was 'Master Jones's', and he was still designing when the last of the Stuart court masques, *Salmacida Spolia*, was staged in 1640. Jones's originality as a stage designer lay in three specific areas: he used well-known art works as the basis for his stage pictures; he created visual focus through the framing of the stage on all sides, and he applied machinery to stage transformations. The results staggered his contemporaries. Surely only a king's theatre could achieve such magnificence, and only those greatly privileged could behold it.

Equally seductive were the costumes which Jones designed. Though somewhat similar for all his masques, they were made repetitively splendid by the use of real gemstones, pearls or precious metals sewn on them, and by the texture of the material, whether coarse buckram in the antimasques, or cloth-of-gold or silk in the main masque. The colours were often brilliant, contrasting or in harmony, and often the masquers wore jewelled half-masks. Even the ugliest character could then provoke a titillating thrill. The Dame of the witches in *The Masque of Queens* was '*naked-armed, barefooted, her frock tucked, her hair knotted and folded with vipers: in her hand a torch made of a dead man's arm, lighted; girded with a snake*'. Less dangerous, but still suggestive were Concord and Good Genius in *Salmacida Spolia*: Concord was a woman in an azure garment with silver trimmings and a skirt of bulrushes, while Good Genius was '*a young man in a carnation garment embroidered all with flowers, an antique sword hung in a scarf, a garland on his head, and in his hand a branch of platan mixed with ears of corn*'.

Sometimes, as with the Dame of the Witches and perhaps Concord's bulrush skirt, the effect was created by an artful semi-nudity, and very many of Jones's dresses for men as well as women are diaphanous and floaty. The effect can be disturbing, as with Prince Henry's costume as Oberon. Designed to display his male beauty, emphasising his thighs, his chest, his buttocks, the effect is also curiously feminine because of the way the delicate cloth reveals as much as it conceals. Jones also discovered how to multiply the effect by having groups of characters dressed alike, so that the impression of beauty was multiplied.

MUSIC

It is impossible to think of the Stuart court masque without thinking of the music. Music suffused the masque performance, and by the 1630s seems to have been virtually continuous throughout. Composers like Robert Dowland, Alfonso Ferrabosco and Henry Lawes provided huge quantities of it, but sadly little survives. Music was essential to the achievement of key moments, especially

Figure 3.12

Inigo Jones, design for the title role in *Oberon, the Fairy Prince* by Ben Jonson, 1611, in which Prince Henry played Oberon

Source: Collection of the Duke of Devonshire, Chatsworth House, Derbyshire/Reproduced by permission of Chatsworth Settlement Trustees/Bridgeman Images

scenic transformations, but also storms, reconciliations and so on. Music reflected – or clashed with – the celestial harmony the Stuart court attempted to radiate. It was pervasive, probably continuing under dialogue, which might also be sung or even performed as some kind of primitive recitative. Singers added their own grace notes.

The music was sometimes lightly syncopated, and sometimes slightly inconclusive or plaintive. For the antimasque, it was usually discordant, clashing and rough, employing plenty of percussion and perhaps brass instruments or bagpipes. A good example is Robert Dowland's music for the witches' dance in *The Masque of Queens* which has survived in his *Varietie of Lute Lessons*. The music shifts constantly between long and short notes, jerking the dancer quickly between stopping and starting. The second witches' dance is even less regular. For the main masque, on the other hand, the music used lutes or violins or harps and was always euphonious, its melodies sweet, its harmonies sensual.

DANCE

The masque's effect was completed by the dances of which there was an exuberant abundance. Harmonious movement was thought to reflect the motion of the stars, and dance was seen as expressing higher values. Rich young people spent hours practising under the eye of a professional dancing master – necessary because court dances were both complicated and fashionable. Balance and grace in dance implied these qualities in the character, and courtiers learned to perform elegance and sophistication. With choreographers like Jerome Herne, Thomas Giles and Thomas Lupo, dance challenged the written text as the primary vehicle of meaning in the masque, because the dance, focused and enhanced by lighting and music, sited the primary experience in the performer's body. The dance was thus performative. The aesthetic pleasure it provided, especially in contrast to the grotesque movements which typified the antimasque, was also the means of communicating that pleasure. The audience gazed, but the dancers gazed too, at each other and at themselves. Even Jonson admitted:

> For dancing is an exercise,
> Not only shows the mover's wit,
> But maketh the beholder wise,
> As he hath power to rise to it.[2]

The questions Clare McManus raises in relation to dance in the masque are highly pertinent: who leads? Who bows? What is the import of lowering the body or straightening the back? And how does this affirm or deny the social hierarchy?

There were three kinds of dance in the court masque: the grotesque antimasque, the harmonious dance of the main masque and the social dance at the end. The antimasque was typified by jerky rhythms, bodies contorted, limbs flung out and eccentric. Jonson describes the witches' dance in *The Masque of Queens* thus:

> With a strange and sudden music, they fell into a magical dance, full of preposterous change and gesticulation . . . contrary to the custom of men, dancing back to back and hip to hip, and making their circles backward, to the left hand, with strange fantastic motions of their heads and bodies.

The dances in the main masque were the opposite, smooth, graceful and charming. They might become quite elaborate, including perhaps chain dances and dances which created floor patterns

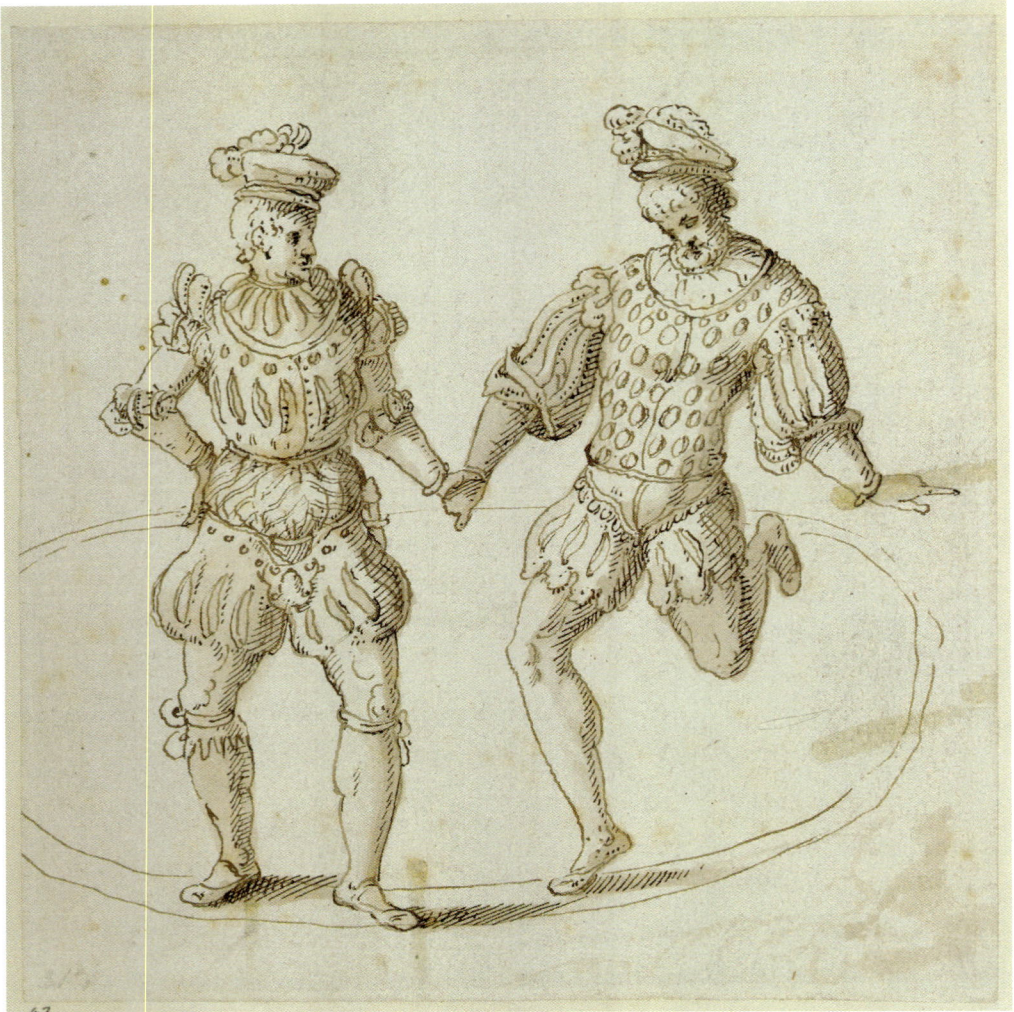

Figure 3.13
Inigo Jones, sketch of dancers for a Stuart court masque

Source: Collection of the Duke of Devonshire, Chatsworth House, Derbyshire/Reproduced by permission of Chatsworth Settlement Trustees/Bridgeman Images

which spelled out the name of the person being celebrated, and sometimes they allowed individual dancers the opportunity to exhibit special skills. One such occasion was at the performance of Jonson's 1618 masque, *Pleasure Reconciled to Virtue*, which the chaplain to the Venetian ambassador described thus:

> They danced the Spanish dance once more with their ladies, and because they were tired began to lag; and the king, who is by nature choleric, grew impatient and shouted loudly, 'Why don't they dance? What did

they make me come here for? Devil take all of you, dance!' At once the Marquis of Buckingham, his majesty's favourite minion, sprung forward, and danced a number of very high and very tiny capers with such grace and lightness that he made everyone admire and love him, and also managed to calm the rage of his angry lord. Inspired by this, the other masquers continued to display their powers one after another, with different ladies, concluding with capers, and lifting their goddesses from the ground. We counted 34 capers in succession cut by one knight, but none matched the splendid technique of the Marquis. . . . The king then honoured the Marquis with extraordinary signs of affection, touching his face.[3]

THE SUPREME MASQUE ARTIST?

The masque required a balance between the contributing arts. But Jonson asserted the writer's primacy, arguing that poetry was superior to the other arts as the soul is superior to the body. Inigo Jones violently disagreed, and in 1631, during work on the masque *Chloridia*, the two quarrelled irreconcilably. Jonson wrote in exasperation:

O shows! Shows! Mighty shows!
The eloquence of masques! What need of prose
Or verse, or sense t'express immortal you?
You are the spectacles of state![4]

Jonson published the text of the masque with his own name ahead of Jones's. Jones objected, whereupon Jonson pilloried him as Vitruvius Hoop, a cooper, one who makes wooden barrels and buckets, in his new play, *A Tale of a Tub*. Jones complained furiously to the king, who ordered the caricature to be emasculated. Vitruvius Hoop became In-and-In Mildmay, and the two artists, who had virtually established the art form, never worked together again. Jones retained royal favour. Jonson wrote no more court masques, though he did create a few more for other members of the aristocracy.

COURT PERFORMANCE: QUEEN HENRIETTA MARIA AND HER WOMEN

Inigo Jones designed not only court masques, but other court performances as well, including *Artenice*, a French pastoral tragicomedy by Seigneur de Racan, which Queen Henrietta Maria produced at Somerset House in February 1625. It was her first year in Britain and relations with her new husband, Charles I, were not easy. Nor were relations between her native France and her new country. Yet this event – a play, not a masque or a dance – had reverberations for British theatre and performance which can hardly be overstated. The queen and her court ladies produced the drama themselves. They played all the parts, speaking the lines (a thing unheard of for women on an English stage) and even donning false beards to play the male roles. Henrietta Maria played Artenice herself. It is clear that this was, in part at least, an assertion of herself and her culture in the face of her new and not particularly sympathetic surroundings. Inigo Jones designed a proscenium arch, perspective scenery, using painted shutters with peasant cottages and a colonnaded temple which parted to reveal the performers. The final image when the shutters finally closed, in a nice piece of meta-theatre, showed Somerset House itself beside the River Thames: perhaps a peace offering after so daring a display to her unbending husband.

If it was a peace offering, she and Charles had indeed become much closer by the time her second performance venture occurred in 1632. This was the inordinately lengthy *The Shepherds' Paradise* by Walter Montague, which received two performances. The queen and her ladies were coached by the King's Men's leading actor, Joseph Taylor, while Inigo Jones again did the sets and costumes. Bellesa, played by Henrietta Maria, was the leader of the Shepherds' Paradise, a female order dedicated to beauty and chastity: the play explored allegorically the place of women in Caroline courtly society.

Henrietta Maria's vital energy instigated a discussion during the later 1630s about women as actors and whether they could 'civilize' the theatre. In Richard Brome's *The Court Beggar* a character actually says, 'women actors now grow in request'. But not for everyone. William Prynne, a fierce Puritan, published a long polemic shortly after *The Shepherds' Paradise* had been performed denouncing women actors as 'notorious whores' and 'impudent prostituted strumpets'.[5] It looked as though this might be a reproof addressed to the queen, though it had been written (but not published) sometime before that performance. No matter. Prynne was brought before the Court of the Star Chamber and sentenced to life imprisonment, fined £5000, expelled from Lincoln's Inn Fields, barred from the legal profession and made to stand in the pillory first at Westminster and then on Cheapside: and at each of these places to have one ear cut off. After some time the imprisonment was commuted, but Prynne was without his ears for the rest of his life.

The queen was defended by many in the theatrical world, and she soon mounted a third independent production of another French tragicomedy, *Florimène*, this time at Whitehall at Christmas 1635. She herself did not perform on this occasion. Unusually, the text of the play is lost, but Inigo Jones's full set of designs has survived, so that it can be seen that he here introduced angled 'book' wings on the raked stage, and that the back shutters opened between acts to disclose three-dimensional cutout pictures of the seasons.

Henrietta Maria continued to assert a distinct female agenda through the 1630s as she searched for a writer of masques to replace the out-of-favour Ben Jonson. Aurelian Townshend, Shirley and Thomas Carew all tried their hands at the *genre* (as did John Milton elsewhere in the only masque some have ever heard of, *Comus*) before she settled on William Davenant whose four masques made between 1635 and 1640, are among the most accomplished of the age.

DAVENANT'S MASQUES

Davenant's masques demonstrate how the form may intervene in ongoing political debates, and how the court may nudge and advise the supreme monarch, as well as mediate between different court factions. In the first, *The Temple of Love* (1635) the mists of misapprehension and ignorance disperse to disclose the pure truth of Henrietta Maria in the temple of chaste love. *Britannia Triumphans* (1638) tries to shore up and revitalise the king whose difficulties both with local politics and with Scotland were becoming threatening: the masque asserts James's courage, piety and wisdom. *Luminalia* (1638) returns to the praise of Henrietta Maria, whose brilliance dispels the darkness as her Catholicism will drive out the Puritans. And *Salmacida Spolia*, the last masque of the Stuart court, which was by chance also the only masque in which both Charles and Henrietta Maria danced, praises his wisdom at a time of crumbling national cohesion and advocates reconciliation which will avoid bloodshed and war.

Figure 3.14
Inigo Jones, set design for William Davenant's *Salmacida Spolia*, the last Stuart court masque, in which both King Charles I and Queen Henrietta Maria appeared

Source: Collection of the Duke of Devonshire, Chatsworth House, Derbyshire/Reproduced by permission of Chatsworth Settlement Trustees/Bridgeman Images

Salmacida Spolia was a response to the crisis in Scotland, and the presence on stage of both the king and the queen implicitly highlighted the urgent themes of unity and harmony. Inigo Jones's final stage picture was based on Paolo Veronese's *Marriage at Cana* with its classical columns framing the busy bridge with people, horses, carriages and so forth. Davenant recorded:

> The second dance ended, and their Majesties being seated under the state, the scene was changed into
> magnificent buildings composed of several selected pieces of architecture. In the furthest part was a bridge
> over a river, where many people, coaches, horses and suchlike were seen to pass to and fro.

There were, however, in both *Luminalia* and *Salmacida Spolia*, undercurrents of unease concerning the queen's mother, Marie de Medici, questioning her residency in Britain, and the potential disruption her dabbling in European politics might have on Charles's Britain. However, as always, the politics was a matter of subtext, something for those who knew to see, but something which most auditors would miss. Politics were not for general consumption, even if the spectacle and majesty were there to awe all.

THE AUDIENCE AT THE COURT THEATRES

Several of the court theatres held over a thousand people, who were admitted by ticket under the fiction that these were invitations from the king. Such was the demand for tickets and the crush getting into the theatre that in the 1630s turnstiles were installed to control matters. Synopses were handed to those who came, and sometimes complete scripts of the coming performance for perusal before, at ten o'clock, a fanfare announced the king's arrival.

The audiences consisted of aristocrats, foreign dignitaries, and courtiers, who usually had their own better seating area and who were led there by a Master of Ceremonies. Inns of Court men and members of the gentry (male and female) also attended, but the audience was probably more mixed socially than one might expect. There was rarely room for all those who wanted to enter, and there was plenty of scrambling, pushing and fighting for standing space, for there were not seats for the lesser spectators. Undoubtedly it was noisy, hot, smelly and boisterous as a thousand or more people squashed into the lamp and candle-lit hall.

The masque might last until two o'clock in the morning, or even later. And then came supper. Suddenly there was a stampede for food, and tables and chairs were frequently knocked over as the hungry people scrabbled for a mouthful. There was not always enough for everyone, partly because of the greed of those who reached the food tables first. It was an unseemly and most un-Stuart-like conclusion to what was intended to be – and in many senses was – a magnificent evening.

But as the crowds dispersed, and through the ensuing days, the masque was the subject of animated debate, and those who had failed to see it envied those who had.

NOTES

1 Sir Dudley Carlton in a letter to Ralph Winwood, January 1605; in Clare McManus, *Women on the Renaissance Stage*, Manchester: Manchester University Press, 2002, p. 1.
2 Ben Jonson, *Pleasure Reconciled to Virtue*, 1618; David Lindley (ed), *Court Masques*, Oxford: Oxford University Press, 1995, p. 123.
3 Clare McManus, *op.cit.*, p. 51.
4 Ben Jonson, 'Expostulation', in Ian Donaldson (ed), *Ben Jonson*, Oxford: Oxford University Press, 1985, p. 462.
5 William Prynne, *Histriomastix*, 1632.

Chapter 33: Theatre when the theatres were closed

THE CLOSURE OF THE THEATRES

On 2 September 1642 Parliament passed an ordinance which stated, among other things: 'It is thought fit, and ordained, by the Lords and Commons in Parliament assembled, that while these sad causes and set times of humiliation do continue, public stage plays shall cease and be forborne'.[1] It is sometimes thought that this was a triumph for a Puritan campaign which had lasted sixty years. It was not. It was a temporary halt, apparently, more like the usual way to mark the death of a monarch than an ideological measure. But the monarch was in arms in Nottingham, and the whole known way of the world seemed to be tumbling upside down.

THE STRUGGLE TO KEEP PERFORMING

In fact, the evidence from the next years indicates that the public still wanted plays, and, especially from 1646 when the first English Civil War was over, the actors wanted to provide them. The Salisbury Court and the Cockpit, the Fortune and the Red Bull were all still standing. But the struggle was arduous and hazardous, as a brief chronology of the following years demonstrates:

4 October 1643: soldiers raid the Fortune Theatre to put a stop to playing there.

1644: the Globe Theatre is dismantled and replaced by housing; maypoles are banned.

1646: Parliament awards pay arrears to the King's Men to compensate for lost earnings.

July 1647: order for the closure of the theatres for a further six months.

4 September 1647: soldiers raid the Fortune Theatre, stop a performance and take the actors to gaol.

6 October 1647: performance of Beaumont and Fletcher's *A King and No King* at Salisbury Court watched by 'a great number of people, some young lords and other eminent persons'[2] is interrupted by sheriffs.

October 1647: an order made permitting the Lord Mayor of London or Justices of the Peace to raid public or private houses where they suspect performances are taking place.

1647: the King's Men publish a folio of thirty-four plays by Beaumont and Fletcher. The sharers of the company participating in this enterprise are: Joseph Taylor, John Lowin, Richard Robinson, Robert Benfield, Thomas Pollard, Stephen Hammerton, Hugh Clark, Theophilus Bird, William Allen and Eyllaerdt Swanston. Interestingly, although most of these were declared royalists, Swanston was known to be pro-Parliament.

1 January 1648: the prohibition on theatres lifted. The theatres re-open.

27 January 1648: at least one hundred twenty coaches set down spectators outside the Fortune Theatre.

3 February 1648: bills are thrown into gentlemen's coaches advertising a performance of Fletcher's *Wit without Money* at the Red Bull.

5 February 1648: John Evelyn notes in his Diary that he saw a tragicomedy performed at the Cockpit.

11 February 1648: a fresh order is made 'for the utter suppression and abolishing of all stage plays and interludes', which threatens both actors and spectators. Actors are redefined as 'rogues', and if they are caught performing they will be whipped. Spectators caught at a performance will be fined five shillings. Theatre auditoria are to be demolished.[3]

December 1648: the King's Men perform Fletcher and Massinger's *The Bloody Brother*, with John Lowin and Charles Hart in the cast. The performance is interrupted and stopped.

1 January 1649: perhaps because of the imminent execution of the king and the consequent danger to public order, soldiers raid the Cockpit and Salisbury Court, and arrest the actors. They enter the Fortune Theatre, but find only rope dancers and clowns, who however are also arrested. Meanwhile the company at the Red Bull, getting wind of what is happening, disappear before they can be held. The Salisbury Court actors were dragged away still in costume. The actor playing the king was mocked by the soldiers who took off and replaced his crown, suggesting how ephemeral was kingship and conjuring visions not just of Charles I but of Jesus on his way to Calvary, especially as the people laughed at the mockery. It is unclear what happened to the Salisbury Court actors, but those from the Cockpit were gaoled for two nights. The spectators at the Salisbury Court apparently included more than one former MP who had been expelled from the House for supporting negotiations with the king.

1649: the interiors of the three offending theatres, Salisbury Court, the Cockpit and the Fortune, as well as the Blackfriars, were all dismantled during this year.

13 November 1650: Charles Cutts, an actor and barber, was caught in his costume and arrested.

1650: William Beeston paid £200 for repairs done to the Cockpit, and assembled a group of apprentices and servants to train as actors; this enterprise was stopped by the authorities.

1652: Beeston acquires the title to Salisbury Court, but is unable to become active here.

March 1653: an attempt to produce Thomas Killigrew's *Claricilla* at Charles Gibbon's tennis court on Vere Street is prevented after soldiers are tipped off. The suspicion is that William Beeston and Theophilus Bird were the sneaks, since they owned the rights to the play.

June 1653: 'rope dancing' is reported at the Red Bull, perhaps as a euphemism for playing; there are signs that the local authorities are turning a blind eye.

1653: a performance in a pub at Whitney, Oxfordshire of *Mucedorus* is halted when the floor gives way under the weight of spectators.

July 1654: performance of William Berkeley's *The Lost Lady* at Knowlton, Kent.

August 1655: Blackfriars pulled down and replaced with houses.

September 1655: Red Bull raided. Costumes and props are impounded and any spectator who cannot pay the on-the-spot fine has their cloak or other 'gage' confiscated.

1655: Hope Theatre demolished.

1656: a new order issued to suppress cockfighting, bear-baiting and stage plays.

1656: group of actors in Newcastle-upon-Tyne whipped as 'rogues and vagabonds'.

May 1659: Edward Shatterell and Anthony Turner prosecuted for playing at the Red Bull: it seems they had paid hush money to the local community, and had supported some good works here, in hope of being left unmolested, but to no avail.

February 1660: John Rhodes leases and refurbishes the Cockpit; he applies for a licence for performances, and assembles a young company, reputedly including Thomas Betterton and Edward Kynaston.

April 1660: Beeston completes the renovation of Salisbury Court, begins to assemble a new group of Beeston's Boys.

23 April 1660: General Monck, negotiating for the return of Charles II, renews the prohibition on the performance of stage plays.

Of course much is omitted from such a chronicle, but it indicates the nature of the actors' problems. Unrecorded here are the performances staged by aristocrats in their own homes. Holland House, Kensington, for instance, saw several productions before its owner, Henry Rich, Earl of Holland, was seized and beheaded, after which the house was used by Cromwell as army staff quarters. The Earl of Northampton was responsible for a number of productions at his home, Castle Ashby, in the 1640s and 1650s. And Mildmay Fane, Earl of Westmoreland, also mounted some fairly elaborate productions, sometimes of his own plays, at his house at Apthorpe. Mention should also be made of George Jolly, an actor in the Caroline theatre, who organised a troupe of English actors to perform on the continent of Europe from 1648 through to 1659. They appeared in Germany, Poland, Sweden, Austria and France, and employed their first female actor in 1654. They used a tennis court as a theatre, as the first Restoration theatre companies would do in London in the 1660s, and presented plays before the exiled King Charles II.

PAMPHLET PLAYS

Plays which were likely to flourish best under these circumstances were short, sharp pieces, and a number of playscripts were published as pamphlets in the febrile atmosphere of the time – though whether they were intended for performance or whether the dramatic form was merely useful for the propaganda purposes of their authors is uncertain.

Pamphlet plays of the early years of the Civil War included *Tyrannical Government Anatomized* (1642) which purported to show the dangers of allowing a woman to have political influence. An implicit attack on Queen Henrietta Maria, this was a John the Baptist-Salomé play which showed female dancing leading to the prophet's decapitation, and King Herod subverted by his womenfolk. Charles's favourite prelate, William Laud, was the butt of *The Bishop's Potion* (1641) in which the archbishop, feeling unwell, sends for his doctor who causes him to vomit up the tobacco patent, the Star Chamber Order against Prynne, his mitre, a bundle of church livings and so forth; and *Canterbury His Change of Diet* (1641) in which Laud appeared as a sort of ogre devouring Prynne and others.

Royalist works included *Crafty Cromwell* (1648), a two-part play in which the Parliamentary leader seized the throne for himself, and *Newmarket Fair* (1649), also in two parts, perhaps written by the journalist John Crouch, which had Cromwell and Fairfax casting lots as to which should be king, and Mrs Cromwell, wearing the queen's jewels, having sex with a lover behind the arras. *The Famous Tragedy of King Charles I* was printed in 1649, the year of his execution, while other pamphlet dramas included the anti-Ranter *The Jovial Crew* (1651) by Samuel Shepherd, intended no doubt to evoke Brome's play of a decade earlier, and the anonymous *The Ghost, or The Woman Who Wears the Breeches* (1653), an animated diatribe against women.

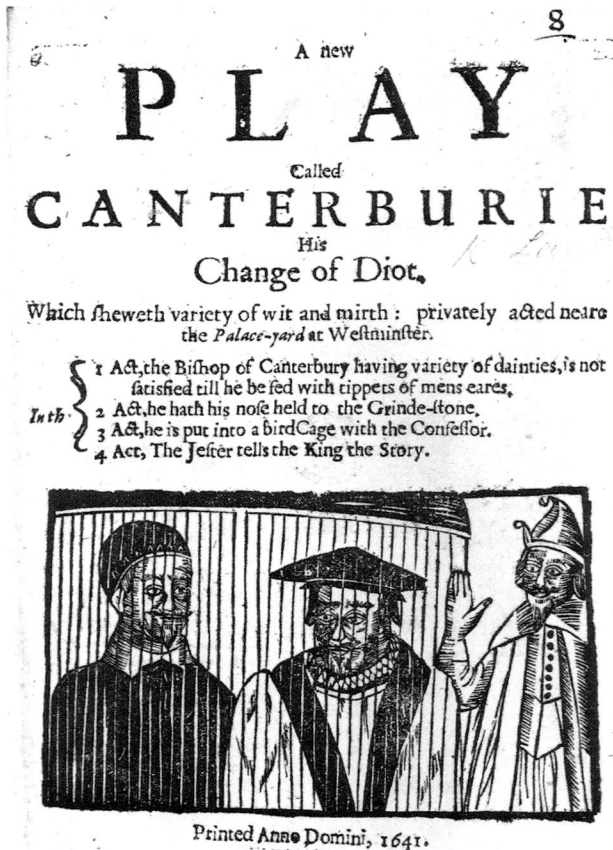

Figure 3.15
Title page of the anti-royalist pamphlet play, probably not intended for performance, *Canterbury His Change of Diet*, 1641
Source: British Library, London

DROLLS

It is possible such plays were, if not performed, read aloud in taverns, raising the question of when recitation becomes performance and querying distinctions between printed and oral cultures. More likely to have been performed were the 'drolls', short farcical dramas deriving from folk plays and jigs suitable for fairgrounds, market squares and inns, as well as grander venues, such as the Red Bull Theatre. These playlets often featured quasi-traditional characters like Bumpkin the huntsman, Hobbinal the shepherd and John Swabber the seaman, and were collected in at least three anthologies, the first by Robert Cox, an actor of pieces apparently performed at the Red Bull, published in 1655. In 1662, *The Wits, or Sport upon Sport* was collected and published by Henry Marsh, and a further collection, also called, confusingly, *The Wits, or Sport upon Sport*, by Francis Kirkman, came out in 1673. One play was a version of the Elizabethan jig, *Singing Simpkin*, another defiantly featured dancing round a maypole, and there were also reduced versions of Jacobean or Caroline masques. A number were filleted from Elizabethan drama, including shortened versions or scenes from Jonson and Beaumont and Fletcher, as well as *Bottom the Weaver* and *The Bouncing Knight*, with Falstaff as protagonist, from Shakespeare.

CLOSET DRAMAS

More sophisticated were the 'closet dramas', full-length plays which probably never saw the light of public performance because of the interdict on the theatres. Usually more philosophical and detached than rabidly partisan, they covered the cautious anonymous play, *The Rebellion of Naples* (1649), John Tatham's anti-usurpation but hardly topical *The Distracted State* (1650), and the strongly republican academic play, *The Tragedy of Cicero* (1651). On the royalist side, there were Thomas Killigrew's *Thomaso, or the Wanderer* about cavaliers in exile, and a series of plays by Cosmo Manuche, such as *The Just General* (1651) and *Loyal Lovers* (1652). Manuche was not a particularly political writer, but he had connections with the Earl of Northampton and may have had plays like *The Banished Shepherdess* (c.1659) with its hints of the plight of Henrietta Maria, staged at the Earl's Inigo Jones-improved Castle Ashby mansion.

Other closet dramas included Gilbert Swinhoe's *The Tragedy of the Unhappy Fair Irene* (1658), in which the chaste Irene is not rescued from the clutches of Mahomet by the Christian hero, and Richard Flecknoe's ambitious attempts to create an English version of Italian opera, which he pursued through *Love's Dominion* (1654), *Ariadne Deserted by Theseus and Courted by Bacchus* (also 1654), and the ambitious *Marriage of Oceanus and Britannia* (1659). But they were never performed, though his suggestions for music and his advocacy of recitative seem to have been influential.

The most interesting closet dramas were undoubtedly produced by the family of the Duke of Newcastle, a conscientious royalist commander and former courtier in Queen Henrietta Maria's favour, who had himself had two plays, *The Country Captain* (1640) and *The Variety* (1641), performed at the Blackfriars by the King's Men. These plays reflected Newcastle's preference for home over the life of the court, and satirised the showy courtiers of the 1630s; they also argued implicitly against one-person rule and for the place of councillors in the affairs of state.

JANE CAVENDISH AND ELIZABETH BRACKLEY

Newcastle encouraged his daughters, Lady Jane Cavendish and Lady Elizabeth Brackley, to write. Their *A Pastorall* (c.1643) appropriated the masque form to deprecate the Civil War with some bitterness, and to lament the threat to woman's place in the countryside. More ambitious was *The Concealed Fancies* (c.1645), written while the authors were living at Welbeck, Newcastle's country seat, when it was under siege by Parliamentary forces and Newcastle himself was in exile in France. The play gives sometimes distressing glimpses of the people, from lord to Jack, the kitchen boy, living in a besieged castle. The young heroine states to her lover near the end of the play, 'O friend, I have been in hell!' and when he replies, conventionally enough, 'No, sure, your goodness cannot that way tell', she replies bitterly, 'O yes, this world doth imitate the other'. All the characters are under strain, and the form itself, almost masque-like, suggests that the possibility of escape is dream-like. The ending is therefore ironically unrealistic: the marriages of the leading characters are blessed by an angel who descends from the heavens, employing sophisticated stage scenery of the type seen in the court theatres. Interestingly for its time, too, the play strongly advocates equality in marriage:

LUCENY: How often, sister, have you read your Bible over, and have forgotten man and wife should draw equally in a yoke?
TATTINEY: I warrant you, sister, I know that text as well as you.

When Presumption announces that he hopes his future wife will obey him, Courtly, on the contrary, wishes that he and his future wife will be as lovers. The play is conducted in lively dialogue, but it is pervaded by a haunting sense of loss and sadness.

MARGARET CAVENDISH

Much more prolific than these two authors was Newcastle's second wife, Margaret Cavendish who published no fewer than nineteen plays in two collections (1662 and 1668). Few of these, if any, received a professional production at the time, the consequence of which is that her work is much less well known than it ought to be. Claiming the public stage for the royalist aristocracy, she was also strongly in favour of women performers. She argued in public in 1667 at Whitehall, the Duke of York's, Hyde Park and the Royal Society for the return of privilege and redress for Cavalier families harrowed by the Civil War.

Cavendish's plays form a refreshing contrast to the predominantly male drama of the first two-thirds of the seventeenth century because they so often revolve round women's desires, needs and concerns, rather than men's. Her best works are perhaps the social comedies often located in the realities of the Civil War and its aftermath. Women's experience of these traumatic events form the subject of *Bell in Campo* in which the heroine, Lady Victoria, rejects the conventional role of soldier's wife and decides to accompany her husband to the war. Where other war wives or widows mourn or pass the time in eating, their identities subsumed in those of their husbands, Victoria puts on her armour, ignores the other women in the war – camp followers and prostitutes – and fights for her cause. *The Sociable Companions*, set immediately after the war, shows women as far more capable in the necessary social rebuilding than men. Witty, compassionate and broadly satirical, the play includes not only the intelligent Jane cross-dressing, but also the male protagonist, Harry Sensible, likewise adopting the attire of the opposite sex.

In *The Female Academy* Cavendish amusingly excludes men from any input into the curriculum of women's education, and this women's viewpoint is often cunningly and sometimes (for the male auditor) disconcertingly evident in her apparently more conventional sex comedies. Thus, in *The Public Wooing* the sparky and handsome Lady Prudence finds herself irresistibly attracted sexually to a wooden-legged beggar in rags. But in the bedroom, like the frog prince of the fairy tale, he is transformed into an elegant husband. And in *Love's Adventure*, also set in the Civil War, Cavendish again makes her heroine cross-dress to attain her ends. Like the heroine of a whole swathe of popular songs and ballads, the energetic and attractive Lady Orphant is taken on as a page to her adored Lord Singularity, and then becomes a soldier in her own right. As in all popular folk tales, she thus wins the heart of the object of her passion, though there seems an unsettling possibility that he may prefer Lady Oliphant as a boy! These plays may sometimes exhibit a lack of theatrical know-how,

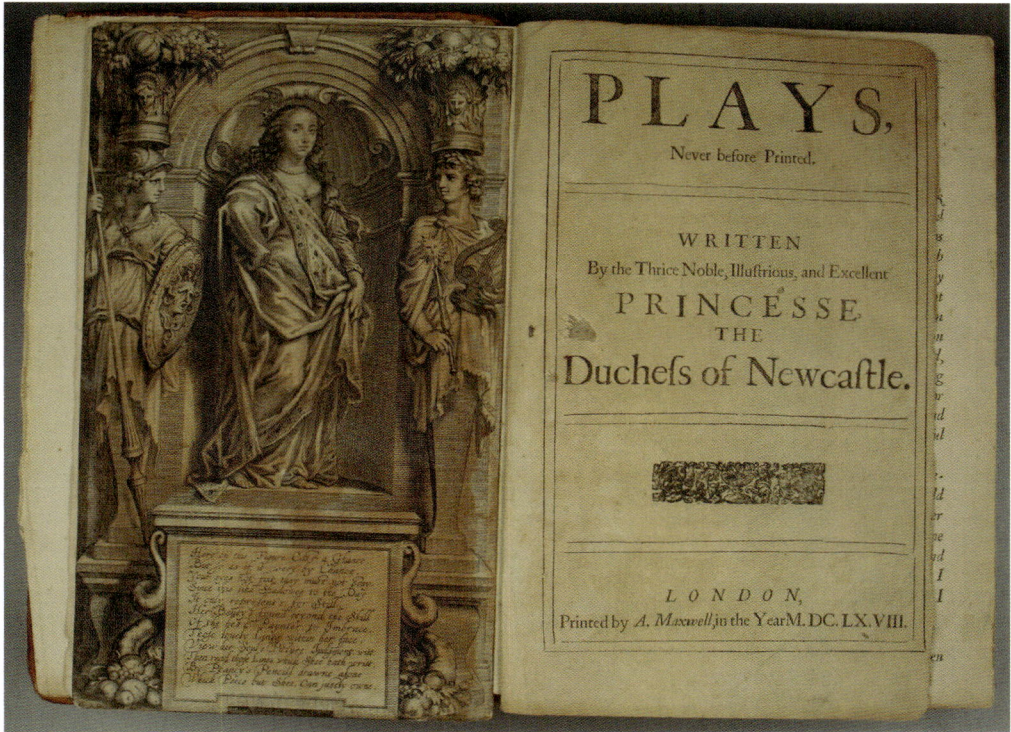

Figure 3.16

Frontispiece to the second volume of *Plays* by Margaret Cavendish, Duchess of Newcastle, 1668

Source: By permission of the Folger Shakespeare Library

but they deserve to be re-integrated into the canon for they certainly offer freshness and an unexpected sharpness to the drama of the period.

DRAMA AT THE COURT OF OLIVER CROMWELL

The first piece of drama which was officially performed during the Commonwealth was James Shirley's unusual but original masque, *Cupid and Death*, which was presented to the Portuguese ambassador in 1653. After an uncomfortable brush with the Parliamentary authorities, when his royalist sympathies cost him £6, Shirley returned to school mastering, though he did write a few masques, perhaps for his pupils. In *Cupid and Death*, the two protagonists swap arrows so that Cupid's darts kill his targets, while Death's reanimate his. The comic confusions which follow may be imagined. The masque includes some dances, choreographed by Luke Channen, plenty of music by Christopher Gibbons and others, and some scenic dexterity. This masque has been revived surprisingly often: in 1659, 1919, 1929 and 1983.

In fact Cromwell was perhaps less opposed to theatre than has been sometimes supposed. The Lord Mayor's shows, banned in the 1640s, were restored during the Protectorate, and when his daughter Frances got married in 1657, the wedding celebrations involved a huge orchestra with forty-eight violins and fifty trumpets, and there was 'much mirth with frolics, besides mixed dancing, a thing heretofore accounted profane', and the fun lasted until five in the morning. And at the wedding of his other daughter, Mary, a few weeks later, not only was there feasting and dancing, but the performance of a masque in which Lord Fauconberg, the bridegroom, appeared as Endymion, and his new bride as Cynthia. And this was followed by a performed playlet in which three country folk discussed marriage.

JOHN TATHAM

The writer most associated with the Commonwealth's Lord Mayor's shows was John Tatham, a would-be dramatist whose opportunities were of course sadly limited. His *The Distracted State* (1651) concerned republican politics and rebellion, written from a royalist perspective, and his later *The Scots Figgaries* is an anti-Scots satire. Whether either of these was ever performed is unclear. Shows he wrote for the London guilds between 1657 and 1664 certainly were performed, and they included both Lord Mayor's shows and triumphal entries.

WILLIAM DAVENANT

The real driving force behind attempts to restart practical professional theatre was William Davenant, erstwhile favourite of the queen who had been imprisoned in the Tower as recently as 1650. He penned an address in 1653, *A Proposition for the Advancement of Morality by a New Way of Entertainment of the People* in which he called for the establishment of a reformed stage which would educate the people through heroic drama. When this seemed to achieve nothing, he changed tack and suggested that the drama could attract the gentry and, with the right plays, encourage their active patriotism. With the Council of State's permission, he mounted *The First Day's Entertainment*, a debate between the cynic, Diogenes, and the comic playwright, Aristophanes, in May 1656 at his own home, Rutland House, in fashionable Aldergate Street. Here he had managed to construct a small stage some eleven feet wide and fifteen feet deep. About a hundred people attended the performance which concluded with a song in praise of Oliver Cromwell.

THE SIEGE OF RHODES

With typical opportunism, Davenant now capitalised on the faint interest he had aroused to present his own operatic drama, *The Siege of Rhodes*. This cleverly chosen subject – the Civil War had seen a plethora of sieges – allowed Davenant to demonstrate all his theatrical experience and expertise, and he staged it at the Cockpit after its premiere at Rutland House. Based on the siege of 1522 by the Turks, it celebrated the a-historical heroism of the British defenders of the island and told the affecting love story of Ianthe and Alphonso. The conception, however, was genuinely original, both in its presentational style and its musical content, and Davenant employed the best composers – Henry Lawes, Henry Cooke and Matthew Locke – to provide the music. This included the new Italian recitative singing as well as instrumental music between the acts and created a strong impression, dignified but more spare than Monteverdi's contemporary Italian operas. As for the staging, he hired John Webb, Inigo Jones's erstwhile assistant, to create a proscenium arch, front curtain, three

Figure 3.17
William Davenant, a driving force in the theatre from the 1630s to the 1660s

pairs of flat wings decorated with designs of rocks and the seashore, and back shutters on grooves. Davenant described the effect fairly enough:

> The curtain being drawn up, a lightsome sky appeared, discovering a maritime coast full of craggy rocks and high cliffs, with several verdures naturally growing upon such situations; and afar off, the true prospect of the city of Rhodes, when it was in prosperous estate, with so much view of the gardens and hills about it as the narrowness of the room could allow the scene. In that part of the horizon, terminated by the sea, was represented the Turkish fleet making towards a promontory some few miles distant from the town.

Webb's designs have survived, and illustrate Davenant's description perfectly. The effects were significant, however, as marking the transfer of the scenic apparatus of the Caroline court theatre to the

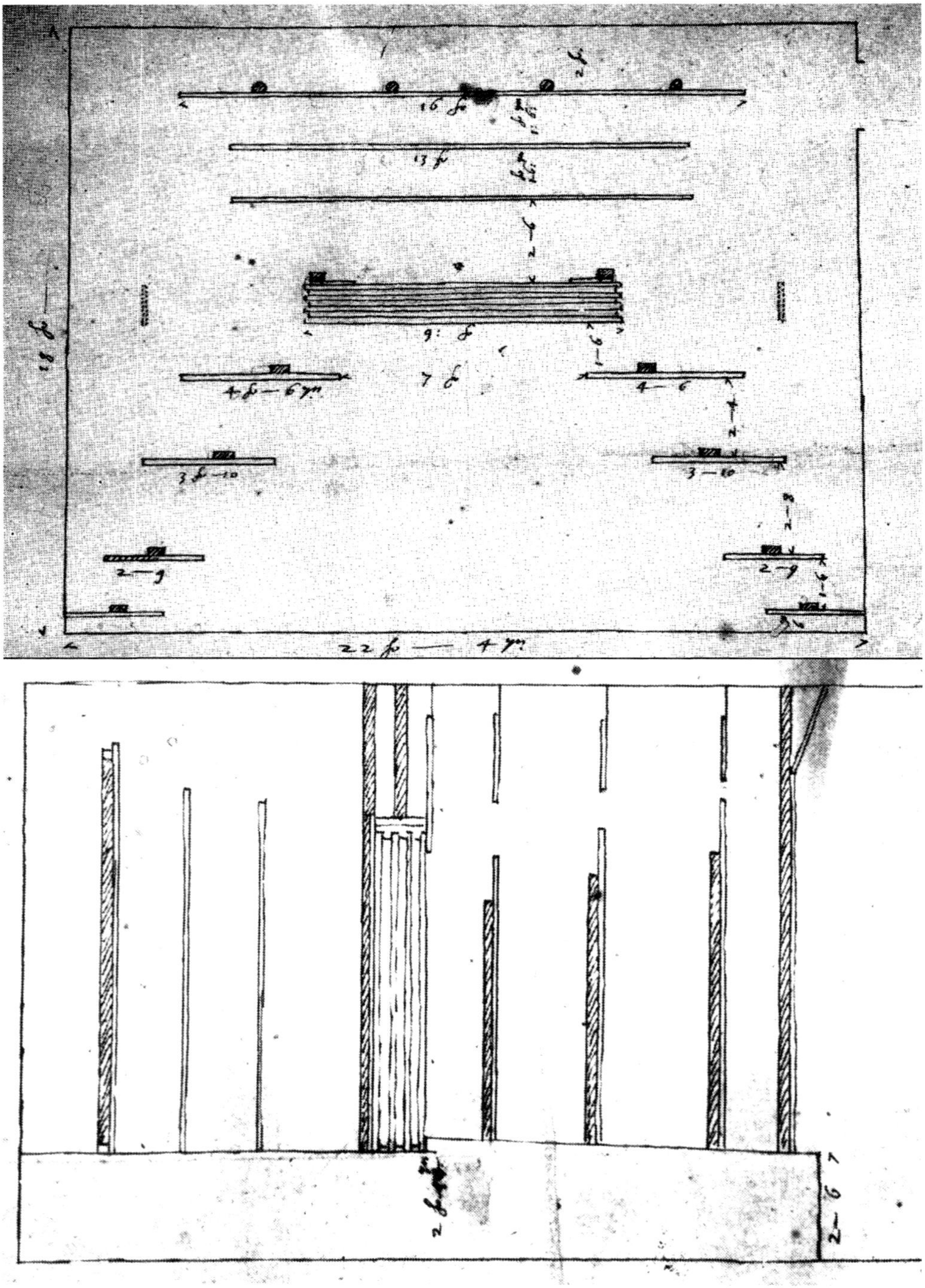

Figure 3.18
John Webb's plan and cross section of the scenery for William Davenant's *The Siege of Rhodes* staged at Rutland House in 1656

nearly public stage. Possibly even more significant for the future, though, was the first appearance of a female performer on the professional stage: Catherine Coleman played the part of Ianthe, the only female in the cast list.

DAVENANT'S PLAYS IN THE LATER CROMWELL YEARS

Davenant tried to follow up this breakthrough with a further would-be historical drama with music, *The Cruelty of the Spaniards in Peru*. He wrote to John Thurloe for permission to stage it at the Cockpit, but it was not until 1658 that permission was granted, which suggests some government doubts. Perhaps the valorisation of Cromwell's imperial project won the day for it. The story concerns the way the natural life of the primitive Peruvians was lost when the greedy invading Spanish arrived, and justice was only restored to these noble savages when New Model Army soldiers in their red coats appeared to put things right, and drive the Spanish out. Scenically the production confirmed the gains made by *The Siege of Rhodes*, and the most stunning effects probably came from the acrobatic performances of some of the cast playing native Americans. There are references to acrobatic acts like 'the sea horse' and 'the porpoise' and one character performs a 'double somerset'. At another moment,

> a rope descends out of the clouds, and is stretched to stiffness by an engine while a rusticair is played, to which two apes from opposite sides of the wood come out, listen, return; and, coming out again, begin to dance. Then, after a while, one of them leaps up to the rope, and there dances to the same air, whilst the other moves to his measures below.

A third Davenant musical extravaganza, *Sir Francis Drake*, also supporting British imperialism, was presented at the Cockpit in 1659. It included recitative and choral singing, and aimed to restore the somewhat tarnished reputation of the Elizabethan seaman.

Davenant almost single-handedly attempted to resurrect the professional theatre in times of trouble, and drag it towards what would be the Cavalier theatre's brilliant final flaring after 1660. And he was to be rewarded when the theatre was encouraged once again by a Stuart king.

NOTES

1 An Ordinance Concerning Stage Plays, 2 September 1642.
2 Jane Milling and Peter Thomson (eds), *The Cambridge History of British Theatre*, vol I, Cambridge: Cambridge University Press, 2004, p. 459.
3 An Ordinance for the Suppression of Stage Plays and Interludes with the penalties prescribed for actors and spectators, 11 February 1648.

Chapter 34: The Restoration narrative

THE RETURN OF CHARLES II

On 28 May 1660, Charles Stuart, son of King Charles I who had been executed in 1649, arrived in England. He stepped ashore and symbolically the monarchy was restored. It was a highly theatrical moment, with huge crowds gathered on the white cliffs of Dover who cheered when he knelt and kissed the ground. He was led up the beach by General Monck with the canopy of state unfurled over his head and carried by flunkies. He received graciously a copy of the Holy Bible. Guns boomed out. Bonfires were lit.

When he came to London, John Evelyn, the diarist, recorded how he was accompanied by

> above 20,000 horse and foot, brandishing their swords and shouting with inexpressible joy; the ways strewed
> with flowers, the bells ringing, the streets hung with tapestry, fountains running with wine; the Mayor,
> Aldermen, and all the companies in their liveries, chains of gold and banners; lords and nobles clad in cloth of
> silver, gold and velvet; the windows and balconies all set with ladies; trumpets, music and myriads of people
> flocking.[1]

Charles II was to perform his role in the regal theatre throughout his twenty-five-year reign.

A NEW SOCIETY

A new national narrative – a cavalier narrative – was needed. The Restoration itself was of course, implicitly and explicitly, a rejection of Puritanism: the returned royalists sought out the surviving 'regicides', and hanged, drew and quartered them; they dug up the body of Oliver Cromwell and two others of his supporters and hanged them, spiking their heads on poles; and when the Great Plague arrived in 1665, they declared it to be God's way of washing clean all traces of the abominable Oliver. The Great Fire of 1666 enabled them to rebuild London in their own image.

The Cavaliers who returned from the continental exile they had shared with Charles had most of their lands and positions restored, and they smartly and smoothly took over many of the levers of power. But they were by no means all powerful, and they had to form some sort of alliance with the now-ousted supporters of the Parliamentary cause, who were often dynamic entrepreneurs and controlled a good deal of the trade and wealth of the country.

Figure 3.19

Charles II's coronation procession to Westminster: performing kingship

Source: Museum of London/Bridgeman Images

The cavaliers therefore required their own forms, their own guidelines and their own style to assert their position. And with this, the theatre, the most public of art forms, could greatly assist. The cavaliers wanted it to affirm their heroism, and they sought in it celebration, a flexing of anti-Puritan muscles in their glad new morning. But it was a brittle brilliance which was both exhilarating and dangerous: it easily turned seduction into rape and horseplay into deadly duelling. The assertive maleness of the culture included an easy misogyny. But it also had an *élan*, and a denial of prudery, which was especially true in the fields of personal and social morality.

THE THEATRE RESTORED

The theatre found a new purpose in developing and exhibiting all this. Public performance reinforced cavalier values: this is the central *motif* in the history of the theatre of this time. At the hub of the renewed theatre stood the king himself. Within two months of his landing in 1660, he asserted his right to control all public entertainments. He created two new theatre companies by Royal Patent, and became patron of the first of them to be established, the King's Company. And he decreed that women's parts should be played by women, not boys or young men. But his interest in theatre went further than such 'political' acts. He helped with casting plays, he encouraged playwrights and even suggested themes and stories for them to dramatise. He asked Roger Boyle, first Earl of Orrery, for a verse tragedy, and received *The Tragedy of Mustapha* (1665). And he helped Dryden with *The Kind Keeper* as late as 1678. He personally gave £1000 to Sir William Davenant, leader of the rival Duke's Company, towards the building of a new theatre at Dorset Garden. And he was an enthusiastic theatregoer, who often attended first performances.

THE FIRST RESTORATION PLAYS

Among the first plays staged after the Restoration were John Tatham's attack on the roundhead Parliament in *The Rump* (1660), John Ogilby's pseudo-masque, *The Entertainment of His Most Excellent Majesty Charles* II (1661), a positive celebration of events, and Abraham Cowley's equally fervent *The Cutter of Coleman Street* (1661).

Cowley was a passionate royalist whose play, set in 1658, dramatises the efforts of the cavalier Sir George Jolly to retrieve his expropriated property: his plan is to marry the widow of the Puritan who obtained it, who had made his money by boiling soap! Meanwhile, the cutter himself pretends to be a Puritan in order to marry the widow's daughter, Tabitha. When Tabitha discovers on the wedding night that he is actually a cavalier and not a Puritan, she becomes considerably aroused: the cavaliers have sex appeal as well as wrongs to right.

Robert Howard's *The Committee* (1662), also set during the Interregnum, shows a committee of low-born, vulgar Cromwellians sequestrating the lands of the upstanding cavalier aristocrats. Among the bullies is the Puritan, Obadiah, played by Cave Underhill, who is made drunk by his resourceful Irish servant Teague, played by John Lacy. Samuel Pepys saw this production: 'a merry but indifferent play', he thought; 'only Lacy's part, an Irish footman, is beyond imagination'.[2]

The king's friends were usually happy to be conscripted into this new project for a cavalier theatre. Sir Samuel Tuke, the first playwright to have a major success after the Restoration with *The Adventures of Five Hours* (1662), was a long-time royalist who had fought at Marston Moor, had lived abroad during the Interregnum and had indeed converted to Catholicism while in France. His play was evidently directly suggested to him by the king. The Earl of Newcastle, the royalist commander who had had plays staged at the Blackfriars Theatre before 1642, and whose family had created many plays during the Commonwealth years, co-wrote *Sir Martin Mar-all* (1667) with John Dryden.

Sir Charles Sedley, notorious libertine and wit, as well as friend and courtier to the king, created a particularly vivid picture of cavalier society in *The Mulberry Garden* (1668), set in the fashionable west end of London. Here the young men and women flirt and fornicate, and the men also go to cock fights, race their horses in the park, play cards and go to the theatre. Set during the Commonwealth, the play's sympathetic characters are constantly in danger politically, though 'to lie in prison for concealing cavaliers will be great merit'. The Puritan father forbids his daughter to marry her hero, a cavalier, but in the end the Commonwealth is brought down, 'the just quarrel of our injured king' is won and the play ends with 'a great shout' which marks 'this all-healing day'.

In Etherege's *She Would If She Could* (also 1668), the silly husband is dressed in someone else's clothes and made a fool of – and we note his name: Sir *Oliver* Cockwood. Even ten years later, Aphra Behn, a staunch royalist, was holding up for our admiration the life of exiled cavaliers during the Interregnum in *The Rover* (1677), while in her *The Feigned Courtesans* (1679) we have perhaps the most devastatingly funny caricature of a Puritan in Mr Tickletext. Furthermore, many of the Restoration's best plays used their author's knowledge of the continental theatre in their dramaturgy, and many continental plays were directly adapted – Molière, for instance, supplied Dryden and Newcastle with the basis for *Sir Martin Mar-all*, Shadwell with *The Sullen Lovers* (1668), Buckingham with *The Rehearsal* (1671), and Wycherley with *The Plain Dealer* (1676).

French models ensured that this would indeed be a new kind of English drama. Many non-political or middling people were tired with the joylessness of the Puritans. Restoration dramas breathed fresh air into the fusty gloom of Puritan society, they gave a taste of liberty and a new tolerance where before all had seemed straight-laced intolerance. The very fact that the theatres were open again was itself part of the narrative. And the brave heroes who were presented in the plays, some of them suffering unjust exile from their native land, offered new models for admiration – characters such as Mustapha in Robert Boyle's *The Tragedy of Mustapha* and Antony in Dryden's *All for Love* (1677), the cheerful but coolheaded Johnson and Smith in *The Rehearsal* and the wits and lovers in the many comedies of the period, the young men in *The Adventures of Five Hours* and *The Mulberry Garden*, Etherege's Courtall and Freeman in *She Would If She Could* and Dorimant in *The Man of Mode* (1676) and Willmore in Aphra Behn's *The Rover*.

The narrative occasionally needed a little steering from Charles II or his agents. The restored Master of the Revels, Sir Henry Herbert, insisted on deletions and amendments from time to time, and actors were discouraged from improvising additions to scripts which had passed his scrutiny. One notorious incident occurred when the King's Company presented the provocatively titled *The Change of Crowns* (1667) by Edward Howard. This was carefully edited by Sir Henry, but when it was performed, John Lacy, the actor, seems to have ad-libbed abuse of the government, in Samuel Pepys's words, 'with all imaginable wit and plainness about selling of places, and doing everything for money'. The company was made to stop performing for a period, and Lacy found himself in gaol.

THE NEW NARRATIVE

Nevertheless, the censorship was not generally oppressive, partly because for the most part play-wrights were happy to uphold the cavalier narrative. Dryden's *The Conquest of Granada* (1670), perhaps the most impressive of all Restoration dramas, shows not only a Restoration, but also the finding of a true heir. In *The Tragedy of Mustapha*, there are discussions of what makes a good king:

SOLYMAN: But a true Prince chiefly by love should reign.
    While in loose knots fear but the body binds,
    We strongly rule by love our subjects minds.
RUSTAN: Yet wisest monarchs by success have proved
    That it is safer to be feared than loved.

The same play reminds its auditors of the horrors of civil war:

    Then the victorious threw their arms away,
    And wept for those whom they did lately slay.
    Some, who had killed their sons, more tears did shed
    For their own guilt, than that their sons were dead.

In Robert Howard's *The Great Favourite* (1668), the king demands, as the beheaded Charles I might have:

    Must Princes' favours then be limited,
    Or judged by common breaths?

though he is urged shortly afterwards by Donna Maria, 'From henceforth, sir, be everybody's king', something the Stuarts were not so adept at achieving.

299 ☐

Figure 3.20
The climax of Sir George Etherege's *The Comical Revenge, or Love in a Tub*, a play very different from the Jacobean revenge plays
Source: Bettmann/Getty Images

A COMICAL REVENGE

In Etherege's *The Comical Revenge* (1664), we hear of a man killed fairly at Naseby; in *The Plain Dealer*, a man who received a scar at Edgehill is favourably compared to one who merely received his in a duel in Bloomsbury. And those who could not accept the new dispensation were characterised as either fools or knaves, like Snarl in Shadwell's *The Virtuoso* (1676), who does not accept the modern theatre: he 'can never endure to see plays since women came on the stage; boys are better by half'. In *The Rover*, Behn mocks such 'politic grave fools' who are unable to accept the new age with its new theatre, and shake their 'empty noddles o'er bamboo' (that is, their walking-sticks). In *Sir Martin Mar-all*, Warner, the clever servant who organises the successful intrigues, turns out to be a true cavalier, a ruined aristocrat, who has been robbed of his rightful fortune by the Cromwellians. All ends for the best, though, and he is rewarded with the hand of his Millicent. It may be significant that whereas the Jacobeans enjoyed *The Revenger's Tragedy*, the Restoration cavaliers preferred *The Comical Revenge, or Love in a Tub*, in which Wheadle informs us that 'to be a cavalier in your heart' is the only way to win a lady. In *She Would If She Could*, Sir Oliver is similarly assured that 'Now you have the mien of a true cavalier, and with one look may make a lady kind, and a hector humble'.

The cavalier's theatrical revenge was, as Etherege had it, a 'comical' one.

NOTES

1 *The Diary of John Evelyn*, 29 May 1660.
2 *The Diary of Samuel Pepys*, 12 June 1663.

Chapter 35: The Royal Patents

NEW THEATRE COMPANIES

At first after the Restoration, and despite General Monck's opposition, the theatrical excitement was palpable. In February 1660 John Rhodes had obtained a licence to stage plays at the old Cockpit. He collected a group of actors and began to create a repertoire, which included *Pericles*, probably the first Shakespeare production since 1642. William Beeston was busily reorganising Beeston's Boys at the Salisbury Court and William Davenant was also clearly expecting to expand his work from the late 1650s. There was intense anticipation.

THE ROYAL PATENTS

And Charles II arrived, clearly keen to support the theatre. However, unlike his ally, Louis XIV across the channel, Charles lacked the funds to subsidise theatres, so he reverted to the idea of the Royal Patent as a means of control. It was awarded to only two companies in London, and none outside the capital. One went to 'our trusty and well-beloved Thomas Killigrew, Esq., one of the Grooms of our Bedchamber', and the other to 'Sir William Davenant, Knight'. They were given

> power and authority to erect two companies of players consisting respectively of such persons as they
> shall choose and appoint, and to purchase, build and erect, or hire at their charge, as they shall think fit,
> two houses or theatres with all convenient rooms and other necessaries thereunto appertaining, for the
> representation of tragedies, comedies, plays, operas and all other entertainments of that nature.[1]

The rest were to be frozen out, and this system of permitting only theatres which had been granted a Royal Patent to operate legitimately lasted for the best part of two hundred years.

OTHER COMPANIES

But those excluded did not simply retire gracefully. True, William Beeston returned to acting and became a noted raconteur of stories and myths about the old, pre-Civil War theatre. But Rhodes kept many of his troupe together, and leaving London took to touring the provinces, occasionally sneaking back to the capital to perform at the Red Bull or the Cockpit. But his enterprise did not last long, and though he tried to keep his foot in the theatrical door, the effort was too much and he died in 1665.

Meanwhile George Jolly had returned from the continent and in November 1660 he established a third London troupe at the Cockpit, largely using actors from Beeston's disbanded company. In December he too received a Royal Patent. In the following years his company performed at the Red Bull and Salisbury Court, but Killigrew and Davenant together persistently objected to his presence in the capital. In 1663 his patent was changed to allow him to perform anywhere in England except London, though he seems to have retained some sort of rights there because Killigrew and Davenant paid £4 per week to keep him away. In 1667 Killigrew and Davenant made out that Jolly had sold them this London licence, and it was revoked. But the company, now based in Norwich, continued to perform. Killigrew and Davenant suggested he establish a 'nursery' to train young actors. Jolly agreed, and established his Hatton Garden Nursery, though he continued to run his own touring company, perhaps in partnership with Edward Bedford, until he died in 1673.

THE FIRST YEARS OF THE NEW COMPANIES

With their Royal Patents granted in August 1660, Killigrew and Davenant wasted no time in moving to production. For a short while they co-operated, their joint company performing in October in the old Cockpit Theatre in Drury Lane. But within a month they had separated. Killigrew concentrated on earning income through performances, but Davenant paused, taking time to fit out his tennis court theatre by Lincoln's Inn Fields, create storage space and prepare scenery. Soon, however, he found himself having to sell shares to keep afloat. Of the fourteen shares in the company, he retained four himself and sold seven. The other three remained in his own control to cover other expenses.

Meanwhile Killigrew's group opened at Gibbons' Tennis Court in Vere Street, near Lincoln's Inn Fields. In May 1663, they moved to a purpose-built theatre in Bridges Street, Drury Lane. They performed here until it burned down in January 1672. They then returned to the Tennis Court until their brand new theatre in Drury Lane was ready in March 1674.

THOMAS KILLIGREW

Thomas Killigrew himself had been a Page of Honour to King Charles I, and an amateur playwright in the 1630s. Now he was a typical middle-aged cavalier who had been in exile and was now hungry to help re-establish the Stuart dynasty. He was the king's more favoured manager: his company became what Shakespeare's had been, 'The King's Company', and its actors, like their Jacobean and Caroline forebears, were 'Grooms of the Chamber' wearing crimson and scarlet livery. He was awarded most of the more experienced professional actors from earlier years, as well as the rights to the lion's share of pre-Commonwealth plays. To begin with he was happy to continue the pre-Restoration conventions of employing young men to play women's roles, and of presenting his stage without scenery or spectacle, just as the old open air theatres had. However, he quickly found himself forced by Davenant's more progressive example to change his ways or lose business.

Figure 3.21
William Sheppard, portrait of Charles II's 'trusty and well-beloved Thomas Killigrew, Esq.', leader of the King's Company after the Restoration

Source: Art Collection 2/Alamy Stock Photo

THE KING'S COMPANY'S ACTORS

In these early years the King's Company seemed strong. Besides reviving the popular Beaumont and Fletcher, they had Dryden as a kind of house dramatist, and Wycherley also gave them all his plays. The company included Pepys's favourite actresses, Rebecca Marshall, Nell Gwynn and Elizabeth Knipp, and in May 1667, he saw Dryden's comedy, *Secret Love*, which pleased him

> infinitely, it being impossible, I think, ever to have the Queen's part, which is very good and passionate, and Florimel's part, which is the most comical that ever was made for woman, ever done better than they are by young Marshall and Nelly[2].

They also appeared together to great effect in Richard Rhodes's *Flora's Vagaries* (1667) and even more triumphantly in Shadwell's *The Sullen Lovers* (1668). Elizabeth Knipp, also adored by Pepys, began as a dancer and singer, but her talents were soon recognised and she did 'mighty well' in Ben Jonson's *The Silent Woman* as well as being the original Lady Fidget in Wycherley's *The Country Wife*.

Around 1670 the company was joined by the probably even more talented Elizabeth Boutell, the *The Country Wife*'s original Margery Pinchwife. She began by playing a series of 'breeches' roles, but soon grew into more complex heroines. She gained a probably unfair reputation for promiscuity ('Betty Boutell, whom all the town fucks', said the scandalous rhyme): she seems to have been reasonably contentedly married to a lieutenant in the army, whom she accompanied abroad when he was dispatched there for military reasons, only to return and resume her acting career. Boutell and Marshall formed an even more popular female partnership on stage with Boutell than she had with Gwynn. Marshall played the passionate and dangerous woman to Boutell's sympathetic *ingénue*. Their finest joint triumph was probably in Nathaniel Lee's stormy *The Rival Queens* (1677), when Marshall was Roxana, domineering and sadistic, and Boutell the pathetic Statira.

Among the King's Company's men, Charles Hart had been a boy player before 1642 and had fought on the royalists' side in the Civil War. Indeed, as an officer in Prince Rupert's cavalry, he had distinguished himself at Marston Moor and Naseby. During the Commonwealth he had been imprisoned for acting in defiance of the ban on the theatres. Nell Gwynn was his lover before King Charles II took her for his own, and she and Hart played a series of 'gay couples' opposite each other to great effect. He was something of a matinée idol, and starred as Almanzor in Dryden's *The Conquest of Granada*, and as Mark Antony in *All for Love*, played Hotspur and Brutus, was Mosca in *Volpone*, and the original Horner in *The Country Wife* and Manly in *The Plain Dealer*. According to Flecknoe

> Beauty to the eye, and music to the ear,
> Such even the nicest critics must allow
> Burbage was once and such Charles Hart is now[3]

while Thomas Rymer wrote of Hart:

> The audience are prepossessed and charmed by his action, before aught of the poet can approach their ears; and to the most wretched character he gives a lustre that so dazzles the sight, that the deformities of the poet cannot be perceived.[4]

Hart was not the only veteran of the king's army whom Killigrew employed. John Lacy and Michael Mohun had also fought for the royalist cause, and Mohun had been seriously wounded. He, too, had been a boy actor before the Civil War and tried unsuccessfully to resume his career in 1659. But he was a founder member of Killigrew's company and developed an impressive line in treacherous and villainous parts: he was the original Pinchwife in *The Country Wife*. Lacy was a skilful rather than a brilliant actor, who also wrote plays and adapted earlier works, such as Shakespeare's *The Taming of the Shrew*. After his provocative improvisations in *The Change of Crowns* by Edward Howard, he was sent to gaol on the king's orders, though Mohun interceded for him and he was soon let out. But he blamed Howard for his incarceration and this so infuriated Howard that he struck Lacy across the face with his glove. Whereupon Lacy picked up a stick and gave him a thorough thrashing.

William Cartwright was another whose career began before 1642. He had been a bookseller and publisher during the Interregnum, and now took older parts, such as Falstaff and Sir Jasper Fidget. Probably the last male player of female roles, Edward Kynaston was reputed to be extremely beautiful ('clearly the prettiest woman in the whole house', spluttered an over-excited Samuel Pepys), though within a year or two of the Restoration he was playing young male roles, when, added Pepys, he 'likewise did appear the handsomest man in the house'. Kynaston's experiences tell us more about the ambience of the theatre of the 1660s and 1670s. Ladies from the audience liked to take him, perhaps in his transvestite costume, into their coaches to enjoy his company in privacy; and he was also known to have been a sexual partner of the Duke of Buckingham. Another rakish actor was Cardell Goodman, for a time lover to Lady Castlemaine, better known as Charles II's mistress, who later 'supplemented his income' by becoming a highwayman.

THE ACHIEVEMENTS OF KILLIGREW AND THE KING'S COMPANY

Killigrew believed it was thanks to his efforts that the whole theatrical establishment after the Restoration was infinitely better than it had been before 1642. He told Samuel Pepys:

> That the stage is now by his pains a thousand times better and more glorious than ever heretofore. Now, wax candles, and many of them; then, not above 3lbs of tallow: now, all things civil, no rudeness anywhere; then, as in a bear-garden: then, two or three fiddlers; now, nine or ten of the best: then, nothing but rushes upon the ground, and everything else mean; now, all otherwise: then, the Queen seldom and the King never would come; now, not the King only for state, but all civil people think they may come as well as any.[5]

The complete truth of this appraisal may perhaps be questioned.

WILLIAM DAVENANT

The second Royal Patent was, perhaps not surprisingly, awarded to Queen Henrietta Maria's old favourite, Sir William Davenant. By now it was clear that Davenant, if not the most talented theatre practitioner of the age, was certainly the most ambitious, both artistically and commercially. His company's patron was the Duke of York – they were 'The Duke's Company'. If Killigrew acquired the rights to most of the pre-Commonwealth plays, Davenant managed to acquire most of Shakespeare, perhaps because of the parentage he claimed. As might be expected from his history, he was both a more active and a more innovative manager than Killigrew. He was who insisted on using female actors for female roles. And he was adamant that his theatre should instal all the old 'engines' devised originally by Inigo Jones to make his scenery moveable and his actors able to 'fly'. According to Dryden, who was soon working with him, 'nothing was proposed to him, on which he could not suddenly produce a thought extremely pleasant and surprising'.

THE DUKE'S COMPANY: THE EARLY YEARS

At first Davenant and the Duke's Company occupied the Salisbury Court Theatre where they performed while their leader prepared another disused tennis court, Lisle's, which like Killigrew's was situated in Lincoln's Inn Fields. In June 1661 his Duke's Company moved into this somewhat cavernous hall, seventy-five feet by about thirty feet wide, and stayed until 1671. In 1668, Davenant had died, and his widow had taken over the Royal Patent. She employed two of her most dedicated company members, Thomas Betterton and Henry Harris, as hands-on managers. Harris seems to have been the handsome public face of the company, while Betterton was its organisational brains. Their decade in charge was largely successful though not without incident. In 1673, for instance, in

Figure 3.22
Sir Christopher Wren designed the fine Dorset Garden theatre on the Thames waterfront where the Duke's Company performed

Source: Heritage Images/Diomedia

a duel scene on stage, Harris stabbed his opponent, played by Philip Cademan, in the eye. It was an accident, but the blade pierced Cademan's brain without killing him. But it destroyed his memory and his power of speech, and he lost the use of his right side. The theatre paid him as a pensioner for over twenty years, until Christopher Rich stopped the payments during his economy drive in the 1696, when Cademan was left without support.

Harris and Betterton oversaw the move to Dorset Garden, near Charing Cross. Probably designed by Christopher Wren, the new theatre was reputed to be the finest of all the Restoration theatres: its 'machinery' and potential for spectacle was as fine as could be procured, and it fronted directly onto the River Thames so that patrons could sail to the door.

THE DUKE'S COMPANY'S ACTORS

The Duke's Company owed much to Davenant's intensity of focus, and the presence in the company of the incomparable Thomas Betterton, as well as new plays by some of the best playwrights of the era, including Etherege, Shadwell, Behn and Otway. Among its actors were Moll Davis, who was the king's mistress before Nell Gwynn, though she was not so good an actress. However, the king showered her with gifts. She gave birth to his daughter, who became Lady Mary Tudor, and when the two separated, Charles generously let her have a large house and a considerable allowance. Her place in the company was taken by Winifred Gosnell. Mary Betterton, *née* Saunderson (she married Thomas Betterton in 1662) was with the company from its inception: she was the first English actress to play Juliet, Lady Macbeth, Ophelia and other Shakespearean roles.

The Company was greatly strengthened in the mid-1670s when Elizabeth Currer and Elizabeth Barry joined. Elizabeth Currer was an extremely beautiful and vivacious woman from Dublin, a popular speaker of Prologues and Epilogues and a natural performer of 'breeches' roles: she featured in at least three such roles in plays by Aphra Behn alone. Elizabeth Barry was to become the greatest actress of her time. During the restoration period, she made her name with superb performances as Harriet in *The Man of Mode* and Hellena in *The Rover*.

PROBLEMS IN PERFORMANCE

However highly skilled the company was, not every performance went as smoothly as it might. Sometimes the actors seemed under-rehearsed, and Pepys overheard Etherege complain that in a performance of *She Would If She Could* that they had fluffed or forgotten their lines. Sometimes they had drunk too much at lunchtime, at others they were guilty of 'corpsing' – that is, laughing during a performance:

> 4th September 1667 – To the Duke of York's playhouse, and there saw Mustapha; which the more I see, the more I like; and is a most admirable poem, and bravely acted; only both Betterton and Harris could not contain from laughing in the midst of a most serious part, from the ridiculous mistake of one of the men upon the stage; which I did not like.

> 5th September 1667 – To the Duke of York's House, and there saw Heraclius, which is a good play; but they did so spoil it with their laughing, and being all of them out, and with the noise they made within the theatre, that I was ashamed of it, and resolved not to come thither again a good while, believing that this negligence,

which I never observed before, proceeds only from their want of company in the pit, that they have no care how they act.

COMPANY ORGANISATION AND FINANCES

The two companies granted Royal Patents by Charles II in 1660 organised themselves on similar lines. At their head was the manager, who might equate to a twenty-first-century 'Artistic Director', except he was also the leading shareholder. Behind him were a number of other 'sharers', usually the senior actors. Below them were the hired actors, or 'hirelings'.

The Restoration theatre companies were profitable businesses on the whole. Income from moneys taken on the door of course varied, but a popular play might gross £100 or more in a single night. Admission prices were not always stable, and for first performances they were considerably increased, but in the 1660s it might cost four shillings (twenty pence) to obtain a place in a Box, two shillings and sixpence (twelve and a half pence) for a place in the pit and one shilling and sixpence or a shilling (seven and a half pence, or five pence) in the galleries. Additional income came from the admittance of some patrons after half time, when they paid half the admission charge. Also, the orange sellers who worked the auditorium paid an annual fee of £100 plus six shillings and eight pence (a third of a pound) per night to sell their fruit and sweets.

Expenditure is more difficult to compute. The builders had to be repaid first – effectively, this was a mortgage. Then the play had to be licensed by the Master of the Revels, who charged £2 for a new work, and £1 for a revival. Publicity and printing cost something, though not a lot. There were also, of course, production costs which could vary greatly, and wages, by far the largest drain on resources. The best actors were paid up to £4 per week, the hirelings obviously less, and new members would receive nothing until they had been in the company for a few months. The playwrights also were rarely paid a fee, but they were usually given a benefit on the third night of the play's run and often a second benefit on the sixth night. There were musicians to be paid – Davenant paid orchestra members up to £1 and ten shillings (£1.50) per day. Then there was a myriad of dancers, specialist entertainers like rope-dancers (who mostly entertained in the intervals), the prompter, the doorkeepers, the scenekeepers (stage hands) and administrators. This expenditure would probably reach at least £25 per day. Sharers were also to be taken into account.

Nevertheless, the value of the shares rose consistently during the first ten or fifteen years after the Restoration. It was only towards the end of the 1670s that audiences began to fall off, and political troubles and controversies began to interfere with the profitability of the theatre.

COMPANY RULES

Actors were contracted to their company and were not permitted to leave without due notice. When Henry Harris tried to change companies, the King ordered him to stay where he was. Contracts stipulated salaries, and though most actors were quite well paid, women's wages were always lower than men's. And neither men nor women were paid when the theatre was closed, as it was when the plague was rife, on Fridays during Lent, if a member of the royal family died or other similar difficulties arose. As for playwrights, they usually sold a single script to a company for the income derived from the third night's performance. In 1668 Dryden signed a contract to provide the King's Company with three plays per year, though he was – perhaps not surprisingly – unable to keep this up and had to back out of his contract. Similar contracts seem to have been negotiated by Nathaniel Lee, John Crowne and other writers, but with not much greater success.

There were also rules for members of the acting companies, such as that no actor might refuse to play the part for which he or she was cast. No costumes were to be taken out of the theatre, and actors were to provide their own costume 'accessories'. The benefit system, in its infancy during the Restoration period, helped actresses in the company, singly or more probably in a group, the apprentices, other particular performers, the playwright, for whom the third performance in a run was generally reserved, and even sometimes a charity.

NOTES

1 Royal Warrant, 19 July 1660.
2 *The Diary of Samuel Pepys*, 24 May 1667.
3 Andrew Gurr, *The Shakespeare Company, 1594–1642*, Cambridge: Cambridge University Press, 2004, p. 229.
4 Thomas Rymer, *The Tragedies of the Last Age*, 1677.
5 *The Diary of Samuel Pepys*, 12 February 1667.

Chapter 36: The Restoration playhouse

A NEW KIND OF PLAYHOUSE

The theatres which were built during the Restoration period created a configuration and physical structure which was to last with comparatively few changes for nearly two centuries. Choosing not to try to recreate the old open popular theatres, Davenant and Killigrew both sought something smaller, more intimate, more select, based on the pre-Civil War Stuart court theatre. It was to be part of the new Restoration narrative.

The first Drury Lane theatre, which opened in 1663, was one hundred twelve feet long and fifty-eight feet wide. Dorset Garden, perhaps designed by Sir Christopher Wren, was longer at one hundred forty feet, but virtually the same width, fifty-seven feet. It could squash into its auditorium a maximum of twelve hundred people. The second Drury Lane, also probably designed by Wren, was one hundred forty feet long, and held a maximum of a thousand spectators. Though widely admired for their splendour, Restoration theatres were actually small.

WREN'S DRURY LANE

From the sectional drawing by Wren, it is clear that the stage area occupied about two-thirds of the building, with only a third left for the auditorium. The stage area nearest to the audience was raked, though not steeply: this was the acting area, and there were two doors by which actors entered and exited. The actors rarely went further back than the proscenium arch, immediately upstage of the doors. Behind the proscenium arch was the 'scenic' stage: Wren's drawing shows clearly the upright flats, or 'shutters', which were pushed in from the wings, to form the backdrop. The furthest right section of the picture was the vista stage, which enhanced the perspective effect of the audience's view. Wren's sketch also shows the auditorium: the raked pit in two sections nearest to the stage, the 'front' boxes behind the pit, the middle gallery above, and the upper gallery above that, with the side boxes in the wall beyond the pit. Wren did not show either the scene dock, which was Davenant's special cornucopia, or the tiring-rooms backstage, one for men, one for women, with their coal fires to keep the actors warm.

BALCONIES

The musicians were generally accommodated in a box above the stage doors, though sometimes for a particularly musical play they might be placed between the stage and the pit. Sometimes actors

Figure 3.23
Cross section of a Restoration theatre, probably a sketch by Sir Christopher Wren of the projected new Drury Lane theatre

appeared above the doors, too, not just for Juliet's balcony scene, but for instance in *Sir Martin Mar-all*, when Millicent and Rose entered '*with a candle, above*' and Rose looked forward to some '*rare music*'. Sure enough, '*Sir Martin appears at the adverse window*', among the musicians, and music was then played, supposedly by Sir Martin.

STAGE

The forestage jutted surprisingly far into the auditorium, but unlike in the Elizabethan open air theatres, there was no floor space for spectators at the sides of this stage. Into the stage itself were cut at least two trapdoors which were used frequently. In Behn's *The Feigned Courtesans*, for example, Tickletext slid down the bucket-rope into a well (that is, through the trapdoor), and reappeared a few moments later '*in the bucket*'. *The Feigned Courtesans* is full of absurd situations and chaotic theatrical gags, demonstrating Behn's mastery of the resources of the particular stage she was writing for: thus, Marcella and Cornelia '*walk down the long garden*' – that is, they entered the scenic stage.

CHANGEABLE SCENERY

The system of changing the scenes derived from Inigo Jones's work on the masques of the pre-Civil War Stuart court, most notably Davenant's *Salmacida Spolia*. Davenant's introduction of the shutter and groove system, however, which he may have aimed to do in his projected public theatre of 1639, turned into a significant innovation in the Restoration public theatre. Before the Restoration, British public theatres had had open stages without pictorial or scenic elements. But not only did Davenant introduce scenery, the scenes themselves, as with the Stuart court masques, were changeable, and were changed in full view of the audience.

Two 'shutters' (huge canvases perhaps fifteen feet square) each formed half the desired back-drop or scenic picture. When they were pushed from the wings opposite each other, they slid to the middle of the stage, where they met, and the picture was complete. To ensure the shutters did meet in the middle, they were slotted into grooves, the lower of which were fixed to the floor, while an upper set held their tops. The system was known as 'shutter and groove' and it lasted, with modifications and improvements, for over two centuries.

The scenes depicted on the shutters were generic or emblematic or decorative, rather than realistic, aiming to focus ideas rather than impart realism to the stage. Behind the proscenium arch there were three or four sets of grooves parallel with the front of the stage. When a stage direction in a script reads '*The scene opens*' it means that the shutters were drawn back into the wings to reveal a new picture – or possibly the vista stage – beyond. When it reads '*The scene closes*', the shutters were pushed to the centre and whatever was behind them could no longer be seen. When the shutters were changed, the wings, or 'side scenes', and the 'borders' across the top of the stage were also changed to be in keeping with – or to contradict – the main picture. Thus, Nathaniel Lee's *Theodosius* (1680) asked for: '*A stately temple, which represents the Christian religion, as in its first magnificence. . . . The side scenes show the horrid tortures with which the Roman tyrants persecuted the church; and the flat scene, which is the limit of the prospect, discovers an altar, richly adorned*'.

THE EMPRESS OF MOROCCO

The first of Dolle's engravings of the production of Elkanah Settle's *The Empress of Morocco* (1673) seems to show the actors just in front of the proscenium arch, and with three sets of wings and borders behind them. In the second picture, the whole effect could be simply a pair of shutters with the scene painted on them, or the pillars could be cutouts, and freestanding, with the ships painted behind them. These scenes were from a particularly elaborate production at Dorset Garden, where the Duke's Company strove to keep up the enthusiasms of Davenant, its founder, even after his death. They also demonstrated the new-found importance of the scene painter and the stage carpenter.

The system also enabled a perspective effect to be achieved on stage, especially when the side scenes were set at an angle. But this raised the fundamental problem built into the system. The stage was now thought of as a picture rather than a space, two dimensional, not three. Perspective is a trick of two-dimensionality, making a picture seem to have three dimensions. But the stage is actually three-dimensional. The search for perspective in the pictorial sense therefore was doomed to failure. So long as the backcloths were symbolic, the problem was manageable. But when, as in *The Empress of Morocco*, the pictures were more or less illusional, difficulties arose. Painted scenes were sometimes extremely dynamic, as in the second picture from *The Empress of Morocco*, but juxtaposed with breathing and moving actors they created as many problems as they solved. It has been argued that this contrast between the real and the painted lent a certain dialectical piquancy to the scene, but this type of painted backcloth is more successful when the subject is a graphic addendum to the action, rather than an attempt to show its location. Thus, illusion and reality clashed in the cavalier theatre in new, unexpected ways. This, however, did not stop many finding the new stages places of wonder and delight. What Davenant and his successors were able to create might have been seen in France, it might have been common in

Figures 3.24 and 3.25
Two scenes from Elkanah Settle's spectacularly staged *The Empress of Morocco*, presented at Dorset Garden theatre, 1673
Source: Private Collection

the presentations of masques in the court of Charles I, but it had never before been seen in the public theatres of England.

CHANGING THE SCENERY

Of course, not every play had new scenery painted for it. Most had a mixture of reused old shutters and new. Changing the scenes was a rehearsed action: the scenekeeper blew his whistle and his fellows, of whom there would probably be ten or more, would set to work. Scene changing soon became an entertaining part of the performance. Spectators cheered as the shutters were drawn in, and clapped when the two halves met. Sometimes the scene change had to be carefully coordinated with the action of the play, as in Otway's *The Soldiers' Fortune* (1680): '*They go within the scene* (i.e. behind the proscenium arch) *where is discovered tables and bottles*' (i.e. the shutters open: they look at the backdrop and walk beyond the first grooves).

BEAU: Why, there's the land of Canaan now in little. Hark you, drawer, dog, shut, shut the door, sirrah – do you hear? – shut it so close, that neither cares nor necessities may peep in upon us.
The scene closes upon Beauguard and Courtine.

FLYING MACHINES

Davenant's most spectacular scenic effects were achieved by the flying machines. He encouraged his writers to create scenes which used this effect, as Lee did in *Sophonisba*: '*Rosalinda rises in a chair, pale, with a wound on her breast; two cupids descend, and hang weeping over her*'. And in Buckingham's *The Rehearsal*: '*The two right Kings of Brentford descend in the clouds, singing, in white garments; and three fiddlers sitting before them, in green*'. 'Flying' actors or vehicles by 'machine' had been seen in London theatres before; but still, Davenant managed to increase the spectacle, or at least give the impression that that was what he was doing. Moreover, the physical business of creating these effects was no easy matter, and no-one except the appropriate stage hand was allowed near when this was happening:

> 'tis impossible to command those vast engines (which move the scenes and machines) and to order such a number of persons as must be employed in works of that nature, if any but such as belong thereunto be suffered to press in amongst them,

as a Royal Proclamation of 1673 put it.

STAGE PROPS

Other practicalities had to be taken account of, too. Stage properties were used when needed on the stage, they were not planted on the set to give the impression of 'reality'. An interesting reflection on the properties used on the Restoration stage is provided by Samuel Pepys, who went backstage in March 1666 when there was no play, and saw 'here a wooden leg, there a ruff, here a hobby-horse, there a crown. . . . But then again to think how fine they show on the stage by candle-light, and how poor things they are to look at too near hand'.[1] The hobby-horse might have been used in *The Rehearsal*, where the cavalry ride into battle on these wicker frames held on by something like old-fashioned braces.

The same principle may have been used for the tub in which Dufoy is imprisoned in *The Comical Revenge*: it is described as 'a tub without a bottom, a shut at the top to be locked, and a hole to put one's head out at, made easy to be borne on one's shoulders'. But props, because they are selected, are frequently more than mere objects. The cup of chocolate brought on in *The Adventures of Five Hours* indicates the character's civilised status, and the sedan chair in which Bellinda arrives at Dorimant's house in *The Man of Mode* fulfils a similar function, while in Behn's *The Forced Marriage*, the betrayer is strangled with her own garter!

COSTUMES

The garter might be regarded as a costume. Though those acting specialised characters, like the kings in white and the fiddlers in green in the spectacular scene from *The Rehearsal*, might be given their costumes, most plays were set contemporaneously, and actors provided many parts of their costume themselves. They almost always supplied hats, wigs, shoes and such accessories. But sometimes a historical or other picturesque production demanded fancier costuming, and John

Downes, the prompter, recalled the Duke's Company's production of Shakespeare's *Henry VIII* when the costumes were provided by the theatre:

> King Henry the 8th, this play, by order of Sir William Davenant, was all new clothed in proper habits: the
> king's was new, all the lords, the cardinals, the bishops, the doctors, proctors, lawyers, tipstaffs, new scenes:
> the part of the king was so right and justly done by Mr Betterton, he being instructed in it by Sir William, who
> had it from old Mr Lowen, that had his instructions from Mr Shakespeare himself.[2]

MUSIC AND DANCE

Costumes, changing scenery, machines which 'fly' characters either down from the ceiling, or up into it, bred a demand for the spectacular, and this found another expression in the music and dance incorporated into productions. Dances of all sorts feature in almost every Restoration play – country dances, social dances, jigs, masked dances, clown dances; and there are many full-blown masques, which may take up a quarter of an hour or more during the play.

It is rarely realised just how much music there was in the Restoration playhouse. Prince Cosimo of Tuscany visited the theatre in 1669, and his amanuensis, Lorenzo Magalotti noted that

> Before the comedy begins, that the audience may not be tired with waiting, the most delightful symphonies
> are played; on which account many persons come early to enjoy this agreeable amusement.[3]

There was more music between the acts: for example, at the end of the first act of *Aureng-Zebe* (1675), '*betwixt the acts, a warlike tune is played, shooting off guns, and shouts of soldiers are heard, as in an assault*', while Act IV of *The Man of Mode* begins with '*the fiddles playing a country dance*'. And of course there was much music during the play – music for its own sake, music for songs, dance music, atmospheric music and so on. In *The Comical Revenge* at least thirteen specific songs are called for, and in *She Would If She Could* there are at least eleven. The theatre orchestra at this time was consequently quite large – up to a dozen violins with assorted flageolets, sackbuts, cornets, oboes and other instruments, including percussion.

STAGE LIGHTING

Finally the lighting in Restoration theatre was important. Lighted candles in hoops hung over stage and audience, and there were more candles in wall brackets. It made the theatre interior rather like a large room with the auditorium and the stage equally well lit, though the scenic vista stages were less bright. Wax candles were preferred in the theatre, being brighter and less smelly, as well as lasting longer than tallow candles. But of course, they were more expensive. The candles were snuffed, or perhaps relit if necessary, between the acts, not during the performance. What this meant was that any scenes supposedly set at night or in a dark place like a dungeon, involved the actors carrying lanterns or candles rather than the lights themselves dimming. Stage directions indicate this. For instance, in Shadwell's *The Libertine*, Maria throws down a letter from her window into the dark street. Don John, not its intended recipient, catches and reads it '*by a dark lantern*'. Then, a few minutes later, when the scene shifts indoors, Flora enters '*with a candle*'. We know from these props that it is night.

This kind of indication for the benefit of the audience who nevertheless can follow the action because it is not in fact being played in the dark, was developed by many theatres through history and across the world before the advent of electricity. But in Aphra Behn's *The Feigned Courtesans* the Restoration theatre can boast an unusually brilliant example of such a scene. Act III of the play takes place on a particularly dark night. Tickletext waits fearfully, clutching his lantern. His enemy Galliard enters. Tickletext mistakes him for his pimp and begins to savour the pleasure he thinks he has to come, when Galliard draws his sword. Tickletext realises who it is, and hastily retreating, bumps into Octavio. '*Octavio strikes him a good blow, beats him back, and draws. Tickletext gets close up in a corner of the stage. Octavio gropes for him as Galliard does, and both meet and fight with each other*'. After further mishaps, Galliard manages to slip away, just as Sir Signal Buffoon enters, gropes forward and stabs his hand on Octavio's drawn sword. He

> hops to the door, and feeling for his way with his outstretched arms, runs his lantern into Julio's face, who is just entering. Sir Signal finds he's opposed with a good push backward, and slips aside into a corner over against Tickletext. Julio meets Octavio and fights him. Octavio falls. Julio opens his lantern and sees his mistake.

NOTES

1 *The Diary of Samuel Pepys*, 19 March 1666.
2 John Downes, *Roscius Anglicanus*, 1708.
3 Count L. Magalotti, *Travels of Cosimo the Third, Grand Duke of Tuscany, Through England During the Reign of King Charles the Second, 1669*, London: J. Mawman, 1821, p. 191.

Chapter 37: Plays on the Restoration stage

NEW PLAYS

The new cavalier narrative demanded new plays to endorse it, even glamorise it. Thus, despite the eighteen-year gap, playwriting resumed in 1660 with gusto, and as early as the fourth season after the reopening of the playhouses, sixteen new plays were staged. In 1676–7, there were twenty-three new plays, so that the need for continually reviving Elizabethan and Jacobean drama quickly lost its urgency.

The new plays took care to show the world the inestimable value of the Restoration court and the cavaliers, a world which of course included the theatre itself. What was significant in such a narrative, and hence in these plays, was its immediacy, its closeness to home, its reference to what these people did here, in London. The actions were seen to be modelled on the 'real lives' of the courtiers and aristocrats, the rakes and libertines of King Charles's court, and stage characters were often directly modelled on particular courtiers. Thus, Dorimant's likeness to John Wilmot, the notorious Earl of Rochester, in *The Man of Mode* was striking; Bayes, in *The Rehearsal*, was assumed to represent Dryden; and Statira and Roxana in Lee's *The Rival Queens* (1677) seemed to be representations of Queen Catherine and Lady Castlemaine.

Then, scenes in plays were set in recognisable, often fashionable London places, as Act V scene 2 in *The Plain Dealer* takes place in 'The Cock in Bow Street', and scenes in *She Would If She Could* are set successively in the Mulberry Garden, the New Exchange, the Bear Inn and New Spring Garden. Following a trend set in the 1630s, some plays took their names from their fashionable locations, such as Sedley's *The Mulberry Garden*, Shadwell's *Epsom-Wells* (1672) and John Dover's *The Mall* (1674).

HEROIC TRAGEDY

Of the new types of drama, the heroic tragedy, which was at its height between 1665 and 1675, was perhaps the most typical of the age. It is probably better to think of it as 'Heroic Drama' rather than 'Heroic Tragedy', the name by which it was known at the time, because it was intended to produce admiration, and even awe, rather than tragedy's more usual pity and fear. Moreover, partly because it was often written in rhyming couplets, it was the form which demands most of our imaginations if we are to enjoy what it has to offer.

It is baroque, exotic, exaggerated, 'stagey'. Its perennial theme is honour, a notion vital to the cavalier mind, and the virtue most prized by its protagonists. It depicts extreme situations and often calls for spectacular scenic effects. It demands not so much a suspension of disbelief or a willing-ness to participate emotionally in the action of the play, as a detached intellect in the spectator, a willingness to weigh up the issues presented and to judge them rationally. Thus, in Dryden's *All For Love* (1677), Antony's apparent vacillation is not to be seen as weakness or foolishness, but rather it points to his intelligence. He listens in Act I to Ventidius, understands his point of view and assents to it. Then in Act II Cleopatra argues her case, and Antony changes his mind and agrees with her, only for Dollabella, Octavia and the children to further change his mind. He listens to the arguments, weighs them up, and responds to them as his reason dictates. And this is set against reason's enemy, appetite, or emotion, the basis for Alexas's appeal to Cleopatra:

> Try
> To make him jealous: jealousy is like
> A polished glass held to the lips when life's in doubt:
> If there be breath, 'twill catch the damp and show it.

This is visceral, not rational.

Often set in distant parts of the world, or in distant periods of history, these plays present a hero who pursues glory and self-aggrandisement through war or adventure. The women, on the other hand, no matter how noble, cannot themselves aspire, and are rather pathetic, as is Sophonisba in Nathaniel Lee's *Sophonisba* (1676):

> The Consul is returned with conquest crowned;
> Triumphant voices rend the echoing ground,
> And to the heavens the trumpets clangours sound;
> Yet I no news of Massinissa hear:
> Should he be slain, which I with reason fear,
> Most lost of women, desperate, undone,
> What couldst thou do? What Gods couldst thou atone?

Such lines do not attempt to imitate everyday speech, they are intended to crystallise a moment, to indicate moral significances or to explicate motives for action. Nevertheless, in this confining of the women's role, the plays lose something of our sympathy. The pervasive attitude to women is typified by Solyman in Boyle's *The Tragedy of Mustapha* (1668):

> 'tis far above a woman's art
> To reach the height of an aspiring heart.

Yet undoubtedly at their best, these heroic plays have an elegance and a formal beauty comparable to baroque music or to some of the churches of Christopher Wren.

DRYDEN'S *AN ESSAY OF DRAMATIC POESY*

Heroic drama was theorised primarily by the dramatist, poet laureate and essayist, John Dryden. Pre-Restoration English drama, lacking the splendid rigour of French neoclassicism, came under

Figure 3.26
Poet, playwright and theatre theoretician, John Dryden

Source: Design Pics Historical/Ken Welsh/Diomedia

attack from French critics and observers, such as Samuel Sorbière, who visited England in 1663, and disparaged English drama's 'irregularity'. Thomas Spratt wrote a lively response to this in *Observations on Mons. Sorbière's Voyage into England* in 1665, the same year in which Dryden withdrew from plague-ravaged London to consider the theoretical base of the new Restoration drama. Dryden finally published *An Essay of Dramatic Poesy* in 1668.

The work purports to describe a boat trip on the River Thames during which four intellectuals, perhaps based on actual intellectuals of the day, argue about drama. The four are Eugenius, who has been identified with Lord Buckhurst, Dryden's patron; Crites, perhaps Robert Howard, a playwright and Dryden's wife's brother; Lisideius, perhaps Sir Charles Sedley; and Neander, whom many have taken to be Dryden himself. The essay therefore proceeds dialectically, with each character putting forward a different viewpoint, though the tone is always rational and civilised. The drift of Dryden's argument lies in his comparison between Shakespeare's power, variety, animation of images and largeness of 'soul', and Corneille's indisputably admirable qualities – which however are seen as irrelevant to Britain. Dryden also compares contemporary English drama with the drama written before 1642, and the results are not all favourable to his own time.

Dryden's intention is to reassess English tragedy in the light of the greater knowledge of French and continental plays afforded by the cavaliers' exile during the Interregnum. He is cosmopolitan enough to value reason and clear ideas, but he also understands the life embedded in the English tradition, with its elaborate plots and comic interludes. He admits these features have no basis in classical authority, but they are successful on the stage. Nevertheless, he feels the time is right to amend the English tradition by the introduction of smoother verse, probably to include rhyme, and neater, more intellectually controlled plots. Shadwell, by the way, disagreed; he suggested: 'Serious love is duller than a rhyming play'. But Dryden, through critical Prefaces to his published plays, as well as his *Defence* of his original essay, refined his ideas, while becoming perhaps less tolerant over the years.

THOMAS RYMER

Dryden's work was largely reinforced by that of Thomas Rymer, an indifferent dramatist but an interesting critic. Rymer clarifies some of the earlier writer's thoughts in his *The Tragedies of the Last Age*, published in 1677. His approach is overtly derived from Aristotle, and he lays emphasis on plot, character and 'thought'. Plot, Rymer demands, must depend on 'probability', that is, it must develop logically. 'Decorum' is what he stresses as far as characterisation is concerned. And he distinguishes between 'historical justice', which is what usually happens in the world, and 'poetical justice', which is what the drama should produce, so that the spectator may be appropriately satisfied. 'Reason', says Rymer, is what must underlie all successful 'fancy'.

BURLESQUE

We find it easy to laugh at the bombast which typifies Restoration heroic tragedy. Should we be surprised, therefore, to discover that the cavaliers themselves were equally able to mock these plays? Shadwell, for instance, in the Epilogue to *The Virtuoso*, mocks the leading characters:

> Though singly they (the heroes) beat armies and huff kings,
> Rant at the gods and do impossible things;
> Though they can laugh at danger, blood and wounds;
> Yet if the dame (heroine) once chides, the milksop hero swoons.

The first Restoration burlesque was probably Davenant's *The Playhouse to be Let* (1663), in which various aspiring theatre entrepreneurs present their cases to be allowed to take over an empty theatre: would-be heroic drama is reduced to farce:

EUNUCH: Ah fickle fortune! who would e're have dreamt this,
   Rome's roaring boys will swagger now at Memphis.

NIMPHIDIUS: Behold, they come who quickly can inform us.

EUNUCH: Nimphidius, mum, be silent as a dormouse.

THE REHEARSAL

The Rehearsal by George Villiers, Duke of Buckingham, and others, is a burlesque which pokes endless, pitiless and hugely comic fun at the heroic tragedy and in particular at its most renowned practitioner, John Dryden. The Prologue forewarns us:

> We might well call this short mock-play of ours
> A posy made of weeds instead of flowers.

It goes on to make plain the authors' aim – to 'reform' the stage through mockery. The action of the play centres on the rehearsal of an absurd 'heroic' drama. The idea of a rehearsal forming the centrepiece of a play was not original with Buckingham, of course: Molière's *L'Impromptu de Versailles* was an obvious forerunner. *The Rehearsal* shows Bayes, the author, directing his play and simultaneously explaining what he is up to to his two humorously sceptical acquaintances, Smith and Johnson. Bayes demonstrates – or, over-demonstrates – the actions to the players. At one point he falls on his nose, and next appears with a 'paper' on it; later, he scratches his head and his wig falls off!

The tone is set by the scene of the action – not Morocco, or ancient Persia, but Acton and Brentford, considerably less salubrious districts of the capital than Sedley's fashionable Mulberry Garden. As the final battle approaches, this localism becomes ever more absurd. The General and the Lieutenant-General urgently formulate the dispositions of their troops:

LIEUT. GEN: Advance from Acton with the musketeers.

GEN: Draw down the Chelsea Cuirassiers.

LIEUT. GEN: The band you boast of, Chelsea Cuirassiers,
    Shall, in my Putney Pikes now meet their peers.

GEN: Chiswickians, aged, and renowned in fight,
    Join with the Hammersmith Brigade.

LIEUT. GEN: You'll find my Mortlake Boys will do them right,
    Unless by Fulham numbers overlaid.

GEN: Let the left wing of Twickenham Foot advance
    And line that eastern hedge.

LIEUT. GEN: The Horse I raised in Petty France
    Shall try their chance.

Prince Volscius pretends to go to Picadilly, but actually heads for Knightsbridge where his army is in hiding. As he is pulling on his boots, he falls in love with Parthenope:

> How has my passion made me Cupid's scoff!
> This hasty boot is on, the other off,
> And sullen lies, with amorous design,
> To quit loud fame, and make that beauty mine.

He 'goes out hopping with one boot on and the other off'. The great hero of the drama, however, is Drawcansir, a parody of Almanzor, the hero of Dryden's *The Conquest of Granada*. Drawcansir has all the traits which contemporary critics deplored in Almanzor, for he is, Bayes claims, 'a fierce hero that frights his mistress, snubs up kings, baffles armies and does what he will without regard to numbers, good manners, or justice'. When he claims:

> I drink, I huff, I strut, look big and stare;
> And all this I can do, because I dare

he echoes Dryden's hero:

> Spite of myself I'll stay, fight, love, despair;
> And I can do all this because I dare.

And indeed, in the final battle which climaxes the play as well as the rehearsal, Drawcansir '*kills 'em all on both sides*'. Johnson and Smith, unable to take any more of this nonsense, sneak away to dinner. The actors, too, melt away. Bayes, left alone, threatens to take his play to the other theatre. But two actors return, and they perform the last dance, if only because it may come in handy in the next play they present.

It may be added that though Buckingham's play is one of the funniest in English, his feud with Dryden was lasting and pursued ruthlessly. He had already, in 1668, had Thomas Killigrew's brother Henry beaten up outside the theatre after Henry Killigrew had disclosed Buckingham's dalliance with the Countess of Shrewsbury. In the duel that followed, the Countess's husband had been left for dead. Shortly afterwards Buckingham's hired thugs murdered Killigrew. In 1679, Buckingham arranged for Dryden to be ambushed and badly beaten, too, though to an extent Dryden was to able obtain his revenge in his most significant poem, *Absolom and Achitophel*, wherein he characterised Buckingham as Zimri,

> A man so various that he seemed to be
> Not one, but all mankind's epitome.
> Stiff in opinions, always in the wrong:
> Was everything by starts, and nothing long.

Is the pen mightier than the sword? The effectiveness of both the poem and the burlesque remain. And Thomas Rymer, writing more than twenty years after *The Rehearsal* was first staged, suggested that

> we want a law for acting The Rehearsal once a week, to keep us in our senses and secure us against the noise and nonsense, the farce and fustian which, in the name of tragedy, have so long invaded, and usurp, our theatre.[1]

OLD PLAYS RENEWED

Most theatres in most places at most periods of history rely on revivals of older plays for their staple fare. And so it was with the Restoration. In many seasons far more plays by Beaumont and Fletcher,

Ben Jonson, Shakespeare and their contemporaries were presented by the Royal Patent theatres than were new 'Restoration' plays. And often then – as now – contemporary writers made new versions of these older works.

For example, Shakespeare seems to have inspired Davenant to create a musical version of *The Tempest*, re-named *The Enchanted Island* (1667). In the interests of neoclassical balance, he added to Shakespeare's cast list Dorinda, a sister to Miranda, and Hippolito, an innocent young man who had never seen a woman (as Miranda has never seen a man). Now the story concerns a love four-some, which almost elbows out of the play Caliban, Trinculo and Stephano, as well as Gonzalo and the courtiers. Neoclassical equilibrium also prompted the considerable expansion of Lady Macduff's part in Davenant's version of *Macbeth* as a counterweight to Lady Macbeth was felt to be necessary.

Equally typical of the period was Nahum Tate's *The History of King Lear* (1681), which usurped Shakespeare's original play on the English stage for at least a hundred and fifty years: the happy ending was more in keeping with Rymer's notion of 'poetic justice' than Shakespeare's terrible end. Tate's version was more rational, too, as well as more intelligible and more ethical. Tate everywhere clarified the characters' motives, thus enabling Cordelia and Edgar to represent some bastion of sense against the unabated appetites of egotism and sexuality. He excised the Fool from Shake-speare's cast and introduced a companion or maid for Cordelia, called Arante.

In Tate's play, Cordelia is not whisked off to France at the end of Act I. She is beloved of Edgar, but when Burgundy rejects her, Edgar is already enmeshed in Edmund's plot and cannot therefore help her. However, once Lear has given up the throne and Regan and Goneril are in power, the peasants begin to rebel:

> The riots of these proud imperial sisters
> Already have imposed the galling yoke
> Of taxes and hard impositions on
> The drudging peasants' neck, who bellow out
> Their loud complaints in vain.

Thus, it is an internal insurrection which Edgar and Albany lead against Edmund, Goneril and Regan, and though (as in Shakespeare), they lose the battle, Edgar's victory over Edmund in the single com-bat, and Goneril's and Regan's deaths, each at the other's hands, enables Edgar to take over the kingdom and marry Cordelia, while the ageing trio of Lear, Gloster and Kent 'will gently pass' their 'short reserves of time' together.

This restructuring does have the effect of keeping Cordelia in front of the audience throughout the play. Tate even gives her own hovel scene to balance her father's, when she and Arante are set upon by ruffians sent by Edmund. And though Tate occasionally slips into rhyming verse, and he cannot resist a typical restoration scene between Regan and Edmund, 'amorously seated, listening to music', the play is sure-footed and in many ways rewarding.

PROLOGUES AND EPILOGUES

One unexpected feature of Restoration dramas is that they are completed by Prologues and Epilogues, spoken by a member of the cast, but probably not in character. They most often beg the audience's favourable reception of the play, and the authors came to be extraordinarily ingenious in discovering new ways to say the same thing. But there was also what might be called a subliminal function to these Prologues and Epilogues, in which the author or the acting company attempts to effect the transition from normal life, the 'real world', to the illusory world of the play, and back again. Tailored for a particular performer, they formed a sort of frame for the special experience the theatre was offering. After the initial music finished, the actor speaking the Prologue would step forward and speak, perhaps mischievously, perhaps winningly, wishing the audience may enjoy the play. At the end of the Prologue, the curtain was drawn back and the drama began. And after it, another actor appeared and spoke the Epilogue, letting us down gently, as it were, back to the 'real world'. Then the final curtain was drawn.

Perhaps in order to fulfil this subliminal purpose, Prologues and Epilogues were often surprisingly informal. Thus, the Prologue to Dryden's *Conquest of Granada*, one of the age's most dignified and decorous dramas, was spoken by Nell Gwynn, who appeared 'in a broad-brimmed hat and waist belt', a joke at the expense of the Duke's Company:

> This jest was first of t'other house's making,
> And, five times tried, has never failed of taking.
> For 'twere a shame a poet should be killed
> Under the shelter of so broad a shield.
> This is that hat whose very sight did win ye
> To laugh and clap, as though the devil were in ye.

In Robert Howard's *The Great Favourite, or The Duke of Lerma* (1668), Nell Gwynn features again, with Pepys's favourite actress, Elizabeth Knipp, performing before 'the King and Court':

KNIPP: How, Mrs Ellen, not dressed yet, and the play ready to begin.
ELLEN: Not so near ready to begin as you think for.
KNIPP: Why? What's the matter?
ELLEN: The poet and the company are wrangling within.
KNIPP: About what?
ELLEN: A Prologue.

According to Pepys, 'Knipp and Nell spoke the Prologue most excellently, especially Knipp, who spoke beyond any creature I ever heard'. He goes on significantly, however: 'The play designed to reproach our King with his mistresses, that I was troubled for it, and expected it should be interrupted; but it ended all well, which salved all'.[2]

A particularly notorious Epilogue, which manifested a kind of daring sexuality, is in Dryden's *Tyrannick Love* (1669). Valeria, played by Nell Gwynn, stabs herself at the end of the play and lies dead on the stage. When the scenekeepers appear to carry her offstage, Nell leaps up:

> Hold, are you mad? You damned confounded dog,
> I am to rise and speak the Epilogue.

She reassures the audience that she is 'the ghost of poor departed Nelly', and a few lines later, this naughty woman, soon to be mistress to King Charles II, promises to haunt the male spectators' most private hours:

I'll come dance about your beds at nights
And faith, you'll be in a sweet kind of taking
When I surprise you between sleep and waking.

Figure 3.27
Nell Gwynn in the Epilogue to John Dryden's *Tyrannick Love*, presented by the King's Company, 1669

In all these, the speaker comes out of character to deliver the twenty or thirty lines the poet has penned. Nell speaks as herself, an actress, not as her character in the play; but she is on the stage, not among the audience. The Prologue is therefore betwixt and between the play world and the real world, at a sort of halfway staging post on the way to the imaginary world of the drama. Prologues and Epilogues overtly attempt to win the audience's favour, by opening a dialogue with them, teasing, or cajoling, or challenging, or flattering them, but always aiming to bring them through the Prologue into the play-world in the right receptive frame of mind, or, alternatively, in the Epilogue, to help them leave it gently, amicably and positively. They are a fascinating threshold which the spectator must cross to receive what is here on offer.

RESTORATION COMEDY

Restoration comedy has often been characterised in the past as 'comedy of manners', but this does very poor justice to the surprising variety and vivacity of the new comedies of the Restoration stage. Besides comedies of manners, there are comedies of situation, comedies of intrigue, sex comedies and comedies of character. Often the comedies embrace more than one of these types, and frequently the plays combine 'high' and 'low' actions, the first set among the aristocracy, the second among their servants. In such plays, it is usual for the aristocrats to speak verse, but for the low-class characters to speak prose.

Love is of course the constant theme of these plays, but not love lost and found, not falling in love, nor wonder and delight. Restoration comedy prefers adulterous love, fickle love, 'the chase', sexual conflict and the cynical manipulation of sexual desire. The actions are pursued by character types, like the 'gay couple' who seek each other through banter, contrariness and insult. Other types commonly met with in these plays include the fop, the miser, the dupe; the countryman who is easy prey for the city slicker; coquettes, snobs, poetasters, lechers, prudes and women of remarkable sensuality. These characters are not intended to be psychologically convincing. If the story itself is thoroughly artificial, we can hardly expect the characters to be realistic. Rather, the characters decorate the story. This may make them seem somewhat flimsy, but they *perform* their parts, they show us typical behaviour, not individual idiosyncrasies.

WOMEN PLAYWRIGHTS

The first woman playwright to have work performed professionally in England was probably Elizabeth Polwheele whose tragedy, *The Faithful Virgins*, was presented by Davenant's Duke's Company possibly as early as 1662. Frances Boothby's tragicomedy *Marcelia* was given by the King's Company in 1669 and two years later Polwheele's *The Frolic*, a not untypical Restoration comedy centring on Rightwit, a rake, and the sparky coquette, Claribell, appeared at Dorset Garden.

WILLIAM WYCHERLEY

These women, however skilful were, of course, amateurs. And some of the best male writers, too, were not professional, such as William Wycherley, who wrote only four plays, and Sir George Etherege, who wrote only three. Wycherley, who was inclined to Catholicism, had a disastrous life: despite the sharpness of his observations of the love-making practices of his contemporaries, his own *affaires du coeur* were largely catastrophic, at one point he found himself in gaol for debt, and at the end of his life in 1715 he was tricked into marrying his cousin's mistress.

His first two plays, *Love in a Wood* (1671), which includes mistaken identities, cunning trickery and plenty of rampant desire, and *The Gentleman Dancing Master* (1673), which he derived from Calderon, a sexually explicit comedy of intrigue sometimes verging on the obscene, show an exuberant promise. In 1675 he fulfilled that promise with *The Country Wife*, still for many the epitome of Restoration drama. It is a masterly comedy about love and marriage, driven lust and demonic jealousy, trust, possessiveness and complacency. Here nothing is what it seems – not vice and not virtue – but it is presented with enormous gusto, energy, excitement and even suspense. The question which academics have debated for decades concerns Wycherley's purpose: is this play a satire on his society? It probably is not. Of course any comedy will point up the distance between intention and behaviour, between what is said and what is done. But here, what makes the play is not some solemn moralistic message or stinging social satire, but the sheer vitality of the action.

Wycherley's last play, *The Plain Dealer*, concerns a sailor, Manly, who hates the hypocrisy of the age but who is nevertheless sucked into the intrigues of his acquaintances. Best known for its 'in-jokes', it contains an extraordinary discussion of the famous 'china' scene in *The Country Wife*. In this sense, it is the Restoration's most inward-looking play: yet in performance, *The Plain Dealer* sparkles.

SIR GEORGE ETHEREGE

Sir George Etherege only wrote three plays, the first of which, *The Comical Revenge, or, Love in a Tub*, made over £1000 in the first month of its life in performance. It is a rumbustious piece, full of music, drunkenness, slapstick and vulgar laughter. One of the plots climaxes in the servant wooer being tied into a tub while his fellow servants dance, sing and mock him in a sort of coarse version of Feste's mocking of Malvolio. In *She Would If She Could*, Etherege paints something darker, a married woman, dissatisfied with her husband, who seeks sexual fulfilment elsewhere. This theme is however treated with the utmost frivolity, as sudden discoveries follow lovers hiding in closets, others concealed under the table and much more.

Etherege's masterpiece is *The Man of Mode*, much revived and frequently the subject of debate (like Wycherley's *The Country Wife*) as to its satirical or moral purpose. What Etherege primarily presents is an incisive view of how people conduct affairs, how passion leads people into unexpected passes, how reason is weak – but not dead – in the face of desire. Dorimant, the central character, is a rake, unscrupulous, a bully, as addicted to sex as Horner in *The Country Wife*. Dorimant is also, however, witty, charming and energetic. He thus poses a problem to the traditional critic. Moreover, the play's ending is deliberately ambiguous as Dorimant seems to agree to Harriet's condition that he must move to the country. Is Etherege avoiding the issues he raises, or is he bringing matters to a kind of harmonious conclusion? Is he encouraging us to be free, or is he warning us to beware of giving in to desire? During the play we ask few such questions, as we are carried along on the switchback of Etherege's chain of attractions.

PROFESSIONAL PLAYWRIGHTS

The times required more than gifted amateurs to meet the day-to-day and week-to-week require-
ments of a healthy professional theatre. Nathaniel Lee, John Banks, John Crowne, Thomas D'Urfey
and Edward Ravenscroft were among the most prolific professional playwrights, and each with
notable successes which contributed to the richness of Restoration drama.

JOHN DRYDEN

Of the professional writers of this period, Dryden was perhaps the most significant, and some of
his work has already been discussed. He broke with his addiction to rhymed heroic tragedy after
Aureng-Zebe (1676):

> To confess a truth, (though out of time)
> (He) Grows weary of his long-loved mistress, rhyme.[3]

But he was still able to turn out extremely attractive comedies, such as *Marriage à la Mode*
(1671), an amusing love comedy set in an unexpectedly serious context of political usurpation
and restoration. If the latter seems somewhat far-fetched, the lovers' carousel is high-spirited as
the characters flirt, swap partners, fail to seal their compacts and finally return to their original
beloveds. It is like a delightful country dance, carried through with wit, elegance and the occasional shameless obscenity, such as Palamede's method of discovering a 'handsome woman': he
carries something like a compass point about him, and when such a lady appears 'it never fails to
point to the north pole'.

THOMAS SHADWELL

Dryden's great rival was Thomas Shadwell, whose politics he abhorred and whom he attacked mem-
orably in his poem, *MacFlecknoe*;

> Shadwell alone, of all my sons, is he
> Who stands confirmed in full stupidity.
> The rest to some faint meaning make pretence;
> But Shadwell never deviates into sense.

Dryden was unfair. Shadwell created a series of excellent fast-paced comedies, packed with farcical
situations and vivid characters. *A True Widow* (1678), for example, is a play of riotous energy. *The
Sullen Lovers* (1668) is a Jonsonian comedy of humours – or is intended to be such – and it certainly
boasts an odd mix of characters, including a group of charismatic cavaliers. But the most surprising
character in this play is Caroline, spirited, intelligent and nobody's fool – a woman depicted in a
thoroughly positive light. *The Virtuoso* (1676) is also a marvellous slapstick comedy. Sir Nicholas,
the 'virtuoso', for instance, tries to learn to swim lying on the table: he has never tried it in water!

The fun made of empirical science in the age of the Royal Society is also highly comic. Sir Formal, an orator, ponders the significance of the mouse in the mousetrap, then falls down the stage trap-door himself. He finds himself in a vault with Sir Samuel Hearty who, incongruously, happens to be dressed as a woman. He, Sir Samuel, has in fact pretended to be pregnant and has, like Sir Formal, been tricked into standing on the trapdoor which has given way and shot him down to the vault. When Sir Formal starts to become amorously inclined, Sir Samuel kicks him and flings him down. This may not be intellectual drama, but it is clearly zestful entertainment.

APHRA BEHN

A third notable professional playwright was Aphra Behn, probably the first British female to earn her living by her pen. Reclaimed by feminist critics in the 1970s, she is now seen as among the most

Figure 3.28
Peter Lely, portrait of Aphra Behn, c.1670
Source: Yale Center for British Art, Yale University, New Haven

impressive of Restoration writers. Of course she was attacked for immorality – a woman encroaching on the male province of playwrighting was not easily accepted – but she defended herself with some spirit, for instance in the Preface to her play, *Sir Patient Fancy* (1678) by turning the criticism round: if such stuff as hers had been written by a man, would it then have been immoral? Her best-known, and probably her best, play is *The Rover* (1677), one of the glories of the Restoration stage, which catches the very essence of the cavaliers: is anything serious to them? 'Oh, that thou wert in earnest', exclaims Hellena, the heroine, at one point. Based on Killigrew's memoirs of his cavalier exile, the play concerns a group of these royalist outcasts. They have reached Naples, and now at Carnival time, they shun earnestness which smacks of Puritanism. Behn depicts an attractive, casual freedom amid the Carnival disguising, a lack of social restraint and a permissiveness, with frank theatricality. Once again, it is the play's sheer exuberance which gives it its power on stage. Significantly, all the characters in the play are young, except the enigmatic ageing courtesan, Angelica Bianca (whose initials, A.B., may or may not be significant): she is not old, however, and is still sexually attractive, unconventional and yet adrift in the social milieu in which she finds herself. She survives only on her wit. Perhaps because of her, the play, despite its high spirits, energy, frivolity even, still holds a kind of nostalgia for those simpler, more hopeful times, before the cynicism and brittleness of London's court society in the 1660s had dissipated such naiveté. The play implicitly questions the relations between these careless men and the women they angle for, it inevitably highlights woman's economic dependency, and hints subtly at the need for greater equality. Behn's instinctive Toryism here seems at odds with the unspoken feminism of the action, her royalism and her libertarianism producing a kind of ambiguity which may make her work paradoxically more powerful.

THE PRINTING OF PLAYS

Many of these plays were printed at the time. The lack of accessible performances during the Commonwealth period led to the widespread printing and reading of plays, and obviously the appetite for printed texts continued. The dazzling variety and exuberance of the plays of the Restoration period show it to have been one of the most exciting in the history of legitimate drama in English. These plays have a narrative strength and vigour which gives them resonance. It is not the characters and it is not the morality (overt or covert) so much as the rhythm of the narrative itself, the sequence of incidents and images, which are performed before us, which convince us of the play's 'truth' – the truth of careless cavalier life which chimes with something in our own experience or perhaps imagination. The energy is the energy of life and has nothing to do with morality or political or social concerns. But it is the energy which makes these plays appealing and attractive. To love Dorimant is not to love philandering or licentiousness, it is to love life, because Dorimant above all has life.

NOTES

1 Thomas Rymer, *A Short View of Tragedy*, 1693; see Curt A. Zimansky (ed), *The Critical Works of Thomas Rymer*, New Haven, CT: Yale University Press, 1956, p. 170.
2 *The Diary of Samuel Pepys*, 20 February 1668.
3 John Dryden, *Aurang-Zebe*, Prologue.

Chapter 38: Restoration actors and acting

WOMEN ON STAGE

The most striking and significant innovation of the Restoration theatre was the introduction of women to the professional stage. First and foremost, this meant that plays about love and marriage, that is, probably, most plays, had a new realism about their performance, a new sort of honesty which most writers rejoiced in. If most of the plays were still written by men, women spoke from the stage as women now, and if the misogyny of the male playwrights was still too common, the actress could use her tone of voice, her gesture, her facial expression to expose masculinist attitudes. The female voice was heard on the stage regularly for the first time.

SEXUALISATION OF FEMALE ROLES

On the other hand, now that female parts were written for female performers, there was a notable sexualisation of female roles. Casting a woman seems often not to have enabled the spectator to understand the woman's position more subtly, but to have greatly aided her objectification, thus endorsing something of the mannish cavalier world view. In Davenant's *The Enchanted Island*, for instance, the audience had enormous fun, and bellowed with masculine laughter, to hear Miranda and Dorinda discuss sex and that strange creature, man. The *characters*' innocence was merely a pretext for male innuendoes about the *actress's* lack of innocence. Provocatively clad young women interacting with lively young men was stimulating enough, but often actresses had simply to pose, perhaps sleeping, *deshabillée* on a rock or a grassy bank. So-called 'breeches roles', when women dressed as men, were especially popular, for a man's costume seemed to display a woman's legs especially provocatively. Aphra Behn provided very many such roles, for instance, in *The Amorous Prince* (1671), *The Rover* and three in *The Feigned Courtesans*. Wycherley has breeches roles in *The Country Wife* and *The Plain Dealer*, Lee in *Sophonisba* and *The Princess of Cleve* (1680), and so on.

The sexualisation of women's roles also provided the occasion for sensational or salacious displays of male violence against the female, especially if the woman's clothes were torn or her skin splashed with blood. Cordelia seized by Edmund's lusting ruffians in Tate's *King Lear* is an example of how the most innocent heroine may be sexualised. Theatre always has a voyeuristic element to it: here voyeurism is taken about as far as it can go. Dim lighting enhanced the eroticism of the stage, and the language of the plays, too, was often highly charged sexually.

FEMALE ACTORS

The titillation inherent in Restoration theatre carried over perhaps inevitably into the actors' social sphere, too. The leading actors of the Restoration stage were stars, the celebrities of their day, who hobnobbed with courtiers and chatted with royalty. Rebecca Marshall, for instance, is credited with introducing Lady Castlemaine, the king's former mistress, to the handsome rope-dancer, Jacob Hall, and Samuel Pepys was clearly star-struck by his acquaintance with some of these actresses. He was more than half in love with Elizabeth Knipp, with whom he flirted and sang duets: he reported her husband to be 'surly' and 'an ill, melancholy, jealous-looking fellow', which was probably true of his reaction to Pepys's attention to his wife. And the actors enjoyed real privileges, too, such as freedom from arrest except with the Lord Chamberlain's special warrant.

But this closeness to the cavalier high society had disadvantages, too. Charles II had suggested, perhaps disingenuously, that the presence of women on stage and in the acting companies would raise the theatre's moral tone. The presence on stage of the most talented of the women actors clearly did raise the artistic level, and indeed the presence of women in the casts enabled the drama to acquire a new kind of realism, especially in its portrayal of the relations between the sexes. But the moral tone was another matter. Men loved to ogle, and playwrights and managers were only too happy to oblige them. After all, 'respectable' women do not become actresses, so therefore actresses are fair game. Women were encircled by predatory males in the theatre, where, as Wycherley implied, the male spectators had virtually *carte blanche* backstage:

> We set no guards upon our tiring-room,
> But when with flying colours there you come,
> We patiently, you see, give up to you
> Our poets, virgins, nay, our matrons too.[1]

Female roles were often presented to titillate during the play. Before it, male spectators came backstage and watched the actresses makeup and put on their costumes. Afterwards they came backstage again. 'How many men do hover about them', Pepys commented. Sexual encounters were unavoidable.

SEXUAL HARASSMENT: REBECCA MARSHALL AND OTHERS

Sometimes this led to outrageous scandals. Hester Davenport, a leading performer with the Duke's Company, who had made a notable impression in the revival of *The Siege of Rhodes*, was fooled into a fake marriage with the Earl of Oxford; after the affair was over, he gave her a hefty payoff.

Rebecca Marshall's experiences were more typical. She was effectively stalked by a man called Mark Trevor in 1665 and 1666, 'as well on the stage as off'. The harassment only stopped when she managed to persuade the Lord Chamberlain to intervene. She had to deal with a somewhat different kind of harassment the next year. On 2 February 1667, Sir Hugh Middleton came into the tiring-room. Rebecca, who was clearly a feisty character, asked him why he was there since he had been heard speaking extremely slightingly about female actors recently. Sir Hugh lost his temper, called her a 'jade' and accused her of lying. He threatened her with a good kicking. As an actress, of course, she had access to the King, and she complained to him. But three days later, as she was starting for home in the evening, she noticed Sir Hugh loitering in her way. She persuaded her sister's husband to accompany her. Nevertheless, she was still jostled by a man as she left the theatre, and when she was nearly home, the man appeared again. Running up to her, he slapped horse dung in her face and ran off. She assumed he was in the employ of Sir Hugh Middleton.

Samuel Pepys, not that kind of violent man, but a great admirer of actresses, certainly found her dark eyes and dark hair almost irresistible. On 3 April 1665, he went to *The Tragedy of Mustapha* by Roger Boyle at the Duke's Playhouse, and sat next to her 'which pleased me mightily'. And in September 1667, he saw a play he thought was called *The Ungrateful Lovers* (though no play of that name has been traced), and again he 'sat by Beck Marshall, who is very handsome near hand'. She was also high spirited. One of her special friends was Nell Gwynn, but Pepys records a fierce spat between the two:

> Mrs Pierce tells me . . . that Nelly and Beck Marshall falling out the other day, the latter called the other my Lord Buckhurst's mistress. Nell answered her, 'I was but one man's mistress, though I was brought up in a brothel to fill strong waters to the gentlemen; and you are a mistress to three or four, though a Presbyter's praying daughter'; which was very pretty.[2]

Rebecca (who, by the way, was not a Presbyterian minister's daughter) was sued for debt more than once and she herself sued the orange-seller, Mary Meggs, 'Orange Moll', in 1669 for abusing her.

THE PLAYER AND THE PART

Life in the theatre obviously had its disturbing social side. But when it came to the business of rehearsing, discipline was strict. The first job of the management when a play had been chosen for performance was the casting. This had its own problems and conventions. Thus, the more experienced actors were obviously more likely to be given the major roles, with the younger actors filling in the less demanding parts. But good or hard-working younger actors were likely to be rewarded with better parts over time. However, this simple approach was tempered by other considerations. Often authors wrote parts with particular actors in mind. Sometimes other powerful outsiders – even the king occasionally – interfered with the process. Moreover, audiences wanted to see well-liked actors in the type of part they had been well liked in previously. Popular female actors especially, such as Nell Gwynn, were often given good parts, whether within their capabilities or not. Furthermore, and inevitably, there was a fair degree of type-casting: Charles Hart was known for his grandeur and majesty; Thomas Betterton was heroic and dignified; and comic roles nearly always fell to such as James Nokes, Tony Leigh or Cave Underhill. The latter's Shakespearean parts, for example, included the Gravedigger in *Hamlet*, Trinculo in *The Tempest* and Feste in *Twelfth Night*. Actors had to be – and most of them were – versatile, they could dance, sing, speak a Prologue or Epilogue clearly and with meaning, and they kept many parts in their head simultaneously. Yet specialisation was no bad thing, and it is no slur on them to find Michael Mohun, for instance, playing a series of comparatively similar sinister parts – Volpone, Iago, Cassius – or Elizabeth Boutell playing sweet, innocent *ingénues*, often opposite the darker, more baleful Rebecca Marshall.

REHEARSALS

At the first rehearsal the play was read through aloud to the company, either by a leading actor or, if he were a good reader, by the author. Nathaniel Lee was an especially convincing reader of his own plays, and indeed Michael Mohun exclaimed after one particularly impressive first reading that it would be impossible for him (Mohun) to make such a vivid impression with his acting, even after rehearsing, as Lee had made with his reading.

After the reading came the distribution of parts – 'cue scripts', exactly like those similarly prepared in the Elizabethan and Jacobean theatres. These contained no more than the lines spoken by that character, plus the three or four words, or 'cues', spoken before each speech. The great advantage of this method was that the actors on stage had to remain utterly vigilant and alert so as to be able to react convincingly and, even more important, so as not to miss their cue. The part was expected to be studied and indeed learned by the actor alone before he or she came to further rehearsals. Rehearsals were held at ten AM on most mornings; all actors were obliged to attend. But the procedures here were not like modern rehearsals, dedicated to teasing out subtexts collaboratively and working out convincing actions. Restoration theatre rehearsals often saw actors working alone or perhaps in small groups on different parts of the stage. In the evening, after the afternoon performance, there might be further rehearsals – songs, dances, going over lines together and so on. Rehearsals might be attended by the author, or even outsiders, who would help the actors, as Bayes does those who are having difficulties with the dance in Buckingham's *The Rehearsal*, and as Pepys did on at least one occasion when he went over Elizabeth Knipp's lines with her.

It might be a month from the handing out of parts to the play's first performance, and at any one time several plays were in preparation. It was only on the morning of the premiere that the whole play was run through by the whole cast together. Meanwhile, the author, or the prompter, had decided such matters as which doors to use for which stage entrances and exits, or which scenery ('shutters') was to be used for which scenes. But most of the actors' moves on stage were the responsibility of the actors themselves. They had to be sensitive to what was happening on stage, and to how their character related to the other characters. There were certain customary practices to help them, such as that the most important character would be centre stage, and other characters would be grouped around him or her, either in a rough semi-circle, or a more or less straight line across the front of the stage. The least significant characters were on the flanks. But there were plenty of exceptions to this, and more formal *tableaux* were likely to be specially arranged.

THE FIRST PERFORMANCE

Saturday was considered the best day for a premiere, and a new play coming on caused not a little excitement in fashionable London circles. Pepys reports over a thousand people turned away from the first night of Etherege's *She Would If She Could*, in February 1668, and in May of the same year, in order to ensure his place at the first performance of Shadwell's *The Sullen Lovers*, he arrived at the theatre three hours before the play was due to start:

> To the Duke of York's playhouse at a little past twelve, to get a good place in the pit against the new play; and there setting a poor man to keep my place, I out, and spent an hour at Martin's, my booksellers, and so

back again, where I find the House quite full. But I had my place, and by and by the King comes, and the Duke of York; and then the play begins.[3]

A new play, if it were successful, might be performed on four or five consecutive nights, and then again with reasonable frequency until its potential appeal had receded. That might be ten or twelve performances. A play judged a failure was removed from the repertoire very rapidly.

ACTING STYLE

Restoration acting took its shape from the cavalier ideal – stately, self-aware, impressive. Colley Cibber wrote of serious actors 'quavering out their tragic notes'. As the stage itself became more pictorial compared with earlier stages, so the acting took on the qualities of the visual, emphasising poses, gestures, concentrating on 'showing' not 'being', so as to complete the stage picture rather than embody the character's life. Approached from a different, but complementary angle, if the play was artificial, it employed an artificial eloquence, which needed artificial or self-conscious acting. Thus Sophonisba instructs her maid, Rezambe:

> Now strike; and bravely act thy tragic part;
> Just here, strike through and through this wretched heart.[4]

Life – and death – are performances, and we must play our parts.

This was a theatre in which staging might be perceived as a series of still pictures, with groups, trios or pairs of actors creating tableau-like moments which dissolved and reassembled in new, meaningful formations. Individual actors moved from one state to another without much need for psychologically convincing transitions. They were extremely close to the audience, and the audience itself was lit by the great chandelier: this produced an unusual kind of intimacy, which was formal but not awesome. In this circumstance, the actor had four chief weapons at his or her disposal.

VOICE

First, the voice. The Restoration actor relied on quite subtle changes in tone of voice. Different emotions produce different tones of voice. To an extent these are simply observable sense, but they were also codified. So anger produced a loud, harsh tone, while fear produced a low, hesitating tone. Always, of course, the voice needed clear articulation, but also a certain coolness and distance, so that the Restoration actor was neither consumed by feelings nor needed to rely on emotion memory. This kind of performance, to be successful, had to *demonstrate* emotion, never 'live' it.

THE ACTOR'S FACE

The second weapon at the actor's disposal in this intimate theatre was the face. In the privileged space of the Restoration theatre, the actor's face was easily visible. Again the resources are fairly clear: one wrinkles one's forehead in puzzlement; in anger the eyes tend to be staring; and so on.

GESTURE

As for gesture, the third weapon, the actor relied on a grammar of gesture, never spontaneity. This is brilliantly illustrated in Etherege's *The Man of Mode* when Harriet and Young Bellair decide to fool their parents that they are in love, a scene in which the principles of Restoration acting are articulated with unexpected clarity:

Y. BELL: Can you play your part?

HARRIET: I know not what it is to love, but I have made pretty remarks by being now and then where lovers meet. . . . I will lean against this wall, and look bashfully down upon my fan, while you like an amorous spark modishly entertain me.

    . . .

Y. BELL: Now for a look and gestures that may persuade 'em I am saying all the passionate things imaginable –

HARRIET: Your head a little more on one side, ease yourself on your left leg, and play with your right hand.

Y. Bell: Thus, is it not?

HARRIET: Now set your right leg firm on the ground, adjust your belt, then look about you.

Y. BELL: A little exercising will make me perfect.

HARRIET: Smile and turn to me again very sparkish.

Y. BELL: Will you take your turn and be instructed?

HARRIET: With all my heart.

Y. BELL: At one motion play your fan, roll your eyes, and then settle a kind of look upon me.

HARRIET: So.

Y. BELL: Now spread your fan, look down upon it, and tell the sticks with a finger.

HARRIET: Very modish.

Y. BELL: Clap your hand up to your bosom, hold down your gown. Shrug a little, draw up your breasts, and let 'em fall again, gently, with a sigh or two. . . . Clap your fan then in both your hands, snatch it to your mouth, smile, and with a lively motion fling your body a little forwards. So – now spread it; fall back on the sudden, cover your face with it, and break out into a loud laughter – take up! Look grave, and all a-fanning of yourself – admirably well acted.

This could almost be from a contemporary manual for actors.

Gesture is seen as the crux of the acting process, and indeed actors were known to practice gestures in front of a mirror, as Melantha does in front of her maid, Philotis, in Dryden's *Marriage à la Mode*:

MEL: Hold you my glass, while I practice my postures for the day. (Melantha laughs in the glass.) How does that laugh become my face?

PHIL: Sovereignly well, madam.

    . . .

MEL: That glance, how suits it my face? (Looking at the glass again.)

PHIL: 'Tis so languissant.

MEL: Languissant! That word shall be mine too, and my last Indian gown thine for 't. (Looks again). That sigh?

PHIL: 'Twill make many a man sigh, madam. 'Tis a mere incendiary.

These gestures, or faces, are for *show*, they are not felt. They are simply gestures.

DEPORTMENT

The actor's fourth weapon, was deportment. Again, much in this area is common sense: one goes hunched in sorrow, one starts in amazement, one stamps about in rage. But actors were trained in dance, and these movements were executed with grace and almost self-consciously. They were trained to observe themselves as they performed. Dramatists gave actors hints about this in their stage directions, and examples from contemporary drama are not hard to find. In *The Man of Mode*,

Figure 3.29
Actors were trained in dance and performed with grace and self-consciousness. This illustration of Thomas Middleton and William Rowley's *Wit at Several Weapons* was printed in 1710.

Source: British Library, London

for instance, Loveit is in a rage. When Dorimant *'offers to catch her by the hand, she flings away and walks on'*. Later, *'she tears her fan in pieces'*. She does this to a rapid rhythm, but with a certain decorousness. In *Marriage à la Mode*, Palamede and Doralice meet: *'she, with a book in her hand, seems to start at sight of him'*. This is truthful as observation, yet also artificial. Movement on stage was dance-like not only in the actor's carriage, but also in the patterns across the floor. Thus, in *The Conquest of Granada*, we find Abdelmelech telling Lyndaraxa, 'That delay, I for denial take', and, says the stage direction, *'is going'*, when he is called back. But with insufficient reason, evidently, for nine lines later he *'is going again'*. Lyndaraxa still tries to persuade him to return, and he *'looks back'*, and then five lines further, he finds himself *'coming back'*. This is clearly stylised, one might almost say choreographed, movement.

CHARACTER

The whole was finally subsumed into concepts of 'character', though here there was divergent opinion about, on the one hand, oddities and eccentricities which made for 'character', as the antiquarian and journalist John Aubrey may have believed, and on the other, the 'outward manifestation' of a person, as the rather more serious Thomas Hobbes argued. Hobbes was a friend of Davenant. His conception, which may have influenced the Duke's Company's leader (though this is hard to determine), was that individual character is a series of dispositions which depend on circumstances. John Locke argued, however, that character was the equivalent of self-consciousness, or, to put it another way, that the self resided in the consciousness of itself.

THOMAS BETTERTON

The greatest actor of the period, Thomas Betterton, exemplified the Restoration style of acting. More will be said of him, but a picture shows him as Hamlet in the closet scene with his mother, when the Ghost of his father suddenly intervenes. It is probably not a 'still' taken from the action, but rather a kind of emblematic tableau. Nevertheless, the moment of the Ghost's appearance might be held for some seconds, while the audience applauded it. In the picture we note the details the artist wanted to point to: Hamlet's stocking 'down-gyved', for example, and the rest of his clothes in disarray. He holds his left arm up, as if to protect himself, but in a gesture which leads our eye inevitably towards the portrait of his father on the wall behind Gertrude. The other arm points to the ghost. His face is startled, with the mouth open and the eyes staring. But still, and in spite of his obvious disturbance, Hamlet's carriage has something admirable about it, perhaps in the straight back and head, thrown back, not cringing in fear. The effect is enhanced by Gertrude's posture and her gesture, and the ghost's stance and gesture. The tumbled chair, upon which we assume Hamlet had been sitting when he saw the apparition, indicates the wider upset.

JOHN LACY

The triple portrait of John Lacy done for King Charles II is another way of illustrating Restoration acting. Here Lacy is seen in three separate roles, and in each he adopts different gestures, expressions and even postures to show the character. On the left, Lacy is shown as Sauney in *Sauney the Scot*

Figure 3.30
Thomas Betterton as Hamlet, his clothes in disarray, his chair tumbled, with the Ghost in armour and Gertrude gracefully shocked. Hamlet's left hand points to the portrait on the wall.

Source: British Library, London

(1667), his own adaptation of *The Taming of the Shrew*. Sawney is an awkward gull who suffers from scrofula, which he is scratching in the portrait. In the centre he is Scruple in John Wilson's *The Cheats* (1663), a finicky but complacently self-righteous character. And on the right he is seen as the self-serving hypocrite, Galliard, in the Duke of Newcastle's 1662 adaptation of his own play, *The Variety* (1641). The detail and the accuracy of the three presentations are worth studying: face, gesture and carriage all illuminate Restoration acting styles.

Figure 3.31
John Lacy portrayed by John Michael Wright in three different roles: as Sawney in *Sawney the Scot*, 1667, as Scruple in John Wilson's *The Cheats*, 1663, and as Galliard in the Duke of Newcastle's *The Variety*, 1662

Source: Art Collection/Alamy Stock Photo

NOTES

1 William Wycherley, *The Country Wife*, Prologue.
2 *The Diary of Samuel Pepys*, 26 October 1667.
3 *Ibid.*, 2 May 1668.
4 Nathaniel Lee, *Sophonisba*, 1675.

Chapter 39: The Restoration audience

THE SEASON

The London theatre season lasted from October through the winter and spring into June; the theatres were generally shut then till the following October, though there might be occasional performances in the summer. There were no performances on Sundays, or on public holidays, other religious days or when there was an outbreak of plague.

THE PERFORMANCE

Performances began at three PM or three-thirty PM and usually lasted approximately three hours. Advertising was by means of bills posted outside the theatre or on posts in the area, by the random distribution of flyers, and through the announcement at the end of the previous day's performance. Word of mouth was also a useful means of publicity – Warner, in *Sir Martin Mar-all*, informs his master that

> There was an ill play set up, sir, on the posts, but I can assure you the bills are altered since you saw them, and now there are two admirable comedies at both houses.

THE SPECTATORS

Pepys sometimes gives the impression that Restoration theatre audiences were almost exclusively made up of courtiers, gallants and wits, with a few delightful and pretty women also present for the gallants' pleasure. When this was not so he was not pleased: 'The house was full of citizens, and so the less pleasant', he remarked on 1 January 1663. In fact the theatres always welcomed a reasonably wide cross section of society. It is true that the side boxes where one could be seen almost better than one could see, were largely taken by peers and courtiers, and the King or his brother when they attended, which was surprisingly frequently, and often gallants sat on the stage, hoping to bask in general admiration. But the best seats were the backless benches in the pit, where the self-appointed critics, sat: the intelligentsia, courtiers, gallants, better-off leisured people or professionals. Often described as the most discerning section of the audience, the pittites were however characterised in Part 2 of *The Rover* by Aphra Behn as

> The dull state-cullies of the pit
> Who have much money, but little wit

and Dryden, in Part 2 of *The Conquest of Granada*, complained that it was only when a masked prostitute appeared in the pit that 'every man who thinks himself a wit Perks up'; as for the play, they 'blindly guess at' what that is about. And Sam Vincent suggested half humorously in *The Young Gallant's Academy* (1674), that 'by sitting in the pit, if you be a knight, you may happily get you a mistress; but if you be a mere Fleet Street gentleman, a wife'. However, the more usual view of the pit is implicit in Etherege's plea for the pittites' indulgence in the Prologue to *The Comical Revenge*:

> And gallants, as for you, talk loud i' th' pit;
> Divert yourselves and friends with your own wit;
> Observe the ladies, and neglect the play,
> Or else 'tis feared we are undone today.

The benches gave a certain egalitarian feel to the pit, encouraging informality where separate seats would have kept individuals apart. Benches were also to be found in the galleries. The view of the stage from the middle gallery was excellent, and this seems to have been preferred by a quieter, less fashionable sort of spectator, the sort of citizen's wives whom Modish and Estridge mock in Sedley's *The Mulberry Garden*.

Above them, in the upper gallery, were to be found commoners, servants and citizens. After the 1670s, the fashionable elite may have attended less frequently as royal patronage waned, and the audience base broadened, but it remained largely Tory and royalist: according to Etherege, 'faction now, not wit, supports the stage'. The fact was that the gallants and courtiers enjoyed seeing themselves portrayed on the stage, and the middle class and lower orders were also fascinated by them. Partly it was simply the difference between this ruling class and the Puritans of the previous decade, but partly it was also the perennial middling people's fascination with celebrity.

AUDIENCE NUMBERS

However, whatever the social composition of the audience, theatregoing was a minority occupation. The theatres seated up to a thousand people, but they were rarely full in London whose population was at least half a million. Thus on Boxing Day, 1677, 514 people attended Drury Lane theatre, sixty in the boxes, one hundred ninety-one in the pit, one hundred forty-four in the middle gallery and one hundred nineteen in the upper gallery. A fortnight earlier, there had only been two hundred fifty-one people present, a mere thirty-eight in the boxes, one hundred seventeen in the pit, sixty-three in the middle gallery and a paltry thirty-three in the upper gallery. It is worth remembering that if the theatre audience was not quite the 'coterie' some commentators have suggested, a disproportionate number of attendances were made by the same, extremely enthusiastic people, like Samuel Pepys, who seems to have visited the theatre at least once a week, often more, over a period of years.

ENTRANCE

Spectators arrived at the theatre, paid at the door and received a ticket to the appropriate part of the auditorium. Once there, they gave up the ticket and entered what was an extremely lively and

Figure 3.32
The audience sitting on the backless benches of the pit in a late seventeenth-century theatre

even convivial scene. For the first performance of a play, entrance was probably a little more complicated, for ticket prices were higher and first performances always set the town talking. On the
afternoon itself there would almost certainly be queues trying to enter.

AUDIENCE BEHAVIOUR

Though Nathaniel Lee despaired of Restoration audiences –

> One half o' th' play they spend in noise and brawl,
> Sleep out the rest, then wake and damn it all –[1]

his condemnation was unfair. Clearly, spectators talked throughout the performance, but that does not mean they could not follow the drama. On the contrary, the pittites understood the conventions of plot, character and presentation, and could always tune back in, as it were, to the drama, after a joke or a gossip with a neighbour. Then they commented vocally and sharply on what was happening on stage. They clapped what they approved of, so that performances were often punctuated with applause, and laughed loudly when amused. And they were sophisticated enough to be able to distinguish between, say, the expression of a sentiment of which they might approve, and the character speaking it, to whom they might object.

There are plenty of contemporary descriptions of this audience. Here is Dryden on doings in the middle gallery (the 'vizard mask' was probably a prostitute):

> Methinks some vizard mask I see,
> Cast but her lure from the mid gallery.
> About her all the fluttering sparks are ranged;
> The noise continues though the scene is changed;
> Now growling, sputtering, wauling, such a clutter.[2]

He continues with a description of the servants in the upper gallery ('They roar so loud'), and ends with a plea to their masters to shut them up so that others may 'hear the play'.

Pepys's description of the audience in February 1667 is less severe and more personalised, and probably gives the fairest impression of the audience of the time:

> the house being very full, and great company; among others, Mrs Stuart, very fine, with her locks done up with puffs, as my wife calls them; and several other great ladies had their hair so, though I do not like it; but my wife do mightily – but it is only because she sees it is the fashion. Here I saw my Lord Rochester and his lady, Mrs Mallett, who hath after all this ado married him; and, as I hear some say in the pit, it is a great act of charity, for he hath no estate. But it was pleasant to see how everybody rose up when my Lord John Butler, the Duke of Ormond's son, came into the pit towards the end of the play, who was a servant to Mrs Mallett, and now smiled upon her, and she on him. I had sitting next to me a woman, the likest my Lady Castlemaine that ever I saw anybody like another; but she is acquainted with every fine fellow, and called them by their name, Jack, and Tom, and before the end of the play frisked to another place.[3]

This suggests an atmosphere almost like a private club, a special group at ease with itself.

Some carried on flirtations here, others made assignations (as Courtall and Freeman do in *She Would If She Could*), and some (the 'vigorous' according to Wycherley in *The Country Wife*) engaged with the masked prostitutes:

> Yet when she says 'Lead on' you are not stout;
> But to your well-dressed brother straight turn round
> And cry 'Pox on her, Ned, she can't be sound!'
> Then slink away, a fresh one to engage.[4]

The social gathering was completed by the orange-women plying their trade and backchatting to the spectators.

A TRUE WIDOW

Shadwell gives a more brutal insight into the theatregoing experience in *A True Widow* (1678). Though the scene is clearly exaggerated for comic effect, it is based, however distantly, in reality. In Act IV of the play, a large group of characters enter the theatre. Two of the young women, Isabella and Gartrude, are masked so that they can watch their gallants' behaviour. When more people arrive, the Door-keeper is told to let in any women outside free, but to make any men pay. Some '*young coxcombs*' come in and begin to '*fool with the Orange-Women*'. The 1st Bully wants to know what the play is, and Prig, '*a rook, a most noisy jockey*', suggests cards in one of the boxes. Selfish, who is '*always admiring and talking of himself*', declares he 'never comes to a play but on account of seeing the ladies'. More characters try to come in:

DOOR-KEEP: Pray, sir, pay me; my masters will make me pay it.
3RD MAN: Impudent rascal! Do you ask me for money? Take that, sirrah.
2ND DOOR-KEEP: Will you pay me, sir?
4TH MAN: No. I don't intend to stay.
2ND DOOR-KEEP: So you say every day, and see two or three Acts for nothing.
4TH MAN: I'll break your head, you rascal!
1ST DOOR-KEEP: Pray, sir, pay me.
3RD MAN: Set it down; I have no silver about me, or bid my man pay you.
THEOD: What! Do gentlemen run on tick for plays?
CAR: As familiar*ly as with their tailors.*

The play within the play begins with a high-flown dialogue between a wife and her lover. This is discussed animatedly by the 'spectators'. The husband returns, the wife and the lover, he having surreptitiously kicked the husband, retire, and the husband vows to enter by the back door. In the audience there is some fooling with the vizarded women, and one man '*sits down and lolls in the orange-wench's lap*'. Meanwhile, Prig plays tricks on other spectators: he '*raps people on the backs, and twirls their hats, and then looks demurely, as if he did not do it*'. In the play, the wife now has two lovers, whom she pretends to her husband are ghosts. They both hide under the table, where they come to blows, standing up with the table hoisted on their backs. Prig's tricks have meanwhile led to two bullies fighting in the auditorium. There is a general *mêlée* and the actors, frightened of the drawn swords, call the play off.

FIGHTS IN THE AUDIENCE

The scene gives us a vivid, if satirical, glimpse into goings-on in the theatre of the time, especially when we realise that such fights were by no means unknown. The playwright Thomas Otway drew on Sir John Churchill, later the Duke of Marlborough, in the theatre when he thought the latter had insulted Orange Betty (Nell Gwynn's original employer). Both Otway and Churchill were wounded, Churchill the more seriously. On 2 September 1675, a Mr Scroop, being the worse for drink, began insulting Sir Thomas Armstrong in Dorset Garden playhouse. He drew his sword. Sir Thomas immediately drew also. They began to fight, and Sir Thomas ran Mr Scroop through the heart and killed him. He 'fell dead upon the place without speaking a word'.

In 1680 at Dorset Garden, a group of drunken men-about-town in the pit shouted insults about, among others, the King's mistress, the Duchess of Portsmouth, and flung lighted brands onto the stage: the King, furious, closed the theatre for several days. In April 1682, a rake named Charles Dering attacked a Mr Vaughan on the Dorset Garden stage, allegedly on behalf of Elizabeth Barry, and was 'dangerously wounded'. The list could be extended.

A SPECIAL WORLD

The Restoration theatre was a special world for the playgoer. Spectators liked to sit on the stage, and to go backstage before or after the performance, despite efforts, including by the Lord Chamberlain, to discourage this. But wherever spectators were seated, they were close to the stage, and the actors were aware of them because of the large chandelier which lit them as brightly as it did the stage. Actors and spectators were on personally familiar terms; yet their meeting here had a formal purpose, the occasion had artistic, not to say political, overtones. It was a special world, almost dream-like, distinct from everyday life yet with its feet planted on surprisingly firm ground. The event of performance provided an experience which mixed informality with occasion in a unique way.

NOTES

1 Nathaniel Lee, *Sophonisba*, Epilogue, 1675.
2 John Dryden, Epilogue, *The King and Queen, at the Opening of Their Theatre Upon the Union of the Two Companies in 1686.*
3 *The Diary of Samuel Pepys*, 4 February 1667.
4 William Wycherley, *The Country Wife*, Epilogue.

Chapter 40: The end of Cavalier theatre

THE CAVALIERS IN 1688

King Charles II died in 1685. By then, the Cavalier theatre had run its course, though politically the Stuart dynasty would not be eliminated from British politics for another sixty years. But the sudden irrelevance of the Cavaliers was demonstrated by their inability to decide what to do four years later, when Charles's heir was threatened with forcible expulsion from the throne. Should they support the Stuart monarch, for whom they had made such sacrifices and to whom they had sworn allegiance? Or should they help to expel him, because he was a Catholic?

THE POPISH PLOT

Historical events in the last years of Charles's reign show the start of the process which undermined the settlement reached at the Restoration. In 1678, one Titus Oates, an uncouth imposter and pathological liar, made a theatrical appearance before the Privy Council and convinced them that a Catholic plot was afoot to murder the king and his supporters, and re-impose Catholicism on the country. This 'Popish Plot' sent the country into a febrile commotion of paranoia. The actor Matthew Madbourne, who was heavily implicated in the plot, found himself in Newgate Gaol, and there, shortly afterwards, he died. Oates swore to the truth of his allegations in front of a magistrate, Sir Edmund Godfrey, who very shortly afterwards was found – melodramatically enough – murdered in a ditch. What more proof of the plot could be needed?

THE EXCLUSION CRISIS

This fabricated rumpus led to what was to be known as the 'Exclusion Crisis', by which Parliament tried to exclude Catholics from the throne, which effectively meant excluding the legitimate heir, James, Duke of York, and inserting one of Charles's bastards, probably the young Duke of Monmouth. In 1679 Parliament brought forward an Exclusion Bill which seemed likely to pass into law. Consequently, Charles dissolved the Parliament and fresh elections were held. The new Parliament was even less supportive of Charles than the old one, however, and when it too seemed on the point of passing its own Exclusion Bill, Charles summoned it to meet in Oxford, away from its London power base. 'Unknown to anyone', writes one historian,

Figure 3.33
Titus Oates, instigator of the 'Popish Plot' of 1678

Source: British Library, London

he had smuggled in the full robes and regalia that he wore to the formal opening and closing of a parliament. When the Commons squeezed into the hall (of Christ Church College), they were confronted by a king in his glory. It was a dazzling piece of theatre. In one sentence, and with one gesture, Charles ordered Parliament dismissed. It was the last Parliament of his reign.[1]

THE CRISIS CONTINUES

The crisis, however, was not done. In 1680 came the 'Meal-Tub Plot', when a group of Presbyterians were accused of raising an army with the aim of establishing a republic. Two years later, Charles's illegitimate son, the Duke of Monmouth, led an anti-Catholic rising against his father, and in 1683 the 'Rye House Plot' to assassinate Charles and his brother failed only because the king had left his lodgings in Newmarket earlier than expected.

This ongoing struggle ostensibly revolved around religion, as most political crises of the century seemed to: it stemmed from the urgent desire to exclude Catholics from all offices, and indeed all influence, in the realm. It split the country. Those who supported the king – a minority in Parliament and probably in the country, too – became known as 'Tories'; those against him were called 'Whigs'. Though there was obviously considerable overlap between the Tories and the old royalists and cavaliers, and between the Whigs and the old roundheads, the new groupings of political forces were not quite the same as in Charles I's time. The Whigs notably derived their strength from the rising entrepreneur class of capitalists, mostly based in London, who – whatever the religious dressing of the arguments – demanded more power to match their growing wealth. The inevitable consequence was that the king must cede more power to Parliament for the new rich held the key to Britain's future.

THE THEATRE AND POLITICS

The vicious politicking had its effects on the theatre. Apart from anything else, it left the king himself with less time for it, and, consequently, the patronage of many courtiers and aristocrats dwindled. Aphra Behn complained in *The Feigned Courtesans* (1679) that there was so much plotting in the real world that there was no space left for stage plots. An early effect of the crisis therefore was a falling away in audience numbers and the pressing need to seek new audiences.

THE CREATION OF THE UNITED COMPANY

The reduction in audience numbers was one cause of the decline of the King's Company, which had initially been the stronger and more experienced of the two set up by the Royal Patent, but in fact, as one historian has expressed it, 'the history of the King's Company in the seventies is an object lesson in how not to operate a theatre company'.[2] In January 1672 they had lost their entire stock of scenery, costumes and everything else in the fire which destroyed their Drury Lane home. When they returned to the new Drury Lane, therefore, they re-started with a considerable handicap.

But by then Killigrew's management was already under fire from some of the senior actors, including Hart, Mohun and Kynaston, and in 1672 Edward Gavill, another actor, was actually arrested for insulting the Patent holder and his friends. In the next three years, the disputes over the payment of wages and also indiscipline in the company, grew. Towards the end of 1675 Killigrew promulgated new rules which were really only the old rules rehashed, but which reveal the state of the company: actors must perform their roles as cast, not swap with, or 'sublet' them to others; they must not miss rehearsals; they were not to take costumes, props or other items out of the theatre building; and they were to meet the treasurer individually, not as a group. They were also censured for rowdiness, drunkenness and smashing windows when on tour.

The 'new' rules made little difference. By February 1676, performances had to be cancelled because of the actors' recalcitrance and their disputes among themselves. Some refused point blank to work for Thomas Killigrew until the King and the Lord Chamberlain intervened. It was not long before Killigrew agreed to hand over the reins to his son, Charles, who then tried to buy the actors' support, paying Charles Hart £100 and Edward Kynaston £60. But Killigrew's father, Thomas, the original Patent holder, still tried to interfere. While the Lord Chamberlain appointed, first, a management committee consisting of Hart, Kynaston, Mohun and Cartwright, and then, when they could not agree, a sole manager in Charles Hart, the Killigrews, father and son, were taking each other to court. Though Thomas kept his shares in the company, his son Charles won the right to manage it in January 1677 – only for the actors to rebel against him a few months later. Charles then decided to ignore the senior actor, and to make a serious effort to win over the younger members of the company, and also to mollify the shareholders. To no avail. And by spring 1678 he was being accused of pawning or mortgaging costumes, scenery and props. In early 1679 the company again closed.

As the political situation in the country was extremely turbulent, with the Popish Plot and the Exclusion Crisis at their height, Killigrew promised the actors extra money if they returned. They did. But he failed to pay them. They went to court and won their case, but by February 1681 the company found themselves quite unable to pay either the actors' wages or the rent on the Drury Lane theatre. There was dissension, debt, ill-discipline and no direction. In March 1682 it was reported that several actors had been wounded in what sounded like a pitched battle on the stage, the older actors against their juniors with drawn swords. The theatre closed.

In the summer, the leading actors, Hart and Kynaston, as well as Charles Killigrew himself, made separate overtures to the Duke's Company, and in May 1682 Charles Killigrew signed the 'Articles of Union' which enabled the Company to be merged into the Duke's. Though Michael Mohun, the actor, complained of the merger to the King himself, and though the shareholders sued Killigrew, it was the end. For Killigrew, the deal gave him a good share of the new United Company's profits, and he also took a nominal non-executive directorship of the company alongside Charles Davenant, Sir John's son. Effective management, however, rested with Thomas Betterton, and William Smith, who had succeeded Harris at helm of the Duke's Company.

The new company now had access to both major London theatres, and though at first they had too many actors, many of them left over the next few years. But the political dangers of the time, and perhaps the lack of any competition, led to stagnation. Thomas Betterton, as manager, and his wife moved into Dorset Garden. Betterton controlled the repertoire, edited or even made new adaptations of the plays to be presented, drafted scenic designs and constantly sought out new opportunities and new styles. Charles II even paid for him to visit France to see what he could bring back for the greater glory of the English stage. But little original was created.

CENSORSHIP

Perhaps this was also partly due to another direct consequence of the political upheavals, a re-energising of the censors. Thus, such apparently Whig, anti-monarchical works as Tate's *The Sicilian Usurper* (1680), an adaptation of Shakespeare's *Richard II*, and Nathaniel Lee's *Lucius Junius Brutus* (1680), were banned after only a very few performances. The latter play contained 'scandalous expressions and reflections upon the government', according to the Lord Chamberlain. It deals with Brutus's expulsion of Tarquin from Rome, and the establishment of a Republic. Tarquin is shown to have violated the constitution, and therefore his overthrow is justified. Some critics have seen parallels between the events of the play and those of the Popish Plot, as when in Act IV, '*the scene draws*' and reveals what the popular imagination may have thought was a typical Jesuit rite: '*the sacrifice: one burning and another crucified; the Priests coming forward with goblets in their hands, filled with human blood*'. And some characters in the play may have resembled contemporary political figures, such as Vinditius, the Titus Oates-like character in the plot. More evocatively, there are certainly echoes of Cromwell, Milton and the Commonwealth to be heard here, and Lee's dramatisation inherently suggests that Roman history was becoming more pertinent than Biblical events, such as Dryden had used in *Absalom and Achitophel*, for parallels with English political problems. His play may seem to lead towards the Augustan age, when the Stuarts and their endless contentions were dying away. It is therefore particularly interesting to note that after *Lucius Junius Brutus* Lee, obviously intimidated, turned to collaborating with the royalist Catholic, John Dryden, for his next play, *The Duke of Guise* (1682): the censor had done his work most thoroughly.

POLITICAL DRAMAS

Though there were other plays upholding the Whig cause against what was perceived as the Catholic danger, such as Settle's *Pope Joan* (1680) and Shadwell's *The Lancashire Witches* (1681), more typical of these fraught years were plays which supported the royalist cause, such as Thomas D'Urfey's *Sir Barnaby Whigg* (1681) or John Crowne's *City Politiques* (1682), which was also, curiously, banned for a time. This is an excellent farcical comedy, with political references thrown in: the absurd Whig and would-be poet, Craffy, is writing 'an answer to *Absolom and Achitophel*', and we hear of Whiggish malpractices and chicanery, but such political satire as it does attempt is usually more general than specific – 'the greatest politicians of our times never write nor read, as you may see by their speeches', says Podesta airily at one point – and if the subject of the play really is 'city politics', they are politics reduced to intrigue, bluster and farcical adventure.

Aphra Behn's *The Roundheads* (1681) is far more specific and violently polemical. It brings onto the stage some of Cromwell's most admired generals – John Lambert, John Desborough, Charles Fleetwood and others, the first time, perhaps, real historical people from the Civil War had been so portrayed. The play focuses on Lady Lambert who falls for the attractions of the fictional cavalier, Loveless. In a climactic scene, as these two are coming together, they hear Lambert approaching. Quickly, Lady Lambert makes Loveless lie on the sofa and covers him with a carpet. When Lambert enters, of course he sits on the sofa. '*Loveless rolls off, and turns Lambert over*'. The play ends with the Restoration of King Charles, when Lady Lambert's only hope lies in Loveless, but whereas Lady Desborough is able to marry her lover, Desborough having been unhistorically killed, Lady Lambert's husband remains alive, and she is not reprieved.

THOMAS OTWAY

Other pro-Catholic plays included *The Royalist* (1682) by Thomas D'Urfey, *The London Cuckolds* (1681) by Edward Ravenscroft, and plays by a failed actor, Thomas Otway (1652–85), who died in penury aged only thirty-two, but whose star blazed brilliantly for a few years at this time. His *The Soldier's Fortune* (1680) depicts a couple of old cavaliers, now down on their luck, and in despair as they see the Whigs returning England to a Cromwellian state. Their poverty shows how their cause has been defeated. In performance this was moving and was capped by James Nokes's masterly comic presentation of the Whig, Sir Davy. More impressive, and indeed one of the three or four genuine masterpieces of the Restoration theatre, was Otway's *Venice Preserv'd, or A Plot Discovered* (1682) which has held the stage ever since it was written. Not closely modelled on the Popish Plot, though obviously referring to it, this tragedy depicts a revolt against the Venetian monarchy

Figure 3.34
The playwright Thomas Otway, author of *Venice Preserv'd*, 1682, the only tragedy of the Restoration stage to have been revived regularly ever since

which is messily foiled. There is a level of political satire – or perhaps malice – in the extremely comic caricature of the Earl of Shaftesbury, the Whig leader, as Antonio, whose sexual peccadilloes are gloriously exposed. On stage, 'when (Tony) Leigh and (Elizabeth) Currer performed the parts of doting Cully and rampant courtesan, the applause was as loud as the triumphant Tories could bestow'. But in fact the play largely avoids contemporary politics as such and focuses instead on the personal motives of the main characters. If it advocates anything political, it seems to be that corrupt stability in a state is preferable to revolutionary extremism.

Venice Preserv'd was a fitting climax to Restoration theatre, perhaps its only tragic masterwork, for the brittle Stuart world of glittering carnality and charming indifference was clearly more suited to comedy. The Stuarts always preferred appearance to substance or reality, which is one reason why their theatre is worthy of our notice. Changeable scenery gave a new prominence to the stage illusion – a term which could hardly have been used before this period, even if it did not mean then what it means today. But the advent of women on the stage seemed to contradict this preference for illusory delights, for the women were certainly real and their flesh and blood reality was there to be enjoyed and admired, especially by their male spectators. The old theatrical contradictions survived, in other words, and still teased and provoked. But now they took fascinatingly new shapes. And if something of the old Elizabethan theatre's open space which invited the imagination to work was gone, yet new kinds of drama, demanding new kinds of imagination, were born.

NOTES

1 Jenny Uglow, *A Gambling Man*, London: Faber and Faber, 2009, p. 519.
2 Judith Milhous, *Thomas Betterton and the Management of Lincoln's Inn Fields, 1695–1708*, London: Feffer and Simon, 1979, p. 31.

Select bibliography

Astington, John H., *English Court Theatre, 1558–1642*, Cambridge: Cambridge University Press, 1999

Bawcutt, N.W., *The Control and Censorship of Caroline Drama*, Oxford: Clarendon Press, 1996

Britland, Karen, *Drama at the Courts of Queen Henrietta Maria*, Cambridge: Cambridge University Press, 2006

Butler, Martin, *The Stuart Court Masque and Political Culture*, Cambridge: Cambridge University Press, 2008

Butler, Martin, *Theatre and Crisis, 1632–1642*, Cambridge: Cambridge University Press, 1984

Cerasano, S.P., and Wynne-Davies, Marion (eds), *Readings in Renaissance Women's Drama*, London: Routledge, 1998

Clare, Janet, *Drama of the English Republic*, Manchester: Manchester University Press, 2002

Findlay, Alison, and Hodgson-Wright, Stephanie, *Women and Dramatic Production 1550–1700*, Harlow: Pearson, 2000

Fisk, Deborah Payne, *The Cambridge Companion to English Restoration Theatre*, Cambridge: Cambridge University Press, 2000

Gurr, Andrew, *The Shakespeare Company, 1594–1642*, Cambridge: Cambridge University Press, 2004

Howe, Elizabeth, *The First English Actresses*, Cambridge: Cambridge University Press, 1992

McManus, Clare (ed), *Women and Culture at the Courts of the Stuart Queens*, Basingstoke: Palgrave, 2003

McManus, Clare, *Women on the Renaissance Stage*, Manchester: Manchester University Press, 2002

Milling, Jane, and Thomson, Peter (eds), *The Cambridge History of British Theatre*, vol 1, Cambridge: Cambridge University Press, 2004

Orrell, John, *The Theatres of Inigo Jones and John Webb*, Cambridge: Cambridge University Press, 1995

Powell, Jocelyn, *Restoration Theatre Production*, London: Routledge and Kegan Paul, 1984

Thomson, Peter, *The Cambridge Introduction to English Theatre, 1660–1900*, Cambridge: Cambridge University Press, 2006

Tomlinson, Sophie, *Women on Stage in Stuart Drama*, Cambridge: Cambridge University Press, 2005

Wiseman, Susan, *Drama and Politics in the English Civil War*, Cambridge: Cambridge University Press, 1998

Interlude: Dramatick opera

The 'dramatick operas' of Henry Purcell, staged in the early 1690s, were an anomalous and unique form of theatre. They were developed after the 'Glorious Revolution' when it was clear the old Restoration comedies of rakes and amoral escapades were no longer appropriate and the drama had not yet found an alternative way. They had a long, if thin, pre-history. The Jacobean and Caroline court masques employed much music and spectacular scenic affects, and these had not entirely been forgotten during the Interregnum. Shirley's *Cupid and Death*, for instance, had been staged at Cromwell's court in 1653, and Davenant had managed to present *The Siege of Rhodes*, which boasted the first use of *recitative* in English, and other extravaganzas with music, before 1660.

MUSIC ON THE RESTORATION STAGE

But the Restoration audiences, although they enjoyed plenty of music during the course of an afternoon at the theatre, preferred their drama spoken. Even *The Siege of Rhodes* was presented as a straight play after 1660. The two theatre companies employed surprisingly large numbers of musicians for pre-performance and interval music and also for supernatural or ritualised scenes. There was, too, the occasional 'musical', such as *The Indian Queen* by John Dryden and Robert Howard (1664), for which John Banister composed a special suite of music. After the new Drury Lane and Dorset Garden, with their potential for scenic effects, came into use in the 1670s, such 'semi-operas' became commoner. *The Empress of Morocco* was presented in 1673, and the production of *Macbeth* in the same year, with flying witches, and much dance, music and singing, partook of 'the nature of an opera'.

In 1674, the Duke's Company mounted a spectacular revival of Davenant's *The Enchanted Island* with new music by Matthew Locke and Pelham Humfrey, and an orchestra including 24 violins, as well as harpsicals and theorboes (large double lutes) and a masque finale of Neptune and Amphitrite. The following year, the same company presented Shadwell's *Psyche*, with music by Locke and Giovanni Battista Draghi and an orchestra of trumpets, drums, cornets, sackbuts, six types of woodwind instruments, strings and continuo, and in 1677 they staged *Circe* by Charles Davenant, with music by John Banister. But in August 1677 Locke died, and Banister followed him in October 1679. The King's Men were sliding towards oblivion, even the resulting United Company struggled and in the 1680s there were few thoughts of musical drama.

ALBION AND ALBANIUS

The nearest the decade came to 'dramatick opera' was perhaps *Albion and Albanius*, with a text by John Dryden and music by Louis Grabu. This aimed to celebrate England after twenty-five glorious years of Charles II's reign. Charles had earlier sent Thomas Betterton, leader of the United Company, to Paris to survey the theatrical scene there, and perhaps bring back either a new opera by Jean-Baptiste Lully, or, better still, Lully himself, to make a work for his court like those he was making for Louis XIV. In fact, Betterton returned with Grabu, a former Master of the King's Music who had retired to France some ten years previously but who now agreed to work on Dryden's triumphantly Tory conception. The result was a somewhat uneasy French-English tone which hardly served the work's original jingoistic purposes. And then Charles II died while the piece was still in rehearsal. When it was finally presented, it was a sad failure. But Betterton saw its potential, which he was prepared to pursue.

CHAMBER OPERAS

Away from the professional theatre, the first chamber operas had been created in English. In 1675, *Calisto*, an imitation Caroline masque with music by Nicholas Staggins and words by John Crowne, was presented at court. In 1682 John Blow created something much closer to a chamber opera, *Venus and Adonis*, based on Shakespeare's poem. This was a through-composed opera, with dance as well as song. Venus was performed by the King's former mistress, Moll Davis, and Cupid by their daughter, Lady Mary Tudor. It was followed by one of the gems of late seventeenth-century music theatre, *Dido and Aeneas*, with text by Nahum Tate and music by Henry Purcell.

DIDO AND AENEAS

There is no clear record for the first performance of *Dido and Aeneas*. Some have argued for a court performance for Charles II in about 1684, but no evidence for this exists. The earliest recorded performance was in 1689 at a girls' boarding school in Chelsea, and even this is disputed. But perhaps the date of its first showing is unimportant for it has remained hugely popular ever since. The action moves nimbly to its climax and consists of brief, contrasting sections. Tate and Purcell's Dido is a sympathetic character in the English tradition, exemplified by Christopher Marlowe's *Dido, Queen of Carthage*, rather than the near-wicked temptress the Europeans usually presented. Though the opera is not without its European influences – for instance, it uses prologue and overture exactly as similar French compositions do – it is by any standards remarkable, its musical structure tight, its characterisation deft and the music itself hauntingly beautiful.

HENRY PURCELL

Surprisingly little is known of Purcell's life. Born probably in 1659 of musical parents, he was a choirboy in the Chapel Royal before becoming a musician and composer in his own right. Before the Glorious Revolution he had a secure place at court, to which as a strong Tory he felt emotionally committed. With the accession of the more philistine William III, less music was called for at court, and musicians and composers looked elsewhere for employment. The theatre was an obvious

Figure 3.35
The ornate setting for Nahum Tate's *Dido and Aeneas* with music by Henry Purcell
Source: DeAgostini/DEA Picture Library/Diomedia

source of work, and in the next three years Purcell was responsible for the music for three 'dramatick operas' presented at Dorset Garden by the United Company. If the dramatick opera can be classed as a *genre* it was, typically, a multimedia extravaganza with a very large quantity of music and notable scenic effects.

DIOCLESIAN

Purcell's first attempt at the form was *The Prophetess, or the History of Dioclesian*, which was presented at Dorset Garden in June 1690. It was an adaptation of a play by Fletcher and Massinger by Thomas Betterton, following up his enthusiasm for *Albion and Albanius*. With its expensive scenery, spectacular effects and sumptuous costumes, Purcell's music and Josias Priest's choreography, *Dioclesian* was highly acclaimed, and to an extent made Purcell's name. The music nicely differentiated the characters: thus, Cupid was represented by the strings, the 'Heroes' by trumpets as well as strings, and Bacchus by the oboes. And though the music was not perhaps very well integrated into the drama, it was still 'radiant and thrilling', according to one modern critic.[1] And the visual spectacle presented was duly amazing, climaxing with a four-level construction, one each for Flora, Pomona, Bacchus and the Sun God, and around each of whom revolved appropriate singers and dancers. The militaristic tone fitted William's endless continental wars, but the Prologue, written by the arch Tory John Dryden was slyly satirical and consequently banned by the Williamite authorities. The production, however, was greatly applauded, and the full score was even published.

KING ARTHUR

The success of *Dioclesian* encouraged the company to try to repeat the formula the next year. Dryden dredged up one of his old scripts, *King Arthur*, originally written in 1684, revised it and gave it to Purcell to supply music. It was performed at Dorset Garden in May 1691. The plot, which derived in no way from the familiar tales of King Arthur and the Round Table and had no Lancelot or Guinevere either, nevertheless attempted to relate to contemporary affairs. Where Arthur had originally been conceived as an embodiment of Charles II, he now represented William, righteously defending Britain from the usurper Oswald, who represented the deposed James II. At the end of the convoluted plot, Arthur defeated Oswald in single combat, and Merlin prophesied a glorious future in a unified Britain. There was more music in *King Arthur* than in *Dioclesian*, and though the full score was never published, great variety and versatility is evident in what has survived: it is at different times urgent, martial, spiritual, jolly and fantastical. It was perhaps Purcell's most successful stagework in terms of the number of revivals it had, at least over the next one hundred fifty years. Most famous was the 'Frost scene', when Cupid descended from the heavens to challenge the Genius of Cold Weather, who rose slowly from below to the steely tremolo of the vibrant strings. The part of Cupid was taken by Charlotte Butler, who was perhaps the first performer to turn their back on the audience at the climactic moment of her scene. Years later, Roger North remembered:

> Purcell's excellent opera of King Arthur, when Mrs Butler, in the person of Cupid, was to call up Genius, she had the liberty to turn her face to the scene, and her back to the theatre. She was in no concern for her face, but sang a recitativo of calling towards the place where Genius was to rise, and performed it admirably, even beyond anything ever heard upon the English stage.[2]

THE FAIRY QUEEN

The Fairy Queen, the third of Purcell's dramatick operas, was staged at Dorset Garden in May 1692, and was probably the most costly of them all. Adapted from Shakespeare's *A Midsummer Nights Dream*, perhaps by Thomas D'Urfey. Purcell's music was at its richest and most wide-ranging, and the scenes were again gorgeous and eye-catching. When Oberon and Titania were reconciled, fountains played, there were statues, columns and cypress trees all round a magnificent broad flight of stairs, while the final masque responded to the vogue for *chinoiserie* with a Chinese garden containing exotic buildings, trees, fruits and birds. It was another gigantic success, though the score was completely lost and only recovered by chance in 1903.

THEATRE MUSIC IN THE 1690S

However, there were no more major attempts at opera by the London theatre companies: they were probably too expensive. Purcell wrote more theatre music: he was one of four composers employed to create music for Thomas D'Urfey's three-part *Comical History of Don Quixote*, the first two parts of which were staged in May 1692 and were very popular. The third part, not performed until November 1695, was much less liked. Purcell also contributed music to new plays like the anonymous *Henry II* and Lee and Dryden's *Oedipus* as well as to revivals such as Aphra Behn's *Abdelazar* and Shadwell's version of *The Tempest*. His last significant success was with a revival of Dryden and Howard's *The Indian Queen* in 1695 when once again music and song were thoroughly integrated into the drama, which was performed by actors who could sing, rather than specialist opera singers.

Purcell died at the age of thirty-six in 1695. His attempts to create a form of English dramatic opera bore little fruit: anyone seeking opera in England in the next three decades would be likely to find performances of German or Italian works.

NOTES

1 Jonathan Keates, *Purcell*, London: Chatto & Windus, 1995, p. 207.
2 John Wilson, *Roger North on Music*, London: Novello, 1959, p. 217.

SELECT BIBLIOGRAPHY

Burden, Michael (ed), *The Purcell Companion*, Faber and Faber, 1995
Herissone, Rebecca (ed), *The Ashgate Research Companion to Henry Purcell*, Farnham: Ashgate, 2012
Holman, Peter, *Henry Purcell*, Oxford: Oxford University Press, 1994
Keates, Jonathan, *Purcell: A Biography*, London: Pimlico, 1996

PART FOUR

THEATRE AND BOURGEOIS SOCIETY

Timeline

	Society and politics	Theatre
1689	The 'Glorious Revolution': James II deposed Accession of William III and Mary II Declaration of Rights	
1690	Battle of the Boyne	Dryden, *Amphitryon* Chris Rich buys shares in Drury Lane
1691	Society for the Reformation of Manners founded	
1692		Murder of William Mountford
1693		Congreve, *The Old Bachelor*
1694	Bank of England established Death of Queen Mary	
1695	Act to prevent the growth of popery	Southerne, *Oroonoko* Actors Co-operative at Lincoln's Inn Fields 'Ariadne', *She Ventures and He Wins*
1696		Manley, *The Royal Mischief* Pix, *Ibrahim the Thirteenth* Anon, *The Female Wits*
1697		Vanbrugh, *The Provoked Wife*
1698		Collier, *A Short View of the Immorality and Profaneness of the English Stage*
1700		Congreve, *The Way of the World* Cibber, *Richard III* Actors Co-operative dissolved Death of John Dryden
1701	Act of Settlement	
1702	Death of William III: accession of Queen Anne	
1703		Rowe, *The Fair Penitent*

1704	Battle of Blenheim	
1705		*Arsinoe*, Drury Lane Centlivre, *The Gamester* and *The Basset Table* Queen's Theatre, Haymarket, opens Subscription raised to build a theatre in Bath
1707	Act of Union between England and Scotland	Farquhar, *The Beaux' Stratagem* Settle, *The Siege of Troy* at Bartholomew Fair
1709		Christopher Rich banned from producing plays
1710		Centlivre, *The Busie Body* Death of Thomas Betterton Wilks, Dogget, Cibber take over management of Drury Lane
1711		Handel, *Rinaldo*
1713		Booth replaces Dogget at Drury Lane Death of Elizabeth Barry Addison, *Cato*
1714	Death of Queen Anne: accession of George I	Death of Chris Rich John Rich becomes manager at Lincoln's Inn Fields
1715	Jacobite rebellion	Steele becomes Drury Lane patent holder Gay, *The What D'Ye Call It*
1718	D'Urfey, *Pills to Purge Melancholy*, published	Centlivre, *A Bold Stroke for a Wife* William Pinkethman opens theatre in Richmond, Surrey
1720	South Sea bubble bursts	Little Theatre, Haymarket, opens
1721	Robert Walpole's first administration	Harper and Lee fairground theatre company formed
1722		Steele, *The Conscious Lover*
1723	'Black Act'	*Harlequin Dr Faustus*, Drury Lane *The Necromancer*, Lincoln's Inn Fields
1724	Execution of Jack Sheppard	Aston's Co at Skinner's Hall, Edinburgh
1725	Swift, *Gulliver's Travels* published	
1727	Death of George I: accession of George II	Edinburgh Company of Players at Taylor's Hall, Edinburgh
1728		Cibber, *The Provoked Husband* Gay, *The Beggar's Opera*
1729		Goodman's Fields theatre opens

1730		Fielding, *The Author's Farce* and *Tom Thumb* Death of Anne Oldfield
1731		George Lillo, *The London Merchant* Anon, *The Fall of Mortimer* banned
1732		End of the triumvirate at Drury Lane Covent Garden theatre opens
1733	Excise Bill defeated	Drury Lane actors rebellion
1734	Hogarth, *The Rake's Progress*	Keregen's theatre opens in York
1735	Bartholomew Fair limited to three days	
1736	Gin Act	Fielding's Great Mogul's Company of Comedians at Little Theatre, Haymarket
1737		'Footmen's riot' at Drury Lane Fielding, *The Historical Register for the Year 1736* Theatre Licensing Act

Chapter 41: A Glorious Revolution

A NEW DISPENSATION

The 'Glorious Revolution' of 1689, which ousted James II from the throne and installed his daughter Mary and her husband William as joint monarchs, effectively ended the old Stuart absolutism and brought the bourgeoisie to power in England.

The Declaration of Rights removed the King's power to suspend the law of the land or to maintain his own army, and asserted that Parliament must meet regularly and frequently. Supremacy shifted to the House of Commons. Nonconformism became acceptable, as a new Toleration Act was passed. In the Prologue to *Bury Fair*, performed in 1689, Thomas Shadwell wrote how he had been 'oppressed' and 'silenced for a Nonconformist poet', but 'now he swears he's loyal as the best', and 'common-sense has won the day'.[1] 'Common sense', compromise, accommodation: these were significant new touchstones, useful especially for merchants, traders and businessmen, supporters of the Whig party, which now began its hold on power which lasted with few breaks for half a century.

POLITICAL DANGERS

But if compromise was newly acceptable, the dethroned James II was still alive and disconcertingly ambitious, at least until William's army defeated him near the River Boyne in Ireland in 1690. Still, for many years, the disloyal (or loyal, according to your belief) toast to 'the King over the water' was privately proposed, and throughout the 1690s there were more or less serious pro-Jacobite incidents or insurrections, like the one which involved John Pate and John Reading, two performers from Lincoln's Inn Fields Theatre in 1695. They were arrested for participating in an affray outside the Dog Tavern, Drury Lane. Having drunk too much, they had lit a bonfire in the street and attempted to force passers-by to drink to 'the king over the water'.

Because the Jacobites were assumed to be Catholic, toleration did not stretch to Catholics. Both Queen Mary and her sister, the future Queen Anne, were staunch Protestants, and the House of Commons passed an Act asserting that a Catholic monarch could never rule over this Protestant nation. In 1695 an Act banning Catholics from entering the British Army, from bearing arms, from establishing their own school or from sending their children to be educated abroad, was passed. In 1704 a further Act restricted Catholics' right to buy, lease or retain land.

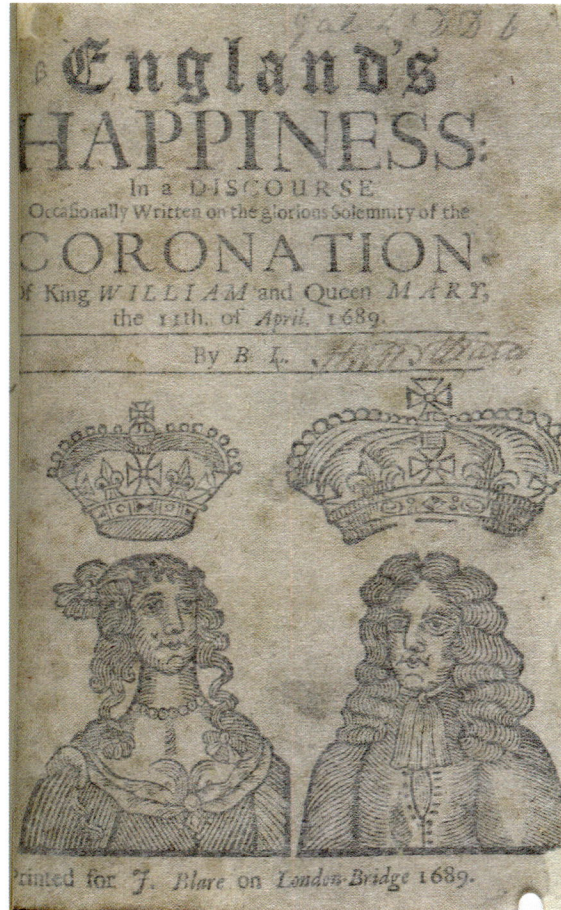

Figure 4.1
England's happiness: King William III and Queen Mary II, 1689
Source: British Library, London/© British Library Board. All Rights Reserved/Bridgeman Images

WILLIAM AND MARY

William and Mary were utterly unlike their Stuart predecessors on the English throne. They were perhaps like contemporary Dutch painting which was superseding the grandiose style of Rubens, van Dyck and Lely, domesticity replacing theatrical grandeur. But still, William III's great project was the shackling of French power: he saw himself as something of a liberator against the tyranny of Catholicism. *Tamerlane* (1701), Nicholas Rowe's version of the Tamburlaine story, is an unashamedly sycophantic portrait of him:

> The scourge of lawless pride, and dire ambition,
> The great avenger of the groaning world

whose purpose was 'to redress an injur'd people's wrongs'. But when Queen Mary died in 1694, and then the Duke of Gloucester, Princess Anne's son and heir to the throne followed in 1700, something of a succession crisis returned. Should James be recalled? Should the now-childless Anne become heir in place of her son? And what would happen when she died? In 1701 Parliament passed an Act of Settlement stipulating that the throne should pass to the Electress Sophia of Hanover or her Protestant heirs if William and Anne were both to die without heirs.

Queen Mary had had an ambivalent attitude towards the drama. She disapproved of Aphra Behn's *The Rover*, but she saw John Dryden's *Amphitryon* (1690) twice, and she commanded a royal performance of William Congreve's *The Double Dealer* (1694). But when she died, William's indifference meant that the theatre lost place at court and was forced into increasing commercialism.

CAPITALISM

This, however, was in line with the times. The founding of the Bank of England in 1694 which issued paper money and financed the national debt (as well as funding William's continental wars), together with John Castaing's establishing of a stock exchange in Jonathan's Coffee House in 1698 after dealers had been ejected from the Royal Exchange for rowdiness, indicate a quite new, dynamic form of capitalism. Britain's future lay in trade underpinned by this new finance capitalism. The importance of money echoes like a refrain through the drama of the period: already in Congreve's *The Old Bachelor*, Heartwell's 'song and dance' are seen to reside in his jingling purse; in Farquhar's *The Constant Couple* (1699), the Smuggler exclaims incredulously: 'Venture your lives? I'm sure we ventured our money, and that's life and soul to me'; in Susanna Centlivre's *A Bold Stroke for a Wife* (1718), Freeman is in the 'good graces' of Mr Tradelove (note the name) because he provided Tradelove with some advance trading information, 'upon which he bought up all the stock he could and . . . he told me he had got (profited) to the tune of five hundred pounds'; and in Richard Steele's *The Conscious Lovers* (1722), we see how a businessman is now as respectable as a landed gentleman: Mr Sealand assures Sir John Bevil, 'give me leave to say that we merchants are a species of gentry that have grown into the world this last century'. The critic John Dennis complained in 1702 that 'discourse now everywhere turns upon interest', but business was deemed to bind society where religion used to divide it. For Widow Lackett in Thomas Southerne's *Oroonoko*, 'business must be followed or lost', while Heartfree in John Vanbrugh's *The Provoked Wife* (1697), assures Constant that 'business must be done, you know'. In Mary Pix's *The Beau Defeated* (1700), the beau is outsmarted by the merchant trader.

NEW IDEAS

Simultaneously popular consciousness, how the world was viewed, was shifting. The Royal Society's democratisation of science ('natural philosophy'), symbolised in the publication in 1687 of Newton's *Principia*, helped to undermine some of religion's fanaticism. Valeria's obsession with 'natural philosophy' in Centlivre's *The Basset Table* (1705), suggests comically how this may indeed become a new fanaticism. And this turning away from religious extremism was reinforced by Hobbes's rational materialism and, more popularly, by John Locke's ideas of toleration, liberty and the significance of property (as opposed to hereditary rights). Locke, in fact, was behind much of the dominant Whig ideology of the period.

CLASS CONSCIOUSNESS

Along with the dynamism of expanding capitalism and new scientific and philosophical ways of looking at the world, a new sort of class consciousness was also emerging. As Lady Reveller remarks in *The Basset Table*: 'A citizen's wife is not to be endured amongst quality. Had she not money, 'twere impossible to receive her'. The poor were getting poorer and the rich richer. The works of Newton and Locke did not seem particularly relevant in the stews and rookeries north and east of Covent Garden, and the theatre had little to say about poverty, except to note its disgrace, as Archer does in Farquhar's *The Beaux' Stratagem*: 'There is no scandal like rags, nor any crime so shameful as poverty'.

Political and cultural power devolved upon the rising middle and upper classes, and they fought for hegemony through their increasingly strident parties, Whigs and Tories. The Tories were handicapped in this struggle by their perceived sympathy for Jacobitism and 'the king over the water'. The Whigs were often dissenters, former radicals or even revolutionaries, but they acquired a veneer of Augustan polish, symbolised by their exclusive but powerful Kit Kat Club. The kind of snobbishness this could lead to is suggested by Valere in Centlivre's *The Gamester* (1705), who renames his servant 'Hector' because it sounds impressive. Whigs believed that freedom was founded in property ownership, and that somehow seemed to excuse a growing selfishness, the relishing of consumption for its own sake and a delight in leisure and pleasure. The age saw a large growth in parks, but also in gaming houses, public baths and brothels – pleasures aimed to cater to men's desires in a male-dominated society.

How far the theatre benefited (or suffered) from this attitude is a matter for argument.

NOTE

1 Thomas Shadwell, *Bury Fair*, Prologue.

Chapter 42: New age, new plays

SHADWELL, DRYDEN AND SOUTHERNE

For playwrights, the 1688–9 Revolution seems to have been a kind of liberation: new plays poured forth over the following decade, taking the drama away from the Restoration celebration of the Cavalier cause and the untrammelled self-indulgence of the rakish victors to something altogether knottier and more problematic.

The first playwrights to follow this path were often the same who had made their names earlier, thus often misleading critics by using the forms of 'Restoration comedy' to different ends. Few plays of the reign of William and Mary can be described as 'Restoration'. Shadwell's *Bury Fair* (1689), for instance, contains more than vestiges of the former style, as well as an old man who 'pretends to have been one of Ben Jonson's sons, and to have seen plays at the Blackfriars'. But *Bury Fair* centres not on a masculine rake pursuing his libido, but on Gertrude, a 'free-spirited lady' who gets the upper hand over any rakes who chase her and fancy marrying her, though she does marry in the end. But her adventures are set against her father's failed second marriage. Marriage itself becomes the centre of the play's discourse, especially as it affects women.

Amphitryon (1690) by John Dryden gives this discussion another dimension. The story of a usurper, Jupiter, who takes Amphitryon's place in Alcmena's marriage bed, investigates not just marriage, but also usurpation in the political sphere. Dryden's political persuasion leads him to see William III as usurping James II's throne, and his play is peppered with ambiguous references to contemporary politics, including a mock 'contract' scene between Phaedra and Mercury which exposes the 1689 Act of Settlement. Because Jupiter takes the shape of Amphitryon, and Mercury the shape of Sosnia, there is plenty of scope for theatrical mistaken identities, but there is also implicit here Alcmena's dangerous female fantasy of a brilliant sexual experience with a godlike lover.

Drama thus begins to enter women's territory in completely new ways. In this context, Thomas Southerne's *The Wives Excuse* (1691) is even more original. Southerne was an experienced playwright whose *Sir Anthony Love* (1690), an excellent 'breeches' comedy, had been a considerable success. His new comedy, however, was a study of marital incompatibility. It was a failure when staged, partly because it sought to extend comedy's horizon of expectation. Southerne's dramatic technique is almost Chekhovian in the way Mrs Friendall's psychological agony is gradually revealed, and like *Amphitryon*, *The Wives Excuse* refuses to offer a consolation 'happy ending'.

Figure 4.2
Thomas Southerne's *The Wives Excuse* was staged at Drury Lane in 1691, though it was not a success. Its discussion of marriage reaches a climax when Friendall's 'gentleman's pleasures' are disturbed

PLAYS OF IDEAS

The theatre of the 1690s is thus no longer the hedonistic playground of a merry monarch and his supporters; it is a platform for debating ideas and especially social and personal power relations. This is true even of such genial plays as Thomas D'Urfey's *The Marriage Hater Match'd*, which features an array of characters including Lady Bumfiddle with a voice 'like a trump-marine', and the sweet young thing, La Pupsey and her little lap-dog, Adonis. But many plays are political, and explore the rights and limitations of kings and subjects (or citizens), or the world of business, as it is through business that the former Puritans emerge as the new Whigs. Most often they concern marital relations.

CIBBER AND VANBRUGH

Colley Cibber's *Love's Last Shift* (1696), for instance, centres on the failed marriage of Loveless and Amanda: he has deserted her ten years ago, but she has remained faithful to him, and now she tries a sexual ruse to win him back. The trick works, and after four acts of overt sexual intrigues, there is a sentimental ending. The play is only partly 'new', however: it is actually dominated by the role of Sir Novelty Fashion, played with huge success by Cibber himself. Sir Novelty is a fop descended

Figure 4.3

Colley Cibber as Lord Foppington in *The Careless Husband*, 1704

Source: Paul Fearn/Alamy Stock Photo

in a direct line from the Restoration's men of mode, and so popular was he that he was 'stolen' by Sir John Vanbrugh to be the central figure in his play, *The Relapse* (1696); or, as Cibber himself put it, Vanbrugh 'did me honour' by making his own play the sequel to Cibber's. In *The Relapse* Sir Novelty has bought himself a peerage and become Lord Foppington. But Cibber reclaimed him in *The Careless Husband* (1704) though in truth by now he had become rather tedious. Significantly, his place as this play's 'character' belongs to Lady Betty Modish, 'a strange giddy creature' full of high spirits who is gradually converted from eccentricity to love and marriage. Her development is the play's most interesting feature, though the eponymous 'careless husband' is also converted from promiscuity to fidelity after his wife finds him sleeping peacefully beside the maid with whom he has just had sex. She places her scarf on his head and departs, and this is enough to make him see the folly of his ways.

Vanbrugh's most popular play, *The Provoked Wife* (1697) is altogether more subtle and satisfying than this. Probably his only original play, his others being adaptations and rewrites, Vanbrugh makes marriage the central focus of the drama and relegates the witty lovers to a subplot in a direct reversal of the practice of most comedy authors of the seventeenth century. Sir John Brute is a Falstaffian Lord of Misrule who is presented on stage as not so much evil as red-blooded. He turns the world upside down, while his wife, Lady Brute's doubts and self-doubts balance his disorderly rumbustiousness: each partner is attractive and repellent. The relationship also implicitly raises the question: if the country can depose its king, can a wife 'depose' her husband? *The Provoked Wife* also contains a spectacularly resourceful scene set in Spring Garden with characters spying on each other, meeting illicitly, being interrupted or discovered in a kind of world outside the world. Its brilliance is sustained by the following scenes with Lady Brute hiding a man in her cupboard, and Sir John 'tumbling' her, and then falling asleep and snoring loudly. Clerical moralists, most notably Jeremy Collier, objected to Sir John's drunken dressing-up as a parson; Vanbrugh was forced to change this so that in later performances Sir John disguised himself as a woman. It was possibly less offensive to the sexist Collier, but it actually made the comedy more resonant.

COFFEE HOUSES AND CLUBS

Cibber and Vanbrugh's closeness – Cibber completed Vanbrugh's *The Provoked Husband*, left unfinished at his death – suggests another feature of this new age, its sociability. Playwrights met at Will's Coffee House, Covent Garden, where Dryden had long held court, and where he collaborated with Southerne and befriended not only Vanbrugh, but also William Congreve, a young playwright from Ireland. The last two were also members of the Kit Kat Club, founded just when court patronage of the arts was diminishing. The Kit Kat Club was initially a dining club meeting at the Cat and Fiddle pub, and it aimed to express and promulgate particular (Whiggish) political and cultural values: the Club's lasting influence may be judged by the fact that Robert Walpole, Britain's first Prime Minister, in office until 1742, was a member. Taste, education and reason, not heredity, were the Kit Kats' central values, and they find expression in Congreve's plays.

WILLIAM CONGREVE

Congreve wrote just five plays in the 1690s and then stopped, though he lived until 1729. The first, *The Old Bachelor* (1693), written when he was just twenty-three, is a *tour de force*. It concerns on

Figure 4.4
Will's London coffee house, symbol of the new bourgeois sociability
Source: Lebrecht Music and Arts Photo Library/Alamy Stock Photo

the one hand the old bachelor, Heartwell, who wants sex but not marriage, and his partner Silvia, who wants marriage before sex; and Fondlewife and his spouse, Laetitia. In a superb comic scene, Fondlewife returns home when Laetitia is entertaining her lover, Bellmour. Success in marriage is the issue here, even if it is sometimes treated flippantly.

Congreve followed this up with *The Double Dealer* (1694), in which 'marriage is the game we hunt', as one character says, and deceit is piled upon deceit in a dizzying sequence; *Love for Love* (1695), chosen to open the new Lincoln's Inn Theatre after the leading actors had broken away from Drury Lane, and after which Congreve was awarded the kind of sinecure any writer would welcome – regulating hackney and stage coaches, for which he received £100 per year; and *The Mourning Bride* (1697), one of the most effective tragedies of these years. But he went further than these in his last play, *The Way of the World* (1699), the complexity and modernity of which is astonishing. It depicts people falling in love with the wrong people, rather like Chekhov's plays, and also like Chekhov's, the characters rarely say exactly what they mean, as when Millament is extremely good-spirited to Marwood, whom she surely has reason to hate. The play addresses questions still difficult to answer, such as, how should ex-partners treat one another? And Mirabell, the hero, is no mere rake chasing a seductive flirt: his relationship with Millament is more profound and articulates something of the difficulty of loving. *The Way of the World* is often taken to be the most accomplished play of the 1690s. Not quite satirical, not quite farcical, it is sharp, funny and yet heart-warming, while the individuality of each character's motives and speech patterns indicates a move towards naturalism which would radically challenge the best actors of the time.

WOMEN PLAYWRIGHTS

The 1690s proved to be one of the most exciting decades for playwrighting also because several women writers appeared. The earliest was anonymous: *She Ventures and He Wins* (1695) was by 'Ariadne', a young lady – in all probability the actress Elizabeth Barry. It is noticeable that there are more female characters than male in the cast list, and that the events of the drama are viewed through women's eyes. The heroine, Charlotte, is the active agent in the plot; Lovewell, whom she desires, is almost wholly passive. Barry herself played Urania, the feisty wife of the would-be philandering squire. When he is tricked into dressing up as a woman to achieve his libidinous ends, she hides him first in a cistern of water, then in the feathers cupboard, and finally, when he is sodden and covered in feathers, has him carried off by 'devils'. It seems like a marvellous practical joke, or else a nightmare come true! The play's use of music is also interesting and contributes to its effect on stage. The first two songs, a serenade and a lament, deliberately contrast with each other. At the end of Act 3 comes the lively duet, 'Oft have you told me', and the play concludes with the beautiful Hymen duet.

The first named female playwright to appear was the witty Catherine Trotter, later to become something of a bluestocking and marry a clergyman. The first two scenes of her *Agnes de Castro* (1695) are played entirely between women, setting the compass for a woman-focused play, while her later *The Unhappy Penitent* (1701) is the 'bloodless tragedy' of a woman, Margaret, who renounces her beloved and enters a nunnery.

DELARIVIERE MANLEY

Delariviere Manley, the Tory daughter of a cavalier soldier, was more controversial. Her first play, *The Lost Lover* (1696) failed because, she said, it was the victim of anti-woman prejudice: she did not utterly condemn the erring heroine. Actually, there is much that is amusing or intriguing in this play, not least some of the less significant characters who are exaggerated and funny, but never maliciously caricatured: Sir Amorous Courtall, for instance, whose fashionable curls actually cover his face, and Orinda, the disdainful poetess who constantly takes snuff. Manley took her next play, *The Royal Mischief* (1696) away from Drury Lane and gave it to Lincoln's Inn Fields, but this tragedy, focused on a woman, and implicitly and effectively confronting patriarchal *mores*,

Figure 4.5
The playwright Catherine Trotter, whose married name was Cockburn (thereafter "Cockburn")

was not much more successful. In *Almyna* (1706), whose heroine's name is almost an anagram of the author's own, Manley again makes a passionate dramatic defence of women's rights and shows how men escape censure for behaviour which brings opprobrium on women. Her strong expressions of female sexuality make Manley both daring and dangerous, especially to the male hierarchy.

MARY PIX

Mary Pix, a convivial woman teased for being overweight, was more prolific than either Trotter or Manley. Her first plays, *Ibrahim, the Thirteenth* (1696), *The Spanish Wives* (1696) and *The Innocent Mistress* (1697), followed quickly upon each other. They dramatise what would now be called gender politics often in outlandish or glamorous settings, and if the plays sometimes seem conventional, the viewpoint and often the details are not. *The Innocent Mistress* contains five separate comic plots, the most telling of which involves a woman who unknowingly falls in love with a married man. *Queen Catherine* (1698), set in the court of Edward IV, and showing the future Richard III in full-blown Shakespearean mode, deformed, ambitious and amoral, provides an unexpected female view of history, while *The Beau Defeated* (1700) contains not only a memorable female quarrel scene between Mrs Rich and Lady de Bassett, in which the latter draws a pistol like a cowboy in a western saloon, but also an aptly named servant, Vermin. *The Conquest of Spain* (1705) contains two plots which show how women's actions and their fates affect politics, rebellion and war. And most strikingly, Pix here conveys the shame and degradation of Jacinta, the general's daughter who has been viciously raped by the king.

THE FEMALE WITS

These plays by women (and there were more: Jane Wiseman's romantic melodrama, *Antiochus the Great*, for example) were versatile and varied, and put women's experience of British life in the late seventeenth and early eighteenth centuries squarely forward. But their work always aroused male resentment. The anonymous author of *A Comparison between the Two Stages* wrote in 1702: 'I hate these petticoat authors. . . . What a pox have women to do with the muses?' and when Mary Pix submitted *The Deceiver Deceived* to Drury Lane Theatre, George Powell, the leader of the company, refused the play but then stole its story and structure and re-wrote and staged it as *The Imposture Defeated*. In late 1696 Drury Lane staged *The Female Wits*, probably composed by a group of the company's actors, which bitingly satirised the women playwrights, especially Manley, who was shown as domineering and insensitive. While the actors appeared as themselves, Trotter became Calista, 'a lady that pretends to the learned languages, and assumes to herself the name of a critic', the overweight Mary Pix was Mrs Wellfed, 'one that represents a fat female author', while Manley became Marsilia, 'a poetess that admires her own works and a great lover of flattery'. The play is framed around a rehearsal of a parody of *The Royal Mischief*, Marsilia largely usurps the position of director, and she and Mrs Wellfed continually drink large glasses of sherry. But beyond this piece of masculine bullying, too many men designated female playwrights whores, their plays licentious and indeed the very concept of female authorship a kind of sexual misbehaviour. The attacks were actually an attack on their right to earn an independent living, for theatre was of course one of the few professions open to intelligent women.

THE EXPERIENCE OF WOMEN

Women's plays dramatised women's issues in a variety of contexts: *The Beau Defeated* focuses on women's experience of London society, *The Unhappy Penitent* on the nature of women's ambition as fundamentally different from men's, and *Almyna* on the fraught feminine relationship between

Zoradia and Almyna. Manley was especially excoriated for her apparently unrestrained expression of female sexuality: in *The Royal Mischief* Homais refuses to

> conceal desire, where every
> Atom of me trembles with it. I'll strip
> My passion naked of such guile, lay it
> Undressed and panting at his feet, then try
> If all his temper can resist it.

After sex with Levan, she muses:

> Where the divine impress has been,
> A pleasing trickling cools through all my veins,
> And tempers into love what else would be
> Distraction.

And Almyna asserts proudly:

> Let vulgar maids by vulgar passions swayed
> Miscall dissimulation modesty;
> My pride of life shall be to own my flame.

The matter is treated perhaps more subtly in other women-authored plays. In *She Ventures and He Wins*, Charlotte asserts unwavering control over her sexual destiny, and Catherine Trotter's women, too, have the potential to decide such matters for themselves. Shekar the favourite mistress in Mary Pix's *Ibrahim the Thirteenth*, has no more inhibitions that Manley's heroines:

> thou knowest my raging fires,
> How passion like a vulture plays upon my heart,
> And the hot flames of love drink up my spirit.

The best male playwrights too were aware of the female circumstance. Mrs Friendall, at the end of Southerne's *The Wives Excuse* speaks for all women trapped in a bad marriage, while Charlotte, in *Oroonoko* (1695), in breeches, is able to manage her own fate. Millament, in *The Way of the World*, asserts: 'I won't be called names after I'm married . . . as wife, spouse, my dear, joy, jewel, love, sweetheart and the rest of that nauseous cant.'

GAY PLAYS

At last a few gay characters are also found in the new drama, though both Lord Simperwell in *The Wives Excuse* and Coupler in *The Relapse* are somewhat leerily presented. But in Thomas Baker's *Tunbridge Walks* (1703), Maiden, 'a nice fellow that values himself upon his effeminacies', is an apprentice who sings, dances and plays a musical instrument. He had been made heir to a

OROONOKO.

Mᵣ SAVIGNY in the Character of OROONOKO.
Oro. I'll turn my Face away, and do it so
Published Nov. 23. 1776 by J. Lowndes & Partners

Figure 4.6
John Horatio Savigny as Oroonoko, c.1776

gentleman who had clearly found him irresistible. In the play, he cross-dresses and enjoys the companionship of women, but he has no wish for sex with them.

COLONIES, SLAVERY AND BLACK PERFORMERS

Women playwrights also expanded the drama's horizons to wider social issues. In 1696, the Navigation Act legislated for all merchandise to and from the colonies to be carried in English ships.

It was a crucial step towards making England a great sea power, with growing trade and settlements in the Americas, India and Africa, from where were shipped pepper, coffee, tobacco, sugar, tea, spices, furs and more. All this, of course, was on the back of the burgeoning slave trade. In 1672 the Royal Africa Company was established, its shareholders including the Duke of York (the future King James II), Prince Rupert, the Lord Mayor of London and many others. Over the following forty years the Company transported over one hundred twenty-five thousand slaves from Africa to the Americas, though only about one hundred thousand of these people survived the Atlantic crossing. Inevitably this meant more black people arriving also in England: there may have been nearly fifteen thousand black people in the country by 1750. They were sailors, pedlars, footpads, servants and stage performers, like the twelve-year-old 'Miss Cross' who sang 'A lass there lives upon the green' in the original production of Thomas Southerne's *Oroonoko* in 1695 and the 'blackamoors' included in the cast of Handel's *Rinaldo* in 1711.

THE EXPERIENCE OF BLACK PEOPLE

The drama of the period took gradual note of the black presence. The protagonist of Aphra Behn's *Abdelazar* (1676) is black, exotic admittedly, but human and attractive to women. In Mary Pix's *The Innocent Mistress* there is reference to Mrs Bantam, who really did keep a coffeehouse near the Guildhall, and Valentine in Congreve's *Love for Love* waxed enthusiastic about 'the buxom black widow in the Poultry', calling her 'a lovely girl, i' faith, black sparkling eyes, soft pouting ruby lips' with 'pretty round heaving breasts, a Barbary shape, and a jut with her bum would stir an anchorite'. Edward Young's tragedy, *The Revenge* (1721) is a kind of Othello story in reverse with the black servant and former prince, Zanga, poisoning the mind of the noble white man, Alonzo, against his innocent wife.

The play which focuses most directly on the black experience is Thomas Southerne's *Oroonoko*, an adaptation of a novella by Aphra Behn. Instructively, his main alteration to Behn's original is to make Imoinda, Oroonoko's beloved wife, white, not black. But the play's two plots indicate how in this society women become commodities as surely as slaves: both are 'disposed of' by their male guardians. 'This is your market for slaves', says Welldon; 'my sister is a free woman, and must not be disposed of in public'. The rowdy English women and the silently suffering slave-wife equally illuminate the colonial experience. The slave trade is not seen as immoral in itself. It is a vital economic activity, but it requires the slaves to be well treated. This of course their owners fail to do: the plantation thrives by 'unheard-of villainy' and 'barbarous treachery'. Oroonoko himself is more 'moral' than the white Christians because the latter are cruel overseers. He is captured royalty, a new version of the 'noble savage' perhaps, and he speaks verse where everyone else speaks prose to indicate his worthiness.

Some of *Oroonoko*'s themes were curiously echoed in Congreve's *The Mourning Bride*. In this play, Osmyn, Heli and Zara are captive 'moors', and Osmyn, like Oroonoko, is of royal blood. He too is wise and cultured, and both he and Oroonoko lose, then find, their beloveds, before both are fettered to await death. *Oroonoko*, however, was the more potent play politically: it was co-opted by the anti-slavery movement and continued to be performed for over a century, the part of Oroonoko being a favourite for leading actors who were prepared to 'black up' throughout the period.

ORIENTALISM AND FEMINISM

Women writers especially also approached the rather more exotic theme of the orient in several plays which combine proto-feminism with orientalism. Trotter's *Agnes de Castro*, Manley's *The Lost Lover* and Pix's *The Spanish Wives* all deal more or less overtly with Islam, and there is always a fascination with features of Moslem life, such as what happens in the women's seraglio. It is sometimes difficult to decide whether this is orientalist or anti-orientalist. Thus, the heroine of Manley's *The Royal Mischief* is a light-skinned Arab who is strong and admirable, but the play also includes an exotic dance by 'Indians' for us to gaze at. The plot of *Almyna* is taken from the newly translated *1001 Arabian Nights*, but the author's attitude is evident in the florid stage direction:

> After a flourish of trumpets and music, Almanzor seats himself on a magnificent throne, Abdalla standing on the right hand, the vizier on the left; Alhador brings the Alcoran wrapped in a piece of very rich stuff and lays it upon a small Indian table before the throne; the grandees ranged on each side of the throne.

We are meant to see this setting as something strange and 'other'. Yet the play recounts Almyna's struggle for women's rights against the Sultan, who is indeed overthrown at the end.

Mary Pix's plays have a similar fascination with the exotic combined with urgent feminist themes. *Ibrahim the Thirteenth* depicts a tyranny being eaten by corruption. But much of the action occurs in the seraglio where Shekar's erotic force challenges the patriarchal authority, and her cleverness undermines the king. But again, the setting contrives to make the whole seem 'other': the play opens with Acmet, the chief eunuch, ordering

> Burn the Sabaean gums and all those rich perfumes
> Where our great Master passes till the room
> Smells sweet as altars laden with incense
> To the heathen gods; spread the gay Persian carpets
> For his royal feet . . .

In *The False Friend*, Zelida, whose 'swarthy veins Carry the royal blood', knows all the poisons when Appamia needs one. And in *The Conquest of Spain*, the fight is against 'the sooty Moors', 'this swarthy brood of hell', while a room is prepared for the lady's seduction:

> The Tyrian purple and the Indian gold
> Curiously interwove by artful hands,
> Large orient pearl and gems of highest values,
> Inferior only to your radiant eyes,
> Are placed in beauteous order all around.

Often these plays demonstrate the difference between bracing English freedom and oriental tyranny and luxury. *Ibrahim the Thirteenth* contrasts the dissoluteness of the Islamic court with the healthier English society; *The Royal Mistress* shows the decline of the Ottoman Empire and the expansion of England, while also exploring women's place in this historical process; and *The False Friend* warns of the terrors of allowing the barbarians to overcome a Christian European state. However, we should also notice how the political turbulence is often echoed in the female characters' distress. These women then assert themselves to raise not only their own fortunes but also those of their communities. Manley explores women's place in the historical process: often these plays show a transformation from chaos or disharmony to a new and better concord through the agency of the woman hero. The contradictions give these plays their fascination.

NEW SUBJECTS AND NEW PERFORMANCES

The playwrights of the 1690s tackled new subjects and used new dramatic techniques, though not always successfully and of course not with the sensibilities or attitudes of the twenty-first century. Yet here was something new, and it was enough to frighten the establishment, the king as well as the church and the moralists, and it asked questions of the performers of the time which were not easily answered.

Chapter 43: The actors' co-operative

THE ACTORS' NEED FOR FREEDOM

The brilliance of the writers of the 1690s partly inspired and was partly inspired by the brilliance of the leading actors. The actors' need for freedom to explore this new repertoire was one reason why in 1695 they broke away from the United Company to form their own co-operative at Lincoln's Inn Fields. But there was at the heart of this a contradiction: was the theatre they were creating based on stylisation, or was it basically naturalistic?

MACHINATIONS AT DRURY LANE

The breakaway was overtly motivated by the repressive, and perhaps corrupt, regime which was asserting itself at Drury Lane. The machinations began in 1687 when Alexander Davenant borrowed money from Sir Thomas Skipwith to buy Charles Davenant's shares in the company. Alexander Davenant quickly ousted the actors, Thomas Betterton and William Smith, from their managerial roles and handed this to his brother, Thomas Davenant. Meanwhile, Alexander Davenant started trading in the shares in such a way as to begin gradually to destabilise the theatre. In March 1690, Thomas Davenant sold his interest in the company to Christopher Rich, law clerk to Sir Thomas Skipwith, and Rich immediately began to try to reorganise the work practices at Drury Lane. Rumblings of discontent began to be heard: actors are conservative in their approach to their job. They felt they did not need the ministrations of a non-theatre man like Rich.

THE BENEFIT SYSTEM

It was at this juncture that Elizabeth Barry, the leading actress in the company, was granted a benefit, that is, she was granted a specific night when she would receive the whole evening's Box Office takings, with only a nominal amount deducted for the evening's running costs. The idea was very quickly seized on by the actors, who realised this could make a considerable difference to their incomes at a time when their salaries were in danger of being cut or perhaps not paid at all. Soon most of the leading players were receiving benefits, and the custom grew that they could choose the play for the evening, and cast it how they liked. Soon they would eagerly beset their friends, acquaintances and any other well-off patrons they were aware of to attend, to swell their receipts. A benefit could provide an actor with half their annual income. The 'distress benefit' to support particular persons who had fallen on hard times, or prisoners, or charitable institutions also became customary.

A STAGE QUARREL

Barry was a fiery and forceful personality, renowned not just for a somewhat promiscuous lifestyle but also for a dangerous quarrel with her fellow female star, Betty Boutell. Both wanted a particular veil from the costume store for the performance of Nathaniel Lee's *The Rival Queens*. It was awarded to Boutell. When they met for the climactic quarrel on stage, the incensed Barry stabbed her rival so ferociously with the blunted stage dagger that it penetrated a quarter of an inch into Boutell's flesh and the blood gushed forth.

THE DRURY LANE ACTING COMPANY

That was in the past. By 1692, with Thomas Betterton, she was heading the United Company, though its debts were sliding towards £1,000. Charles Killigrew, Drury Lane shareholder, attempted to remove the incompetent Alexander Davenant, but without success, and Davenant's gambling with the company's assets increased. Meanwhile, Betterton lost virtually his life savings when the India trading company of Sir Francis Watson, in which he had invested heavily, collapsed. His share in the acting company remained, but his dissatisfaction with Rich's management and Davenant's financial dealings, together with the loss of his savings, led him finally to dispose of his shares and return to receiving a salary. He had tried to rally the sharing actors, but without much success, and at least two died that year. One was Tony Leigh, the comic actor whose last triumph had probably been in Dryden's *Amphitryon*. His double act with James Nokes in this production had been conspicuously acclaimed: Leigh, as Mercury, assumed the shape and person of Sosnia, played by Nokes. In a scene reminiscent of the medieval *Jack Juggler*, Sosnia is gradually persuaded that Mercury actually is him – but then who is he? The implications are terrifying and hilarious simultaneously.

THE MURDER OF WILLIAM MOUNTFORD

Another death was that of William Mountford. Mountford, a good-looking young leading actor with a wide range and a sharpness and clarity about his work, was murdered after a performance of Lee's *The Rival Queens* in which he played Alexander opposite the beautiful Anne Bracegirdle's Statira. Bracegirdle had been besieged by a veteran of the Battle of the Boyne, one Captain Richard Hill. He offered her marriage, but she rejected him. Hill enlisted his friend Lord Mohun, a noted young swordsman, and a number of his fellow soldiers, and after spending the afternoon watching *The Rival Queens*, attempted to waylay and kidnap Bracegirdle on her way home. But the actress's screams, reinforced by those of her mother, who clung on to her daughter round the waist, were enough to drive off Hill and his confederates. Hill now suspected that Mountford, Bracegirdle's stage lover, was also her real lover, and he and Mohun decamped to where Mountford lived. They hung about in the street, waiting for Mountford's return, despite an attempt to get rid of them by Mountford's landlady. When finally he appeared at midnight, the two desperadoes intercepted him, there was an altercation and Hill drew his sword and stabbed Mountford. He and Mohun ran off, while Mountford was carried indoors to his pregnant wife by the actor George Powell. The theatre surgeon was sent for, but it was too late. Mountford died the next morning. Hill escaped abroad; Mohun was acquitted by the House of Lords.

THE ACTORS REBEL

While the acting company was devastated by these losses, Alexander Davenant's incompetence and dishonesty was reaching a peak and in October 1693 he fled to the Canary Islands with plenty of Drury Lane's reserves. The theatre faced an exceptionally serious crisis. Killigrew and Skipwith tried to persuade Betterton to resume the management, but he refused and Rich now took full control. Though he was very much a minority shareholder, Rich began to intervene at all levels of the theatre's operations, cutting the number of performances and trying to transfer the best parts from the established actors to younger – cheaper – players. Most of the actors rebelled, but Betterton, hardly happy himself, persuaded them to accept Rich's new conditions. In the autumn of 1694, however, less than a year after Rich had assumed control, the actors petitioned the Lord Chamberlain, the Earl of Dorset, with a long list of grievances. Not all the actors signed the petition: Joe Haines the comedian, John Verbruggen, a leading juvenile player, and the young Colley Cibber, ambitious but as yet still very junior, all held back. Rich and his shareholders counter-petitioned. The Lord Chamberlain chaired a meeting in December at which no agreement was reached.

Then, on 28 December 1694, Queen Mary died, and the theatres were commanded to shut until Easter 1695. Though there were attempts to reconcile the warring factions during this period without performances, it was too late. Betterton and his supporters had started to refurbish Sir William Davenant's old 1660 premises at Lisle's Tennis Court in Portugal Row, Lincoln's Inn Fields. They sweet-talked not only King William III, but also their old friend, the Earl of Dorset, now Lord Chamberlain, to grant them a licence to perform, so that when the theatres reopened in April 1695, there were again two theatre companies in London, Drury Lane, under Christopher Rich, and the New Theatre, Lincoln's Inn Fields, run by an actors' co-operative.

THE NEW THEATRE AT LINCOLN'S INN FIELDS

The leader of the co-operative was Thomas Betterton. He was supported by the two leading actresses, Elizabeth Barry and Anne Bracegirdle, as well as other actresses, Mary Betterton, Elizabeth Bowman, Betty Boutell, Eleanor Leigh, and male actors such as Edward Kynaston, Cave Underhill, William Bowen, Thomas Dogget, John Bowman and others. There were over twenty of them in the company at the 'New Theatre' (or 'Betterton's Booth' as it was sometimes slightly called). In the auditorium there were boxes on one side and across the back, with a sunken pit and a single gallery. The stage jutted out in front of the proscenium wall with its doors for actors' entries, and beyond this, marked off with a curtain, was a not-too extensive scenic stage. Colley Cibber's later remark, that it was 'small and poorly fitted up', need not be taken too literally – he was a member of the opposition, after all – but it probably contains some truth.

THE NEW COMPANY BEGINS ITS WORK

The actors started with their supporters' goodwill. The 'people of quality' had subscribed generously towards the new venture, especially after the 'importuning and dunning' they had received from the actors, contributing to the tune of twenty and sometimes forty guineas each. On the first night, the audience, which included the King, energetically clapped each actor who stepped onto the stage.

In the new dispensation, Betterton was to be paid £200 per year with four other men on salaries ranging from £100 to £200, while Barry was the best-paid woman at £100 per year. These were good salaries, especially in a company with no capital and, as a co-operative, no investors either. Betterton drew on his experience as a manager, and he was supported by his sharers, including four of the women, but the putative democratic organisation was probably never rigorous enough, especially in its financial oversight. The sharers were expected to attend rehearsals, read new plays, order costumes, oversee the wardrobe, the getting and storing of props, the management of painters, musicians, singers, doorkeepers and they also, of course, acted the main parts in every play presented. It was a huge burden.

The repertory was ambitious. The company opened with Congreve's new play, *Love for Love*, which was a smashing success, and the repertoire soon came to include *She Ventures and He Wins*, Manley's *The Royal Mischief*, Vanbrugh's *The Provoked Wife* and a series of plays by Mary Pix, including *Queen Catherine*, *The False Friend* and *The Beau Defeated*. Betterton was also able to indulge his enthusiasm for spectacle, including productions of Motteaux's opera *The Loves of Mars and Venus* with an orchestra of trumpets, kettle-drums, violins and hautboys, and later a musical version of *Measure for Measure*. This included 'a masque of the loves of Dido and Aeneas', though their connection with Shakespeare's Angelo and Isabella was never obvious. The end of Act Two was not untypical of the show: there was a great storm, a cave arose, witches appeared and there was a dance of six Furies, after which they sank through the stage, and the cave flew off into the sky. In fact, of course, though Congreve worked closely with the company, which probably helped his plays, the company depended on revivals of Shakespeare and other 'old' dramatists.

THOMAS BETTERTON

Thomas Betterton's performance as Hamlet has already been noticed. He actually played the part from 1661 until 1709, surely a record no other actor has matched; according to Pepys in 1668, it was 'the best part, I believe, that ever man acted'. At the moment pictured when the Ghost appeared in Gertrude's bedroom, Betterton's Hamlet actually appeared to go 'pale as his neckcloth', according to one witness, and Cibber described how

> he opened with a pause of mute amazement; then rising slowly to a solemn, trembling voice, he made the ghost equally terrible to the spectator as to himself; and in the descriptive part of the natural emotions which the ghastly vision gave him, the boldness of his expostulation was still governed by decency, manly, but not braving; his voice never rising into that seeming outrage, or wild defiance of what he naturally revered.[1]

Not all Betterton's audiences were so appreciative: Anthony Aston, for instance, suggested that 'when he threw himself at Ophelia's feet, he appeared a little too grave for a young student lately come from the University of Wittenberg'.[2]

Born in 1635, and making his Restoration debut with Rhodes's short-lived company, Betterton quickly transferred to Davenant's Duke's Men where he made an immediate impression, especially in Shakespeare, whose plays seemed, according to one contemporary, to have been made for him. He played Macbeth, King Lear, Othello, Henry VIII and Brutus with outstanding success, and the compassion with which he killed Desdemona, when 'he betrayed such a variety and vicissitude of passions as would admonish a man to be afraid of his own heart', was both agonising and pitiful.[3] Cibber indicated his range by noting both 'the fierce and flashing fire' of his Hotspur and the 'settled dignity' of his Brutus.[4] Yet he was not prepossessing physically. His legs were short, his feet large, and he neither danced nor sang. His voice was perhaps his strength: with it he 'enforced universal attention, even from the fops and orange girls',[5] and he preferred 'attentive silence' in the spectators to any applause.[6] He stayed at the top of his profession for over forty years, during which time he created over a hundred original roles. His method began with working dispassionately to understand the role, and only then to find its emotional heart. But then this emotional centre was presented in a totally controlled manner.

ELIZABETH BARRY

This was similar to his co-star, Elizabeth Barry's method. She was the daughter of a Cavalier who spent time in the Tower of London at the pleasure of Oliver Cromwell. She was brought up in Sir William Davenant's household, and learned not only from the Davenants, but also from John Wilmot, Earl of Rochester, and from Mary Betterton. Rochester, the greatest poet and the most notorious rake of the Restoration period, became her lover. From September 1675 to July 1676 he 'taught' her to act – though what he knew about acting is hard to discover, and his teaching seems to have consisted of making her repeat speeches parrot-fashion after him thirty or forty times, until he was satisfied. She may have learned more from Aphra Behn when she played Hellena in *The Rover*, the part which made her a star. She always thereafter tried to discuss her part with the author.

Her acting began with the face, passed to gesture or action and finally appeared as spoken words. Her speech was slightly drawled and she opened her mouth more on the right-hand side. But she had presence, dignity, even majesty, and no-one could wring pity from an audience more expertly than she. Though 'indifferently plump', she was equally good in roles requiring sexual ardour, such as Homais in *The Royal Mischief*. She was savagely satirised for this in *The Female Wits*, and at a time when actresses were becoming celebrities, it left her and her peccadilloes exposed to plenty of gossip and malicious wit. Yet she had what is probably the actor's most precious gift, the ability genuinely to listen to her partners on stage, and to adjust her playing to theirs. She tutored the young Princess – and future Queen – Anne in speaking, and by the time the co-operative was functioning she was formidable, assertive and well-off.

ANNE BRACEGIRDLE

Barry forged a significant partnership with Anne Bracegirdle: she was the strong, self-confident partner where Bracegirdle was the pert *ingénue*. Brought up by the childless Bettertons, Bracegirdle made her stage debut in 1680, aged nine. By 1688 she was a fully fledged member of the United Company, a youthful, witty comedienne, bubbling with vitality and sometimes eroticism. Perhaps her greatest creation was Millament in *The Way of the World*, when, according to Colley Cibber, 'all the faults, follies and affectation of that agreeable tyrant were venially melted down into so many charms and attractions of a conscious beauty'.[7] And when she sang, John Downes, the prompter, wrote, she 'caused the stones in the street to fly in men's faces'.[8] She had a long and passionate affair with Congreve, but she never married, though she, like Elizabeth Barry, was

Figure 4.7
Elizabeth Barry by Sir Godfrey Kneller
Source: Courtesy the Garrick Club, London

attacked in *The Female Wits* and in gossip and pamphlets. She retired in 1708 but lived a further forty years after that.

ACTORS IN THE CO-OPERATIVE

The co-operative had plenty of other fine actors. Edward Kynaston was still there, the former boy player of women's parts, now a handsome man in his fifties and – as was enviously observed – still with all his teeth. He too had the gift of acting 'in the moment', 'as if he had himself, that instant,

Figure 4.8
Anne Bracegirdle in *The Indian Queen*, 1695
Source: Courtesy the Garrick Club, London

conceived' his actions, as Colley Cibber recorded. Elizabeth Bowman was a strong, versatile actress, playing the second youthful leads, having only made her debut in 1692. The comic roles were initially entrusted to the temperamental Thomas Dogget, who however left the company after little more than a year, but who was clearly a brilliant performer.

STYLISATION AND NATURALISM

Yet the contradiction at the heart of the co-operative's achievement remained. Descended from the Restoration actors, these players were often studied in their performances, sometimes almost to the point of mannerism. They tended to regard a longish speech as like an aria in an opera, and they were encouraged by Charles Gildon to practice gesture and movement in front of a mirror.

The plays often demanded 'acting out' as when Brisk prepares to make his addresses to Lady Froth in *The Double Dealer*, or when in *The Provoked Wife* Rasor recalls for Madamoiselle the doings

Figure 4.9
King Lear, 1710. Note the use of gesture and movement and the contemporary costume.

in Spring Garden, thereby exciting himself sexually. Characters were often thought of as externally conceived types. One poet wrote:

> The frowning bully fills the tyrant's part:
> Swollen cheeks and sagging belly make a host,
> Pale meagre looks and hollow voice, a ghost;
> From careful brows and heavy downcast eyes,
> Dull cits and thick-skulled aldermen arise.[9]

Ladies of tragedy were submissive, chambermaids chattered. This conception of character could be justified by reference to the ideas of Thomas Hobbes, who thought of character as a kind of social mask, a matter of outward show. It led in performance to self-awareness and stylisation, as can be seen in Betterton's Hamlet: the schematic arrangement of the picture and the studied gestures may not exactly replicate what happened on stage, but they indicate the stylised nature of the production.

Encouragement for this approach can be found in many of the plays of the period. In Shadwell's *Bury Fair*, Tom stands 'jutting out his bum'. When Lord Foppington called for his enormous, over-fashionable periwig in Vanbrugh's *The Relapse*, two servants brought it on, heaving and sweating, in a sedan chair. In *The Old Bachelor*, Heartwell's feet refuse to obey him as he knows he should not linger outside Silvia's lodgings. And in the second scene of Trotter's *Agnes de Castro*, the Princess is discovered '*sitting in a melancholy posture*'. These are all theatricalised and conventionalised performative tropes.

CHARACTER

Just at this time, however, in France, Bernard Mandeville was asking: what if you remove the Hobbesian mask? What is underneath? And he suggested that what was underneath was egoism, a desire to impress, an urge towards power or domination and a selfish hunger for gratification. Greed, consumption, self-interest – these were actually everywhere in late seventeenth- and early eighteenth-century society, even when it may have been fashionable to preach moderation, or even abstinence. Most especially, Mandeville concluded that people tried to conceal their sexual proclivities and desires. Life was not what it seemed; in other words: it had what might be called a 'subtext'.

It was this subtext which some authors were able to access in their works. In some plays, for example, the author uses the aside to make the subtext clear, as Congreve does in *Love for Love* when Scandal explains Angelica's comment:

ANGELICA: If you speak truth, your endeavouring at wit is very unseasonable.
SCANDAL (*aside*): She's concerned, and loves him.

Vanbrugh, in *The Mistake*, uses the aside to explain Lopez's hidden intention to gull his master:

LOPEZ (*aside*): Are you thereabouts, i'faith? Then sharp's the word; egad I'll own the thing, and receive his bounty for't. – (*Aloud*) Why, sir – not that I pretend to make a merit o' the matter, for, alas! I am but your poor hireling, and therefore bound in duty to render you all the service I can; – but – 'tis I have done't.

Similarly, an approach which is aware of hidden desires is needed to capture Lady Bountiful's hypocrisy as well as her intellectual vitality in *The Provoked Wife*; and Friendall, in *The Wives Excuse*, needs more than a stylised approach if we are to understand him properly: he is a would-be rake, but he is also a weakling and a coward.

The actor's dilemma, naturalism or stylisation, was never clearly resolved at this time, but it may partially explain why several of the best writers of the 1690s, including Congreve, Vanbrugh, Trotter and Manley, virtually retired from stage writing. John Dennis tried to articulate the problem: 'when a good comedy does come to be writ, it can never be liked because it can never be acted'.[10] In other words, the actors lacked the capacity to combine the traditional stylisation of the Restoration with the naturalism the new writers' works demanded.

TWO COMPANIES AS RIVALS

Meanwhile, competition between the artistic co-operative and Rich's Drury Lane company was sharpening. Betterton and his fellows had been applauded on their first appearance, while their rivals at Drury Lane appeared in disarray. They were, according to one commentator, 'for the most part learners, boys and girls', which hardly did justice to a company which included George Powell, John Verbruggen, Colley Cibber, William Pinkethman and Joe Haines, as well as Frances Maria Knight, Jane Rogers and Susanna Mountford, soon to be Susanna Verbruggen. The latter, for example, was 'a fine, fair woman, plump and full-featured',[11] and Colley Cibber remembered her as vivacious, good at accents, and asserted that 'nothing, though ever so barren, if within the bounds of nature, could be flat in her hands'. But still, the company found the going hard.

As their rivalry hotted up, each group tried to spike the other's guns. For instance, they commissioned special Prologues and Epilogues, and produced plays which were intended to undercut or pre-empt the other house's productions. Drury Lane staged burlesques and introduced variety turns, such as singing or conjuring or rope dancing, between the acts of a play; Lincoln's Inn Fields moved towards double bills. Where Lincoln's Inn Fields relied on string players – John Eccles and John Lenten – for their music, Drury Lane used 'organists', Jeremiah Clarke, Daniel Purcell and John Blow. When John Verbruggen crossed swords with young Thomas Skipwith, he left Drury Lane to join Lincoln's Inn Fields; meanwhile the discontented Thomas Dogget was moving in the opposite direction.

Manley's *The Lost Lover* was a failure at Drury Lane. When the actors laughed at the apparently overwrought and melodramatic nature of her next play, *The Royal Mischief*, she withdrew it from that theatre, even though it was in rehearsal there, and handed it to Lincoln's Inn Fields. Drury Lane responded with the furious satire, *The Female Wits*, which ridiculed not just the female playwrights but also the actors. In it, Marsilia (Delariviere Manley) is seen directing Frances Maria Knight to imitate Anne Bracegirdle: 'Dear Mrs Knight, in this speech, stamp as Queen Statira does, that always gets a clap . . . run off, thus . . . now stamp, and hug yourself, Mrs Knight. Oh! The strong ecstasy!'

THE END OF THE RIVALRY

Vanbrugh's *The Relapse* was a success for Drury Lane, and so, comparatively, were Cibber's *Love's Last Shift* and Southerne's *Oroonoko*. But when they produced Powell's *The Imposture Defeated*, stolen from Pix's *The Deceiver Deceived*, Congreve led a party from Lincoln's Inn Fields which included Pix to try to hiss it down. However, Rich had a stronger financial base than his rivals, as well as much more scenery, costumes, and other stock, and in 1697 he remodelled Drury Lane, shortening the stage by four feet, and increasing the number of boxes, as well as the space in the pit. He believed his theatre would triumph.

The novelty was gradually wearing off the Lincoln's Inn Fields venture. Dryden suggested it was becoming 'like ancient Rome, majestic in decay'. The actors were getting older, some were tired of managing as well as acting, and discipline in rehearsals was becoming lax. Though audiences at both theatres were falling off, Drury Lane was now the more profitable. At Lincoln's Inn Fields, Betterton sighed for Davenant's day. It was noticed that the small part players on stage would whisper together during a scene, or signal to their friends in the audience. The actors were becoming 'insolent' to the play.

In 1700, the Lord Chamberlain, Lord Jersey, dissolved the co-operative and appointed Thomas Betterton sole Manager of the company.

NOTES

1 Colley Cibber, *An Apology for His Life*, London: J.M. Dent, 1938, p. 57.
2 Anthony Aston, *A Brief Supplement to Colley Cibber, Esq.; His Lives of the Late Famous Actors and Actresses*, 1748, in A.M. Nagler, *A Source Book in Theatrical History*, New York: Dover Publications, 1952, p. 216.
3 Richard Steele, *The Tatler*, 4 May 1710.
4 Colley Cibber, *op.cit.*, p. 59.
5 Anthony Aston, *op.cit.*, p. 217.
6 Colley Cibber, *op.cit.*, p. 62.
7 *Ibid.*, p. 92.
8 John Downes, *Roscius Anglicanus*, 1708.
9 'A Description of the Playhouse in Dorset Garden', sometimes attributed to Joseph Addison.
10 John Dennis, *The Comical Gallant*, Preface, 1702.
11 Anthony Aston, *op.cit.*

Chapter 44: Immorality and profaneness

JEREMY COLLIER'S *SHORT VIEW*

One reason for the theatre's loss of some of its best writers at the end of the 1690s was the bombshell lobbed in 1698 by Rev Jeremy Collier: a long pamphlet entitled *A Short View of the Immorality and Profaneness of the English Stage*.

Collier was a 'non-juror', that is, having sworn an oath of allegiance to James II, he refused to take a new oath to William and Mary. Consequently, he lost his living, and indeed when he refused to be silent about his opposition to the Glorious Revolution, he was gaoled. It was as an outlaw in 1696 that on the scaffold at Tyburn, he blessed two conspirators who had plotted to assassinate King William in 1696, and he continued to argue that England needed saving and that this would only happen through the restoration of the authority of the monarchy and the church. His *Short View* was thus part of a larger campaign, embarked on because he was 'convinced that nothing has gone farther in debauching the age than the stage poets and the playhouse'.

Collier begins with the brash assertion: 'The business of plays is to recommend virtue, and discountenance vice'. He argues that virtue arises from authority, in particular the authority of the Bible, a view strongly at odds with the age's apparent levelling tendencies: it was the descendants of the Levellers, the Whigs, who had deposed James II and installed William and Mary on the throne. Collier saw the contemporary stage practice as part of this levelling tendency: he believed that the theatre should be governed by the moral structure and authority of the godly state, and not answer to the Whiggish moral compromise of secular and pragmatic forms. The *Short View* is thus a covert attack on the legitimacy of William III's crown.

It was exemplified by Collier in the stage's 'smuttiness of expression . . . swearing (and) profaneness', and was especially to be rejected when 'poets make women speak smuttily'. He argued that *Hamlet* would be a better play if Shakespeare had allowed Ophelia to keep her modesty when mad, and attacked the treatment of women in Otway's *The Orphan* and Dryden's *The Spanish Friar* as well as *Don Quixote* by Thomas D'Urfey, *The Relapse* by Vanbrugh and Congreve's *Love for Love*. There is misogyny in what Collier writes: looking at bodies on the stage, the carnal gaze, unnerves him, and never more so than when he thinks of women spectators watching other women's sexual behaviour. 'The smut and scum of thought rise uppermost', he insists.

Collier believed that 'it was upon account of these disorders that Plato banished poets his commonwealth', and he urged poets to aim platonically for ideal truth rather than historical truth. He wished to apply Rymer's view of tragedy to all drama, and having defined the theatre's aims to his

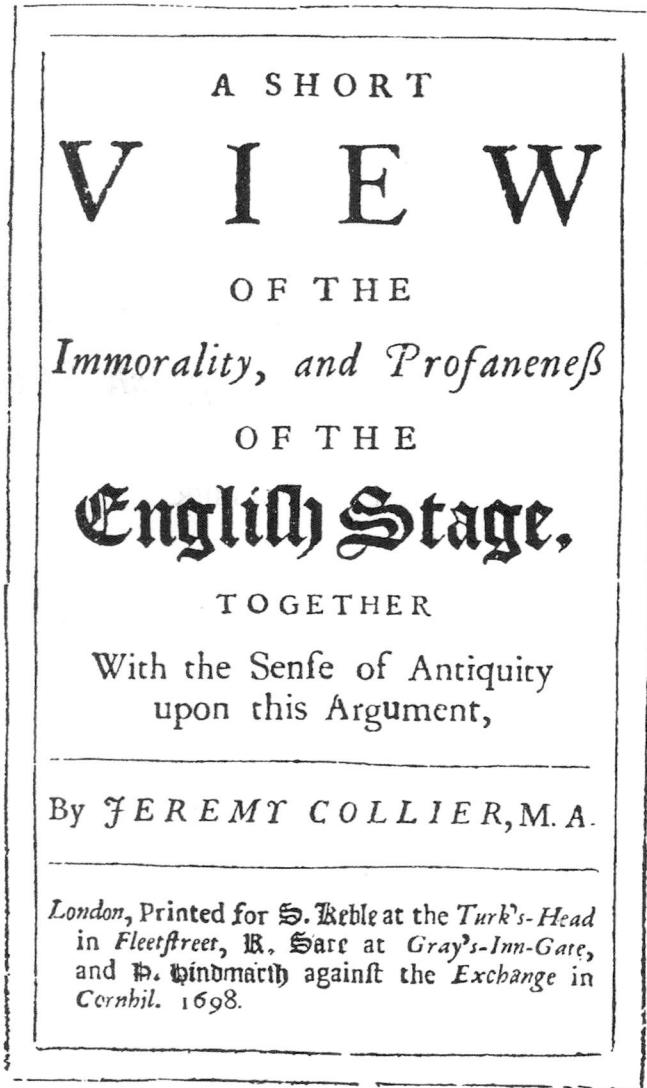

A SHORT

VIEW

OF THE

Immorality, and Profaneß

OF THE

English Stage,

TOGETHER

With the Senſe of Antiquity
upon this Argument,

By *JEREMY COLLIER*, M.A.

London, Printed for S. Keble at the *Turk's-Head*
in *Fleetſtreet*, R. Sare at *Gray's-Inn-Gate*,
and H. Hindmarth againſt the *Exchange* in
Cornhil. 1698.

Figure 4.10
Title page of Jeremy Collier's *A Short View of the Immorality and Profaneness of the English Stage*, 1698

own satisfaction, he then berated those playwrights who fulfilled their own aims rather than his. He further objected to disrespect for the clergy: he attacked Congreve's *The Old Bachelor* because 'almost all the characters are foul and nauseous',[1] and because of the four women in the cast list, three were whores; but perhaps his real discomfort stems from the fact that in the play Bellmour dresses up as a Puritan to seduce Laetitia; and he vociferously objected to Rake's 'drunken atheistical catch' at the end of Act 3 of *The Provoked Wife* when his real objection was probably to the fact that Vanbrugh had Sir John Brute disguise himself by dressing as a priest.

WIDER OPPOSITION TO THE THEATRE

Collier, despite his extensive knowledge of contemporary plays, in truth opposed the theatre as such. He saw its function not as entertainment or as a way of releasing the imagination, but as part of society's structure for regulating behaviour and morality. In this, he asserted, it had failed. And Collier was not alone. As far back as 1693, *The Athenian Mercury* argued that 'the two worst things in our modern plays' were 'their swearing and cursing and their contempt of sacred orders'. The anonymous *A Reflection of our Modern Poesy* argued in 1695

> What place so much debauched as is our stage
> Which next the pulpit should correct the age?
>
> . . .
>
> In our theatres we daily see
> Vice triumph o'er dejected honesty.

And Richard Willis, in an *Occasional Paper*, writes of the 'many gross immoralities and particularly lasciviousness and profaneness' in 'our plays, especially our modern ones'.

SOCIETY FOR THE REFORMATION OF MANNERS

Equally dangerous for the theatre was the foundation in 1691, with the backing of Queen Mary, of the Society for the Reformation of Manners. Part of a trend away from sacramental religion, and towards a more general emphasis on moral precepts, this organisation, based in the Strand, was a haven for Nosey Parkers who wanted to stamp on anything they disapproved of. In 1697, at the end of one phase of his war with France, William III found supporting this society a convenient way to deflect attention from his decision not to reduce taxation. As the Society grew with his backing, he even declared his support for Jeremy Collier, who was thus able to emerge from hiding.

VANBRUGH'S REPLY TO COLLIER

Vanbrugh and Congreve, the playwrights most under attack, hit back. Vanbrugh published *A Short Vindication of* The Relapse *and* The Provoked Wife *from Immorality and Profaneness, by the Author*, but his case was flawed by contradiction. He accepted that 'the business of comedy is to show people what they should do', and this involved, he argued, showing reality – if his play were to 'make their (his characters') faces too fair, they (the public) won't know they are dirty, and by consequence will neglect to wash 'em'. The argument is fair enough as far as it goes: because people swear, in his play he shows characters swearing. But his defence of his presentation of Sir John Brute was quite different. This character, he stated, was 'a visible burlesque', that is, *not* a true representation.[2] The contradiction seems to leave his defence considerably weakened.

CONGREVE'S REPLY TO COLLIER

Congreve's defence in his *Amendments of Mr Collier's False and Imperfect Citations* also lacked some intellectual rigour. He suggested that by picking out licentious and lewd moments from larger plays, Collier had demonstrated only 'his own impurity', and those moments he had objected to 'were sweet enough till tainted by his breath'. It was hardly convincing, but the dispute was actually irresolvable: Collier was a moral absolutist, with Plato and the Bible at his back; Congreve and Vanbrugh were moral relativists, relying on Aristotle and empirical reason. Collier's attack was weakened because he failed to recognise any difference between reality and theatre, but both sides agreed on the moral base of artistic production, and also that the theatre needed to be regulated. The question was, how? George Farquhar concluded sourly in *The Adventures of Covent Garden* that 'Mr Collier showed too much malice and rancour for a churchman, and his adversaries too little wit for the character of poets'. Farquhar's plays, however, betrayed more clearly which side he was on. In *The Constant Couple* he urged the 'reformer of the times' to be 'less severe in your censures, less rigid in your precepts and more strict in your example', while in the Preface to *The Twin Rival* she called Collier an 'enemy' of the theatre, who designed to 'take away its life'. Colley Cibber responded in *The Careless Husband* a few years later:

LORD MORELOVE: Plays now, indeed, one need not be so much afraid of, for since the late short-sighted view of 'em, vice may go on and prosper; the stage dares hardly show a vicious person speaking like himself for fear of being called profane for exposing him.
LADY EASY: 'Tis hard indeed, when people won't distinguish between what's meant for contempt and what for example.

THE BATTLE CONTINUES

The battle raged for the next decade and saw forty or more pamphlets published including two defences of his work by Collier himself. The general tone of the arguments rarely rose much above that of William Bissett's in *Plain English*, published in 1704, which denounced the London theatres as 'those two famous academies of hell, those nurseries of all vice, those incorrigible brothels . . . where Satan's seat is, where he keeps his headquarters'. The most convincing argument against Collier was put forward by John Dennis in *The Usefulness of the Stage* in which he linked Collier's high church Jacobitism with the old Puritans, endorsed the stage's use of wit and depiction of life and the passions and contradicted Collier's view that satire was morally destructive, claiming rather that it was morally instructive. Whereas for Collier *The Double Dealer* encouraged vice, for Dennis it castigated hypocrisy.

THE FUNCTION OF THEATRE

A series of books also sought to question the aim and function of the theatre, and to analyse its essence. James Drake's *The Ancient and Modern Stages Survey'd* and James Wright's *Historia Histrionica, An Historical Account of the English Stage*, were both published in 1699. Wright's book, like Dryden's *Essay of Dramatic Poesy*, is cast as a dialogue, in which Truman, an old playgoer from the Restoration period, argues with Lovewit, a contemporary critic, that the old idea of drama as ritual, as a way of marking socially significant happenings as mystery plays, processional pageants and so on did, had been debased by the entertainments of the two theatres with Royal Patents. It was a view which chimed with Collier's.

THE AUDIENCE

The contrary argument was that theatre had to move with the times, and produce what its audiences wanted. This was not always clear, however. There is some evidence that theatre attendances were declining in the late seventeenth century. Though this was probably true as compared with the beginning of the century, it may not hold for the period from 1682. From 1695 two theatres were operating, though both were on a financial knife edge and both needed more than courtiers and well-heeled aristocrats to survive. They therefore sought a more middle-class clientele, while trying, not always successfully, to protect their aristocratic patrons by the class divisions strictly retained in the configuration of the auditorium. The auditoria in both theatres illustrated the typical divisions of bourgeois society: often gallants still sat on stage; in the boxes were aristocrats and their ladies; the pit housed the gentry, professional people and the intelligentsia; in the first gallery were citizens, business figures, tradespeople and their wives; and in the upper gallery sat servants and common people.

THE AUDITORIUM

The custom of gallants sitting on the stage was gradually dying out, to the relief of most, though actors were known to encourage it on their benefit nights. The boxes remained the property of the upper classes, though mostly women. Vanbrugh's Lady Brute was perhaps typical. She loved

> to sit in the forefront of a box, for if one sits behind there's two acts gone perhaps before one's found out. And when I am there, if I perceive the men whispering and looking upon me, you must know I cannot for my life forbear thinking they talk to my advantage. . . . I watch with impatience for the next jest in the play, that I may laugh and show my white teeth.

Cibber's Sir Novelty Fashion, one of the few men who sat in a box, also liked to be watched by the rest of the audience.

The pit contained more men, including occasional aristocratic youths. Henri Misson, a French visitor, captured something of the sociability of the pit at Drury Lane in 1698. It was, he wrote,

> filled with benches without backboards, and adorned and covered with green cloth. Men of quality, particularly the younger sort, some ladies of reputation and virtue, and abundance of damsels that hunt for prey sit all together in this place, higgledy-piggledy, chatter, toy, play, hear, hear not.[3]

One account from 1699 probably exaggerates the liveliness of the pit, but contains an element of truth. A 'drunken lord' enters with his followers. They start to quarrel 'and put the whole house into a hurly-burly':

> then you'll see fine work indeed; the whores tumbling over the seats, and the poor squires and beaus tumbling after 'em in a horrible fright and disorder; the whole pit's in arms in a minute, and every man's sword drawn to defend himself.[4]

This is partially contradicted by the journalist Tom Brown, who in 1710 wrote of the playhouse as 'an enchanted island . . . frequented by persons of all degrees and qualities whatsoever'. In the pit he saw a fashionable young man who dare not

> stir his head, nor move his body, for fear of incommoding his wig, ruffling his cravat, or putting his eyes or mouth out of the order his maitre de dance set it in, whilst a bully beau comes drunk into the pit, screaming out, 'Damn me, Jack, 'tis a confounded play, let's to a whore and spend our time better'. Here the ladies come to show their clothes which are often the only things to be admired in or about 'em.[5]

The first gallery contained 'citizens', probably the descendants of the Puritans who had supported the overthrow of James II and who were now potential Whigs. The upper gallery was the place for the lower classes whose behaviour, like that of the pittites, was not always seemly. At Drury Lane in December 1700 a group of 'French Scaramouche dancers', performing between the acts of the main play, were forced off the stage when spectators in the upper gallery started hurling oranges and other missiles at them.

AUDIENCE FACTIONS

The audience was also often infiltrated by factions, determined either to support the play or 'hiss it off'. Thus, in one part of the audience 'sit the poet's friends, which are resolved to carry him off, right or wrong', and in another part of the house, the opposing faction, 'straddling upon the seats, hollowing, clapping and flouncing, making an impertinent clatter and noise, and using many insolent and indecent actions'.[6] George Granville in *The She Gallants*, produced at Lincoln's Inn Fields in 1695, records a group of enemies of a play spreading out all over the auditorium, 'some in the pit, some in the boxes, others in the galleries but principally on the stage', disrupting the performance as they 'cough, sneeze, talk loud, and break silly jests, sometimes laughing, sometimes singing, sometimes whistling, till the house is in an uproar'. William Congreve himself led a claque to Drury Lane in 1697 to hiss down George Powell's *The Imposture Defeated* which he had plagiarised from Mary Pix, while some years later the actress Jane Rogers, incensed that Anne Oldfield had been preferred for a leading part, led her friends Richard Steele, Henry Brett, Jonathan Swift, Alexander Pope and others to the theatre on the first night where they caused such a rumpus that the guards had to be called.

WOMEN IN THE AUDIENCE

It is noticeable that these audiences included a large number of women. Beaumont in Pix's *The Innocent Mistress* avers that 'plays and romances' are 'the seducers of women'. Women even formed their own claques sometimes, as when one such group tried to shout down *The Double Dealer* in 1693 for its bawdiness. Many women disguised themselves at the theatre by using a vizard mask, usually made of black velvet and covering the whole face, partly simply to be private, partly to hide their responses, particularly to bawdy plays, partly also for the adventure of anonymity. Vizards then became a useful accessory for the prostitutes who worked the theatres.

PROSECUTIONS

Inspired by Collier's diatribes, the reformers now set out to destabilise the theatre and its audiences. In 1697 the Lord Chamberlain had demanded that the Master of the Revels be much more vigilant in censuring immorality in plays, and in February 1698, just before Collier's *Short View* was published, the House of Commons had moved to suppress 'immorality and profaneness' on the stage. Now Collier's supporters took courage to prosecute the published text of Congreve's *The Double Dealer*, compelling the author to make alterations to it. The king, too, made clear his disapproval of actors speaking profanities, and the Grand Jury of Middlesex, perhaps emboldened by this, demanded that *The Double Dealer* and D'Urfey's *Don Quixote* be banned. When Congreve's play was presented again, it was in an expurgated version.

Informers began to visit theatres, sometimes flourishing notebooks ostentatiously, ready to take down any oaths spoken or blasphemies uttered with a view to later prosecution. The theatres, of course, noticed:

> Now sour reformers in an empty pit,
> With table books, as at a lecture, sit,
> To take notes, and give evidence 'gainst wit.[7]

Note that the pit was 'empty' here. Spectators were being driven away. In 1700 Betterton, Barry, Bracegirdle and others were found guilty at the Court of the King's Bench for speaking 'the most abominable, impious, profane, lewd and immoral expressions contained in the plays acted by them'.[8] They were fined £5 each and bound over not to repeat the offence. The plays cited were *Love for Love*, Edward Ravenscroft's *The Anatomist* and *The Provoked Wife*. It might be added that the Drury Lane actors were found not guilty of the same offence after performances of *Volpone* and *Sir Courtly Nice*. In November that year, John Hodgson, actor, was also fined for profanity on the stage. In 1704, however, Queen Anne was constrained to accept that actors could not be prosecuted for speaking lines from any play passed by the Master of the Revels.

By 1699 there were nine separate societies for the reform of manners, and that number was doubled by 1701. Prostitutes and vizards were, as may be imagined, a particular target for these people. Consequently in 1698, the Grand Jury of Middlesex tried to ban vizards at plays; in 1700 the Lord Chamberlain also tried; and in 1704 no less a person than Queen Anne added her voice to the clamour for a ban on vizards. All failed, and women continued to mask their faces as and when they wanted to.

A LASTING CAMPAIGN AGAINST THE THEATRE

But the negativity unleashed by Collier took years to spend itself. Something of it can still be heard in 1726 in the fiery Nonconformist preacher, William Law's denunciation – 'a player cannot be a living member of Christ' – in his *The Absolute Unlawfulness of the Stage Entertainment Fully Demonstrated*,[9] and perhaps even distantly fifty years after that in Francis Burney's novel, *Evelina*. When the eponymous heroine attends a performance of *Love for Love* at Drury Lane, she reflects that 'though it is fraught with wit and entertainment, I hope I shall never see it represented again; for it is so extremely indelicate'.[10]

Was this then Collier's victory? It is true that Congreve, Vanbrugh, Trotter and Manley hardly wrote anything more for the stage. Trotter indeed became a supporter of Collier. But when Congreve staged *The Judgment of Paris* at Dorset Garden in 1702, the audience was treated not merely to a classical beauty contest, but to each of the contestants appearing nude in a highly erotic show. And in 1704, Congreve and Vanbrugh together opened the new Queen's Theatre in Haymarket. They did not write new plays for it, though, and for the next two decades English drama was marked by a retreat from the positions of the 1690s, and by reticence and tranquillity.

NOTES

1 All quotations from Jeremy Collier, *A Short View of the Immorality and Profaneness of the English Stage, Together with the Sense of Antiquity upon this Argument*, 1698.
2 All quotations from John Vanbrugh, *A Short Vindication of the Relapse and the Provok'd Wife, from Immorality and Profaneness*, 1698.
3 Henri Misson, *Misson's Memoirs and Observations in His Travels over England*, 1719, in A.M. Nagler, *A Source Book of Theatrical History*, New York: Dover Publications, 1952, p. 208.
4 A.M. Nagler, *A Source Book of Theatrical History*, New York: Dover Publications, 1952, pp. 235–236.
5 *Ibid.*, p. 247.
6 *Ibid.*, p. 235.
7 Nicholas Rowe, *Tamerlane*, Epilogue.
8 Jane Milling, 'Abominable, Impious, Prophane, Lewd, Immoral; Prosecuting the Actors in Early Eighteenth Century London', *Theatre Notebook*, 61 (3) (2007), pp. 136–137.
9 Roy Porter, *Enlightenment*, London: Penguin, 2000, p. 97.
10 Frances Burney, *Evalina*, vol 1, Letter XX.

Chapter 45: London theatre in the reign of Queen Anne

QUEEN ANNE'S REIGN

Queen Anne was surely one of the least charismatic of England's monarchs, yet her reign was in several ways tumultuous. Her kingdom was at war almost all the time, and the theatre too went through upheavals and strife.

Anne inherited William III's wars with France, now Europe-wide and called the War of Spanish Succession after the death of the old king of Spain in 1700. John Churchill, Duke of Marlborough and husband of Anne's dearest friend, led the British Army to famous victories at Blenheim in 1704 and Ramillies in 1706, but they did not end the war. Taxes rose, press gangs operated and trading patterns were dislocated. Anne meanwhile supported the Church of England and believed in decency and good manners. She had little interest in the theatre. Politically she supported the Tories, but she was supposedly 'above Party' (Marlborough was a Whig), and she was the last monarch to preside over the cabinet. When her favourite Tories were installed in government in 1710, she accepted Marlborough's dismissal as Commander-in-Chief with little demur. Almost the last act of her reign was the Peace of Utrecht, which ended the war at least for a time, and brought England the beginnings of an empire, mostly in the Americas, and a monopoly of the slave trade – two outcomes which would influence much of the later eighteenth century.

UPHEAVALS AND STRIFE

As for the theatre, perhaps Christopher Rich at Drury Lane sensed victory in 1700 when his rivals, the Actors Co-operative at Lincoln's Inn Fields, lost some of the Lord Chamberlain's favour and became a more conventional company. He increased the capacity of his theatre by reducing the forestage, extending the pit and installing more boxes.

Rich at this time seems to have controlled both the Royal Patents, which had been amalgamated on the foundation of the United Company in 1682. But the Patents were losing traction as shares in them were traded as commodities, and there were increasing questions about what exactly they referred to. Did they cover 'illegitimate' acts, variety turns, dance or song? Both companies came to rely increasingly on these extra turns in their presentations to attract wider audiences.

Lincoln's Inn Fields still attempted to offer a more sophisticated programme to appeal to its Kit Kat Club and other intellectual patrons. But the company, lacking sufficient capital, were struggling. John Verbruggen, one of the company's most reliable actors, complained that Betterton, Barry and

Bracegirdle were paying themselves too much, at the expense of the rest of the company. There were even whispers of Betterton embezzling funds, though it seems probable that he was more extravagant than dishonest. Some actors, like William Pinkethman and Thomas Dogget, resorted to working in the London fairgrounds to supplement their official earnings. In 1703, Pinkethman even leased Dorset Garden for a season of popular plays, including *The Cheats of Scapin*, *The Comical Rivals* and *The Humours of Harlequin*, together with rope dancing, vaulting, dances and more, and later opened a theatre in Richmond, Surrey.

Betterton proposed a new United Company, and when this was not accepted he offered to lease Drury Lane at a higher rent than Rich was paying. Since Rich in any case frequently defaulted on the rent, Charles Killigrew and some of the other Drury Lane Theatre's shareholders made clear they were minded to accept Betterton's offer. But they reckoned without the litigious and ruthless Rich. Claim and counter-claim flew through the courts, Rich paid off some of the rent due, mollified some shareholders and hung onto his theatre. As his biographer notes, 'an impartial observer has to admire Rich's legal skills and business acumen, while continuing to question his ethics'.[1] In September 1703 Rich, while still contriving to cut some of his employees' wages and delay paying others, negotiated a new lease for Drury Lane.

ARSINOE

Meanwhile the playwright-architect, Sir John Vanbrugh, in close contact with Betterton, proposed to build a new theatre in the Haymarket. In answer to this challenge to Rich strengthened his company, luring Dogget and Powell back from Lincoln's Inn Fields, and giving new contracts to the Irish comic actor, Richard Estcourt, and the attractive singer and actress, Letitia Cross.

In January 1705 he attempted to pre-empt the glory that was promised by Vanbrugh's new Queen's Theatre by mounting his own spectacular opera, *Arsinoe*, with libretto by Pierre Motteaux and music by Thomas Clayton. This has often been regarded as the first proper opera in English since it adopted *recitative* from Italian opera rather than spoken interludes.

The stage designs for *Arsinoe* by Sir James Thornhill have survived. They give a good impression of theatrical scenery at the start of the eighteenth century. The first scene, for example, a garden by moonlight, shows a backdrop painted on a pair of shutters, depicting a fountain playing in the garden of a country mansion with mountains beyond. The side scenes, or wings, are quite heavily decorated with foliage and trees, and Arsinoe is seen sleeping on a sort of *chaise-longue*. The moonlight effect might have been created by special coloured glass placed over the wing candles and footlights.

Rich used his connections with the upper classes to obtain financial backing for this production, and the subscribers must have been gratified by its success. It was performed fourteen times in the following months.

VANBRUGH'S QUEEN'S THEATRE IN THE HAYMARKET

The new Queen's Theatre was designed to be magnificent. Seating nearly a thousand spectators and lavishly decorated and appointed, it had a deep scenic stage to allow for grandiose spectacle, a shallow forestage and an orchestra pit. With gilded cornices and sturdy columns, its high ceiling carried a fantastic painting of Queen Anne surrounded by the Muses floating in the cosmos. Unfortunately,

Figure 4.11
Arsinoe, 1705: Sir James Thornhill's sketch for the moonlit garden
Source: Victoria and Albert Museum, London

this ceiling caused severe problems with the theatre's acoustics, which greatly reduced the appeal of its productions for a considerable time.

In November 1704, even though it was still unfinished, the theatre opened with an impressive concert attended by Queen Anne herself. Her interest may have been slight, but her presence at this opening still outraged the followers of Jeremy Collier and the Society for the Reformation of Manners. Nevertheless, her attendance endorsed London fashionable society's approbation. Many of them had subscribed to its establishment at the rate of £100 per subscriber, which enabled them to attend all future productions free. But besides the poor acoustics, the location in the Haymarket turned out to be too far to the west for the comfort of Vanbrugh's target audience, the aristocracy and the intelligentsia.

The first production, the Italian opera, *The Loves of Ergasto* by Jakob Greber, opened in April 1705. It was not a success. For the following season, Vanbrugh reverted to straight drama productions. He brought in Betterton's Lincoln's Inn Fields company, Betterton, now seventy years old, handing over the management to Vanbrugh in a move of dubious legality. But Vanbrugh acquired a new licence from the queen, brought Congreve into the management and opened a season which consisted largely of revivals, with two new plays by Mary Pix. But the programme failed to draw audiences, and the venture was soon in financial difficulties. Congreve left, while Vanbrugh, having been awarded the contract to build Blenheim Palace for the Duke of Marlborough, handed the management over to Owen Swiney, Christopher Rich's associate.

CHRISTOPHER RICH IS BANNED

There were again moves in 1706 to unite the two companies, but the actors – and Christopher Rich himself – objected. Swiney and Rich quarrelled. Most of the Drury Lane actors, including Colley Cibber, probably their leader, moved to the new Queen's Theatre, leaving Rich with virtually no performers. He hired a group of opera singers, but by the autumn of 1707 the singers too were in revolt against his high-handed and pettifogging ways.

In December the Earl of Kent, the Lord Chamberlain, ordered the union of the two companies (which some wags compared to the forcible union of Scotland with England): Drury Lane was to concentrate on drama and the Queen's on opera. The actors once again came under Christopher Rich. And once again his oppressive treatment provoked a petition to the Lord Chamberlain. At last the Earl of Kent took drastic action. He used the fact that Rich, against his specific orders, had deducted more than the agreed amount from the actors' benefits, to close Drury Lane, and ban Christopher Rich from exercising any Royal Patent he might control. Rich expected the order to be rescinded, but it was not. Finally, after some months, Rich removed virtually the whole stock of Drury Lane's costumes, props and other moveables, and decamped to Lincoln's Inn Fields, whose lease he had also managed to obtain. But he was still banned from producing plays. He started on a large-scale rebuilding of Lincoln's Inn Fields, but the prohibition remained in force, and he was unable to open it for performances.

WILLIAM COLLIER AT DRURY LANE

William Collier MP now obtained the lease on Drury Lane Theatre. Installing Aaron Hill as manager, he opened the theatre with a company made up of the remnants of Rich's troupe. But this arrangement, too, soon became embroiled in squabbles and internecine troubles. Hill left Drury Lane in June 1710. Collier then engineered a take over of the Queen's Theatre, ousting Swiney who returned to Drury Lane while Hill became manager of the Queen's. Now it was Collier's turn to recognise his own limitations, and in 1711 he sublet Drury Lane to three actor-sharers, Robert Wilks, Thomas Dogget and Colley Cibber. They were to concentrate on drama, while Queens' would focus on opera. It was this disposition, with some modifications, that was to end the fevered contentions for control of the theatre during the reign of Queen Anne.

THE END OF AN ERA

By 1700, the star actors were ageing and stepping back from the stage. After 1705 Thomas Betterton was no longer the force he had been, and in 1707 Anne Bracegirdle retired, though she lived on in retirement for more than thirty years. That summer John Verbruggen left the company in ill health and died in 1708. Elizabeth Barry retired in 1709 and died in 1713. Betterton himself died in 1710. Farquhar, too, had died in 1707 and Vanbrugh, Southerne and Congreve were all virtually silent, though Vanbrugh lived till 1726, Congreve till 1729 and Southerne survived till 1746.

Of their younger contemporaries, George Powell died in 1714, the year in which Thomas Dogget retired. Dogget was a small Irishman, a passionate Whig, who was known mostly for comic, low-life characters, such as Ben in *Love for Love* and Fondlewife in *The Old Bachelor*, as well as a comic Shylock in *The Merchant of Venice*. His singing and dancing meant that he was always in demand, despite being somewhat temperamental. He retired to Kent, and in 1715 he founded what is now the oldest rowing race in the world, Dogget's Coat and Badge, and died in 1721.

George Powell had managed rehearsals and chosen the plays for Rich's Drury Lane from 1695. Two years earlier he had been stabbed on stage by his fellow actor, Samuel Sandford, when the latter picked up the 'wrong' dagger for their scene. He had charisma as an actor, but he was erratic, and his love of strong drink spoiled his work. According to Anthony Aston, when he played Alexander, 'he maintained not the dignity of a king, but out-Heroded Herod, and in his poisoned mad scene, out-raved all probability'.[2]

Figure 4.12
Thomas Dogget dancing: Dogget became a star in the fairground theatres and an actor-sharer at Drury Lane

A NEW GENERATION

The repertory system had kept younger actors back, for theatrical custom was that once an actor had been cast in a role, they would retain it till they either voluntarily relinquished it, retired or died, which is how Betterton managed to continue playing Hamlet into his old age. Young actors had had to wait for good parts to fall vacant.

But customs and acting styles were evolving. *The Spectator* argued that character in man was visible, and that it showed in a person's demeanour and deportment, their clothes and their attitude. This emphasis on outward qualities led to a tragic style which tended to be mannered, the emotion often seeming vehement but studied. What we would recognise as emotional truth was rarely to the fore. Indeed, realism of that order was in no way demanded of the actor, and if we find it extraordinary that Anne Oldfield could play Marina, the virgin daughter of Cato, when nine months pregnant, the eighteenth-century spectator did not. Audiences then looked for a different kind of truth. The artificial quality of tragic acting manifested itself in comedy as poise, wit and ease, qualities which made their performance amusing and becoming.

YOUNGER ACTORS

The best exponents of the new style included Robert Wilks, an elegant, flamboyantly actorish Irishman who took over William Mountford's parts after the latter's murder. Handsome and vivacious, he had, according to Colley Cibber, 'sometimes too violent a vivacity'.[3] Joseph Addison thought his Hamlet seemed more angry than frightened when his father's Ghost appeared. He could be awkward, too. At a rehearsal for Centlivre's *The Busy Body* he threw his script into the pit, exclaiming that 'nobody could bear to sit to hear such stuff' and it was 'a silly thing wrote by a woman'.[4]

William Pinkethman was a comic actor noted for his irrepressible *ad-libbing* and playing to the gallery, which perhaps suited his Harlequin if not every part he played. Collie Cibber, playwright and Whig, despite a poor voice, stiff movement and a scrawny figure (at least when he was young), successfully created a group of amusing grotesques, though when he played his own Richard III, one observer wrote that he 'screamed through four acts without dignity or decency', so that at the end the audience 'were not better pleased that so execrable tyrant was destroyed than that so execrable an actor was silent'.[5] Aaron Hill compared the performance to 'the distorted heavings of an unjoined caterpillar'.[6] Somewhat younger was the dignified Barton Booth, a pupil of Betterton, whose Oroonoko was a noble savage. His masterpiece, according to Cibber, was Othello, in which he was 'torn and tortured by the most distracting passion that can raise terror or compassion in the spectator'.[7] When he played Hamlet's father's Ghost, he wore cloth shoes so that he would not be heard as he approached the stage.

ANNE OLDFIELD

Among the women, Hester Santlow, a dancer as well as an actor, who married Barton Booth, Jane Rogers, the original Anne in Cibber's *Richard III* and Isabinda in *The Busy Body*, who became Wilks's partner, and Mary Porter, a fiery figure renowned for her tragic impetuosity, were all impressive. But the greatest star was Anne Oldfield. Vanbrugh gave her first part, but it was not until she played Leonora in *Sir Courtley Nice* in 1703 that her talent was properly recognised and not until

Figure 4.13
Portrait of Anne Oldfield by an unknown artist
Source: Art Collection 3/Alamy Stock Photo

she created Lady Betty Modish in *The Careless Husband* the following year that it was clear that here was a major theatrical force. Tall, with large expressive eyes which she fluttered to devastating effect, she was renowned for the sexy way she would toss her head. William Chetwood described his reaction to her performance as Calista in Rowe's *The Fair Penitent*: 'Her excellent clear voice of passion, her piercing flaming eye, with manner and action suiting, used to make me shrink with awe'.[8] Anne Bracegirdle, noting the new star, tactfully retired though she was only thirty-six.

Anne Oldfield was also a significant person in her own right. She was the prominent Whig and Kit Kat Club member, Arthur Maynwaring's partner, a connoisseur of fine art and a witty conversationalist. After her death at least three volumes purporting to be her personal memoirs were published, though how authentic any of them were must be open to doubt. For many years she was the highest paid performer in England, her income often rising to nearly £500 when benefits and other emoluments were added. Here was a woman who retained her independence of mind and spirit, and stayed firmly in control of her own destiny.

THE TRIUMVIRATE

In 1711, Wilks, Cibber and Dogget formed a triumvirate to take over the management of Drury Lane. The year before Anne Oldfield had been invited to become a sharer with them when the company was still based at the Queen's Theatre in the Haymarket, but Dogget vehemently objected to women in such positions, and Oldfield was instead granted a thirteen-year contract at £200 per year plus benefits. Settled at Drury Lane, it seems that Wilks was responsible for the day-to-day business of the company, including rehearsals and publicity; Dogget, 'naturally an oeconomist', according to Colley Cibber, was in charge of the finances; and Cibber, besides choosing new plays and arranging the repertoire, also kept the peace between his two quarrelsome colleagues.

NOTES

1 Paul Sawyer, *Christopher Rich of Drury Lane*, London: University of America Press, 1986, p. 41.
2 Anthony Aston, *A Brief Supplement to Colley Cibber, Esq.; His Lives of the Late Famous Actors and Actresses*, 1748, in A.M. Nagler, *A Source Book in Theatrical History*, New York: Dover Publications, 1952, p. 216.
3 Colley Cibber, *An Apology for His Life*, London: J.M. Dent & Sons, 1938, p. 295.
4 Joseph Donohue (ed), *The Cambridge History of British Theatre*, vol 2, Cambridge: Cambridge University Press, 2004, p. 83.
5 Elaine M. McGirr, *Partial Histories: A Reappraisal of Colley Cibber*, Basingstoke: Palgrave Macmillan, 2016, p. 118.
6 Aaron Hill, *The Prompter*, 19 November 1734.
7 Colley Cibber, *op.cit.*, p. 296.
8 Felicity Nussbaum, *Rival Queens: Actresses, Performance and the Eighteenth Century British Theater*, Philadelphia: University of Philadelphia Press, 2010, p. 108.

Chapter 46: Augustan drama

THE AUGUSTAN AGE

The 'Augustan Age' is generally reckoned to cover the first four decades of the eighteenth century. Named for the Roman Emperor Augustus, during whose reign admirable good sense was supposed to have dominated public discourse, it showed itself now in a concern for dignity, calmness and attention to external appearances. Writing and culture was seen as a social gesture between friends, or potential friends, which emphasised intelligence, good manners and proper sentiment at the expense of boorishness. It was adopted by the upper crust of society – the Earl of Shaftesbury, the Duke of Newcastle, Archbishop Tillotson as well as intellectuals like Isaac Newton and John Locke and writers like the old schoolboy chums, Richard Steele and Joseph Addison. They valued 'wit', which Locke opined must be tempered by 'judgment', and which led to their brilliance in satire and irony. These, however, were to be tempered with sentiment, the ability to feel, though in practice sentiment easily tipped over into sentimentality. It was manifested dramatically when, for example, the good apprentice and the bad apprentice meet in the gaol at the end of George Lillo's *The London Merchant* and weep together, or when, in Steele's *The Conscious Lovers*, Bevil Junior asserts sententiously and also perhaps tearfully, 'To hope for perfect happiness is vain'.

CRITICAL APPROACHES

Augustan attitudes could also lead to a kind of static neoclassicism. Addison disliked the physicality of the theatre and argued for a cerebral drama. He was also, of course, influenced by Jeremy Collier's moralistic preaching, though he was hardly alone in this. Colley Cibber maintained Collier had 'a very wholesome effect' on playwrights, and Steele, whose earliest published work was entitled *The Christian Hero*, was, he said, 'a great admirer' of Collier, 'and took it into my head to write a comedy in the severity he required'.[1] Steele wanted to touch the spectator's heart with a model of good behaviour. Obviously, he rejected Restoration plays like *The Man of Mode*, seeing them as vulgar and even offensive.

In *The Tatler* and *The Spectator* Steele and Addison developed a coherent approach to the stage through a series of reviews, ushering in a new form of dramatic criticism, one which asserted the morality of drama, and advocated a kind of anti-political politics of moderation. John Dennis, the often curmudgeonly critic who disliked Steele personally, rejected this approach. He saw their sentimental comedy as mere flattery of the middle class, untruthful and morally cowardly. Comedy,

Dennis argued, should have no truck with pathos or sentiment: showing models of good behaviour was actually the opposite of its purpose, which was the exposure of vice and folly upon the stage so that it would be recognised for what it was in life.

Perhaps more significantly, if not surprisingly, Augustan values turned out to be very close to Whig values – integrity, stoicism, patriotism and toleration, the opposite of 'enthusiasm': 'Enthusiasm makes villains martyrs', exclaims Nicholas Rowe's Tamerlane. Addison endorsed the view of the classical philosopher, Epictetus, that the world was 'a theatre, where everyone has a part allotted to him', though he also agreed that the future of the country rested with the *bourgeoisie*.

THE JUDGMENT OF PARIS

Members of the Kit Kat Club, very Augustan, encouraged music and opera. In search of an English opera, Congreve wrote a libretto, *The Judgment of Paris*, and a group of wealthy aristocrats put up two hundred guineas, half of which formed the First Prize, to be awarded to the composer who could best set it to music. In June 1703 four settings, by John Weldon, John Eccles, Daniel Purcell and Gottfried Finger, were staged in a single day at Dorset Garden. Four times the actresses who played goddesses disrobed to tempt Paris in a scene of unabashed nudity and eroticism. The enthralled audience was invited to vote for the best composition: Weldon won (though when the BBC re-staged the competition in 1989, the audience vote went to Eccles's version).

HANDEL AND OPERA

English operas which followed included *Arsinoe* (1705) and *Camilla* (1706). *Rosamund* (1707), with music by Thomas Clayton and libretto by Joseph Addison, was intended to be something more substantial than these. Based on the story of Henry II's mistress, who is finally cast off as the king is reconciled to his Scottish wife, Addison saw it as an allegory of the Union of Scotland and England. Despite a spectacular backdrop depicting Vanbrugh's vision of the still-uncompleted Blenheim Palace, the opera was an utter failure which embittered Addison against the form. However, *Thomyris, Queen of Scythia* (1707), the first opera in England to use a *castrato*, was more successful and so too was *Pyrrhus and Demetrius* (1709), in which the English singers sang in English, but Italians in Italian. *Idaspe* (1709) was sung entirely in Italian, and then, after *Almahide* in 1710, George Frederick Handel's first opera, *Rinaldo*, was staged in 1711. It was a runaway hit, some songs in it capturing the popular imagination enough to enter the popular repertory, such as the March which reappears in *The Beggar's Opera* as the tune to the Gang's 'Let us take the road'. Its popularity greatly vexed Addison and Steele, who were especially incensed by the flock of sparrows and chaffinches which were released halfway through the show, and flew about, messing spectators' heads for the rest of the evening.

Handel settled down to enjoy English life, finally taking British citizenship in 1727 and staying till his death in 1759, while Italian opera became all the rage. It brought with it more *castrati*, such as Carlo Broschi, known as Farinelli, and Francesco Bernardi, or Senesino, with their angelic, other worldly, yet somehow unnerving voices. Handel quarrelled with Senesino, because the latter seemed more popular than he, yet he continued to write superb roles for this wilful and sexually compelling singer. This quarrel, however, was nothing compared to that between the female *divas*, Faustina Bordoni and Francesca Cuzzoni, each paid £2,500 for the 1727 season, each living in the height of

Figure 4.14
Sheet music title page: *The Judgment of Paris*: a pastoral composed for the music-prize, London: 1700, by Daniel Purcell
Source: Houghton Library, Harvard University

luxury, and each cat-like in her jealousy of the other. Each was supported by her own 'claque', who wore the favour of their idol and hissed and booed every appearance of her rival. Performances were interrupted and disrupted, and on one occasion the two singers came to blows on stage. Yet the aristocracy could not get enough of opera, which by the way also provided unequalled profits for pickpockets, as Filch tells Mrs Peachum in *The Beggar's Opera*.

Figures 4.15
Rivals in artistry and in the lavish pay they received: Francesca Cuzzoni

Figures 4.16
Rivals in artistry and in the lavish pay they received: Faustina Bordoni

Handel, who had founded the Royal Academy of Music to present his operas at the King's (formerly Queen's) Theatre in the Haymarket, in 1729 went into management there with John James Heidegger, a well-known entrepreneur of London's secret pleasures. Their 'English' Italian opera was supported by George II, and for the next four years their popularity with their class audience soared. But in 1733 they were challenged by the Opera of the Nobility at Lincoln's Inn Fields, established by Frederick, Prince of Wales, and his friends in a deliberate provocation by the Prince against his hated father. The group even 'stole' Francesca Cuzzoni from Handel. Handel moved to Covent Garden, whereupon his rivals moved into the King's. Handel's company was bankrupted, and the composer turned from opera to oratorios. Soon after, the Opera of the Nobility was dissolved. Remnants of the two companies united for a last season in 1737–8, but the opera craze in London was over.

THE REPERTOIRE: REVIVALS

As with any theatre at any period, the theatre of the time of Queen Anne relied heavily on revivals of old plays. When the Battle of Blenheim was won, it was announced from the stage of Drury Lane prior to a performance of Aphra Behn's *The Emperor of the Moon*. Ben Jonson was probably the most performed 'old' dramatist after Shakespeare. Shakespeare was frequently mightily tricked out. The 1704 production of *Macbeth* had special vocal and instrumental music composed for it by Richard Leveridge and included 'several sonatas on the violin by Signior Gasparini' and 'entertainments of dancing by Monsieur Du Ruel'. When Betterton played Macbeth for what must surely have been almost the last time in December 1707, there were included 'several new scenes proper to the play' as well as a new vocal epilogue by 'Signior Cibberini', perhaps a pseudonym for Colley Cibber.

Cibber's own most memorable contribution to the revivals of Shakespeare was his rewriting of *Richard III* (1700). His short but effective version of Shakespeare's play drags in pieces from *Henry VI* Part 3, *Henry IV* Part 1, *Henry V* and *Richard II* but still contains much of Cibber's own work, such as the pathetic scene when the Princes bid farewell to their mother before being escorted away to the Tower, and the unforgettable line: 'Off with his head! So much for Buckingham!' Actors and audiences alike loved Cibber's version, and there are still vestiges of it to be seen in Laurence Olivier's famous 1955 film.

GEORGE FARQUHAR

Only two original dramatists from the first decade of the eighteenth century made a lasting mark, George Farquhar and Susanna Centlivre. Farquhar came to England from Ireland a failed actor but with the aim of becoming a playwright, and his work has never dropped out of the repertoire. His early *The Constant Couple* (1699) might almost be a pre-Congreve comedy, though it already incorporates some delicious scenes involving misunderstandings and disguise. But he developed his technique rapidly and his last two plays, *The Recruiting Officer* (1706) and *The Beaux' Stratagem* (1707) have always been deservedly popular. The former uses favourite dramatic motifs, such as recruitment to the armed forces and female cross-dressing particularly effectively, and indeed Sylvia, as a man, not only makes the stage her own but also encourages some intriguing gay byplay. *The Beaux' Stratagem* is a brilliantly constructed comedy which has at its heart the knotty problem of marital relations. Farquhar's plays glimpse a kindlier world than almost any that preceded his work,

Figure 4.17
George Farquhar's *The Recruiting Officer*, 1706. Sergeant Kite makes fun of Bullock. KITE: 'I have seen one of these hussars eat up a ravelin for his breakfast, and afterwards pick his teeth with a palisado'. BULLOCK: 'Ay, you soldiers see very strange things'.

Source: Lebrecht Music and Arts Photo Library/Alamy Stock Photo

which perhaps makes his satire, as with the parallel he draws between highwaymen and beaux, sting more potently. Farquhar died at the age of twenty-nine in poverty and distress.

SUSANNA CENTLIVRE

Susanna Centlivre, a strolling player who is reputed to have met and been befriended by a Cambridge University student, who dressed her as his male friend and took her to his college lectures, wrote a total of nineteen plays. Her reputation has suffered unfairly because she was frequently belittled or cheated by contemporary male dramatists and critics. Thus Colley Cibber objected to her comedy, *Love at a Venture* (1706), but then cribbed it for his own play, *The Double Gallant* (1707). Her pair of early comedies about the evils of gambling, *The Basset Table* (1705) and *The Gamester* (also 1705) are both potent social dramas and elegantly theatrical, but they were violently attacked by the Society for the Reformation of Manners. *The Gamester* was one of the last productions to star the three great names of the late Stuart stage, Elizabeth Barry as Lady Wealthy, Thomas Betterton as her suitor and Anne Bracegirdle as Angelica.

Centlivre's best play is probably *The Busy Body* (1710). In line with normal patriarchal expectations, one supposes the eponymous busybody will be a woman – after all, it is old women who are busybodies, is it not? But the busybody here is a man, a highly originally conceived comic character called Marplot. Mary Pix may have collaborated with Centlivre on this play, but as with all Centlivre's work, there is a sly gender consciousness at work in it. Indeed her plays often seem to question whether marriage, for example, is a sustainable idea at all. Centlivrre is notable for her inventiveness in creating comic set pieces, and the fact that her best plays largely dropped out of the repertoire was the loss of later generations of playgoers. She is certainly the equal of George Farquhar, and more prolific as well as more versatile. Both these writers' work, however, is original: it is less overtly satirical than some comedies, but it contains an unusual warmth and humanity.

STEELE'S SENTIMENTAL COMEDY

Meanwhile Richard Steele was producing plays as patterns for a new, post-Collier comedy: 'agreeableness of behaviour', 'innocence and virtue', leading perhaps to something 'charming' and 'natural'. These included *The Funeral* (1701), *The Lying Lover* (1703), and *The Tender Husband* (1705), each sentimentally urging tolerance and moderation. But the latter play actually includes a scene which Steele's prudishness probably prevented him from noticing. Lucy Fainlove, disguised as a man, attempts to seduce Mrs Clerimont in what is clearly a lesbian love scene. Titillating it certainly is, and surely provides little of the 'moral instruction' Steele protested he believed in.

For whatever reason, Steele's next comedy took nearly twenty years to reach the stage, and in the meantime his friend Joseph Addison had produced a comedy of his own, *The Drummer* (1716), though it is not much more rewarding than Steele's comedies. Finally, in 1722, Steele's *The Conscious Lovers* was presented, a play which focuses on *bourgeois* values, contrasting the industrious merchant with the idle gentry. At its centre is the respectful and obedient hero, young Bevil, who today seems smug and self-absorbed, but *The Conscious Lovers* was much admired in its time.

TRAGEDY: NICHOLAS ROWE

Augustan tragedy is rather more arresting, perhaps particularly that of the Shakespeare scholar and Poet Laureate, Nicholas Rowe. He wrote a series of plays, including *The Ambitious Stepmother* (1700), *The Fair Penitent* (1703), *Jane Shore* (1714) and *Lady Jane Grey* (1715), which developed what came to be known as 'she-tragedies'. In vogue during the reigns of Mary II and Anne, and capitalising on the availability of great women actresses, notably Elizabeth Barry and Anne Oldfield, these plays showed good women as victims of social or historical forces too strong for them.

Other playwrights created 'she-tragedies': Trotter in *Agnes de Castro*, Congreve in *The Mourning Bride* and Mary Pix in *Queen Catherine*, for example, but it was Rowe who crystallised the form and its chief concerns. She-tragedies depicted passive women suffering, a situation not without a *frisson* of sexual titillation, gender stereotyping ('How hard is the condition of our sex', laments Calista in *The Fair Penitent*), and the objectification of women. But it is Rowe's placing of these matters in *bourgeois* society that gives his work its originality. *The Fair Penitent* is, says its Prologue, 'a melancholy tale of private woe'.

JOSEPH ADDISON

The superficially more heroic tragedy of *Cato* (1713) by Joseph Addison, is situated similarly in 'private' life. *Cato* appears to deal with public issues: opening just two weeks after the signing of the Treaty of Utrecht, which the Whigs vehemently opposed, it actually seems to endorse both Whig

Figure 4.18
Illustration from Nicholas Rowe's influential 1710 edition of Shakespeare's plays: Macbeth watches the procession of future Kings of Scotland presented by the Weird Sisters

Source: British Library, London

and Tory positions – a sure sign that this is not where its heart lies. Everyone can support heroic resistance to tyranny like Cato's, and understand that empires fall as well as rise. The play's heart lies in its private, not public, response to events. In this, it is, like Rowe's tragedies, a quintessentially *bourgeois* production. 'Content thyself to be obscurely good', says Cato, and the trail Addison blazes here was to be followed by Aaron Hill in *The Fatal Extravagance* (1720) and Ambrose Phillips in *The Briton* (1721).

Addison was so nervous before *Cato*'s first performance that he had bottles of Burgundy and champagne brought to his Box to drink while watching. But the play was superbly successful. At its end, Bolingbroke, the Tory leader, presented Barton Booth, who had played the hero, with fifty guineas to signify his approval.

GEORGE LILLO

Another unexpectedly successful tragedy was George Lillo's *The London Merchant* (1731). Written in prose not verse, the *bourgeoisie* is placed firmly at its centre: 'merchant' means businessman. The play may be set in Elizabeth times, but the fate of the Spanish Armada seems to depend on the availability of a bank loan. What Lillo refrains from examining is how business unleashes greed. He fails to ask how Barnwell or Millwood's greed is so different from Thorowgood's. But his picture of the inexperienced Barnwell's nervousness before his first sexual experience is thoroughly convincing, and Millwood, the vixenish villainess, may be melodramatically drawn but is still a good antidote to the suffering heroines of the she-tragedies. As the first tragedy of a young would-be businessman, *The London Merchant* long retained its popularity, and it became a tradition to present it every Shrove Tuesday, that being an apprentice's holiday. It was an ironic apotheosis for the sometimes starchy Augustans.

NOTE

1 Sir Richard Steele, *Mr Steele's Apology for Himself and His Writings; occasioned by his expulsion from the House of Commons*, 1714, p. 48.

Chapter 47: Theatre practice in the first half of the eighteenth century

COMMERCIAL THEATRE

Theatre was by 1700 a thoroughly commercial enterprise, and the struggle to attract spectators was often extremely fierce. Shakespeare was sensationalised, music suffused the hall, and there was the promise of slapstick and high jinks. To provide all this, companies, with thirty or more members, as well as an often extensive orchestra, were growing larger. The whole programme began at six PM, but even before that the orchestra played. Then came the prologue which, after more music, led to the play, during which there were extensive *entr'actes*. The play finished with an epilogue, and after that there was more music and an afterpiece, lasting probably forty-five minutes.

THE AFTERPIECE

The afterpiece was effectively the second half of a double bill, and as such it remained as a fixed item in the theatre's typical evening programme for perhaps two centuries. Prompted by a mixture of theatrical competition and audience demand, Betterton first attached an afterpiece to the main play in 1696 at Lincoln's Inn Fields, probably to gain a competitive advantage over Christopher Rich's Drury Lane. The competition can be seen still operating years later, when in 1714, both theatres mounted afterpieces based on *The Comedy of Errors*, one by Christopher Bullock at Drury Lane, the other by Charles Johnson at Lincoln's Inn Fields, and both entitled *The Cobbler of Preston*.

It was also becoming obvious at the end of the seventeenth century that many would-be patrons were being lost because the hour of performance, six PM, though this suited the idle and better-off spectator, meant that tradespeople and others, who worked all day, missed the opening. The afterpiece gave them their money's worth.

Afterpieces were of many sorts. Descended from the drolls of the Commonwealth and Restoration periods, they were most usually farces. Many were original, but many too were squeezed out of older plays, either as more or less self-contained excerpts, or as abridgements of whole plays. Frequently they were at least part-improvised, and usually they relied on broad, even slapstick, comedy with few pretensions to sophistication. Pantomimes, dances and musical entertainments were other forms of afterpieces. That they could be powerful vehicles for satirical invective was also shown particularly by Henry Fielding in the 1730s.

ENTR'ACTES

Between the acts of the play were the *entr'actes*, turns which might range from a comedian to an Italian opera soloist, from a French dancer to a troupe of trained dogs. Lincoln's Inn Fields spectators enjoyed variously tumblers, performing monkeys and Madame Subligny, a French dancer, while Drury Lane offered 'the Devonshire Girl', one Evans who vaulted off and on a moving horse, and spectacular scenes from operas. Christopher Rich even considered bringing an elephant on stage, and was only deterred when informed that the stage boards might give way under the beast's weight. Derided by one commentator in 1702 as 'caperers, eunuchs, fiddlers, tumblers and gypsies', these 'illegitimate' entertainers nevertheless provided farcical *entr'actes* which point forward to pantomime:

> What a rout here was with a night-piece of Harlequin and Scaramouche, with the guitar and the bladder! What jumping over tables and joint-stools! What ridiculous postures and grimaces! and what an exquisite trick 'twas to straddle before the audience, making a thousand damned French faces, and seeming in labour with a monstrous birth, at last my counterfeit male lady is delivered of her two puppies, Harlequin and Scaramouche.[1]

MUSIC AND MUSICIANS

It is not clear where the musicians, of whom there might be more than twenty, were positioned: perhaps in side boxes, perhaps above the stage, or even perhaps between the stage and the pit.

Eighteenth-century theatre was suffused with music. Before the play began the musicians performed two pieces, the 'first music' and the 'second music'. People actually attended the theatre merely to hear this introductory music and then left, having a percentage of their admission money refunded. After the prologue was spoken, there was the overture, and often also 'curtain music'. During the play, music often featured between the acts, and during the action it was used to enhance, express or even contradict the mood of the play. Moreover, many old plays, including Shakespeare's, had songs added, often specially composed songs, and contemporary plays, too, demanded a musical dimension. Thus, Farquhar's *The Recruiting Officer* includes a particularly attractive version of the old English folk song, 'Over the hills and far away', while Congreve inserted a song into Rowe's *The Fair Penitent*. In Cibber's *Love's Last Shift*, music is played in the park; in Pix's *Queen Catherine*, Act V opens with 'an overture of victory' for Edward IV. Music also often stimulated dance, as in Manley's *The Royal Mischief*, when the 'Indians' dance to music, and Centlivre's *The Gamester*, which ends with 'a country dance'.

THE STAGE

The stage was still part of the main hall, actors and spectators, as it were, together. The audience was close to the action – indeed spectators still sometimes sat on the stage. But the proximity allowed actors to speak directly to the audience, or, when cliques of followers or opponents were present, to speak to some and ignore others. Behind them were suggestive or pictorial settings on the vista stage which was occasionally entered but was rarely part of the action since it was lit only dimly with candles behind the wings. Thus, in Vanbrugh's *The Mistake* Don Carlos *'goes to the scene and returns'*, and in Pix's *The Conquest of Spain*, Jacinta *'exits to the scene'*. Doors, which could be locked or knocked on, let the actors onto the stage: Mellefont and Maskwell, in Congreve's *The Double Dealer*, enter *'from different doors'* and in Centlivre's *The Stolen Heiress*, Euphenes and Count Gravello enter *'at several doors'*.

The flats and side wings were decorated with pictures, which were not scenery in the modern sense, though they could be useful, as in Farquhar's *The Beaux' Stratagem*, when Grub *'goes behind the side-scene and listens'*. There was a convention, too, that an actor could exit through a door from a scene in, say, a drawing room and re-enter through the same door, but now be understood to be on the street: in Farquhar's *The Constant Couple*, Lady Lurewell and Clincher Senior *'come down'* from the previous scene set in the street, and *'the scene changes to a dining room'*. The trapdoor, of course, was also a permanent feature of the stage.

SCENERY

Most plays depended on emblematic scenery which did not attempt any kind of realism. For example, cutout waves across the stage behind the actors were a conventional means of representing the sea. Most scenes were painted on flats which were pushed by stage hands into place behind the actors along grooves nailed to the floor and more grooves above to contain the top edges of the flats. The scenes were likely to be generic rather than specific. Thus, Act II of *The Recruiting Officer* opens in *'an apartment'*; for scene 2, *'the scene changes to another apartment'*. Both scenes were generalised, not specific, and the side scenes would remain the same. Of course, mistakes could happen:

> At the Haymarket, the undertakers forgetting to change their side scenes, we were presented with a prospect of the ocean in the midst of a delightful grove; and though the gentlemen on the stage contributed to the beauty of the grove by walking up and down between the trees, I must own that I was not a little astonished to see a well-dressed young fellow, in a full-bottomed wig, appear in the midst of the sea, and without any visible concern taking snuff.[2]

The shutters could be drawn back to reveal not just a picture, but the beginning of the action, as in Susanna Centlivre's *The Basset Table*, when *'the scene opens, and discovers Valeria with books upon a table, a microscope, putting a fish upon it, several animals lying by'*, and in *A Bold Stroke for a Wife*, when *'the scene draws and discovers Sir Philip upon a bench with a woman, masked'*. Scene changes could be wonderful or absurd, as Aaron Hill in 1734 noted, perhaps sarcastically: 'I have seen houses move, as it were, upon wings, cities turned into forests, and dreary deserts converted into superb palaces'[3]. But this stage could accommodate practicable furniture: *She Ventures and He Wins* has an *'arbour'* behind which Sir Charles and Sir Roger retreat, and into which Charlotte and Juliana go, and in *Rinaldo*, there were two cutout dragons which spat fire and smoke.

THE SPECTACULAR

Eighteenth-century audiences greatly enjoyed spectacular scenic effects, and stage managers were not averse to meeting this enthusiasm. Thunder and lightning, for instance, according to *The Spectator*, 'are often made use of at the descending of a god, or the rising of a ghost, at the vanishing of a devil or the death of a tyrant'.[4] In 1714, it was reported that Drury Lane had acquired a new thunder machine, 'more deep and sonorous than any hitherto made use of'. Moreover, they had new lightning, too, able 'to flash more briskly than heretofore'.

Clouds, suspended from the flies, were often used, even for indoor scenes. They were 'voluminous' and 'furbelowed', and there were different clouds, presumably less fluffy and darker coloured, for storm scenes, and the gods usually descended from the heavens, as in plays from Dryden's *Amphytrion* (1690) to Carey's *Chrononhotonthologos* (1734). But not always happily. At Covent Garden on 1 October 1736, during a performance of *The Necromancer*, the wires holding the 'flying machine' snapped, and four actors crashed to the stage. Three were badly injured; the fourth, James Todd who was playing the Miller's Man, fractured his skull and died the next day. Spectators were at first amazed at what they assumed was deliberate, then realised the truth, and several of them fainted. There was, according to *The Gentleman's Magazine*, 'great confusion upon this sad accident'.

LIGHTING

The main stage lights were the chandelier, or chandeliers, which illuminated audience and actors equally, and there were candles in brackets on the auditorium walls, as well as lights behind the side wings and footlights across the front of the stage. For a night scene, the chandeliers might be raised, or even extinguished, and lanterns employed by the actors. For special effects, coloured glass might be placed in front of burning candles.

The candle snuffers, of whom there were several, tiptoed about the theatre, making sure the lighting was as it should be, but prepared also to be summoned to the stage to perform as extras in a large-scale scene.

COSTUME

Cibber boasted that Drury Lane spent good money on costumes, but Downes, the long-serving prompter at the theatre, suggested that it was rare for plays to be 'new cloath'd'. Nevertheless, Richard Steele urged that 'the first dramatic rule is, Have good clothes', and suggested that 'heroes die unpitied, if ill-dressed'.[5] This often seemed to mean, according to Joseph Addison in *The Spectator*, clapping 'a huge plume of feathers on (the hero's) head' which might rise 'so high that there is often a greater length from his chin to the top of his head than to the sole of his foot'.[6] Women on stage, he continued, were often encumbered by a 'broad sweeping train' which necessitated a boy following her about and arranging the train whenever she stood still.

In Shakespeare's plays, actors usually wore contemporary costume: Hal and Poins watching while Falstaff takes Mistress Quickly on his knee are dressed as eighteenth-century gentlemen, complete with full wigs if not sprays of tall feathers clapped upon their heads (Figure 4.19). In the Roman plays some attempt was made to create togas for senators, but the women still wore contemporary

Figure 4.19

Henry IV Part 1: Falstaff with Mistress Quickly on his knee overlooked by Prince Hal and Poins, 1710

Source: British Library, London

hooped skirts, and Aaron Hill, manager at Drury Lane in 1709–10, complained of careless costuming, actors going on stage in coats which were too long or without buttons, wigs done up with packthread and 'patchwork inconsistencies'. Audiences seemed content to accept a miscellaneous jumble in the costuming of plays.

MAKE-UP

Actors wore make-up in this theatre, partly to offset the dimness of the lights, but partly also because it was socially fashionable. Usually a white oil-based foundation covered the whole face, and was overlaid sometimes with a pink blush, but often with patches, which were thought to bring out the ladies' pallor more effectively. The lips were painted, too. But this was only a beginning, as an anonymous poem of 1699 suggests:

> The royal consort next consults her glass,
> And out of twenty boxes culls a face:
> The whitening first her ghastly looks besmears,
> All pale and wan the unfurnished form appears;
> Till on her cheeks the blushing purple glows . . .

A few lines later, the poem describes a young *ingénue*'s make-up:

> Her ruddy lips, the deep vermilion dyes;
> Length to her brows the pencil touch supplies,
> And with black bending arches shades her eyes.
> Well pleased, at last the picture she beholds,
> And spots it o'er with artificial moulds.[7]

Men used the same means, though most men were not so pale. In John Gay's *The What D'Ye Call It*, Dock makes up Nettle on stage, giving him a '*ruddy complexion*' and '*making whiskers with burnt cork*'. Most actors carried their own 'powder knife' to scrape together powders from chalk, antimony (a bluish colour for highlights) or paint sticks. These were mixed together with lard, tallow or pig's fat and smeared on the face. For a white actor playing a black character such as Othello or Oroonoko, soot, burnt nuts or fruit stones, or charcoal or even burnt ivory might be used.

THE PROMPTER

A key figure was the prompter. He acted as both company manager and stage manager, organising rehearsals and running them, deciding on exits and entrances, poses, processional movements and explaining and shaping speeches for the actors. He edited the script, writing cuts and revisions into his master copy from which he worked, and he was responsible for the writing out of the actors' parts.

He also ran the show itself from his leather armchair in the wings, unless an actor was absent when he might perform the role himself. He was assisted by stage hands, messengers and candle snuffers (in practice often the same people). The messengers, or call-boys, called the actors to appear on cue. For scene changes the prompter blew a whistle to signal the stage hands to stand by. The whistle was peremptory and authoritative. Aaron Hill wrote: 'I have seen heaven and earth pass away and chaos ensue; and from thence a new creation arise, fair and blooming, as the poet's fancy; and all by the powerful magic influence of this wonder-working whistle'.[8]

The stage hands who performed these transformations, like the candle snuffers, were often also part of any stage army, or crowd or mob.

The prompter also had a bell, which was rung as a cue for the musicians to commence playing, both at the end of a scene or act and also during an act. Aaron Hill again notes:

> by the tinkling of this bell, if a lady in tragedy be in the spleen for the absence of her lover, or the hero in the dumps for the loss of a battle, he can conjure up soft music to soothe their distress; nay, if a wedding happens in a comedy, he can summon up the fiddlers to dispel care by a country dance.[9]

GETTING THE SHOW ON

The theatre season began in September after the summer break. Usually the first performances were of old plays re-rehearsed. New plays would be introduced to the repertoire only gradually.

The author who submitted his play to the theatre was in the usually conservative hands of the manager – Colley Cibber in Drury Lane's case. He might or might not read the play, but if he accepted it for production, the first step would be for the play to be read aloud to the company, usually by the author. If the actors were not happy with it, the play could still be refused. It was cast by the manager, or the prompter (or both), with the author rarely having much say in the matter. In Fielding's *The Author's Farce*, it is the prompter who casts the drama.

Parts, with cues, were distributed, and the rehearsal process was a comparatively leisurely affair. A tragedy might take five weeks or more to rehearse, though a comedy usually took less time, and an afterpiece might only be in rehearsal for two weeks. But since so many pieces were being prepared at any one time, concentration on one of them was by no means exacting. There might be up to three collective readings while the actors were learning their parts, as well as one or two script-in-hand rehearsals.

Once parts had been learned, one or two more general rehearsals were called by the prompter, who had the power to fine actors for absence or lateness, as well as other misdemeanours. At Drury Lane, full cast rehearsals were generally controlled by Cibber or Wilks, but both the prompter and the author were also crucial figures in rehearsals. Swift watched a rehearsal at Drury Lane in 1713, when the actors had to be prompted 'every moment'. In this case Addison was involved in the direction, but Swift chiefly remembered Anne Oldfield calling out 'in the midst of a passionate part', 'What's next?'[10] These rehearsals were generally held in the mornings, though occasionally in the evenings after a performance. Their purpose was never to work through the minutiae of the author's subtext or similar matters, they were largely functional, fixing exits and entrances, and deciding general stage positions, processions and so forth. There may have been some attention paid to voice, intonation, gesture and similar matters, but the prompter often coached individual actors in these areas outside general rehearsals.

Plays usually premiered on Saturday, but still, Aaron Hill noted sourly, 'it seldom happens that a play is well acted the first night which . . . ought to be the most exact of all'.[11] Sunday was set aside for making necessary adjustments and corrections.

NOTES

1 Staring B. Wells (ed), *A Comparison Between the Two Stages*, Princeton: Princeton University Press, 1942, p. 28.
2 Quoted in George C.D. Odell, *Shakespeare from Betterton to Irving*, New York: Dover Publications, 1966, p. 301.

3 *The London Magazine*, vol 3, 1734, p. 582.
4 *The Spectator*, 20 April 1711.
5 Richard Steele, *Prologue to the Mistake by John Vanbrugh*, 1705.
6 *The Spectator*, 18 April 1711.
7 Quoted in A.M. Nagler, *A Source Book in Theatrical History*, New York: Dover Publications, 1952, p. 243.
8 Aaron Hill, *The Prompter*, 19 November 1734.
9 *Ibid.*
10 Quoted in Tiffany Stern, *Rehearsal from Shakespeare to Sheridan*, Oxford: Clarendon Press, 2000, p. 219.
11 Aaron Hill, *op.cit.*, 6 May 1735.

Chapter 48: Provincial theatre, 1660–1740

THEATRE BEYOND LONDON REVIVES

After the debilitating disruptions of Civil War and a puritanical commonwealth, theatre beyond the west end of London gradually stirred into energetic life.

Many London actors seemed happy to tour in the summer, sometimes as members of *ad hoc* groups, sometimes when the whole company from their theatre debouched, generally to the Home Counties. But there were permanent companies based outside London, too, such as the Duke of Norfolk's Men in East Anglia which flourished between the 1690s and the 1720s. At one time this company was led by Thomas Dogget, later to be part of Drury Lane's management triumvirate. Other companies were less well founded, such as that set up by Thomas Clarke, Cardell Goodman and James Gray, all members of the King's Men, in 1679 when that London company was tottering towards its own destruction. Another was Larina Violante's company. Her husband was a tightrope dancer, who had accidentally hanged himself during a performance. She, too, was a noted rope dancer, but she also taught acting. She appeared in Scotland in 1719 and in Dublin ten years later where she was reputed to have discovered the great actress Peg Woffington.

STROLLING PLAYERS

Actors wanting to join a company of strolling players usually met the manager in a pub, probably around Covent Garden. They might be paid a nominal sum and join the company wherever they were in England, usually being expected to walk there, and then to play whatever parts needed to be covered. For members of smaller companies who probably gave most performances as one-night stands in villages, travel was almost continuous, and must have been extremely tiring on the roads of the time. They often carried the scenery or bundles of costumes on their backs, though the more reputable companies may have had a cart or even a coach to travel in.

A company would arrive in a village or town, parade down the main street beating a drum or singing together, and handing out playbills. They performed in guildhalls, market halls, but also in pubs, barns and stables, perhaps using the pigsty as a dressing room. Hogarth's *Strolling Actresses in a Barn* reveals much. Often they had to erect their stage and perhaps a whole booth to house it; these were often put up even inside market halls or barns.

Companies could be small. Five men and two or three women might be all that could be afforded, and there was plenty of doubling and cross-gender casting. Charlotte Charke, cast as Plume in *The*

Figure 4.20
William Hogarth, Strolling Actresses in a Barn, 1738, engraving from an original painting destroyed in 1874

Recruiting Officer, was forced to play Sylvia, Plume's lover, as well, when the cast actress failed to appear. Elizabeth Elrington once played both Polly and Lucy in *The Beggar's Opera*; how she managed their duet is not recorded. One actor reported by Sybil Rosenfeld, in a single evening appeared as King Richard, then sang two comic songs, played in an interlude, danced a hornpipe, spoke a prologue and appeared as Harlequin.

These actors were paid only after all the expenses of the performance had been cleared. Then they shared whatever was left, though the manager usually ensured he received four or five shares. It meant that sometimes actors went without pay, though the manager always took the 'saddle' – what he thought was his due. Actors depended heavily on benefit nights, which were contracted in advance. They were always responsible for publicity, and for their benefit they would try to knock on every door, distribute bills to every shop and create as much interest as possible in the town.

Their audience might be drawn from the country around, as well as from the village or town of the performance. Occasionally companies were invited to perform at the country seat of the local nobility. Quite often the actors would join audience members at the pub after the show. Holiday crowds were best, most likely to appreciate the actors' efforts, and also most likely to pay. So the companies were inevitably drawn to race meetings and fairs.

THEATRE IN BARTHOLOMEW FAIR

Of the fairs, Bartholomew Fair in Smithfield was still the greatest, and shortly after the Restoration it expanded to a two-week carnival, with an increasingly exhilarating theatrical element. It became a kind of 'fringe' for the London theatres, operating in the summer when they were closed, and it took on a truly carnivalesque flavour, an unofficial site for theatrical audacity and oppositionism. Often parodying official culture, defying what the 'mob' saw as political or religious repression,

Figure 4.21
William Phillips, the 'Prince of Merry Andrews' whose 'pleasant humours, various adventures, cheats, frolics and cunning designs' delighted Bartholomew Fair goers for many years from the 1690s

it created grotesqueries and insisted on laughter and spontaneity. Much of this happened outside the theatre booths as well, in the freak shows, the rope dancing and revelry. But the theatre of the fairgrounds offered a kind of escape to another, more vivid world, painted in the vibrant colours of dissent, disrespect and desire.

This explains the desire of the authorities to ban the fair, or at least its theatrical components, especially after Jeremy Collier's harangues. It was consistently harassed and harried, and as consistently its practitioners and popular audiences resisted. In 1717 Bartholomew Fair was limited to three days and stage plays banned, but in a year or two it had sprouted again into a two-week carnival and the theatre booths were back. That same year, 1717, William Pinkethman and some of his booth company were arrested at Southwark Fair, and William Bullock and Francis Leigh were also taken from their booths, but their prosecutions failed, at least in the case of those who were actors with a Royal Patent company.

This ushered in what Sybil Rosenfeld called the fairgrounds' 'theatrical heyday', but it lasted for less than two decades. In 1735 Bartholomew Fair was again limited to three days, and plays were again prohibited. They returned the following year, but in 1737 came the Licensing Act which put harsh new pressures on the theatre at all levels. The three-day fairs became less attractive and less profitable as a summer alternative available to actors in the main London theatres: they turned more and more to performing in newly built provincial theatres, leaving the fairgrounds to a different kind of operator.

THE FAIRGROUND BOOTH

The typical booth of the time was a temporary wooden building erected only for the duration of the fair. Tall and quite narrow, it was yet surprisingly large, measuring up to fifty feet in length on ground for which the proprietor or manager paid about £5 rent for the fortnight. Booths were often placed in an innyard: thus, two favourite pitches in Smithfield were the Crown Tavern by Hospital Gate and the George Inn yard. On the front of the booth was a raised platform upon which the actors in costume paraded, sang songs, cracked jokes and performed acrobatics and other feats to draw the crowds. Behind or above them hung vivid coloured show cloths depicting the drama within, and a trumpeter on the parade blew to announce the beginning of the show. Entry was through a door below the parade platform.

SPECTACULAR FAIRGROUND SHOWS

Inside, most booths made some attempt to cater for the audience's taste for the spectacular. One account from 1699 describes how this stage

> beholds gods descending from machines, who express themselves in a language suitable to their dignity; it traffics in heroes; it raises ghosts and apparitions; it has presented the Trojan Horse; it has seen St George encounter the dragon and overcome him. In short, for thunder and lightning, for songs and dances, for sublime fustian and magnificent nonsense, it comes not short of Drury Lane or Lincoln's Inn Fields[1].

The most famous fairground spectacular was given in 1707 in Mrs Mynn's magnificent booth at the Crown Tavern, Smithfield, which Elkannah Settle suggested she should call 'Ben Jonson's Booth' to dignify it with the great dramatist-poet's name. This was Settle's *The Siege of Troy*. A typical stage direction will convey the extravagance:

> The scene opens and discovers Paris and Helen, fronting the audience, riding in a triumphant chariot, drawn by two white elephants, mounted by two pages in embroidered livery. The side wings are ten elephants more, bearing on their backs open castles, umbraged by canopies of gold; the ten castles filled with ten persons, richly dressed, the retinue of Paris; and on the elephants necks ride ten more pages in the like rich dress. Beyond and over the chariot is seen a picture of the city of Troy, on the walls of which stand several trumpeters, seen behind and over the head of Paris, who sound at the opening of the scene.[2]

The splendours of Inigo Jones's 1630s court masques have finally reached the popular showground.

Of course most booth shows were less flamboyant than this, not least because in few of the temporary structures was there much room backstage. Most could not manage more than about two pairs of flats, though 'flying' was always popular and the most modest of booths tried to cater for it.

MANAGEMENT OF TRAVELLING COMPANIES

Mrs Mynn was one of the most determined and capable fairground theatre managers, who operated from about 1690 to her death in 1717. Her company actually toured throughout the year without any base, and her success may be measured by the fact that when she died she left £4000 to her daughter, Hannah Lee, who continued to manage the company. Such itinerant troupes which visited fairs on their travels were complemented by whole companies from legitimate theatres, such as the Lincoln's Inn Fields company which brought their production of *The Constant Lovers* to Bartholomew Fair in 1719, or the company from the Little Theatre, Haymarket, which transferred their production of *The Beggar's Opera* to the fair in 1728. Other companies mixed strollers with legitimate players.

Mrs Mynn was a determined sole manager, and there were others, especially from the legitimate theatres who were prepared to control a company alone, including Thomas Dogget and William Pinkethman. More usually companies were controlled by a pair of managers, such as Hippisley and Fielding or Harper and Lee, though few pairs stayed together for long as these two did. Different combinations of managers also led to some trios, like Miller, Mills and Oates, who worked together for a number of years, but also led to an exciting sense of unpredictability about the fairground theatres. The most successful managerial pairing was probably that of Hannah Lee with John Harper. In 1721 Harper joined Mrs Lee's troupe, and soon they became business partners, their company lasting well into the 1730s. They produced the first pantomime to be seen in the fairground, and in several years in the 1730s supported two impressive booths in Southwark Fair.

FAIRGROUND ACTORS

Harper was a round-faced, plump comedian who was also renowned for the lightness of his dancing. His later career took him to stardom in the legitimate theatre where he was especially admired for his Falstaff, played without padding. Other well-known actors of the first part of the eighteenth century who appeared in the fairgrounds included James Quin, Charles Hulett, Mary Elmy, Hannah Pritchard, Henry Giffard, Theophilus Cibber and Thomas Walker, the original Macheath at Lincoln's

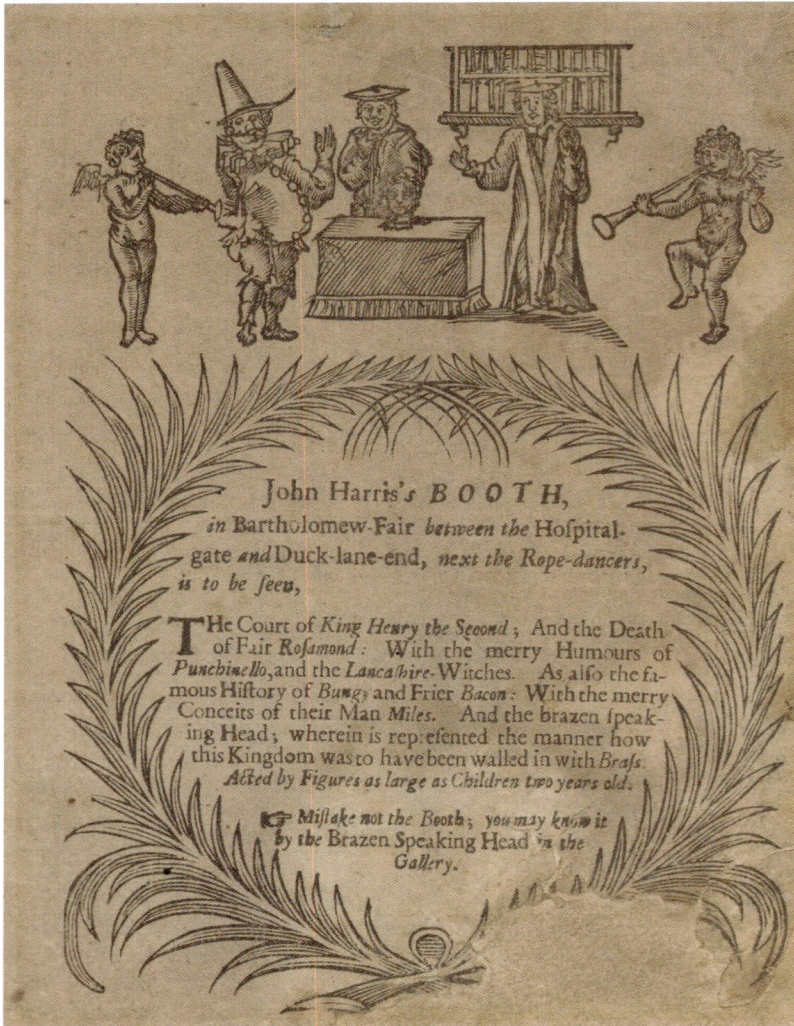

Figure 4.22
Flyer for John Harris's booth at Bartholomew Fair

Inn Fields. Equally or more popular in the fairground were comic performers, such as John Edwards, Merry Andrew in Pinkethman's company, and Jubilee Dicky Norris, who formed a double act with William Bullock, he being short and stocky while Bullock was tall and thin. Early examples of pantomime dame characters were also seen, such as John Egleton's Wicked Witch of Cornwall in *The Fair Maid of the West*, at Southwark Fair, played by Harper at Bartholomew Fair the following year. The standard of acting was often, but not always, high. There is a report of Dogget's company around 1702 performing with 'starched' movements and 'singing miserably', though Dogget's own performance, in 'a hobledehoy of a dance', dressed in 'old woman's petticoats and red waistcoat', was of a different quality: 'it would have made a stoic split his lungs if he had seen the temporary harlot sing and weep both at once'.[3]

THE REPERTOIRE OF THE FAIRGROUNDS

The play was a droll version of *Friar Bacon and Friar Bungay*, in which the characters were 'jumbled confusedly together', there was '*a flying shoulder of mutton*' and '*singing and dancing devils*'. How much was improvised is difficult to judge, but clearly a proportion of such drolls followed no script. A 'droll' was a short, usually action-packed and comic playlet, lasting perhaps half an hour, or it might be a scene from or a condensation of a longer play. What was important for the droll was that it was fast-moving, comic, surprising and probably crude. The most popular drolls were based on traditional tales and folklore – Dick Whittington, the Blind Beggar of Bethnal Green, Jane Shore, Robin Hood; but filleted versions of current theatrical 'hits' such as *The Recruiting Officer* or *The Beggar's Opera* were also appreciated, while others were based on Biblical legends, like *Jephthah's Rash Vow* or *Judith and Holofernes* and classical myths like *The Siege of Troy*. Drolls could yoke together the strangest couples: in 1733 at Southwark Fair Theophilus Cibber and company presented a show which united *Tamerlane* and *The Miser* in a forty-five-minute play. If politics ever intruded into this fast-moving, make-believe world, it was of the coarsest kind. There were rough anti-Catholic pieces seen at the time of the Popish Plot in 1680, and the later *Wat Tyler and Jack Straw* had the merest veneer of conformist politics. Rather, we see Jack Straw praise his beloved:

> Whiter than new-peel'd turnips is her skin,
> Her breath far sweeter than the smell of gin;[4]

and the end is signalled when the king spouts a final patriotic tirade.

The popular audiences loved it, and even the Prince of Wales paid several visits over the years to Bartholomew Fair's play booths. We hear of 'the mob' being 'wonderfully pleased, as well as greatly astonished' by what they saw, and women in the audience 'cracking nuts and looking round for admirers'. In many booths, the majority of spectators simply stood in the pit; benches around the sides, perhaps elevated on trestles, served for 'boxes'. The shows, which might last an hour, ran continuously from noon or one PM until nearly midnight, one show following another as rapidly as one audience could be shifted out and another one brought in. There were occasional accidents – in 1725 at Southwark Fair, a gallery in Lee and Harper's booth collapsed: one man was killed by the spikes, another badly injured his leg. But what these entertainments provided was a time out of time, when the quotidian world was forgotten and fantasy and imagination ran free.

NORWICH THEATRES IN THE SEVENTEENTH CENTURY

The most theatrically active provincial city in England after the Restoration was Norwich, the base of George Jolly in the 1660s. In the next decades, two companies, led by John Coysh and Robert Parker respectively, appeared frequently here, usually at the Red Lion, where the performing space included pit and boxes and was warmed by two open fires. Parker, a regular at Bartholomew Fair, may have been based in Newmarket and performed during race meetings there. In 1687, a new company, or perhaps Parker's old company under the new leadership of John Power, played in

Norwich, first at the Red Lion and then from 1692 at the Angell. The group had about twenty members, and they gave the proceeds from one show at Christmas 1694 to the poor. By this time Coysh's company had become the Duke of Norfolk's. It included at different times Thomas Dogget, Tony Aston and Thomas Keregen. In 1697, Dogget, now their leader, ousted Power from the Angell, but two years later, during a performance, the gallery, probably overcrowded, crashed down, killing a young woman and injuring many.

NORWICH THEATRES, 1700–1740

In 1702, John Power's company, now the Duke of Grafton's Servants, returned with renewed energy, performing *Timon of Athens*, *Love for Love* and *The Provoked Wife* and being invited to perform for Queen Anne at Windsor in 1706. The Duke of Norfolk's were also still active. In 1710 they presented Davenant's operatic version of *Macbeth*, as well as plays by Shakespeare, Behn, Dryden, Farquhar, Centlivre and others. They flourished throughout the 1710s, but faded thereafter. It is not clear whether it was they who performed the anti-Jacobite drama, *The Earl of Mar Marred*. The Earl of Mar was a leader of the Jacobite army of 1715. A faction in the audience cheered, stamped and shouted at this, but others in the gallery hissed King George, swords were drawn, the ladies shrieked, but calm was eventually restored.

In the 1720s, two new companies appeared, sparking a new rivalry. Thomas Keregen now had his own troupe, which performed in 1723 at the White Swan, and that same year Henry Tollett brought a company to the King's Arms. Tollett's company, which may have been the same as the Duke of Grafton's, seems to have almost settled in Norwich. In 1728 it was almost certainly they who performed a particularly notable version of *The Beggar's Opera*, outclassing even the original London production according to some who saw both. They continued in Norwich well into the 1730s, when another company belonging to a female manager, Mrs Schoolding, was also seen. These Norwich companies all also toured beyond the city. They were frequently seen at Ipswich's Shire Hall, for instance, where there was another terrible disaster in 1729, the exact nature of which seems lost, though it is known that many people were hurt. Norwich companies also appeared in a warehouse at Yarmouth and in Colchester's moot hall.

YORK

Thomas Keregen moved away from Norwich in the 1720s to York, where performances had been recorded since at least 1705 at the Merchant Taylor's Hall. A company led by an actor called Ager was based here through the 1710s, and in 1715 the Duke of Norfolk's Servants, including Thomas Keregen, appeared. In 1721, Keregen left them to form his own company in York, where he soon supplanted Ager's group. Through the 1720s, though based in York, his company toured widely, appearing at race meetings in Leicester, Nottingham and Newcastle, but developing a circuit which also included Scarborough, Leeds, Beverley and Hull. In 1731 Keregen was in a position to organise longer subscription seasons in York and to pay the actors wages, rather than insist they survive on the fickleness of sharing. In 1733 he applied to make the tennis court in Lord Irwin's Yard into a permanent theatre, which the Corporation warmly welcomed: 'A commodious playhouse in this city may very much conduce to the entertainment of the nobility and gentry resorting to this city and encourage them to spend their winter seasons here'.[5] The new theatre opened in 1734 with a programme of two plays per week over twenty-six weeks, the opening production being *Henry IV Part 1*. Subscribers were asked to pay a guinea and a half for a box for the season or a guinea for a place in the pit.

Keregen's theatre was however closed by the terms of the 1737 Licensing Act, though it seems the company continued to play illicitly in different venues in the city, winked at by the authorities. They advertised and charged for a 'concert' and presented plays free in the 'interval'. In 1741, Keregen died. The company was taken over by his widow, who continued not without male challenges, until her death, by which time she had had constructed a New Theatre in Mint Yard, the site of the present Theatre Royal, York.

BATH AND THE SOUTH WEST

In Bath in the 1690s, a stable by the Abbey Gate served as a theatre, and there were also performances in the Guildhall and Harrison's Assembly Rooms. In 1703, the Drury Lane company visited the city when Queen Anne was there. It was then that Anne Oldfield first showed glimpses of her future greatness, for Susanna Verbruggen was too ill to travel, and Oldfield took her parts.

The following year John Power's company, the Duke of Grafton's from Norwich, visited Bath, and in 1705, presumably on their initiative, a subscription was raised to erect perhaps the first provincial purpose-built theatre in England on the corner of Borough Wells and Vicarage Lane. The company continued, though standards seem to have deteriorated, with tawdry decor, shoddy acting and thin audiences reported. They toured as far afield as Exeter, Worcester, Gloucester and to villages round about, and their *Beggar's Opera* was notably successful in 1728. In 1730 Power's widow was still in charge.

In Bristol matters were more turbulent. The authorities there were not sympathetic to theatre, and the enormous popularity of *The Beggar's Opera* led them to restrain the theatres as 'public nuisances and nurseries of idleness and vice'. The people rioted in protest, and in 1729 John Hippisley, Peachum in the original *Beggar's Opera*, opened a new theatre at Jacob's Well in the city.

Further west records are scant, though Monmouth in south Wales received a touring company in 1724 which performed Otway's *The Cheats of Scapin* in the town, and at other race meetings and fairs in south Wales.

RICHMOND

In 1718 William Pinkethman built a theatre in Richmond, Surrey, convenient for the Prince of Wales, and for his company's annual visits to the London fairs, and four years after his death in 1726, Thomas Chapman either reopened it or erected another theatre there.

SCOTLAND

Scotland was perhaps slower than England to develop its own theatre tradition. The country's religious struggles continued for decades after 1660, the Covenanters still struggling for their rights, and, after 1690, many Scots finding their loyalties lying with the Jacobites. After the Glencoe

Massacre of 1692, there were risings in Scotland in 1694 and 1696. Later that decade famine bestrode the land. The Darien Scheme, which seemed to offer a way forward, collapsed disastrously in 1700, and the Alien Act of 1705 followed by the Act of Union in 1707 further undermined any nascent Scottish theatrical culture.

In 1663 an amateur performance of *Marciano* by William Clarke was performed in the tennis court at Holyrood House in Edinburgh, and there were further occasional performances, for instance Thomas Sydserf's *Tarugo's Wiles* also in Edinburgh in 1668 and Archibald Pitcairn's angry pro-Jacobite *The Assembly* in 1692. In 1679, three actors from London King's Men joined a company in Edinburgh managed by Thomas Serfe, though for how long is unknown. But London drew many Scottish theatre practitioners, like Catherine Trotter in the 1690s, and David Crawford and Newburgh Hamilton in the following years. After the Union there was a craze for Scottish 'entertainments' in London, and these spilled over sometimes into the theatre, as in Susanna Centlivre's *The Wonder! A Woman Keeps a Secret* which features Gibby, a Scottish servant 'in highland dress', and the Unionist Colonel Briton (note the name), who protests: 'the kirk starves us Scotsmen. We are kept so sharp at home, that we feed like cannibals abroad'.

THEATRE IN EDINBURGH

In Edinburgh itself, a company of strolling players performed in 1715 at Holyrood and Old Magazine House, Canongate. Four years later Larina Violante appeared, rope dancing, tumbling and teaching elocution. She mounted a production of Molière's *The Cheats of Scapin*, probably in Otway's version, with a group of students for which Allan Ramsay wrote a Prologue. In 1729 Ramsay's *The Gentle Shepherd*, originally written in support of the 1715 Jacobite Rising, now adapted as a ballad opera, was given by the students of Haddington Grammar School at Taylor's Hall.

In 1724 Tony Aston's strolling company arrived in the city. They performed at Skinner's Hall, to the chagrin of the kirk. 'A company of stage-players are acting plays . . . filled with horrid swearing, obscenity and expressions of double meaning',[6] which, considering their repertoire included *Love for Love*, was unexpectedly apposite.

It was Lady Morrison who finally managed to engineer Aston's expulsion. She lived beneath Skinner's Hall and complained the audience was in danger of coming through her ceiling. In spite of Ramsay's *Hints in Defence of Dramatic Entertainment*, Aston's troupe was ejected. They were replaced for the Edinburgh theatregoer, however, by the Edinburgh Company of Players who based themselves in Taylor's Hall in Cowgate. They claimed to possess a Royal Patent, and gave performances for charity, as well as touring both the east coast of Scotland as far north as Aberdeen and down into England's north east. Led by John Ware, who would later appear at Drury Lane, their repertoire included Shakespeare, Vanbrugh, the inevitable *Beggar's Opera* and plays by Henry Fielding. But in 1736 they lost their Royal Patent and closed.

Ramsay himself energetically started a new company, who performed in Carrubber's Close, giving *The Recruiting Officer* and *The Virgin Unmasked*, but within months the 1737 Licensing Act came into force. The company, which included the nomadic Henry Giffard of Bartholomew Fair and Goodman's Close Theatre, London, tried to defy the law by mounting Adam Thomson's ballad opera, *Buckram in Armour*, but they were forced to close. Attempts to present plays free in the 'intervals' of concerts were also tried, but with only mixed success.

Figure 4.23
Portrait of the poet Allan Ramsay, Scottish theatrical *animateur* in the first decades of the eighteenth century

Source: Ian Dagnall/Alamy Stock Photo

PROVINCIAL THEATRE AND LONDON THEATRE

Many Scots still turned to London where a number of playwrights enjoyed some success, the most prominent being James Thomson, author of *Sophonisba* (1730), *Agamemnon* (1738), the anti-royalist *Edward and Leonora* (1739) and *Tancred and Sigismunda* (1745), and David Mallet, who wrote the Jacobitical *Eurydice* (1731) and the anti-Walpole *Mustapha* (1739). Thomson and Mallet, both supporters of the Prince of Wales, collaborated on *The Masque of Alfred* (1740), which was premiered at the Prince's private mansion and concluded with the new song, 'Rule, Britannia'.

Early eighteenth-century theatre in the fairgrounds, the provinces and Scotland all demonstrated the potential of a different theatre beyond the wealthy west end of London and beyond the legitimate and accepted drama. It was the beginning of an alternative theatre which was to persist throughout the coming centuries.

NOTES

1 Sybil Rosenfeld, *The Theatre of the London Fairs in the 18th Century*, Cambridge: Cambridge University Press, 1960, p. 14.
2 Henry Morley, *Memoirs of Bartholomew Fair*, London: Hugh Evelyn, 1973, pp. 370–371.
3 William Hone, *The Every-Day Book,* London: Hunt and Clarke, vol 1, 1826, p. 1240.
4 Sybil Rosenfeld, *op.cit.*, p. 142.
5 Linda Fitzsimmons, 'The Theatre Royal York', in *York History*, York: York Educational Settlement, n.d., p. 169.
6 James Buchan, *Capital of the Mind*, London: John Murray, 2003, p. 103.

Chapter 49: Theatre in the reign of George I

A DIVIDED INHERITANCE

As Queen Anne lay ill and dying, the nation's political classes were (as they often are) feverish with uncertainty: should they bring back the expelled Stuarts in the shape of the 'Old Pretender', or stick with their earlier determination to bring in the Elector of Hanover? In the event, while the Tories dithered, the Whigs imported the ageing George I, his poor English, his two mistresses, one fat, one thin and all. At his coronation there were protests, but here was a battle-hardened soldier who fought the Turks in the 1690s and who shared a name with England's patron saint. The fact that he always preferred Germany to his new kingdom only gradually became apparent.

But the split in the country was real enough. The Tories turned to the king over the water. Their leader, Bolingbroke, fled to the Old Pretender in France, but the Whigs won the 1715 General Election and consolidated their alliance with the new king. The Jacobites, however, increasingly erratically supported by the Tories, were not eradicated. James II had died in 1701. An invasion of Scotland had been defeated in 1708. Now the Jacobites planned to return to claim 'their own', only for their new planned rebellion to be betrayed by Bolingbroke's mistress to the Whigs at home. Though the 1715 rebellion therefore made little headway, rumblings continued to come from Jacobite supporters through the ensuing decades.

Partly they were supported by disaffected Catholics who, in spite of much religious toleration, were still excluded and oppressed. The Church of England acquired a new, higher class of parson and bishops entered party politics. The Society for the Reformation of Manners was still enthusiastically prosecuting those it disapproved of, but mainstream clergy lived well, and did little, leading inevitably to Wesley's mission and the rise of Methodism. This was also a response to grim social conditions – cities, including London, sordid, evil-favoured and brutal, with gambling and gin-drinking rife, and three in four babies born not surviving. Extreme poverty neighboured obese wealth.

THE WHIGS AND DRURY LANE

Party politics took a particularly poisonous form at this time. The Tories, shorn of their Stuart allegiances, turned to the Prince of Wales, the king's detested son, while the Whigs boasted they stood for business, property and freedom, by which they meant economic freedom. They sought stability, and an end to continental wars, which they associated with the Tories, but were unsure how to achieve these goals. One way seemed to lie with the South Sea Company, a trading monopoly like the East India Company, and bought shares in it with borrowed money. When this led to its unavoidable crash in 1720, those 'in the know', including politicians, escaped with minimal damage, while those less well-off like Colley Cibber and John Gay paid most of the price. The man who disentangled the mess for his friends was Robert Walpole who now became in effect Britain's first Prime Minister.

Walpole was never popular but he was a skilful politician, and the fact that George I was often in Germany, while the Stuart Pretender was also abroad, gave him a new sort of status: he became a kind of bourgeois pseudo-king. His 'reign' saw trade greatly expanded as his economic liberalism took hold. Economic liberalism is not usually helpful to personal liberty, however, and the near-deification of property rights led to frenzied activity, both in the money markets, depicted brilliantly in Susanna Centlivre's 1718 comedy, *A Bold Stroke for a Wife*, and in civil society, exemplified in the so-called Black Act of 1723 which introduced over fifty new capital offences. Soon, if a child stole a handkerchief, he could be hanged on the gallows. Walpole, using the Jacobite threat for excuse, suspended *habeas corpus* in 1722, and also outlawed working people's combinations. No wonder the lower classes found themselves moving towards the Jacobites, for by the end of the 1720s Britain was in some senses little better than a police state.

Figure 4.24
Susanna Centlivre's *A Bold Stroke for a Wife* was presented at Lincoln's Inn Fields in 1718
Source: Art Collection 3/Alamy Stock Photo

Figure 4.25
Interior of a coffee house, where homosociability was given full rein

The situation was partially ameliorated by a new sociability, the founding of new clubs and societies, the opening of coffee houses and pleasure gardens, and the publishing of many new newspapers. Though most of this was for men only, it was a force for democratic good, opening up the rigid class system.

Theatre, too, was a force for sociability. When Queen Anne died, the theatres were closed for six weeks, during which time Drury Lane was refurbished. More significantly, William Collier's licence lapsed with her death, and the triumvirate in charge invited Richard Steele to replace him, and Steele, an outspoken Whig, was granted a personal patent for Drury Lane Theatre in January 1715, and indeed was knighted later that year. From this time, Drury Lane was identified as a Whig house, and the triumvirate of Cibber, Wilks and Booth attained a stability which their political mentors were quite unable to match. The nearest they came to controversy was probably the production of Susanna Centlivre's *Gotham Election*. Inspired by the 1715 election, which had provoked such mayhem that the Riot Act had been passed, it mocked the politicians' election pledges, nepotism and the buying and selling of votes, and climaxed with a riot. It was banned, and not performed till 1724.

STABILITY AT DRURY LANE

'In the twenty years, while we were our own directors', Cibber boasted, 'we never had a creditor that had occasion to come twice for his bill',[1] though this was partly due to their notorious miserliness

Figure 4.26
'A Just View of the British Stage, or Three Heads Are Better Than One', satirical print by William Hogarth, 1724. The triumvirate, Barton Booth, Robert Wilks and Colley Cibber, sit at the table, imagining a new farce.

when it came to expenditure on new costumes, furnishings or whatever. The obverse of this was that the three 'directors' cast themselves in all the best roles – Booth was Othello, Cibber Iago and Wilks Cassio; Wilks was Hamlet, Booth was the Ghost; Booth was Brutus, Wilks Antony; Booth was Lear, Wilks Edgar; and so on. In 1717 they staged Cibber's violently anti-Catholic, anti-Jacobite *The Non-Juror*, loosely derived from Moliere's *Tartuffe*, with Cibber as the villainous Doctor Wolf who turns out to be a Papish priest. When he is unmasked, Mr Heartly, played by Wilks, declares: 'To guard our freedom, George must fill the throne'. George himself attended the production, though he probably understood little since his English was appalling, but he allowed Cibber to dedicate the play to him, much to the Tories' fury. They immediately mounted *The Per-Juror* at Lincoln's Inn Fields, which, however, flopped pathetically.

Drury Lane's worst upset during George I's reign probably came as a result of Whig political infighting in 1719. Walpole and the Duke of Newcastle, the Lord Chamberlain, being at loggerheads,

Newcastle turned his ire on Sir Richard Steele, a prominent Walpole supporter. Steele believed his Royal Patent enabled him to bypass the Lord Chamberlain or the Master of the Revels in his conduct of the theatre's affairs. Now Newcastle demanded to see the theatre's accounts. Steele refused permission. Newcastle, furious, ordered Steele to sack Cibber, another strong Walpole supporter. When Steele protested, Newcastle had Cibber flung into gaol and Drury Lane Theatre closed. Wilks and Booth, the managers still at liberty, quickly agreed to jettison Steele. Cibber was freed, and a new licence given to the triumvirate. In 1722, however, Walpole reinstated Steele as the patent holder, though exactly what Steele did for his sufficient emoluments is not clear. Nevertheless, now, perhaps to seal the reconciliation, the company mounted Steele's most significant comedy, *The Conscious Lovers*.

THE NEW LINCOLN'S INN FIELDS

At the same time, around 1720, the other patent house, Lincoln's Inn Fields, was undergoing a crisis of its own. Christopher Rich had sat on his suspended Royal Patent from 1709, biding his time until Queen Anne was safely in her grave. Then he moved. He persuaded Sir James Craggs, a Tory minister, to intercede on his behalf, and George, reminded that Charles II had granted two theatres patents in 1660, agreed that Rich's patent suspension should be lifted. At last Rich was back where he wanted to be. But his joy was short-lived. During the autumn, as the finishing touches were put on his newly reconstituted theatre, he slipped and fell while descending from his coach, injuring his leg. The leg became gangrenous, Rich was incapacitated, and in November he died, leaving the renewed patent to his sons, John and Christopher Moyser Rich.

The new Lincoln's Inn Fields theatre which their father had created had a frontage eighty-nine feet long along Portugal Street; its sides were not completely parallel but each stretched back to a depth of about forty-five feet. Built of brick with stone facings, it included side and front boxes, a pit and two galleries. Its apron stage jutted into the auditorium, and was flanked by mirrors – excellent for actresses to admire themselves in, according to one wag – and was finely decorated, and held above a thousand spectators. There were also rooms for painting, a carpenter's workshop, a wardrobe, a barber's room, a tailor's room and offices. The ceiling was painted with Apollo and the Muses above the apron stage, and a group of eminent theatrical personages, including Shakespeare, Ben Jonson and Thomas Betterton, over the audience.

The new theatre made its way only shakily in the face of Drury Lane's uncompromising competitiveness, and in 1717 the Rich brothers handed over the management of their theatre to two of the actors, Christopher Bullock and Theophilus Keene. But the theatre continued to lose money. In 1719 Keene died. Bullock tried to continue on his own, but by 1720 the position was unsustainable. Sir Richard Steele, relieved at this point of his Drury Lane duties, was mooted as a replacement, but in the event John Rich returned and began a much more successful period in the theatre's history.

In 1723, he mounted Elijah Fenton's blank verse tragedy, *Marianne*, and later the same year Johan Christoph Pepusch's *The Union of the Three Sister Arts*, a perhaps over-solemn attempt to combine music, poetry and visual art. Unexpectedly heavy for an afterpiece, it still proved popular with theatregoers, and by 1725 Rich felt secure enough to order another major refurbishment of his theatre.

THEATRICAL STAGNATION

Part of the reason for Lincoln's Inn Fields' improved circumstances resided in the cartel arrangements Rich had made with Drury Lane after their troubles. The two companies agreed to co-operate to the extent that quite often they performed on alternate nights so as not to undercut each other's audience, and they further agreed not to poach each other's actors, which of course gave increased power to the two managements. The upshot was a period of stagnation artistically, as both houses consolidated their positions. Some new plays were accepted for production, but too often the production failed to materialise. Perhaps the triumvirate were losing their touch, but perhaps their timidity was the result of a political climate in which the South Sea Company had crashed, the Jacobites were still apparently threatening and statutes like the Black Law were being enacted.

Figure 4.27
Robert Wilks in one of his most admired roles, Sir Harry Wildair in George Farquhar's *The Constant Couple*
Source: Performing Arts Images/ArenaPAL

THE END OF THE TRIUMVIRATE

Meanwhile claques, probably mostly Tories, began to target Colley Cibber, partly because of his closeness to Walpole. Cibber's plays, and often his appearances on the stage, became the cue for booing and hissing. Cibber was a successful manager, a playwright of skill and tenacity, an actor of above average competence, and he possessed energy and commitment to Drury Lane. But there was something about him which infuriated people. Alexander Pope made him the king of all dunces in his mock-epic, *The Dunciad*. Now, Cibber's plays, first *The Refusal* (1721), then *Caesar in Egypt* (1724), were hooted from the stage. When *The Refusal* was first booed, Cibber spoke from the stage, trying to mollify his detractors, and was loudly applauded. But the next night, when the play was Cibber's *The Rival Fools*, the booing and hissing began again. Indeed Wilks, playing the lead, was pelted with oranges, or wooden balls painted orange. Cibber's plays were withdrawn from the repertoire for a while.

When George I died, Cibber took the opportunity to mount a lavish *Henry VIII* with magnificent coronation procession reminiscent of George II's recent crowning, and followed this with a triumphant rewriting of Vanbrugh's last unfinished play, *Journey to London*, retitled by Cibber *The Provoked Husband* which ran for nearly thirty successive performances. Cibber's fortunes appeared to be rising again.

But not for long. Barton Booth had retired from the stage in 1727. He died in 1733, the year after Robert Wilks died. Cibber himself, perhaps disheartened, retired in 1732, and though he occasionally reappeared during his long retirement, the years of the triumvirate were over.

NOTE

1 Colley Cibber, *An Apology for His Life*, London: J.M. Dent & Sons, 1938, p. 226.

Chapter 50: Pantomime and ballad opera

THE FIRST PANTOMIMES

Pantomime was the first genuinely original form thrown up by the Georgian theatre.

In 1716 John Weaver, a 'little dapper cheerful man', and the choreographer at Drury Lane, presented a series of 'Italian night scenes' as afterpieces. John Rich, at Lincoln's Inn Fields copied him, and presented *A New Italian Mimic Scene between a Scaramouche, a Harlequin, a Country Farmer, His Wife and Others* with himself appearing as Harlequin under the name of 'Lun'. The following year, Weaver presented *The Loves of Mars and Venus*, performed 'after the manner of the ancient pantomimes', and *Perseus and Andromeda*, danced 'grotesquely by Harlequin and Columbine'. Harlequin gazed at a picture of Columbine, realised she was out of his reach and made to kill himself. But the chair he stood on to hang himself turned into a magician, who gave Harlequin a magic sword. With this he effected a series of marvellous transformations, not least of himself into a dog which entered Pantaloon's house, and urinated on the master's leg. He escaped with Columbine, but was chased, caught and was about to be hanged – but his magic sword enabled him to escape.

Even this brief description indicates the workings of the Georgian pantomime. It was a mix of quaint dance and mime, low comedy and spectacular transformations. Further pantomimes expanded the form. In *The Cheats, or The Tavern Bilkers*, Weaver brought pantomime nearer to home, but it was in 1723 that the *genre* was crystallised. In November that year, Drury Lane mounted *Harlequin Dr Faustus*, which showed Harlequin's mischief after he signed the pact with Mephistophiles: he cut off his own leg, and replaced it with another which flew in from the sky, he put asses' ears on Punchinello, Pierrot and Scaramouche, and at the end he was carried away by fiery devils. At Lincoln's Inn Fields a month later, John Rich mounted a similar piece, *The Necromancer*, which included Hero and Leander singing of their love before Harlequin was hauled off by dragons.

HARLEQUIN SORCERER

Rich, the gauche and youthful inheritor of Christopher Rich's patent, found the perfect vehicle for his talent by anglicising Harlequin. His pantomime star ascended throughout the 1720s and for decades beyond. In 1725, he was in *Harlequin Sorcerer with the Loves of Pluto and Proserpine*. This consisted of an overture, followed by a vision of witches in a moonlit wilderness. They

Figure 4.28
John Rich as Harlequin in *The Necromancer*, 1723
Source: University of Bristol/ArenaPAL

sang, till Harlequin suddenly leapt in among them on a long pole. There was a dance, with the witch's broomsticks clattering out the time, before Harlequin was seen serenading Columbine. But Pantaloon, Columbine's crusty old father, discovered him and gave chase. After miraculous escapes, acrobatics, transformations of characters and scenery and, of course, plenty of dance and song, Harlequin was reduced to exhaustion, lightning flashed and four devils in flame-coloured stockings surrounded him. And then, amazingly, the whole tableau rose up and was borne away into the sky.

THE STRUCTURE OF EARLY PANTOMIMES

The format was set. Its first section was a classical story, perhaps from Ovid's *Metamorphosis* or similar source, in verse and song, often a pastiche of Italian opera. But before long a magician intervened, and the characters were changed into Harlequin, Columbine, Pantaloon, Punchinello, Scaramouche and other British versions of characters from the Italian *commedia dell'arte*, whose tricks, jokes and adventures were danced or mimed.

PANTOMIME DANCE AND MOVEMENT

The dance was not balletic, it was 'grotesque'. Harlequin, with his small, rapid, running steps, his jumps with hands and feet flying out, his 'postures' and his flourishing of his hat was the protagonist. But the others, too, had their characteristic movements: Pierrot's were straight and graceful, Punchinello's head went back and forth like a hen's, Scaramouche took long strides with ridiculous solemnity. Famous Harlequins were John Rich, Theophilus Cibber and Henry Woodward, but sometimes the androgynous Harlequin was played by a woman – Hester Santlow, Barton Booth's wife, was a particular favourite at Drury Lane. Harlequin always wore a black mask, which was perhaps diabolical, or perhaps simply 'other'. Francis Leigh and Louis Layfield were famous Scaramouches, and le Roussau probably the best early Pierrot. Children, too, sometimes appeared in these roles. Alongside the stage actors not involved in the action narrated the story.

PANTOMIME MUSIC

Pantomimes were quintessentially musical. There were arias, as well as *recitatives*, ensembles and choruses. Several comic songs were sung, and between the vocal items there were instrumental pieces which accompanied the performers' mimes. In pantomime, the music was virtually continuous from beginning to end.

SPECTACLE IN PANTOMIME

Spectacle was the final essential element. An enormous snake appeared, with gold and green scales, red spots and fiery eyes: when a soldier drew his sword to fight it, the audience roared with laughter. A forest grew from nothing before the audience's eyes. Blossom appeared, then fell off the branches. Fruit grew in its place. The wonders seemed never ending. Pope, not a fan of pantomime, nevertheless enumerated others in *The Dunciad*:

> Behold a sable sorcerer arise,
> Swift to whose hand a winged volume flies;
> All sudden gorgons hiss and dragons glare,
> And ten-horned fiends and giants rush to war.
> Hell rises, heaven descends; and dance on earth,
> Gods, imps and monsters, music, rage and mirth,
> A fire, a jig, a battle and a ball,
> Till one wide conflagration swallows all.

These myriad marvels were always and hilariously interspersed with basic slapstick comedy and smutty jokes. Amid the miracles, the leading characters, Harlequin and Columbine, were servants, not gentry or aristocrats. Pantomime was carnivalesque, the everyday world was turned upside down.

JOHN RICH AS HARLEQUIN

Pantomime was the making of John Rich, who was an accomplished dancer and contortionist. His most famous exploit as Harlequin was his birth. He hatched out of an egg. One spectator wrote:

> From the first chipping of the egg, his receiving of motion, his feeling of the ground, his standing upright, to
> his quick Harlequin trip round the empty shell – through the whole progression every limb had its tongue,
> which spoke with most miraculous organ to the understandings and sensations of the observers.[1]

THE WHAT D'YE CALL IT

Then ballad opera burst upon the scene, an altogether more spiky form. It was created almost single-handedly by John Gay, a Tory poet and friend of Swift, Pope and others, whose earlier plays were often puzzling. *The What D'Ye Call It* (1715) was a 'tragi-comical pastoral farce' which mocked contemporary theatrical pretensions using parody, burlesque and bathetic rhymed verse. A play within a play in which 'reality' and 'fantasy' constantly collide in disconcerting fashion, it also contains some delicious absurdities, such as a 'chorus of sighs and groans' when Kitty's proposed marriage falls through, and a chorus of haymakers, singing, when the marriage has been resurrected, 'A wedding, a bedding; a wedding, a bedding'. All this was brilliantly performed by Rich's Lincoln's Inn Fields company with alarming solemnity. Alexander Pope noted gleefully that the spectators 'received it at first with great gravity and sedateness, some few with tears; but after the third day they also took the hint, and have ever since been very loud in their claps'.[2]

THREE HOURS AFTER MARRIAGE

Three Hours after Marriage (1717), which Gay wrote with Pope and John Arbuthnot, concerns Dr Fossil who discovers three hours after marrying that his wife is serially unfaithful. Sometimes cynically anti-women, including a misogynistic attack on women playwrights, the play, which again violates every dramatic convention, is nevertheless riotously funny about the culturally pretentious. Produced by Colley Cibber with himself as Plotwell, the comedy was enhanced because Cibber failed to realise that Plotwell was a caricature of himself.

BALLAD OPERA

Excellent as these plays were, they did not prepare Gay's audience for *The Beggar's Opera*, the original 'ballad opera', which was premiered on 29 January 1728. A ballad opera is one which uses popular existing tunes and sets new words to them, in an operatic three-act structure. The popular music is the key to the form. Old tunes known since childhood are reassuring, comfortable, but they also create resonances with a wilder world, releasing the imagination into the unpredictable carnival of popular culture, and the world turned upside down.

THE BEGGAR'S OPERA

When Gay presented his playscript to Cibber at Drury Lane, Cibber rejected it. Rich took it up at Lincoln's Inn Fields, but with some trepidation. Quin, his leading actor, turned down the part of Macheath, and the cast Rich employed were largely his second string. But even on the first night, after a certain puzzlement in the audience, the piece was received with overwhelming applause, and it became immediately the greatest hit ever seen in the British theatre. Tickets could hardly be acquired at any price.

The Beggar's Opera presents a deliberately sideways view of society, wry, sometimes contemptuous, always fascinated. Peachum's first speech sets the ironic tone:

> A lawyer is an honest employment, so is mine. Like me too, he acts in a double capacity, both against rogues, and for 'em; for 'tis but fitting that we should protect and encourage cheats, since we live by them.

To 'peach' is to betray, to 'impeach', to arraign. Peachum, a fence and procurer, relies on betraying his friends and employees, and, if possible, arraigning them, the timing for his treacheries depending entirely on the financial needs of his 'business': he is thoroughly *bourgeois*. Yet his attitude and that of his arch enemy and antagonist, the aristocratic highwayman, Macheath, are almost exactly the same. Macheath's romantic glamour is shattered when it is revealed that he has four more wives, besides Polly and Lucy. Women are for Macheath what cash is to Peachum. Civilisation is a mere veneer over acquisitiveness and greed.

Part of the success of *The Beggar's Opera* came from the ribald mockery of upper-class opera, especially in its ending which ridiculed neoclassical poetic justice. But there was also a good deal of spleen vented at the Whig political establishment, Peachum and Lockit being to the audiences of the time perfect fits for Walpole and Charles 'Turnip' Townshend: 'Like great statesmen we encourage those who betray their friends'. Their friends are the gang who are liberal businessmen, their workings being enterprising capitalism, their spirit thoroughly *bourgeois*. If they defy the law, it is because the laws are unjust, and thwart them in their enterprise – highway robbery, which some said was Walpole's policy. Who are the crooks in this society?

Money ensures that you can purchase lighter handcuffs when you find yourself in gaol, and the ending under the gallows takes a final swipe at the law's fiercest symbol, so venerated by the Black Law. The parallel between, on the one hand, Macheath and the much-admired robber, Jack Sheppard, who escaped so brilliantly and so often from gaol, and Peachum and the thief-taker and swindler, Jonathan Wild, on the other, has been made many times. When Sheppard was hanged a crowd of over twenty thousand attended, weeping and crying. When Wild was hanged few mourned, though he had been most of his life an apparently thoroughly respectable *bourgeois* trader, even if this facade masked a cheating, lying criminal.

POLLY PEACHUM: LAVINIA FENTON

The drama's favourite scene was the meeting of Polly and Lucy in Newgate Gaol: their jealousy and quarrel reminded watchers of the fatuous rivalry between the operatic singers, Cuzzoni and Faustina, which was repeated in 1736 over this work, when Kitty Clive and Susanna Cibber quarrelled violently over who should play Polly in a new production. Polly, charming even as she

Figure 4.29
Lavinia Fenton, who scored an extraordinary success as Polly Peachum in *The Beggar's Opera*, 1728

parrots conventional romantic clichés, was played by the inexperienced though talented Lavinia Fenton. Within days of the opening, her picture was available in the shops, her life was written (or fictionalised), poems were published to her and her 'sayings' were collected. She received gifts from male and female admirers alike, and it was soon clear that the Duke of Bolton, estranged from his wife, was viewing her with more than an ordinary playgoer's feelings. It was therefore no surprise when in June 1728, Fenton ran away with the Duke. She lived with him, bore him children, and finally, when the first Duchess died in the 1750s, married him to become a Duchess herself. The other star was Thomas Walker who played Macheath. He had more experience than Fenton, but soon he too was being imitated by apprentices and swooned over by young women.

Figure 4.30
Two versions of the same scene from The *Beggar's Opera*: Lavinia Fenton as Polly Peachum points with her right hand into the scene where the action is.

Figure 4.31
Two versions of the same scene from *The Beggar's Opera*: All of Lavinia Fenton's attention is on the seated Duke of Bolton, whom she would eventually marry.

Source: National Gallery of Art, Washington, Paul Mellon Collection and Yale Center for British Art, Paul Mellon Collection, Yale University, New Haven

THE BEGGAR'S OPERA'S POPULARITY

The Little Theatre on the Haymarket immediately mounted a production of their own of *The Beggar's Opera*; it was seen in more than one version in the fairgrounds, and in 1730 in Dublin it was performed by children. It remained extraordinarily popular, and later in the century, there was a production with the men's parts taken by women and the women's by men. Indeed Macheath was a favourite part for many actresses. And the work's popularity was never dimmed. Nigel Playfair's June 1920 revival ran for 1469 performances until 1923.

POLLY

Gay hastily wrote a sequel, *Polly*, set in the West Indies, with Macheath as a pirate, and noble Jamaicans facing white interlopers. But Walpole banned it without performance, the first time he had struck at cultural criticism of himself or his administration, and a significant move against the increasingly dynamic and politically engaged theatre of the 1730s.

MORE BALLAD OPERAS

Meanwhile, ballad operas proliferated like breeding rabbits. Thomas Walker's *The Quaker's Opera* appeared before the end of 1728; the next year saw Charles Johnson's, *The Village Opera*, Charles Coffey's *The Beggar's Wedding*, William Chetwood's *The Lovers' Opera*, James Ralph's *The Fashionable Lady, or Harlequin's Opera* and Allan Ramsay's *The Gentle Shepherd*; and 1730's crop included Colley Cibber's *Love in a Riddle*, Gabriel Odingsells's *Bayes' Opera*, Henry Fielding's *The Author's Farce* and Charles Coffey and John Mottley's *The Devil to Pay*. Ballad operas continued to pour out in the ensuing years and decades. Even in the twentieth century, new ballad operas continued to appear, such as Ewan MacColl's *Johnny Noble* (1945). But none matched the original *Beggar's Opera*.

NOTES

1 Raymond Mander and Joe Mitchenson, *Pantomime: A Story in Pictures*, London: Peter Davies, 1973, p. 8.
2 V.C. Clinton-Baddeley, *The Burlesque Tradition in the English Theatre After 1660*, London: Methuen, 1973, p. 45.

Chapter 51: After *The Beggar's Opera*: London theatre in the 1730s

THE END OF THEATRICAL STAGNATION

After 1728, the theatre became more open to new work and experimentation. The long stagnation of the 1710s and 1720s were over. But this in turn led to new confrontations which culminated in the 1737 Licensing Act.

QUARRELS IN THE ROYAL FAMILY

The confrontations were epitomised in the royal family. Frederick, Prince of Wales, quarrelled violently with his bullying father, George II, and set up a rival court with some encouragement from the 'Patriot' Tories, led by William Pitt. The poor often supported the Tories and the Jacobites. Frederick dabbled in drama himself and wrote a play, *The Modish Couple*, under the pseudonym, 'Charles Bodens', which was given at Drury Lane in 1732. It was perhaps an example of the subversion which Walpole increasingly felt threatened by. His Excise Bill of 1733 was met with unexpected fury: was a freeborn Englishman's pleasure to be taxed? He blamed the ensuing civil disturbances on the Jacobites. The Gin Act of 1736, too, which heavily increased the duty on gin and required its retailers to obtain an expensive licence, provoked outrage and popular riots.

DANGERS OF THE THEATRE

To Walpole, even the theatre seemed to be dangerous. It was not so much that plays were politically motivated, though some were; it was that experimental theatre, improvisation, burlesque, satire, even irony, were all perceived as undermining a political authority bent on control. Take Charles Johnson's *Hurlothrumbo*, performed at the Little Theatre, Haymarket in 1729 for over thirty nights. This strangely named play was a kind of nonsensical farce with the author in the leading part, playing his violin, dancing and stilt-walking. What was it about? Or Robert Baker's *Rehearsal of a New Ballad Opera Burlesqued, Called The Mad House* (1736), which purported to show the story of a young lady confined to a mad house to prevent her marrying a poor man. Or Henry Carey's plays, like *Chrononhotonthologos* (1734), in which the King of the Antipodes walked on his hands and wore his crown on his feet, or *The Dragon of Wantley* (1737), a 'low' story, but with mock highbrow music, and a dragon which was killed with 'a kick on the backside'.

Perhaps more worrying was the theatre's propensity for cross-dressing and consequent homo-sexual fantasies. So-called 'breeches roles', in which an actress played a boy, or a woman masquer-ading as a boy, were particularly popular: men enjoyed ogling the women's legs, while cross-dressed women were surely the equal of men. The most notorious cross-dresser of the period was Charlotte Charke, Colley Cibber's youngest child whose apparent masculinity was incorrigible. Moreover, she was a further threat because of her tendency to assemble and manage her own theatre company, a position more fitted, it was generally thought, to a man. It was her company which staged *The Deposing and Death of Queen Gin* (1736) by 'Jack Juniper, a distiller's apprentice turned poet', just a month before the Act came into force.

Figure 4.32
The prison scene from Henry Carey's extravagantly titled *Chrononhotonthologos*: the king of the Antipodes upside down with his crown on his feet

DRURY LANE AFTER THE TRIUMVIRATE

The success of *The Beggar's Opera* was also perhaps an implied criticism of the Whig-supporting Drury Lane. In 1732, the triumvirate which had controlled the theatre for so long negotiated to obtain the Royal Patent which had been Richard Steele's, and then they broke up. Wilks and Booth were replaced initially by John Ellys, a painter, and John Highmore, who had acted as an amateur, but whose chief contact with the theatre had been as a spectator. These two, with no professional experience between them, could now outvote Colley Cibber. Cibber, whom Walpole had decided should be Poet Laureate, lent his share of the patent to his son, the actor and would-be impresario, Theophilus. The upshot was a fiasco. They agreed on nothing, the 1732–3 season was disastrous, and then, in March 1733, to Theophilus's amazement and fury, his father sold his share to Highmore.

Highmore was now the absolute master of Drury Lane. The actors, and Theophilus Cibber in particular, were seething. They had the idea that, because the patent to present plays and the lease on the theatre were two separate matters, they could take the ground from under Highmore by obtaining the theatre's lease. The Lord Chamberlain, the Duke of Grafton, however, refused to help them, and it was obvious that the legal position was unfathomably murky. All through the summer of 1733, therefore, there was a wary and contumelious standoff.

THE ACTORS' REBELLION

In September, however, Theophilus Cibber and most of the actors made their move. They opened a season of their own at the Little Theatre, Haymarket, leaving few actors behind to form a skeleton company. The outraged Highmore tried to force them back, even having the popular comedian, plump John Harper, arrested as a rogue or vagabond. The charge failed utterly to stick. The rebel actors countersued Highmore to repossess the Drury Lane theatre, and surprisingly they won. Highmore sold out to Charles Fleetwood in March 1734, the actors returned to Drury Lane and Theophilus Cibber became company manager. But bitterness remained. Cibber, arrogant and self-centred, was not popular, and the two factions, those who had been loyal to Highmore, and those who had rebelled, could not simply forget their differences. Moreover, they had to woo back their audience. There is some evidence that they now formed a cartel with John Rich at Covent Garden to cushion their plight.

LONDON THEATRES

London had by now at least six regular theatres to bewilder the politicians. Besides Drury Lane, the other patent was Rich's new theatre in Bow Street, Covent Garden, around the corner from Drury Lane. The building, which cost in excess of £6000, seated well over a thousand spectators. It had a steeply raked stage in front of the vista stage, and an equally raked pit. The auditorium was horseshoe-shaped, with two tiers of boxes, including at the sides of the apron stage, and two galleries. Then there were the King's (formerly Queen's) opera house in the Haymarket, Lincoln's Inn Fields, now available to hire from John Rich, the Little Theatre, Haymarket, and the theatre at Goodman's Fields.

Figure 4.33
Theophilus Cibber leads his fellow actors in the revolt against John Highmore's rule at Drury Lane, 1733
Source: The Metropolitan Museum of Art, New York. Harris Brisbane Dick Fund, 1917

Of these, the Little Theatre was the most controversial, operating as it did without a patent. It opened in 1721 after John Potter, a carpenter, had built it on the site of a pub, the King's Head, opposite Vanbrugh's King's. It was small and rather basic, with a single gallery as well as boxes and a pit. For Potter it was a speculation: he let it to whoever wanted to rent it, amateurs, touring companies or even providers of non-dramatic entertainments. A few actors seem to have been readily available for work here, including William Mullart, James Lacy, Charles Steppelaer, Michael Dove and Mrs Nathaniel Clarke, most of whom were also regulars in the fairground booths. But attempts to form a permanent company, such as Aaron Hill's in 1721, soon foundered. In 1729 Theophilus Cibber took the theatre for a summer season, presenting among other plays, Essex Hawker's experimental *The Country Wedding* (1729), and five years later his sister, Charlotte Charke managed a company for the summer, presenting *The Beggar's Opera* in Roman dress, and *Hurlothrumbo*, with Charke as Lord Flame.

The final permanent theatre operating in the 1730s was in Ayliffe Street, Goodman's Fields, near the city, where Thomas Odell, an official in the Lord Chamberlain's office curiously enough, converted a shop into a small theatre. He met fierce opposition from local businessmen and magistrates, who urged that it would draw 'tradesmen's servants and others from their lawful occupations and corrupt their manners'. But it opened. It was small with only one gallery, but splendid decorations including mythological and literary figures painted around the walls and George II over the pit, guarded by the figures of Peace, Liberty and Justice, seen trampling down Tyranny and

Oppression. The Lord Chamberlain, however, ordered it closed in 1731. Odell brought in Henry Giffard, an actor, who redesigned it but did not close it, and turned it into a generally well-run, if unadventurous theatre. The repertoire seems usually to have consisted of plays by Vanbrugh, Congreve, Farquhar, Otway and Shakespeare.

There were also sporadic theatrical appearances elsewhere in the capital. In 1730, Russell's Great Theatrical Booth, probably a temporary construction, was to be found in Tottenham Court; the next year a play was presented in the Great Room in the York Buildings, near the Strand; and in1732 there was some kind of theatre in Bowling Green, Southwark.

ACTING

Perhaps, too, the power of the actor frightened that pseudo-actor, the politician. In 1741, Luigi Riccoboni, the great Italian *improvisatore*, wrote: 'If after forty-five years experience I may be entitled to give my opinion, I dare advance that the best actors in Italy and France come far short of those in England'.[1] If this were true, it was partly at least because the best playwrights of the time provided challenging parts for them, such as the stoic heroes and heroines of tragedies like *Cato* and *Jane Shore*. But Riccoboni may have been referring more particularly to the comic opportunities early eighteenth-century plays afforded, such as Farquhar's Scrub in *The Beaux' Stratagem*:

> he carries his hands in his pockets, just so (walks in the French air) and has a fine long periwig tied up in a bag

or Fielding's Lappet and Lovegold in his version of Molière's *The Miser*, when they 'both burst into tears'. These are old, but highly charged *lazzi*, but Susanna Centlivre provides perhaps even richer possibilities, as for Sancho, a pedant in *The Stolen Heiress* (1705) originally played by Thomas Dogget:

> Your beaus wear their hats (offering to put it on) no, hold, thus, sir; (clapping it under his arm); your conceited
> wit, thus; (putting it over the left eye) and your travelled wit, thus; (over the right eye without a pinch) your
> country squire, thus, (putting it behind his wig).

An even better sequence comes from Centlivre's *The Wonder! A Woman Keeps a Secret* (1714), after Violante and Don Felix have quarrelled:

(He pauses, then pulls a chair and sits by her at a little distance, looking at her some time without speaking. Then draws a little nearer to her.) Give me your hand at parting, however, Violante, won't you? *(Here he lays his hand upon her knee several times.)* Won't you, won't you, won't you?

VIOLANTE *(half regarding him)*: Won't I do what?
DON FELIX: You know what I would have, Violante. O, my heart!
VIOLANTE *(smiling)*: I thought my chains were easily broke. (Lays her hand into his.)
DON FELIX *(draws his chair close to her, and kisses her hand in a rapture)*: Too well thou knowest thy strength! O, my charming
    angel! my heart is all thy own!

Either of these might have come from a Charlie Chaplin film or from the absurdist existentialism of Samuel Beckett.

THEORISTS OF ACTING

Theorists of acting, however, were more concerned with the representation of emotion. Charles Gildon, early in the century, had recommended a kind of emotion memory. When emotion was required, the best actors 'kept their own private afflictions in their mind and bent it perpetually on real objects and not on the fable or fictitious passion of the play which they acted'.[2] Aaron Hill, who argued for an 'acting academy', created a sort of taxonomy of emotions for use by the actor. Starting from the premise that there were six basic emotions – joy, sorrow, fear, scorn, anger and surprise – he believed that these could be combined to express further emotions, such as love, a

Figure 4.34
James Quin as Falstaff

Source: Heritage Images/The Print Collector/Diomedia

mixture of joy and fear, pity, a mixture of fear and sorrow, jealousy, a combination of fear, scorn and anger, and so on. In contradistinction to Gildon's idea, he asserted that the actor needed 'power to put on, at will, the marks and colours which distinguish' the emotions.

Hill mechanistically also declared that there were four steps in the acting process: first, the imagination must assimilate the idea; then, visible expression of the idea must occur in the facial expression; third, the body must adopt the appropriate stance or gesture; and finally all this inevitably finds its outlet in either action or speech or both. He also castigated actors who 'relaxed' as soon as they had finished speaking, 'looking round and examining the company of spectators with an ear only watchful of the cue, at which, like soldiers upon the word of command, they start suddenly back to their postures'; and he deprecated costumes which were largely emblematic, that is, actors, especially those in smaller parts, in contemporary clothes, with the addition of, perhaps, a helmet

Figure 4.35
Theophilus Cibber as Pistol in Shakespeare's *Henry IV* Part 2

or a Roman toga. In truth, speech was often drawled, with volume the only means of indicating heightened emotion ('ranting'), and the tragic 'strut', one leg shooting out in front of the other thoroughly unnaturally, replacing walking.

STARS OF THE THEATRE

Yet undoubtedly some actors were able to move their audiences profoundly. These included James Quin, the biggest star of the 1730s, who turned down the role of Macheath in *The Beggar's Opera*. He was also branded on the hand for killing Williams, a fellow actor: Quin had humiliated him on stage, and he had waylaid Quin on the way from the theatre. The ensuing fight resulted in Williams's death and Quin's confession and conviction. Quin also quarrelled with Theophilus Cibber, whom he regarded as jumped-up and arrogant. But his acting was cool and mannered, his voice grave and rhetorical, suggesting hidden depths in his character.

Theophilus Cibber was charismatic and energetic. He owed his prominence to being the son of his father, perhaps, but he was good at physical comedy, his Pistol especially being a notable grotesque. The third star of this stage was the young Charles Macklin, another man with a hot temper who had also killed a fellow actor. He attempted an acting style considerably more natural than most of his contemporaries. Other actors adorning this stage included Richard Charke, the attractive singer-actor who foolishly married Colley Cibber's daughter, Charlotte, and after some years fled to the West Indies; comic John Harper, whose Falstaff was regarded as funnier than Quin's, but less well sustained; and 'Jubilee Dicky' Norris whose squeaky voice and comic timing made him much loved.

THE FEMALE STARS

Among women, the most impressive was probably Molly Porter, whose 'tragic rage' was renowned. Porter had been held up by highwaymen one night going home from the theatre, but she had drawn her own pistols and driven them off. Kitty Clive (*née* Raftor), who appeared in ten of Henry Fielding's plays, was clever and sassy. She married but separated from her husband in less than two years, thereafter controlling her own destiny sagaciously in a notoriously masculined age. Her Portia was especially admired, partly because in the trial scene she caricatured well-known members of the judiciary.

Christiana Horton, supposedly the most beautiful woman in London, was a coquettish comedy specialist. Susanna Cibber, sister of the composer Thomas Arne and wife of Theophilus Cibber for a short time before deserting him for the actor William Sloper, was extremely moving in tragic or pathetic roles. Sarah Thurmond was a veteran of 'heavy' parts, while Eliza Haywood was a sharp comic actress. Haywood was a butt of Fielding in *The Author's Farce* in which she is lightly disguised as Mrs Novel, for she did write erotic novels as well as plays, including the excellent comedy, *A Wife to Be Let* (1723), and *The Opera of Operas, or, Tom Thumb the Great* (1733) written with William Hatchett and with music by Thomas Arne.

THE ACTOR-AUDIENCE RELATIONSHIP

The close proximity of audience and actor resulted in a powerful relationship between stage and auditorium which helped to give this theatre its characteristic *timbre*. Kitty Clive, for instance, more than once was seen to wink at a friend in the pit, but then when a woman there fainted it was Clive who dashed into the wings, poured a glass of cold water and handed it down to the sufferer. When the woman recovered, Clive was warmly applauded. Other actresses were known to curtsy to any lords of their acquaintance in the boxes. Actors certainly responded to audience comments and even heckles, as when Anne Oldfield curled her lip at an offending spectator and murmured, 'Poor creature!' at him, mortifying him and provoking applause from the other pittites.

CLASS-STRUCTURED AUDIENCE

The price of admission was not cheap: five shillings for a box, three shillings in the pit, two shillings in the first gallery, and one shilling in the upper gallery were usual. The prices, of course, reinforced the class structuring of the audience: persons of rank occupied the boxes, the lesser gentry, self-styled wits and the intelligentsia sat in the pit, citizens, tradespeople and their wives and daughters stayed in the lower gallery, while servants and labourers remained in the upper gallery. But things were not quite as staid as this implies. For one thing, many spectators paid by the act, with the door-keeper making a round of the auditorium to collect money almost every act. Archer in Farquhar's *The Beaux' Stratagem* records his shame at this: he was

> obliged to sneak into the sidebox, and between both houses steal two acts of a play, and because we han't the money to see the other three, we come away discontented, and damn the whole five.

A TURBULENT EGALITARIANISM

This helped to create what was actually a sort of turbulent egalitarianism which contradicted the social propriety inherent in the pricing, confronting the sobriety, deference and order that implied. First of all, the lights in the auditorium remained on throughout the evening, so that people could see each other. Indeed they dressed up and ogled each other. Theatre was a social occasion, when people gazed, argued, flirted and negotiated business deals and sporting bets. It was also a place of secret assignations: Clerimont is invited to meet his unknown admirer there in Pix's *The Beau Defeated*, for example. The atmosphere was ribald and pleasantly dangerous, which Lappet, Harriet's maid, captures entertainingly in Fielding's adaptation of Molière's *The Miser*:

> About a month ago my young lady goes to the play in an undress, and takes me with her. We sat in Burton's box, where, as the devil would have it, whom should we meet with but this very gentleman! her blushes soon discovered to me who he was; in short, the gentleman entertained her the whole play and I much mistake if ever she was so agreeably entertained in her life. Well, as we were going out, a rude fellow thrusts his hand into my lady's bosom; upon which her champion fell upon him and did so maul him! My lady fainted away in my arms; but as soon as she came to herself – had you seen how she looked on him! Ah! sir, says she, in a mighty pretty tone, sure you were born for my deliverance: he handed her into a hackney coach, and set us down at home.

The plays might be hissed or booed, for political as well as for personal or capricious reasons. Audience members were quite likely to call out to an actor to speak up, or to denigrate 'foreign' characters or unpatriotic sentiments. They demanded their favourite performers appear, and they

Figure 4.36
William Hogarth, The Laughing Audience
Source: The Metropolitan Museum of Art, New York. Harris Brisbane Dick Fund, 1917

stopped the play if a member of the audience needed assistance or a quarrel broke out. At Lincoln's Inn Fields in 1721, one arrogant aristocrat walked across the stage in the middle of the play to speak to a friend on the far side of the audience. He was thrown off by the actors, a scuffle developed involving many spectators in the pit and the mêlée took long to be calmed. The upshot was that soldiers were ordered into the theatres, where they stood guard at the doors, ready to intervene if trouble threatened.

THE FOOTMEN'S RIOTS

But they failed to stop the riots of 1737. At Drury Lane Charles Fleetwood decided to stop the practice of footmen being admitted free to the upper gallery if they were accompanied by, or had spent time reserving a place below, for their masters. The footmen vociferously objected, refused to be quiet when the pittites turned on them and soon there was a regular fight. A magistrate was brought, the Riot Act was read (despite some footmen threatening to 'knock his brains out' if he continued), and some semblance of peace was restored. But a few nights later, the banned footmen returned with staves and cudgels, broke down the door which was shut on them, and stormed back to 'their' gallery. In the pitched battle, some thirty people were injured, and eighteen footmen were arrested and gaoled. But Fleetwood's policy was reversed, and the footmen received back their favoured treatment.

FIELDING'S SCANDAL SHOP

More threatening than either the dangerous anarchy of the theatre audiences or the unnerving unintelligibility of the experimental drama were the activities of the theatre's most original and sharpest talent, Henry Fielding. Fielding created a series of dramatic works which defy the categories of critics: burlesque, parody, satire, ballad opera, farce – none quite matches the exuberant inventiveness of Fielding's best pieces, in which satirical vigour is matched by comic relish. His earliest plays were more or less conventional. It was when he linked himself to the Little Theatre on the Haymarket that his work became exceptional, and the theatre acquired the nickname, 'Fielding's Scandal Shop'.

    The Author's Farce (1730), a kind of knockabout comedy of manners, ran for forty-two nights, and was soon paired with *Tom Thumb*, a raucous Aristophanic rude gesture at the country's (and the theatre's) 'great men'. To the absurdly pretentious royal court comes the conquering hero, a 'young beginner' of 'inferior size', Tom Thumb, played by a slim young actress, Miss Jones. How many self-proclaimed heroes were similarly slight and tiny? The play ends as ridiculously as it began after Tom Thumb has been unfortunately gobbled up by a cow:

(*The Ghost of Tom Thumb rises.*)
GHOST: Tom Thumb I am – but am not eke alive.
    My body's in the cow, my ghost is here.
LORD GRIZZLE: Thanks, O ye stars, my vengeance is restored,
    Nor shalt thou fly me – for I'll kill thy ghost. (Kills the Ghost.)
HUNCAMUNCA: O barbarous deed! – I will revenge him so. (*Kills Lord Grizzle.*)
MR DOODLE: Ha! Grizzle killed – then murderess, beware. (*Kills Huncamunca.*)
QUEEN: O wretch! – have at thee. (*Kills Mr Doodle.*)
MR NOODLE: And have at thee too. (*Kills the Queen.*)
CLEORA: Thou'st killed the Queen. (*Kills Mr Noodle.*)
MUSTACHA: And thou hast killed my lover. (*Kills Cleora.*)
KING: Ha! Murderess vile, take that. (*Kills Mustacha.*)
    And take thou this. (*Kills himself and falls.*)

The King's dying speech, however, boasts that he 'fell the last'. If Rich and Cibber were Fielding's particular targets in these two plays, Walpole, the country's 'great man', was certainly also in his sights. Tom Thumb's ghost, by the way, was one of Fielding's first, but it was certainly not the last, and the joke of 'killing' it would be repeated. His fondness for ghosts was said to have almost ruined the stage of the Little Theatre because he had so many trapdoors cut into it for ghosts to rise through.

By 1732 he had expanded *Tom Thumb* into *The Tragedy of Tragedies* and this he now paired with a new afterpiece, *The Welsh Opera*, which took his abuse of Walpole to new levels of bitterness. In this ballad opera-style entertainment, a dysfunctional family, easily recognisable as George II, Queen Caroline and Frederick, Prince of Wales, employ a servile butler, a lightly disguised Walpole, to organise their needs. The success of *The Welsh Opera* stimulated Fielding to expand it, too, and it became *The Grub Street Opera*. But at this point Walpole intervened and the piece was banned.

FIELDING AT DRURY LANE

By now Fielding's enormous popularity led him into the embraces of a nervous Drury Lane, where his most intriguing work was probably *The Covent Garden Tragedy*, though it was certainly not his most successful since it received just a single performance. Set in a brothel, its bad taste is scabrous and its morality uncompromising. 'A naughty, riotous masterpiece', according to Fielding's early twentieth-century editor, W.E. Henley, it is centred on the bawdy-house madam, Mother Punchbowl, a queen in her own court, and a mother to her family of willing ladies.

Fielding's career at Drury Lane, however, was short. The actors' rebellion against the manager, John Highmore, interrupted it, and they moved to the now-vacant Little Theatre. Fielding sided with Highmore. He wanted to be at the heart of English theatre, but also he disliked Theophilus Cibber. As the latest Drury Lane debacle played out, Fielding was left in an untenable position.

THE GREAT MOGUL'S COMPANY OF COMEDIANS

In 1734 he was back at the Little Theatre with a company drawn from those disaffected with Drury Lane, where he produced *Don Quixote in England*, revised from an earlier script dating back to the late 1720s, notably by the inclusion of a wryly contemptuous election scene.

But it was only when he formed 'The Great Mogul's Company of Comedians' two years later that he really hit his stride. He himself was the 'Great Mogul', an ironic response to the self-important managers of the major theatres, Rich, Fleetwood and Cibber, all of whom had rejected his work at some time. With his efficient assistant, James Ralph, he brought together an excellent company of actors, including Kitty Clive, Eliza Haywood, William Mullart and his wife, Elizabeth Mullart, James Lacy who went on to work with Garrick, and Charlotte Charke, Colley Cibber's cross-dressing disowned daughter. *The Author's Farce*, in which she had had a part, had satirised her father with vicious relish, and now, in Fielding's new production, *Pasquin*, she again made fun of him.

PASQUIN

Pasquin is a jesting but bitter satire on government corruption but it takes the form of a play rehearsal – or rather, two plays, a tragedy and a comedy. Queen Common-Sense is opposed to

Queen Ignorance. They fight, and Queen Common-Sense is defeated and killed. But her enemies' triumph is truncated by her return as a ghost. Queen Ignorance and her attendants flee. This is another rehearsal play and one in which more ghosts appear, including one who is sent away again because his person has not yet been killed. The play had as long a run as *The Beggar's Opera*, thousands were turned away according to one newspaper, and the Prince of Wales himself, no friend of the king or the government, attended, thereby associating Fielding willy-nilly with the court opposition and the antagonistic Rumpsteak Club. *Pasquin*, however, is more than mere anti-Whiggery. It is a different kind of play, something beyond the reach of the patent theatres, and truly original. It was accompanied as an afterpiece by *Tumble-Down Dick*, an uncompromising satire of Rich's Covent Garden pantomimes.

THE HISTORICAL REGISTER FOR THE YEAR 1736

At the end of his highly successful season in 1736 Fielding announced plans to build a brand new theatre of his own and started seeking financial support for the venture. But before his plans could take any discernible shape, the new season was upon him. His major offering this year was *The Historical Register for the Year 1736*, in which, he promised, 'a pack of politicians, a pack of patriots, a pack of ladies, a pack of beaus' would appear, along with 'Mr Medley, an author, Mr Sourwit, a learned critic, Lord Dapper, a great critic . . . and Mr Ground-Ivy, a Laureate', this last another swipe at Colley Cibber. It was, like *Pasquin*, enormously popular, but also, with its afterpiece, the 'merry tragedy' of *Eurydice Hiss'd*, very dangerous. It contained an extraordinary *tour de force*, performed by Charlotte Charke as Mr Hen, the auctioneer, caricaturing London's most famous auctioneer, Mr Cock, and Charke's cross-dressing added swirling layers of meaning to the character. 'Mr Hen' auctions not knick-knacks or even antiques, but abstract qualities, such as political honesty, patriotism, modesty, which nobody bids for, all the wit of the pantomime, a clear conscience, 'as new', interest at court, which sells for £100, and so on. Finally, the Walpole-like Quidem arrives, pours out gold onto the table which is 'snatched up' by all the other characters, and dances out. And everyone dances after him. They are all dancing to Walpole's tune.

FIELDING'S AESTHETIC

Fielding was a perhaps unique anarchist radical Tory. His political seriousness, doubted by some later critics, is proved many times, for example in his treatment in *Pasquin* of Walpole's Excise Bill. As Brecht made Hitler a small-time gangster and clown in *The Resistable Rise of Arturo Ui*, so Fielding, in his own very different way, does with Walpole. 'Great men', like Walpole, always need exposing. So do theatre managers like Cibber. Both are indefatigable manipulators of people.

But Fielding's grotesque is richer than mere contemporary satire. He developed a highly productive dialectical relationship between the main play and the afterpiece. He also refused to set his script as it were in stone. He adapted it, changed or expanded it according to context and circumstances, and indeed there seems some likelihood that by the time he had his own Great Mogul's company, the actors were permitted, perhaps encouraged, to improvise. By these means he constructed a plural vision which confounds the distinctions between actor and character, reality and metaphor, practice doing and actual doing. This gets to the heart of how theatre functions, the endless elusive process which oscillates between response and renewal, the negotiating of which is a large part of the pleasure of theatre.

Southerne in *The Wives Excuse*, the anonymous makers of *The Female Wits* and Gay in *The What D'Ye Call It*, had all put their toes into these waters, and contemporary Prologues and Epilogues often nudge the spectator towards a recognition of such theatricality. But it fell to Fielding to consistently create a theatre in which the spectator generates rather than receives meanings. His techniques deliberately draw attention to the different planes on which the performance operates, and highlights their seeming incompatibilities. Fielding's theatre allows, even encourages, the spectator to experience the process of theatre-making, and thus enables meanings.

This was a highly original aesthetic, albeit one still being worked out. But it never reached its final fruition. In the summer of 1737 the Licensing Act became law, and the career of Fielding the playwright and theatre manager was effectively arrested.

NOTES

1 Luigi Riccoboni, *An Historical and Critical Account of the Theatre in Europe*, London: T. Walker and R. Dodsley, 1741, p. 176.
2 David Thomas and Arnold Hare (eds), *Restoration and Georgian England*, Cambridge: Cambridge University Press, 1989, p. 168.

Chapter 52: 1737

In 1737 Robert Walpole's government passed the Theatre Licensing Act, and at a stroke brought to an end the burgeoning theatrical culture and achievements of Betterton and Congreve, Centlivre and Oldfield, *The Beggar's Opera*, Harlequin and the whole historical register. It was an Act of cultural vandalism probably unequalled in British history.

THE LEGAL POSITION

It is true that the laws governing the theatre were by that date in an unholy muddle. Who was responsible for the plays performed and the theatre companies who performed them? The Lord Chamberlain? The Master of the Revels? The holders of the Royal Patents? Sir Richard Steele certainly believed it was the patentees, as his dispute with the Duke of Newcastle in 1719 showed. And there was no agreement either on what should be permitted. Should any censorship cover politics? What about manners or morals? Or blasphemy, or bad language? In fact, the quarrel between the Duke of Newcastle and Steele was more to do with Whig Party political infighting than the passing of plays for performance. There was very little attempt at censorship in the 1720s. It was perhaps unnecessary anyway, with the highly conservative policies of the patent theatres, and Cibber's position especially as a political jackal. But by the 1730s there were at least five and sometimes six different theatres operating, only two with Royal Patents, and any of them could erupt into dangerous oppositionalism at any time. Many people advocated a stronger censorship regime, Cibber and John Dennis among them.

THE AUTHORITIES TAKE ACTION

The first intimation that the authorities might be willing to institute a new stricter regime came with the banning of *Polly*, John Gay's sequel to *The Beggar's Opera*. In this case, whatever the protocol should have been, the Lord Chamberlain himself, Lord Grafton, ordered John Rich directly not to stage it.

Two years later, the anonymous *Fall of Mortimer*, which ran for fifteen performances at the Haymarket Little Theatre, caused a greater stir. The play is about a weak king, too like George II, and his advisor, Mortimer, whose close friendship with the queen enables him to bamboozle the king into doing his bidding. The parallel with Walpole's friendship with Queen Caroline was unmistakeable. The play shows Mortimer/Walpole guilty of bribery, fixing juries, using execution as a political

Figure 4.37
Robert Walpole, Prime Minister: the Stature of a Great Man, or the English Colossus
Source: Library of Congress, Washington, D.C.

weapon and even attempting rape. He is, however, stopped in his career by the people, who overthrow him in an act of revolution. The government threatened but did not itself strike. Instead a Grand Jury pronounced the play guilty of seditious libel. Some of the actors refused to continue, but the play was recast and advertised again. Consequently the High Constable and his men raided the theatre, and though the actors managed to escape, some at least were caught and gaoled, and the theatre itself was closed. John Potter, landlord of the theatre, himself cancelled the next production, *The Restoration of Charles II* by Walter Aston, although it was already in rehearsal. The implications of the play, that to replace one government, in this case the Cromwellian Commonwealth, with another, that of Charles II, was permissible and even admirable, were simply unacceptable.

THE 1735 PLAYHOUSE BILL

In the next years, while Walpole was busy with the Excise Bill and the putative Gin Act, the theatre's unruliness grew, and in 1735 the Whig MP, Sir John Barnard, introduced a Bill to Parliament intended to tame it. This so-called Playhouse Bill was also part of the city's campaign against the opening of Goodman's Fields, which Barnard feared might interfere with his money-making business there. He proposed to limit the number of theatres in London to two and to give greater powers of censorship to local magistrates. Walpole, as determined a centrist as most Prime Ministers, wanted censorship to remain with the Lord Chamberlain. The Bill fell.

UNREST IN SOCIETY AND THE THEATRE

The country itself was increasingly restive, with the Edinburgh Porteous Riots, protests against the Gin Act and anti-Irish disturbances, as well as damagingly vituperative party politics. In February 1737, the Drury Lane afterpiece, *Eurydice*, was disrupted by rioting spectators – the inspiration for Fielding's *Eurydice Hiss'd* – and a few days later the first performance of the subversive *A Rehearsal of Kings* was prevented by a further riot among playgoers. Fielding's *Historical Register for the Year 1736* and *Eurydice Hiss'd*, meanwhile, were alarmingly popular. The government newspaper, *The Daily Gazetteer*, launched an attack on Fielding not unlike the attacks Stalin's *Pravda* newspaper mounted on his artist-enemies, Meyerhold, Shostakovich and others, in Russia two hundred years later.

THE 1737 BILL

In May 1737 Fielding announced his new plans: a production of the banned *Polly*, faintly reworked as *Macheath Turned Pirate*, and an afterpiece called *The King and Titi*, almost certainly an attack on George II and his relations with his son, Frederick, Prince of Wales, into whose ambit Fielding was being drawn. The next day, Walpole introduced the Theatre Licensing Bill into Parliament. To support the need for greater control of the theatre, he read aloud in the House of Commons passages from an apparently treasonous and abusive play, *The Festival of the Golden Rump*, which was an especially venomous attack on the king, who was renowned for the size of his backside. It was said that the Prime Minister had been handed the play personally by Henry Giffard, manager of Goodman's Fields Theatre. Some suspected that this was no more than Giffard currying favour with the government at a particularly dangerous time for alternative theatres, though there was no proof of this. At any rate he was paid £1000 for his trouble, though the ensuing Licensing Act would close Goodman's Fields. A few voices were raised in Parliament against this blatant attack on free speech and ancient freedoms. Fielding himself protested at the bill's 'encroachment on British liberties'. But in June the Act was passed into law.

It provided that only theatres with a Royal Patent should be permitted to present plays and that all plays and adaptations were to be submitted at least fifteen days in advance of their first performance to an Examiner of Plays, with a penalty of £50 for failure to comply.

THE EFFECTS OF THE LICENSING ACT

It seems that Fielding may have been prepared to continue, at extreme risk to himself, but Potter, perhaps at the government's behest, entered his own Little Theatre, dismantled Fielding's sets,

THE FESTIVAL OF THE GOLDEN RUMP.
Rumpatur, quisquis Rumpitur invidia.

Figure 4.38
The Festival of the Golden Rump, a scurrilous attack on George II who was known for the size of his backside
Source: The Trustees of the British Museum

and dumped bricks and earth on the stage. The Great Mogul was finished. Indeed the theatre in Britain was emasculated. Only Drury Lane and Covent Garden were now allowed to operate; variety of fare on the London stage disappeared; actors were put out of work; and serious writers turned away from the stage. Theatre in the provinces seemed to be banned altogether. Fielding himself may finally have been bought off by Walpole, who perhaps financed his retraining for the law. Apart from a few puppet shows, he mounted no further dramas. Puppets were one form which escaped the censor; 'concerts' which added 'free' drama performances in the 'intervals' between musical pieces, were another. Most writers, however, including Fielding himself, diverted their energies into the novel. The effects on the theatre were devastating and long-lasting. The tradition of playwriting, once literature's finest form, the chosen *genre* of Marlowe, Shakespeare, Middleton, Dryden, Congreve, Centlivre and now Fielding, was effectively smashed.

The Whigs' vaunted 'freedom' turned out to mean economic freedom, freedom to make money, not cultural freedom, freedom to put the theatre at the centre of social intercourse.

Select bibliography

Brown, Ian (ed), *The Edinburgh Companion to Scottish Drama*, Edinburgh: Edinburgh University Press, 2011

Cordner, Michael, and Holland, Peter (eds), *Players, Playwrights, Playhouses*, Basingstoke: Palgrave Macmillan, 2007

Donohoe, Joseph (ed), *The Cambridge History of British Theatre*, vol 2, Cambridge: Cambridge University Press, 2004

Engel, Laura (ed), *The Public's Open to Us All: Essays on Women and Performance in Eighteenth Century England*, Newcastle-upon-Tyne: Cambridge Scholars, 2009

Freeman, Lisa A., *Character's Theater: Genre and Identity on the Eighteenth Century English Stage*, Philadelphia: University of Pennsylvania Press, 2002

Loverre, Kathryn (ed), *The Lively Arts of the London Stage*, Farnham: Ashgate, 2014

Nussbaum, Felicity, *Rival Queens: Actresses, Performance and the Eighteenth Century British Theater*, Philadelphia: University of Pennsylvania Press, 2010

O'Brien, John, *Harlequin Britain: Pantomime and Entertainment 1690–1760*, Baltimore: John Hopkins University Press, 2004

Paulson, Ronald, *The Life of Henry Fielding*, Oxford: Blackwell, 2000

Roberts, David, *Thomas Betterton: The Greatest Actor of the Restoration Stage*, Cambridge: Cambridge University Press, 2010

Shevelow, Kathryn, *Charlotte: The True Story of Scandal and Spectacle in Georgian London*, London: Bloomsbury, 2005

Thomson, Peter, *The Cambridge Introduction to English Theatre, 1660–1900*, Cambridge: Cambridge University Press, 2006

White, Jerry, *London in the Eighteenth Century: A Great and Monstrous Thing*, New York: Vintage Books, 2013

Interlude: Eighteenth century amateur theatricals

THE AIMS OF UPPER-CLASS AMATEURS

The eighteenth century was marked by an unprecedented leap in the wealth, and the leisure time, of the upper classes, and one way this new abundance was consumed was in the creation of dramatic performances. Indeed a veritable craze swept through the mansions of the rich in the second half of the century, which sometimes showed the professional theatre as a tawdry roughhouse.

The performances had to be private, since they would otherwise contravene the terms of the 1737 Act, but in part they embodied upper-class opposition to the rowdy audiences and the dilution of serious programming at the patent theatres, an attempt to reclaim ownership of the theatre, though it never quite threatened the supremacy of Covent Garden and Drury Lane.

The aristocratic amateurs staged a serious repertoire extremely well. And because the performances were open to fellow aristocrats and gentry, as well as to the servants and agricultural workers employed on the estate, or in the surrounding countryside, audiences of several hundred were not uncommon. Bold in themselves, the performances also provided a *frisson* of delight and perhaps exhibitionism for the ladies. Indeed they raised delicate questions, much debated, about upper-class female participation, though this was widely allowed so long as the entertainments were private.

CHILDREN ACTING

Children had long acted in private and the eighteenth century offers plenty of examples of that continuing. Hogarth's 1732 painting, *A Scene from 'The Indian Emperor'*, shows the children of the Conduit family presenting an excerpt from Dryden's play to an august gathering of adults, while performances like that of Addison's *Cato* by the boys of Mr Rule's Academy at Sadler's Wells in 1762 shows another side of youth drama.

SOME UNLIKELY PERFORMANCES

There were also very private amusements, such as Garrick's rewriting of *Julius Caesar* for the Hoadly family in 1746, when Brutus became Brutarse, Cassius Cassiarse and Lucius Loosearse. Then there were absurd extravaganzas like the hiring of Drury Lane by Francis Delavel, a raffish minor aristocrat and close friend of Samuel Foote, to present himself and his family in *Othello*. The family had

Figure 4.39
William Hogarth, A Scene from *The Indian Emperor*, 1732, performed by the children of the Conduit family, engraved by Robert Dodd, 1792

Source: The Metropolitan Museum of Art, New York. Harris Brisbane Dick Fund, 1917

experience of performing both at their London home and their Northumberland mansion, but this venture cost them at least £2,000, and if the House of Commons adjourned for it, and the star-spangled audience was headed by the Prince of Wales and the Duke of Cumberland, it was, according to Foote's biographer, 'a triumph of celebrity over art'.[1]

AMATEUR PERFORMANCES IN BIG HOUSES

The main run of amateur theatricals in big houses started after this. In 1760 the Earl of Sandwich mounted theatricals, an interest he continued sporadically till 1786. In 1761 Lord Holland began a determined sequence of performances at Holland House where in 1768 his barn was converted into a theatre. There were performances under the Earl of Mulgrave at his Harley Street mansion from 1768, Sir Watkins Williams Wynn at his house in north Wales, Wynnstay, from 1770 till 1787, and the Duke of Marlborough at Blenheim Palace in 1773. Wynn's son continued his father's tradition at Wynnstay between 1803 and 1810. In 1774 General John Burgoyne mounted his own two-act masque, *The Maid of the Oaks*, at the wedding of his wife's nephew, a work later expanded to five acts and presented at Drury Lane with noted settings by de Loutherbourg. By the 1780s the craze was at its height, with performances in more than a dozen big houses, as well as others like William Fecter's at the Assembly Rooms in Dover, which lasted until 1798.

THE EARL OF BARRYMORE AT WARGRAVE

Perhaps most famously of all, the Earl of Barrymore presented plays at his home, Wargrave, where by 1788 he had built a large, impressive theatre in which his amateurs mixed with professionals from the local theatre in Reading. They all rehearsed under the direction of John Bannister, a protégé of David Garrick, and Barrymore also employed Carlo Delpini to coach his company in pantomime.

They rehearsed from nine in the evening till four in the morning, the scenery was striking and the repertoire as good as Drury Lane's: it included Vanbrugh's *The Confederacy*, Garrick's *Miss in Her Teens* and Inchbold's *The Midnight Hour*. In 1790, when the Prince of Wales attended a performance at Wargrave, Barrymore reconstructed his theatre, basing it now on the Vanbrugh's Queen's in the Haymarket. But by 1792 he had overreached himself and was declared bankrupt, his theatre finished.

FURTHER ARISTOCRATIC THEATRES

Almost equally extraordinary was the Duke of Richmond's theatre at Richmond House. In April 1787 Parliament adjourned so that the many members involved in Richmond's *The Way to Keep Him* could fulfil their roles. This company, which included Lord Derby, was coached by Elizabeth Farren who would go on to marry Derby after his current wife died. Other notable aristocratic amateur theatres were those of the Petre family at Thorndon Hall, West Horndon, and the Margravine of Anspach, who built her own theatre at her estate in Hammersmith and mounted productions there from 1793 until her death in 1806.

'THE CLOSET'

Some amateur theatricals were less noticed than these. House parties, or even simply families, sometimes organised theatrical performances in private homes. Jane Austen, who had absorbed amateur performance from her childhood in Steventon Rectory, performed at Manydown House at Christmas 1808, besides describing an amateur production in *Mansfield Park*. Such ventures enabled women, otherwise so assiduously ignored, to take responsibility for creating productions in their own domestic space, and often of their own dramas. It provided space for women's personal development, and some of women's most significant drama, including that of Joanna Baillie, sprang from this form of 'closet drama'.

LOWER CLASS AMATEUR THEATRE

Many amateurs belonged to classes lower than the aristocracy. Officers camped at Coxheath in the 1780s and 1790s put on plays. In 1802 the Pic-Nic Club took the concert room in Tottenham Street, hired a professional to direct them, and performed, in spite of opposition from Sheridan and others. Further performances were noted at Chatsworth in the 1830s and Burton Constable in the 1840s, and Dickens, comic as well as patronising, described 'private theatres' in *Sketches by 'Boz'* before going on to found his own notorious company.

But by the mid-nineteenth century amateur theatre no longer threatened the mainstream.

NOTE

1 Ian Kelly, *Mr Foote's Other Leg*, London: Picador, 2012, p. 212.

SELECT BIBLIOGRAPHY

Rosenfeld, Sybil, *Temples of Thespis*, London: Society for Theatre Research, 1978

PART FIVE

THEATRE AND ENLIGHTENMENT

Timeline

	Society and politics	Theatre
1737		Theatre Licensing Act
1739	David Hume, *Treatise of Human Nature* published	
1740		Debut of David Garrick at Goodman's Fields
1741		Macklin appears as Shylock in *The Merchant of Venice*
1742	End of Robert Walpole's premiership	
1745	Jacobite rebellion	
1747		Start of Garrick and Lacy's management of Drury Lane
1755	Johnson, *A Dictionary of the English Language* published	
1756	Outbreak of Seven Years War	Murphy, *The Apprentice* Home, *Douglas*
1757	Battle of Plassey	
1759	Battle of Quebec Death of Gen Wolfe	
1760	Death of George II: accession of George III	
1761		Death of John Rich
1762		Bickerstaffe, *Love in a Village* Half-price riots, Drury Lane

1766		Garrick and Colman, *The Clandestine Marriage* Foote granted Royal Patent for Little Theatre, Haymarket Wilkinson becomes manager at York Theatre
1767		Thomas Harris and three others take over Covent Garden Royal Patent granted for a theatre in Edinburgh
1768	*Encyclopaedia Britannica* published	Royal Patents granted to theatres in Bath and Norwich
1769		Shakespeare Jubilee, Stratford-upon-Avon
1771		Cumberland, *The West Indian*
1772		Foote, *The Nabob*
1773		Goldsmith, *She Stoops to Conquer* de Loutherbourg designs *Alfred*, Drury Lane
1775		Mrs Siddons debut at Drury Lane
1776	American Declaration of Independence Adam Smith, *The Wealth of Nations* published	Sheridan and others take over Drury Lane Theatre
1777		Sheridan, *The School for Scandal* Death of Samuel Foote
1779		Death of David Garrick
1780	Gordon Riots	Cowley, *The Belle's Stratagem*
1781		Theatre Royal, Glasgow, opens
1783	William Pitt the Younger becomes Prime Minister	
1785		O'Keeffe, *Omai, or A Trip Round the World*, design – de Loutherbourg, Drury Lane Mrs Jordan debut at Drury Lane
1786		Carstairs, *The Hubble-Shoe*
1787	Warren Hastings impeached First performance of Mozart, *Don Giovanni*	
1788		Theatre at Richmond, Yorkshire, opens
1789	Outbreak of French Revolution George III's first episode of 'madness'	Reynolds, *The Dramatist*

1791	Tom Paine, *The Rights of Man* published	Stephen Kemble becomes manager, Edinburgh Theatre Royal Drury Lane theatre burns down
1793		Inchbald, *Every One Has His Fault*
1795	Pitt's 'Two Acts' against Treasonable Practice and Seditious Meetings	
1797		Lewis, *The Castle Spectre*
1799		Sheridan, *Pizarro*
1800		Morton, *Speed the Plough*
1801	Attempted assassination of George III in Drury Lane Theatre	
1802		John Philip Kemble becomes manager at Covent Garden
1804	Napoleon Bonaparte becomes Emperor of France	
1805	Battle of Trafalgar: death of Nelson	
1808		Covent Garden theatre burns down
1809		Drury Lane theatre burns down O.P. Riots, Covent Garden
1810		Whitbread takes control of Drury Lane
1812	Napoleon defeated in Russia	Opening of new Drury Lane theatre Mrs Siddons retires
1815	Battle of Waterloo	
1816		Death of Sheridan

Chapter 53: After 1737

BANNED

The 1737 Theatre Licensing Act changed the nature of the British theatre utterly. A foretaste of what might happen occurred in 1739 when Henry Brooke's *Gustavus Vasa*, about the sixteenth-century liberation of Sweden from Danish rule, became the first play to be banned outright. Walpole believed the villain was a portrayal of himself. The action prompted Samuel Johnson's first published work, a sarcastic *Vindication of the Licensers of the Stage* in which he suggested that the lives of civil servants would be made easier if the British people were forbidden from expressing any opinions about anything whatsoever and that reading and writing should not be taught to children.

A DIFFERENT AGE

It is true that after Robert Walpole's loss of power and the defeat of the Jacobites in 1745, politics in Britain cooled down. Argument became rooted in the production of wealth, trade and manufacture at home, and the expanding empire abroad. The Jacobites were important only because support for them was still to be found among the dispossessed, and social unrest or riots were usually – sometimes correctly – blamed on Jacobites. They no longer seriously endangered the state.

   The population grew, especially in towns, and inventions like Arkwright's water frame and Hargreaves' spinning jenny, together with developments in transport, such as canals, meant increases in prosperity for many. Not for all, of course: the poor were still with us, and their needs and dreams found new spokespersons in John Wesley and George Whitefield, progenitors of Methodism which soon became a well-organised and enthusiastic grouping. But politically, under the influence of the belligerent and empire-building William Pitt, Earl of Chatham, Britain settled into a period of domestic peace and foreign warmongering.

   For almost the whole of the second half of the eighteenth century and on until 1815, the British army and navy were fighting the French. The Empire initially was focused on America, and Wolfe's victory in Quebec, for instance, was celebrated in more than one stage play; but the 1776 American Revolution turned the empire-builders' energies eastwards to India.

THE ENLIGHTENMENT

The American Declaration of Independence was a typical document of the 'Enlightenment'. It was premised on the principle that the law's only purpose was to enable people to live their lives as they chose. The watchwords were 'life', 'liberty' and 'property'. Property freed a person to do good, and liberty was applied equally to political, social and economic affairs. The 'free market' was the bringer of universal happiness, and logic and reason were tools for improving the world.

Scepticism and the scientific method endorsed enlightened ways of thinking, and new discoveries and new knowledge were collected in the *Encyclopaedia Britannica*, published in 1768. Wingate, in Arthur Murphy's *The Apprentice* (1756) asks: 'Why should not a man know everything?' Old forms of religion were displaced by something more rational, moral values came to revolve around taste and what was possible, and happiness replaced salvation as the goal of life. 'The pursuit of happiness' was indeed written into the new United States of America's Constitution in 1776.

This was, on one level, a rationalisation of selfishness, but the enlightened man was supposed to be moderate and convivial. London had over a hundred coffee houses where intellectual and cultural intercourse thrived. Clubs were often located in coffee houses or pubs, and many people belonged to one or more club, as the lawyer in Samuel Foote's *The Minor* (1760) belonged to a Tuesday nightclub at the Magpie and Horseshoe in Fetter Lane, and Marlow in Oliver Goldsmith's *She Stoops to Conquer* (1773) was 'a great favourite' at 'the Ladies' Club' in town. The lower orders, too, had their clubs: in Murphy's *The Apprentice* (1756), it is a 'spouters' club', where young men practiced acting, while in David Garrick's *Miss in her Teens* (1747), Fribble belongs to a club of 'young bachelors' which meets three times a week to drink tea and chat.

CULTURAL POWER CHANGES HANDS

Cultural power followed political power from the court to the *bourgeoisie*, symbolised in the publication in London alone of fourteen different newspapers. Act two of Elizabeth Inchbald's *Every One Has His Fault* (1793) is set in a 'coffee or club-room in a Tavern', where newspapers are available for patrons' use. These spread enlightened ideas of science, commerce and the arts, even if their gossip columnists, like Crowquill in Hannah Cowley's *The Belle's Stratagem* (1780), were as unscrupulous as their twenty-first-century counterparts in obtaining scandal. Women, too, participated in this culture: they walked about freely, they joined in mixed coffee house debates and were novelists, essayists, historians, translators, literary critics, biographers and of course theatre managers, actresses and playwrights.

EMOTION AND FEELING

Enlightened thought opposed absolutism, superstition and enthusiasm, and suggested emotion was a poor basis for decision-making. Foote's comedy, *The Minor*, makes fun of Methodist 'enthusiasm', while many plays show the folly of allowing emotion too much sway. But 'feeling' was not excluded. Harry 'silently weeps' when he parts from Rover at the end of the first act of John O'Keeffe's *Wild Oats* (1791), and at the height of the climactic confusion in Garrick and Colman's *The Clandestine Marriage* (1766), Mrs Heidelberg exclaims approvingly: 'My brother feels, I see!' In Richard Brinsley Sheridan's *The School for Scandal* (1777), the apparently admirable Joseph Surface is called 'a man of sentiment' while his profligate brother Charles has 'no sentiment'. Sheridan thus cleverly problematises a seemingly facile notion.

THE INSPIRATION OF CLASSICAL GREECE

The Enlightenment seemed to liberate man from dogma, tradition and authority. Human perfectibility became conceivable. But the reconciliation between reason and religion was not so easily managed, and there was a turning back to ancient Greece for inspiration. The classical world was admired for its serenity and probably influenced architecture most overtly – the British Museum and Woburn Abbey, for instance.

The theatre was keen to be part of this 'high' culture and not for nothing was the leading theatre practitioner of the age, David Garrick, frequently referred to by the name of classical Rome's most famous actor, Roscius. The redesigned Covent Garden, as well as many provincial theatres of the period, were designed in pseudo-Grecian Palladian style. The Greek and Roman republics provided a model for a polite and rational society governed by the rule of law, and hymned in the stately and considered verse of Homer and Virgil. Polybius, the Greek historian, described the rise of the Roman republic and advocated the kind of separation of powers which underpinned the American Constitution.

A PERFORMATIVE CULTURE

Much of the public culture of the time, like that of Greece or Rome, was performative and theatrical: the staging of politics, for instance, or public executions at Tyburn with their rowdy crowds; the public displays of the British army or navy, with uniforms, parades and military camps; and the finale to this kind of cultural statement – Nelson's grand funeral in January 1806.

CENSORSHIP

The theatre itself, which should have been a leading player in the public consciousness, was shackled by the 1737 Act. For instance, the censor excised the following lines from Charles Macklin's *A Will and No Will* (1746):

> The statesman's skill, like mine, is all deceit.
> What's policy in him – in me's a cheat.
> Titles and wealth reward his noble art,
> Cudgels and bruises mine – sometimes a cart.
> 'Twas, is, and will be, to the end of time,
> That poverty, not fraud, creates a crime.

Audiences learned to read subtexts, rather as Moscow audiences learned in Stalin's Russia. In 1738 at a performance of *Richard II* at Covent Garden, they applauded loudly and boisterously when Northumberland said:

> The king is not himself, but basely led
> By flatterers.

They assumed a reference to Walpole. Later, the line 'The Earl of Wiltshire hath the state in farm' was greeted with even louder shouts and cheers.

Figure 5.1
Horatio Nelson's grand funeral procession, January 1806
Source: Heritage Images/Diomedia

TRAGEDY AND COMEDY

Despite the admiration for ancient Greek Apollonian poise, and despite counsel such as John Gregory's to his daughter, that tragedy's 'sorrows will soften and ennoble your heart', tragedy was not in tune with the times.[1] Tragedy explored extremism, notably emotional extremism, and comedy, an apparently rational form, was preferred. But what form comedy should take was the subject of much debate. Oliver Goldsmith, in an article in *Westminster Magazine* in December 1772, compared 'laughing' and 'sentimental' comedy, the latter of which, he declared, was the prevailing mode. It was 'a new species' in which 'the virtues of private life are exhibited', and which was concerned with the 'distresses' of mankind rather than its faults or follies. Goldsmith objected to this new species, which was derived from Richard Steele's attempts to circumvent Jeremy Collier's moralising strictures earlier in the century. He wrote:

> In these plays almost all the characters are good, and exceedingly generous; they are lavish enough of their tin money on the stage; and though they want humour, have abundance of sentiment and feeling.

'These sentimental pieces do often amuse us', he admits; 'but the question is, whether true comedy (laughing comedy) would not amuse us more'.[2]

The fact that tragedy and traditional ('laughing') comedy were both out of fashion explains, first, why dramatic works written after 1737 often seem disappointingly thin: 80% of all new plays licensed in the forty years after 1737 were 'afterpieces', that is, short lightweight entertainments or farces; and second, the fact that the theatre of this period belonged to actors more than playwrights, and audiences enjoyed performances more than plays.

DAVID GARRICK AND 'THE PARADOX OF THE ACTOR'

The British theatre's foremost practitioner between 1740 and his retirement in 1777 was David Garrick. His brilliance amazed many including the sophisticated members of a *salon* in Paris which he visited in 1764. Denis Diderot described how he

> put his head between two folding doors, and in the course of five or six seconds his expression . . . change[d] successively from wild delight to temperate pleasure, from this to tranquillity, from tranquillity to surprise, from surprise to blank astonishment, from that to sorrow, from sorrow to the air of one overwhelmed, from that to fright, from fright to horror, from horror to despair, and thence . . . again to the point from which he started.[3]

This exhibition led directly to Diderot's formulation of the paradox of the actor – that he portrayed intense feelings and emotions while actually experiencing nothing. 'Actors impress the public', Diderot asserted, 'not when they are furious, but when they play fury well'.[4] It was a paradox which was to continue to engage actors and critics for a long time, but it is worth noting the Apollonian cast of the idea. For Apollo, the theatre was not a matter of sweat and tears, but one of considered imitation.

OTHER AMUSEMENTS

Meanwhile, and perhaps unsurprisingly, the public which had filled up to six theatres in London before 1737, now often found other amusements. Pleasure gardens, from Vauxhall and Ranelagh to less fashionable places proliferated, not only in London but in towns and cities beyond. Here people might watch or listen to singers, bands, puppets, and peep shows; there were pavilions, 'Turkish tents', and platforms for dancing; people dressed up and walked the perfumed paths among trees, lawns, birds and bushes, and indulged in headily romantic behaviour – or misbehaviour. Food – cheesecakes, syllabubs – was served, and ale and wine drunk, and there was entertainment from tumblers, rope-dancers, performing animals and opera singers. Could theatre match this?

Another way of spending leisure time and money was to attend lectures such as George Alexander Stevens's 'Lectures on Heads', illustrated with life-size model heads on sticks and including comic and satirical references to well-known contemporaries. Lessons on subjects such as oratory, a notably Grecian art, were offered. Perhaps the most remarkable school for this was established in 1753 by the actor Charles Macklin in the piazza in Covent Garden where his 'British Institution' was to be found in 'a magnificent coffee room'. Evoking 'ancient Greek and 'Roman' models, as well as modern French and Italian ones, he not only taught public speaking, but also gave public lectures on matters such as whether men or women were more eloquent and whether plays should be read before being seen. *The Kept Mistress*, an anonymous afterpiece of 1756, revolves around oratory.

Figure 5.2
Two sketches by Johann Zoffany of David Garrick as Abel Drugger in Ben Jonson's *The Alchemist*, which suggest Garrick's versatility

Source: Ashmolean Museum, University of Oxford/Bridgeman Images

and the craze is manifest in publications such as John Lawson's *Lectures Concerning Oratory* (1758), *A Course of Lectures on Elocution* (1763) by Thomas Sheridan, father of the playwright, and John Walker's *Pronouncing Dictionary of English* (1774). Samuel Foote, who mocked 'oratory' in several plays, gained some notoriety with his own alternative entertainment, the 'tea party', which evaded the censors by offering patrons, not a performance, but 'a dish of tea'.

THE PLACE OF THEATRE

Besides these, London offered multifarious other diversions: masquerades, concerts and music-making, the assembly rooms, art exhibitions and more. But even in the world of the Enlightenment, theatre remained fascinating. Actors, and especially actresses, were role models and gossip factories. Their lives offered moral example and cultural awareness. And the theatre was discussed in newspapers, journals, pamphlets and stationers' windows.

Figure 5.3
The rotunda in Ranelagh pleasure gardens, 1751
Source: British Library, London

Even in its pinched form, theatre offered a site for the articulation of social and political tensions. All classes met here.

> 'Tis such a concourse, such a staring show!
> Mobs shout above, and critics snarl below.[5]

People in the second half of the eighteenth century regarded the theatre as a public place for argument, laughter, scandalmongering, assertion of rights, eating and drinking, defiance of authority, flirting, fixing sexual assignations and indulging all forms of sentimentality. Indeed, such was their self-assertion and demanding insouciance, it seemed that they wanted actually to 'own' the theatre.

NOTES

1 John Gregory, 'A Father's Legacy to His Daughter, 1774', in Vivien Jones (ed), *Women in the Eighteenth Century: Constructions of Femininity*, London: Routledge, 1990, pp. 48–49.
2 Oliver Goldsmith, *An Essay on the Theatre, or, a Comparison Between Laughing Comedy and Sentimental Comedy*, 1772, passim.
3 Denis Diderot, 'The Paradox of Acting, c.1773', in Toby Cole and Helen Krich Chinoy (eds), *Actors on Acting*, New York: Crown Publishers, 1970, p. 168.
4 Denis Diderot, *op.cit.*, p. 168.
5 Gillian Russell, *The Theatres of War: Performance, Politics and Society, 1793–1815*, Oxford: Clarendon Press, 1995, p. 124.

Chapter 54: The patent theatres, 1737–77

CRISIS IN FLEETWOOD'S DRURY LANE

After 1737 Drury Lane Theatre slid into crisis. Charles Fleetwood, the gout-stricken Staffordshire landowner who was the proprietor, increasingly used it to finance his gambling, and he even inveigled actors to leave rehearsals and accompany him to illegal boxing matches. Despite an excellent company, including by 1742 Charles Macklin, Denis Delane, Hannah Pritchard, Kitty Clive, Peg Woffington and a young David Garrick, the debts continued to mount, and when Fleetwood tried to raise admission prices, the public reacted furiously. After four weeks of paying the higher prices, they interrupted the performance by calling for Fleetwood. When he refused to appear on stage, they began tearing up the benches, flinging missiles and threatening to mount the stage and destroy the scenery, as if they owned the theatre. The riots reached such a pitch that soldiers with fixed bayonets were brought in.

Fleetwood had to back down. But now he thought to cut the actors' salaries to make savings. The outraged actors, led by Charles Macklin, petitioned the Lord Chamberlain for permission to perform elsewhere. While the Lord Chamberlain pondered their request, the actors agreed not to allow Fleetwood to persuade them individually to return to Drury Lane: solidarity was to be maintained at all costs. But the Lord Chamberlain refused their petition, and the actors, one by one, including David Garrick, did return to Drury Lane. All except Macklin, whom Fleetwood refused to reinstate.

MACKLIN AGAINST GARRICK

Macklin was incensed, especially with Garrick. His friends formed a claque to disrupt Garrick's performances. They booed and hissed his appearance on stage, and flung rotten eggs and apples. Garrick and Fleetwood mustered their own ruffians, and when Macklin's men again began their disruption, Garrick's defenders sprang into action. A fight across the auditorium ensued, and Macklin's men were driven off. Garrick continued the performance, but his quarrel with Macklin was never mended.

GARRICK AND LACY TAKE CHARGE AT DRURY LANE

Meanwhile Fleetwood was engaged in a series of extraordinary deals, involving among others two bankers called Richard Green and Newton Amber. He sold his patent, while still ensuring himself

£600 per year, brought James Lacy into the management and escaped to Europe where his creditors could not reach him.

Lacy had been assistant at Covent Garden, and had mounted his own 'Oratory' performance which had evaded the 1737 Act by pretending to be a 'lecture' with several different speakers – that is actors. For this he had been sent to Bridewell Prison. He had also been involved in the opening of Ranelagh Pleasure Gardens in 1734. Now he found himself in charge of Drury Lane. His first initiative was to bring back Macklin as artistic manager.

It was not a good appointment, and it ended when the Jacobite Rebellion of 1745 caused a run on the banks. Green and Amber were ruined, and Lacy was left struggling. Susanna Cibber and Garrick were meanwhile negotiating a partnership to take over the theatre, but in 1747, Garrick linked with Lacy, leaving Cibber out of the management, just as thirty-five years earlier Dogget and Susanna's father-in-law Colley Cibber had excluded Anne Oldfield. And again like Oldfield, Cibber was awarded a generous contract.

THE NEW PARTNERSHIP

Lacy became business manager and Garrick assumed the artistic direction in the new dispensation. Garrick took an annual salary of £500 in addition to his half share of the profits because he continued to act. In the summer of 1747 Drury Lane was refurbished, and Lacy and Garrick settled into the management which lasted till Lacy's death. It brought stability as well as high achievement to the theatre, but it was never a happy partnership. Garrick and Lacy simply did not much like each other, and there were several run-ins which threatened their collaboration. But probably both realised that in spite of all they were better together than apart.

DIFFICULTIES AT OTHER THEATRES

The King's Theatre, Haymarket, was having as difficult a time. It found presenting purely opera unviable, and in 1748 turned to comic operettas and burlesques. But when the leading singer, John Francis Croza, fled after being arrested for debt, it shut down completely for several years. Meanwhile Henry Giffard at Goodman's Fields Theatre, having advertised concerts with dramatic interludes included for free, and having presented amateurs and students, and having indeed introduced David Garrick to the London public, had finally been forced to close his unlicensed theatre.

JOHN RICH AND COVENT GARDEN

Covent Garden, however, was secure under the shrewd and successful management of John Rich. He travelled to France to learn the latest staging techniques which he imported into Covent Garden. Charles Churchill, in *The Rosciad*, a long poem about the London theatres and its leading actors, describes the strength of this theatre, and in particular of Rich, or Lun as his stage name billed him, who starred in pantomime as Harlequin:

> Harlequin comes, their chief! – see from afar
> The hero seated in fantastic car!

> Wedded to novelty, his only arms
> Are wooden swords, wands, talismans, and charms!
> On one side Folly sits, by some called Fun,
> And on the other, his arch-patron, Lun.

GARRICK'S EARLY CAREER

Garrick had arrived in London in 1737 – not a good year for the theatre! He made a sensational debut anonymously as Richard III at Giffard's Goodman's Fields, and was immediately recognised as a new force in the theatre. But London was gripped by fear of the Jacobite rebels, and Garrick left to act professionally in Dublin.

Theatrical connections with Dublin were many and varied at this time. Thomas Sheridan managed Dublin's Theatre Royal, and actors from Dublin frequently became leaders of the profession in England: Macklin, Peg Woffington, Henry Woodward, George Anne Bellamy and Spranger Barry were just some of these, so that this was hardly a step back for Garrick.

Figure 5.4
William Hogarth, David Garrick as Richard III
Source: Walker Art Gallery, Liverpool

GARRICK'S REFORMS

Back in London, Garrick was able to begin to put in place some of the reforms which were to help make his reputation. He wrote two decades later:

> And may the stage, to please each virtuous mind,
> Grow every day more pure, and more refined;
> Refined from grossness, not by foreign skill,
> Weed out the poison, but be English still.[1]

As may be inferred from these lines, Garrick's reforms were aimed to attract the rising middle class. Samuel Johnson, in his Prologue at the opening of the 'new' Drury Lane in 1747, had noted the management's hopes, as well as the paradox at the heart of the theatre's problem:

> Ah! let no censure term our fate our choice.
> The stage but echoes back the public voice.
> The drama's laws the drama's patrons give,
> For we that live to please, must please to live.[2]

Garrick's reforms were many, but most significantly, he was able to transform performed drama from a predominantly static, aural medium to something more dynamic and more visual. To his contemporaries this seemed to make his acting more 'natural' and as such was widely admired, though pictures show that Garrick's style would seem to later generations extremely stylised.

Moreover, he aimed to create programmes which were better integrated: his hand may be seen, for example, in the pairing of *The Merchant of Venice*, in which Macklin presented Shylock as a human being and no longer merely clownish, with Macklin's own afterpiece, *Love à la Mode* (1759), in which four suitors, the Scot Sir Archy Macsarcasm, the Irish Sir Callaghan O'Brallaghan, the English Squire Groom and the Jewish Beau Mordecai, contest for the hand of the heroine, Charlotte, just as in Shakespeare's play the suitors contest for Portia's hand.

THE FRENCH EXAMPLE

The Comédie Francaise in Paris had finally ended the practice of allowing rich spectators to sit on stage during a performance, and Garrick followed their lead by enforcing this reform at Drury Lane in 1763. He employed the French scenic artist, Philippe Jacques de Loutherbourg, who changed the appearance of drama here for good, including the way scenes were presented, costume was apprehended, and lighting was used. Garrick's theatre sought an integrated production whole. And he engaged the charismatic French dancing master, Jean Georges Noverre, to bring a new quality to English stage movement.

NOT EVERYTHING CHANGES

The reforms, of course, did not change everything. This was still the stage on which an actress like Sarah Ward, in the most pathetic scene in *The Fair Penitent*, could fiddle with the bow on her glove, which had come loose, rather than notice the emotion the character might be feeling. Other actresses frequently winked at beaux in the audience, or curtsied to lords in the side boxes, and indeed gentlemen were known to enter onto the stage to squeeze a favourite actress in front of the noisy crowd. Actors still pointed their performances round 'clap traps', and those with smaller parts often paid little attention to the stage action.

REHEARSALS IN GARRICK'S THEATRE

Rehearsals, to which actors were still summoned by a drum beaten around the coffee houses and back ways of Covent Garden, were few, most actors simply learning their lines by themselves from cue sheets divided into 'lengths' of forty-six lines and given to them by the prompter. Garrick may have insisted on more general rehearsals, but they were only comparatively more thorough.

At rehearsals, the prompter was still the pivotal figure. He sat at a table and controlled proceedings, having his 'call-boy' on hand to make sure actors made their proper entrances, and keeping the keys to the props cupboard and the wardrobe. He was also responsible for integrating the music, copying (or getting an underling to copy) the parts in 'lengths' for the actors, and for seeing to the publicity. The prompter was so busy and so crucial to the workings of the theatre, that neither Thomas Dibdin, the prompter at Drury Lane, nor Richard Cross, his deputy, who appeared as himself in Kitty Clive's *The Rehearsal* (1750), were often able actually to leave the theatre building.

THE THEATRICAL FUND

Garrick also played a significant role in another reform, the establishment of a Theatrical Fund for needy actors, who had fallen on hard times. Though the first move came in 1766 from the Covent Garden company, Garrick and Lacy at Drury Lane soon opened their own fund, and Garrick acted as steward when the two funds were merged. And he was instrumental in having the combined fund incorporated in an Act of Parliament in 1776.

THE SUCCESS OF GARRICK'S REFORMS

Garrick's reforms prompted one commentator in 1750 to declare significantly that 'the British can now vie with the Athenian drama when in its severest state of purity'. But the question remained: how far could he claim the theatre for his own?

DRURY LANE THEATRE

When Garrick assumed control, Drury Lane's exterior was rather grand, though its interior was still uncomfortable and rough. The stage was more than forty feet wide and nearly thirty feet deep, fifteen of which were in front of the proscenium where the curtain hung. It was on this forestage that most of the action happened. Behind it was the rather dim 'vista' stage and in front a small orchestra pit. The pit itself, like the stage, was slightly raked and contained backless benches upon which there were marks every twenty-one inches supposedly to indicate an individual's allowed space. Spectators, however, could 'squash up' when the play was popular. The galleries also contained benches, though there were chairs in the boxes. Backstage was a maze of corridors and dressing rooms, offices, store cupboards and the green room and workshops.

The stage was thus an empty space in the middle of a busy world, both a dreamland and an actual place, neither realistic nor illusional. This was its strength, and perhaps its appeal.

DRURY LANE: THE AUDIENCE

At six o'clock the entertainment began, but crowds waited long before this. Because there was no way of reserving a seat, and no inclination to form an orderly queue, people arrived perhaps two or even three hours early, and when the doors were opened there was a mighty shoving and jostling, and sometimes worse, to get in. Servants pushed for their masters, and kept a place for them inside, then retired to the upper gallery when their masters appeared. Guardsmen were often positioned on stage to discourage would-be rioters.

Just before the performance commenced, the chandeliers were lowered and the candles trimmed, the stage floor was swept, and the music began. The programme, which might last till midnight, was something of a variety show: the main play was punctuated by musical interludes, there was at least one afterpiece as well as a succession of other 'turns', almost always including specialised dance performances.

The audience came and went during all this. Besides watching the play, they chatted, flirted, displayed themselves, greeted each other, and noticed scandalous goings-on in the boxes. Whores cruised the passageways and fruit sellers offered their wares. The auditorium was structured by class, and tensions between, say, the gallery and the boxes were often marked by rowdy assertiveness. Garrick himself seemed puzzled how to please them all. His epilogue to Murphy's *All in the Wrong* (1761) articulates his bewilderment:

> What shall we do your different tastes to hit?
> You relish satire (*to the pit*), you *ragouts* of wit (*to the boxes*),
> Your taste is humour and high-season'd joke (*to the 1st gallery*),
> You call for hornpipes, and for hearts of oak (*to the 2nd gallery*).

But there were also similarities between the denizens of every part of the auditorium – everyone cheered, jeered, heckled and laughed. Some came to be seen as well as to see: Loveless in Sheridan's *A Trip to Scarborough* (1777) finds watching the audience more satisfying than watching the play, while Mrs Hardcastle's scintillating hairstyle in Goldsmith's *She Stoops to Conquer* (1773) 'in a side-box at the playhouse would draw as many gazers as my Lady Mayoress at a City Ball'.

Whatever the different social strata's motives and behaviour, all agreed that the theatre belonged to them as much as to the players, and they asserted this conviction every evening. Garrick's drive to attract the middle class was not so much misconceived as too partial. When he played Lothario opposite Quin's Horatio in Covent Garden's *The Fair Penitent* in 1747, 'the shouts of applause . . . were so loud, and so often repeated, before the audience permitted them to speak, that the combatants seemed to be disconcerted'.[3] Whose theatre was it?

In 1751, when many disliked Edward Moore's *Gil Blas*, they hissed, threw fruit (Hannah Pritchard was hit by an apple) and, despite Garrick's objections, brought its run to an end. Wingate, the hero's father in Arthur Murphy's *The Apprentice* (1756), states bluntly that actors must expect to have their eyes 'knocked out with withered apples' thrown by audience members.

RIOTS AT *LES FÊTES CHINOISES*

In 1755 the audience again asserted itself. Early that year Garrick had appealed against those who threw fruit, potatoes and other missiles and pointed out that a young lady had been badly injured by a huge flying cheese weighing nearly half a pound. Later that year he presented Noverre's *Les Fêtes Chinoises* at a time when war with France was threatening, and the audience erupted. Though King George II attended the first night, there were hisses during the performance and shouts of 'No French dancers!' At the second performance, some spectators in the gallery and pit tried to stop the show, while those in the boxes defended it. In the mayhem, a man was thrown from the gallery into the pit where he, and the man he landed on, were both killed. Those in the boxes leapt into the pit, swords were drawn and after the spilling of some blood the evening ended inconclusively.

A few nights later Garrick himself appeared in *Much Ado about Nothing* on the same bill as *Les Fêtes Chinoises*. He was mocked as a Francophile, and the gallery tore up benches and hurled them into the pit, smashed the chandeliers and tried to reach the stage. Rioting continued until midnight, when Lacy appeared and agreed to end *Les Fêtes Chinoises*'s run. But the box patrons objected to this. Violence continued sporadically in the coffee houses and on the piazza of Covent Garden.

Even when Garrick addressed the audience from the stage, the situation got no better. Some box patrons entered the pit and threatened the life of one protester, who was only saved by Garrick's personal intervention. A further performance was agreed, but this was stopped by rioters who invaded the boxes and the stage (even though it was sprinkled with tacks and dried peas), missiles were thrown and heads – and legs – were broken. Only the entrance of the magistrates accompanied by a troop of constables stopped the riot, though some rioters later went to Garrick's house and smashed his windows. It took weeks for matters finally to calm down.

THE FOOTMEN'S RIOTS

Four years later, footmen in the gallery rioted when they objected to the play, *High Life below Stairs* as well as to Garrick's attempt to end the practice whereby they were given free seats in the gallery in return for holding their masters' seats in the pit. In 1763 when both patent houses tried to end the practice of allowing spectators in at half price after half time, further protests and riots took place for several weeks at both houses, and ended with the theatres backing down and reinstating the half-price concession.

DIFFICULT AUDIENCES

In 1770 a significant proportion of the Drury Lane audience, who supported the radical John Wilkes, objected to the production of *A Word to the Wise* by a prominent government supporter, Hugh Kelly. Again two sides faced each other, and Garrick was permitted neither to withdraw the piece

Figure 5.5
Covent Garden half-price riot, 1763: spectators clamber onto the stage protesting against the management's attempt to end the half-price concession

nor continue with it. When Kelly tried to address the audience, he was pelted with rotten fruit and had to retreat. The audience was finally dispersed, having been given their money back.

Three years later when Charles Macklin appeared at Covent Garden as Macbeth in an unexpected tartan costume, he was booed and heckled, and even asked to kneel to the audience. This time, however, it was not ideological or political objectors behind the mayhem, but friends and supporters of 'Gentleman' Smith, who had been usurped in this role by Macklin.

THE AUDIENCE AND THE THEATRE

All these examples show how audiences strove to own the theatre. The drama's laws the drama's patrons gave, indeed! Yet audiences were also usually sharply aware of proceedings on the stage, and they responded openly and emotionally. They also, of course, gazed on the beautiful bodies moving, dancing, apparently making love in front of them, and admired the actors' skill and refinement. The Prologues and Epilogues flattered them and besought their help, drawing them into the performance and helping them to genuinely collaborate in the evening's events. The theatre space was extremely intimate, and 'soliloquies' were occasions when a character could talk frankly and confidingly with the audience, as Mrs Oakly does in Colman's *The Jealous Wife* (1761), or George in Arthur Murphy's *The Citizen* (also 1761).

The fact of the audience is thus crucial to an understanding of eighteenth-century theatre. The auditorium was a site for argument, clamour and self-advertisement, but also deep absorption.

PATRIOTIC DRAMA

The practitioners' preferred way of engaging with politics and society was probably through patriotic displays. Garrick provided plenty of these at Drury Lane: he revived *Alfred*, the patriotic masque by James Thomson and David Mallett, in 1751, and in 1755, when war with France was imminent, *Britannia*, with words again by Mallett and music by Thomas Arne.

In 1760 King George II died and the theatres were shut, but his grandson, George III, was crowned next year, and both Drury Lane and Covent Garden mounted spectacular coronation

Figure 5.6
The Farmer's Return, 1762: engraving by James Basire the Elder

Source: The Metropolitan Museum of Art, New York. Harris Brisbane Dick Fund, 1932

shows. Garrick also presented a curious afterpiece, *The Farmer's Return from London* (1762) in which the rustic Farmer John returns home after visiting London for the coronation. He is amazed by the big city, the lights, the crowds, but the play is unexpectedly ambiguous: it appears to support the war with France which George III and his first minister, the Earl of Bute, opposed.

In 1771, after new prominence had been given by the establishment to the Order of the Garter, Garrick presented *The Institution of the Garter, or Arthur's Round Table Restored*, a lavish spectacle of patriotic sentiment; whereupon Covent Garden, under the management of George Colman the Elder, presented *The Fairy Prince, with the Installation of Knights of the Garter*. It was part of the friendly rivalry which prevailed between Garrick and Colman, and preferable to their earlier rivalry, when each had tried to outdo the other with *entr'actes* and dance features, as well as staging 'The Battle of the Romeos' in 1750, when the two theatres staged *Romeo and Juliet* simultaneously, with Garrick and Spranger Barry competing as Romeo, and George Anne Bellamy and Susanna Cibber as Juliet.

DRURY LANE ENLARGED

The stability of its management allowed Drury Lane to be enlarged twice during Garrick's steward-ship, first in 1763, when the stage was extended and the auditorium increased in capacity through-out; and in 1775 when the Adam brothers gave it a splendid new frontage as well as considerable improvements within. In 1763, when the extensions were completed, Garrick and his wife left for a two-year Grand Tour of Europe. George Garrick, his brother, and George Colman, the playwright, joined Lacy in running the theatre while Garrick was away.

THE COVENT GARDEN ROYAL PATENT

Meanwhile, in 1761 John Rich had died, leaving the Covent Garden patent to his widow and John Beard, his son-in-law. Beard was a singer and musician, and he soon introduced a series of musical comedies and operettas by Isaac Bickerstaffe, Charles Dibdin and others. But in 1767 Beard sold his share to four purchasers, including Colman, the actor William Powell, John Ruth-erford and Thomas Harris. They were a fractious group, whose quarrels culminated in Colman trying to lock Harris and Rutherford out of the building. When they forced their way in, they expelled Colman and refused him access for three weeks until he obtained a sheriff's warrant. In 1769 Powell died, and in 1774 Macklin sued Colman for the damage he had suffered during the audience uproar which had attended his performance as Macbeth. Colman gave up, and sold his share to Harris, the former soap manufacturer who now became the long-serving sole manager of the theatre.

END OF THE GARRICK–LACY PARTNERSHIP

In 1774 James Lacy, Garrick's partner at Drury Lane died. He left his share of the theatre to his son, Willoughby Lacy, a demanding and pettish young man whom Garrick found extremely difficult to deal with. Perhaps it hardly mattered because Garrick himself retired in 1776. At that 'awful moment', he made a graceful speech and left the theatre. But his retirement was not long: he died just three years later.

THE REPERTOIRE

This theatre may have been alive, but the repertoire of plays it presented was in some ways disappointing. New plays tended to be inward-looking, and farce and pantomime were more popular than new plays, which often depended on intertextuality and meta-theatre. But they were formally timid and their subject matter unoriginal. The best comedies celebrated *bourgeois* life, but too often they were prolix and the language ponderous.

The 1737 Act meant the repertoire was largely filled with old plays. Shakespeare, Otway, Congreve, Cibber, Rowe and Farquhar were continuously recycled, often in cleaned-up versions, like Garrick's *Country Girl*, which replaced Wycherley's *The Country Wife*. Garrick's Pinchwife is Marjorie's guardian, not her husband.

SHAKESPEARE

Shakespeare, too, continued to be rewritten, but with cheap editions of his plays increasingly available, and organisations such as the Countess of Shaftesbury's Shakespeare Ladies Club springing

Figure 5.7
Nicholas Rowe's *Tamerlane* at Drury Lane
Source: The Trustees of the British Museum

Figure 5.8

David Garrick and Hannah Pritchard in *Antony and Cleopatra* at Drury Lane

Source: By permission of the Folger Shakespeare Library

up, he became something of a symbol of sound English common sense. A monument was raised to him in Westminster Abbey in 1740. There had been a danger Shakespearean scholarship and Shakespeare's plays on the stage were becoming divorced, but Garrick's work helped to prevent that, and also incidentally to raise the status of the theatre and actors.

Garrick wanted to restore Shakespeare but he also wanted to make him accessible to an eighteenth-century audience. Consequently, his *Macbeth* omitted the Porter's scene as well as Lady Macduff, but included flying musical witches and added a new dying speech for the hero, written by Garrick himself. His *Hamlet* considerably reshuffled the play and had Hamlet's sortie to England prevented by the arrival of Fortinbras and Laertes's journey to France cut short. His *Midsummer Night's Dream* became *The Fairies*, with no Bottom, no 'rude mechanicals' and of course no play of *Pyramus and Thisbe*. But he mounted the first production of *Antony and Cleopatra* since Shakespeare's time, and he put Shakespeare squarely at the centre of Drury Lane's repertory.

PROBLEMS FOR WOMEN PLAYWRIGHTS

Among contemporary playwrights, women faced particular problems. In Kitty Clive's *The Rehearsal* (1750), it is clear that no-one expects a woman to write a play, and the aged Sir Albany Oldlove takes it upon himself to teach Mrs Hazard her business. Yet Frances Sheridan, Richard Sheridan's mother, wrote several comedies, including *The Discovery* (1763) and *The Dupe* (also 1763), both of which were successful at Drury Lane.

SOME MALE PLAYWRIGHTS

Among male playwrights, Dr Samuel Johnson's *Mahomet and Irene* (1749) made him more money than anything else he had written, and also introduced him to the enticing 'white bosoms and silk stockings' of the actresses, which made 'his genitals quiver'.[4] Arthur Murphy was prolific but rarely sharp. He was a passionate royalist who was probably jealous of Garrick, with whom he had a stormy relationship. Garrick's own plays, such as *The Lying Valet* (1741), *Miss in her Teens* (1747) and *The Irish Widow* (1772), are smoothly wrought but, as Robertson Davies noted, show 'no growth' in his practice. George Colman the Elder, Oliver Goldsmith, Samuel Foote and Richard Cumberland were all capable of good scenes and engaging characters without ever enough to excite later ages.

CONTEMPORARY THEMES IN DRAMA

Their plays do address a number of contemporary themes, if rarely very profoundly. Garrick and Colman's *The Clandestine Marriage* (1766) and Garrick's *Bon Ton* (1775) assert the superiority of the upright Englishman. Emerging class differences, notably the differences between the aristocracy and the rising middle class, find expression in a play like Colman's *The Jealous Wife*, in which the heroine, Harriet, is courted by an effete but nasty aristocrat, a 'sporting rake' and an honest but foolish middle-class young man: the middle-class young man wins her hand. In Samuel Foote's *The Nabob* (1772), the social hierarchy is upset by the intrusion of a returning empire-builder: in the end, Mr Oldham frees the family from Sir Matthew Mite's grasp, thus demonstrating the power of business over both upstart insistence and birth and privilege. Charles Macklin's *A Will and No Will* (1746) and Richard Cumberland's *The West Indian* (1771) explore further the world of eighteenth-century capitalism: they revolve around wills and the laws of roguery (*A Will and No Will*) or a box of diamonds (*The West Indian*).

Comedies about marriage proliferated. The 1753 Marriage Act had raised the age of consent for a woman from twelve to twenty-one, protected her assets from predatory males but also given increased authority over young people to their parents. In Colman's *The English Merchant* (1767), a Scottish Jacobite returns from exile to take charge of his daughter's marital destiny, though he had had no part in her earlier education. In *Three Weeks after Marriage* (1776) by Arthur Murphy, while the parents deliberate on their younger daughter Nancy's possible husbands, their elder daughter's three-week-old marriage to Sir Charles Rackett, arranged by them, is an utter disaster.

Popular plays like *The Clandestine Marriage* and *The Jealous Wife* explored some of the realities of marriage, *She Stoops to Conquer* asks disconcertingly whether a refined virgin or a whorish barmaid would make the better wife, and in Colman's *Polly Honeycombe* we watch the Honey-combe's cloying fondness for each other as they discuss disposing of their daughter 'like a piece of merchandise'.

THEATRICALITY

Self-conscious theatricality sometimes gives dynamism to these plays. In *She Stoops to Conquer*, for example, Kate's acting gives the play a delicious dimension of performativity. In Macklin's *A Will and No Will* (1746), besides a discussion of Macklin's playwriting skills by two of the actors, Shark informs Bellair that 'the farce is now in the very height of the plot, and it is impossible you can have your mistress till it be ended'. In Murphy's *The Apprentice*, the drama-mad but now reformed Dick exclaims, 'it'll be like a play if I reform at the end'. And this is the end. In Clive's *The Rehearsal*, Clive herself plays the author of the piece in rehearsal, while Richard Cross, the prompter, plays Richard Cross, the prompter. Similarly, in *The Minor* (1760) by Samuel Foote, Mr Foote plays Foote, and Mr Pearse plays Pearse.

These examples indicate the eighteenth-century comedy's richest vein, and suggest that it might have more to offer than has sometimes been recognised.

NOTES

1 David Garrick, *Mrs Pritchard's Farewell Epilogue*, spoken on 25 April 1768 at Drury Lane.
2 Samuel Johnson, *Prologue at the Opening of Drury Lane Theatre*, 1747.
3 *The Life of Mr James Quin, Comedian*, 1766, p. 88.
4 Jeffrey Meyers, *Samuel Johnson: The Struggle*, New York: Basic Books, 2008, p. 5.

Chapter 55: Garrick and acting: Romantic realism

GARRICK, THE ENGLISH ROSCIUS

Theatrically the third quarter of the eighteenth century was dominated by David Garrick, as manager, as playwright, but above all as actor. His style has been characterised as 'romantic realism', which, as Shearer West has pointed out, does not exclude convention or contrived attitudes. Nor does it mean identification with, or 'living', the part.[1]

Garrick amazed a *salon* full of intellectuals in Paris in 1764, and stimulated Denis Diderot to consider 'the paradox of acting'. He deduced that the best actor (that is, Garrick) stays in control of both himself and his part, that while the actor 'watches, studies and gives us the result', 'it is we who feel'. What the 'Roscius of England' exhibited, in other words, was a creature of his imagination.[2]

JAMES QUIN

English acting by 1740, when Garrick made his amazing debut, had fallen into a rusty conservatism, characterised somewhat exaggeratedly by Aaron Hill:

> The puffed, round mouth, an empty, vagrant eye, a solemn silliness of strut, a swing-swang slowness in the motion of the arm, and a dry, dull, drawling voice that carries opium in its deadly monotony.[3]

The personification of this was James Quin, whose style too often relied on the rhetorician's: he tended to stand and speak, employing a few predictable gestures as he did so. Smollett in *Peregrine Pickle* describes Quin's performance thus: 'His utterance is a continual sing song, like the chanting of vespers, and his action resembles that of heaving ballast into the hold of a ship'.[4] According to the playwright, Richard Cumberland, Quin 'rolled out his heroics with an air of dignified indifference', using 'very little variation of cadence, and in a deep full tone, accompanied by a sawing kind of action, which had more of the senate than of the stage in it'.[5] And Charles Churchill said:

> His eyes, in gloomy socket taught to roll,
> Proclaimed the sullen habit of his soul.[6]

But there was much more to Quin than these commentators allowed. John Hill asserted that Quin's speaking was 'perfection', and that he had gravity, but also humour and even boisterousness.[7] All agreed he was excellent as Falstaff, as Henry VIII and as Sir John Brute.

Figure 5.9
James Quin as Coriolanus
Source: BAMS Collection/Arenapal.com

JOHN HILL'S THEORY OF ACTING

John Hill's remarks are especially valuable. Hill was a failed actor and a failed playwright, but a thoughtful commentator and theorist of acting, whose ideas influenced Diderot. He probably came closer to pinning down Garrick's elusive genius than anyone. In his analysis of acting, he empha-sised, first, the actor's need to understand: 'a good understanding is as necessary to a player, as a pilot is to a vessel at sea'. Second, he urged what he called 'sensibility', by which he meant both emotional capaciousness and acting 'in the moment'. He noted how Garrick ran through 'the sev-eral artful transitions . . . from one passion to another' in Farquhar's *The Beaux' Stratagem*, and yet 'how wholly does he devote himself to each in its turn, as if no other, of whatever kind, had ever claimed any power over him!' Finally Hill called for 'fire' in the actor, 'rapidity of thought and vivacity of disposition'. And these three elements – understanding, sensibility and fire – were what enabled the actor 'to delude the imagination, and to affect the heart'.[8]

CHARLES MACKLIN AND NATURALISM

Even before Garrick, an important practical influence on 'romantic realism' in acting was exerted by Charles Macklin. In 1741 Macklin upset traditional theatregoers and excited the unconventional when he appeared as Shylock in *The Merchant of Venice*. He had visited London's Jewish quarter and read Josephus's *History of the Jews* as well as *The Old Testament*, and now he produced something striking, novel and – according to his contemporaries – realistic. This Shylock was no longer a minor comic figure, but someone at the centre of the action, in whose 'malevolence there is a

Figure 5.10
Johann Zoffany, Charles Macklin as Shylock, 1768
Source: The Holburne Museum, Bath/Bridgeman Images

forcible and terrifying ferocity'. But still this was a performance far from what we would recognise as 'realistic'. One witness described the scene when Shylock realises Jessica has left him:

> He comes on hatless, with disordered hair, some locks a finger long standing on end, as if raised by a breath of wind from the gallows, so distracted was his demeanour. Both his hands are clenched, and his movements abrupt and convulsive. To see a deceiver, who is usually calm and resolute, in such a state of agitation, is terrible.[9]

Even allowing for the fact that eighteenth-century behaviour was more demonstrative than our own, this was hardly naturalism.

Yet it was new, and its biggest impact came from Macklin's almost everyday way of speaking Shakespeare's lines. It was this that formed the basis of his teaching, David Garrick being one of his early pupils. Macklin remembered how he had initially been rejected at Covent Garden perhaps twenty years before: 'I spoke so familiar and so little in the hoity-toity tone of the tragedy of that day, that he told me I had better go to grass for another year or two'.[10] Now he asked his students to speak a line perfectly naturally, as if at home, and then for the stage to use the same rhythm and intonation, but to heighten them. Sense and emotional flow superseded sonority and attention to classical poetic rhythms in speaking the text.

GARRICK AND PEG WOFFINGTON

Macklin asked the actress Peg Woffington to help Garrick with the part of Farquhar's Sir Harry Wildair, and before long the two had moved into Macklin's house as co-students and lovers. The idyll only lasted so long. Macklin and Garrick quarrelled vehemently over the actor's rebellion against Charles Fleetwood, and by 1747, when Garrick took over the management of Drury Lane, he cut loose from Woffington and never acted with her again.

DAVID GARRICK'S ACTING

Garrick was a small man, with penetrating eyes, but elegant and graceful. He tried to counter his lack of height by wearing shoes with the heels built up. His stage presence was noted for its energy. He was a very physical actor, 'alive in every muscle and feature', as Cumberland noted,[11] though Peter Thomson has noted that this might turn into 'bustle, bustle, bustle. A German visitor, however, commented that it was

> refreshing to see his manner of walking, shrugging his shoulders, putting his hands in his pockets, putting on his hat, now pulling it down over his eyes and then pushing it sideways off his forehead, all with so slight a movement of his limbs as though each were his right hand.[12]

Hone records how at a splendid dinner party Garrick's place was noticed to be empty. The guests

> were drawn to the window by the convulsive screams and peals of laughter of a young negro (sic) boy, who was rolling on the ground in an ecstasy of delight to see Garrick mimicking a turkey-cock in the courtyard, with his coat tail stuck out behind, and in a seeming flutter of feathered rage and pride.[13]

Even in such a situation, Garrick was acting 'in the moment'. Instances could be multiplied. Samuel Derrick described his Jaffier in Otway's *Venice Preserved*:

> the mad confusion which is seen in his visage, the pangs which heave his breast on representing to himself his friend in tortures, the resolution of stabbing Belvedira, prevented by the gleam of love, which for a moment may be seen to glow in his face, but afterwards eclipsed by returning rage.[14]

The intensity here was repeated in many performances. In *Macbeth*, in the banquet scene, Garrick's Macbeth hissed so fervently at the murderer, 'There's blood upon thy face', that the unfortunate actor blurted out: 'Is there, by God?' instead of the murderer's actual words – ''Tis Banquo's then'.

EMBODYING EMOTION

Garrick was able to embody emotion, to physicalise the abstract, in remarkable ways. Descartes suggested that passion in the soul was expressed in the body, and that is exactly what Garrick seemed able to do. Intensity also manifests itself on stage by an actor who pays attention to what his fellows are doing and saying, which Garrick did from his earliest stage appearances:

> When three or four are on stage with him, he is attentive to whatever is spoke, and never drops his character when he has finished a speech, by either looking contemptuously on an inferior performer, or suffering his eyes to wander through the whole circle of spectators.[15]

From Macklin Garrick learned the value of a conversational tone, but his characters were never laid-back. The lines were broken by the patterns of emotion, as in natural speech, rather than by grammatical punctuation. His pronunciation was not perfect, and his pauses became legendary, but they were usually filled with meaning: it is probable that he was 'taking aim' at his next action, which Meyerhold termed 'pre-acting'. Arthur Murphy described how, as Virginius in Samuel Crisp's *Virginia* (1754), Garrick stood by the stage-door

> with his arms folded across his breast, his eyes riveted to the ground, like a mute and lifeless statue. Being told at length that the tyrant is willing to hear him, he continued for some time in the same attitude, his countenance expressing a variety of passions, and the spectators fixed in ardent gaze. By slow degrees he raised his head; he paused; he turned around in the slowest manner, till his eyes fixed on Claudius; he still remained silent, and after looking eagerly at the impostor, he uttered in a low tone of voice, that spoke the fullness of a broken heart, 'Thou traitor!' The whole audience was electrified.[16]

CHARACTER

Character for Garrick seems to have been somewhat akin to Locke's definition of it as 'self-consciousness', often revealed therefore in gesture.

> To die, to sleep;
> To sleep, perchance to dream – (*pause – gesture*) ay, there's the rub.

Garrick understood what Thomson has called the 'particularity' of character, thereby escaping the mechanistic conceptions of earlier theorists. He seemed intuitively in tune with Jean-Jacques Rousseau when the latter exclaimed, 'If I am not better, at least I am different!'

THE STAGE PICTURE

Finally, Garrick understood the significance of the stage picture. When Tom Jones and his friends visit Drury Lane in Fielding's novel, they apprehend the play pictorially. Garrick was friends with Hogarth, Zoffany and other artists who painted him many times in action, and he was as influenced

Figure 5.11
Sir Joshua Reynolds, David Garrick as Lord Chalkstone in his own drama, *Lethe, or Aesop in the Shades*, originally performed in 1740

Source: Courtesy the Garrick Club, London

by their pictorial compositional skills as they were by his. It would perhaps be possible to imagine a Garrick production as a series of signifying still pictures, and certainly his responsiveness to rhythm seems at least partly dependent on the pictures he wished to create.

GARRICK'S HAMLET

Garrick's art was above all conscious of itself, calculated to make the effects he desired. He boasted that he could 'speak to a post with the same feelings and expression as to the loveliest Juliet under heaven'.[17] Yet audiences felt the specificity of each performance. Many detailed descriptions of Garrick in particular scenes have come down to us. Here are two of them, which give a flavour of his acting at its best. First Georg Christoph Lichtenberg's moment-by-moment account of Garrick's Hamlet's first encounter with the Ghost:

> Suddenly, as Hamlet moves towards the back of the stage slightly to the left and turns his back on the audience, Horatio starts, and saying: 'Look, my lord, it comes', points to the right, where the ghost has already appeared and stands motionless, before anyone is aware of him. At these words Garrick turns sharply and at the same moment staggers back two or three paces with his knees giving way under him; his hat falls to the ground and both his arms, especially the left, are stretched out nearly to their full length, with the hands as high as his head, the right arm more bent and the hand lower, and the fingers apart; his mouth is open: thus he stands rooted to the spot, with legs apart, but no loss of dignity, supported by his friends. . . . At last he speaks, not at the beginning, but at the end of a breath, with a trembling voice: 'Angels and ministers of grace defend us!' . . . The ghost beckons to him: I wish you could see him, with eyes fixed on the ghost, though he is speaking to his companions, freeing himself from their restraining hands, as they warn him not to follow and hold him back. But at length, when they have tried his patience too far, he turns his face towards them, tears himself with great violence from their grasp, and draws his sword on them with a swiftness that makes one shudder, saying: 'By heaven! I'll make a ghost of him that lets me!' That is enough for them. Then he stands with his sword upon guard against the spectre, saying: 'Go on, I'll follow thee', and the ghost goes off the stage. Hamlet still remains motionless, his sword held out so as to make him keep his distance, and at length, when the spectator can no longer see the ghost, he begins slowly to follow him, now standing still and then going on, with sword still upon guard, eyes fixed on the ghost, hair disordered, and out of breath, until he too is lost to sight.[18]

GARRICK IN *THE ALCHEMIST*

Garrick was unusual for his time in that he was as much a master of comedy as of tragedy. Here he plays the apparently unrewarding part of Abel Drugger in *The Alchemist* by Ben Jonson:

> Abel Drugger's first appearance would disconcert the muscular economy of the wisest. His attitude, his dread of offending the doctor, his saying nothing, his gradual stealing in farther and farther, his impatience to be introduced, his joy to his friend Face, are imitable by none. Mr Garrick has taken that walk to himself, and is the ridiculous above all conception. When he first opens his mouth, the features of his face seem, as it were, to drop upon his tongue; it is all caution; it is timorous, stammering, and inexpressible. When he stands under the conjuror to have his features examined, his teeth, his beard, his little finger, his awkward simplicity, and his concern, mixed with hope and fear, and joy and avarice, are above painting.[19]

GARRICK COACHES ACTORS

Garrick, though he enjoyed being centre stage, also spent much energy coaching, teaching and directing his company. To young actors he emphasised hard work and 'study', recommending reading, including 'other books besides those of the theatre', and getting out into the world. He took other actors through their lines, showing how he thought they should be spoken, and if this made them to some extent his imitators, it also ensured coherence in the production and a uniform level of performance. And he was not pedantic. Having coached Henry Woodward patiently as Bobadil in *Every Man in His Humour*, he then missed a rehearsal. When he returned and found Woodward had varied his performance, he exclaimed 'Bravo!' and encouraged Woodward to develop his own ideas further.

SUSANNA CIBBER

Garrick's first leading lady was the singer and actress, Susanna Cibber, whose 'sensibility and sweetness of voice' Tobias Smollett praised. 'She has, besides', Smollett added, 'an elegance of person and expression of features, that wonderfully adapt her for the most engaging characters of your

Figure 5.12
Johann Zoffany, David Garrick and Susanna Cibber in *Venice Preserv'd* by Thomas Otway

best plays'.[20] She was equally at home in sentimental comedy and in tragedies such as Rowe's *Jane Shore*. However, not all was perfect with her. As Ophelia in *Hamlet*, she was once seen three times to stand up in the play scene to curtsey to particular audience members.

PEG WOFFINGTON

Her rival at Covent Garden was Garrick's early beloved, Peg Woffington. Beautiful and nimble-witted, she was known for her shapely legs which perhaps led to her noted popularity in 'breeches' parts. One such was Harry Wildair in Farquhar's *The Constant Couple*, which became perhaps a

Figure 5.13
Peg Woffington, c.1750, a fine actress and early love of David Garrick

Source: Heritage Images/Diomedia

delicate assault on male gender domination as she swaggered and laughed through this masculine role. She had a somewhat squeaky voice, and a sharp temper, shown when she stabbed her female rival, George Ann Bellamy, with a blunted stage dagger on stage.

HANNAH PRITCHARD

Garrick's best stage partner was probably Hannah Pritchard, though she was several inches taller than him, and grew very stout in her later years. Though Dr Johnson belittled her pronunciation and accused her of never reading more than her own part in any play, her best performances gave the lie to this. She was generally agreed to be Garrick's equal in their lively, funny and perennially popular *Much Ado about Nothing* and as his Lady Macbeth, she was also brilliant, according to Thomas Davies:

> When she snatched the daggers from the remorseful and irresolute Macbeth, despising the agitations of a mind unaccustomed to guilt and alarmed at the terrors of conscience, she presented to the audience a picture of the most consummate intrepidity in mischief. . . . In exhibiting the last scene of Lady Macbeth, in which the terrors of a guilty conscience keep the mind broad awake while the body sleeps, Mrs Pritchard's acting resembled those sudden flashes of lightning which more accurately discover the horrors of surrounding darkness.[21]

KITTY CLIVE

Kitty Clive, Fielding's favourite actress in the 1730s, created the roles of Lady Freelove in *The Jealous Wife* and Mrs Heidelberg in *The Clandestine Marriage*. She could be difficult, but was irresistible in the right comic role, hoydenish and ready for a romp. She was, said Samuel Foote, 'the best actress in her walk that I, or perhaps any man living, has seen . . . peculiarly happy in hitting the humours of characters in low life'.[22]

FRANCES ABINGTON

More formidable was Frances Abington, a brilliant actress but yet another awkward, not to say wilful, person. She was painted by Sir Joshua Reynolds as the Comic Muse, and gained particular kudos for creating the part of Lady Teazle in Sheridan's *The School for Scandal*, though she was forty years old by then. Despite running battles with both her managers, Garrick and Sheridan, her Box Office appeal was undeniable, and her popularity such that the pretty cap she wore as Kitty in *High Life below Stairs* was taken up by fashionable young women and called 'the Abington'.

MARY ANN YATES

Intense and highly talented, Mary Ann Yates was the last of this series of leading ladies. She was probably the most effective woman at tragedy between the retirement of Hannah Pritchard and the appearance of Mrs Siddons, and to some, she too was the equal of Garrick. But he found her temperament, like so many of these outstanding actresses, hard to deal with. Were they flighty, or merely trying to assert their rights against a dominant manager?

Figure 5.14
Frances Abington as Lady Betty Modish in Colley Cibber's *The Careless Husband*

OTHER ACTRESSES

Another excellent tragedy actress was Ann Barry, wife of the actor Spranger Barry. Jane Hippisley was perhaps Garrick's earliest leading lady and the first Kitty in his *The Lying Valet* and Biddy in his *Miss in Her Teens*. When he formed his first company at Drury Lane, Jane Hippisley was a member of it. More worldly, perhaps, was George Anne Bellamy, an Irishwoman who wrote her autobiography in no fewer than six volumes. And a younger star was Jane Pope, who took over Kitty Clive's roles, and created the part of Polly in *Polly Honeycombe*.

HENRY WOODWARD

Among the male actors of the time, pride of place should probably go to the Irishman, Henry Woodward. He was the author of pantomimes, and a notable Harlequin, described by Charles Churchill:

> Woodward, endowed with various tricks of face,
> Great master in the science of grimace
> . . .
> A speaking Harlequin, made up of whim,
> He twists, he twines, he tortures every limb,
> Plays to the eye with a mere monkey's art,
> And leaves to sense the conquest of the heart.[23]

But he was a more versatile actor than this suggests. A notable Mercutio and a versatile Bobabdil, he created among other parts the barber in Murphy's *The Upholsterer*, a wonderfully lugubrious character (the reader must imagine the long pauses in the dialogue):

(Enter Razor, with suds on his hands.)
QUIDNUNC: Friend Razor, I am glad to see thee – well, hast got any news?
RAZOR: A budget! I left a gentleman half shaved in my shop over the way; it came into my head of a sudden, so I could not be at ease till I told you.
QUIDNUNC: That's kind, that's kind, friend Razor – never mind the gentleman – he can wait.
RAZOR: So he can, he can wait.
QUIDNUNC: Come now, let's hear – what is't?
RAZOR: I shaved a great man's butler today.
QUIDNUNC: Did ye?
RAZOR: I did.
QUIDNUNC: Ay.
RAZOR: Very true.
(Both shake their heads.)
QUIDNUNC: What did he say?
RAZOR: Nothing.
QUIDNUNC: Hum – how did he look?
RAZOR: Full of thought.
QUIDNUNC: Ay, full of thought – what can that mean?

RAZOR: It must mean something.

(Staring at each other.)

QUIDNUNC: Mayhap somebody may be going out of place.

RAZOR: Like enough – there's something at the bottom, when a great man's butler looks grave; things can't hold out in this manner, Master Quidnunc! Kingdoms rise and fall – luxury will be the ruin of us all – it will indeed.

(Stares at him.)

And so on.

RICHARD YATES

Quidnunc was played by Richard Yates, Mary Ann Yates's husband. He had appeared both in the provinces and at Bartholomew Fair, though he was reputed to be poor at learning lines. He was in the company at Goodman's Fields when Garrick made his debut there and was Hamlet when Garrick played Osric. He was best known for comic roles, however, not only Harlequin in pantomimes but also Feste, Touchstone and Shylock.

TWO IRISH ACTORS

Spranger Barry, an Irish actor who worked for years in Dublin, was Covent Garden's Romeo when Garrick played the same part at Drury Lane. The competition between them was intense over twelve consecutive nights. Barry was ideally suited to Romeo, being handsome and charismatic: he was supposed to be better than Garrick in the first half of the play, though Garrick came into his own in the final scenes of the tragedy. Another Irish actor was William O'Brien, Laertes to Garrick's Hamlet. Romantic, an expert fencer, his promising career was cut short when he eloped with Lady Susan Fox-Strangeways, whose outraged family then sent the couple away to America.

OTHER ACTORS

William Powell was a protégé of Garrick, who played Romeo, King John and Jaffier in *Venice Preserved*. But Garrick turned against him, describing his King John as 'bouncing, strutting, striding, straddling, thumping, grinning, swaggering, staggering, all be shit'. He joined Colman and some others to take over the Covent Garden patent in 1767, but died two years later before he had time to prove himself in the position.

John Palmer also died young, aged forty. A success as Mercutio, Palmer was best remembered for his creation of Sir Brilliant Fashion, the exquisite in Murphy's *The Way to Keep Him*. William Lewis, who was 'mercurial' as Mercutio, was an actor of inexhaustible energy:

> No greyhound ever bounded, no kitten ever gambolled, no jay ever chattered (sing, neither bird nor man in question ever could) with more apparent recklessness of mirth than Lewis acted. All was sunshine with him: he jumped over the stage properties as if his leap-frog days had just commenced; danced the hay with chairs, tables, and settees, and a shade was never upon his face, except that of the descending green curtain at the end of the comedy.[24]

Robert Baddeley was the last actor to regularly wear the royal livery, which members of the Royal Patent theatre companies were entitled to, while Henry Mossop was an emotional but rather vapid actor, renowned as the leader of the 'teapot school': he stood on stage with one hand on his hip and the other gracefully curved like a teapot spout.

JOHN MOODY

John Moody was a man of no little courage who defied the rioting audience during the half-price disturbances in 1762. He dealt with one on-stage intruder who was trying to set light to the scenery, and when the angry hordes demanded an apology, he said he was sorry if saving their lives had given offence. This only further enraged them, and they demanded he go on his knees and apologise properly. Retorting in a loud voice, 'By God, I will not', Moody stalked off the stage. The crowd then forced Garrick to agree not to employ him again, but he fronted the chief rioter, one Fitzpatrick, an Irishman like himself, and frightened him into writing to Garrick to ask for his reinstatement in the company, a demand Garrick happily complied with.

NED SHUTER

The two best known comic actors of the period were probably Ned Shuter and Thomas Weston. Shuter was often drunk, but had a mad, irrepressible humour caught by Charles Churchill:

> From galleries loud peals of laughter roll
> And thunder Shuter's praises – he's so droll.[25]

He donated large portions of his salary to the disapproving Methodists, whose precepts he struggled to follow, and it was said his brilliant reading of the absurd threatening letter in Goldsmith's *The Good-Natured Man* was what made this play the success it was.

THOMAS WESTON

Thomas Weston worked a good deal with Samuel Foote at the Haymarket Theatre. He drank too much, was frequently in debt and quarrelled with his fellows consistently. Some idea of his comic style is indicated by James Northcote:

> It was impossible, from looking at him, for anyone to say that he was acting. You would suppose they had gone out and found the actual character they wanted, and brought him upon the stage without his knowing it. Even when they interrupted him with peals of laughter and applause, he looked about him as if he was not at all conscious of having anything to do with it, and then went on as before.[26]

'Romantic realistic' acting at its best was described by George Christoph Lichtenberg in his account of Weston as Scrub opposite Garrick as Archer in *The Beaux' Stratagem*:

> While Garrick sits there at ease with an agreeable carelessness of demeanour, Weston attempts, with back stiff as a poker, to draw himself up to the other's height, partly for the sake of decorum, and partly in order

to steal a glance now and then, when Garrick is looking the other way, so as to improve on his imitation of the latter's manner. When Archer at last with an easy gesture crosses his legs, Scrub tries to do the same, in which he eventually succeeds, though not without some help from his hands, and with eyes all the time either gaping or making furtive comparisons. And when Archer begins to stroke his magnificent silken calves, Weston tries to do the same with his miserable red woollen ones, but, thinking better of it, slowly pulls his green apron over them with an abjectness of demeanour, arousing pity in every breast. In this scene Weston almost excels Garrick by means of the foolish expression natural to him.[27]

NOTES

1 Shearer West, *The Image of the Actor*, London: Pinter, 1991.
2 Denis Diderot, 'The Paradox of Acting' in Toby Cole and Helen Krich Chinoy, *Actors on Acting*, New York: Crown Publishers, 1970, pp. 162–170.
3 Aaron Hill, *The Prompter*, quoted in E.R. Wood (ed), *Plays by David Garrick and George Colman the Elder*, Cambridge: Cambridge University Press, 1982, p. 6.
4 Tobias Smollett, *The Adventures of Peregrine Pickle*, Oxford: Oxford University Press, 1969, pp. 274–275.
5 Ian McIntyre, *Garrick*, London: Penguin, 1999, p. 125.
6 Charles Churchill, *The Rosciad*, 1761.
7 John Hill, *The Actor*, London, 1750, p. 99.
8 John Hill, 'Understanding, Sensibility and Fire' in Toby Cole and Helen Krich Chinoy (eds), *op.cit.*, pp. 123–131.
9 A.M. Nagler, *A Source Book in Theatrical History*, New York: Dover Publications, 1952, p. 358.
10 Toby Cole and Helen Krich Chinoy, *op.cit.*, p. 120.
11 Richard Cumberland, *Memoirs*, New York: Brisban and Brannan, 1807.
12 A.M. Nagler, *op.cit.*, p. 365.
13 William Hone, *The Every-Day Book*, vol 2, London: Hunt and Clarke, 1827, p. 61.
14 Samuel Derrick, *The Dramatic Register*, 1752, p. 68.
15 Ian McIntyre, *op.cit.*, p. 62.
16 *Ibid.*, p. 218.
17 Toby Cole and Helen Krich Chinoy, *op.cit.*, p. 132.
18 A.M. Nagler, *op.cit.*, pp. 368–369.
19 Stanley Wells, *Shakespeare and Co*, London: Penguin, 2006, pp. 154–155.
20 Tobias Smollett, *op.cit.*, p. 272.
21 Ian McIntyre, *op.cit.*, p. 145.
22 Ian Kelly, *Mr Foote's Other Leg*, London: Picador, 2012, p. 147.
23 Charles Churchill, *op.cit.*
24 George Taylor (ed), *Plays by Samuel Foote and Arthur Murphy*, Cambridge: Cambridge University Press, 1984, p. 27.
25 Charles Churchill, *op.cit.*
26 Donald Sinden (ed), *The Everyman Book of Theatrical Anecdotes*, London: J.M.Dent & Sons, 1987, p. 47.
27 Peter Thomson, *On Actors and Acting*, Exeter: University of Exeter Press, 2003, p. 105.

Chapter 56: The Scottish Enlightenment and theatre

THE SCOTTISH ENLIGHTENMENT

The Enlightenment was at its most dynamic in Scotland in the second half of the eighteenth century, after the defeat of the Jacobites. It was spearheaded by two scholars, outstanding not just in British but in European philosophical thought, David Hume, a moral philosopher whose ideas remained inspirational for centuries, and Adam Smith, whose *The Wealth of Nations* is considered the first work of modern economic theory. They advocated moderation and rationality.

But the theatre played an unexpectedly important role in its inception, and a drama also marked its inevitable demise.

THE SCOTTISH THEATRE AFTER 1737

Hume's *Treatise of Human Nature* was published in 1739, while the Edinburgh theatre was still struggling with the consequences of the 1737 Licensing Act. A few 'concerts' were given, with 'free' drama performances in the intervals, such as those mounted by Thomas Este under the patronage of the Duke of Hamilton in Taylor's Hall, but it was not till the defeat of the Jacobites that the Canongate Concert Hall opened on a regular basis in 1747, giving two or three 'concerts' per week.

AFTER THE 1745 JACOBITE REBELLION

Scotland was not cut off from England by the Jacobite rebellion, but Scots were often regarded by the English as a nation of Jacobites. In 1746, Sadler's Wells staged an anti-Scottish ballet, *Culloden*. In Edinburgh in 1749, when the song 'Culloden' was sung in the Canongate Concert Hall, a regular battle developed in the auditorium between English soldiers and supposed Jacobite sympathisers: apples and snuff boxes were thrown, and even pieces of benches from the gallery. As late as the early 1760s James Boswell reported the Covent Garden audience, on seeing two men in Highland dress in the pit, hissed, threw rotten apples at them and yelled: 'No Scots! No Scots!' Scots were thus in a sense on their own.

SARAH WARD AND WEST DIGGES

Scottish theatre struggled. The Canongate Concert Hall was established after a dispute among Este's company at Taylor's Hall in 1745. Sarah Ward, an actress from Keregen's York Company who would go on to perform at many theatres across Britain, including both Covent Garden and Drury Lane, led a group of discontented performers, together with her lover West Digges and Lacy Ryan, to a new venue in November 1747. It was the first 'permanent' theatre in Scotland, situated in what is still Playhouse Close, Edinburgh, but its early years were troubled: money was lost, partnerships split, Ward herself left and returned, left again and returned again, and tours to the north and east of Edinburgh met with little success.

DOUGLAS BY JOHN HOME

However, in 1756, this theatre produced what became Scotland's greatest theatrical success of the century, and a marker for the Enlightenment, *Douglas* by John Home.

Garrick had rejected *Douglas* for Drury Lane, whereupon a group of progressive Scottish intellectuals decided to give the script a public reading. David Hume took the part of the villain, Glenalvon, William Robertson was Randolph, John Home himself was Douglas, Alexander Carlyle Old Norval, Adam Fergusson Lady Randolph and Hugh Blair Anna. All except Hume were clergymen, but 'Moderatists' who were trying to introduce European mainstream values. For Hume, the project induced 'sociability' and demonstrated the civilising power of the passions. He thought of the mind itself as 'a kind of theatre', while the stimulation to the imagination imparted by drama chimed precisely with Adam Smith's notions of psychology articulated in his *Theory of Moral Sentiments* published in 1759.

But the project sparked a fire which became the Scottish Enlightenment. Pamphlets were published with titles such as *An argument to prove that the Tragedy of Douglas ought to be publickly burnt by the Hands of the Hangman*, and *Douglas, A Tragedy, weighed in the balance and found wanting* which accused the play of 'impiety, profaneness, error, immorality and vice'. Attempts were made to excommunicate David Hume, and Alexander Carlyle was arraigned before the Presbytery of Dalkeith.

The 'enlightened' fought back: Fergusson published his own pamphlet, *The Morality of Stage-Plays Seriously Considered* and contrarily, the ferocity of the opposition stimulated a reaction in favour of the drama. *Douglas* was presented at the Canongate Concert Hall in December 1756, with Digges as Young Norval, and Sarah Ward as Lady Randoph in probably the greatest success of her career. According to one observer, 'the applause was enthusiastic; but a better criterion of its merits was the tears of the audience which the tender part of the drama drew forth unsparingly'.[1] The drama's success is supposed to have prompted the Scotsman's triumphant question of his English counterpart: 'Whaur's yer Wullie Shakespeare noo?' Within three months *Douglas* was presented at Covent Garden (not Garrick's Drury Lane) to considerable acclaim.

Douglas is a tragedy which resonates because Scotland's wounds from the '45 rebellion were still raw. It has been called the first Romantic drama, with its dark sense of inexorable fate, its submerged Oedipal longings and its wild Scottish landscape. But it is probably better to see it as a late example of neoclassical tragedy, since it observes the 'unities' and its catastrophe happens offstage. David Hume certainly saw it as such, declaring its author the successor to Sophocles and Racine. As for the wild landscape, Edmund Burke had suggested that 'crags, precipices and torrents, windswept ridges, unploughed uplands (were) the very acme of taste' in 1757.[2]

Figure 5.15
John Home, author of *Douglas*, 1756

Source: New York Public Library

JOHN HOME'S LATER CAREER

But John Home was still subject to the proceedings of the Presbytery. He resigned his living at Athelstaneford and became secretary to the Earl of Bute, later George III's first Prime Minister, and tutor to the future king. He continued to write, but none of his later plays, which were all staged at Drury Lane, and included *Agis* (originally written in 1747 and rejected by Garrick), *The Siege of Aquileia* (1760), *The Fatal Discovery* (1768) and *Alonzo* (1773), met with much success.

THEATRE IN EDINBURGH AFTER *DOUGLAS*

The success of *Douglas* not only gave a decisive shot of confidence to Scotland's leading thinkers, it also strengthened Scotland's theatres. When Samuel Foote appeared in Edinburgh in the spring of 1759 he was warned he would fail, but he returned with a heavy purse gained from full houses. The summer season at the Canongate Theatre that year was under the management of David Beat, an active Jacobite in 1745, and ran from June to August with three performances each week. Included in the programme was the Scottish play, *The Coquettes, or The Gallant in the Closet* by Eleonore Cathcart, based on a work by Corneille. Cathcart was a cousin of James Boswell, who directed the production and probably edited the anonymous *A View of the Edinburgh Theatre during the Summer Season 1759*. Dedicated to West Digges, whose relationship with Sarah Ward was now over, this record of the quarrels, gossip and debates surrounding the theatre in Edinburgh show its burgeoning vigour.

This was exemplified the following summer when the theatre presented Towneley's *High Life below Stairs*, which had already aroused the wrath of London's footmen. In Edinburgh it was the sedan chair carriers who took offence, their riot only ending when the City Guard were called in.

GEORGE ANNE BELLAMY AND A SCOTTISH REPERTOIRE

Digges had by now taken up with George Anne Bellamy, who certainly helped to raise standards in Beat's company. In Thomson's tragedy, *Tancred and Sigismunda*, originally presented at Drury Lane in 1745 starring Garrick and Susanna Cibber, Bellamy played opposite West Digges and this Scottish work soared to new heights of popularity. Subsequently Bellamy's repertoire always included Scottish drama – *Macbeth*, *Douglas*, even an adaptation of *Ossian*.

Other Scottish plays were now mounted: James Baillie's *Patriotism* (1763), supporting the controversial Scottish Prime Minister, the Earl of Bute, Andrew Erskine's cross-dressing farce, *She's Not Him and He's Not Her* (1764) and John Wilson's Scottish history play, set in the reign of Scotland's James II, *Earl Douglas, or Generosity Betrayed* (1764), and though in 1764, Digges's creditors forced him to flee Edinburgh, Tate Wilkinson, a versatile provincial actor and later manager, took over as leading man for the season.

CONTROVERSY AND DEBATE

By now the theatre was not only fashionable in the Scottish capital, it was a centre of intellectual and political controversy and debate. The conflicting demands of the need for union with England and the simultaneous requirement to assert a national culture became overlaid by something of a generational clash. When the favourite of the younger playgoers, George Stayley, was not cast in a role they thought should be his, and he was sacked from the company, they rioted, tore up the seating and demanded the leading actor, now James Aicken, go on his knees on stage and apologise to them. Aicken refused and fled through the back door of the theatre. The City Guard arrived, but were beaten back, and the young rioters tore up the scenery and set fire to the Green Room. The theatre was closed, and the company went on a long tour to the north of England and the Scottish provinces.

Figure 5.16
George Anne Bellamy
Source: Bibliothèque nationale de France, Paris

EDINBURGH THEATRE ROYAL

Meanwhile, an Act of Parliament in 1767 for the building of Edinburgh New Town to the north of the Royal Mile included provision for a theatre, to be granted a Royal Patent. But the battle between new and old Scotland was not finished. The managers of the nearby Orphan Hospital, for example, opposed the building because they thought 'the said erection will be attended with bad consequences for the orphans by leading them into habits of idleness and dissipation', and even when the theatre was built they worried that it exposed the orphans to 'too much communication with those who frequent the playhouse (and) the loose company who (were) known to haunt and frequent' it.[3]

But Pitt's man in Scotland, the 'enlightened' Henry Dundas, saw that the theatre was built at the north end of North Bridge, and it opened in 1769. David Ross, formerly an actor at Covent Garden where he had fallen out with John Beard, was appointed the company's new leader. But no sooner was the theatre opened than the bridge onto which it abutted collapsed, and the theatre had to be built all over again.

It reopened in 1772, but building it twice had significantly increased the debts, leading to cost-cutting and the employment of cheaper, less experienced actors. The problems were compounded by Heartley, the prompter's frequent drunkenness.

One remedy Ross sought was to arrange for Samuel Foote to return. He had a lease for performing at the Little Haymarket Theatre in London during the summer; now he was tempted to come to Edinburgh in the winter. But the experiment failed, Foote's repertoire being too London-oriented, and he sold out to the returning West Digges, now with yet another female partner.

In 1773 Digges tried to extend the Theatre Royal's reach to Glasgow, but soon he found he was unable to manage two theatres simultaneously and Ross took over in Glasgow. By 1777 Digges was back in the debtor's gaol, Ross was attempting unsuccessfully to sue Samuel Foote, and Wilkinson had returned to Edinburgh. Finally, in 1781 Ross sold his Glasgow interest to John Jackson.

EARLY GLASGOW THEATRES

The struggle for a theatre in Glasgow was no less fierce than in Edinburgh. 'A Pantomime Entertainment called *Harlequin Captive, or the Dutchman Bit*' was performed at Burrell's Close in September 1751, but an attempt to erect a permanent theatre in 1752 in Castle Yard, near Glasgow Cathedral, was thwarted by zealous Methodists who set fire to the building before a play could be presented. And a similar event accompanied the attempt to establish a theatre in Alston Street ten years later, when George Anne Bellamy was contracted to open it. When it was burned down, Bellamy had a temporary booth erected where she appeared to highly appreciative audiences.

THEATRES ROYAL IN EDINBURGH AND GLASGOW

For the next two decades, the Edinburgh Theatre Royal was controlled by a series of managers: from 1768 for three seasons a strolling actor called Williams was in charge, but from 1773 David Ross was again the manager. He was succeeded by Tate Wilkinson and in 1780 by another actor, John Bland. But in 1781 Jackson amalgamated the Edinburgh and Glasgow companies and obtained a Royal Patent for a new Glasgow theatre in Dunlop Street next to a pleasure garden.

SCOTTISH TOURING COMPANIES

There had also developed recognised circuits for touring companies, like Corbet Ryder's, which visited, besides Glasgow and Edinburgh, Perth, Montrose, Dundee, Aberdeen and other places. How successful companies like this were is difficult to judge. Aberdeen, for instance, struggled to sustain a permanent venue for theatrical performances: in 1768, a new theatre was built in the New Inn, ten years later one opened in Show Lane, and in 1780 one opened in Queen Street. Dundee had a booth theatre between 1755 and 1767, and later a theatre at Yeoman Shore. In Perth, theatre companies used first the Guildhall, then by the 1780s Glover's Hall, where Corbet Ryder's group performed.

Another group led by George Sutherland performed here regularly, too, and in 1792 they staged a spectacular local drama, *The Siege of Perth, or Sir William Wallace* by John Maclaren. Robert Burns, the poet, saw Sutherland's troupe in Dumfries and declared Sutherland 'a man of genius'. Burns was not the author of a poem which eulogises such companies:

> Where is the place that mair o' life ye'll learn
> Than 'hint the scenes in some auld kintra barn,
> Where two-three hungry, ragged spouter blades
> Mang kintra folk do ply their kittle trades?[4]

Often itinerant troupes like Sutherland's or Ryder's, which by the way employed English actors as often as Scots, augmented their numbers with local amateurs. The Enlightenment helped to make amateur theatricals, especially in the Edinburgh area and the Borders, popular among the better-off and the intelligentsia, and performances were encouraged in Scottish schools, too.

SCOTTISH FOLK PLAYS

All this was in spite of the kirk's attitude. However, it is also true that the kirk sponsored dramatic activity of its own, especially some of the traditional folk plays which were still performed. Linlithgow's *The Marches Day*, for example, performed annually and published in 1771, uses Scots dialect and valorises local trades, in a manner rather reminiscent of the theatrical 'Common Ridings' which still persist in some of the Border towns today.

More intriguing, perhaps, are Gaelic plays like *The Hag of the Mill-Dust* from the western isles. Here an old couple argue and fight with sticks. When the old man knocks down and apparently kills the old woman, he howls loudly. But when he touches her, she stirs. He touches her again, then again, until she stands up, and the pair embrace, howling again, but now joyously.

SCOTTISH DRAMA

There was thus a gradual *rapprochement* between enlightened thought and more traditional Scottish ways, and the mainstream theatres in Edinburgh and Glasgow began to introduce something more distinctly Scottish into their repertoires alongside English favourites. Scottish plays produced included Henry Mackenzie's tragedies, *The Prince of Tunis* (1773) staged by Digges in Edinburgh, and *The Shipwreck* (1784) and his comedy, *Force of Fashion* (1789), though John Wood's history play, *The Duke of Rothsay* (1780) went unperformed. Then there was the prolific actor-playwright, Archibald Maclaren, who wrote plays such as *The Conjuror, or The Scotsman in London*, first staged in Dundee in 1781, and performed in Edinburgh two years later, *The Coup de Main* (1783), *The Humours of Greenock* (1788) and *The Highland Drover* (1788). This last is set in Carlisle, but gains much of its humour from the linguistic misunderstandings between Gaelic and English speakers, and it was presented at Covent Garden in 1805. Maclaren moved to England, where he continued to write, notably *The Negro Slaves or The*

Blackman and the Blackbird (1799), an anti-slavery drama whose hero, the Scot MacSympathy, confronts an English slave owner.

Scottish women began writing plays, too. Some did not have their work performed, including Gioia Marishall (or Jane Marshall), whose *Sir Harry Gaylove*, an indictment of the patriarchy and arranged marriages, was published in 1772, and three plays by Lady Eglantine Maxwell Wallace, though her *Ton, or The Follies of Fashion* was presented at Covent Garden in 1788.

THE HUBBLE-SHUE

Most interesting was *The Hubble-Shue* (1786) by Christian Carstairs, an extraordinary metatheatrical *tour de force* in two scenes, perhaps unfinished, which evokes some of the baffling absurdity of *Alice in Wonderland*. 'A bizarre anarchic comedy' according to Edwin Morgan,[5] the play begins with a zany dinner party but somehow transfers to the theatre where it is supposedly delayed for half an hour. Mrs Kennedy tries to fill the time with a song, but the audience boos and throws oranges until the scene descends into a dire storm at night with a drunken coachman who crashes his coach. The play also manages to include an attack on imperialism and racism – a little black girl's father is eaten by a crocodile, and she is 'rescued' by a fashionable English gentleman.

It is not clear whether *The Hubble-Shue* was ever actually produced: its wild fantasy and illogicalities are hardly in keeping with enlightened rationality. Its creation marks perhaps, the beginning of the end of the Scottish Enlightenment, though not, of course, of Scottish theatre.

ERSKINE JOHNSTON

There were also excellent Scottish actors, the best of them probably Erskine Johnston, 'the Scottish Roscius' who was admired in England as well as Scotland. Perhaps the high point in his career came when he appeared as Young Norval in *Douglas* in full highland dress, which had been banned since 1746. His Scottish audience rose and applauded him with unabashed fervour. He appeared with success at both Covent Garden and Drury Lane in the first decade of the nineteenth century, and in 1808 just failed to obtain the Edinburgh Royal Patent. He did become manager of Glasgow's Queen Street Theatre in 1814, but this venture ended in bankruptcy.

THE NATION AND THE UNION

The Enlightenment had helped to ease the tensions between the union and Scottish national aspirations, but tension could still be seen in the fortunes of the Scottish Royal Patent theatres. In 1792, at a performance of *As You Like It* at the Theatre Royal in Dumfries, the oldest theatre still operating in Scotland, sympathisers with the French Revolution, still smarting from the defeat of Culloden, objected to the playing of 'God Save the King', and caused a minor riot. Robert Burns, the poet, remained seated during the anthem. Two years later in Edinburgh, at a performance, perhaps itself provocative, of *Charles I, or The Royal Martyr*, 'God Save the King' was again met with loud voices of dissent and calls for the Scottish song, 'Maggie Lauder'. In the play, Cromwell's anti-royalist speeches were applauded, and when 'God Save the King' was repeated, fighting broke

Figure 5.17
Erskine Johnston as Young Norval in *Douglas*
Source: Paul Fearn/Alamy Stock Photo

out between officers of the army and the better-off patrons on one side and the commoner people on the other. Soldiers had to be called to restore peace.

There was irony, then, in the extremely warm reception afforded to Mrs Siddons, the leading English actress, when she appeared in 1784 as Lady Randolph in *Douglas* in both Edinburgh and Glasgow. In Edinburgh the Scottish General Assembly was only able to transact its business on days when Mrs Siddons was not appearing, while in Glasgow, she so impressed the audience that there was deep silence in the theatre at the end of her scene, broken by an awed voice: 'Tha's no bad'. Other English stars welcomed in Scotland included Siddons's brother, John Philip Kemble and Dora Jordan, though the latter was less popular partly thanks to publicly vented disagreements with the manager, John Jackson.

La. RAN. Eternal providence ! What is thy name?
My name is NORVAL : and my name he bears.

DOUGLAS

Figure 5.18

Sarah Siddons as Lady Randolph in *Douglas*

Source: Florilegius/Alamy Stock Photo

STEPHEN KEMBLE'S SCOTTISH VENTURES

Jackson went bankrupt in 1791, and Stephen Kemble, another Englishmen, brother to Mrs Siddons and John Philip Kemble and already managing the Theatre Royal, Newcastle-upon-Tyne, became manager. But he was obstructed by the actress Harriet Esten, mistress to the Duke of Hamilton, and he moved to the 'Circus' at the top of Leith Walk. This venue, however, had no Royal Patent, and Kemble was forced to leave Edinburgh.

In 1794 Esten herself left for Covent Garden, and Kemble returned, managing the theatre until 1800. Though not particularly successful, in 1795 he extended his control to the Aberdeen theatre, and in 1799 acquired a northern England circuit as well. In 1800 he therefore relinquished his post in Edinburgh, and Jackson, who had published the first *History of Scottish Theatre* in 1793, returned, this time in partnership with the actor, Francis Aicken.

By now Scottish intellectual life needed a new stimulus. Walter Scott and Scottish romanticism was about to emerge.

NOTES

1 Ronnie Young, Ralph McLean and Kenneth Simpson (eds), *The Scottish Enlightenment and Literary Culture*, Lanham, MD: Bucknell University Press, 2016, p. 125.

2 Roy Porter, *Enlightenment*, London: Penguin, 2000, p. 314.

3 Minutes of the Orphan Hospital of Edinburgh (NRS: GD 17/2), 13 June 1768 and 12 February 1770.

4 Ian Brown (ed), *The Edinburgh Companion to Scottish Drama*, Edinburgh: Edinburgh University Press, 2011, p. 37.

5 Edwin Morgan, *ScotLit 20*, Spring, 1999.

Chapter 57: Mavericks

Theatre after 1737 strained to escape its legal constrictions, and perhaps the first genuine mavericks of British theatre emerged, edging towards a theatre embracing Dionysian, as well as the prevailing Apollonian, qualities.

ISAAC BICKERSTAFFE AND BURLETTA

One was surely Isaac Bickerstaffe, an Irish former soldier who had been discharged from the service under sadly suspicious circumstances. He had aspirations to make drama, and when John Beard inherited the Covent Garden Royal Patent from his deceased father-in-law, John Rich, Bickerstaffe's chance arrived.

He had already written *Thomas and Sally* (1760) with music by Thomas Arne, a short piece about a young woman who resists the importuning of the local squire and is rescued by the return of her sailor lover. It was perhaps the first 'burletta' in English, though it is rarely credited as such. The definition of 'burletta' is slippery. It was a new form, a short piece of music theatre, lasting about half an hour, 'a poor relation to an opera', according to Mrs Hazard in Catherine Clive's *The Rehearsal*. An example is the piece being rehearsed in that play. Sheridan's excellent *The Duenna*, with music by two Thomas Linleys, father and son, is perhaps another example. At their best, burlettas included jokes and clowning; they were pacey, sexy and included attractive popular music; and they were perhaps most useful as a means of evading the limitations imposed by the 1737 Act.

Bickerstaffe created a series of the best of them: *Love in a Village* (1762) with music by Arne, including the ever-popular song, 'The Miller of Dee'; *The Maid of the Mill* (1765) this time with music by Samuel Arnold, based on incidents from Samuel Richardson's novel, *Pamela*; and *Daphne and Amintor* (1765) with music by various composers. These works changed the direction of British musical drama away from ballad opera, towards something more lyrical and fully orchestrated.

In 1767 Bickerstaffe began a successful partnership with Charles Dibdin, and together they produced *Love in the City* (1767) which was later adapted into the hugely successful farce, *The Romp* (1781), and *Lionel and Clarissa* (1768).

CHARLES DIBDIN

Dibdin himself went on to create the libretto as well as the music for further burlettas – *The Recruiting Sergeant* (1770), *The Deserter* (1773) and the very popular *The Waterman* (1774) in which Tom

Figure 5.19

Johann Zoffany, Isaac Bickerstaffe's *Love in a Village*, 1762, with Edward Shuter, John Beard and John Dunstall

Source: Yale Center for British Art, Paul Mellon Collection, Yale University, New Haven

Tug rows to victory in Dogget's Coat and Badge race, thereby winning the heart of his darling. Dibdin was for several decades an extremely popular composer. His work, according to Roger Fiske was 'wholly *galante* in style', but 'his knowledge of counterpoint was rudimentary and his harmony unadventurous'.[1] To make up for this, however, his work was intensely dramatic, often clever and occasionally dynamic.

BICKERSTAFFE AND SCANDAL

Bickerstaffe's later work became more interesting, but in 1772 he was caught up in a whirlwinding scandal after he had propositioned a guardsman for sex. When the guardsman threatened to tell his superiors, at a time when homosexual acts were punishable by death, Bickerstaffe foolishly pressed money as well as a watch, seals and a ring, into his hands to try to buy his silence. It was in vain, and Bickerstaffe fled to the continent, where he remained, often in the direst poverty, for the rest of his life. The scandal was inflamed by a scurrilous lampoon, *Love in the Suds*, by William Kendrick, which went so far as to implicate David Garrick in a homosexual relationship with Bickerstaffe.

EXPLORING IMPERIALISM

Before his exile Bickerstaffe had written *The Padlock* (1768) for Garrick at Drury Lane, in which appears the spry, witty, defiant, self-possessed black servant, Mungo, an unusually positive depiction of a black person for the period. The padlock of the title keeps Don Diego's wife imprisoned: Mungo is instrumental in obtaining her release. *The Sultan, or A Peep into the Seraglio* (1775), with music again by Charles Dibdin, was written for the actress Frances Abington and became a significant success. The piece concerns Roxalana, an English slave, who becomes the Sultan's favourite and convinces him of the English virtues of love and freedom. Under her tutelage, he breaks the Islamic ban on wine-drinking, renounces his harem and marries Roxalana: British values (and the charm of British female sexuality) prove stronger and finer than those of Islam.

THE NABOB

These works explore, however naively, the emerging problems of imperialism and its associated racism. They may be set beside a major work by another maverick, *The Nabob* (1772) by Samuel Foote. A nabob was any Briton who returned from India greatly enriched and now sought place and status in society at home; or, as Thomas says in Foote's play:

> These new gentlemen, who from the caprice of fortune, and a strange chain of events, have acquired immoderate wealth, and rose to uncontrolled power abroad, find it difficult to descend from their dignity, and admit of any equal at home.

The classic nabob was Sir Robert Clive, victor of the Battle of Plassey, who brought home £230,000 in Dutch bills, £41,000 in bills on the East India Company, £30,000 in diamonds, £12,000 in other bills, and more. He claimed to be 'astonished' at his own 'moderation', though he was brought before the House of Commons to explain his conduct.

Foote's play recreates Clive as Sir Matthew Mite, though he reserves some of his sharpest arrows for the corrupt bankers and financiers who were warping London life. Sir Matthew buys out persons whose property he desires for four times its value, enmeshes the sinking fortunes of the aristocratic family he wishes to marry into, and heartlessly discards his old school friend whose existence only serves to publicise Mite's own humble origins. In the end, the honest merchant frees his brother from Mite's stranglehold, implicitly demonstrating how commerce trumps both nabobery and birth and privilege.

SAMUEL FOOTE'S EARLY CAREER

Foote first appeared in London in the 1740s, a would-be actor and author who began to make a name for himself as a mimic and impressionist. In 1747, he staged a series of morning performances, the first 'matinées' in Britain. These he billed as 'meetings' or 'encounters' when he served a dish of chocolate or tea to his auditors. Really they were one man shows, monologues spiced with satirical topicalities, 'diversions' which evaded the 1737 Act. Later Foote tried something similar with mock auctions. And in 1749 or 1750 he teamed up with the poet Christopher Smart and toured a drag-act round the pubs of London late at night, Smart as 'Mother Midnight', Foote as his niece, Dorothy, clad in sumptuous dresses and presenting mostly risqué and suggestive material.

By then, however, he had begun to write plays, and he became a prolific author of shortish satirical farces, in many of which he starred himself. These included *The Knight* (1749), *An Englishman in Paris* (1753), *The Englishman Returned from Paris* (1756) and *The Commissary* (1765), a hilarious satire on those profiteering from the European wars.

THE MINOR

In *The Minor* (1760) Foote addresses the 'enthusiasm' of the zealots of Methodism and their 'field orators' like George Whitefield. The play suggests that such preachers are like actors, and perhaps as insincere. In the production at the Little Theatre on the Haymarket, Foote played himself, Foote, but also Shift, who in the play plays Smirk, and also Mother Cole, a bawd. The conflation of dramatic

Figure 5.20

Samuel Foote as Mother Cole in *The Minor*, 1760

characters with 'real' people was dizzying. Mother Cole was an incarnation of the well-known London brothel-keeper, Mother Douglas, Squintum represented Whitefield who was renowned for his squint. There were in other words, layers of reality, like a hall of distorting mirrors, and as Mother Cole mouths Methodist pieties while selling her 'girls', sex and religion become indistinguishable.

The play caused enormous offence and controversy. Whitefield's supporters wanted it stopped, the Lord Chamberlain hesitantly ordered some cuts to the text, but it seemed to the antagonists he was endorsing Foote's attack. More significant, perhaps, was Foote's renewed sexual ambivalence. The tradition of cross-dressing involved women playing 'breeches' parts, not men playing women, and Foote's persistence in this was not only socially challenging, it would lead him into trouble later.

For now, his performances amazed the town. Churchill described him in *The Minor*:

> By turns transformed into all kinds of shapes,
> Constant to none, Foote laughs, cries, struts and scrapes;
> Now in the centre, now in van or rear,
> The Proteus shifts, Bawd, Parson, Auctioneer.

FOOTE'S ACCIDENT AND THE HAYMARKET ROYAL PATENT

From the mid-1750s Foote had starred in productions at the Little Theatre, Haymarket, during the summer when Drury Lane and Covent Garden were dark. It had no Royal Patent and was in constant danger of being closed, but its small, intimate auditorium was particularly fitted for his style of work. In 1762 he took over as manager and his summer seasons became more popular every year.

But 1766 an extraordinary tragedy struck Samuel Foote. In February of that year he was staying with aristocratic friends at Methley Hall in Yorkshire. They dared the notoriously unathletic Foote to mount a particularly mettlesome stallion. No sooner was Foote in the saddle than the horse reared up and flung him off. He broke his leg horribly in two places. At that date there was no cure for such an injury, and a surgeon was sent for from London. When he arrived nearly three days later, Foote must have been near death. But his leg was amputated above the knee and without anaesthetic, and extraordinarily enough, Foote survived. Indeed in less than six months, he was back on stage, acting again, but now with a wooden leg.

The good that came out of this for Foote was that his guilty but still influential friends pulled the right strings, and in July 1766 he was awarded a Royal Patent for the Little Theatre to run from 15 May to 15 September every year.

FOOTE'S LAST YEARS AND SCANDALOUS END

The one-legged Foote now himself became an object to be stared at – a peglegged superstar! He wrote new plays for his loyal company, still with leading roles for himself: *The Devil upon Two Sticks* (1768), *The Lame Lover* (1770) and *The Maid of Bath* (1771), based on the romance of Richard Sheridan, the playwright, and Elizabeth Linley, his first wife, a play that lurks behind Sheridan's own *The Rivals*.

His last play, *A Trip to Calais* (1775), led him to the ultimate scandalous notoriety. It was not that in the play, when it was finally put on under the title *The Capuchin*, Foote, dressed again as a woman, kissed another man on the mouth on stage; rather it was the satire aimed at Elizabeth

Chudleigh, Lady Kingston, which landed him in trouble. She had appeared in the original text thinly disguised as Lady Crocodile. The Lord Chamberlain had refused the play a licence. Foote threatened to publish it, for the Lord Chamberlain had no power to censure printed material. Hearing this, Lady Kingston offered Foote a bribe not to publish, and when Foote refused the offered cash, Lady Kingston charged him with extortion. At the same time her friend William Jackson, publisher of *The Public Ledger*, accused Foote of homosexuality.

He had some evidence. Foote's coachman, Jack Sangster, had accused Foote of a homosexual assault upon him. Gossip flared. An obscene poem, purporting to describe the incident, entitled *Sodom and Onan*, was published. Foote himself denied the accusation, but it came to a sensational trial, the outcome of which, surprisingly enough, was the acquittal of Foote. His friends in high places had never stopped supporting him.

But Foote's health was broken. He tried to continue performing, but collapsed on stage. His doctor sent him to Brighton to recuperate, but he died there in October 1777.

The place of Samuel Foote in the history of the theatre of the period is marginal, but it is also original. His work was not classical, at least as the Enlightenment understood the term, but it was laughter-making, Dionysian rather than Apollonian.

NOTE

1 Roger Fiske, *English Theatre Music in the Eighteenth Century*, Oxford: Oxford University Press, 1986, p. 349.

Chapter 58: Philippe Jacques de Loutherbourg and the stage picture

STAGING IN THE 1740S AND 1750S

In the 1740s and 1750s, conventional staging and lighting, essentially still the system devised by Inigo Jones in the early seventeenth century, came to be seen by many as dated and inadequate. Actors still performed in front of painted scenes which ran in grooves, the upper grooves being concealed by flown clouds, or painted perspective ceilings, or swags of drapery. Occasionally this was varied by drop scenes attached to rollers and let down from above, but even the painting on these was emblematic and conventional, stock pictures of generic locations. Lighting was by chandeliers which illuminated stage and auditorium alike, and perhaps footlights and lights on battens in the wings. Mostly candles were used, though occasionally oil lamps were preferred.

As for costume, most characters wore contemporary English clothes, sometimes adding an emblematic helmet, turban or cloak, though there were also 'shapes' which actors adopted: a Roman 'shape', for example, or a Turkish 'shape' with a turban, or a Spanish 'shape' with a cloak and a sword. But still Smollett complained in 1750 of Hamlet appearing as an undertaker, and Lothario from *The Fair Penitent* as a mountebank.

The problem was compounded by carelessness and inefficiency. Too often, stage hands brought in shutters which failed to match, or allowed 'flown' clouds to hang in a lady's boudoir; one scene might 'open' before the stage was cleared from the previous one; or the chandeliers were noisily lowered for the candles to be trimmed by snuffers on long poles, and then cranked back up again, during the performance.

ATTEMPTS TO IMPROVE SCENERY AND LIGHTING

David Garrick wanted the enlightened taste of *bourgeois* audiences to govern the stage spectacle, and in 1759 he introduced transparent back scenery in the pantomime, *Harlequin's Invasion*, allowing dim figures to be seen through the backcloth; at the same time, he installed coloured silk screens which could be turned on their axis to reflect their various colours for the audience.

However, it was after his return from the continent that he systematically addressed the means of presentation. He worked for new scenes for every production, and managed to affect several lighting improvements which he learned in France. He introduced reflectors behind candles in the wings and footlights, and curved metal shields which could be drawn over a flame to dim or even smother it. He also turned to French oil burners with circular wicks surrounding an empty centre, which when placed inside a tubular glass chimney, greatly intensified the illumination. This enabled the chandeliers, whose lights were a constant annoyance to spectators, to be downgraded or even dispensed with entirely.

PHILIPPE JACQUES DE LOUTHERBOURG

As for the scenic side of production, Garrick found himself excited by the ideas of the French painter, Philippe Jacques de Loutherbourg, whose canvasses depicted rocky landscapes in atmospheric light. He hired him, initially for the enormous fee of £100 per month, later modified to £500 per year. De Loutherbourg's conception was the integration of all the visual aspects of the production, and he demanded absolute authority over all relevant areas – scenery, lighting and costume. He was perhaps the first real designer in the British theatre, for he employed others to execute his ideas – John French, Thomas Greenwood or Pierre Roger.

ALFRED

Despite some input into *The Pygmy* at Drury Lane at the end of 1772, de Loutherbourg's first major work for Garrick was for the 1773 revival of Mallett and Thomson's *Alfred*, the patriotic masque which included 'Rule Britannia' among its musical numbers. Though the plot, so far as there is one, is exceedingly dull, de Loutherborg's contribution was wildly applauded. *St James's Chronicle* described the representation of the 'Grand Naval Review' thus:

> The view of Spithead and the fleet is taken from the saluting battery, which we here see mounted with cannon. Every ship of the line is a beautiful perfect model, with rigging, etc., complete, dressed with their proper suits of colours, and carrying their regular number of guns; the Isle of Wight, in the background, forms a just and beautiful relief; the royal yacht is seen sailing into the harbour, under a salute of battery and the whole fleet. Numberless and various kinds of vessels are beheld under weigh, with their sails full, making their different tacks, amongst which is readily distinguished the model of the beautiful cutter belonging to the Duke of Richmond, remarkable for its blue and white striped sails. The deception of the sea is admirable.[1]

A CHRISTMAS TALE

Alfred was followed by *A Christmas Tale*, which Garrick himself adapted from a French piece which de Loutherbourg had already staged in Paris. Here de Loutherbourg unloosed some of his most famous and extraordinary effects, such as the forest scene in which the leaves on the trees gradually turned from green to blood red, an effect achieved by the use of coloured silks stretched over the side-scene lamps on a pivoted frame. When the frames revolved, a different colour covered the lamp which was projected onto the stage. Finally, the palace itself tumbled into ruin as it was consumed by fire. '*The scene grows dark; flames of fire are seen through the seraglio window; all but Floridor quit the place, shrieking*'. Then '*the seraglio breaks into pieces and discovers the whole place in flames*'. It was sensational, and received ecstatically by spectators.

Figure 5.21
Philippe Jacques de Loutherbourg, Act V Scene 2, *Richard III*, Drury Lane, 1772
Source: Victoria and Albert Museum, London

DE LOUTHERBOURG'S LATER PRODUCTIONS

The list of de Loutherbourg's triumphs at Drury Lane could be extended. In 1775 in *Queen Mab* he staged a regatta not unlike the grand Naval Review in *Alfred*. In 1776, in Hannah Cowley's *The Runaway*, he created a thoroughly realistic waterfall through the play of light and shadow, and the same year, in Sheridan's *The Camp*, he staged further deceptively realistic scenes, this time of military manoeuvres by the use of mechanical puppets and painted scenery.

> Different battalions marched through the camp, lit by the soft glow of an autumn evening: by a kind of magic peculiar to himself, (de Loutherbourg) makes the different battalions, composed of small figures, march out in excellent order, into the front of their lines, to the astonishment of every spectator.[2]

In *The Wonders of Derbyshire* (1779), audiences were taken through the scenic wonders of that county in a series of views of Chatsworth House, Matlock at sunset, Dovedale in the moonlight and the Derbyshire landscape at dawn. They were scenes which realised on the stage something of what de Loutherbourg had tried to achieve in his easel paintings.

DE LOUTHERBOURG AND LIGHTING

In a few years, de Loutherbourg had achieved Garrick's aim to transform the stage spectacle. He had developed to the furthest possible point lighting by candle or oil. He had employed transparent scenes, coloured silks to illuminate either stage or backcloth, lamps on battens above the proscenium, and he had used a gauze across the front of the stage to create a fog effect. He had also introduced new more convincing effects of lightning through the use of lycopodium powder which could produce a 'flash' effect.

OMAI, OR A TRIP ROUND THE WORLD

In 1781 de Loutherbourg's permanent contract at Drury Lane came to an end, but he continued to live in England, and indeed did some of his most striking work at Covent Garden. This was exemplified in 1785 in *Omai, or, A Trip Round the World*, a pantomime by John O'Keeffe with, according to O'Keeffe, 'beautifully wild' music by William Shield. The somewhat flimsy story was based on Captain Cook's voyages in the south Pacific, and de Loutherbourg used sketches made on the spot by Cook's fellow traveller, John Webber, in his designs. The use of transparencies was especially noted and enabled the stage to present with a new realism the moon shining, fire and the explosion of volcanoes. *The Times* revelled in the 'superb scenery, enchanting music and sheer fun' of the production.

THE EIDOPHUSIKON

Perhaps even more exciting was his establishment in his house of a miniature theatre he called 'The Eidophusikon'. The auditorium held one hundred and thirty people who paid five shillings each to

Figure 5.22
Philippe Jacques de Loutherbourg's Eidophusikon
Source: The Trustees of the British Museum

view the small stage, eight feet by six. The first programme de Loutherbourg devised for this little theatre consisted of a series of 'moving pictures', including a view of London from Greenwich Park as the sun rose, the city of Tangier with a distant view of the Rock of Gibraltar in the noonday heat, and sunset near Naples in Italy, followed by moonlight over the Mediterranean. Finally, there was a highly dramatic view of a shipwreck in a mighty storm. The whole was accompanied by music on the harpsichord by Michael Arne and singing by Mrs Arne. The Eidophusikon continued in operation till at least 1786 and was long remembered, especially by ambitious stage designers and scenic decorators.

DE LOUTHERBOURG'S THEATRE

De Loutherbourg's lighting reforms complemented his scenic ideas. His use of freestanding stage pieces was not original: Sir James Thornhill had used something similar in *Arsinoe* as long ago as 1705. But de Loutherbourg allied this to a particular vision of picturesque landscapes, often exotic or historical, including, for example, mountains which could actually be climbed in full view of the spectators. His various depictions, his British navies and his distant views of the South Seas or of unexplored regions of Britain, could be revealed quickly and efficiently thanks to his enhanced and advanced stage machinery. It was this combination of the visionary and the practical man of the theatre which held the key to de Loutherbourg's success.

THE SEPARATION OF STAGE AND AUDITORIUM

Perhaps its most worrying consequence was its demand for an increasing passivity in the spectator. Christopher Baugh has pointed out that whereas Inigo Jones was an architect, de Loutherbourg was an easel painter. Jones's inclusive and intimate theatre was becoming lost as space became pictorial, to be viewed from outside. It is true that de Loutherbourg's paintings also, in a sense, became three-dimensional, but still, under his influence, the theatre was dividing into two halves. This is seen in the visual demands playwrights could now make on designers. Thus, Elizabeth Inchbald opened *Lovers Vows* with the direction: '*A high road, a town at a distance; a small inn on one side of the road, a cottage on the other*', and Thomas Morton opened *Speed the Plough*: '*In the foreground a farmhouse – a view of a castle at a distance*'.

The practical effect of this separation was to force the performer back from the forestage into the lighted scenic world, which in turn necessitated reformation in the costuming of plays. Stage, lighting and costume 'improvements' compelled actors to be more precise in their movements and gestures, because, being further back, they were under a new kind of scrutiny. And because it was no longer much used, the forestage itself was allowed to shrink and eventually to be eliminated altogether, though that development was still some decades away.

DE LOUTHERBOURG'S LEGACY

Philippe Jacques de Loutherbourg may not have been a true revolutionary himself, but he refined, focused and made concrete previous scattered ideas and hopes. After him, the scene painter became a vital lynchpin in the theatrical operation: whereas Covent Garden had only two scene painters in 1767, by 1785 it had ten and in 1794 twenty-seven, though not all permanently employed. The designer, too, became a not uncommon member of a theatre company. John Inigo Richards was one such. He worked from an initial script to create a maquette for realisation. The practice grew up that once the maquette had been accepted by the author, stage carpenters and painters, as well as 'wardrobe-keepers' and others, went to work, and often actors in costume would parade on the 'set' so that the author could approve the effect before the first performance. Theatre practice was transformed.

NOTES

1 Christopher Baugh, *Garrick and Loutherbourg*, Cambridge: Chadwyck-Healey, 1990, p. 32.
2 James Morwood, *The Life and Works of Richard Brinsley Sheridan*, Edinburgh: Scottish Academic Press, 1985, p. 88.

Chapter 59: The provincial circuits

ANTERLIWT

By 1800 there were over four hundred theatres in Britain. Most people, therefore, did not experience theatre by way of Drury Lane or Covent Garden: they went to local performances.

These might still be, as in some remote areas of rural Wales, especially the north east, given by small groups of travelling players, perhaps at special feasts and seasons. Known as *anterliwt* (interludes) and performed in the Welsh language on farm carts, these shows were not unlike the Scottish Gaelic folk dramas. They involved stock characters in realistic settings getting up to all sorts of roguish, ribald and satirical pranks, and part-improvised knockabout. The performers often roped in locals for small roles or as chorus, particularly as traditional songs and dances were a feature of the shows. Typical was 'Peppers Black', a traditional boisterous danced song dating from at least 1650. The most famous *anterliwt* performer-composer was Twm o'r Nant (Thomas Edwards), nine of whose comedies survive. But it seems the form fell victim to the spread of repressive Methodism and hardly survived into the nineteenth century.

Beyond this, and other companies of strolling actors who simply went where they thought they could attract an audience, provincial performances were given by *ad hoc* temporary touring companies, usually from one of the London patent theatres, and by locally organised companies based in a particular provincial town or city, and touring regularly a predetermined circuit.

THE CIRCUITS

Circuits consisted of two or more venues in different but geographically related towns to which the company would return regularly – probably annually – and stay for several weeks, till their repertoire, or their audiences, were exhausted. Then they moved to the next venue on the circuit. Gradually, over years, permanent theatres were built or constructed at each of these regular stopping places.

Most circuits were organised round local events and festivities – race meetings, fairs, assizes and so on, when the town was likely to contain more people who might be seeking diversion. Provincial cities were not big enough to be able to support a year-round theatre operation.

THE NEW THEATRES ROYAL

The theatres of these early circuits, sometimes known as 'Long Rooms', were comparatively small, and led to a demand for something larger, and soon new Theatres Royal, often twice the size of

Long Rooms, and with appropriate patents, were springing up outside London. In ten years no fewer than seven Theatres Royal were established in England: in Bath and Norwich in 1768, York and Hull in 1769, Liverpool in 1771, Manchester in 1775, Chester in 1777 and Bristol in 1778. As this process continued and accelerated, a Theatre Representation Act was passed in 1788, which permitted local magistrates to licence theatres outside London for up to sixty days, excepting only the University cities and wherever the king was residing.

THE PROVINCES AND LONDON

Circuits were encouraged by improvements in travel and by the development of municipal authorities. Provincial cities were both more aware of London culture and more able to evolve their own cultural amenities, which meant that provincial theatre was always more than a pale copy of what happened in the capital. It articulated its own concerns. Indeed, the relationships between provincial Theatres Royal and Drury Lane and Covent Garden were complex. Less overtly commercial, the provincial houses nevertheless gladly accepted visits by London 'stars', while retaining their own individuality because of the patronage of their own local gentry who were pleased with the accolade of their theatre as 'Royal'. Covent Garden and Drury Lane often tried to poach provincial actors, not always successfully, and they jealously guarded their original playscripts from any borrowing or stealing. Local theatres, however, also sometimes fell foul of local tradespeople because their activities seemed to draw off limited local spending power.

THE THEATRE AT RICHMOND, YORKSHIRE

The theatre at Richmond, Yorkshire, built in 1788, survives as a living example of the eighteenth-century country playhouse. Alarmingly small, it nevertheless has a focus which actors over centuries must have blessed. It was abandoned as a theatre in 1848, and used as an auction room, a wine store and for other purposes, until a local schoolteacher at the time of the Second World War began investigating it, and it was soon found to be uniquely complete and undamaged. Today it is alive again, a living theatre, run by the Georgian Theatre Royal Trust, and embodying answers to some of the tantalising questions about the theatres of this period.

On either side of 1800, Richmond was a key town in a north of England circuit which linked it with Northallerton, Ulverston, Kendal, Ripon, Beverley, Whitby and Harrogate. The theatre company would stay up to two months in each of these towns in turn, wintering either in Whitby or in Kendal and Ulverston jointly.

There is no evidence, sadly, that they ever performed in Grassington, thirty miles to the south west of Richmond, where there was a tiny barn theatre run by the local carrier, Robert Airey and the village schoolmaster who taught the amateur actors pronunciation – 'fattygewed' for 'fatigued', 'paggyantry' for 'pageantry', and so on.

THE BATH-BRISTOL CIRCUIT

Most touring companies took a few days to travel from one venue to the next, usually travelling by wagon, a mode of transport not without danger. In 1758 a theatre wagon caught fire on Salisbury Plain and the company's scenery, props and other moveables were all destroyed.

Figure 5.23
The Georgian theatre at Richmond, Yorkshire, after refurbishment in 2004
Source: Mike Kipling Photography/Alamy Stock Photo

The richer Bath-Bristol circuit company travelled by long coaches called 'caterpillars' which could hold twelve persons as well as their luggage. This company for years served only Bath and Bristol: in September and October they performed on three-week nights in Bristol, and Saturday nights in Bath; from November to May three nights in Bath and Mondays in Bristol; and in the summer they performed mostly in Bristol, though this was sometimes varied to include appearances in Wells, Cheltenham and other southwest cities.

The Bath-Bristol company was also responsible for most of the theatre seen in south Wales. In 1807, though, Swansea opened its own Theatre Royal on Bank Street, with Andrew Cherry, a minor playwright and comic actor from Drury Lane, as manager. He staged a pantomime, *Mother Goose*, in 1809 and employed, at different times, John Bannister, a youthful Edmund Kean and an equally youthful Sheridan Knowles, later a successful playwright. Cherry's company toured to Carmarthen, Haverfordwest and Waterford, but Cherry died in 1812 and was not replaced, so that south Wales relied again on receiving productions from Bristol and Bath.

NORTHERN CIRCUITS

The circuit based in York in the 1750s included Beverley and sometimes, strangely, Newcastle-upon-Tyne, but later it became more settled with Beverley retained alongside Leeds, Pontefract, Wakefield, Doncaster and Hull.

Newcastle itself was host to two companies in much of the 1750s and 1760s, one run by Thomas Bates which played in Newcastle in January and February, moving to Stockton in May, Durham in July, Sunderland in August and North Shields from October to December. Bates's comic actor, James Cawdell, took over in 1783. He built a new theatre on Pipemakers Stairs in North Shields, and then another in South Shields in 1791. When he fell ill a few years later, he handed his circuit over to Stephen Kemble.

The better-known Heatton and Austin company prospered especially after Michael Heatton's place was taken by Charles Whitlock, who married Mrs Siddons's sister. Joseph Austin, meanwhile, had been at Garrick's Drury Lane before moving into management. By the 1780s their circuit encompassed Newcastle in the winter, Lancaster and Preston, and often Warrington and Whitehaven as well, in spring and summer, and Chester in the autumn. Austin and Whitlock were still the managers when the new Theatre Royal opened in Newcastle on 1 January 1788, an event marked by the loud ringing of the bells of St Nicholas and St John's churches. But after 1800 Stephen Kemble took over this circuit which now included Durham, North and South Shields, Sunderland, Alnwick and Berwick-upon-Tweed.

SOUTHERN CIRCUITS

The Thornton Company covered much of the south of England for thirty years from 1785 and embraced at various times – never all in a single year – Newbury, Andover, Henley, Farnham, Reading, Guildford, Horsham, Dorking, Chelmsford, Gosport, Windsor, Arundel, as well as South end, Croydon, the Isle of Wight and even Oxford. Thornton's great rivals were the Collins-Davies Company, based in Hampshire and Wiltshire. They often wintered in Salisbury, were in Southampton from July to September, and visited Chichester, Winchester and other towns at other times during the year.

PURPOSE-BUILT THEATRES

Circuits usually had a purpose-built theatre, often a Theatre Royal, as a headquarters, but performed in 'long rooms', barns or the like in other places. However, as the century wore on and the theatre's popularity grew, more and more purpose-built theatres were erected. An incomplete list of theatres built in the period would include:

    1758 – Norwich
    1765 – York
    1766 – Bristol, Bath
    1768 – Edinburgh
    1772 – Horsham, Liverpool
    1774 – Birmingham
    1775 – Manchester

1777 – Boston (Lincolnshire), Chester
1779 – Sunderland
1780 – Canterbury
1781 – Plymouth
1782 – Portsmouth
1783 – South Shields
1784 – Whitby
1785 – Winchester
1786 – Margate
1787 – Farnham, Penzance
1788 – Richmond, Harrogate, Newcastle
1789 – Guildford
1790 – Kendal, Lichfield, Canterbury, Faversham
1791 – Rochester, Chatham, North Shields
1792 – Newbury, Chichester, Ripon, Durham, Dumfries
1793 – Windsor
1795 – Henley
1796 – Ulverston, Gosport
1798 – Maidstone
1800 – Northallerton

Many of these theatres were small and intimate, as Richmond's is today. None came anywhere near the size of Drury Lane or Covent Garden, but Newcastle's Theatre Royal held well over a thousand spectators, and York's was also large.

However, even the most modest interior was often housed in a splendid building. Weybridge, a town of only 700 inhabitants, had a 'barn-like' theatre, with a single box inside, but still managed a proper portico at the front. Plymouth Theatre Royal had a massive portico. Birmingham Theatre Royal, which had a coffee room added in 1777, was enlarged in 1780 when an impressive portico was added.

CROYDON

Earlier in the century, conditions were significantly more primitive. At Croydon, gallery spectators had to ascend an outside ladder to enter. But by 1800 the reconstructed theatre was a 'perfect bijou, small but compact', with 'All the World's a Stage' painted over the proscenium.[1] It is true that a rough and muddy path past pig sties had still to be negotiated by pit and gallery patrons, but the theatre was highly appreciated – 'respectable in every way', according to the *Monthly Mirror*, whose correspondent, however, had probably not needed the assistance of a burly porter to carry him past the pig farm.

NEWBURY

At Newbury the old theatre had to be entered up an unlit narrow lane, but in 1792 a new theatre was opened in nearby Speenhamland with four pillars supporting an impressive portico bearing the royal arms. Other new theatres included what Fanny Burney called a 'pretty little theatre' in Chel-tenham,[2] and Gosport's 'very elegant' one, which had a central archway where patrons entered an interior of a 'splendour superior to any other provincial theatre'.[3]

WINCHESTER

Winchester's 1785 edifice achieved a probably more extraordinary grandeur:

> The front of the stage is a grand arch, supported by two noble pillars of the Ionic order, near 14 feet high, most beautifully gilt and ornamented; in the centre is the bust of Shakespeare, over which is the following motto: 'Omne tulit punctum qui miscuit utiledulce' and on either side are the arms of the city and country. The pillars that support the green boxes and gallery are superbly painted in imitation of a blue sky, with some well-fancied clouds, in the centre of the ceiling is a ventilator, and at the four corners Thalia and Melpomene, as the comic and tragic muses, Apollo as an emblem of the opera, or music, and Pierrot as the representative of pantomime; the panel next the ceiling is decorated with festoons of flowers, and the whole house is finished with a style of excellence.[4]

CHARACTERISTICS OF PROVINCIAL THEATRES

These purpose-built theatres varied widely in all sorts of ways, but they raised standards and attracted the public, and soon acquired expected features, such as green decorations with red hangings in the boxes. The theatre in Richmond still adheres to this. In the York Theatre, 'the interior (was) coloured orange, green and white, and the seats covered with crimson cloth'.[5] Lighting was by candles in candelabra and wall brackets: in Birmingham, these were tallow, except on special occasions when they would be replaced by wax candles.

Theatres were heated by stoves or open fires, such as can still be seen at Richmond, but which were surely fire hazards, as were the candles. Plenty of theatres burned down. Birmingham lost its concert hall on Moseley Street, which gave plays gratis in the intervals of its concerts, in 1782, and the Theatre Royal in the city centre ten years later, both to fire. Manchester's Theatre Royal burned down in 1789, after less than fifteen years' existence.

The other problem with theatres built to accommodate touring companies was that they stood empty for too long, and consequently deteriorated too quickly. They were hired out for lectures and concerts or to demonstrate phantasmagoria or orreries, and several were so constructed that a floor could be laid at stage level over the pit, and thus be transformed into a ballroom. But maintenance of buildings far away from a company's headquarters was rarely a high priority.

MANAGING PROVINCIAL COMPANIES

Running a company which appeared at a theatre, performed for some weeks and then moved on to another theatre, was a complex and ever-changing business, and the managers had to juggle staging the plays, acting, finding space and time to rehearse, paying salaries and other expenses, working out the logistics of each tour, organising publicity, transporting scenery and props as well as actors, and more. Many managers, as leading actors, married their leading ladies, though not always with happy results, as Fisher, manager of a Suffolk circuit, discovered when he tried to impose some discipline on his unruly troupe. His wife was sexually involved with his comic actor, one Scraggs: whenever Scraggs felt his manager was being too demanding, he threatened to runaway with Mrs Fisher, and indeed did so more than once, only to accede to Fisher's (and Mrs Scraggs's) impassioned entreaties to return.

Some theatres or companies went from one manager's care to another's, as happened in the first decade of Manchester's Theatre Royal. This fine theatre, centre of a Lancashire circuit, was initially managed by Joseph Younger and George Mattocks in 1775. But Younger departed in 1777, and in 1781 Austin and Whitlock took over. James Miller became manager in 1783, only for Mattocks to return in 1785.

TATE WILKINSON AT YORK

Other companies were more stable. The York circuit managed by Tate Wilkinson is the best-known example of this, partly because in 1795 Wilkinson published four volumes of memoirs, *The Wandering Patentee*. Wilkinson was the son of a former chaplain to the Prince of Wales, and early in his career appeared at both Drury Lane and Covent Garden. He was most closely associated, however, with Samuel Foote at the Little Theatre, Haymarket. He was at Bath from 1758 to 1760 and then had a spell on the Plymouth-Exeter-Portsmouth circuit, before acting at York for Joseph Baker. In 1766 he took over this company as manager and remained there into the nineteenth century, developing a tight company ethos centred around three major theatres, York, Sheffield and Hull, with various other Yorkshire venues along the way. Energetic and commercially sharp, he made the York Theatre Royal the envy of many.

It was a 'golden age' in York, with up to thirty regular members of the company, many of whom stayed for years, and including as many as eight married couples, as well as his prompter, the appropriately named Earby, his carpenter, Bearpark, and his faithful finance officer, Swalwell. Gruff, convivial and thoughtful, Wilkinson stayed in charge till his death in 1803, when his son John took over. But his was an altogether less happy reign, and the York circuit quickly disintegrated once Tate Wilkinson was gone.

JOHN PALMER AT BATH

York's only rival was Bath Theatre Royal, headquarters of what was generally regarded as the most artistically accomplished company outside London, which also had up to thirty acting members for many years. John Palmer became proprietor in 1766 and in 1771 appointed William Keasberry, an actor in the company, manager. When he extended his proprietorial empire to include the equally profitable Bristol Theatre Royal, Keasberry took into joint managership William Wyatt Dimond, the company's leading actor, noted for reversing Hamlet's traditional 'business' when the Ghost appeared in the closet scene: instead of, like Betterton, starting out of his chair, Dimond sank back into it, then dropped to one knee before the regal figure. Dimond's career had begun at Garrick's Drury Lane, and he continued to act after Keasberry's retirement in 1795. He was largely responsible for the building of Bath's new theatre in Beauford Square in 1805, and he remained as joint manager and proprietor till his death in 1812. Palmer did not die until 1817.

Figure 5.24
Portrait of Tate Wilkinson by Stephen Hewson

Source: Courtesy York Museums Trust

SAMUEL BUTLER AT RICHMOND

Richmond, Yorkshire, was also a highly successful theatre thanks to Samuel Butler's company. A jobbing actor, by the age of 23 he had became the third husband of his manager, Tryphosa Brockell. She was exactly twice his age, and soon he was running things. By the 1790s his company had more than twenty regular performers, including his second wife as his leading lady, and when he died in 1812, she took over as manager. It was only with her death in 1818 that the company began to fall apart.

HENRY THORNTON

Henry Thornton, a hugely energetic theatre builder, whose empire stretched from Hampshire in the west to Essex in the east, was a larger-than-life character, who had begun life as an actor and had had a spell as prompter in Portsmouth. As an actor he had played parts like Macheath, Belcour in *The West Indian*, and Shakespearean characters such as Edmund in *King Lear* and Petruchio in *The Taming of the Shrew*. He was renowned for his inability to learn lines, but was an adept improviser and indeed was not above importing speeches from other plays when his memory for the correct lines failed. On one occasion, he realised he had 'died' before he had passed on a letter necessary for the furtherance of the plot. Whereupon he rose from the ground, stated unabashedly, 'One thing I had forgot through a multiplicity of business. Give this letter to my father: it will explain all', and promptly 'died' again.[6]

He wrote innumerable rhyming Prologues and Epilogues, and later in life, when he played Pantaloon rather than Harlequin, he suffered terribly from gout. He married into a theatrical family – his wife, too, was his leading actress – and his company was prolific and successful enough by the 1790s to be able to split into two and sometimes even three discrete groups, playing in separate theatres, perhaps miles apart, for weeks at a time. His wife died in 1816, and he went into partnership with Edward Dawson, who, however, simply ran off with the company's wages. Thornton retired, and died in 1818.

JAMES SHATFORD

Another 'character' was James Shatford, who took over the lucrative Devizes-Warminster-Salisbury circuit from Collins and Davies. The son of a Gloucestershire doctor, Shatford began life as a strolling actor. A lithe and handsome juvenile lead, he started his own company touring in Bedfordshire, Berkshire and Huntingdonshire till he teamed up with Henry Lee. Ten years his junior, Lee had performed at Drury Lane and then been in management in Birmingham and Devonshire. It was as 'Shatford and Lee' that they ran the Salisbury Theatre and circuit. Shatford was an eccentric: he sometimes shaved only half his chin, he dressed quirkily and had an obsession with umbrellas, which he hated. Sociable but fiercely efficient, he grew stout and came to performing 'heavy' comic parts such as Falstaff, before he died in 1809.

OTHER MANAGERS

Others to be remembered for their contribution to this often-neglected provincial theatre were Roger Kemble, father of Mrs Siddons, John Philip Kemble and their siblings. He joined John Ward's company, which had a large, loose circuit around Birmingham in the 1740s and 1750s. He soon married Ward's daughter and took over the company management, though in truth it was the strong-willed and effective Sally, his wife and mother to the Kemble dynasty, who ran things.

They were one of the earliest companies to tour Wales, and indeed it was while they were performing at Llandrindod Wells that Sarah, later Mrs Siddons, was born in 1755. The company continued to tour Wales for many years: they were at Monmouth in 1775 and presenting Farquhar's *The Constant Couple* at Carmarthen in 1776.

A later Welsh company was established by Henry Masterman, which toured to, among other places, Neath, Swansea, Abergavenny, Cardiff and Carmarthen, and included at different times Thomas Dibdin and Charles Mathews. Swansea's theatre in Wind Street was operating in 1785, when William Keasberry's company performed there.

Another father to future theatrical greatness was William M'Cready, whose son became a leading star of the early Victorian period. He took over the Birmingham circuit – Worcester, Northampton, Shrewsbury and other towns – after the Birmingham Theatre Royal burned down in 1792.

SARAH BAKER

Sarah Ward in Edinburgh and Sally Kemble in Birmingham were two highly efficient women managers, and there were others, like the clergyman's daughter, Tryphosa Brockell, who married an actor, Henry Miller, in 1749 and after his death married the company manager, J. Wright. When Wright died in 1771, Brockell took over the company, which became the foundation of the York-Richmond circuit. Her children by both marriages became actors.

Perhaps the most notable manageress was Sarah Baker, who ran the Kent circuit from the 1770s until nearly her death in 1816. The daughter of a fairground showman-actor who had also appeared at Sadlers Wells, and herself both puppeteer and actress, Baker's circuit was based around Canterbury, Folkestone, Maidstone and Faversham. She actually built six theatres all more or less to the same plan so that scenery from one could easily be transferred to the others. Tough-minded and clear-sighted, she attracted many London stars to her theatres, including Edmund Kean, G.F. Cooke, Dorothy Jordan and Joseph Grimaldi. Her leading actress was her sister, who was also a dancer and company wardrobe mistress, and her prompter and cashier was Bonny Long, who was reputed to have ten fingers and no thumbs.

OTHER WOMEN MANAGERS

Other women managers' careers are often harder to track. Betty Martin, who seems frequently to have 'married' her acting partners, was one such. Originally Irish, she toured England with Richard Elrington in the early1740s. Later she joined Ward's company in the midlands as Mrs Elrington, and in 1750 appeared at Covent Garden. She ran her own company in Manchester, Liverpool and Buxton in the 1750s, and also toured Northern Ireland. She returned to Wales, now as Mrs Workman, then appeared in Mansfield where she became Mrs Wilson. She was a member of Whitley's Company in the 1760s and finally at Leeds in 1767, after which she may have retired.

Mrs Herbert ran the company in her husband's name which toured in Lincolnshire, and there were at least two lesser-known strolling companies with women managers, those of Mrs Fawkes in the middle of the century, and Mrs Sturmer in the 1780s and 1790s.

LONDON ACTORS AND THE PROVINCES

One of the boasts of the provincial theatre was that it provided a training ground for future Drury Lane and Covent Garden luminaries. Thus, Mrs Siddons and Robert William Elliston spent early years at Bath, Mrs Siddons's brother, John Philip Kemble, and Dorothy Jordan worked at York,

Edmund Kean and Thomas Dibdin began at Richmond, and William Charles McCready started at Birmingham.

Many London-based patent theatre actors spent at least some summers guest-starring at provincial theatres, and once the circuits were reasonably defined, this became a significant part of a leading actor's income, and a mainstay of the Georgian provincial theatres. Mrs Siddons was an inveterate tourer, and Ned Shuter, Mary Ann Yates and Elizabeth Farren spent time at York, John Quick, Joseph Munden, Stephen Kemble and G.F. Cooke all worked with the Thornton Company, and Munden and Cooke also performed at Newcastle. This is the merest tip of an enormous iceberg. Master Betty appeared in several provincial theatres after his triumphs in London and as his star waned. Many leading players made returns to the places where they had begun – Kean to Richmond, J.P. Kemble and Dorothy Jordan to York, and so on.

The provincial company certainly received a short-term gain from all this, but also perhaps some longer-term problems. After a week of sell-out houses when Mrs Siddons performed, the following weeks saw Box Office takings often fall alarmingly, and then stay low. The company's relations with the local community probably suffered, too, and its internal dynamics were likely to be dislocated by a star, who tended to stand centre stage and allow the other actors to be their satellites. On the other hand, F.C. Wemyss, acting Jaffeir in *Venice Preserv'd* at Richmond to the Belvedira of Mrs Renaud from Drury Lane, was hugely encouraged when she commended him: 'as we left the stage, at the end of the first act, her expression of "Very well indeed, sir – excellent", enabled me to proceed with that confidence which, in an actor, is the sure forerunner of success'.[7]

PROVINCIAL ACTORS

Local companies grew their own stars. Abraham Bennett, for instance, was highly popular in Richmond, while in York George Inchbald, juvenile lead, and John Emery, comic, were local stars. Thomas Grist was loved in Manchester, James Wheeler, a singer and actor notably successful as Macheath, in Portsmouth and Plymouth, Ralph Wewitzer, who played foreigners and Jewish parts, and Elizabeth Richards, who graduated from Thornton's company to the Bath theatre, were others, though some of these, including Emery, Grist and Wewitzer did finally move on to London.

Comic actors and clowns were especially popular. Goddard, originally from Birmingham, was at Weymouth around the turn of the century where he became George III's favourite performer. But he lacked staying power, and 'kept floundering from one petty theatre to another'. Nevertheless Walter Donaldson, an experienced actor himself, considered that in certain parts, Geoffrey Muffincap in *Amateurs and Actors* by Richard Brinsley Peake, for example, he had 'not met with any actor to be compared' to Goddard.

It is difficult to judge the artistic standards of many of these companies, which probably varied from excellent to poor. Fidelity to the text was frequently lost, and actors clearly learned to improvise. Rehearsal practices, too, varied from company to company, but no company rehearsed much, and when they did it was probably in an empty theatre at night when they were tired. Entrances and exits were planned, and crowd movements sorted out, but many performances were extremely static, with the actors lined across the stage, and much of the work was done privately, for instance between wives and husbands.

Besides, once an actor had been cast in a part, he 'possessed' it, and expected to play it for the rest of his career, which sometimes meant increasingly exciting performances, but also often led to complacency, not to mention annoyance when a visiting star appeared and took over the part.

There was certainly bad acting – drunkenness, laughing during performances, telling jokes and acknowledging audience members. Dan Egerton of Thornton's Company always 'read' rather than acted his part. Platt, an experienced actor at Chester, playing Thoroughgood in *The London Merchant* opposite a new young actor as George Barnwell, forgot his lines. Taking his young partner to the front of the stage, he begged the spectators to excuse the failure, which was due to the novice's inexperience. As the audience clapped, Platt walked off, leaving the young actor to improvise his way out of the situation as best he could.

Sometimes provincial actors combined acting with other work: Mr and Mrs Ratchford, dancers in Thornton's company, taught dancing at places where they were also performing. Charles Whitlock, company manager, never gave up entirely his other career as a dentist.

ACTORS' PAY AND CONDITIONS

Provincial actors were poorly paid and relied on their benefits to make a tolerable living. Benefits were held for most actors at most venues, usually on Saturday nights. Married couples shared a benefit. Actors frequently thanked their audiences profusely at the end of the benefit performance, though Wilkinson stopped this tradition at York. Benefits were also held for all sorts of causes – for the company hairdresser, for example, or the local militia, or even just for 'the poor'.

Actors often lodged with local shopkeepers for the duration of a stay in a town, because the shop made an excellent sales centre for tickets to benefit performances. But they – or the managers – also stayed with private landladies, many of whom took a genuine interest in their welfare. One single actress left her toddler daughter in the care of the landlady every day while acting, and the landlady always fed her – 'mostly porridge' – along with her own children. Visiting stars were more likely to stay in the local inn.

Amateurs were also brought in to play small parts, or fill out crowd scenes, as when Richmond Theatre hired willing locals to be slaves in Colman's *The Africans* in 1810. Whether they 'blacked up' or not is unclear. Ambitious amateurs were also known sometimes to pay a fee to act with the professional company.

SCENE PAINTERS AND CARPENTERS

Scene painters and carpenters were often local. George Cuitt was a local Yorkshire artist who painted scenes for Richmond, and the scenery was made by the local carpenter, one Coatsworth. Joseph Halfpenny was a local artist working for York Theatre Royal; Tobias Young, inspired by de Loutherbourg, worked at Reading Theatre; and the versatile and noted artist, William Cave, worked for both Winchester and Gosport Theatres.

Other scene painters, like 'Little' Harvey, were company members: Harvey travelled with Thornton's Company, perhaps as a sort of stage manager. But his counterpart with Butler's Richmond Company, Dunning, was scene painter and actor – a notably athletic Harlequin, for example.

THE PROVINCIAL REPERTOIRE

The repertoires of these companies were enormous. In three months at Whitby in the winter of 1799–1800, Butler's Company performed seventy-six different programmes. The same company performed over a hundred different 'pieces' (comedies, farces, pantomimes, ballad operas and so on) between March 1810 and March 1811. Managers were always desperate to obtain copies of new successful London plays, buying them from the managers of Drury Lane or Covent Garden, or even pirating them surreptitiously.

This enormous repertoire included large numbers of contemporary plays, comic operas, Gothic dramas, sentimental comedies, heroic dramas and, most popular of all, Sheridan's plays. To these were added older plays, especially Shakespeare's, though his plays were almost always heavily adapted. *Henry IV*, for example, became essentially a play about Falstaff, *King Lear* was adapted even from Nahum Tate's version, *Richard III* was played in Colley Cibber's version and the comedies usually included new songs. In *The Merchant of Venice*, for instance, Jessica sang 'What would be this dull town to me if Lorenzo was not there?' to the tune of 'Robin Adair' and 'How wanton thy waters her snowy feet lave' to the tune of 'Mary of Afton Water'.

Spectacle and special effects were always highly prized. Consequently all companies presented pantomimes, like that at Derby in 1782 when the Magician was seen descending on a cloud, and extravaganzas like Morton's *Columbus*, which called for an Indian procession, the Temple of the Sun being destroyed by a hurricane, an erupting volcano and the triumphal entry of Columbus himself.

Among new plays premiered in the provinces were Frederic Reynolds's adaptation of Goethe's *The Sorrows of Young Werther*, titled *Werter*, and interesting plays by women who probably struggled to get a hearing in the noisier London theatre, Ann Yearsley's *Earl Godwin*, first seen at Bristol Theatre Royal in 1789, Catherine Metcalfe's *Julia de Roubiqué*, Bath 1790, and Margaret Holford's *Neither's the Man*, Chester 1798.

LOCAL PLAYS

The provinces also spawned their own local plays, such as the very early Gothic drama, *The Fiend in the Air, or The Glastonbury Apparition* by a Glastonbury author named Stroud, at Glastonbury in 1773. The same year saw *The Merry Midnight Watch* by David Ogborne, a comedy set in Chelmsford, staged in Chelmsford.

At least two anonymous dramas centring on local history were presented in Bath, *The Inflexible Captive* in 1775 and *Bladud* in 1777, while an obscure playwright named Benson wrote local plays for different venues, such as *Britain's Glory, or A Trip to Portsmouth* for Portsmouth Theatre in 1785, and *All Alive at Windsor* for Windsor a year or two later. Windsor Theatre's manager between 1778 and 1789, Francis Godolphin Waldron, also wrote dramas about the town's history. *Apollo's Holiday* by Cawdell was a Newcastle-set comedy performed at Newcastle Theatre Royal in 1792, an anonymous play set in Birmingham, *My Grandmother*, was presented at Birmingham Theatre Royal in 1795, and *The Maid of Liverpool, or The Royal Tar* was staged at Liverpool's Theatre Royal in 1799.

Then there were plays like *The Whitby Lasses*, staged by Butler's Company in Whitby in the 1790s, which was almost certainly the same, but with a few names changed, as *The Beverley Lasses* presented by the same company in the same season at Beverley. *The Pretty Girl of Gosport* staged at Gosport at about the same time, may have been similar.

TOPICAL PLAYS

Provincial theatres also kept up with the news. When Manchester Theatre Royal staged Alexander Fyfe's *The Royal Martyr* in 1777, they added overt references to the scandalous recent trial of Elizabeth Chudleigh, Duchess of Kingston, for bigamy. *British Bravery, or Taking the Island of Trinidad* about the French war in the Caribbean, was an original pseudo-documentary presented at Newbury in 1797, while *Harlequin's Invasion*, an original pantomime including a representation of a sea battle between the English and the French, was staged at York in 1809.

COMMAND PERFORMANCES

Local companies were happy to receive 'commands' for specific performances from those on whom they relied – local aristocrats, officers of the local regiment, the freemasons' lodge or the local school. Lady Caroline Herbert bespoke a performance at Wakefield in 1775, and Lady Armitage did the same a year later. In 1782 York Theatre Royal put on a performance for the High Sheriff and Gentlemen of the Grand Jury and another for the Ladies and Gentlemen of the Card Assembly.

AN EVENING'S PROGRAMME

It is worth remembering that performances in provincial, as in London theatres included 'specialty' and other acts between plays, and between acts of plays – fencing displays, tightrope or slack wire walking, and 'phantasmagoria', the excitement of which was bolstered by the need to blow out the candles and render the auditorium dark. William West, the Covent Garden ballet master, danced solo at Gosport – and, presumably other places – in 1811. Bath's special acts included Signor Rossignol doing bird imitations in 1783 and 1800, Moses Kean, 'the one-legged dancer' in 1789, Bryson's Musical Children in the same year and the Band of the Bohemian Silver Miners in 1803.

Most provincial theatres gave three performances per week. Doors opened at six PM, the performance began at seven and after eight most theatres admitted patrons at half price. Some offered subscription tickets, effectively season tickets, at reduced rates. There were moves to segregate audiences by class more effectively: aristocratic patronage needed safeguarding, but theatres could not manage without poorer spectators. In Norwich, separate entrances for different parts of the theatre were mooted before the end of the century, and in 1813 in Birmingham, Robert Elliston let it be known that Friday nights offered better-off patrons the 'best company'. (Horatio Nelson who visited the Birmingham Theatre Royal more than once in August 1802 with Sir William and Lady Hamilton seems not to have needed such refinement.)

PROVINCIAL AUDIENCES

People were smaller then than they are now, but still they were squeezed into very small spaces on popular nights. Plenty of women attended the theatre, and audiences were lively and demanding. At Liverpool, slave traders objected to a performance of *Oroonoko*. In York, some ladies objected to a performance of *The Provok'd Wife* on the grounds of indecency, sportsmen opposed *Love à la Mode* because it satirised racegoers, and one man objected to *The Author* because he thought it reflected on his father. Performances of all these were consequently cancelled.

Figure 5.25
Audience at the Theatre Royal, Plymouth, built in 1781. The serenity of this scene may be compared with the scene 'at the pit door' to a London theatre at almost exactly the same time (see Figure 5.39), though the provincial audiences were not always as tranquil as this one seems.

Source: Private Collection/The Stapleton Collection/Bridgeman Images

Audiences judged plays for themselves rather than accepting London verdicts, and in Birmingham there was a theatre journal for independent criticism, *Theatrical John Bull*. In many theatres, the gallery was liable to contradict the Box Office patrons' opinions. It would be too much of a generalisation to assert that aristocratic patrons preferred a sophisticated farce to Shakespeare, whereas the galleries' preferences were the opposite, but there is some truth in this. It is also true that in Manchester, the noisy but jolly gallery was said to be particularly fond of murders and relished plenty of bodies.

SOLDIERS AND SAILORS AS SPECTATORS

Members of the army and navy were known as eager theatregoers. Garrison towns saw officers seated in the pit while lower ranks filled the galleries: no love was lost between the groups. It is worth recording that several theatres in these towns failed after the Battle of Waterloo and the disbandment of much of the army.

Sailors of course frequented the theatres of Portsmouth and Plymouth, though Plymouth had two theatres, one for sailors and another for the gentry. Sailors were notably enthusiastic but rowdy. One group at Portsmouth, seeing the characters on stage drinking, dropped from their gallery perch and joined them, stopping the action until the actors sent for 'real' drink from a nearby pub, which they then amicably shared. Another time at Portsmouth sailors were recruited as extras for a battle scene, and their 'acting' soon became real, the fighting genuinely dangerous, much to the seated spectators' admiration.

AUDIENCE BEHAVIOUR

But spectators in provincial theatres were rarely as riotous as London audiences. In Newcastle in 1775 an actor was hit by an apple, and in 1790 a man who threw a bottle was fined fifteen shillings. In Richmond there was a 'riot' in the theatre three months after it opened in 1788, but in fact it seems this was little more than a fuss caused by a drunken spectator. Richmond's gallery contained 'kicking-boards' which can still be seen today to allow the less well-off patrons to vent their emotions harmlessly if noisily.

In 1788 the management of Birmingham Theatre Royal published the following notice:

> A reward will be paid by the manager to any person who will discover the ruffians who have thrown, or shall hereafter throw, bottles, plates, apples, etc, at the actors and upon the stage and after the performance.[8]

This does not imply that many people were indulging in such behaviour. The sailors at Portsmouth certainly threw apples, oranges, potatoes and even bottles at the stage from time to time, and it is also true that upper-class patrons, including ladies, sometimes barracked, hissed or whistled as noisily as their lower-class contemporaries. But on the whole, people in the English provinces wanted theatres because they wanted to watch plays.

NOTES

1 Paul Ranger, *Under Two Managers*, London: Society for Theatre Research, 2001, p. 31.
2 Claire Tomalin, *Mrs Jordan's Profession*, London: Penguin, 1995, p. 79.
3 Paul Ranger, *op.cit.*, p. 33.
4 *Hampshire Chronicle*, 23 May 1785.
5 Linda Fitzsimmons, 'The Theatre Royal, York', in *York History*, York: York Educational Settlement, n.d., p. 183.
6 J.C. Trewin, *The Pomping Folk*, London: J.M. Dent & Sons, 1968, pp. 56–57.
7 Francis Courtney Wemyss, *Twenty-Six Years of the Life of an Actor and Manager*, New York: Burgess Stringer, 1846, p. 40.
8 John E. Cunningham, *Theatre Royal: The History of the Theatre Royal, Birmingham*, Oxford: Ronald, 1950, p. 42.

Chapter 60: The London theatres of Sheridan and Kemble

SHERIDAN AND PARTNERS TAKE OVER DRURY LANE

In 1776 David Garrick sold his share in Drury Lane to a consortium of Richard Sheridan, Thomas Linley and Dr James Ford, who soon after acquired Willoughby Lacy's share, too, so that they could assume full control. They had to get past Garrick's final performance, attended by the king. The excitement, the crowd, the febrile atmosphere were such that the actors had to leave the stage temporarily while the doors were opened to relieve the crush and most spectators could be seated.

It was autumn when the new management really took control. George Colman the Elder wrote *New Brooms!*, a topical comedy specially for the opening. Set in the theatre itself, the scene opened in Playhouse Passage, with '*various people going to the play*'. Later, the new Irish manager comes on stage to recite Shakespeare:

> As in a theatre the eyes of min,
> After a well-graced actor laves the stage,
> Are idly bint on him that inters nixt –
> O the devil! this passage is rather *mal-a-propos*.

How strong Sheridan's Irish accent was is unclear, but his period of management was marked by scandals, financial problems and a very few artistic achievements.

RICHARD BRINSLEY SHERIDAN

Born in 1751, Richard Sheridan was the son of a prominent and successful Irish actor and theatre manager, Thomas Sheridan, and his wife, Frances, a well-regarded novelist and playwright. Educated at Harrow, in 1772 he eloped with a beautiful singer, Elizabeth Linley, whose father was to become his partner at Drury Lane and composer for his musical dramas. He even fought a duel over her. Now, with one hit, *The Rivals*, under his belt – though the first performance of this comic masterpiece had been fraught with problems which had led both to recasting and rewriting – at the age of twenty-five, he was virtually the master of the English theatre.

DRURY LANE IN 1776

Drury Lane was at this time still essentially an intimate theatre, and it was during Sheridan's period of proprietorship that it was transformed into a large-scale commercial enterprise. In 1776, the forestage still projected into the auditorium, and the pit was still the preserve of a 'terrible, fierce, maddening crowd'.[1] Prices for a seat ranged from five shillings in a box to sixpence (or a shilling) in the gallery, and like all theatres it operated a repertory system: that is, each night it presented a different programme, usually including a modern or 'old' play, as well as a pantomime or after-piece (or both), and interludes with dancing, music or singing, and lasting five or six hours. The season ran from September to the following June, with performances on three or four evenings per week.

One theatregoer remembered visiting Drury Lane at this time when he was a child. As he entered the auditorium, the 'theatrical fruiteresses' were advertising their wares: 'Chase some oranges, chase some numparels, chase a bill of the play'. 'Chase' was cockney for 'choose', and 'numparels' were 'nonpareils', tiny chocolate and sugar balls. He continued:

> The boxes at that time, full of well-dressed women of quality, projected over the pit; and the pilasters reaching down were adorned with a glistering substance . . . (which) . . . appeared a glorified candy! – The orchestra lights at length arose. . . . once the bell sounded. It was to ring out yet once again. . . . The curtain drew up – and the play (began).[2]

Actors were tightly contracted. Their main terms included provision for no pay for absence through sickness and forfeits for failure to attend rehearsal. The contract also laid out conditions for the taking of benefits, and George Frederick Cooke's contract at the end of the century included 'time for study'. But actors could be fined for standing on stage in rehearsal when not required, and for not wearing the correct costume in performance. Even the stage doorkeeper could be fined for allowing an undesirable person backstage.

THE SCHOOL FOR SCANDAL

The early months of the new management were not successful, until Sheridan's new play, *The School for Scandal*, scored a brilliant triumph. Its success was needed, for Colman now posed a potential threat, having taken over the Little Theatre, Haymarket, in 1777, while a new Examiner of Plays, John Larpent, had been appointed. Larpent's unpredictable and scandalous ways with censorship have been well documented by David Worrall, and he was a constant danger to the new Drury Lane. His political connections and reactionary conservatism certainly did not chime with Sheridan's views, for Sheridan had by now become fast friends with the prominent Whig, Charles James Fox, who was to marry one of the theatre's dressers.

SHERIDAN AS THEATRE MANAGER

Sheridan was an incorrigible, infuriating mix as a person. On the one hand he was witty, handsome, lively company and a brilliant speaker. In 1779, when Garrick died, Sheridan closed Drury Lane and acted as chief mourner at his funeral. On the other hand, he was feckless, shifty and even dishonest. He failed to answer letters, he was manipulative and a scandalmonger, who drank too much, and he was a flirt who was effortlessly unfaithful to his wife.

As manager of a theatre Sheridan was irremediable. He had no business sense, was absent for long stretches yet still insisted on interfering when he wanted to, and he failed to pay bills, including

Figure 5.26
John Hoppner, portrait of Richard Brinsley Sheridan
Source: Fine Art Images/Diomedia

failing to pay the salaries of his actors. He appointed his vain and rancorous father as a kind of stage manager, but then removed him. As early as 1778 the theatre's finances were in a precarious state, houses were poor and the actors smouldering. Within a year of Garrick's death, Sheridan was failing to pay his widow what was due to her from his debt to her husband.

THE KING'S THEATRE

He was also a wheeler-dealer. In partnership with Thomas Harris, proprietor of Covent Garden, he bought the King's Theatre, Haymarket, then in the hands of Richard Yates and his wife Mary Ann and James Brookes. Yates's proverbial meanness was epitomised in the story of how he fell into a vat of lamp oil, was pulled out by a pulley and hung on a peg over the vat, dripping oil till it had all been recovered. Sheridan and Harris soon sold the King's to William Taylor. He had the theatre redesigned and refurbished but the cost was such that he was arrested for not paying his bills, and though the theatre struggled on with a series of temporary licences issued by the Lord Chamberlain, in 1785 it was refused further extensions and the theatre went dark.

RICHARD SHERIDAN, MP

In 1780, the year of the dangerous Gordon Riots, and as the American colonies slipped away, Sheridan was elected to Parliament. A Whig, he fought for a series of causes, including Parliamentary reform, curbing the abuses of imperialism, advocating peace not only in America but also with France, and Catholic emancipation. But his position as an MP also elevated him to prominence in the fashionable world, he became a close confederate of the Prince of Wales and Drury Lane became of secondary interest to him. It was useful chiefly as a cash cow to enable him to pursue his other life, and in 1782 he appointed an actor, Thomas King, to manage the company on a day-to-day basis. The story of Sheridan's Drury Lane descended into a string of episodic escapades.

COVENT GARDEN UNDER THOMAS HARRIS

Nearby, Covent Garden Theatre was on an apparently much sounder footing under the steady proprietorship of Thomas 'Jupiter' Harris. He had been there since 1767, approachable, shrewd and hard-working, and remained till well into the nineteenth century, a rare example of theatrical stability though it was not without incident, such as the quarrel with George Colman recounted earlier.

THE ROYALTY THEATRE

In 1787 the Patent theatres were faced with another threat when John Palmer, already proprietor of Bath and Bristol Theatres Royal, obtained a licence from a magistrate to open the Royalty Theatre, to the east of Covent Garden and Drury Lane, near the Tower. Sheridan and Harris took immediate action, and Palmer's enterprise was virtually stillborn. He returned to Bath.

JOHN PHILIP KEMBLE AT DRURY LANE

Meanwhile, Thomas King resigned his post at Drury Lane, asserting loudly that he could no longer work with the unpredictable and treacherous Sheridan. John Philip Kemble, Sarah Siddons's brother and a leading actor with the company, was appointed in King's place. Kemble soon afterwards married the daughter of Hopkins, the prompter (he had been expected to marry Elizabeth Inchbald), and tried to recover the theatre's reputation.

He was meticulous, disciplined and hard-working, with a special enthusiasm for Shakespeare. He was probably the first manager to understand the importance of the production overall: his biographer described how Kemble 'set himself seriously to prepare the play for representation'. He did not

> order the prompter to write out the parts from some old mutilated prompt copy lingering on his shelves; but himself consider(ed) it attentively in the author's genuine book: then to examine what corrections could be properly admitted into his text; and, finally, what could be cut out in the representation, not as disputing

Figure 5.27
Sir Thomas Lawrence, John Philip Kemble as Hamlet

Source: Heritage Images/Diomedia

the judgment of the author, but as suiting the time of the representation to the habits of his audience, or a little favouring the powers of his actors, in order that the performance might be as uniformly good as it was practicable to make it. The stage arrangements throughout the play were all distinctly marked by him in his own clear exact penmanship, and when he had done his work, his theatre received, in that perfected copy, a principle of exactness, which was of itself sufficient to keep its stage unrivalled for truth of scenic exhibition.[3]

As for rehearsals, Kemble worked hard to instil discipline into his company. Actors still largely prepared their roles by themselves, and much stage business, and indeed the rhythm and intonation of speeches was traditional and seemingly unalterable. But Kemble spent significant time marshalling and choreographing crowd scenes. He also became increasingly interested in scenic effects and had an antiquarian's interest in period costume.

But despite Kemble's best efforts, salaries still went unpaid, and actors felt free to take time off when the proceeds of their benefits were swallowed up in 'running costs'. The theatre's greatest asset, Mrs Siddons, began refusing to co-operate: even her £30 per week was not forthcoming.

A NEW DRURY LANE

At this point, the building itself was condemned as unsafe. The company moved to the King's Theatre, and a new, huge Drury Lane holding three thousand six hundred and eleven spectators was built over two years. Surely it would provide enough income both for Sheridan's extravagance and for the actors' salaries. So much was spent on the lavish interior that nothing was left to finish the outside, intended to be in the Enlightened style of 'Grecian Ionian'. It was to be called the Grand National Theatre, but the name failed to catch.

When the company moved back into Drury Lane in 1794, Sheridan discovered that the patent he had bought at such expense was in fact the temporary licence Queen Anne had granted to William Collier; now he had to return to the Rich family descendants and buy the genuine patent at further unexpected expense.

Meanwhile, in 1789 James Ford had decided he had lost enough money and sold his interest in Drury Lane. It was a difficult time, with Kemble's idealistic traditionalism set against Sheridan's irresponsible risk-taking. Kemble shut the theatre as a mark of respect when the French king was executed. Sheridan was livid, though whether from progressive principle or because of the loss of income was unclear. His pro-revolutionary sentiments did not prevent him the next year from staging the flamboyant spectacle, *The Glorious First of June* which recreated Lord Howe's naval victory over the French, the proceeds going to the widows and orphans of the sailors who lost their lives in the engagement. Perhaps it was patriotism, too, which led him to produce what he claimed to be a new-found work by Shakespeare, *Vortigern and Rowena*, in 1796. Kemble, too, seems to have been fooled by this absurd forgery by one William Ireland. It was received with disbelieving scorn.

For such spectacles as these, Kemble turned to William Capon, on whom the influence of de Loutherbourg was easily detectable. Capon responded by producing vast realistic pictures of buildings like the Palace of Westminster and the Tower of London, exact copies of their originals on huge unwieldy canvases, and they delighted Kemble.

KEMBLE RESIGNS

Kemble's reign, however, was coming to an end. He found himself in trouble in 1796 after he sexually assaulted a dancer-actor in the company, Marie-Thérèse de Camp, whose screams brought help to her and humiliated him. He was forced to make a public apology, and later that year he resigned his post, though he continued to act. (Strangely, when de Camp later married Kemble's brother, he gave her away.)

COVENT GARDEN IN TROUBLE

Meanwhile, fresh trouble was brewing for Harris at Covent Garden. When he decided to raise the house charge on actors for their benefit nights from £160 to £180, Joseph Holman, backed by John Fawcett, Joseph Munden, Alexander Pope and others, challenged Harris. There was a suspicion among them that Harris and Sheridan were again operating a cartel, that any conditions one manager imposed, the other would support, so that the actors in dispute were trapped. They turned to the Lord Chamberlain, but he was unsympathetic. Their protest had failed. Harris sacked Holman but accepted the others into a revamped company which now included George Frederick Cooke as leading tragic actor.

AN ATTEMPTED ASSASSINATION

Sheridan's bumpy ride at Drury Lane continued. In May 1800, the king and queen commanded a performance of Colley Cibber's 1702 comedy, *She Would and She Would Not*. The king did not usually attend Drury Lane: he preferred Covent Garden where Harris's Pittite Toryism chimed better with his ideas than Sheridan's notorious Whiggism. But he wanted to see Dorothy Jordan perform. As the royal party were entering their box, James Hadfield, a spectator in the pit, shot at them with a pistol, narrowly missing the king. There was a scuffle, the would-be assassin was collared, and the king came to the front of the box to show he was unharmed. By then, Sheridan had cobbled up a new verse to 'God Save the King', and it was sung lustily by actors and spectators together three times.

Figure 5.28
The attempt on King George III's life at Drury Lane Theatre, 15 May 1800
Source: Library of Congress, Washington, D.C.

AT COVENT GARDEN

A year later all was changed. In another blow to Drury Lane, William 'Gentleman' Lewis, the acting manager at Covent Garden, retired and John Philip Kemble was invited to replace him. Kemble bought a sixth share in Covent Garden and took his sister, Sarah Siddons, with him. He set out to build 'a palace for Shakespeare', working with Harris's newly appointed ballet master, James Byrne. Byrne's innovative choreography matched the classical splendour and colourful pageantry of Kemble's new Shakespeare productions, the vastness of the theatre encouraging spectacle, and helping to form Kemble's final stately acting style.

NOTES

1 Adrian Poole, *Lamb, Hazlitt, Keats: Great Shakespeareans*, vol 4, London: Bloomsbury, 2010, p. 21.
2 William Hone, *The Every-Day Book*, vol 2, London: Hunt and Clarke, 1827, p. 1252.
3 A.M. Nagler, *A Source Book in Theatrical History*, New York: Dover Publications, 1952, pp. 414–415.

Chapter 61: Defining the nation: Plays and playwrights of the late eighteenth century

The repertoire of the patent theatres in the last quarter of the eighteenth century contained many more revivals of Shakespeare and other 'old' plays than original works. But there were original plays being written which tried to define the nation at a time of great social and political stress.

THE PLAYS OF SHERIDAN

The playwright from this period who has always been rightly admired is Richard Brinsley Sheridan. *The Rivals* (1775), after a bumpy start when it was disrupted by a claque organised by Matthews, Sheridan's vanquished rival for the love of Elizabeth Linley, was an extraordinarily brilliant first play by a twenty-three-year-old. It was also largely autobiographical, from its setting in Bath where he had courted Miss Linley, through the secretive love affair, the duel, elopement and more, but it is infused with an attractive combination of high spirits and irony, and Sheridan creates characters who are both absurd and sympathetic.

Not the least of its virtues is that it is extremely funny. When Falkland boasts how he saved Lydia from drowning, she remarks, 'Well, I should never think of giving my heart to a man because he could swim!' Mrs Malaprop may not be the only character in the canon who garbles her words – coins 'malapropisms' – but the fact that her name attaches to this comic trick is well deserved. Captain Absolute's apparent good breeding inspires her compliment: 'He is the very pineapple of politeness', and when later Lydia asks her what is the matter, she responds: 'Why, murder's the matter! Slaughter's the matter! Killing's the matter! – but he can tell you the perpendiculars!'

Sheridan followed this with the less consequential *St Patrick's Day* (1775) and one of the best musical plays of the period, *The Duenna* (1775). He then adapted Vanbrugh's *The Relapse* for *A Trip to Scarborough* (1777) before producing his masterpiece, *The School for Scandal* (1777). When this was produced, the applause and laughter were so terrific at the climax of the 'screen' scene that one passer-by, the twelve-year-old Frederic Reynolds, thought the building was collapsing. The satire on scandalmongering is acute and surely applies to more societies than Sheridan's. Mrs Candour asks: 'What news do you hear? – though indeed it is no matter, for I think one hears nothing else but scandal'. Society itself, in other words, is the school for scandal. This is partly because too much attention is paid to the surface of things. Not for nothing is the central family surnamed Surface: we are to ask, what is beneath the surface? The answer lies in the way power is manipulated through a society both complacent and corrupt.

Figure 5.29
The 'screen' scene from Sheridan's *The School for Scandal*, Drury Lane, 1777
Source: De Agostini Picture Library/Getty Images

ENGLAND: THE SUBJECT OF PLAYS

This in turn points to the central concern of many playwrights of the period: England, English values and her social and political trajectory. She seemed an island of contradictions. The squirearchy's grasp on political power was threatened by the merchant class's economic power; the growing wealth of the rich was set against the growing poverty of the poor; and sublimity of aspiration was challenged by the extremes of physical squalor.

The debate, and the plays, were conducted with decorum. The boisterousness of Shakespeare, or even Fielding, was rejected, and the theatre tried to tell stories which in their way of telling would help to define the nation rationally, and this in itself would contribute to public discussion. It was a kind of recreated classicism. Apollo was the god to whom these playwrights did homage, perhaps unconsciously, just as Josiah Wedgwood did in manufacturing Greek-style pottery and contemporary architects in building Palladian mansions.

ENGLISH VALUES

At the easiest level, many plays simply asserted the virtues of England, from Garrick's *The Irish Widow* (1772): 'The poorest man in England is a match for the greatest if he will but stick to the laws of the land' to Thomas Morton's *Speed the Plough* (1800): in England 'an upright heart is too potent for tyranny' and George Colman the Younger's *John Bull, or An Englishman's Fireside* (1803) which William Dunlap called 'a bold illustration of national character, and a noble lesson of high morality'. There were also extravagant pageant-like celebrations of national victories, like James Cobb's *The Glorious First of June* (1794), Thomas Dibdin's *The Mouth of the Nile, or The Glorious First of August* (1798) and the theatrical outpourings over Nelson's victory and death like Drury Lane's *The Victory at the Battle of Trafalgar and the Death of Lord Viscount Nelson* (1805).

But not every play was so secure. Sir William in Elizabeth Griffith's significantly titled, *The Times* (1779), ruminates: 'Why, sir, there have been no *men* born at least for these last thirty years – all monkeys and macaronis. No hearts of oak now, Belford – all dwindled into aspens', while Irwin's experiences on his return to England after nine years' absence in Elizabeth Inchbald's *Every One Has His Fault* (1793) is thoroughly negative: 'Is this my native country? Is this the hospitable land which we describe to strangers? No – we are savages to each other; nay worse'.

INDIVIDUAL IDENTITIES

Something of an identity crisis emerges here and it affects individuals, too. In George Colman's *The English Merchant* (1767), the Scottish Jacobite's daughter has lost her identity in London while her father is in exile abroad, while in Morton's *Speed the Plough* Harry's identity has been displaced and he is uncertain who he is. More comically, when Lord Scratch asks Vapid in Frederic Reynolds' *The Dramatist* (1789) who he is, Vapid answers: 'Who am I? – here's a question! in these times, who can tell who he is?'

THE CRITIC

The best plays of the period use performativity and self-referential modes to create a sort of hallucinatory effect which sometimes seems almost postmodern. Sheridan's *The Critic* (1779) is a brilliant case in point. Descended ultimately from Buckingham's *The Rehearsal*, the tragedy being rehearsed here keeps tripping over Sheridan's play so that we are taken on a dizzying ride through different levels of reality. Thomas King, playing Puff, on stage with Sneer, played by John Palmer, and Dangle, played by James Dodd, discusses his reaction to an as-yet unperformed drama:

> Mr Dodd was astonishingly great in the character of Sir Harry. That universal and judicious actor, Mr Palmer, perhaps never appeared to more advantage than in the colonel; – but it is not in the power of language to do justice to Mr King: indeed he more than merited those repeated bursts of applause which he drew from a most brilliant and judicious audience.

THE BELLE'S STRATAGEM

Hannah Cowley's *The Belle's Stratagem* (1780) is almost as effective, though in a slightly different manner. It, too, is descended ultimately from an earlier play, in this case *The Beaux' Stratagem* by George Farquhar, but it treads more dangerous ground by exploring the attractions of virtue compared with those of vice, ladylike behaviour with prostitution, and in its final scene at the masquerade, when mistaken identities, sexual desire and the losing of the self are mingled together, it achieves an unnerving dreamscape extremely rare in drama.

THE DRAMATIST

A third play which unsettles the spectator is Reynolds's *The Dramatist*. 'People always applaud most where they least comprehend', Vapid the dramatist eagerly informs Ennui, and this certainly applies here. It received a noisy premiere at Covent Garden punctuated by 'roars of laughter'.

Vapid spends the play organising the action to fit his conception of drama, so the characters are also characters in his play, which is not quite Reynolds's play. When Marianne hides him behind her sofa, 'here's an incident', he exclaims. He knows he needs 'a trap for applause' and he hides in the china closet in an arch echo of Wycherley's famous scene in *The Country Wife* – though hardly to the same effect. Lady Waitfor't (surely descended on the wrong side of the blanket from Lady Wishfort) bemoans that she has been 'ruined by a writer of epilogues', whereas Marianne, coming into money, vows to build Vapid a theatre.

Vapid's half-made, imagined drama, perhaps the concept of drama itself, is the hinge upon which the actual drama turns. Drama itself, the act of making a play, its performance and its reception, are what drives *The Dramatist*.

WOMEN PLAYWRIGHTS

Many of the best plays of the time were by women. Hannah Cowley has already been mentioned. In a series of provocative dramas, she experiments with form and opens questions of women's rights through her female protagonists. If her plots sometimes seem conventional, the fact that they are driven by a heroine rather than a hero contradicts this.

Almost equally effective as a dramatist was the actor, Elizabeth Inchbald, who also wrote stimulating dramatic criticism. Her comedies make strong pleas for tolerance and she fiercely attacks the masculine drive to subdue and control women.

There were plenty of other women playwrights towards the end of the eighteenth century. The plays of Elizabeth Griffith, Mariana Starke, Ann Yearsley and Frances Brooke have been partially recuperated, but they still deserve to be better known. Fanny Burney is usually recognised as a novelist though she wrote several plays, and Hannah More, once close to Garrick, would finally exchange playwrighting for philanthropy.

The sisters, Sophia and Harriet Lee, both wrote plays. Sophia's *A Chapter of Accidents* (1780) was successful enough to enable them to found a Seminary for Young Ladies in Bath, and Harriet went on not only to reject an offer of marriage from William Godwin, the recently widowed husband of Mary Wollstonecraft, but to write three plays, as well as novels, herself.

Later, Joanna Baillie wrote a number of essentially eighteenth-century comedies, though her major contribution to the drama was in her Romantic tragedies, discussed below; and Marie-Thérèse de Camp also wrote comedies, the best of which, *Smiles and Tears* (1815), is a curious, but not unattractive, splicing of eighteenth-century comedy with nineteenth-century melodrama.

PROBLEMS FOR WOMEN PLAYWRIGHTS

Considering this list it is surprising that there was still noticeable prejudice against female authors among male theatre managers, but Hannah Cowley wrote in 1795 that critics

> will allow me, indeed, to draw strong character, but it must be without speaking its language. I may give vulgar or low bred persons, but they must converse in a style of elegance. I may design the coarsest manners, or the most disgusting folly, but its expression must not deviate from the line of politeness.[1]

In 1787, an actress in the York Theatre Royal company, Mrs Belfille, wanted to produce Elizabeth Inchbald's new play, *Such Things Are*, and gained Inchbald's agreement. But the two women were overridden by the theatre manager, Tate Wilkinson, whose managerial priority was not to be gainsaid. When Inchbald was submitting plays to George Colman, manager of Covent Garden Theatre, she was conscious that he wanted a paternal relationship with her, whereas she sought something more equal. His 1778 version of Fletcher's 1612 *Tragedy of Bonduca*, showed how women weaken the nation, especially relevant when the troops camped on Coxheath waiting to fight the French were the object of female attentions.

WOMEN'S PERSPECTIVES

In fact, women brought a distinctive perspective to the stage. At the end of Cowley's *The Runaway* (1776), Bella, realising marriage may be in the offing, responds: 'Oh mercy! I won't hear of it! *Love*, one might manage that perhaps – but *honour*, *obey* – 'tis strange the ladies had never interest enough to get this ungallant form mended'. The opening scene in Burney's unperformed *The Witlings* (c.1779) is set in a milliner's shop and shows young women working for their living. Inchbald's *The Wedding Day* (1794) mocks male vanity throughout. Her ironic humour is seen, too, in *Lovers Vows*, when Anhalt sighs: 'Woman herself is a problem', forcing the spectator to ask – to whom?

These writers question the dominant patriarchy. Inchbald shows up its absurdity in *Every One Has His Fault* (1793) when Lord Norland bursts out: 'As my child, was she not most bound to obey me?', while in Elizabeth Griffith's *The Times*, Lady Mary strikes for some kind of freedom: 'Why must I be treated like a picture for a drawing-room, not to be hung up without its companion?'

Most disconcertingly, perhaps, these plays encourage us to gaze not at passive and obedient maidens, but at active and self-possessed women. The actresses of course were complicit in this, being both glamorous and independent. The finest point this reached, perhaps, was the case of Dorothy Jordan, mistress to the Duke of Clarence. When he came to the theatre, the audience could gaze at him gazing at her.

FRAUGHT TIMES

Whatever the Duke of Clarence's desires, this was a fraught time in Britain. America won her independence and the French Revolution terrified many. At home, all sorts of currents seemed opposed to tranquillity. There were strong demands for universal male suffrage. Opponents of the state showed they were capable of disciplined destructiveness in the Gordon Riots of 1780. And the endless wars discomposed the participants and the press-ganged, agitated those left behind, relatives, lovers, friends, workmates, and adversely affected taxes and trade. In 1787 the king had his first attack of 'madness'. And all this was compounded by the freezing over of the Thames, by bad harvests and economic depression. In the 1790s it seemed you could either argue for a rational re-ordering of society, as Tom Paine did in *The Rights of Man*, or you could introduce a 'White Terror', which was William Pitt's way when he introduced the Two Acts, against Treasonable Practices and Seditious Meetings.

HISTORY PLAYS

Some turned to history for reassurance. In 1789, as the French Revolution warmed up, Kemble presented *Henry V* at Drury Lane, significantly subtitled 'The Conquest of France' and *Henry VIII* with his sister Sarah Siddons as Katherine. Colman's *Bonduca* suggested that England needed a strong general like his hero, Caratach. Ann Yearsley delved into the long distant past for *Earl Godwin*, though this had a very different attitude to women.

Robin Hood, more legend than history, was a favourite with a certain kind of sturdy patriot, and hero of Dibdin's 1783 musical and Leonard McNully's of the following year which boasted music by William Shield. Covent Garden's 1795 pantomime, William Pearce's *Merry Sherwood, or Harlequin Forester*, with lyrics by John O'Keeffe and music by William Reeve, was 'a patriotic endorsement of the moral values of "manly" England versus "effeminate" France'.

This, however, did not go uncontested. Thomas Holcroft's *The Noble Peasant* (1784) with music by William Shield, also used the Robin Hood legend, but to rather different ends.

INDIA

'Manly' England, of course, was at the heart of empire. India came to replace the lost colonies of America in the British imperial mind, and there were plenty of people in late eighteenth-century British society who had returned from the subcontinent. These included not just the nabobs whom Foote dissected so pitilessly, but others presented more sentimentally and more constructively, such as Mariana Starke's Eliza and Louisa Moreton in *The Sword of Peace* (1788), or Beauchamp in Matthew Lewis's *The East Indian* (1800), as well as lower class, and considerably less enriched, agents of colonialism, like Jack Rover in O'Keeffe's *Wild Oats*. Others were simply recipients of nabob aggrandisement, like Miss Neville in Goldsmith's *She Stoops to Conquer*, whose jewels had been left her by her uncle, 'the India Director', or Angela in *The Castle Spectre*, upon whom are lavished 'the treasures of India'.

The fear that imperial gains of this sort might destabilise Britain's economy also grew, and can be seen not just in Foote's *The Nabob*, but also in *The School for Scandal*, Burney's *A Busy Day* and other plays. Such fear was a strong contributing factor in the 'orientalism', or 'othering' of societies and places seen as different and probably exotic, and it powers works like James Hook's *Oriental Magic, or Harlequin Nabob* (1778) and James Cobb's *Ramah Droog* (1798).

In these plays, Indian or eastern regimes are presented as despotic or barbaric, pursuing practices such as 'suttee', or widow-burning, which is the subject of Mariana Starke's *The Widow of Malabar* (1791). Alternatively, they may sap British masculinity, as in Cowley's *A Day in Turkey* (1791), in which the effeminate oriental Turks confront the European Russians, who intriguingly seem to uphold British values, or Cobb's *Love in the East* (1788), though here there is an implication that the Calcutta-based empire-builders are also weakened by contact with the failed French colonisers whom they have defeated.

Orientalism justifies conquest, and plenty of plays glorify imperial victories, often with extraordinary topicality, such as Murphy's *The Upholsterer* (1757), produced in the same year as the Battle of Plassey. Feeble is going to bed when Quidnunc bursts in upon him:

QUIDNUNC: Brother Feeble, I give you joy – the Nabob's demolished.
(Sings 'Britons, strike home, revenge', etc.)
FEEBLE: Lackaday, Mr Quidnunc, how can you serve me thus?
QUIDNUNC: Suraja Dowla is no more.
(Sings 'Rule, Britannia', etc.)
FEEBLE: Poor man, he's stark mad.
QUIDNUNC: Our men diverted themselves with killing their bullocks and their camels, till they dislodged the enemy from the octagon, and the counterscarp, and the bunglo.
FEEBLE: I'll hear the rest tomorrow morning – oh, I'm ready to die –
QUIDNUNC: Odsheart, man, be of good cheer – the new Nabob, Jaffier Ally Cawn, has acceded to a treaty; and the English company have got all their rights restored in the Phirmaud and the Hushbulhoorams.

Similar triumphalism accompanied the series of plays purporting to reveal the events of the long campaign against Tipu Sultan, the 'Tiger of Mysore', in the 1790s.

IMPERIALISM

Such conquests required the skill and courage of intrepid British manhood, and sometimes womanhood, too, as in Mariana Starke's *The Sword of Peace* (1788). But in reality these imperialist conquerors were under no illusions: the empire was there to supply Britain with raw materials at minimal cost, and to provide profitable markets for British manufactured goods. Sometimes this necessitated appallingly brutal measures, which when scrutinised in Britain seemed shocking and ultimately unacceptable. Thus, a Regulating Act of Parliament in 1773 tried to control the East India Company's more flagrant activities, and Warren Hastings, the unrepentant Governor-General of India from 1773 to 1785, was impeached in 1787, though after his lengthy trial, he was acquitted in 1795.

PIZARRO

Hastings's leading opponent, who made an impassioned attack on his administration, was Richard Brinsley Sheridan, and eventually he wrote a play which reflected not only on Hastings but on imperialism in general. *Pizarro* was adapted from Kotzebue's German original about the conquest of Peru, and first performed at Drury Lane in 1799 with a star-studded cast, including John Philip Kemble and his brother Charles, James Aicken, Dorothy Jordan and Sarah Siddons. It remained a favourite in British theatres for more than half a century.

Pizarro was Sheridan's first play for over twenty years and his last. It tells the story of the gallant indigenous people of Peru resisting invasion by marauding Spaniards, and it is unequivocally on the side of freedom and revolution. The story is naturally epic in scope, but Sheridan had no available models for epic drama. *Pizarro* seems to be conceived more as a spoken opera, though the ritual sacrificial offering, the warriors' Song of Victory and Rolla's stirring address on liberty to his troops would fit any epic play.

Figure 5.30
John Philip Kemble as Rolla in *Pizarro* by Richard Brinsley Sheridan, 1799
Source: By permission of the Folger Shakespeare Library

It offers stern reflections on British imperialism, by implication on the repression of Bengali people and the Jamaican and Windward maroons, not to mention the Irish, and many read it as an allegory of contemporary politics. The cruel Pizarro was likened to Hastings, with Peru as camouflage for India. Later, it was more convenient to see Pizarro as Napoleon, and he was even taken for William Pitt, Sheridan's Parliamentary opponent, who instituted the 'White Terror'. But the play may be relevant to any country under the heel of a foreign imperial power and seeking its own freedom. It is able to convey both the exoticism and the reality of empire.

In performance, the epic theme was reinforced by the costumes – Mrs Siddons as Elvira appeared almost like a Wagnerian Valkyrie, dressed in armour and a huge plumed helmet. De Loutherbourg produced magnificent scenery for '*a wild retreat among stupendous rocks*'. Later, a fallen tree formed a precarious bridge over a '*torrent*' across which Rolla escaped with Alonzo's child in his arms, pursued by soldiers. Perhaps this scene was in Bertolt Brecht's memory when he wrote *The Caucasian Chalk Circle*. Such moments, especially as acted by the stately Kemble and Siddons, made this play the epitome of enlightened Apollonian classicism.

SLAVERY

If India provided one immense tranche of Britain's growing wealth, slavery provided another. This was the time of growing agitation against the slave trade. In 1800 the Haymarket staged John Fawcett's *Obi, or Three-Fingered Jack, the Terror of Jamaica*, which told the story of an escaped slave, and in 1808, the year after the slave trade was outlawed, the same theatre presented George Colman the Younger's *The Africans, or War, Love and Duty*, which unexpectedly entangles the slave trade with ruthless capitalism.

INKLE AND YARICO

Colman's earlier *Inkle and Yarico* (1787) explores the same territory more provocatively. Yarico, a black princess, and her servant-confidante, Wowski, fall into reciprocal love with Inkle, an ambitious young trader, and his servant, Trudge. When Inkle tries to sell the loving Yarico for a slave, he is denounced as a scoundrel. His attempt to exculpate himself refers to his father's teaching:

> As I grew up, he'd prove – and by example – were I in want, I might e'en starve, for what the world cared for their neighbours; why then should I care for the world? Men now lived for themselves. These were his doctrines: then, sir, what would you say, should I, inspite of habit, precept, education, fly in my father's face, and spurn his councils?

Unbridled capitalism, in other words, is without feeling, but if it adds a moral dimension, slavery is abolished.

Yarico is a typical long-suffering female victim, yet there are further ambivalences here. According to the stage direction, the first act takes place in America, whereas Elizabeth Inchbald's introduction to the 1808 edition of this highly popular play urges that this was a mistake for Africa. Thus the conventional slave trade would be depicted. But what if the original setting in America was correct?

The action would then take place just after the American colonies had obtained their liberation, and Yarico and Wowski may be runaway slaves themselves.

BLACK WOMEN CHARACTERS

Another interesting feature of this play is the presence in it of two beautiful black women. The stage often bridled at such representations. *Oroonoko*, Thomas Southerne's late seventeenth-century play based on Aphra Behn's novel, was adapted and frequently revived in the cause of abolition, but with Oroonoko's beloved Imoinda presented as a white woman. In 1807, the Drury Lane pantomime, *Furibond, or Harlequin Negro*, was set on a slave plantation in the West Indies, and then in London. The play's white heroine, Columbine, is wooed by the slave-owner. But she prefers one of his slaves, Harlequin. Her choice of the black slave over the white slave-owner is salutary, and Harlequin's plea in favour of abolition exemplary.

BLACK SERVANT CHARACTERS

Partly because of the slave trade, there were plenty of black people in Britain at this time. Many of them were servants, and we see black servants in plays like Murphy's *The Way to Keep Him* (1761) and in Garrick's *The Irish Widow* (1772). Matthew Lewis's *The Castle Spectre* (1797) has three black servants, while Mite in Foote's *The Nabob* has four. In Burney's *A Busy Day* (1801), a hotel waiter is outraged that he must respect Eliza Watts's black servant, though perhaps it should be added that the black servants in these examples are actually probably from the Indian subcontinent.

SKIN COLOUR

Problems with skin colour as such also surface sometimes. In Samuel Foote's *The Cozeners* (1774), a black woman tries to pass for white. More extraordinary is Henry Bate's comedy, *The Blackamoor Washed White* (1776), in which the heroine's father decides to sack his white servants and replace them with black ones. The young lady's lover disguises himself as a black in order to elope with her, and the first act ends with the embarrassing line: 'O that I should ever live to see the day when white Englishmen must give place to foreign blacks'. Whether because of the play's racialism or because Bate had had a dangerous altercation with a Mr Fitzgerald, who had hired a large claque of ruffians to drown out the drama, the production met with successive nights of raucous mayhem, missiles flying, drunken fights in the auditorium and no heed paid even to King George III's pleas for the play to be permitted to continue. After three nights it had to be taken off.

RACISM

Racism, which was never far away in any of these plays, is also entangled with national identity, and there were periodic protests against Jews in theatre audiences. Plays sometimes reflected this. In Sheridan's *The Duenna*, the heroine's father conspires with a Jew against his own daughter. In O'Keeffe's *The Young Quaker* (1783), a Jew claims he will be a second father to the young woman he wishes to seduce. And in the Drury Lane afterpiece, *Mordecai's Beard*, the protagonist's beard is greased with pig's fat and converted, though Mordecai himself remains a heathen.

BRITAIN AND CLASSICAL ANTIQUITY

All these plays about slavery, race and skin colour tell us something of the problems and anxieties connected with characterising 'Britishness'. Yet finally it may have been an unscripted performance which defined most precisely the contradictions embedded in the nation.

Classical serenity seemed a positive counterweight to the problems of gender, empire and racism. Or it would if it could be resurrected. The difficulties inherent in this were highlighted in Foote's *The Nabob*. Here the antiques and 'curious remains' which Mite has brought from Italy, and which have won him membership of the prestigious Antiquarian Society, turn out to be the merest bric-a-brac.

SIR WILLIAM HAMILTON

This was a wry glance at the Dilettanti Society which had been formed in the 1730s to sponsor deeper understanding of the classical world. Its members included at different times Horace Walpole, David Garrick, Joshua Reynolds and Sir William Hamilton. The painting of the actress Dorothy Jordan, in company with Euphrosyne, one of the three Graces, escaping the satyr, symbolised what the Society stood for – high culture unadulterated by Dionysian laughter, coarse jollity or heated indignation.

Sir William Hamilton, while Ambassador to the Kingdom of Naples, had found all kinds of exquisite treasures of ancient culture, and had shipped many back to Britain. He had also married the somewhat louche Emma Hart, who was widely regarded as the acme of classical beauty. She was painted over and over again by artists such as George Romney, often as a classical character such as Iphigenia, or Circe, or Ariadne.

LADY HAMILTON'S 'ATTITUDES'

From this, Lady Hamilton graduated to poses, or 'attitudes'. She was not alone: in *The Dramatist*, Ennui is told that to win the lady he desires he needs 'a new dress – bold looks – a few oaths and much swaggering'. The stage direction reads: '*Ennui puts himself in attitudes*', which suggests a new contradiction – theatricality against vapidity.

Lady Hamilton's 'attitudes', however, were copied from figures found on the ancient vases her husband had collected. Sir William had constructed a small stage outlined with a golden frame within which his lady presented something between a peep show and a playlet. She wore a Grecian costume, adding perhaps a shawl or hat or other prop to define the specific 'attitude' and to aid the transition from one to another. Each 'attitude' was elucidated by a commentary from Sir William.

He explained that the 'attitudes' represented, first, a character from the classical world, and second, a specific emotion. Sometimes Emma used a child to fill out her tableau. Thus, as Niobe she clasped the child to her breast while defying the heavens. As Medea, she grasped the child's hair and brandished a sword. But sometimes she was alone: particularly popular with her male audiences was the highly eroticised maenad, representing imagination and desire. One pose melted

Figure 5.31
Two views of Lady Hamilton's 'Attitudes'

Figure 5.32
Two views of Lady Hamilton's 'Attitudes'

into another, rapid yet relaxed, elegant yet sensual, posture united with passion in a mesmerising sequence.

This performance embodied the epitome of national aspiration to the Apollonian sublime, even while Lady Hamilton conducted her noisy, Dionysian, adulterous affair with the nation's favourite hero, Horatio Nelson. The contradictions perhaps defined the nation.

NOTE

1 Folger Collective of Early Women Critics, *Women Critics 1660–1820*, Bloomington: Indiana University Press, 1995, p. 201.

Chapter 62: Siddons and acting: Romantic classicism

AN ACTORS' THEATRE

The theatre at the end of the eighteenth century belonged to the actors. Kemble was a more significant presence than Sheridan. This is illustrated by the fact that, as Frederic Reynolds admitted, it was the actress Dorothy Jordan, not the playwright or the theatre manager, who saved his comedy, *Better Late Than Never* from failure when it was staged at Drury Lane in 1790.

It was made even clearer, perhaps, when Mrs Siddons was preparing to play Lady Macbeth for the first time. Sheridan hurried into her dressing room. Having heard she intended to put the candle down on the table in the sleepwalking scene, he begged her not to. She refused, saying she needed both hands for the action of washing. Sheridan pointed out that Mrs Pritchard had never put down the candle. Siddons, who had studied somnambulism, was adamant. And after the extraordinary acclaim which greeted her performance, Sheridan came creeping back. Later she remarked mordantly, 'he most ingeniously congratulated me on my obstinacy'.

With brighter lighting in the theatres, an actor's movements and gestures became plainer and therefore carried more meaning. It was less easy for a lazy actor to generalise, and it forced everyone on stage to concentrate. This pressure was further intensified as the theatres became larger: they required bigger and probably fewer gestures, and less but clearer movement. They also required greater clarity in speech because of the cavernous acoustics. The good actor's performance was probably simpler but more vivid.

This was the challenge posed to that generation of actors who worked between the periods of dominance of Garrick and Kean, between the first performance in 1777 of *The School for Scandal*, and that of *Pizarro* in 1799. Their enlightened classicism was tinged with romanticism, and their pre-eminent representative was Sarah Siddons.

SARAH SIDDONS: THE EARLY YEARS

Born the eldest child of theatrical parents, Sarah Siddons served an acting apprenticeship in provincial theatres, though the small size of many of these may not have been an ideal preparation for her future work in Drury Lane. At the age of eighteen she married a mediocre actor, Henry Siddons, who was charming and good-looking, but also a somewhat ineffectual character, though he did write a book on acting, based largely on what he thought his wife was doing. She bore seven children, and they were mostly cared for by their mother, despite the fact that she was also the family's chief breadwinner. She continued to act even when pregnant, as many actresses had to do at that time.

She made her London debut at Garrick's Drury Lane at Christmas 1775, playing Portia in *The Merchant of Venice*. But it was a disaster – she was overcome with nerves and her performance was feeble. She returned to the provincial theatre, and seven years later, in the autumn of 1782, she returned to Drury Lane. She played the name part in *Isabella, or The Fatal Marriage* by Thomas Southerne, and her performance was met with tumultuous applause. She was hailed as the epitome of the tragic actress, and from this her career never faltered.

SARAH SIDDONS'S LADY MACBETH

She was helped to her success by her striking appearance. She was tall, slim, physically well coordinated and had dark compelling eyes. She had had a mind-boggling moment when she had been first asked to play Lady Macbeth when she was still very young. After the household had retired to bed she began to learn the lines. Suddenly her imagination caught fire at the terror and potency of the murderous events. She sat in silence till, overwhelmed with horror, she fled upstairs to bed, where her husband lay peacefully asleep. She was even frightened of the rustling of her own clothes. Too scared even to undress, she lay awake on her bed as the night ticked by. She had understood viscerally that acting was more than merely learning and repeating lines from a script.

Lady Macbeth became one of her most memorable roles. Hazlitt saw her play the part decades later and wrote:

> We can conceive of nothing grander. It was something above nature. It seemed almost as if a being of superior order had dropped from a higher sphere to awe the world with the mystery of her appearance . . . she was tragedy personified. . . . To have seen her in that character was an event in anyone's life not to be forgotten.[1]

Her first appearance reading Macbeth's letter set the tone. 'They (the witches) made themselves – ' pause, then speculatively, almost amused, ' – air'. Then, 'Glamis thou art, and Cawdor', and with hardened voice, 'and *shalt be* what thou art promised'. This was a determined, adamantine woman, yet when she came some minutes later to recall how she had given suck to her babe, an unexpected tenderness crept in. This weak moment in her resolute strength would have pleased that most demanding theatrical taskmaster, Stanislavsky.

Later Macbeth asks doubtfully, 'If we should fail?' 'We fail', she retorted decisively. No querulous – 'We fail?' – here. 'But screw your courage to the sticking-place and *we'll not fail*', each syllable hammered out. She stood ramrod straight. Body and thought were in concert, indeed the body itself might have been doing the thinking.

In the famous sleepwalking scene, her big eyes were wide open, but blank. She glided here and there, almost tossed by the storm in her mind. 'Out, damned spot', came in a hollow, tormented voice. She listened for something. Then, 'One! Two!' and in a weird whisper, 'Why then, 'tis time to do't'.

Figure 5.33
Robert Smirke, Sarah Siddons as Lady Macbeth
Source: By permission of the Folger Shakespeare Library

MRS SIDDONS'S METHOD

Most of the hallmarks of Siddons's brilliance are noticeable here. She works in great detail, from one bit, or unit, to the next, letting each make its own impact; but each is controlled by the through line of the characterisation. She speaks clearly whatever the circumstances. Her movement is distinct, bold or faint, lively or stately, and the energy is always there, even in the pathetic or muted moments. She knows that a certain reserve may convey more than greater flamboyance, but she does not act mechanically – this is not remembered rehearsal. It is interesting to know that Siddons did not like her dressing room door closed during a performance, even when she had long periods off stage: she wanted to follow every detail so that she could be alert to any unexpected nuances that might appear.

MRS SIDDONS IN TRAGEDY

Her most admired parts were all in tragedies – Calista in *The Fair Penitent*, Belvedira in *Venice Preserved* and Lady Randolph in *Douglas*, and among Shakespearean roles, besides Lady Macbeth, Volumnia in *Coriolanus* and Queen Katherine in *Henry VIII*. Her Katherine was poised and dignified, occasionally flavoured with imperious contempt, but as she lay dying, she presented a peevish old lady, hands fluttering over the counterpane, fretful yet never without at least a shred of her former majesty. As Volumnia, she enjoyed her son's triumph with her head held high in a mixture of pride and grandeur. And as she walked the scene, her stately self-possession gradually deserted her and she became almost drunk with glory. 'Her action lost all grace', wrote one spectator, 'yet became so true to nature, so picturesque and so descriptive, that pit and gallery sprang to their feet, electrified by the transcendent execution of the conception'.[2]

Siddons emphasised how much her performance owed to painstaking application and thorough study; yet she also, apparently, 'felt' the part. This may be less of a contradiction than it appears. Only when an actor deeply comprehends the character is it possible to so identify with it that each performance is unique, a genuine response to the situation as it appears at the specific moment. Siddons mastered the knack of what some actors call 'flying' – almost improvising from a base of understanding.

'UNITY OF DESIGN'

Macready described Siddons's performance in Edward Moore's *The Gamester* tellingly when he spoke of her 'unity of design, the just relation of all parts to the whole', and continued:

> Throughout the tragedy of The Gamester, devotion to her husband stood out as them a inspring of her actions, the ruling passion of her being; apparent when reduced to poverty in her graceful and cheerful submission to the lot to which his vice had subjected her, in her fond excuses of his ruinous weakness, in her conciliating expostulations with his angry impatience, in her indignant repulse of Stukely's advances, when in the awful dignity of outraged virtue she imprecates the vengeance of Heaven upon his guilty head. The climax to her sorrows and sufferings was in the dungeon, when on her knees, holding her dying husband, he dropped lifeless from her arms. Her glaring eyes were fixed in stony blankness on his face; the powers of life seemed suspended in her; her sister and Lewson gently raised her, and slowly led her unresisting from the body, her gaze never for an instant averted from it; when they reached the prison door she stopped, as if awakened from a trance, uttered a shriek of agony that would have pierced the hardest heart, and rushing from them, flung herself, as if for union in death, on the prostrate form before her.[3]

The passage is revealing for its explanation of Siddons's method. First, she has a 'unity of design', what Stanislavsky called the 'Supertask', which is the overarching imperative determining the whole creation. But this is split down into its component parts, or, in Stanislavsky's terminology, 'bits' and 'tasks', each conceived as a single unit which coheres on its own terms, but each of which also fits into the overall 'design' of the part.

Figure 5.34
Sir Joshua Reynolds, Sarah Siddons as the Tragic Muse, 1784

Source: Yale Center for British Art, Paul Mellon Fund. Yale University, New Haven

MOMENTS OF STILLNESS

And there is more to Siddons's achievement even than this in the building of a character, for what Macready's description leaves out are the moments of stillness which she incorporated into what she did. These poses, almost 'attitudes', which existed like individual vertebrae in the spine of the part, frequently derived from either fine art paintings or Greek or Egyptian sculptures and aimed to crystallise specific moments or emotions. Thus, in the scene above, when she reached the prison door, she 'stopped', frozen for a moment in the horror of the situation.

As Hermione in *The Winter's Tale*, she appeared 'one of the noblest statues that even Grecian task ever invented':

> Upon the magical words pronounced by Paulina, 'Music, awake her; strike', the sudden action of the head absolutely startled as though such a miracle had really vivified the marble; and the descent from the pedestal was equally graceful and affecting.[4]

Finally it should be noted that Mrs Siddons deepened her work by playing the same parts over many years and opposite different partners. She never stayed solely in Drury Lane, but in many summers toured the provinces where she met and performed with all sorts of different companies.

CELEBRITY

Mrs Siddons quickly became a celebrity. Details of her clothes, her salary, her private life were pored over, and her admirably chaste life as wife and mother gave her greater sway over her adoring public. These included King George III and Queen Charlotte, who attended Drury Lane to watch her despite their abhorrence of Sheridan's politics. Her first benefit performance at Drury Lane in 1783 broke all Box Office records, and often patrons left the theatre after her part was over, too shattered to stay for the comic afterpiece.

After discussing Kemble, Cooke, Kean and others, Byron asserted that 'Mrs Siddons was worth them all put together'. And it was as the sublime Tragic Muse that Joshua Reynolds painted her in one of his most famous works.

MRS SIDDONS'S FAREWELL

Her final performance in 1812 was as Lady Macbeth. The house was crowded and overcrowded, and at the end of the sleepwalking scene, Lady Macbeth's last, the applause simply continued until she reappeared to make a farewell speech, after which the audience would not permit the play to continue, but departed into the night. The following year she gave some well-attended public readings from Shakespeare, and when she died in 1831 her coffin was followed to the graveyard by many thousands of mourners.

DOROTHY JORDAN

Mrs Siddons's only rival was Dorothy Jordan who was, however, a very different kind of actor. They did act together sometimes, in *Cymbeline* for instance, and *Pizarro*, but Jordan's special gift was for comedy and she was indeed painted by John Hoppner as the Comic Muse just as Siddons was painted as the Tragic Muse.

Jordan made her Drury Lane debut in 1785 as Peggy in *The Country Girl*, and soon caught the eye of the king's third son, the Duke of Clarence, with whom she had a long and mostly happy affair, bearing him ten children. Like Siddons, she acted through her pregnancies, though she could have relied on Clarence for her needs.

She was quite short, with a mobile and expressive face and a quick, lively smile. She was boisterous, lively, energetic, had a delightful speaking voice and a warm, infectious laugh. Like all the best actors she had the gift of seeming spontaneous, making each performance seem absolutely original.

She was seen to notable advantage in 'breeches' parts, including Shakespeare's Rosalind and Farquhar's Sir Harry Wildair, a part written for a man, but often played by a woman since Peg Woffington first decided to try it. Jordan's performance was certainly sexy and spiced with a hint of lesbianism as 'he' (Wildair) pursues Angelica. More conventionally she was appreciated and admired as Priscilla Tomboy in Charles Dibdin's *The Romp*, Miss Hoyden in Sheridan's *A Trip to Scarborough* and Miss Prue in Congreve's *Love for Love*. Leigh Hunt's description of her in *The Country Girl* tells much:

> Though she was neither beautiful, nor handsome, nor even pretty, nor accomplished, nor 'a lady', nor anything
> conventional or comme il faut whatsoever, yet was so pleasant, so cordial, so natural, so full of spirits, so
> healthily constituted in mind and body, had such a shapely leg withal, so charming a voice, and such a happy
> and happy-making expression of countenance, that she appeared something superior to all those requirements
> of acceptability, and to hold a patent from nature herself for our delight and good opinion.[5]

For all her charm, she had a steely courage and never accepted coercion or ill treatment from colleagues or theatre managers, though doubtless her assertiveness was assisted by the presence in the background of her powerful lover. In 1811, however, he cast her off, and though she continued acting till 1814, her last years were clouded by one of her son's financial disasters, and she died in poverty in France in 1816.

JOHN PHILIP KEMBLE

The greatest male stars of the period were Mrs Siddons's brother, John Philip Kemble, and George Frederick Cooke. Kemble, a Catholic at a time when Catholics were still excluded from many areas of British life, wrote plays when he was young. But soon acting seemed a more profitable way forward: he was handsome and athletic, though he was also serious by nature, even solemn, even pompous, and it was this probably which prevented him from becoming a truly great actor.

He suffered from asthma which may explain why he gradually became grander and more statuesque. It is possible that in a less rumbustious age his talents might have shone more brightly. Once when a child in the gallery was screaming through his performance, he came to the front of the stage and announced: 'If the play be not stopped the child cannot possibly continue'. And the O.P. Riots of 1810 showed him far out of kilter with most of his contemporaries.

His widely admired Hamlet presented a gentle, wistful Prince, who boldly praised his father – 'he was a man, take him for all in all' – but melted into tenderness on 'I shall not look upon his like again'. When the Ghost descended through the stage trap, Kemble instituted a move much copied by later Hamlets: he knelt behind the trap in filial compassion. His costume also provoked comment from traditionalists. He wore contemporary court dress in black velvet, a star on his breast with pendant ribbon of some imagined chivalric order, and a mourning sword and buckles. His long hair was powdered and fell to his shoulders.

He also gained plaudits for the classical Roman parts – Cato, Brutus and Coriolanus. But Leigh Hunt for one could not stomach this. Of his Brutus he wrote:

> This artificial actor does so dole out his words, and so drop his syllables one by one upon the ear, as if he was measuring out laudanum for us, that a reasonable auditor . . . has no alternative between laughing and being disgusted.[6]

Not all assented to this. His Coriolanus, for example, was greatly admired. It was still mannered and grandiloquent, and depended on the idea, which has some traction, that restrained passion can move a spectator as effectively as one more extravagantly expressed. But some found it once-paced, and he failed utterly to see the street fighter in Coriolanus.

This was due perhaps to his method, which was cerebral. It sometimes led to too deliberate an action, as when he took scrupulous care to arrange 'the disposition of his mantle', but it also produced some memorable results. His Jaques, in *As You Like It*, for instance, was noted for its 'exquisite colouring and embellishment'. But it also relied too much probably on the 'supertask'. Kemble aimed to discover a 'ruling passion' which informed every scene, and when played with intensity, could become relentless. But this neo-Platonist approach showed Kemble as a man of his 'enlightened' time. He never believed in 'living' the part.

GEORGE FREDERICK COOKE

His younger contemporary, George Frederick Cooke, was in many ways Kemble's opposite. A fascinating and brilliant actor with a *penchant* for strong drink and an overdeveloped sense of *amour propre*, he quarrelled frequently, married serially and was imprisoned for debt. Square-jawed and hook-nosed, with a wide mouth and eyes set far apart, he may have looked more like a pugilist than an artist, but his performances could be electrifying.

As Richard III,

> he entered on the right hand of the audience, and with a dignified erect deportment, walked to the centre of the stage, amidst their plaudits. His appearance was picturesque and proudly noble: his head elevated, his step firm, his eye beaming fire . . . (when he spoke) the high key in which he pitched his voice, and its sharp and rather grating tones, caused a sensation.[7]

At his best, Cooke displayed an original imagination and a commitment to hard work which enabled one writer to assert of his Hamlet, 'the beauties are so many, that ill-nature and envy must stand up, and say to all the world, "This is an actor" '.[8]

'Ill-nature and envy' were the demon drink which ruined Cooke's life as well as his career. From early on there are reports of him failing to appear when he had been billed. Thus, at Newcastle in 1788, when he was to appear with Mrs Jordan, he simply could not be found, and his part had to be read by a novice actor. In 1802, when appearing as Orsino in *Twelfth Night* at Covent Garden, he arrived, but was so drunk he was hissed from the stage. 'When the tragedian was intoxicated', wrote a contemporary, 'he was overbearing, noisy and insufferably egotistical, asking questions and answering them himself. Thus: Who am I? Sir George Frederick Cooke, sir. What am I, sir? The Tragedian, not Black Jack, sir'.[9]

Figure 5.35
Thomas Sully, George Frederick Cooke as Richard III
Source: Pennsylvania Academy of the Fine Arts, Philadelphia

It was a shame. He had, one commentator wrote, 'a piercing, pleasant voice, a flexible countenance, and a judicious deportment, without any of that unnecessary *rant* so much in use upon
the stage'. He found the humour in Richard III when that character was usually played as wholly
villainous, and he had the rare ability to act *with* his partner on the stage: 'he never loses sight of
the character, or the situation of the other performers who are engaged in the scene with him'.[10]

He was totally involved even when not speaking and understood the importance both of the overarching conception of the part and the need for convincing detail in the playing. When sober, Cooke, it was agreed, had no equal.

A late triumph was his Falstaff, which seemed to rescue that favourite character from the hands of clowns. A correspondent to the *Bristol Gazette* noted:

> Falstaff has been too commonly turned loose upon the stage to make sport for the galleries. . . . Mr Cooke rescued him . . . and we saw again the man of powerful sense and pregnant wit, debauched and unprincipled indeed: but glorying in the predominance of his fascinating powers over the fancy and affections of a discerning and accomplished prince. To this end his vapouring and his lying, his bullying and his cowardice conduce: and this important point was carefully kept by Mr Cooke.[11]

OTHER ACTORS

Other actors who enriched the late eighteenth-century stage included the fat, convivial John Palmer, proprietor of the Bath and Bristol Theatres Royal, and the original Joseph Surface; James Dodd, who made his debut in 1765 and specialised in fops and simpletons; and John Bannister, son of the actor and singer, Charles Bannister, who trained to be an artist with de Loutherbourg before becoming a special protégé of Garrick. 'Gentleman' Smith was another protégé of Garrick. Tall and handsome, he once fought a duel with Charles Macklin, though neither was hurt.

Tom King, Garrick's assistant and later Sheridan's manager at Drury Lane, was a hard-working, reliable actor who created the parts of Belcour in *The West Indian*, Sir Peter Teazle in *The School for Scandal* and Puff in *The Critic*. John Henderson was perhaps the most brilliant of them all, but he was a mighty drinker, too: he took sixteen glasses of gin most mornings. He was thickset and ugly, but he possessed real charisma, as well as energy and intelligence. Sadly he died before his fortieth birthday in 1785. Another superb actor who died young was Charles Holland who took over several of Garrick's parts, including Hamlet and Richard III, but contracted smallpox and died in 1770. Robert Baddeley, the last actor to wear the royal livery as normal dress, had a Magic Lantern Show at Marylebone Pleasure Gardens around 1770.

PLAYWRIGHTS AND ACTRESSES

Among women who made their mark as actresses at this time were two playwrights, Elizabeth Inchbald, who was friendly with Kemble and Mrs Siddons and had a productive career at Covent Garden, and Elizabeth Griffith, who played Juliet, Cordelia and Calista among other roles at Drury Lane.

ELIZABETH FARREN

Some actresses found fame in other ways. Elizabeth Farren, a former child actress, was an extremely beautiful woman, and a clever actor. She played Berinthia in *A Trip to Scarborough* and, later, Lady Teazle in *The School for Scandal*. Her 'perfect intimacy with the better born . . . made her the accomplished woman of fashion she represented', one critic commented, and she had 'all the indescribable little charms which give fascination to the woman of birth and fashion'.[12] She was courted by many, including the actor John Palmer, but fell for the Earl of Derby,

Figure 5.36
Sir Thomas Lawrence, portrait of Elizabeth Farren

Source: The Metropolitan Museum of Art, New York. Bequest of Edward S. Harkness, 1940

who was estranged from his wife. When she refused to give in to him unless he divorced his wife, stalemate was reached, but the pair continued together, apparently chastely, for nearly twenty years until the Countess of Derby did die, when Elizabeth Farren married her Earl and entered the aristocracy herself.

MARY ROBINSON

Mary Robinson had not quite the same fortune. She made her debut as Juliet, stringently coached by Garrick himself, but still accompanied by extreme nervousness, and she later played Perdita in *The Winter's Tale*. She was the lover of several prominent people, including Charles James Fox and Sheridan, but most notably the Prince of Wales, who after *The Winter's Tale* styled himself archly her 'Florizel'. He was only sixteen when she became his mistress in 1778, and in consequence she, too, became a celebrity and the object of much gazing. After the affair was over, she became a friend of Marie Antoinette, and she wrote novels, poetry and an illuminating memoir, as well as *A Letter to the Women of England on the Injustice of Mental Subordination*, which argued forcefully against male domination and for the right of women to voice their opinions.

CHILD ACTORS

For a brief period in the early nineteenth century, child actors became fashionable, most notably Master William Betty, who aged thirteen starred at Drury Lane and Covent Garden as Hamlet, Richard III, Young Norval in *Douglas* and other parts. When he played Hamlet, Pitt adjourned the House of Commons so members could attend the theatre. Untutored, but heavily coached and managed by his hard-bargaining father, he rose to a salary of a hundred guineas a night briefly. It is hard to say how talented this 'Boy Wonder', or 'Young Roscius', was. He seems hardly to have understood most parts he played, but he was energetic, 'pretty' and precocious, a haunting melding of childish innocence and forbidden eroticism.

His success seems to have inspired the appearances of other children, such as 'the Infant Billington' and Anne Moody who played Peggy in *The Country Girl* at Covent Garden aged eight. In the 1820s William Robert Grossmith, the forebear of George Grossmith of Gilbert and Sullivan's Savoy operas, was another 'Young Roscius', who travelled the country under his father's management with a miniature stage, suitable for erection in Assembly Rooms and other halls. William Robert was later joined by his younger brother Benjamin, and their partnership lasted into the 1840s, after which one became a maker of artificial limbs and the other a missionary, though their histrionic gifts obviously continued into future generations of the family. Female child stars of these decades like Jean Davenport and Clara Fisher were probably more attractive to the voyeur than the serious theatregoer.

THE MUSE AND THE SATYR

The theatre around 1800 thus focused sharply the anxieties around performing. The child performers seem oddly perverse, while the women were exposed to predatory males, especially aristocratic men. Hoppner's painting of Dorothy Jordan as the Comic Muse reveals the danger: Jordan turns away from the grinning satyr towards something close to the sublime, but she is caught between the two. Priscilla Wakefield's 1798 warning echoes balefully in the green rooms and corridors of the contemporary theatres:

> The profession of an actress is indeed most unsuitable to the sex, in every point of view; whether it be
> considered with respect to the courage requisite to face an audience, or the variety of situations incident to it,
> which expose moral virtue to the most severe trials.[13]

Figure 5.37
James Northcote, William Betty as Hamlet before a bust of Shakespeare
Source: Yale Center for British Art, Paul Mellon Fund, Yale University, New Haven

But the stage did offer women a rare platform to articulate their own experiences and fulfil their intellectual ambitions.

Put crudely, the theatre and the actors were caught between the desire for poetic elevation and the need for aristocratic patrons. The fact that the careers of Kemble and Mrs Siddons, and perhaps Elizabeth Farren, undoubtedly raised the status of the theatre did not mean that the contradiction was resolved.

Figure 5.38
John Hoppner, Dorothy Jordan as the Comic Muse, 1786, perhaps a riposte to Reynolds's painting of Sarah Siddons as the Tragic Muse

Source: Yale Center for British Art, Paul Mellon Fund, Yale University, New Haven

NOTES

1 William Hazlitt, *The Examiner*, 1816.
2 Stanley Wells, *Great Shakespearean Actors: Burbage to Branagh*, Oxford: Oxford University Press, 2015, p. 57.
3 J.C. Trewin, *The Pomping Folk*, London: J.M. Dent & Sons, 1968, pp. 29–30.
4 James Boaden, *Memoirs of the Life of John Philip Kemble, Esq*, London: Robert H. Small, 1825, p. 435.
5 Robert Tanitch, *London Stage in the Nineteenth Century*, Lancaster: Carnegie Publishing, 2010, p. 6.
6 *Ibid.*, p. 32.
7 Arnold Hare, *George Frederick Cooke, the Actor and the Man*, London: Society for Theatre Research, 1980, p. 2.
8 *Ibid.*, p. 43.
9 *Colburn's New Monthly Magazine*, vol 41, p. 4458.
10 *The Monthly Mirror*, vol 1, p. 371.
11 Arnold Hare, *op.cit.*, pp. 196–197.
12 *Bentley's Miscellany*, vol XVIII, 1845, p. 59.
13 Priscilla Wakefield, 'Reflections on the Present Condition of the Female Sex, 1798', in Vivien Jones (ed), *Women in the Eighteenth Century: Constructions of Femininity*, London: Routledge, 1990, p. 126.

Chapter 63: Whose theatre?

A SATURNALIA

Around 1800 probably in excess of twelve thousand people visited the theatre weekly. Hundreds would gather early, especially on popular nights, and when the doors finally opened there was a brutal scrum involving shoving, elbowing, fisticuffs and brute strength to pay and enter the gallery. For pickpockets, it provided almost unparalleled opportunities, and entry to the pit which was not much more civilised, also offered prime rewards. Once inside, spectators sang, whistled, stamped their feet, hollered their friends (or enemies), ate, drank and generally enjoyed themselves as raucously as they liked. It was soon hot, stuffy and smelly – almost a Saturnalia.

Noise, disrespect and vice were everywhere. People flaunted themselves, made assignations, told lewd jokes. There were prostitutes to suit all tastes and pockets. Especially in the side boxes, watching the play was not a priority. As one journalist wrote in 1808:

> The spectators in the theatre, especially the fashionable part, have their several ends to answer by coming hither. Young women come to show themselves – old ones to show their daughters – men come, one to see those they love, and others to be loved by those who see them. In short, in the side boxes and the private boxes, the stage is the last consideration.[1]

Box patrons often arrived late, attendants shouted for seats for them, doors slammed, parvenus and toffs sat on the box parapets with their backs to the stage, gossiping. M.P. Andrews described 'an over flowing house':

> Here, Box-keeper, are these my places? No,
> Madam Van Bulk has taken all that row;
> Then I'll go back – you can't – you can, she fibs,
> Keep down your elbows, or you'll break my ribs:
> Zounds, how you squeeze! Of what do you think one made is?
> Is this your wig? No, it's that there lady's.
> Then the side-boxes, what delighted rows!
> Peers, poets, nabobs, Jews and 'prentice beaux.
> Alderman Cramp, a gouty rich old cit,
> With his young bride, so lovingly will sit;

While a gay rake who sees the happy pair,
A bliss so wonderful resolves to share.[2]

Between the acts there were intervals of at least five minutes, frequently longer, when music was played, the 'Second Music', the 'Third Music' and so on, sometimes specially composed. During these intervals, it was common for rakes in the pit to get onto the stage, behind the curtain, in order to watch and perhaps molest the female dancers as they limbered up. When the curtain rose, they scampered away, frequently accompanied by hisses from the galleries.

Figure 5.39
The Pit Door, 1784

Source: The Metropolitan Museum of Art, New York. The Elisha Whittelsey Collection, The Elisha Whittelsey Fund, 1969

SPECTATORS' DEMANDS

However rowdy or apparently uninterested, the spectators still expected to be taken notice of. When Mrs Jordan returned to Drury Lane after illness and some scandalous grumbling about her finances in 1791, the audience booed and hissed her. She came to the front of the stage and protested her case, which the audience accepted, and she was permitted to proceed. In 1796 at Drury Lane, they objected vociferously to the execrable performance of an actor called Medley, cast as Skirmish in *The Discovery*, and insisted he be replaced and the play represented with the new actor.

In 1801, Kemble decided to dispense with the clown, Joseph Grimaldi. When the audience at *Blue Beard* noticed that his comic sword fight had been omitted, they loudly demanded an explanation. Kemble, who appeared before them, was unable to satisfy them, and boos and catcalls continued until well after the end of the play. Sheridan, who happened to be in the house that night, was furious. He called the whole company together and demanded an explanation. When he heard it, he sent immediately to Grimaldi's home to request his attendance at tomorrow morning's rehearsal. When he arrived, Sheridan gave him a pay rise.

A few years later an angry dispute between Kemble and John Braham, the singer, erupted. Each addressed the audience to explain the row, the audience cheering and counter-cheering for an hour, at which point Braham walked out. In 1805 London tailors protested against the performance of the play, *The Tailors*.

COOKE'S TRIALS

As might be expected it was G.F. Cooke, caught between the bottle and the public, whose travails were the worst in this respect. When he missed a performance at Covent Garden at the start of the 1801 season, the audience protested till they were promised their money back. When he did appear, they booed and hissed until he apologised from the stage. Later he appeared in *Hamlet*:

> The Ghost was drunk and found so much difficulty in expressing his 'mission' and in keeping himself above ground that the pit 'rose at him' indignantly, to which he replied with a motion of defiance whereupon a row ensued which for some time interrupted the progress of the tragedy.[3]

PLAYS WITHDRAWN

The same treatment was given to plays which displeased. *The Blackamoor Washed White* was hooted off the stage after three performances in 1776. Mary Robinson's play about women gambling, *Nobody*, aroused the ire of women spectators in particular. They hissed and their servants in the gallery supported them, and the play was taken off again after three performances. *Virginia* by Frances Plowden quickly displeased the audience in 1801. By the second act the booing completely drowned the actors' voices, and Kemble was forced to come forward and agree not to present it again.

OTHER DISTURBANCES

Sometimes there seemed even less reason for riot. Drunken spectators at Covent Garden in 1801 hurled fruit, glasses and even bottles at each other till guardsmen with fixed bayonets intervened.

In 1806, during a performance of *Coriolanus*, Mrs Siddons was hit by a flying apple core. When Kemble demanded why, he was told it was aimed not at the great tragedienne, but at the snobs in the side boxes.

An intervention by the authorities was especially resented. When, in 1805, in obedience to a new decree from the Bishop of London, the King's Theatre in the Haymarket brought the curtain down at midnight in the middle of a ballet, the audience screamed their dissent. Francis Gould the manager and his ballet master appeared and apologised. It was not enough. Spectators flung chairs out of the boxes, wrenched up the pit benches, broke the chandeliers, and smashed the orchestra's instruments. It is true Gould successfully sued some of the ringleaders of this 'riot', but the spectators' behaviour begged the question: whose theatre was this?

PRICES AND PROBLEMS

In 1791, when Drury Lane prices were increased, discontent surfaced quickly, but Kemble explained why he had had to raise them, and the spectators, however unhappily, accepted his explanation. The following year, however, when Covent Garden tried the same thing, protests were more vehement, and Harris had eventually to back down. And twelve years later, Thomas Gilliland published a pamphlet, *Elbow Room*, in which he objected to the increase in 'private' boxes at Covent Garden, and asserted that the theatre was different from other commodities, that the public had rights, partly because of the monopoly status of Drury Lane and Covent Garden. Theatre provided a public, not a private space.

FIRE AND THE THEATRES

These theatres were also extraordinary fire risks. The floaty drapery of Mrs Siddons, statuesque as Hermione, were set alight one night by the lamps nearby: a quick-thinking stage hand doused the flames before they took hold. In 1802, in *The Country Girl* at Drury Lane, Mrs Jordan's skirt caught fire up to the waist, and she was forced to conclude the scene in her petticoat only.

Theatres themselves caught fire, too. In June 1789 the King's was set ablaze. The firemen were too drunk to attend, and several houses next to the theatre were also destroyed. Arson was suspected, perhaps at the instigation of Pietro Carnivalli, leader of the orchestra, who was at daggers drawn with the theatre's deputy manager. The opera was taken to the Pantheon, but that too burned down in 1792.

COVENT GARDEN: DESTRUCTION AND REBUILDING

In September 1808, Covent Garden theatre caught fire. What started it is unclear: probably wadding fired from a gun became trapped in scenery, but whatever the cause, the flames quickly spread. Firemen trying to enter the blazing building were crushed by falling masonry. Others were scalded to death by steam from their own hosepipes. All the scenery, properties and stage armour were utterly destroyed as were priceless Handel, Arne and other manuscripts, Handel's huge organ and John Philip Kemble's unique library. Mrs Siddons lost a veil given to her by Marie Antoinette worth a thousand pounds. The flames were said to have risen four hundred fifty feet into the air, and seven nearby houses and a pub were also gutted. On the house roofs for miles around people stood gazing at the catastrophe.

Figure 5.40
Covent Garden in flames, 1808: fire hoses play on the blaze while men try to rescue the theatre's artefacts in sacks

Source: The Trustees of the British Museum

Immediately, an appeal for money to rebuild was launched: the insurance paid about £50,000, about £75,000 was raised by public subscription and the Duke of Northumberland donated £10,000. Despite there being still a considerable shortfall, on 30 December 1808 the Prince of Wales led a procession of freemasons through streets lined by Life Guards and military bands to Covent Garden where he laid a new foundation stone.

DRURY LANE BURNS DOWN

Before the building was anything like complete, however, in February 1809, the other patent theatre, Drury Lane, was also razed to the ground by fire. 'The awful grandeur of the conflagration defies description', wrote one who saw it.[4] Sheridan sat in the Covent Garden piazza with a bottle of wine, watching it go. When somebody voiced surprise that he should be sitting there, he replied: 'Is a man not permitted to drink a glass of wine beside his own fireside?'[5]

THE NEW COVENT GARDEN

The new Covent Garden opened exactly a year after the destruction of the old one, in September 1809. Designed by Robert Smirke, it took the Parthenon in Athens as its inspiration with a portico featuring allegorical statues of Comedy and Tragedy, as well as Greek gods, Sophocles and

Shakespeare. Within it featured white-veined marble and red porphyry, as well as more classical statues, and it held over a thousand people more than its predecessor. It soon became clear, however, that while the experience provided would be improved for Box patrons – especially private Box patrons who did not wish to be watched – that for the lowest classes would be worse. Visibility and audibility were both reduced for them. Nevertheless, the gap in finances needed to be closed. The obvious way to do this was through raised prices.

COVENT GARDEN RE-OPENS

The grand reopening of Covent Garden was set for 18 September 1809, and big crowds gathered early around the building. When the Duke of York arrived he was greeted with irreverent good cheer: 'Wotcher, Charley', 'Charley is my darling', and so on. Inside, just before the curtain rose, the audience burst out, apparently spontaneously, with 'God save the king and 'Rule, Britannia', though there were also cries of ''Old prices!' and 'Down with the pigeonholes' as the new cramped and divided gallery places were already nicknamed. And the new specially written Prologue was drowned out by roaring, hissing, hooting spectators. The din continued almost unabated through the evening. Kemble's Macbeth faced a special barrage of hostile jeering, and when Macduff killed him on stage, the wags in the audience cheered especially noisily.

At the end of the evening, the disturbance continued. The lights were turned down and the stage trapdoors opened to deter the rioters, but they continued their boisterous disapproval. The Riot Act was read. The response was, 'No police in the theatre!' The protesters did not disperse till after two AM.

The rioters thought they were defending their traditional rights and customs. The theatre was a public place where people came to see and be seen. The new auditorium prevented this. It was impossible to see into the private boxes, and the popular places had been reduced because of the expansion of boxes. Besides which, people objected to the salaries offered to such performers as the Italian opera singer, Angelica Catalani.

THE RIOTS WORSEN

On the second night, banners and placards were smuggled into the theatre. One read: 'National Theatre: Fair Prices: English Drama: No Catalani'. People stood on benches, clapped, shouted, sang and whistled. Horns were blown, handbells shaken and rattles twirled. The din was frightful. The actors continued, but in the equivalent of mime. Many in the audience stood with their backs to the stage. Others imitated animals – donkeys braying, dogs barking. Two men brought in a coffin inscribed 'Here lies the body of New Price, an ugly child and base born'. The 'O.P. Dance' was invented: it consisted of large groups of protesters stamping rhythmically with their boots or sticks, and shouting 'O.P.' at the designated moment.

When Kemble addressed the crowd, asking what their behaviour meant, they bawled: 'Off, off, off! Damn you, can't you read? O.P.! Old prices!' and stamped, blew their trumpets, thwacked their sticks on the floor, rattled their frying pans, pokers and fire tongs, and unloosed real pigeons from the so-called 'pigeonholes' in the new gallery. A self-appointed spokesman jumped onto the stage and pointed to the boxes, with their lordly occupants and their louche young ladies.

Figure 5.41
John Philip Kemble facing the O.P. rioters
Source: Victoria and Albert Museum, London

A PAUSE

Kemble paused the performances for some days and had an independent audit of the theatre's accounts published. It only inflamed things. Kemble was paying himself, Catalani and others far too much; he was greedy and arrogant; actors should be the public's servants, not their bloodsuckers.

RIOTING RESUMES

When the theatre reopened the protests continued with greater ferocity. Handbills were printed and distributed, commemorative medals struck and cockades made. Witty and artistic banners appeared, and people arrived in grotesque or bizarre costumes, in military uniform or in drag. New jokes, rhymes and songs were created, like the parody of the national anthem:

> God save great Johnny Bull,
> Long live our noble Bull,
> God save John Bull;

> Send him victorious,
> Loud and uproarious,
> With lungs like Boreas,
> God save John Bull.[6]

The dances expanded. The O.P. Dance now concluded with a shout of 'Down O.P.s!' and the dancers sat down all together with their backs to the stage, sang 'Rule Britannia' and 'God Save the King', followed by three cheers for John Bull and three groans for John Kemble. And there was a new dance, the Rattlesnake Minuet, a sort of conga with the dancers snaking in a long line around the auditorium and clashing sticks. There were mock sword fights, races across the pit benches, even wrestling contests. Aristocratic patrons came to watch the antics in the pit, not the action on stage.

TROUBLE ON THE STREETS

There was trouble in the streets around the theatre, too. Cabbies were stopped and their allegiance demanded: 'O.P. or N.P.?' One night about three hundred rioters marched to Kemble's house from the theatre and called him out. He did not appear, so they flung clods of earth and coins at the house, and smashed some of the windows. The authorities at least attempted to quell street violence, though they did not interfere with activities in the theatre.

WHO WERE THE RIOTERS?

The rioters considered themselves representatives of John Bull, defending the rights of true-born Englishmen. 'Up with King George and down with King John' was their slogan. And they came from virtually every stratum of society, indicating, by the way, the wide popularity of theatre at this time. There were upper-class protesters: one evening the denizens of the boxes beat back a group of marauding constables, and often elegant ladies were to be seen dancing in their boxes. But there were also plenty of 'labourers', shopmen, clerks, footmen in livery, coal heavers and apprentices.

MANAGEMENT COUNTERATTACKS

By mid-October, the management was counterattacking. They hired two prize fighters, Daniel Mendoza and Dutch Sam, to beat up the protesters, but the protesters defended themselves. Blood spattered the pit benches, and Leigh Hunt opined that 'the pit has been metamorphosed into a pugilistic arena, where all the blackguards of London, the Jew prize-fighters, Bow-street runners, hackney-coach helpers, and vagabonds returned from transportation have ranged themselves on the side of the management'.[7] The fact that Mendoza was Jewish added a rancid streak of anti-Semitism to the mix.

James Brandon, the theatre doorkeeper, also brought in Joseph Grimaldi, who almost halted the protests when he appeared, but had no effect on his second appearance. Kemble himself published a leaflet threatening legal action, and though the government refused to send in the army, Brandon was able to bring in enough constables to press individual charges. At Bow Street court, cases were heard against a woman for brandishing a child's rattle, a man for sneezing, coughing and howling 'unnaturally' and a man for wearing a hat with 'O.P.' written on it.

POLITICAL RADICALS

The climax came with the arrest and charging of Henry Clifford, a well-known radical Catholic barrister. A large group of protesters marched in his support, and the magistrate acquitted him. Clifford then countersued Brandon for wrongful imprisonment and won his case. He became an instant hero.

Clifford was not the only Radical involved. Other well-known dissidents supporting the O.P. protests included Thomas Tegg, Francis Place, William Hone, John Lambert and Sir Francis Burdett, the Radical MP for Westminster. They published articles and pamphlets, like John Fairbairn's *Remarks on the Cause of the Dispute between the Public and Managers of the Theatre Royal, Covent Garden*, they helped to defend protesters in the court free of charge and they formed a Committee to raise funds for those 'unjustly prosecuted'. They were nevertheless the object of government spying operations. Sir Richard Ford, spymaster and Bow Street magistrate, kept them under close surveillance and planted at least one government spy, James Powell, among them. Still, they gained the rioters' trust.

It was these Radicals who articulated best the deeper causes of the O.P. riots. They asked: Who owns Shakespeare? Was not the purpose of the Royal Patent to open the best in theatre to all the people? Was not the size of the new theatre a way of killing personal interaction? Who gained from the profit motive now seen to be driving the theatre? And did not the higher prices merely entrench class divisions and underwrite the lechery of the rich?

By December the disturbances had become more dangerous. The stage itself became the target for all kinds of missiles, including hard peas which caused havoc among the dancers. At the same time it became clear that the theatre was losing serious sums of money.

KEMBLE CAPITULATES

On 14 December, Kemble met Henry Clifford at the Crown and Anchor, the Radicals' favoured tavern. The next night Kemble stood on the stage and publicly apologised for raising the prices, as well as for employing pugilists and other aggressive acts. After a meeting at Francis Place's house, prices were returned to 1808 levels, James Brandon, the belligerent doorkeeper was sacked, and most of the Boxes changed so that their occupants could be seen at all times. The following year, after more disturbances, every box was changed.

THE RECKONING

After a memorial dinner at the Crown and Anchor hosted by the group of political Radicals, to which Kemble was invited, it was clear the 'war' was over, though desultory protests did continue through 1810. The rioters appeared to have won. Shakespeare belonged to everybody.

But change was afoot. The patent theatres' devotion to classical drama loosened, as the 'minor' theatres boomed. The patent houses' answer was to go 'downmarket' and stage extravaganzas and pantomimes of their own and reduce their productions of Shakespeare, new drama and other work which their patents gave them the rights to.

THE END OF SHERIDAN'S DRURY LANE

Meanwhile, as Drury Lane lay in ashes, Samuel Whitbread, scion of the famous brewing family, offered help. Sheridan invited him onto the board, and fundraising was begun. But soon it was clear that the theatre's debts reached nearly half a million pounds. Sheridan's presence on the board was obviously a liability. Reluctantly, he resigned. Under Whitbread, the money was raised to build a new Drury Lane, and this opened in October 1812, with a new young actor, Robert Elliston, playing Hamlet.

The next years, however, were calamitous. Sheridan, though no longer on the Drury Lane board, was arrested for debt in May 1814. Samuel Whitbread bailed him out, but Whitbread himself was finding running the huge Drury Lane theatre too much, and he too was sued for debt. In a fit of depression, he cut his own throat with a razor in July 1815. Sheridan, now very ill, tricked the Prince of Wales into lending him money. By July 1816, the bailiffs were in possession of his house, there was hardly a stick of furniture left and he was arrested in his bed. But before these proceedings could work themselves out, he died.

Sheridan was buried in Westminster Abbey on 13 July 1816. A theatrical era was over.

NOTES

1 Robert Tanitch, *London Stage in the Nineteenth Century*, Lancaster: Carnegie Publishing, 2010, p. 21.
2 M.P. Andrews, 'Epilogue to Frederic Reynolds', in *The Dramatist*.
3 Arnold Hare, *George Frederick Cooke: The Actor and the Man*, London: The Society for Theatre Research, 1980, p. 151.
4 William Hone, *The Every-Day Book*, vol 2, London: Hunt and Clarke, 1827, p. 1249.
5 Thomas Moore, *Memoirs of the Life of the Right Honourable Richard Brinsley Sheridan*, vol 2, London: Longmans, Rees, Orme, Brown, Green, 1825, p. 368.
6 Thomas Tegg, *The Rise, Progress and Termination of the O.P. War*, London: Thomas Tegg, 1810, p. 52.
7 *Covent Garden Journal*, vol 1, 1810, p. 150.

Select bibliography

Baer, Marc, *Theatre and Disorder in Late Georgian London*, Oxford: Clarendon Press, 1992

Baugh, Christopher, *Garrick and de Loutherbourg*, Cambridge: Chadwyck-Healey, 1990

Bhattacharya, Nandini, *Reading the Splendid Body*, London: Associated University Presses, 1998

Brewer, John, *The Pleasures of the Imagination*, London: Routledge, 2013

Buchan, James, *Capital of the Mind: How Edinburgh Changed the World*, London: John Murray, 2003

Engel, Laura (ed), *The Public's Open to Us All: Essays on Women and Performance in Eighteenth Century England*, Newcastle-upon-Tyne: Cambridge Scholars, 2009

Fiske, Roger, *English Theatre Music in the Eighteenth Century*, Oxford: Oxford University Press, 1986

Hare, Arnold, *The Georgian Theatre in Wessex*, London: Phoenix House, 1958

Luckhurst, Mary, and Moody, Jane (eds), *Theatre and Celebrity in Britain 1660–2000*, Basingstoke: Palgrave Macmillan, 2005

McIntyre, Ian, *Garrick*, Harmondsworth: Penguin, 1999

Moody, Jane, and O'Quinn, Daniel (eds), *The Cambridge Companion to British Theatre, 1730–1830*, Cambridge: Cambridge University Press, 2007

O'Quinn, Daniel, *Staging Governance: Theatrical Imperialism in London, 1770–1800*, Baltimore: John Hopkins University Press, 2005

Porter, Roy, *Enlightenment: Britain and the Creation of the Modern World*, London: Penguin, 2000

Ragussis, Michael, *Theatrical Nation: Jews and Other Outlandish Englishmen in Georgian Britain*, Philadelphia: University of Pennsylvania Press, 2010

Ranger, Paul, *Under Two Managers: The Everyday Life of the Thornton-Barnett Theatre Company, 1785–1853*, London: Society for Theatre Research, 2001

Rosenfeld, Sybil, *The Georgian Theatre of Richmond, Yorkshire*, London: Society for Theatre Research, 1984

Russell, Gillian, *The Theatres of War: Performance, Politics and Society, 1793–1815*, Oxford: Clarendon Press, 1995

Thomson, Peter, *The Cambridge Introduction to English Theatre, 1660–1900*, Cambridge: Cambridge University Press, 2006

West, Shearer, *The Image of the Actor*, London: Pinter, 1991

Worth, Katherine, *Sheridan and Goldsmith*, Basingstoke: Palgrave Macmillan, 1992

Interlude: Garrick's Shakespeare Jubilee

Five years late, and in the autumn of one of Britain's wettest years, the bi-centenary of Shakespeare's birth was celebrated at Stratford-upon-Avon.

THE IDEA FOR A JUBILEE

The idea was David Garrick's. The little market town, with a population of about three thousand, invited him to present a statue of Shakespeare and a portrait of himself to adorn their new Town Hall, and with it they offered to make him a freeman of the town. Garrick was excited, honoured and stimulated, and proposed the 'jubilee' with himself as steward in response. His suggestion was accepted and preparations were immediately set in train.

PREPARATIONS

Garrick worked hard and conscientiously over the summer of 1769. Gainsborough painted his portrait, songs and glees, mostly by Garrick himself, were set by composers from Thomas Arne to Charles Dibdin, and an octagonal wooden rotunda, holding up to a thousand people, was erected on the bank of the Avon, approximately where the Memorial Theatre would be built more than a hundred and fifty years later. Medallions were struck, ribbons prepared and souvenirs carved from the wood of the mulberry tree believed to have been planted in New Place garden by Shakespeare himself. If all were genuine, the tree must have been considerably larger than most mulberries!

But not everyone in Stratford was happy, and some in London were distinctly unhappy. These included Garrick's grumpy Drury Lane partner, James Lacy, and the irrepressible Samuel Foote, who knew a target for satire when he saw one. But in spite of doubts and mockery, and a horribly sodden summer, the grandiose event went ahead, lasting for three days from 6 September.

THE JUBILEE BEGINS

From the beginning of the month, aristocratic and fashionable people had been flocking to Stratford, along with tradespeople, hairdressers, cooks and a large cohort of sedan-chairmen from Bath. Prices sky-rocketed.

On the opening day, at five AM, Drury Lane's musicians dressed as waits sang Dibdin's setting of 'Let Beauty with the Sun Arise' outside Garrick's lodging. Cannon were fired, church bells rang out and the fife and drum band of the Warwickshire Militia paraded through the town. Garrick was presented with the freedom of the town in a specially carved box of mulberry wood. The public breakfast was followed by a performance in Stratford Parish Church of Arne's oratorio, *Judith*. Later seven hundred guests had dinner in the rotunda, which was then hastily cleared for the Assembly Ball held that night.

THE SECOND DAY

On the second day rain put a heavy damper on the serenaders, the cannons and the bells. Moreover, Garrick's barber cut his chin badly while shaving him; in any case, Garrick had awoken with a cold. The rain continued to fall. The pageant of two hundred and seventeen of Shakespeare's characters who were to parade through the town in costume was cancelled.

At twelve noon, however, Garrick's Shakespearean Ode was recited in the rotunda by the author and steward of the festival. He spoke against the orchestral music of Thomas Arne, which swelled up as the choir sang between Garrick's verses. It was a triumph, the high point of the three days. At its climax, praise of the River Avon, the doors of the rotunda were flung open to disclose the river, now bubbling, brown and furious, as the rain continued to pour down. But the audience was highly enthusiastic.

The Ode was followed by the Oration. Garrick spoke for minutes, praising Shakespeare exorbitantly, and ending by appealing for anyone in the audience who had been equally moved by any other poet. A man in a greatcoat, actually Thomas King, primed and in character, came forward

Figure 5.42
David Garrick reciting the Ode in honour of Shakespeare at the Jubilee, surrounded by the musicians of the orchestra

Figure 5.43

David Garrick speaking the Oration at the Jubilee, with Shakespearean characters around him and a languid Bard, looking rather like Garrick, on the pedestal. Moments later, the rain undermined the temporary building, the benches in the auditorium collapsed and the audience was hustled out.

Source: The Metropolitan Museum of Art, New York, Harris Brisbane Dick Fund, 1953

to denigrate Shakespeare. But this rehearsed scene was interrupted as the overcrowding of the rotunda, together with the water in the meadow and under the temporary construction, began to undermine the building itself. Benches collapsed and several people were hurt. The audience was hustled out.

The building must have been repaired, for later in the afternoon it was the venue for the public dinner, the highlight of which was a huge turtle, weighing over three hundred pounds, which was consumed while appropriate music played. But the fireworks which were due to follow had to be abandoned – they were soggy and impossible to light.

In the evening the masquerade did go ahead, and the masqueraders in their fancy costumes squelched through the mud to get there. They danced till dawn as the rains outside went on and on, and the Avon threatened to burst its banks. At dawn, duck boarding was laid down and the revellers departed, some ladies being carried piggy-back by their partners, others falling into the endless floods.

THE THIRD DAY

On the third and final morning, the weather forced the pageant to be cancelled again, though the horse race went ahead on a waterlogged course. This, however, was the last act of the extraordinary, financially disastrous Jubilee, in which not a word by Shakespeare had been spoken, and none of his plays performed.

AFTER THE JUBILEE

Yet it was not quite the end. George Colman the Elder opportunistically made a small comedy out of it, *Man and Wife, or The Shakespeare Jubilee* which was presented at Covent Garden, though without great success. Much more popular was Garrick's own drama, *The Jubilee*, in which he was able to repeat the most successful parts of the festival, rejigged for the Drury Lane stage, and at last to present the pageant of Shakespearean characters. Despite the carping of his enemies and the satire of others, *The Jubilee* proved very popular and was given over ninety performances that season.

This curious event, which first made Stratford-upon-Avon into a tourist trap and was perhaps the earliest British outdoor arts festival, made a deep and positive impression on many of Garrick's contemporaries. And it was a crucial moment in the history of British theatre and performance: it is from this event that Shakespeare's overwhelming significance, as well as his enduring popularity, may be dated.

SELECT BIBLIOGRAPHY

McIntyre, Ian, *Garrick*, Harmondsworth: Penguin, 1999
Stochholm, Johanne M., *Garrick's Folly: The Stratford Jubilee of 1769*, London: Methuen, 1964

Glossary

Above Stage balcony or other raised area usually at the rear of the stage.

Ad-lib Impromptu words invented on the spot and spoken by an actor; lines not authorised by the playwright.

Afterpiece Short, usually light play, presented after the main play in an evening's entertainment.

Anti-hero The protagonist of a play who is neither courageous, virtuous nor sympathetic.

Anti-masque Comic or burlesque (q.v.) prelude to a masque (q.v.).

Attitude Performer's pose which crystallises a specific idea or emotion.

Auditorium Area inside a theatre designated for spectators.

Balcony Small raised acting area at the rear of the stage, especially in the Elizabethan open air theatre; often referred to as 'above' (q.v.).

Ballad opera Musical dramatic form in which new words were set to traditional or popular airs and sung between conventional dialogue.

Bauble Clown's stick with miniature head, usually modelled on the clown's own features, at its end.

Below Area beneath the stage which the audience is aware of; often accessed by a trapdoor in the stage.

Benefit performance Performance when the income received from audience admissions was given to a particular person: authors expected the third performance of a play to be for their benefit, and towards the end of any season most actors expected at least one benefit; other beneficiaries might be charities or other organisations. Benefits were granted at the management's discretion.

Blank verse Dramatic speech in the form of unrhymed verse, whose lines are formed in iambic pentameters.

Borders Hanging flats or drapes which went across and behind the top of the proscenium opening to provide the upper part of the stage picture.

Bottling Obtaining money from spectators by passing around a hat or other receptacle (the 'bottle').

Box Office Place where a spectator may purchase entry to the theatre; or where a spectator may reserve a place in advance.

Breeches role A role in which a female actor appeared in male costume.

Burlesque Dramatic form which makes fun of the pretentious and the pompous by imitating and exaggerating what it mocks; often with a metatheatrical (q.v.) element.

Burletta Short musical drama.

Business Any activity performed by an actor not specified in the playscript; also called 'byplay' (q.v.).

Byplay Stage action not authorised by the playwright.

Call boy Prompter's assistant.

Castrato Male soprano.

Claque Group of spectators paid to applaud – or boo – a particular performer or performance.

Closet drama A play not intended for the public stage, usually only read or performed privately.

Circuit Sequence of regular venues played by itinerant theatre companies.

Cross-dressing An actor of one gender dressed in the costume of the other gender.

Cue Word or words or action or effect which acts as the trigger for the following speech or action; in a dialogue, the last two or three words of one speech form the *cue* for the next speech.

Cue script The script given to an actor at the commencement of rehearsals, which contained only that actor's part and the cues (q.v.) for each speech.

Discovery A character, object or interior scene revealed by the drawing of a curtain or opening of a door.

Doorkeeper Person taking admission money from spectators entering the theatre.

Doubling The practice of a single actor playing two or more parts.

Droll Short, farcical play popular during the Commonwealth, but also as an afterpiece (q.v.) when the theatres re-opened after the monarchy was restored.

Dumb show Mute enactment of some crucial or symbolic action which explicates either the plot or its significance or both.

Entr'acte Entertainment presented between the acts of a play.

Epilogue Speech or short scene given after the main play's final scene.

Flats See shutters.

Fly gallery Area above the stage, concealed by the borders (q.v.) from where painted clouds could be hung or actors flown down onto or drawn up from the stage.

Flying Applied to an actor's performance when it appears to 'take off', the words and actions seemingly entirely spontaneous.

Footlights Lights arranged across the front of the forestage (q.v.), to light the performers but shielded from the audience.

Forestage That area of the stage in front of the proscenium arch (q.v.)

Gag Comic stage trick or joke.

Gauze Curtain hung across the stage which when lit from in front appeared opaque but which could be seen through when lit from behind.

Green Room Room offstage where actors wait to be called onto the stage.

Grooves Wooden tracks on the stage floor and at the height of the shutters (q.v.) within which the shutters moved, and which held them in place.

Groundlings Spectators who stood in the yard of an open air theatre.

Hangings Curtains at the back of the stage in indoor theatres.

Heavens Room above the stage in the Elizabethan open air theatre where machinery was housed and from where spectacular entrances and exits could be made. The heavens formed the ceiling over the stage and may have been painted blue like the sky, with clouds or stars.

Humanist Student of classical civilisation, not, as may have been the case in later centuries, a non-believer.

Humour A person's disposition to behave according to their physiological and metabolic make-up; put simplistically, earth, air, fire and water were thought to be the elements of the world, and they were thought to be replicated in human bodily fluids; the predominance of one fluid over the others led towards the four basic temperaments – sanguine, choleric, melancholic or phlegmatic.

Interlude Short play, often comic and unpretentious; also, any short item performed between weightier presentations.

Jig Afterpiece, featuring dance and song, having usually a simple, farcical plot.

Lazzo Italian word for a piece of comic stage business.

Length Single sheet of forty-six lines of a character's role, part of a cue script (q.v.).

Long room Small, narrow provincial theatre.

Maquette Scale model of a stage set.

Masque A mostly amateur performance, frequently spectacular and usually including music, dance and often poetic speech.

Medley Form of presentation consisting of a series of only loosely connected scenes, in a variety of styles.

Merry Andrew Clown, often performing solo.

Metatheatre Theatre which draws attention to its own artificiality, or theatricality, or to the circumstances of the performance.

Mimesis On-stage imitation of human behaviour, often silent.

Miracle play Dramatisation of the lives and deeds of saints.

Morality play Dramatisation of a moral lesson, often with characters embodying abstract qualities, such as Everyman, Mercy or Idleness.

Motley Clown or Fool's parti-coloured costume.

Mumming Disguised playing of games or interludes (q.v.); also may refer to a dumb show (q.v.) when actors keep 'mum'; or to a folk play.

Mystery play, mystery cycle Short play, or series (cycle) of short plays, or pageants, performed in sequence, which tell stories from the Bible.

Natural A simpleton.

Neoclassicism The attempted reincarnation of a classical Greek or Roman aesthetic, including dramas structured by the unities of place, time and action, literary decorum and monumental effects.

Orchestra Circular or semi-circular space between stage and audience, originally used for dancers; later for musicians.

Orrery Clockwork mechanism designed to show the movement of the planets and the stars.

Pageant Staged show without complex plotting, often celebratory, sometimes spectacular; also used of a wagon upon which a show was presented.

Pantomime Dramatic form originally featuring English versions of *commedia dell'arte* characters; spectacular, comic, musical, the form evolved continuously over three hundred years.

Pastoral Play depicting country life, originally the life of the shepherd.

Patent The Patent theatres were those with a Royal Patent (q.v.). Between 1660 and 1843, the main Patent theatres were Drury Lane and Lincoln's Inn Fields, replaced by Covent Garden around 1730.

Pit The front ten or so rows downstairs in the auditorium. Comprising backless benches, the pit provided places for those who considered themselves most interested and responsive to the drama.

Place-and-scaffold Open performance space, usually circular, with two or more booth stages erected around the perimeter.

Platea Central unlocalised acting space in a place-and-scaffold (q.v.) performance arrangement.

Pratfall Comic tumble onto the backside, usually with the effect of deflating or confounding the pratfalling performer.

Prologue Speech or short scene given before the play proper begins.

Props, or properties Articles used on stage, being smaller than any items of furniture.

Proscenium arch The physical frame at the front of the main stage area.

Quête Processional movement of players at the end of a traditional drama during which alms are collected.

Rake The slope of the stage down towards the audience in some theatres.

Rhetoric Speech designed to persuade its auditors of some abstract truth; usually marked by linguistic elegance or subtlety.

Rope dancer Tightrope or slack wire performer.

Royal Patent The grant of a Royal Patent permitted the holder to stage plays professionally, and to charge spectators an entry fee. Charging spectators or paying performers without a Royal Patent was illegal from 1660 to 1843.

Scenekeeper Stage hand.

Sharers Those with a financial interest in a theatre company.

Shutters The painted backdrop to the stage in indoor theatres consisted of two equal pieces, or 'flats', which parted in the middle when drawn apart, and came together when pushed from the wings. Each half was known as a shutter.

Slapstick Clown's stick with split end which, when used to slap, makes a resounding crack; the word came to be applied to any physical buffoonery.

Station Site of performance of mystery plays (q.v.) or pageants (q.v.)

Stock character A character conceived according to dramatic convention or tradition rather than psychologically.

Strolling Itinerant; applied to groups of actors ('strollers') who moved from place to place performing where they could find an audience.

Subtext The hidden meaning beneath the words of the text.

Tableau Static grouping of actors on the stage.

Tableau vivant Static pictorial arrangement of performers to represent an incident or idea.

Tiring-house Dressing room, 'tiring' being an abbreviation of 'attiring'.

Tragicomedy Dramatic form introduced in the early seventeenth century in which the intrigue brought one or more of the characters close to death before the happy ending.

Transformation scene A scene in which the stage picture was entirely changed, usually effected by machinery as well as stage hands.

Type casting The casting of an actor in the same kind of role over a series of plays; or the casting of a particular actor in a role because the actor seems to resemble the character in some way.

Vice Archetypal character from the morality plays (q.v.): the Devil's henchman or servant.

Vista stage Extension at the back of the main stage intended to give distance to the scene; rarely approached by the actors.

Walk-up Platform outside a fairground booth theatre where performers in costume acted, sang or harangued the crowd in an endeavour to attract them inside. The entrance to the theatre inside was often over the walk-up.

Wing piece Freestanding unit of scenery at the side of the stage, used to block the audience's view of 'off-stage'. The faces of wing pieces were usually decorated with pictorial scenes; often they had three or five faces which could be revolved when the scene changed.

Index